UNDERSTANDING THE CHRISTIAN FAITH

UNDERSTANDING THE CHRISTIAN FAITH

CHARLES D. BARRETT
Wofford College

PRENTICE-HALL, INC., Englewood Cliffs, N.J. 07632

Library of Congress Cataloging in Publication Data

BARRETT, CHARLES D (date)
  Understanding the Christian faith.

  Bibliography: p.
  Includes index.
  1. Theology, Doctrinal—Popular works. 2. Religion. I. Title.
BT77.B343   230   79-24858
ISBN 0-13-935882-X

Editorial/production supervision and interior
  design by Frank J. Hubert
Cover design by Wanda Lubelska Design
Manufacturing buyer: John Hall

PRENTICE-HALL INTERNATIONAL, INC., *London*
PRENTICE-HALL OF AUSTRALIA PTY. LIMITED, *Sydney*
PRENTICE-HALL OF CANADA, LTD., *Toronto*
PRENTICE-HALL OF INDIA PRIVATE LIMITED, *New Delhi*
PRENTICE-HALL OF JAPAN, INC., *Tokyo*
PRENTICE-HALL OF SOUTHEAST ASIA PTE. LTD., *Singapore*
WHITEHALL BOOKS LIMITED, *Wellington, New Zealand*

To Jim and Helen Barrett,
   who gave me life and a faith by which to live it,
and to Sally, Sandra, and Christopher,
   who do a lot to keep both life and faith interesting

To Jim and Helen Barrett,
   who gave me life and a faith by which to live it,
and to Sally, Sandra, and Christopher,
   who do a lot to keep both life and faith interesting

Contents

PREFACE   xi

ACKNOWLEDGMENTS   xv

prologue   CHRISTIANITY: AN HISTORICAL INTROIT   1

part one
A FAITH AMONG FAITHS   7

I.   RELIGION AS AN APPROACH TO REALITY   9

What Religion Is Not	12
What Religion Is	18

II.   RELIGIONS AND LIFE STYLES   30

Religions Born of Nature: The Style of the Swinger	32
Religions Born of Reason: The Style of the Square	38
Religions Born of History: The Style of the Shaper	46

III.   PUTTING CHRISTIANITY ON THE MAP   60

Christianity as a Historist Faith	61
Faith as Time-Consciousness and Involvement in History	76
The Christian View of the Self-World Relation	81

vii

IV.   THE CHRISTIAN PROJECT   95

Stories, Styles, and Standards   99
Modes of Service   111
Ties That Bind: The Christian Vision Projected (A Preview)   119

part two
FAITH AND THE WORD   127

V.   FAITH AND KNOWING: THE WORD AS RELATION   129

Two Well-Explored Routes: Revelation and Reason   132
Two Rejected Paths: Gnosticism and Agnosticism   134
Faith and Knowing: A Summative Postscript   166

VI.   FAITH AND RELATING: THE WORD AS REVELATION   177

The Meaning of Revelation   178
The Scope of Revelation: The Reason-Revelation Question Revisited   180
The Question of Revelation's Nature and Form   197
The Bible and the Word of God: The Question of Revelation's Medium and
  Norm   204
Revelation as the Realization of a Relationship   217
A Summary and Concluding Critique   220

VII.   FAITH AND BEING: THE WORD AS CREATION   230

What Creation Does Not Mean   232
What Creation Means   237
Creation as a Painful Process (The Problem of Evil)   246
Creation's Human Dimension   260

VIII.   FAITH AND BECOMING: THE WORD AS REDEMPTION   273

Redemption's Setting and Purpose: Creation and the Creator's Image   274
Redemption's Necessity: The Sin of the Creature and the Judgment of the
  Creator   278
Redemption's Source: The God Who Is Alive   287
Redemption's Realization: Jesus the Christ   300
Redemption and Becoming   314

IX. FAITH AND COMMUNITY: THE WORD AS RECONCILIATION 322

Redemption's Appropriation: The Holy Spirit 323
Redemption's Existential Effects: Liberation and Reconciliation 327
Redemption's Ecclesiastical Effects: The Church as Corporation, as Sect, as
  Community 339

X. FAITH AND CARING: THE WORD AS PROMISE 366

Redemption's Ethical Effects: The Ways of Law, Liberty, and Love 367
Redemption's Eschatological Effects: Caring and Hoping 375
The Christian's Destiny: Not-So-Final Thoughts on Final Things 388

EPILOGUE 399

SELECTED BIBLIOGRAPHY 401

INDEX 411

Preface

THIS IS A SELF-CONFESSED TEXTBOOK. And while I am making
a clean breast of it, let me also confess what has prompted so brazen
an attempt to counter a trend which has placed theological textbooks on
virtually everybody's list of endangered species.

The trend itself has done much of the prompting. As a teacher of an
introductory course on the Christian faith, I have found it difficult in
recent years to find books which deal with both the subjective (personal)
and the objective (doctrinal) aspects of that faith. And on the rare occasions when such books have appeared on publishers' lists, I have often
wished that those books went a couple of steps further—far enough to
set Christianity within the context of the major religious options available to people in these times; and far enough to discuss, at least in an
introductory way, the peculiarities of the religious approach to life. Only
a book with the breadth of a textbook could be expected to touch so
many bases, and so the textbook format seemed a logical choice for the
endeavor whose results follow.

The dearth of works of sufficient breadth to service an introductory
course of the scope mentioned has done much to produce this text. But
of greater importance, perhaps, have been the convictions which have
led me to consider such breadth important. First, it seems to me that our
superficially secular age has blinded many people to the religious presuppositions which inform both the prevailing culture and the challeng-
ing counter-cultures which shape contemporary life. Whatever one's
attitude toward religion, it seems important that that attitude be informed by an understanding of the peculiar role religion plays in providing the value-assumptions and integrative imagery of the cultural options open to us. Regard for this role seems to require that a textbook
pay some attention to the practical and social functions of the religious
approach to reality.

Just as distressing as the blindness born of one-dimensional secularism has been what I consider a failure on the part of the theological profession to mount an adequate response to such blindness. Theology books continue to be published in great profusion, but more and more they tend to be in-house affairs, technical in approach, narrow of focus, esoteric in theme or language. Certainly such shop-talk is necessary among theologians. Still, one wonders if the growing concentration on theology of this nature has not done much to make theology the cultural equivalent of the Dodo bird. The great theological spirits of a generation ago—the Niebuhrs, Maritain, Gilson, Tillich, Barth, Herberg, *et al.*—addressed not only fellow theologians but the Church and the enlightened public generally. Most of these thinkers were both apologists and theological generalists, and they accordingly succeeded in winning at least a hearing in the larger culture. But the failure of the counter-culture theologies of Altizer, Hamilton, and company to win anything more than a negative notoriety for their responses to culture seemed to signal the end of efforts by theological generalists to be culturally responsible and responsive. The works of Harvey Cox, Peter Berger, and James Cone, among Protestants, and those of Michael Novak, Andrew Greeley, and Hans Küng, among Catholics, are certainly responsive to developments in culture, but it seems significant that none of these writers except the European among them, Küng, has attempted anything like a *Systematik*. They seek to address a broad audience, but mostly in particular and pragmatic, as opposed to general and systematic, terms.

The general American pragmatism and the antitheological bias of the American churches may do much to explain these developments. But one wonders increasingly just how pragmatic the current pragmatisms, whose perspectives are so slender and short-term that they conduce to both tunnel vision and myopia, really are. One need only mention Harvey Cox's *The Secular City* to make it clear that even the premier theological minds of an age may come a cropper if they seek to find in the particular and immediate trends of culture the primary manifestations of the will of God. Cox's particularistic pragmatism in *City* should not be blamed, perhaps, for his inability to foresee the ecological and energy crises—no theological generalist foresaw them either—but such inability should at least remind theologians that their main contribution to the improvement of the human situation may consist in the provision of a general critical and constructive perspective rather than in the development of particular analyses and solutions.

These, then, are the main convictions and concerns which have moved me to write a textbook. That theological generalism which came into being with St. Paul's letter to the Romans and which remains very alive in the Europe of Küng, Wolfhart Pannenberg, and Jürgen Moltmann, seems in America to have become a dying art. This book is a modest contribution toward a revival of that art, not on the sophisticated level of the Europeans just named, but rather on a level which speaks to college students, lay theologians, and seminarians.

But if the book is designed to be general, and to be basic, this does not mean it is designed to be bland. It attempts to be, on the contrary, a general survey of the implications of consciously provocative and particularistic definitions of religion and faith. While a serious attempt has been made to make the discussion of issues as comprehensive, consensual, and informed by tradition as possible, my own personal perspective has inevitably defined, and in some cases recast, the theological issues. It seems to me that such personal involvement is essential to the writing of any text which is itself to be a work of theology rather than a work of journalism. Theology is in my view something *done,* not something merely reported or memorized. A theological textbook should therefore take on, as part of its pedagogical job, the task of provoking thought no less than that of providing information. Only as it serves as a springboard for class discussion, and as a treatise whose ideas instructors and students alike can complement and quarrel with, can this book succeed in its main objective, which is to promote the *study* of theology by provoking the *doing* of theology.

Because of these pedagogical concerns I have sought to make the book dialectical rather than catechetical in approach and tone. A catechetical approach I define as one which provides correct or proper answers for pre-given questions. A dialectical approach, on the other hand, is one which approaches possible answers in a way which keeps questions alive. It is important, I think, that beginning students learn the limits of theology as well as its usefulness, and that they learn and have to deal with its persistent questions even as they become acquainted with the perspective(s) it affords for approaching these questions.

Because my text is aimed at beginning students, I have chosen, where the choice had to be made, to err in the direction of oversimplification rather than that of obfuscation. To those whose scholarly palates find some of my generalizations distasteful, I offer apologies in advance. And from those readers who still think I am speaking at points in the unknown tongue, I beg forbearance, tolerance, and an awareness that jaw-breaking words may sometimes be preferable to circuitous and mind-boggling phrases and clauses. Teachers of virtually all disciplines know that what the layman calls jargon the informed person considers a sort of shorthand; I trust, therefore, that teachers who use this book as a text will amplify and clarify some of its more technical terms and definitions in accord with the needs and questions of their students.

To mention fellow teachers is to bring to mind the enormous debts I owe to so many members of the teaching profession: teachers of the past who instructed and inspired me, and colleagues both past and contemporary who have encouraged and put up with me. From both groups, my own teachers and my colleagues in teaching, I have learned much— enough, indeed, to know that many of the things in this book which I would like to ascribe to originality should rather be attributed to a short and deficient memory. Though I have tried to acknowledge my debts via footnotes wherever possible, I am painfully aware that there are many omissions of proper acknowledgment. Long as it is, the list of acknowledgments which follows would be much longer if all such debts were properly recognized.

Though I am in basic agreement with Mark Twain's remark that one should not say "we" unless one is a member of royalty or has a tapeworm, I have nevertheless opted for "we" rather than "I" in the text of the book for two reasons. The first has just been suggested: much that might appear to be my own is in fact not simply my own but a product of long-forgotten conversations, lectures, or readings, and I wish, by the use of "we," to express my sense of indebtedness to these. The second reason is that, in many instances at least, the "we" form constitutes an attempt on my part, and an invitation to the reader, to adopt a standpoint which is more consensual than personal. While I must, and do, accept responsibility for those points at which I fail to reflect consensual viewpoints fairly and adequately, I still feel that the effort to be consensual is important to the theological enterprise. Theology is essentially a community endeavor, I believe, and as such it requires a willingness to empathize and "think in the plural." To the extent that speaking in the plural may encourage such thinking in the plural, it seems to me worthwhile.

                                                            C. D. B.

Acknowledgments

THE DEBTS INCURRED in the preparation and production of this book are almost beyond numbering. Their number, even so, is exceeded greatly by their importance to the completion of the project. In full awareness that gratitude is a totally inadequate way to repay debts of such magnitude, I still would tender it, in lieu of nothing, to the following institutions and persons:

To Wofford College, for an atmosphere conducive to free inquiry and creative pursuits and for a summer grant which greatly facilitated the completion of the manuscript;

To Prentice-Hall, Inc., and especially to Charlie Place, Alice Dworkin, and Frank Hubert of the Prentice-Hall editorial staff, for constant encouragement and invaluable assistance;

To the National Council of the Churches of Christ in the U.S.A., for permission to quote from the Revised Standard Version of the Bible, copyrighted 1946, 1952, © 1971, 1973 by the Division of Christian Education of the NCCC. (Except where otherwise noted, all quotations of Scripture are from the RSV.);

To Piet Hein and his business manager, Bett Quistgaard, for permission to use the brilliantly witty picture-verses called "Grooks" which enliven a number of the book's pages;

To my colleagues in the Department of Religion of Wofford College, John M. Bullard, William W. Mount, and Donald J. Welch, for the collegial congeniality and scholarly stimulation which make the department an exciting place in which to work, think, and write;

To Mrs. Everett (Mildred) Thompson, who constantly exhibits an astounding ability to keep thirty or so "bosses" happy and who made me especially happy by her painstaking typing and her indomitable and often inspiring good humor;

To my talented friend and former student, Rick Miller, whose etching so aptly illustrates the discussion in Chapter VIII of the Fall's consequences;

To my good friends Gene Norris and Donald and Trisha Britt, who read substantial portions of the manuscript and made valuable suggestions for its amendment;

To my valued colleague and friend, Ed Minus, and to dear friends Capers and Nancy Cross, each of whom read much of the manuscript and must be credited with numerous improvements in its clarity and logic.

To colleagues John Bullard, Bill Mount, John Harrington, Jim Keller, Dan Hank, and Edmund Henry for constructive and helpful reactions to portions of the manuscript;

To Mrs. Dallas (Sally) Hutcheson, for helpful comments regarding Chapter I and the project as a whole;

To students and former students Jim Barrett, Robert Cannon, Jimmy Harper, Reggie Rowell, Mark Taylor, and Robert Wisnewski for helpful critiques of portions of the manuscript;

To the thousand or so students who over the past fourteen years have listened and responded to virtually all of the ideas herein, and who have evoked or produced quite a few of them;

To my mother, brothers, and sister, who kindly left unexpressed their wonderment that I would launch a venture of this size;

To my wife, for adding to her innumerable chores those of proofreading, indexing, and typing letters;

And most of all to Sally Cross Barrett, Sandra Cross Barrett, and Robert Christopher Barrett, for being themselves and for putting up with me when I have been too much myself over the past months.

prologue

Christianity:

An Historical Introit

IN THE YEAR 6 B.C., or thereabouts, a child was born to a couple from Nazareth in the Roman province of Palestine. Though tradition characterizes the circumstances of his birth as extraordinary, the child's upbringing in his home town in the subprovince of Galilee seems to have been much like that of most children of the time. Both his circumcision on the eighth day, as required by religious law, and his faithful attendance at synagogue during later years suggest that he was imbued by his parents with a strong sense of loyalty to the traditions of their faith, Judaism.

Despite his devotion to the spirit of Judaism and a profound acquaintance with that faith's scriptures, this young man, whose name was Jeshua, or Jesus, soon found himself in conflict with the guardians of Jewish orthodoxy. Both his brashness—he claimed authority to represent God, even though he was not of the priestly tribe of Levi—and an unorthodox style of living, in which he consorted with sinners and outcasts, alienated him from both religious and political leaders, inciting anger in the former and suspicion and fear in the latter.

After a short (one- to three-year) career marked by continual controversy and mounting conflict, Jesus of Nazareth was tried in a Roman court and executed on a Roman cross. Though some of the charges against him seem to have originated among the religious authorities, the charge of which he was convicted was subversive activity against Rome. That he was executed by the barbaric mode of crucifixion indicates not only that his "crime" was considered particularly heinous but also that his fate was intended to serve as an example to other would-be subversives.

A short time after Jesus' execution something remarkable occurred among the small band of followers who had considered him a prophet. Wretched in their bereavement, they suddenly became joyous. Their

1

new joy, they announced, came from their discovery that Jesus still lived, that he was still in their midst and promised to be with them always. In the power of their sense of his presence and promise, they formed a tight-knit community shaped by their care for one another and by their zeal in debating with the authorities and in enlisting new recruits for their cause.

For most of the next three centuries the fortunes of this group—who soon called themselves Christians because their faith in Jesus' resurrection had convinced them that he was the Christ, or Messiah—ebbed and flowed. Though they were frequently the target of religious ostracism and political persecution, they persevered and their number multiplied rapidly. Finally, in the fourth century, they received political recognition and sanction—first through the Constantinian Edict of Toleration (313), then through the emperor's adoption of Christianity as his own faith and as the favored faith of the empire.

The fortunes of Christianity entered the ascendant just as the fortunes of imperial Rome began to go into eclipse. In 408, when Alaric the Goth pushed his troops to the gates of Rome itself, it was not the emperor (who had discreetly fled) but the Bishop of Rome who met with him to negotiate the fate of the city. It was a mark of the success of the Church's missionary endeavors that Alaric himself was by this time a Christian (albeit an heretical, Arian one) and was willing therefore to hear and heed the Roman pontiff's petitions that the city be spared.

The flight of the emperor before the barbarian invaders and the courage of the Roman bishop in going out to meet them serve as effective symbols of the transition of the Eternal City from the seat of imperial power to that of ecclesiastical authority. The Church replaced the empire as the one strong, unifying force in the Mediterranean world. Constantine had already, in the fourth century, established a second and rival capital—Constantinople—to rule the distant eastern provinces. This led not only to a considerable attrition of Rome's political prestige and prominence but also to actual civil war between the ruling powers—Constantine's sons and their successors—who occupied the two capitals.

Although this state of affairs served in the short term to strengthen the Church's hand as the one universal presence in the empire, over the longer term it was ominous for the Church as well as the State. Theological as well as political differences grew up between the Eastern (Greek-speaking) and the Western (Latin-speaking) churches of Christendom. The controversies incited by these differences led ultimately to the great schism of 1054, which made the one Catholic Church into two—the Roman and the Byzantine (known to westerners today as the Eastern Orthodox Church).

The medieval (literally, "middle-aged") period (1000–1500) was for both the Eastern and Western churches a time of continued growth and consolidation. The missionary strategy of earlier centuries had been one of accommodation. Missioners found pagan tribes attached to local tribal deities and for the most part completely incapable of thinking of God in terms of universality and transcendence. They sought to wean the tribal chieftains and their people away from their native polytheism by substituting for their traditional village deities a local saint, real or mythical, who embodied the virtues and devotion the Christian God demanded. This practice, which accounts in part for the large number of saints' days in the Roman Church's present liturgical calendar, left much work to be done as the great missionary era reached its crest and celebrated its nominal conquest of Europe.

The work required to make pagan converts Christian in more than name was more educational than evangelistic in nature. The successes of the Church's evangelists meant that it now was faced with the great task of civilizing and Christianizing its new communicants. In an image of the time itself, the Church was compared to Noah's Ark; it was said of it that, as with the Ark, the stench on the inside would have been unbearable but for the storm on the outside.

The accomplishment of the medieval Church has been consistently underestimated by many modern historians, largely because, enthralled by the antimedieval prejudices of the Age of Enlightenment, they have chosen to remain ignorant of the immense challenges faced and met by the Church of that day. Consider just some of those challenges: massive, almost universal, illiteracy; wide-ranging and peace-disturbing barbarism and tribalism; recurrent famine and pestilence; and thick, almost impenetrable superstition. Under the circumstances the Church could deservedly be congratulated for simply retaining its unity and viability; in point of fact, it did much more, educating the illiterate through "audio-visual aids" (statuary, stained glass windows, memorable creeds); civilizing the barbarians and establishing the Truce of God* among the tribes; caring and praying for the sick and hungry; and founding monastic schools and universities.

Although the results of such remarkable initiative and energy did not add up to an architectonic masterpiece, as some Catholic romantics would have us believe, they nevertheless were impressive. And had the Church retained the resiliency and powers of accommodation and response shown in the early Middle Ages, it very possibly could have forestalled the next great calamity in its history. The powers of love, understanding, and tolerance that it had used to win the hearts of outsiders unfortunately were not used in dealing with the waywardness of some of its own members. First the Albigensians, Cathari, and Waldensians of Italy and southern France, then the Wycliffites of Britain and the Hussites of Bohemia, and finally the arch rebels Luther and Calvin, all came to feel the Church's scathing and potent wrath. The tragic historical result has been the badly shattered, strife-torn church of subsequent centuries.

The issues that separated, and continue to separate, Protestant from Catholic are discussed later in this book. Although the book mainly describes those features of Christian faith in which all Christians share, it is lamentably true that any accurate description of the total Christian phenomenon would have to include references to conflicts, and even wars, in which Christians have been set against other Christians.

Martin Luther did not envision, nor did he sanction, the chaotic disunity and discord among Christians his Reformation set off. Pope Leo X, had he foreseen the tragic divisions and strivings to which his course of action contributed, surely would have dealt differently with Luther. Perhaps it is only as the Church can begin again—as it did at the begin-

---

*Instituted by the great Cluniac (monastic) reform movement of the tenth and eleventh centuries, the Truce of God restricted the times during which Christians could go into combat to certain days of the week (essentially Monday through Wednesday) and forbade combat of any sort on holy days.

ning of the Christian era and again at the beginning of the medieval period—to focus on and respond to a history larger than its own, that it will come to realize anew that it is one Church called to serve one Lord toward the accomplishment of one aim: the establishment of God's rule on earth.

part one

A
FAITH
AMONG
FAITHS

I. Religion as an Approach to Reality

WHATEVER ELSE IT IS, religion also is the art of putting together a world.[1]

The word "religion" itself implies this. Derived from the Latin root *religo*, meaning "to tie together," the English word indicates a type of relating which conditions the human psyche much as a ligament (a word descended from a kindred Latin term) conditions the body. Just as a ligament joins parts of the human anatomy, so a religion joins the human self to its world and defines the lineaments of the world to which the self is joined.

The principal realities religion ties together to compose a human world are facts and values. When analyzed carefully (a philosopher might say "phenomenologically"), both of these realities are perceived to be constructions of thought. A "fact" is a *representational* thought: it represents, or purports to represent, an actual state of affairs. A "value," on the other hand, is an *interpretive* thought: it assigns positive or negative meaning to a fact or constellation of facts.

One of the writer's major assumptions in this book is that "religion" arrived on the world-scene when animals first gained the capacity to assign values to facts. A related assumption is that the animal named "homo sapiens" arrived on the scene at exactly the same instant. "Religion" and "humanity" are thus the products of a single origin; both were born with the advent of the valuing process.[2]

The startling idea that humanity and religion have been united since birth seems to have occurred long ago to an ancient storyteller and mythmaker.* The story that records his insight is found in the book of

---

*Myth, as we shall define and use the term in this book, does not mean a fiction or fantasy but rather a story that tries to convey, in concrete human terms, a sense of divine (infinite and transcendent) reality. Because human language and the human imagination

9

Genesis, Chapter Three. Here we are told that the Lord God, having made a special creature to watch over the rest of creation for him, imposed only one limit on that creature: that he or she should not eat of "the tree of the knowledge of good and evil."

Perhaps the best analysis of this story yet made is that of Paul Tillich.[3] Tillich argued that the story should not be read as a literal account of an episode in the life of the first human couple. It rather should be interpreted as an attempt to explore and illuminate a crucial occurrence in the life of each individual human being.[4] Tillich characterized this occurrence as the "loss of dreaming innocence."

Each of us, Tillich contended, passes through an age of innocence. During this phase of our development our humanness, though real, is not complete, for we have not yet actualized one capacity which is essential to full humanity—the capacity to accept responsibility, in a complete and self-conscious way, for our own situation.

This state of proto-human existence Tillich dubbed "dreaming innocence." It is that period in our lives when we live in a kind of dream, protected both from life's harsh realities (the "facts" of our situation) and from the necessity to take responsibility for (to place a "value" on) these realities. We have not yet eaten, as it were, from "the tree of the knowledge of good and evil," so we have become neither self-conscious (that is, aware of our own "nakedness"—see Gen. 3:7) nor conscious of our eminent vulnerability, and responsibility, within an alien, nonhuman environment (an environment that gives us bread only "in the sweat of our brow"—Gen. 3:19).

The stage in actual human development that best accords with Tillich's age of dreaming innocence is that of adolescence. At this juncture in life, the youth experiences uneasiness about his or her personal status in the order of things. He vacillates between being sick of home and being homesick, with home generally winning only because it offers a harbor for an occasional, much-needed rest from psychic turbulence.

At last there comes a time when the youth must break away. The moment may come quietly with a succession of not unexpected events (graduation, the beginning of a career) or cataclysmically (pregnancy out of wedlock, the death of a parent on whom one was financially or emotionally dependent). In either case the self comes to a position of self-reliance and accountability (a fullness of humanity or "adulthood") not previously experienced.

---

itself are finite, and because myths, whatever their ultimate source, are restricted to the terms of human language and imagination, the task myths try to accomplish is in a sense impossible. But, as we shall see, great myths continue to fascinate human beings and, in ways not totally understood, continue to instruct and excite their minds.

With the arrival of independence and accountability, not only the self but also its situation changes. The world itself takes on a different aspect. The self must now decide not only what to do with itself but also what to make of its situation. Both responsibilities require that it begin the lifelong job of evaluating realities. The very birth into adulthood imposes on the individual what we earlier defined as the essentially religious task of putting a world together, of relating facts to values in a comprehensive and life-supportive way.

Most of this relating goes on subconsciously. Religion is, in the first instance, a *primary* mode of relating to reality. As such it is characterized by immediacy, spontaneity, and responsive creativity. In other words, it is more a matter of making do and coping than of thinking through and planning.[5] It may thus be as much a matter of "things I learned at my Mother's knee and other joints" as of things learned by conscious intent and endeavor.

Religion functions on another level as well, and we do not intend to deny or demean the position of those who view religion as a matter of self-conscious discipline and intentional activity. It appears, however, that religion on that level is a *secondary* phenomenon which appeared on the human scene at a much later time than did that religion which is as old as our humanity.

Cutting through these different levels of religion is an important common quality. Whether religion is understood as an immediate relationship to reality or as a mediated and consciously chosen relationship to it, it has to do in any case with who and how we are—that is, with the very self-concept and life style that motivate and direct us as we live. It is this quality in religion, its closeness to home and our corresponding psychic dependence on it, that produces problems for those who study religion academically. You, O Reader of This Book, are presumably such a student. Yet you may not feel at all ready for what you are setting out to do. Religion may be so much a matter of your own immediacy, of your own identity or intended life style, that to study it seems to you as hard, perhaps even as threatening, as a pilgrimage into psychoanalysis.

Let us begin, then, by facing this problem as frankly and directly as possible. Let us begin by recognizing that the process of thinking through ("studying") the perspectives and processes by which we make do and cope has it dangers. It is, indeed, hard to use a hammer while focusing on it instead of the nail, and it may be equally hard to *remain* religious while *studying* religion.[6] "Studying" after all implies a willingness to take what Martin Heidegger called a "step backward" (*Schritt zurück*), a temporary and purposive suspension of one's immediate commitment to what is to be studied. But can we really afford such a step where religion is concerned? Can we really afford to "step back"

and look analytically at the very faith which is the fiber of our being—
which, that is, holds reality together for us?

Occasionally one encounters persons for whom such a step into study
is not to be recommended. The greater danger, however, appears to lie
in the other direction. Analytical, even critical testing of faith's fiber
seems to be conducive to a healthier, fuller faith and the absence of such
testing to a thoughtless, flabby contentment with parental and peer
conditioning, or with trying to live the faith of others after them.

That a religious commitment can in fact thrive as a result of self-
examination should not surprise us, especially if we have taken seriously our earlier correlation of religion with humanity. They were born
simultaneously, we noted, with the advent of the valuing process.
Should it surprise us, then, to find that our human tendency to question
and to probe may be an ally and not an enemy of our religious tendency
to relate and to evaluate? Questioning, to be sure, may have certain
dissolvent effects, but are these effects not necessary (*pace* Unamuno)[7] to
any unity that corresponds to the vitality and vibrancy of reality? To take
a biblical example: Should Jesus have left the faith of Nicodemus un-
questioned,[8] simply so that the latter's comfort and complacency might
go undisturbed? Indeed, does the breakthrough from dreaming innocence itself not imply the rupture of a certain womb-like faith, a "being
born again" into a human identity and a religious commitment that are
distinctively our own—made so, in part at least, by the birth-pangs of
intellectual questioning and existential doubt?

That the writing of a book such as this is undertaken at all indicates
that the writer has come to a particular resolution of questions like these.
It is our assumption that a serious study of religion may in fact enrich
and enliven faith; at the very least, it should broaden and challenge it,
posing for it questions which reside in the essentially religious nature of
human existence. But at no point should such a study try either to
impose a faith or to pose as a faith. Its task is far more humble—namely,
the fostering and enhancing of human understanding.

WHAT RELIGION IS NOT

Definition involves a process of elimination. To determine what a thing
is, I must determine what it is not. If I am to define a common house
key, for example, I must recognize that it is not a lock even as I recognize
that its positive definition depends on the existence of a lock. So with
religion. We have noted that religion is not to be equated with the study
of religion. But neither is religion to be identified with a great many
other human activities. How is religion distinguished from these other
activities?

I'D LIKE –

I'd like to know
what this whole show
is all about
before it's out.

From Grooks *by Piet Hein. Copyright 1966 by the author.*
Used by permission of Mr. Hein.

Let us begin by simplifying the task. Let us note that human activities (at least as they are classified in the Western tradition) generally fall into two types or classes: *arts* (inclusive of all types of *practical* activity) and *sciences* (embracing all forms of *theoretical* activity).[9] In what follows we shall argue that religion is best defined as an art, and that it is accordingly to be distinguished both from the sciences in general and from the one science which most resembles it, philosophy.

Religion Is Not a Science

Religion is not a science primarily because it is a practical activity, whereas the activities of science are primarily theoretical. But just what is a practical activity, and how is it to be distinguished from a theoretical one?

Let us begin by admitting that theoretical activities can be eminently practical in terms of their long-range effects. Some years ago the Soviet Union penetrated outer space well ahead of the United States by concentrating on the practicalities of developing a rocket technology. In the process, however, Soviet scientists neglected the study of theoretical mathematics, and, because such abstract studies proved essential to *computer* technology, the U.S.S.R. eventually lost the race to the moon.

Theoretical activities, it is obvious, can have practical effects. But such effects are really accidental, and not intentional, results of such activities. The first distinction that we may draw, therefore, between religion as a practical activity and science as a theoretical one is that religion is directly tied to practical questions of human well-being (let us call them *value* questions), whereas science is mainly concerned with more abstract questions of pure truth (*fact* questions). Science may determine, *quâ* science, that the *facts* of atomic physics make atomic fission possible; it cannot, however, within the bounds of its own work, make the *value* judgment that atomic fission should be utilized for the good of humankind. To make such a judgment is to make a step toward, if not into, religion.[10]

The basic distinction between the practical cast of religion and the theoretical interest of science leads to further important differences between them. For example, because it pursues the truth *for its own sake*, science must assume a stance of impartiality and objectivity in all it undertakes. But because it seeks to use truth *for the sake of human beings*, religion must evoke passionate commitment and personal, subjective involvement from its adherents. Moreover, because what is true in and for its own sake must be *universally* true—must, in other words, be essentially replicable in all times and places, given the same empirical conditions[11]—science must tend to disallow the significance (if not the reality itself) of the uniquely personal and occasionally eccentric experiences on which the religious sensibilities thrive.

Religion and science differ no less in their *methods* than in their operational attitudes or presuppositions. Science's method is schematic and self-conscious. It follows a standard protocol or procedural scheme: hypothesis—design and performance of experiments to test hypothesis —observation of experimental results—confirmation or modification of hypothesis. By contrast, religion's style of operation (the closest thing it has to a method) is informal, unstructured, personal, and existential. Although its "method" may involve thought (even self-conscious thought), such thought can never be divorced from the feelings and involvements of the total self, but rather is an extension of them. Its thought thus becomes something in the nature of a prayer, an act of prayerful contemplation, or an elaboration or critical examination of convictions.[12]

Religion and science differ also in their *languages*. The language of science is neat, hard, precise, abstract, and syntactic. Its intention is to state as clearly and precisely as possible the conclusions reached by processes of scientific analysis and synthesis. For that reason science is in large part mathematical and statistical, for these forms of language lend themselves more readily than verbal forms do to precision of expression.

The aim of religious language, by contrast, is not precision so much as incision. It is designed not so much to describe the hard surfaces of reality as to penetrate those surfaces in search of significance within and beyond them. Religious language therefore tends to be symbolic, emotive, paratactic, mosaic, and confessional—terms whose meanings are sufficiently distant from our ordinary language to make a closer look at them advisable.

Religious language is first of all *symbolic*. Poetry, metaphor, and myth are its milieu. This is true mainly because religion functions as the conveyor of reality's inherent relationality to the human psyche. To accomplish this, religion must depend not so much on precise, unitary words as on congeries or congregations of words, themselves related in such a way that their total meaning is more than the sum of their particular meanings considered separately. Words so arranged (or ideas, images, objects, or events so arranged) comprise *symbols*. According to N. O. Brown,

> Symbolism is mind making connections (correspondences) rather than distinctions (separations). Symbolism makes conscious interconnections and unions that were unconscious and repressed.... symbolism is on the track of... a lost unity: the lost continent, Atlantis, underneath the sea of life in which we live enisled ... the unity of the whole cosmos as one living creature, as Plato said in the *Timaeus*. [13]

As Brown's definition suggests, religious symbolism's impact on the self is generally emotive. The Latin root of the words *emotive* and *emotional* is a composite term meaning "to move out." In saying that religious language is emotive, therefore, we mean to indicate that it in some way moves us out of ourselves into a larger reality. Far from locking us up in some inner world of feeling, faith's symbols evoke emotions which open doors for us and usher us into dimensions of reality we had not encountered before. The feelings that accompany such moments of opening and entering are quite powerful, but, despite their power to attract attention to themselves, they should be understood as indicators of reality's impact on us, not as experiences to be sought in and for themselves.

Because religious language is so rich a mixture of concrete symbolism and induced emotion, it has well been described as *paratactic* in form. [14] The word "paratactic" opposes in meaning the word "syntactic." "Syntactic" language, which is our legacy from Greek science and philosophy, is the sort of straightforward, logical language one encounters in daily newpapers and popular magazines and books. It may be described as "chain" language: its sentences and paragraphs serve as links connecting each other to a common topic or theme. In contrast to syntactic language, paratactic language leaves a great many transitions or connections unmade. Its gifts to the mind are not well-forged chains but collections of beads that require stringing by an alerted imagination.

The distinction between syntactic and paratactic forms of language may be illustrated by comparing the teaching tactics of the two premier instructors of the Western mind: Plato and Jesus. Most of Plato's works were written in the form of dialogues between Plato's own teacher, Socrates, and some of Socrates' pupils. These dialogues are filled with wit and irony, but if one does not permit these qualities to distract or confuse (for example, by taking Socrates' witticisms literally), one will be struck by two other things as well: first, that the dialogues are lengthy, and second, that they follow a continuing though sometimes tenuous thread of connecting ideas on a unifying theme.

The teachings of Jesus contained in the synoptic gospels* are strikingly different in form from those of Plato. There is no extended dialogue and no thread of transitions from one of the teacher's pronouncements to the next. Each pronouncement stands as a brief, independent unit, and frequently the unit closes with a question (*Which man was neighbor to the man who fell among thieves?* [15] *Which of you, if his child asks him for bread, will give him a stone?* [16]). Quite clearly the teacher seeks, through such staccato speaking and questioning, to throw the pupil off balance, to force him or her to view matters from new angles and put things together in new ways. The *paratactic* (broken, unconnected) form of the language thus has a clear purpose: to involve the pupil himself or herself in the learning-relating process which constitutes an authentic tying-together or religion.

The *symbolic* language of religion is porous, *paratactic,* so that it can be *emotive,* forcing the human spirit to move out into new ways of relating to reality. Religious teachers do not say all that could be said, precisely so that their pupils may be drawn into the essentially religious act of putting things together for themselves. The watchword of religious teachers could thus be a word of Jesus': "Let those who have ears to hear, hear . . . ."[17]

For those who do hear the language of religion, its symbolism is in fact not incoherent, despite its paratactic quality. The religious view of reality and the language that conveys it form for the religious person a kind of *mosaic* or tapestry. Individual elements (symbols, parables, hymns, rituals, creeds, and so on) may seem to lack meaning when standing alone, but when tied with other elements and with the realities represented by the various elements they take on body, life, and significance.

---

*The synoptic gospels are Matthew, Mark, and Luke. The term "synoptic" comes from a Greek verb meaning "to see together." Its application to these gospels indicates that they are quite similar in their vision and interpretation of the career of Jesus.

The result is often a replacement of piecemeal perceptions of life by a new, wholistic perception in the power of which even menial tasks and experiences become charged with meaning.[18]

In the end, precisely because it is symbolic, emotive, paratactic, and mosaic, and because these qualities enable it to affect the entire self, religious language is concretely *confessional*. It issues from the heart, from the whole being, not merely from the cerebrum. It is the expression or confession ("testimony") of a concrete or corporate person[19] whose life has been struck by faith's symbols and moved out of itself into a newly constructed perspective on reality. Perhaps no words better fit this experience than those of St. John's blind man made well: "I used to be blind; now I can see!"[20]

Religion is not science. It is not science because science is fact focused, and religion is value focused; because science is impersonal in mood, and religion is personal; because science builds on universal (reproducible) evidence, and religion, as often as not, on unique experiences; and because science's language is abstract, objective, syntactic, theoretical, and cerebral, while religion's is symbolic, emotive, paratactic, mosaic, and confessional.

Religion Is Not Philosophy

Despite its obvious differences from science, religion is frequently confused (or even fused) in popular thought with one particular science—the queen mother of the sciences, philosophy.

Such confusion or fusion is understandable. Historically, Western philosophy evolved from religion,[21] and substantively the two share many of the same concerns. Even so, religion and philosophy are distinctive ways of relating to reality, and religion ought not be equated with or reduced to philosophy.

If religion may be called the art of putting a world together, philosophy may be deemed a *science* that seeks to do the same.[22] Though similar in function and objective, the two are conspicuously different in their modes and categories of operation. Religion, like all of the arts, is practical, while philosophy, like all of the sciences, is largely theoretical. The truth (fact) question is paramount for philosophy, and the purpose (value) question is primary in religion. Although both are synthetic in aim, the main aim of the religious synthesis is living the good life, while that of the philosophic system is discovering and demonstrating the real (the whole) truth.

The tendency to equate religion with philosophy has a natural source in the common heritage of the two. As the name (*philein*, to love, plus *sophia*, wisdom) implies, philosophy originated in a love affair between thinkers and their thoughts.[23] The thoughts of the first philosophers were so intoxicating and absorbing that some of them came to view their thoughts as supreme realities and pursued their discovery with religious fervor. Plato (like Pythagoras before him) could therefore require a kind of monastic discipline of those who desired to join him in pursuing wisdom.

Early (especially Platonic) philosophy was a kind of intellectual religion.[24] Its aim was the salvation of the mind through its reunion with the eternal ideas in which its fulfillment lay. As the mind was drawn out (e-ducated*) by its contact with such ideas, it became fit to inhabit that eternal realm to which the ideas themselves belonged.

Classical philosophy was thus closely allied with religion.[25] But as Nietzsche and others[26] have demonstrated, that alliance meant a transfiguration and truncation of primordial religious impulses. Under philosophy's aegis human life came more and more to be identified with the life of thought, and the words "man" and "mind" came to be equated.[27] As far as the larger world was concerned, those things which were reproducible in thought were deemed most real, and those which were intractable to thought (for example, historical events) or transcended its universal forms (for example, the ecstatic visions of poets or prophets) were held to be less so, if indeed they were deemed real at all.

Classical philosophy thus transformed religion by reducing it to theoretical, or mentally digestible, proportions. But in the process it eviscerated, emasculated, and all but embalmed it. This is the danger that always attends liaisons between philosophy and religion: the philosopher is strongly tempted to confuse the electrocardiogram with the heartbeat itself and to substitute mind-pleasing theories for life-enhancing therapies. Thus, although philosophy can be a powerful and effective adjunct to religion, it generally makes a poor substitute for it.

WHAT RELIGION IS

Religion is not science, and it is not philosophy; on the other hand, it *is* an art of some kind. These are the generalizations we have so far made about its nature. We must now ask what it means to call religion an "art," and what its more positive relationships to science and philosophy are.

Essentially, as we have seen, religion means relationship. It means involvement in and with the entire ecosystem. The insight of modern

---

*From the Latin roots *e* or *ex*, meaning "out of," "from," and *ducere*, "to draw" or "to lead." See "Religions Born of Reason" in Chapter II.

physics, that each of us is related to and affected by both the universe's smallest subatomic particle and its largest heavenly body, merely echoes a sense of reality's togetherness which has long been celebrated in religious rituals.[28]

Such a view of religion scarcely seems to fit a description of it as an art. Art is commonly conceived to be a form of conscious and deliberate activity, and when religion is understood as a mode of primal, preconscious relationship it hardly seems compatible with the artistic enterprise. This observation has led some—notably the late great Friedrich Schleiermacher[29]—to distinguish religion from the arts no less than from the sciences. Religion, in Schleiermacher's view, is born of our human receptivity rather than our activity. It is a "sense of absolute dependence" and belongs, therefore, to a sphere transcending both art and science, since both of the latter describe modes of human activity in which, far from being totally dependent (receptive and determined), humans are at least relatively independent (free to modify their environment).

To a point our understanding of religion accords with that of Schleiermacher. Religion is indeed a product of a sense of absolute dependence. But against Schleiermacher we would argue that the self who receives this sense is not passive or inert in receiving it but actively involved, reciprocally related in some way, with the sense's ultimate Source. As a result, the sensing of a prior togetherness with the universe comes across as also a positive act of putting things together.

It may seem pretentious, and to some even heretical, to say that we human beings have a hand in putting together the universe. But we would argue that, on one level at least, we do precisely that. For though we *inherit* a universe of being, we actively participate in fashioning our own personal universes of meaning. It is our contention here that religion includes participation in *both* universes. For, as Teilhard de Chardin maintained, "Man, the centre of perspective, is at the same time the *centre of construction* of the universe."[30]

What we intend here may be clarified by the experience of working artists and other creative persons. Such people report that they sometimes feel themselves to be mere instruments of the visions and perceptions that take form through their work. At the same time they maintain that they never seem more alive, more active, or more genuinely themselves, than when they are the captive instruments of such moments of inspiration. Somehow, through such moments, a sensed togetherness becomes a projected and thus a communicated (and thus a somewhat modified!) togetherness.

The sense of all-togetherness and the art of putting a world together appear to be inseparable but distinguishable moments or elements

SIMPLY ASSISTING GOD

I am a humble artist
moulding my earthly clod,
adding my labour to nature's,
simply assisting God.

Not that my effort is needed;
yet somehow, I understand,
my maker has willed it that I too should have
unmoulded clay in my hand.

From Grooks *by Piet Hein. Copyright 1966 by the author.*
Used by permission of Mr. Hein.

within the religious phenomenon. Moses found in the burning bush not an object separate from and alien to him but a project that reached out to him, kindled his conscience, and led him into active involvement in the affairs and fortunes of his long-neglected people.[31] His new religious awareness (his new sense of relatedness to his fellow Israelites) produced his sense of duty ("Go down, Moses... Tell Pharaoh to let my people go"); the sense of the togetherness of things led to a daring effort to put them together differently.

If we say religion is an art, we do so because it expresses the sort of creative responses to, and projections of, reality that are characteristic of the arts. But we also must recognize that religion has a distinctive place among the arts. It might best be called a primal art, an art indigenous to human life as such, as contrasted with the learned or acquired arts. Religion, like the arts generally, is practical, not theoretical; it survives and thrives only as a project to be lived and languishes when made a mere object of thought or of passive enjoyment.[32] At the same time religion stands on the frontier of the arts: it depends not so much on human creativity as on receptivity and openness to the universe. It is precisely these qualities which make it so profound and prolific a source of artistic vision and inspiration.

Religion and Science

Religion as Schleiermacher perceived it could scarcely converse with natural science, let alone conflict with it. It belonged to a sphere of reality beyond that of scientific interest and investigation. Religion as we have described it belongs no less than science to the sphere of human activities. Have we not, therefore, reopened the possibility of head-on conflict between science and religion?

The answer to that question must be a qualified "yes." We have indeed opened the possibility of such a conflict even as we have shown how unnecessary it is. Conflict between science and religion is possible because both are modes of human activity; but such conflict is not necessary because these modes of activity are, as we indicated above, so markedly different in aim and method. True, the celebrated Scopes trial[33] brought to a climax a history of controversy between faith's defenders and fact's pursuers which was perhaps inevitable, given the degrees of passion and illiteracy on both sides. But this inevitability can be traced to the intensity of feeling and the narrowness of vision in the participants themselves, not to anything inherent in the nature of religion *quâ* religion or science *quâ* science. Had people on the two sides understood the true proportions of religion and science, the debate would have lost much of its heat and acrimony and might have become an occasion on which each side could have learned something from the other.

That conflict between science and religion is not necessary but may nevertheless occur is clear from the fact that some of our planet's religions seem to favor and even to promote science, whereas others are antiscientific. An incident of the 1950s illustrates this. A group of Western scientists working at that time on a polio vaccine found, in a remote province of India, a certain species of Rhesus monkey which proved useful in their experiments. Their efforts to capture these monkeys were interrupted when the people of the province learned that the monkeys were being captured not to be revered but rather to be killed. The popular uproar that followed this discovery eventually led the provincial government to prohibit the scientists' efforts to capture more monkeys.

The actions of the Western researchers on the one hand and of the Indian provincials on the other reflect ethical attitudes traceable to sharply different religious perspectives. Schooled in the biblical notions that God transcends the natural order and that he places humans in charge of the subhuman world, Western scientists look on nature as fair game in the effort to improve the human prospect. The Hindu perspective of their Indian counterparts, on the other hand, extols the sanctity of nature and sees the Rhesus monkey, among other animals, as a repository of ancestral spirits. One view obviously sees science as divinely permitted (if not indeed mandated) while the other sees it as a virtual act of sacrilege.

In practice, then, it appears that religion may be either science's antagonist or its ally. Despite their involvement in occasional heated controversies—especially those surrounding the names and theories of Copernicus, Galileo, and Darwin—the religions of the West (Judaism and Christianity) have on the whole been pro-science in attitude and effect. Even in its conflicts with Copernicus and Galileo, the Christian establishment acted not from antiscientific motives but rather from the standpoint of a different and older science. Science had been so accepted by Christian scholars and so thoroughly harmonized with the Christian revelation that it had assumed an aura of sanctity of its own. But its support among Christian thinkers came more from their appreciation for Aristotelian common sense than from their religious principles.[34]

The Darwinian controversy came at a time when the scientific establishment itself was neither so Christian nor so monolithic as the established science of the Middle Ages had been. Nevertheless that controversy, like those of the medieval era, did not pit religion against science but rather an older science, which had been harmonized with traditional religion, against a newer one, which had not. The real issue was between a Newtonian world view, which both deistic and orthodox Christians found acceptable, and a Darwinian perspective, which seemed to undermine the sense of cosmic design that Newton himself had not only accepted but preached.[35]

The point at which each of these great controversies came closest to being an outright conflict between science and religion was in the popular perceptions of them. For those Christians who perceived Genesis as a scientific account of the world's origin and composition, and for those popularizers of science who saw the works of Copernicus, Galileo, and Darwin as religious testaments, the conflicts probably seemed necessary and unavoidable. To such champions of religion, Genesis and other religious documents answered not only the religious questions whence, why, and whither but also the scientific queries when, where, and how. For such camp followers of science, science's success in answering its questions had reduced to virtual irrelevance the questions of religion.

Our analysis of the essential and operational differences between science and religion suggests, however, that the entire controversy between the two proceeds from false assumptions. Religious persons who are threatened by science may perceive science as a rival to religion in dealing with value questions. Insofar as science has in fact become such a rival, their apprehensions are justified; but they should recognize in such instances that what they are threatened by is no longer science but actually a rival (and probably a specious) religion. On the other hand, scientific persons who are repelled by religion may well be so because religion purports to answer the fact questions that interest science. To the extent that a given religion does this, their reaction is quite proper; but they should recognize that what they actually are dealing with is not religion properly so-named, but rather a pseudoscience.

If religion and science do not in fact speak to the same questions and if they do not therefore *have to* come into conflict, neither is it *necessary* that they avoid conversation with each other. The religions of the West and the sciences born in the West owe much to each other. Historically, Western science owes a great debt to the Western religions, for the latter, with their idea that God exists beyond nature, not *in* it or *as* it, have left nature open to scientific perusal and exploration. Materially, religion must constantly be indebted to science, for the latter frequently uncovers facts which are useful in implementing the values religion promulgates.

Far from being contradictory, religion and science may well be complementary in function. Religion may give science room to breathe by creating in the popular mind a world view and value system which

FRANK AND ERNEST   by Bob Thaves

Reprinted by permission of Newspaper Enterprise Association (NEA).

SEPARATING ONESELF FROM RELIGION OR RELIGIOUS PRESUPPOSITIONS MAY BE MORE DIFFICULT THAN PEOPLE SOMETIMES ASSUME IT TO BE.

support scientific endeavors, and science may supply religion important insights and implements with which to serve its ideals.

Religion and Philosophy

Philosophy, as we have seen, is that science which most nearly approaches religion in objective. Having looked earlier at qualities which distinguish the two, let us now consider what positive relationships connect them.

Though devoted to a common objective—the creation of, and habitation in, universes of meaning which harmonize with the real universe—religion and philosophy approach that objective differently, as we have seen. But both their common purpose and their different methods can and should make them allies and not antagonists.

Religion can contribute to philosophy its own depth of involvement in life. That primordial condition of relatedness from which religion obtains its name was for many centuries the main staple in Western philosophy's diet. Classical and medieval philosophy were completely focused on the religious arts of living (or being) and dying. Religion has contributed, and still can contribute, a profundity of subject matter to philosophy which the latter can expect to find nowhere else.

Religion's aim is life, life enriched and enhanced, and philosophy's aim is the truth about life. Therefore, as religion can offer philosophy, for its study, concrete lives as they are lived, so philosophy can offer religion avenues to the truth about itself. Philosophy can thus elucidate or clarify religion even as religion informs or inspires philosophy. To paraphrase a famous dictum of Immanuel Kant's: Philosophy without religion is shallow; religion without philosophy is blind.

Most college students find the philosophical approach to religion a new venture. Whatever has been learned about religion to this point has been learned by rote, hearsay (the bull sessions at camp or on campus), ritualistic routine, or diluted reports in the popular press. Clearly reasoned analysis has not been applied to religious ideas and activities; indeed, many have been schooled by parents and others to think that such analysis in matters of religion borders on sacrilege. As we noted above, such fears of a liaison between philosophy and religion are not altogether groundless. But too radical a separation of the two may constitute an even graver danger. Life itself is all of a piece, and when thinking head and believing heart do not converse, the result can be spiritual schizophrenia. The course we propose to take in this book, therefore, is one which applies a philosophic method (analytical thought) to a religious subject matter. Such an approach should afford us not only a degree of academic objectivity but also an opportunity to indicate that faith can be simultaneously full bodied and clear sighted.

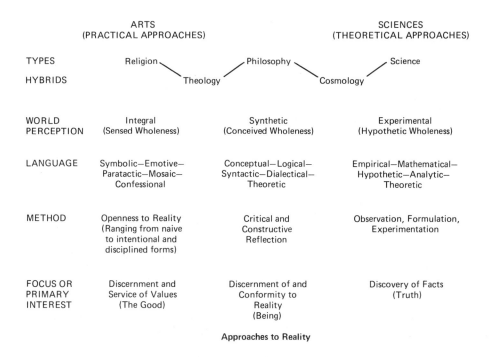

	ARTS (PRACTICAL APPROACHES)		SCIENCES (THEORETICAL APPROACHES)
TYPES	Religion	Philosophy	Science
HYBRIDS	Theology	Cosmology	
WORLD PERCEPTION	Integral (Sensed Wholeness)	Synthetic (Conceived Wholeness)	Experimental (Hypothetic Wholeness)
LANGUAGE	Symbolic—Emotive— Paratactic—Mosaic— Confessional	Conceptual—Logical— Syntactic—Dialectical— Theoretic	Empirical—Mathematical— Hypothetic—Analytic— Theoretic
METHOD	Openness to Reality (Ranging from naive to intentional and disciplined forms)	Critical and Constructive Reflection	Observation, Formulation, Experimentation
FOCUS OR PRIMARY INTEREST	Discernment and Service of Values (The Good)	Discernment of and Conformity to Reality (Being)	Discovery of Facts (Truth)

Approaches to Reality

QUESTIONS TO GUIDE STUDY AND DISCUSSION

At the conclusion of each chapter in this book you will find questions designed to help you organize and think about the chapter's main themes. Concisely developed answers to these questions should provide you with a brief outline of each chapter's main ideas, an outline which may prove useful in class discussions or for later study and review.

1. On what basis can it be argued that "religion" and "humanity" are the products of a single origin and that, therefore, where you find one you will always find the other? On what grounds might this argument be disputed?

2. What does it mean to say that religion is a "primary" (as opposed to a "secondary" or "mediated") way of relating to reality?

3. Why is it difficult to *study* religion? Are there other reasons, besides that mentioned in the text, that religion is difficult to study? Explain.

4. How does an "art" differ from a "science"? Why is religion better called an art than a science?

5. In what ways are religion and philosophy alike? In what ways are they different? Do you agree with the writer that religion and philosophy may enrich each other and that together they may provide a more comprehensive understanding of life? Why or why not?

6. What relationship should pertain between religion and science? What have been the major causes of conflict between them?

7. What can religion offer philosophy? What can philosophy contribute to the quest for an authentic religious faith?

NOTES TO CHAPTER I

1. It is of course far more, though for our purposes it suffices to describe it in the terms used here. For further, far more elaborate discussions of religion's nature see the works by Eliade, Otto, Söderblom, and Van der Leeuw in the Selected Bibliography.

2. That religion and values are concurrent or concomitant in their emergence does not mean that they are identical. It is our assumption in what follows that religion is the source of values and not vice versa, though values do comprise religion's "evidence" or "footprints." This judgment follows from the ontological observation that human beings *relate*, or stand in a condition of relatedness, before they *evaluate*. This relatedness makes human beings potentially religious before the establishment of the relationship between facts and values makes them actually religious. Religion as potency (or potential religion) thus precedes the valuing act, which is the act by which religion becomes actual.

3. A German thinker who was forced into exile by Adolf Hitler, Tillich became America's most renowned theologian while teaching at Union Theological Seminary, Harvard University, and the University of Chicago. He developed the idea of dreaming innocence in Volume II of his *Systematic Theology* (Chicago: University of Chicago Press, 1957), pp. 33–36.

4. The story is what Tillich called a "symbol," in that it emerges from and illuminates human experience across cultural and generational lines.

5. This is where some pejorative definitions of religion—for example, Harvey Cox's in *The Secular City*, rev. ed. (New York: The Macmillan Company, 1966)—fail to read the nature of religion correctly. Cox identifies religion with the development of a closed metaphysical system or world view. In later writings (*The Feast of Fools, The Seduction of the Spirit*) Cox himself acknowledges the fallacies in so limited a definition.

6. This is a point that was made with particular force by such existentialist writers as Dostoyevsky, Nietzsche, and Kierkegaard. Perhaps the most sustained single statement of it is in Miguel de Unamuno's *The Tragic Sense of Life*, a fierce denunciation of what Unamuno called "the dissolvent effects" of all rational treatments of religion.

7. See note 6.

8. The Gospel according to St. John, chapter 3.

9. We have here chosen to follow the European rather than the American understanding of the term "science." In the German use, for example, even the humanities are deemed to be "sciences," albeit of culture rather than of nature. In the European use, "science" obviously retains its older generic meaning of *knowledge*, whereas in America it is identified with a particular *method* by which knowledge is sought.

10. It is in any case a step into the *art* of ethical judgment, a type of activity which can never reach the degree of certainty possible to the natural sciences.

11. This is one of the fundamental tenets in what may be called the *faith* of scientists; for it is true that science, no less than religion, rests on a faith. The chief difference between these faiths appears to be that science's faith rests on certain fundamental intellectual axioms, whereas religious faith is born of certain innate proclivities and life-shaping experiences.

12. This "religious" thought may take many directions and entail many types of mental activity: the quakings of a guilt-ridden conscience, the affirmations of a faith stance (in creeds or sermons), and the thought which seeks to explicate faith in rational terms (in theology) are but a few examples.

13. *Love's Body* (New York: Random House, Inc., 1966), pp. 81–82. Copyright © 1966 by Norman O. Brown. It is religion's habit of "making connections," according to R. G. Collingwood, that clearly distinguishes (but should not separate) it from science: "A person who sees that the whole of life, regarded as a whole, is the sphere of religion, and that the same whole, regarded as made up of details, is the sphere of science, must see that it is possible to be religious without ceasing to be genuinely scientific and scientific without ceasing to be genuinely religious." Copyright © 1968 by Lionel Rubinoff. Reprinted by permission of TIMES BOOKS, a division of Quadrangle/The New York Times Book Co., Inc. from R. G. Collingwood: *Faith and Reason*, edited by Lionel Rubinoff, p. 145.

14. Cf. Erich Auerbach, *Mimesis: The Representation of Reality in Western Literature*, trans. W. R. Trask (Princeton, N. J.: Princeton University Press, 1953), chaps. 1, 5, and 12.

15. Luke 10:36.

16. Matthew 7:9; compare Luke 11:11.

17. Matthew 11:15, 13:9, 43; Mark 4:9, 23; 7:16; Luke 8:8, 14:35.

18. Nowhere is this sense of the meaningfulness of life in even its most menial aspects more clearly expressed than in a book of meditation composed by Brother Lawrence, a seventeenth-century lay monk of the Carmelite order. In this book, entitled *The Practice of the Presence of God*, Br. Lawrence tells how he learned through his work as a monastery kitchen helper that it can be a significant religious experience simply to "pick up a straw to the glory of God."

19. A "corporate person" is a social-religious community united by common values and a common (covenant) loyalty to its deity and self-depicted (in its folklore, literature, and so on) in terms analogous to those commonly used in speaking of individual persons. Although the most fully developed ancient example appears to have been the self-concept of the early Israelites (cf. H. Wheeler Robinson, *Corporate Personality in Ancient Israel* [Philadelphia: The Fortress Press, 1964], especially pp. 1–20), the idea has been used in contexts as far removed as that of Plato's *Republic* (in which he views the state as a kind of person "writ large") and that of contemporary America, which personifies itself as Uncle Sam.

20. John 9:25. The translation used here is that of J. B. Phillips, *The New Testament in Modern English*, revised edition. Copyright © J. B. Phillips, 1958, 1960, 1972. Used by permission of Macmillan Publishing Co., Inc. and Collins Publishers.

21. See F. M. Cornford, *From Religion to Philosophy: A Study in the Origins of Western Speculation* (New York: Harper & Brothers, Publishers, 1957); and H. Frankfort and others, *Before Philosophy* (Chicago: University of Chicago Press, 1946).

22. Our point here is amplified beautifully by Teilhard de Chardin: "Like the meridians as they approach the poles, science, philosophy and religion are bound to converge as they draw nearer to the whole." B. Wall, trans., *The Phenomenon of Man*, p. 30. English translation copyright © 1959 by William Collins Sons & Co., London, and Harper & Brothers, New York. Original edition copyright 1955 by Editions du Seuil, Paris.

23. In the twelfth century Peter Abelard wrote, "Did they [the ancient philosophers] not apply the name of wisdom or philosophy as much to the religion of life as to the pursuit of learning, as we find from the origin of the work itself, and likewise from the testimony of the saints?" H. A. Bellows, trans., *The Story of My Misfortunes* (New York: The Macmillan Company, 1922), pp. 26–27. Copyright 1922 by Thomas Alexander Boyd.

24. Some of the major characteristics of this religion will be described in our discussion of religious styles of life in Chapter II.

25. This alliance was so close that Socrates himself was convicted and executed for, in effect, converting the Athenian orthodoxy (Olympian polytheism) to an heretical counter-religion (rational monotheism). See B. Jowett, trans., "Apology," *The Works of Plato* (New York: Random House Inc., 1928), pp. 67–81.

26. See F. Nietzsche, *The Birth of Tragedy from the Spirit of Music,* trans. W. Kaufmann (Garden City, N. Y.: Doubleday & Co., Inc., 1956), especially chaps. 11–25; F. M. Cornford, *From Religion to Philosophy;* and H. Frankfort and others, *Before Philosophy.*

27. So Aristotle: "Reason more than anything else *is* man." "Ethica Nicomachea," Book X, chap. 7, in W. D. Ross, trans., *The Basic Works of Aristotle* (New York: Random House Inc., 1941), p. 1105. Copyright, The Clarendon Press, Oxford, England.

28. This is why G. van der Leeuw writes that, for early humans, "there is actually no 'environment' in the strict sense of the word," and that "Man . . . interweaves his own life with the greater and mightier continuity of Nature." J. E. Turner, trans., *Religion in Essence and Manifestation,* (London: George Allen & Unwin, Ltd. and New York: Harper & Row, Publishers, Inc., 1963), vol. I, pp. 57, 68. Copyright © 1938 George Allen & Unwin, Ltd. In a similar vein Erich Neumann observes that "the world of the dawn man is very largely an interior world experienced outside himself, a condition in which inside and outside are not discriminated from one another." Neumann goes on to describe this condition of unity with the world as "uroboric," "because it is dominated by the symbol of the circular snake [whose mythical name was Uroboros], standing for total nondifferentiation, everything issuing from everything and again entering into everything, depending on everything, and connecting with everything." *The Origins and History of Consciousness,* trans. R.F.C. Hull, Bollingen Series XLII. Copyright 1954 by Princeton University Press. The cited matter is found in the later Torchbook edition (New York: Harper & Brothers, Publishers, 1962) on p. 276.

29. Schleiermacher (1768–1834), who is sometimes called the father of liberal Protestant theology, is most notable theologically because he changed theology's focus from one attending chiefly to objective statements of faith (in scripture, creeds, dogmas, and the like) to one which pays attention to the "religious emotions" of believers themselves. The essentially romantic note in his viewpoint was expressed in verse by a romantic contemporary, William Wordsworth, in the final stanza of "The Tables Turned":
> Enough of Science and of Art;
>   Close up those barren leaves;
> Come forth, and bring with you a heart
>   That watches and receives.

30. *The Phenomenon of Man,* p. 33. Emphasis in original. For more on the identity and point of view of Teilhard, see Chapter III, pp. 66–67.

31. Exodus 3:1–4:18.

32. As a poet put it, "Heaven gives its glimpses only to those/ not in position to look too close." Robert Frost, "A Passing Glimpse," *The Complete Poetry of Robert Frost* (New York: Holt, Rinehart & Winston, 1969), p. 248.

33. In 1925 John T. Scopes of Dayton, Tennessee was prosecuted and convicted for teaching the theory of evolution in violation of a state statute. William Jennings Bryan, a three-time nominee for president, was the prosecuting attorney, and the famous trial lawyer Clarence Darrow was defense counsel. Because of the issues involved, the trial attracted international attention.

34. "It is safe to say that even had there been no religious scruples whatever against the Copernican astronomy, sensible men all over Europe, especially the most empirically minded, would have pronounced it a wild appeal to accept the premature fruits of an uncontrolled imagination, in preference to the solid inductions, built up gradually through the ages, of men's confirmed sense experience. . . . Contemporary empiricists, had they lived in the sixteenth century, would have been first to scoff out of court the new philosophy of the universe." E. A. Burtt, *The Metaphysical Foundations of Modern Physical Science,*

2nd, rev. ed. (London: Routledge & Kegan Paul, Ltd., 1950), p. 25. U. S. Rights: Humanities Press, Inc., New Jersey.

35. See Ian G. Barbour, *Issues in Science and Religion* (New York: Harper & Row Publishers, Inc., 1971), p. 38; and John Dillenberger, *Protestant Thought and Natural Science* (Garden City, N. Y.: Doubleday & Co., Inc., 1960), chaps. 4, 5, 8.

II. Religions
and Life Styles

RELIGION EXPRESSES ITSELF in styles of life. Life styles reflect particular ways in which human selves and societies tie facts and values together. The Christian life style is but one of many, not all of which arise from self-conscious religions.[1] It is the purpose of this chapter to distinguish or at least to begin to distinguish the Christian life style from its major rivals. We shall try to do this briefly and accordingly shall set and acknowledge certain limits on the attempt. First, we shall deal only with broad categories or "families" of religion; second, we shall describe these families in general terms and therefore must neglect minor, though still important, features within and among them; and third, we must emphasize that what we describe in this way is an abstraction from concrete instances and is seldom if ever found in its pure form.

The term "life style" as we use it here means a mode or manner of living determined by a ruling principle or principles. Diverse though they are, the religions of humankind seem to fall generally into three large families, each built on a different reigning principle and each producing a distinctive style of life. Our primary aims in this chapter are to describe these life styles, to examine their religious roots, and thereby to construct a kind of map on which to locate the Christian faith.

We begin by assuming that all religions are *not* the same. Our discussion of religion and science in Chapter I made it clear that the values served in some religions favor science, whereas those espoused by others inhibit science's acceptance and development. This difference indicates that the world's religions tie reality (the "facts") together from the standpoint of different values and that these variations in standpoint have profound effects on practical life. Scientific endeavor is not only accepted but applauded in the West because Western religions have given the values served by science a prominent place in popular consciousness. In the East, on the other hand, science has frequently been suspect in the popular mind, largely because it cuts against the grain of values promoted by the traditional Oriental faiths.

All religions, then, are not the same. Despite the efforts of honorably motivated groups and individuals to argue otherwise, it is simply not true that "we're all working for the same thing" or "we all serve the same God."[2] The clash between religions in general and science in general may be without warrant in the nature of religion and science themselves, but the differences between one concrete faith and another are, on the level of beliefs affirmed and values emphasized, real and obvious.[3]

For clarity's sake we need to stress that the differences among religions, while distinct and discernible, are not simple. There are cases in which values extolled by one religion are considered vices by another,[4] but such cases are rare. Generally, the basic differences between religions are matters of emphasis rather than of exclusion. Hinduism, for instance, emphasizes reverence for nature far more than Christianity does. But this does not mean that nature is despised or deprecated in Christianity. It simply means that, in the Christian view, nature is not to be valued on a par with God's revelation of himself in Christ or with the advancement of human equality and justice.

One final word needs saying before we set out to explore and map the contours of earth's religious families. In the course of human history, there has been much intermarriage among religious families. As a result we must warn the reader that the map we are going to draw has (like all maps) only a limited usefulness. The religious families whose major traits we describe are rarely if ever found in pure form; the earth's actual empirical religions are almost invariably mongrelizations in which elements from the three families—religions of nature, religions of reason, and religions of history—have gone through multiple forms and phases of coalescence and merger.

Of what use, then, is a map of the sort we intend to draft? Generally such a map can, we believe, acquaint us with the major features ("landmarks") that distinguish the great religious traditions from each other. Practically speaking, such an acquaintance should make it possible for us to encounter persons who come out of religious traditions other than our own with appreciation rather than apprehension. And, as far as the specific goals of this book are concerned, acquaintance with our map should, as already noted, help us locate Christianity within the broad spectrum of the world's faiths.

We assume that our map can, for all its limits, be useful. But what features must it include to be of optimum usefulness? As the conventional cartographer equips his map with a legend elaborating a system of uniform symbols, so must we. Basically, what we shall seek to provide with regard to each of the major religious families are answers to the following questions:

1. **The Situation Question:** Where (that is, under what circumstances) did (or does!)[5] this religious perspective originate, and what circumstances contribute(d) to its growth and development?

2. **The Problem Question:** What problem preoccupied the original adherents to this perspective, and what problem is this perspective designed to solve or address?

3. **The God Question:** In what source is a solution to the preoccupying problem sought, or from what source is it expected? Who or what, in other words, is this perspective's god?

4. **The Man Question:** What is the meaning of human life in this perspective? What self-image is controlling for it, and what style of life is normative?

5. **The Sin Question:** What does sin mean from this point of view? What life styles are considered deviant or evil?

6. **The Salvation Question:** In what does salvation from sin consist, and how is it pursued?

7. **The Time Question:** What significance, if any, do the currents of time have in this tradition? How does its particular life style shape and otherwise affect life's "stuff," time?

RELIGIONS BORN OF NATURE:
THE STYLE OF THE SWINGER

By far the oldest of the human religions are those born of nature. As their family name indicates, such religions originate within societies for whom nature is a close and constant companion. The *situations* within which these religions emerge and within which they grow and develop are dominated by natural entities and forces.

Reconstructing the conditions of life within which primitive people lived is extremely difficult, if not impossible, for twentieth-century city dwellers. Even back-to-nature cultists who inhabit agrarian communes experience a reality quite different from that which faced the ancient hunter and farmer. The difference, of course, is that modern Western naturists are such by choice, not by necessity. No matter how firm their resolve, they live in the knowledge that the door to the city, and to an entirely different life style, is always open.

No such door was there for primitive denizens of nature. The presence of nature was for them inescapable and its pressure inexorable. An alternative existence was not conceivable, let alone practicable. Nature was the constant surrounding reality, the matrix which contained and restricted them no less than a spider's web confines the wayward housefly.

The *preoccupying problem* of nature dwellers was that of accommodating themselves and their style of life to the routines, rhythms, and aberrations of nature. At issue in this work of accommodation, ultimately, was their very survival. Unless they could come to terms with the natural environment which confined them, the tribe and its culture would surely perish.

The source of their problem was at the same time for primitive people the source to which they looked for a *solution*. If they were to perish, it would be because nature had proved too much or provided too little for them. If they were to survive, they would owe it to her benevolence. It was to nature, after all, that they had to look for the food for their table, the clothes on their children's backs, the thatch for their roof. When nature withheld these gifts life itself was at peril. Nature, who in the course of time was personified as the Earth Mother (*Terra Mater*) or the Great Mother (*Magna Mater*),[6] thus took on the visage of a *god*. And well it might, for it bestowed all the gifts and posed all the threats associated with the nature child's quest for survival.

Whatever *self-image* people in such surroundings have is ill defined. It is the general view of anthropologists that self-consciousness as we know it did not exist in prehistoric cultures. There were, however, certain *roles* which the members of the family or tribe were expected to play. Although the details of these roles are not important for our purposes, we should note that such role expectations were derived in general from an image of human beings as nature's children and as kinsfolk of other animate beings. The relation to nature was primary at every juncture in their thinking and behavior.

As nature's children, practitioners of nature religion are expected to mind their mother. Her apron strings are never cut, though they may be lengthened or loosened to some degree. Basically, therefore, the *life style* of the naturist must be one of accommodation. The nature mother's moods and rhythms must be read, sensed, and followed. The naturist must be in effect a swinger, nature's dance partner, one who catches and swings to her rhythms, attunes himself or herself to her cycles, and senses and satisfies her moods.

We urbane moderns sometimes register astonishment at the means used by the *Farmer's Almanac* and other rural journals to forecast the weather. We are even more astounded by the remarkable accuracy of their forecasts. Their ability to read the lore of nature—to see in the bushier tails of squirrels, for example, a hard winter approaching—is but a small reminder of a time when nature was people's chief teacher. The learning acquired in this primitive time was entirely without benefit of books, of course, but its impact was far greater than that of most book learning, for life itself, and not just a livelihood or a quality of life, was at stake in it.

Sin in such a setting is in every case mortal sin, for the survival of the entire clan or tribe is imperiled by it. Indeed, the first revelation that sin has been committed may coincide with a drought or a flood or some other natural calamity. Such frowns on Mother Nature's normally benign visage can only mean that she has been offended. When she inflicts suffering, her children must have done something to upset her—must, therefore, be guilty of sin.

So reason the children of nature, or so we may imagine. But in what have they sinned, so to aggrieve Mother Nature? Their behavior reflects—and we must depend largely on traces of their behavior for evidence, since they have left us few written records—that sin for them was *religious* in nature.

Here we need to recall briefly what "religion" means. As we determined earlier, religion is essentially a condition of relatedness or relationship. The most important relationship, for our naturist or "swinger," is that to nature itself. When we say that sin is "religious" for them, therefore, we mean that it involves a violation of this crucial relationship. Sin occurs when members of the tribe, wittingly or unwittingly, try to cut the umbilical cord tying them or the tribe to the Earth Mother. In everyday life and practice this could happen in any number of ways, whether by intention or misadventure. In any event, if we may take the naturists' own myths and rituals as evidence, they seemed to see in sin a certain loss of accord, a disruption of the proper rhythm, between themselves and the Great Mother.

For naturists then, sin is essentially *unrhythm,* discord, a loss of harmony with nature. Accordingly, *salvation* from sin consists in a restoration of such harmony or rhythm.

The forms or rituals used by the nature religions to accomplish such a restoration are practically innumerable. Their number and variety are not as important to us, however, as their usual features. Their common elements disclose quite clearly the relationship which naturists believed to exist between the sacred world and human beings.

The common ingredient in many of the rites and myths of naturism is an understanding of divinity in terms of the recurring rhythms of living organisms. The cycle of birth, maturation, decline, and death found in every living organism is rooted, according to the myths of naturism, in the nature and the acts of the gods themselves. An ancient Canaanite myth illustrates this. According to this myth (variations on which are found in most agrarian cultures), Baal, the Canaanite god of rain, is busy constructing a temple to the supreme god, El, when he is accosted by Mot, the god of drought. Mot kills Baal, then kidnaps the corpse and takes it to his own underground lair. There ensues a period when living things languish and die as Anath, Baal's consort-goddess, mourns the loss of her lover. The goddess's grief is followed, however, by an angry resolve which drives her to invade Mot's underground realm, slay him, and resurrect Baal. Her grief and anger then give way to a joy of recovery which brings the entire natural order back to life.

One need not look too deeply to see in the basic lines of this myth a description of the prevalent natural phenomena in Canaan and surrounding areas. Anath is but a name for Mother Earth, and Baal, whose name comes from a common Canaanite word meaning "lord" or "husband," is described in the myth itself as the giver of rain, that inseminating fluid without which the arid earth of Canaan could never become fertile. Baal's demise at the hands of Mot corresponds clearly to the succession of the wet season by the dry one, and his resurrection by Anath represents in turn the conquest of drought by the returning rains.

Though the two-stage conflict it describes does find in the gods a means of explaining the major seasonal changes known in the arid Middle East, we sell the myth short if we make it no more than an ancient dramatization of recurring weather phenomena. It clearly goes beyond that to make our larger point, that the nature and acts of the gods are viewed by naturists as analogous to the life-and-death cycles of natural organisms and of nature as a whole.

Something else this myth does is even more intriguing: it provides the basic model by which nature religions define and seek *salvation*. The salvation of Baal consists, according to the myth, in his rescue by and his reunion with Anath. But Anath represents Mother Nature. The myth thus points, through its story of Baal's redemption, to the source of redemption for all. Salvation, according to naturism, is to be found only in a reunion or reestablishment of the proper relationship with nature. The children of nature must somehow get back in the swing with nature if they are to survive.

The means by which such redemption is sought by naturists are myriad. We can look at only a few of these here and shall choose those most consonant with our main objective, the description of nature religion's essence.

Central to a number of naturism's salvation rites is a view of sex as sacred. The gods themselves (recall Baal and Anath) are perceived in sexual terms. It is their procreative intercourse which makes for fertile fields and child-bearing wives,[7] and temple rites and seasonal festivals are aimed at encouraging such intercourse. Shrines and temples are therefore staffed by priests and priestesses,* sexual intercourse with whom is presumed to effect a certain sympathy,[8] and consequently a similar intercourse, among the gods.

Father Baal and Mother Earth are thus thought to bestow their blessings through sexual union. But sex is not the only means by which the worshipper of nature may seek union with his or her deity. One finds even today in the Middle East a certain holy personage called the dervish, whose vocation is to dance himself into a stupor or trance, out of which he utters oracles that, whether intelligible or not, are believed to be messages from God. In like fashion ancient Baalites and Dionysians wandered about in minstrel bands and danced themselves into states of ecstatic communion with the gods who reside beyond consciousness.[9]

Not far removed from the ancient orgiast and the perennial dervish are the drug cultists, both ancient and modern. Though they seek it not so much by acting as by permitting themselves to be acted on, their objective and that of the dancer and orgiast are virtually the same. The aim of their drug taking is (to use the modern phrases) to "blow their minds" or (more elegantly) to undergo an expansion of consciousness. In any event, their normal everyday mentality must go, to be replaced by an ecstatic union with divine vitalities which that mentality has kept at bay.

Although sacred sex, dervishlike dancing, and drug-induced trances are fairly extraordinary means to communion with the nature deities, the lives of common folk too have a sacred dimension in naturist cultures. The tribal community's drug is wine, and in its communal festivities it seeks in the juice of the vine a means of entry to the presence and favor of the gods.

However one may evaluate primitive people's pursuit of communion through intoxication,[10] it is extremely difficult, if common sense alone is one's criterion, to fault its logic. Our primitive cousin's reasoning may have gone something like this: I drink the wine, and I become spirited; therefore a spirit must inhabit the wine and must, through it, have come to inhabit me; perhaps the wine itself is the very blood of Dionysus (or of Baal), for it seems to fill me with a life and spirit beyond my own!

Through drink, as through dance, drugs, and sex, naturists pursue their quarry: life in union with subterranean but superhuman vitalities which keep them alive and make their environment surge with life—life in union, in other words, with the divine powers of nature. Not just

---

*The modern term "temple prostitute" would have been deemed not only inappropriate but sacrilegious by practitioners of these nature faiths. Far from prostituting themselves, these temple officiants were perceived by the faithful as pursuers of a sacred vocation.

their rituals of worship and oblation but also their culturally supported patterns of life express this pursuit. In planting and harvesting no less than in worshipping and auguring, naturalists accommodate themselves to the rhythms and routines of nature. They are well called swingers, then, these denizens of the open country, for the tempo of their lives is thoroughly determined by their efforts, conscious or unconscious, to swing with nature.

Nowhere is the all-pervasiveness of nature's influence more clearly indicated than in the way naturists perceive and relate to *time.* Time is a crucial category in the description of any life style, for time is the human name for the stuff (the "duration") of life itself. A style of life is really nothing more than a way of approaching, using, and conceiving this stuff of life. The controlling tempo, or way of accommodating to life's duration or time, may therefore be a crucial indicator of a culture's reigning values or principles.

How, then, do naturist cultures and religions organize time? As one would expect, they organize it around nature. These cultures are the inventors and celebrators of calendar time, with its notation of and accommodation to the annual, seasonal, lunar, and diurnal rhythms of natural bodies (sun, moon, tides, and so forth). Time in this arrangement is cyclical, curling back upon itself, repeating the past again and

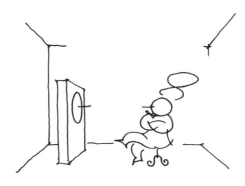

TIME

Does time exist?
I gravely doubt it.
But gosh, what should we do
without it?

From Grooks 3 *by Piet Hein. Copyright 1970 by the author.*
Used by permission of Mr. Hein.

again, bringing nothing new into being. Naturist cultures express this theologically in myths like that of Baal, Mot, and Anath cited above, or by similar tales of Dionysus and Ceres or Isis and Osiris, all of which view time (the passage of the "seasons" of various lengths) as a cyclical reflection and product of the life, death, and rebirth of the gods; and they express it liturgically by the various festivals of the seasons, which are designed to enlist the gods' aid (through rites of spring, for example) or to thank them for aid already given (as in festivals of harvest).

Because it is so totally subservient to the natural processes, time in the naturist perspective is essentially inhuman or subhuman in character. The events to be celebrated in time are natural events, not human (or "historical") events. The naturist's attitude toward time thus reflects that, in any contest between the two, all distinctively human aspirations and acts must give way to the massive movements of nature itself. The well-being and life objectives of the individual are thus of little consequence. What counts is what endures, and what endures are the ceaseless rhythms and motions of the natural order.

RELIGIONS BORN OF REASON:
THE STYLE OF THE SQUARE

If the gods of nature religion live mainly below ground and evoke the devotion chiefly of country folk,* the gods of reason are gods of the city, and of a city set on a hill—a very particular hill named Olympus.

There is of course no actual city located on that range of mountains in northern Greece know as Olympus, but the religious loyalties of Greek city dwellers did lie there, and the Olympianization of the gods is considered by many to have been a prerequisite to the emergence of a city culture. As long as the gods who controlled people's loyalties and destinies dwelt underground, the ground itself was sacred and humans dared not take liberties with it. But if the gods resided only on the high ground, if they could be localized indeed on the very highest ground known to Athenians and Spartans and Thebans, then the city builders could "break ground" and build their more stately mansions.

The Olympian gods were not merely the passive patrons of the emerging city-state; they were its active promoters too. If their passivity on remote Olympus made the city's emergence possible, their eventual sanctioning presence on the high ground of its acropolises made its

*The original meanings of the English names for devotees of the nature deities are quite significant in this regard. The word "pagan" comes from a late Latin term, *paganus*, which meant a country dweller or country townsperson. The name "heathen" goes back to the old English *haethen* which meant a field dweller or dweller in the heath.

peculiar style of life practicable. The Olympian gods, despite their quirks and in-house feuds, were essentially the gods of form and order, of balance and limit. No qualities were more crucial to the life style of the city than those of order, pattern, and regularity. By sanctioning these values, the gods of Olympus helped the city builder tame the unwieldy drives and antisocial urges of countryfolk-come-to-town,[11] and thereby did much of the civilizing work essential to urban life.

The history of the emergence of cities, romantic and fascinating though it is, must not detain us here. We are interested only in the city as the *situation* in which a particular type of religion, and a corresponding style of life, grew up. If we ask why the city should foster religions based on reason and gods virtually equated with it, we must look for an answer primarily in the most obvious feature of city life: the congregation and congestion of large numbers of people.

The most abundant resource the city offers to civilization is people. The cry of the cannibal, "I just get fed up with people sometimes," is the occasional cry of the city person as well. For while the countryman is pressed and harassed on every side by Mother Nature, the overwhelming problem of the city culture has to do with *human* nature. City life is preeminently social and commercial, not natural and agricultural. As a result the big problems of urban existence are people problems: problems of transportation and traffic, of human intake (education, consumption) and output (production, trash and sewage disposal), of employment and division labor, of law enforcement and crime prevention.

What have such problems to do with reason, and with religions born of reason? Again, as in our review of nature religions, we find that the originators of a perspective look to the source of a problem for clues to its solution. As the naturist saw in nature both a menace and a messiah, so the rationalist looks to something in the human condition for his or her salvation from problems posed by that condition.

The essential *problem* posed by the human condition in a city setting was perceived by the sensitive spirits who produced reason religion to be a form of a larger quandary known to philosophers as the problem of the one and the many. Whereas the earliest Greek philosophers, naturalists all, had asked the question "What *one* substance underlies and composes the *many* beings in the world?" the later philosophers of the city state asked, "What single power can make *one* harmonious city out of *many* citizens, with all their conflicting interests and desires?"

The first self-conscious formulators of this question were Greek thinkers called sophists, and the most thorough and thoughtful answer to it came from Plato. The one power that can unify the *polis* or city, Plato argued, is reason, for reason is the principle of order. It is so in the individual: In each person the intellect or reasoning power is the means by which options are examined, emotions controlled, motives explored and purified, and courses of action planned and ordered. And it must be so as well in that congregation of individuals called the city. Here, too, unless cool reason prevails over hot emotion, chaos will overtake order, destroying both individual integrity and the stability of the body politic. But where, in the city, can reason be found? In the individual, reason or intellect is innate: standard equipment, as it were. But cities are not individuals, not even organisms for that matter, just vast artificial constructs brought into being by the interplay of human interests. Where is the *mind* of such an artificial structure?

Some of the sophists of ancient Athens answered that the mind or ordering power of the city should be the popular will. To get the mind of the city, they argued, just add together the minds of all of its free inhabitants. To Plato, however, this answer seemed an appallingly unperceptive prescription for political disaster. He had watched as the popular will had sought to destroy, and had in fact silenced, the keenest mind in Athenian history, that of Socrates. The location of city-governing reason in the popular will, he believed, could lead only to the death of genius on the altars of gossip and political expediency.

The reason which should govern the city, Plato theorized, does not lie on the horizontal plane but on the vertical one. Government should be of the people and for the people but not by the people. It rather should be by the philosophers, for the philosophers alone had, through years of arduous study and preparation, entered the inner sanctum of divine Reason.

It is almost as difficult for participants in a modern democratic society to enter into the world of thought that led Plato to these conclusions as it is for urban Americans to penetrate the world view of primitive naturists. We may gain some slight insight into Plato's thought processes, however, if we recognize how enthralled he had become with certain discoveries of an earlier philosopher named Pythagoras. Pythagoras (for whom the famous Pythagorean theorem is named) was a mathematical genius who had theorized that "all things are made of number." This sounds absurd to us until we realize that it seems to have meant to Pythagoras something similar to what modern physicists mean by holding that the clue to an understanding of nature's workings lies in their measurability (that is, their reduction to a language of number!).

Plato himself was not a physicist—not even as much of one as Pythagoras may have been.[12] But what impressed him about Pythagoras' number theory was that it seemed to be entirely an invention of the human mind and to depend in no way on sense verification for its logical consistency and cogency.

This discovery appears to have struck Plato with the force of a revelation. If there are in fact ideas (of mathematical and kindred sorts) which derive purely from other ideas[13] and not in any way from sense experience, then such ideas (Plato reasoned, not illogically) must be inborn, must indeed have been divinely implanted. There is thus a divinity in human ideas and an even higher divinity in the mind which can contain and educe them. The human mind is thus for Plato what later came to be called a *scintilla divinitatis*, a spark of divinity.

What reason is it that must govern the city, in Plato's vision? It is a human reason attuned to, indeed at one with, divine Reason; in other words, it is the reason of the true philosophers, who have spent their lives divorcing themselves from that sensory order which deludes and controls the "popular will" and who have devoted themselves to pursuing that genuine wisdom born of divine Reason.

One might gather from this statement of his general position that Plato desired that all humans—at least all those of the city-dwelling variety—be made into philosophers. But the author of *The Republic* was far too well acquainted with human realities to believe that possible. In its rational aspect human nature does afford all of its possessors an opportunity to be "lovers of wisdom" (or "philosophers") but in their everyday doings most people neither hear nor march to the ethereal music heard by the philosophic ear.

What Plato does expect, at a minimum, of all citizens of a just state, is that they follow the dictates of reason. Citizens in the lower echelons of society—in the warrior, merchant, or artisan classes—may learn these at second-, third-, or fourth-hand. No matter: the crucial thing to the well-being of the state is that they learn them somehow and that they follow them. Reason religion, like nature religion, has as its basic and most immediate concern the well-being not of individuals but of a group. The city is to reason religion what the tribe is to naturism: its crucible, its patron, and its chief beneficiary.

City life and culture make possible the transposition of religion into a somewhat higher key than it could attain in a purely agrarian environment. The mode of relatedness which dominates the lives of city dwellers is not natural and mundane but economic and urbane. The umbilical cord binding the city dweller to Mother Nature may still be real, but it is lost to view, hidden by all kinds of social conventions and economic artifices: entrepreneurs, markets, manufacturing, and monetary exchange, to name a few.

The *style of life* and *self-image* of city dwellers are pervasively affected by their dependencies on such conventions and artifices. The latter may so blind people to their ultimate dependency on nature that only a natural catastrophe or a Malthusian[14] crisis can again alert them to it. On the other hand these conventions may make them conscious of certain other facets of the situation. In particular they may alert them to realities of social expectation and possiblities for individual improvement which could never become conscious objects for tribal people.

The life style and self-image of the citizen, both of which are dictated to a large extent by social expectation, could be described in contemporary Americanese as *the style and image of the square.* The square is that person who is, above all, socially reliable. Like the geometrical figure from which he or she takes the name, the square is stable, balanced, constant, dependable. He or she is capable of being the building block, the proverbial pillar, of the social order.

One may study the ethical theories of those founders of the reason religion, Plato and Aristotle, to find the basic rules of the square's existence. The constant axiom from which all those rules spring is "In all things, act moderately: find the golden mean, the balance point between extremes." By definition, something a square never does is tip over, fall over the edge of rational sobriety into excess.

The life style of the reason religionist is preeminently, then, one of balance. The kinship of the English words "rationality" and "ratio" reflects something of the impact that the ideal of balance has had on the Anglo-American and Indo-European cultures. "Ratio" is primarily a mathematical term pertaining to proportions. That it is, quite literally, the basis for our words "rational" and "rationality" is a clear indication that in our culture "to be rational" means "to be balanced," "to maintain a sense of proportion."[15] The square is thus, to employ a geometrically ironic figure, a *well-rounded* person, one with a highly developed sense of proportion. The life style he or she favors and practices is that of the solid citizen who never loses his or her balance, or confident commitment to the fortunes of the city.

In an environment so determined by law and order, balance and equity, *sin* can only mean the absence or opposites of these qualities. Acts of sin may take many and varied forms, but all the forms express disorder, lawlessness, imbalance, and, as their bottom line, irrationality. Plato portrayed the self as a chariot drawn by the wild horses of appetite and emotion but steered by reason. If reason should, for whatever reasons, loosen the reins on the wild steeds of desire and interest, the self would lose its balance, or, to return to the metaphor, the chariot would tip over or even be torn apart.[16] Sin can thus have disastrous effects for the individual.

But the individual is not sin's only, or even its main, victim. Society, too, and the innocent within society,[17] suffer when sin goes unchecked. Sin is primarily disorder, and disordered individuals produce disordered societies, whether by antisocial behavior (crime) or unsocial lethargy (social irresponsibility).[18] The rationally governed urban leader therefore opposes in principle all policies and actions, in both the private sector and the public one, that could lead to an excess of reaction or inaction by the populace. Balance and proportion (ratio!) are the main desiderata in making social policy.

If balanced persons and an ordered and equitable society are the main aims of reason religion, how are these aims to be achieved? How, in other words, are the sins of disorder and irrationality to be controlled and overcome? The answer lies in the city dweller's three r's of *salvation*: restraint, regulation, and reason.

The call for law and order which became a watchword in the urban centers and suburbs of the United States in the 1960s and early 1970s was partly[19] a call for *restraint* from the champions of urban orthodoxy. The prescription whose application they demanded has almost always been one of the city dweller's favorite nostrums. Periodically through the centuries, as again in America in this century, great crowds of country folk have come to the city in pursuit of economic improvement. Such immigrants bring with them little appreciation for the traditions of the city and for the restraints and regulation that those traditions impose. In living out their accustomed life styles of vital rhythm and emotional expression, they inevitably clash with these traditions. A pressure-cooker effect may result. As the uncouth countryfolk express themselves with typical vigor, they arouse more and more resentment in the normally cool city dweller. This resentment breeds attempts at restraint ("law and order"), and restraint produces an equally resentful reaction. This leads to a still tighter screwing down of the pressure-cooker lid and ultimately to the blowing of the lid—that is, to the sorts of urban explosions and conflagrations that America experienced in the 1960s. But despite such results urban traditionalists may continue to emphasize the importance of restraint, for without it, they fear, the life style of the city itself would be endangered.

Although restraint is the most basic weapon in the square's arsenal, it is also the crudest, and he or she prefers more urbane tactics when possible. Perhaps as good a catch-all name for these as any is the word *regulation*. Squares are very regular persons. They live very organized, regulated lives. And for good reason: suppose all city dwellers chose at whim, for example, which side of the street they would drive on, or at what hour they would arrive at work. The results would be incalculable, but the odds favoring a socially destructive chaos would increase enormously.

Regulation is as indispensable to city life as restraint is; only through its continued practice can a well-managed city be maintained. Nevertheless restraint and regulation are sources of peril as much as of promise if they are not accompanied and governed by the one power that can restrain the restrainers and regulate the regulators—the power of *reason*.

Reason itself is the ultimate savior within the perspective of rational religion. But how is the salvation which reason offers to be made effective in people's lives?

For reason religion there is finally just one salvation ritual, and its name is education. The word itself is instructive. Traceable to Latin roots meaning "to draw out" or "to lead out," "education" expresses or assumes two ideas which are central to Plato's conception of salvation. The first is that reason is the common property of all human beings—that it is innate, coming with the condition of humanity itself. The second is that this property can stand, indeed demands, "drawing out," educing, developing.

From his day to this, Plato's premises have controlled much of the educational theory and practice of the West. Western democratic idealism is built particularly on the twin notions that all persons are endowed with rational capacities which fit them for self-government and that educational institutions have as one of their principal obligations the fullest possible development of these capacities.[20]

One of the more profoundly religious premises of Plato's theory of reason has not enjoyed the wide and perennial acceptance of the two ideas just noted, but it is worthy of our attention here as a clear indication that what Plato advocated was a full-blooded religion and not just a fervently argued secular philosophy. We refer to Plato's belief in the mind's intrinsic immortality and divinity, and its corresponding qualitative difference from all things mortal and physical, including the human body that houses it.

This conviction of Plato's, that the mind is a spark of divinity encased or entombed in the body, gives his philosophy of human salvation an existential earnestness it otherwise would lack. It means that at stake in the individual's quest for salvation is not merely temporary happiness but eternal blessedness itself. Platonic salvation/education has eternal significance, for through it the mind is "drawn out" of the body and so out of temporality's darkness into eternity's light.

Plato's famous allegory of the cave offers a particularly good illustration of this theory of education as salvation. Most of us, he maintained,[21] are like cave dwellers who are duped into believing that the shadows we see on our cave's walls are realities. These shadows (which he suggests are to be equated with physical objects) have no enduring reality. Only as we are drawn out of the cave by education can genuine and eternal realities become the focus of our lives. Then we begin to see what is really important and to place the long-range goal of the mind's well-being ahead of temporary considerations such as physical satisfaction.

To summarize: in the reason religion's classic model, that of Platonic philosophy, salvation has both social and personal meaning. On it depend both the political well-being of the city and the eternal destiny of the individual mind or soul. Both the good person and the good society are required to submit to restraint and regulation under the aegis of reason. Reason becomes powerful and effective in the lives of citizens through education, the development of rational capacities that are inborn and immortal.

From an undercurrent in his doctrine of salvation came one of Plato's main points regarding the character of *time*. Actually there was a marked ambivalence in his attitude toward time, and his theory of the soul's immortality contributed only to the negative aspect of that attitude. Though it would be desirable that all minds be saved from their miasmal state of bondage to the physical order, such salvation is in fact the exception, not the rule. The hold of the physical is so strong and so obscures the attractiveness of spiritual truths that, at death, the mind can scarcely take its flight to the spiritual realm. It is thus destined to fall back into a different form of bodily life. This process, which Plato called metempsychosis (literally, "transmigration of the soul"; freely, "reincarnation"), is bound to recur again and again until the mind is sufficiently developed to return to the divine domain which is its true home.

It is this cycle of continuing recurrence which shapes Plato's conception of time. From the standpoint of the individual mind or soul, time is a meaningless repetition of bodily careers, each one very like those that precede and succeed it. Reason stands at the center of this circle of repetitions, but it does so as the circle's prisoner, and when properly informed it can only yearn to break out and reunite itself, beyond time's grasp, with the divine Mind.

So far Plato's attitude toward time was purely negative. For the individual spirit, Platonic religion advocates a kind of mystical escapism in which time is to be escaped if at all possible. Continued temporal existence can only mean to the individual mind a dreary bodily entrapment, repeated *ad infinitum* via the cycle of death and reincarnation.

But time has a somewhat more positive aspect as well, in Plato's view. Though it does not make life meaningful, it does at least make it bearable, for time is in any event one of the works of divine Reason. The alternative to a world regulated by time, it appears, would be no world at all, a state of pure chaos, a hellish and thoroughly uninhabitable reality. Time is eternity's "moving shadow," its forming image or regulatory principle, which, however inferior it may be to the eternity it imitates, at least manages to form and shape physical reality into a semblance of that eternity. Therefore time has preliminary or penultimate value, for it makes the material universe habitable by rational beings.

This rather sketchy treatment of classical rationalism's view of time makes one thing apparent: reason religion takes at least one significant step beyond nature religion, in that it does not totally subordinate human acts and aspirations to the massive rhythms and movements of nature. In Plato the human mind at last brings these massive movements into conscious focus and realizes that it is more than they are, or that it is at least not reducible to them. With this discovery a new religious possibility came into being, and countless new human possibilities were not long in the offing.

RELIGIONS BORN OF HISTORY:
THE STYLE OF THE SHAPER

A deep-running hostility marks the history of relations between religions of nature and religions of reason.[22] The values celebrated by the two are in important respects antithetical. Reason religions celebrate the rule of the mind, nature religions that of bodily rhythms.[23] Open spaces are sacred to the naturist, city life to the rationalist. Naturists generally find human company a blessing; large families, kinship ties, and tribal festivals are occasions for rejoicing. Rationalists, on the other hand, tend to see in aggregations of people a problem demanding efficient management.

The differences between the two perspectives could be further elaborated. But what we really wish to note here is that, despite their deep divergences, in one important way naturism and rationalism agree and do so in clear opposition to the religions of history. Neither reason religion nor nature religion finds positive meaning in time, while the religions of history find in the course of time, or at least in certain crucial temporal events, a sustaining revelation of the purposes of God.

Frederick the Great of Prussia is said to have asked his barber on one occasion for a proof for the existence of God. The barber's reply was spontaneous and brief: "The Jews, your majesty. The Jews are the best proof I know of the existence of God."

The barber had a point, which he quickly made clear to his royal patron. At the time of Frederick's rule of eighteenth-century Prussia, the Jews had been without a homeland for some seventeen centuries. In medieval Europe they were even denied the right to own landed property, and during the Inquisition they were driven bodily from England, Spain, and other European countries. Yet, despite all, the Jews remained an identifiable community. Only a miracle of divine Providence could have sustained their community integrity, Frederick's barber argued, against such geographic, political, and economic odds.

Divine Providence may indeed have been the source of Judaism's continued vitality through the centuries. Divine Providence is an elusive force, however, whose presence cannot be verified by the historian's methods. What can be verified is that the Jews were kept together, and kept loyal to their singular faith, by a lively sense of shared history.

The Israelites began to acquire this sense for history quite early in their life as a people. During King David's time (the early tenth century B.C.), historians of their national life began to compile the lore of the past and to compose on the basis of it a national literature. Much of this inherited material was shrouded in legend,* but they found in it nonetheless a perspective which gave the national life purpose and meaning.

In the sixth century B.C., Jerusalem fell captive to the Babylonians and most of its leading citizens were taken into exile by the conquerors. As a result the national consciousness embodied in Israelite literature underwent a severe test. For many of the exiles the loss of their homeland and the destruction of Jerusalem, their holy city, meant a crisis of faith.[24] Such a crisis indicates to us that their faith had over the centuries become attached to sacred spaces. But more important, it indicated to them that they must take a new look at the meaning of their faith.

The priestly group who attended the exiles in Babylon had brought with them sacred scrolls recounting the people's ancient traditions. Jerusalem and its temple were not portable and could not make the pilgrimage into exile, but these very portable scrolls, the priestly caste argued, contained all that was essential to the faith of Israel. Israel's God is not confined to temples made with hands, or to holy cities or holy lands, but is present with his people in all times, places, and conditions of being, within the words of the Torah (literally, "the teaching") which recount the sacred events of Israelite history.

The significance of this discovery by Israel's priests for subsequent history would be hard to overestimate. With this discovery there emerged in human consciousness, even before Plato conceived it on different grounds, the idea of a God not bound by space or other physical limitations; and from this the prophets of Israel concluded that the true God was to be sought not in shrines or other sacred *places* but rather in the remembrance and reenactment of sacred *events*. Henceforth, ac-

---

*The word "legend," like the word "myth," has had a bad press in fact-conscious America. Legend does have positive value for historians, however, in that it serves as a valuable gauge by which they can measure the impact of a historical figure on the minds of contemporaries. The historical legend may thus serve historians in a way analogous to that in which a map's legend serves map-readers: as the map's legend orients its reader to the space to which the map applies, so the historical legend may orient the historian (albeit less precisely) to the time from which it emanates.

STYLE	ORIGINATING LOCALE	PROBLEM	GOD (RULING PRINCIPLE)	MAN	SIN	SALVATION	TIME	DEVOTEES (EXEMPLARY)
NATURISM	Country	Survival	Mother Nature and Consorts (e.g., Dionysus, Baal)	Swinger	Unrhythm	Rhythm	Cyclical (Mother Nature at cycle's center)	"Pagans" "The Heathen"
RATIONALISM	City	Order	Reason (e.g., Apollo The Logos)	Square	Disorder	Education	Cyclical ("Rational soul" at cycle's center)	Rationalists Stoics
HISTORISM	History	Integrity (Identity)	Lord of History (Yahweh, Allah)	Shaper	Rebellion (Irresponsibility)	Conferral of Responsibility (Grace)	Linear (Progressive)	Jews, Christians, Moslems

Styles of the Self

cordingly, God can be conceived as transcendent, mobile, and universally accessible to all beings capable of recalling his mighty acts in history.

The *situation* from which history religions spring, then, is one of time rather than one of space. Neither the rhythms of country space nor the rational regularities of city space are to control human behavior, according to this perspective, but rather the remembrance of, and reaction to, certain incursions into time by God himself. It is significant, therefore, that the most sacred *place* of all in Israel's history, Mt. Sinai, the holy mountain from which God first declared himself to them as a people, is neither physically described nor geographically located in their literature, and scholars to this day are not sure where it is. No better indication of what is important to this faith could be found than this: that, although their locale is completely ignored, the *events* of the Sinai covenant's establishment are thoroughly and repeatedly described.

The *problem* peculiar to so spaceless a religious stance is (as our Prussian barber recognized) that of getting and keeping one's bearings. There are, quite literally, no landmarks, no visible or mapped territorial boundaries from which to gain a sense of identity and from which to launch a program of activity. As a result the community is always in danger of forgetting its own name and nature, of merging into other communities which are solidly and geographically identifiable.

The source of Israel's problem was thus its own nature as a people of history rather than one united by blood ties, geographic boundaries, or commercial interests. Its very earliest name, Habiru, root of the word "Hebrew," indicated that it was a homeless, spaceless people, a group of wanderers or gypsy shepherds consigned to follow their flocks from oasis to oasis across the Arabian wilderness. Indeed, as long as they led a desert existence, as long as the spaces they traversed were hostile and unappealing, the problem of losing their identity was not grave. In the first place, simple survival in so hostile an environment meant that they had to keep together as a people. In the second, the wilderness really afforded no options, no settled and civilized communities to tempt and entice younger generations, luring them from the way of the fathers into pagan life styles.

It was only when Israel settled down, and particularly when it became a nation among nations, that the problem of cultural disintegration assumed threatening proportions. Indeed for a time, as we have noted, the people seem to have learned from their naturist neighbors to tie their religious faith to a holy land and to think of their God as a kind of super-Baal who could out-Baal the deity of the Canaanites.[25] In such times, only the voices of lonely prophets seemed to speak out for the true faith, to recall Israel to the rock from which it was hewn, and to remind it of what one of them viewed as the people's "honeymoon in the wilderness" with God.[26]

In so preaching, these prophets expressed the essential genius of Israel's faith and pointed to what was in their view the sole solution to its problem of identity. In prodding the nation to recover and reenact that sacred history which had brought it into being, they voiced their belief that Israel's identity could cohere and endure only within that history.[27]

That history was essentially a *covenant* history. The word "covenant" denotes a special relationship of choice and response established between two parties. It was Israel's belief that it was the choice of God to be his people. Its history was a Cinderella story: Israel had been a poor chimney sweep of a people, held in bondage by the king of Egypt, but had been made by God's choice "a kingdom of priests and a holy nation."[28] Its deliverance from slavery (known as the Exodus, a Greek term meaning "the way out") thus constituted a point-of-turning in its history. In this astonishing event God had shown his inestimable and wondrous favor to a people who could in no way deserve it. Behind his choice of Israel lay some intention the people could not fathom, but that the choice was real they could not doubt.

Israel was constituted then through a birth or new birth of freedom and believed that this liberating historical event was the work of God himself. Who was this *God*, who had so mercifully intervened in history?

He was so awe inspiring, this God, that Israel believed his name to be beyond utterance. When in one of his most memorable manifestations he appeared to Moses before the Exodus, Moses had asked to know his name.[29] The answer, which in most English translations is rendered simply "I am who I am," might more literally be read "I cause to happen what I cause to happen." To an inordinately curious Moses, God refuses to surrender the inmost secret of his being. He instead declares himself to be a God known only through his acts in history. "Go down, Moses," he says: "if you would know who I am, go down to Egypt and learn who I am from what happens, for it is I, only I, who cause to happen what happens."

The fact that Moses asks for God's name and receives instead a promise of divine action reveals a great deal about the nature of the religions born of history. As Thorlief Boman has demonstrated,[30] the Hebrew message regarding God's deeds in history lays more stress on verbs than on nouns. Nouns are static words, incapable of capturing or expressing the meaning of a God who is dynamic, one who continually acts to change the face and the course of history. Verbs, on the other hand, change form; they express variations in activity and time and are therefore better suited to the message of a God who acts, constantly trans-forming history into his story.

It is no accident, then, that the name Israel finally settled on as most expressive of God's being is not a name or noun at all but a verb. In the Hebrew Bible (the Christian "Old Testament"), this word is left un-vocalized even today, indicating that in orthodox Jewish belief it is still considered unutterable. In its unvocalized or consonantal form it simply reads YHWH, which is a third person singular form of that same verb used in recording the divine response to Moses (the verb translatable "I am" or "I cause to happen").

Most contemporary scholars believe that a fairly literal vocalization of this Hebrew term would read YAHWEH, although the scholarship that produced the King James version of the Bible and other older English translations favored YAHOWAH, or Jehovah. Virtually all of today's translations beg both the vocalization question and the meaning ques-tion by rendering the term with the rather innocuous and ambiguous noun phrase "the Lord."

Though "the Lord" does lose many of the rich connotations and much of the awesome mystery inherent in the Hebrew sense of deity and in the verb name that conveys that sense, it does express a central Hebrew conviction—namely, that God is in control of history. A "lord" is known for his commanding presence. Yahweh, in the view of the Old Testament, has clear command of history, using both the acts of Israel and those of its enemies to his purposes and for his glory.[31]

Israel, as the first historist faith,* sees God chiefly as the prime mover and manager of history. *Humans,* in its view, are to be understood mainly as Yahweh's agents and collaborators in this activity. Made in the Lord's image, they too are movers and managers, or shapers, of history.

The initiative in history clearly lies with God. He is the one who "in the beginning" sets history on its course no less than the planets in their orbits. The role of humans in history is that of fellow-actors or reactors who respond to divine initiatives and overtures. It follows that what it means to be human is far less fixed and clear in the history religions than in the reason religions and the nature religions. Naturists find a recur-ring regularity in nature's rhythms to which they can become habituated; similarly, rationalists believe the laws of reason to be as fixed and immutable as the truths by definition of mathematics. Historists swim, as it were, in a river of time whose banks are hard to see, and they

---

*The historist faith or "historism" is not to be confused with "historicism," that rela-tivistic philosophy which reduces history to the one dimensional terms accessible to secu-lar historiography. As a religious perspective, historism stands to historicism much as "naturism" stands to philosophic naturalism, that philosophy which defines truth exclu-sively in terms of natural causes and effects.

must learn to fathom the deeps of God's intentions for history in daring and creative ways.

The *self-image and style* of the historist may be compared to those of actors in an improvisational theater, who must learn to work both creatively and responsively, providing stimulation for fellow actors and in turn responding to their creative initiatives. No written or memorized script is available to guide or channel their acts and words. Rather, they must trust themselves to the moment, to the historical situation, and seek in it the design and intention of God, the prime Actor.

The mode of relating which dominates and defines history religion is *dramatic.* In the Bible even nature becomes a player in the divine drama, as serpents,[32] bushes,[33] donkeys,[34] lilies of the field,[35] and mustard seeds[36] all have something to say. But the drama's chief players, without question, are just two: God, and the one creature fashioned in God's image, the human being.

Looked at as a whole, the biblical drama (which is seen by historists as a kind of simile for the entire drama of history) could be described as a tragicomedy. Tragedy occurs whenever acts which are grand or noble in intention produce self-destructive results. From Genesis 3 onward, the Bible is full of such tragedies: Adam and Eve would be "as gods" but end by worshipping the image of God in themselves rather than the real God;[37] Cain would make God an offering but ends by placing his relationship to Mother Nature ahead of those to Father God and brother Abel;[38] the builders of Babel's tower (probably an allusion to the ziggurats or prayer towers of Babylon) would go up on high to communicate with God but end up unable even to communicate with each other.[39] The higher people's aspirations are, it seems, the greater their capacity to disappoint. Even Jacob, the patriarch whose renaming gave Israel itself its name,[40] was not immune. Though his name meant originally "may God protect," it later came to mean, no doubt from his character as much as from the circumstances of his birth, a "heelsneak."[41]

The name "Israel" itself expresses the ambiguity and the potential for tragedy inherent in the relationship between God and his chosen co-star in history. Though it can be rendered "may God rule," "Israel" may also be translated "he who wrestles with God." In view of its actual history, this name could represent both Israel's prayer that God might rule its life and that of all people and its actual performance as one who wrestled with, and frequently against, God.

These ambiguities in the chosen people—beautiful, potentially ennobling prayers betrayed by perfidious and shabby performances— make them all the more effective, in the biblical story, as dramatic foils for the story's other major actor, God himself. Though his ways are past finding out, the rightness of his intentions and the righteousness of his deeds are never in question. This means that, though people's deeds taken in and by themselves could make history a tragedy, it is ultimately destined, by God's choice, to be a comedy.

Comedy differs from tragedy essentially not as laughter differs from tears but as ultimate harmony differs from ultimate discord. The action of tragedy pits one actor against another, or even against himself or herself; the movement is toward disunity, strife, and division. The action of comedy, on the other hand, however much it may play actor against actor for comic effect, ends in a climactic reunion of estranged parties. For every comedy, and not just for one of Shakespeare's, all's well that ends well.[42]

Though it is a very basic ingredient in the faith of historists, their confidence that the drama of history will have a happy ending is not a case of Pollyannas whistling their way through a graveyard. History is no mere comedy, they know, but tragicomedy, whose tragic component is made very real and very grave by one reality—that of human *sin*.

The literature of historism portrays sin in many lights and as taking many forms. But the root of sin is in every case religious: it inheres, that is, in a false way of putting things together, of connecting values and facts, of relating God and the world.

Humans' principal mistake, as historists see it, lies in worshipping the creature instead of the Creator, the product instead of the process, gods who are nouns instead of the God who is a verb. People would rather *have* than *be* and *do;* they prefer lives of security and stability to lives of activity on the stage of an improvisational theater in which the props and the plots keep rearranging themselves. As a result they become *historically irresponsible,* unable to respond to God the Improviser, that God who acts and speaks through the dramas, great and small, of history.

From the historist point of view, the name of sin could well be historical irresponsibility, a condition of impotence or even wilful rebellion in the face of history's demands and challenges. Such a condition is never something that people can blame on beings other than themselves. The condition of sinfulness clearly results from a *decision* to put one's life together in a way which runs counter to the realities of creation. This means that, however they might prefer to deny it, people are ultimately responsible for their own irresponsibility.

The meaning of sin is portrayed in dramatic form again and again in the Hebrew scriptures. In the account of sin's introduction to the world in Genesis 3, Eve stands poised between the word of a God beyond her and the word of nature (taking voice in the serpent) beneath her. In choosing to take her bearings from the voice from below, from the world that would convince her that she can be "as god" herself,[43] she seeks to take over history, as it were, and in the process to depose the true God of history. Her decision to eat of the tree of the knowledge of good and evil indicates that she, like a good naturist, would seek the source of values and the meaning of time in natural objects and thereby would displace the Creator with the creature.

The psychological forerunner of a physical loss of identity is insecurity, and the actions of Eve assume added meaning when we realize that her act may involve an attempt not only to determine who she is (what powers or potential she has) but also to secure herself against the terrors of an unknown future. The way history keeps coming at us is from out of the future, and life with the God of history means moving into the uncharted territory encompassed in the word "future." Sin—Eve's and that of all the rest of us*—is, from the standpoint of historism, an effort to make ourselves immune to the challenges and threats of the future. It is simultaneously an abandonment of freedom and an abdication of responsibility, for freedom in its positive aspect is nothing but "response-ability," the ability to respond to the demands and promises of history as they come out of the future into the present.

If, in historism, sin means the loss of responsibility in the face of a future that constantly presses in on us, *salvation* means the recovery of such responsibility. But once it is lost how can one recover the ability to respond?

Perhaps the difficulty of this problem can be imagined more keenly if one thinks of oneself as a divorced person who has been profoundly hurt by a former partner in marriage. All lines of communication have been ruptured by callous and thoughtless deeds. How, in such a situation, is one to regain an ability to respond, assuming that the other person wishes to renew communication?

The problem is all the greater if what is desired is not merely a power to respond temporarily but a power to reestablish a continuing relationship of response. From the perspective of the religions of history, just such a continuing relationship is the objective of salvation. How, then, is such a relationship to be established?

The answer that historism supplies is that of a divine love which is both long-suffering and sovereign. Though God is the offended party in the covenant relationship, he takes the initiative, forgiving rebellious humans and re-enlisting them as actors in the dramas of history. Like the prophet Hosea, whom he commanded to court and marry a prostitute, the God of history will not leave human beings alone, despite their

---

*The original meanings of the names "Adam" and "Eve" indicate that the authors of the Genesis accounts probably thought of them as representative, and not just as primal, figures. In the Hebrew "Adam" means "man" and "Eve" means "life." The story of Adam and Eve may thus be read as the (highly symbolic) story of man(kind) and its life.

waywardness; instead he keeps coming at them, keeps nudging them out into the river of time and making them buoyant enough to contend with that river's depths and shoals and currents.

Historism's salvation strategy rests on a strong sense that God takes the initiative in drawing human beings into a relationship of response to history. The obvious implication is that history is worth responding to. Why is history worth responding to? The historist answers, "Because history is the arena of God's own activity; it is essentially his story, the realm in which divine purposes are to be achieved."

With this answer we come upon the key to historism's attitude toward *time*. Here time is not, as in naturism, a mere snake chasing its own tail, a meaningless though perpetual rerun of occurrences in nature. Nor is it, as in rationalism, an inferior and parasitical image of some eternal order beyond itself. It is rather a realm with direction and purpose which is to culminate in a sociohistorical reality called the Kingdom of God.

Unlike naturism and rationalism, historism is not escapist in its attitude toward time. Time is not an endless retracer of its own tracks or of the tracks of natural bodies or immortal souls. It is not something to flee in favor of the subhistorical rhythms of nature or the superhistorical realms of pure reason but rather something to be lived, redeemed, and transformed into a city with foundations, whose ultimate shaper is God.[44]

Rare indeed are the instances in history in which any of our three religious styles has found pure expression. In ages of reaction and reform, priests and puritans of all three traditions have worked zealously to purge their respective belief communities of elements of nonconformity. Such efforts have in practice always met with some degree of failure, doubtlessly because the human beings who are the targets of the efforts are themselves complex manifolds of forces, moved by natural vitality, directed by reason, and enmeshed in and taught by history. Now one, now another, of these forces may be in the ascendant at any given time, in any given individual or culture. But the triumphant principle is never totally able to banish the other two, and they remain real though subordinate factors in the situation.

No religious perspective can remain viable in such circumstances unless it realizes its own relativity and proves itself resilient and responsive in the face of the changes effected by the constant interplay among the vital, rational, and historical elements in reality. Historism's sole legitimate claim to superiority, if indeed it has any, lies in its character as a perspective from which such historical changes can be appreciated and analyzed, and from which they can be shaped toward the ends of human growth and fulfillment. Authentic historism can thus have no interest in stifling or denying the impulses from which rationalism and naturism spring. It rather must be concerned that these impulses be directed toward the accomplishment of human autonomy and dignity within history.

QUESTIONS TO GUIDE STUDY AND DISCUSSION

1. In what ways can an outline or "map" of humanity's major religious families and life styles be useful? In what ways may it be misleading?

2. Why is it difficult for people of modern technological cultures to empathize with the devotees of nature religion?

3. Why can the practitioners of nature religion be called "swingers"? What does this term suggest regarding their understanding of themselves, God, sin, and salvation?

4. Why do the families of religion discussed in this chapter generally define sin in religious, rather than moral, terms? What is the difference between a religious understanding of evil and a moral understanding?

5. How did the Olympianization of the gods relate to the advancement of Greek city culture?

6. Why are followers of reason religion appropriately called "squares"? What does this term indicate about their views on human life, the nature of deity, and the meaning of sin and salvation?

7. Discuss the relationship between the cultural history of the Jews and the emergence of history religion. What were the major impediments to Judaism's evolution as a history-based faith, and how did its efforts to cope with these impediments influence the shape of its faith?

8. What examples of the religious life styles discussed in this chapter can you find among individuals and cultures (or subcultures) with which you are acquainted? To what extent does increased study of and knowledge about given individuals and cultures make you less willing to classify them exclusively as members of a single "family"?

9. Of the three life styles studied, which has the greatest appeal to you? Why?

NOTES TO CHAPTER II

1. A self-conscious religion is one that knows and identifies itself as a religion. But there are religions, or ways of putting life together, that are not self-conscious or do not recognize the religious character of what they do. Communism is one of the more organized examples of this sort of religion; "implicit," less organized examples would be modern hedonism (for example, the *Playboy* philosophy) and nontheistic (for example, Sartrean) existentialism.

2. From this fact Harvey Cox draws the proper practical implication: "The Christian must consciously respond to Moslems and Hindus—to a larger, highly diverse, indeed world-wide family of faith. . . . The borrowing we need today, however, should not mean that the historical particularity of a living religion is dissolved in some universal pabulum. Theology should discard both the ideal of an abstract universal science and that of a global religion unsullied by the stain of concrete history. Religion at its best is one of the guardians of human eccentricity." *The Seduction of the Spirit* (New York: Simon & Schuster, Inc., 1973), p. 151.

3. As H. W. Robinson notes, there is even virtue in such conflict, for "only as a religion has to meet the challenge of its opposite does it discover its own nature and potential strength." "The Religion of Israel," *A Companion to the Bible*, ed. T. W. Manson (Edinburgh: T. & T. Clark, 1939), p. 293.

4. The Gnostics and Manichaeans of the Roman era quite clearly renounced, for example, the positive value placed on material realities by Judaism and Christianity.

5. New religions are in fact constantly being born in the world. Examples include the drug cults of the 1960s, built around figures like Timothy Leary, the Black Muslim faith founded by Elijah Muhammad, the maniacal messianism of the Charles Manson "family," and the Unification Church of Sun Myung Moon.

6. Cf. Van der Leeuw, *Religion in Essence and Manifestation*, trans. J. E. Turner (London: Allen & Unwin, Ltd., and New York: Harper & Row Publishers, Inc., 1963) Vol. I, pp. 91–100, especially p. 92: "The Mother . . . is anything but a theoretical invention intended to explain the world process. She is Form, just barely outlined; and everywhere that Nature gives or takes something, there is the Mother." Copyright © 1938 George Allen & Unwin, Ltd.

7. According to Van der Leeuw (*Religion in Essence*, Vol. I, p. 57), women and fields are scarcely separated in the primitive consciousness: "Woman is a tilled field, the tilled field a woman." This identification may have its roots in the intermeshing dependence on women and fields, respectively, which primitive peoples experienced. The tending of fields and flocks made large families—especially large numbers of healthy male children—very necessary. There thus was a direct connection between fertile wives and harvestible fields.

8. Because they seek to induce such sympathy and thereby to control the behavior of the gods, these rites are described by some modern anthropologists as exercises in "sympathetic magic." For a discussion of various forms of such magic, cf. Sir James Frazer, *The Golden Bough* (New York: Macmillan, 1951), pp. 12–55.

9. These bands appear to have been the (somewhat disreputable) precursors of the later prophets of Israel. Cf. R. B. Y. Scott, *The Relevance of the Prophets* (New York: Macmillan, 1953), pp. 45–59.

10. Here it should be noted that early Christianity's strongly negative evaluation of drinking and dancing was probably based more on theological than on moral grounds. Dancing, drinking, and even going to the theater were associated with pagan festivals and were ways of pursuing redemption through pagan gods. They were therefore idolatrous, that is, violations of the commandment that one should have no god save Jehovah, and this, not moral questions about human well-being, was the crucial reason for renouncing them.

11. For early dramatic treatments of the essential antipathy and the historic struggle between the nature religion of Dionysus and the reason religion of the newly emerging city states, see *Antigone* by Sophocles and *The Bacchae* by Euripides.

12. We cannot tell about Pythagoras; none of his writings, if indeed he composed any, is extant. For a brief but informative treatment of his thought's impact on philosophy, physics, and mathematics, however, see R. G. Collingwood, *The Idea of Nature* (New York: Oxford University Press, Inc., 1960), pp. 49–55.

13.   The derivation of these ideas appears to proceed thus: First, sense experience relates the mind to a physical thing; then the mind constructs an image and a concept of this thing; the mind proceeds similarly with other things. To this point all of the mind's ideas appear to derive directly from sense experience. But then the mind creates other ideas in order to relate and organize its sense-derived ideas. These ideas—for example, number, ratio, space, time, cause, justice, love—are the mind's own creations, expressions of its own nature, and ultimately (according to Platonic reasoning) expressions of a higher, divine order of reality.

14.   Thomas Robert Malthus, whose name provides the basis of the adjective "Malthusian," was a nineteenth-century British economist who argued that poverty is unavoidable because population growth occurs by geometrical progression though provisions for subsistence increase only arithmetically. Occasional catastrophe (or Malthusian crisis) is therefore inevitable as nature, human avarice, and the like impose limits on population through famine, disease, and war.

15.   The significance of such mathematical terms in both ordinary language and clinical theories of mental health would make an interesting subject for study. We speak of mentally ill persons as being "unbalanced," for example, and in Freudian theory normalcy comes about through the ego's maintenance of a degree of proportion between the demands of the id and those of the super ego.

16.   In a similar vein a latter-day reason religionist named Sigmund Freud portrayed the self as a triadic being composed of animal instincts (the id), social inhibitions (the super ego), and rationality (the ego). The ego in this model is something like a rope in a tug of war between the animal and the social dimensions of the self. If the rope snaps, the self loses not only its individual integrity but also its social usefulness.

17.   During the 1960s a number of riots occurred in the major industrial cities of the United States. For the most part these expressed the frustrations and the just anger of the inhabitants of the cities' black ghettos. But one sadly ironic short-term consequence of the riots was that the people who suffered most from them were the ghetto residents themselves. This irony, which seems to accompany most revolutions, helps explain the rationalist's deep-seated fear of any form of excess, even that which seems justly motivated.

18.   It often has been observed that nothing produces tyranny more quickly and effectively than anarchy. The cries of "law and order" which arose in America during the sixties were in part code words designed to protect racist traditions and institutions, but they were in part, too, the perennial watchwords of city dwellers, frightened as they are by the prospect of anarchy.

19.   See note 18.

20.   The religious cast this takes has been noted and emphasized by J. Paul Williams in *What Americans Believe and How They Worship*, rev. ed. (New York: Harper & Brothers, Publishers, 1961). Williams himself suggests that "Governmental agencies must teach the democratic ideal *as religion*" (p. 488) and nominates the public school for the role of a kind of established church to that end (p. 490). Emphasis in original.

21.   In *The Republic*, Book VII.

22.   The celebrated fable of the town mouse and the country mouse goes back at least to Aesop (sixth century B.C.) and has had countless retellings, clearly signaling both the antiquity and the persistence of the rivalry between naturists and city dwellers.

23.   An old philosophic pun states one version of this fundamental distinction: "An idealist [read "rationalist"] says 'No matter'; a materialist [one type of naturist] replies 'Never mind.'"

24.   This crisis finds poignant expression in Psalm 137, doubtless a psalm composed during the Babylonian exile or in painful remembrance of it:

"By the waters of Babylon,
    there we sat down and wept,
        when we remembered Zion. . . . [the Temple's site in Jerusalem]
    How shall we sing the Lord's song
        in a foreign land?"

25. Cf. Elijah's encounter with the prophets of Baal to determine whether Baal or Yahweh was in fact the Lord of rain: I Kings 18:17–40.

26. Isaiah 51:1; Hosea 13:4–5. The phrase "honeymoon in the wilderness" is B. W. Anderson's in *Understanding the Old Testament,* 3rd ed. (Englewood Cliffs, N. J.: Prentice-Hall, Inc., 1975), p. 289.

27. This belief persists today. In the award-winning play *Fiddler on the Roof,* the staunchly Jewish protagonist, Tevye, concludes his musical tribute to "tradition" with the memorable line, "Without our traditions, our lives would be as shaky as—as a fiddler on the roof!" Taken from *Fiddler on the Roof* by Joseph Stein. © 1964 by Joseph Stein. Used by permission of Crown Publishers, Inc.

28. Exodus 19:6.

29. Exodus 3:13.

30. J. L. Moreau, trans., *Hebrew Thought Compared with Greek* (Philadelphia: The Westminster Press, 1960), especially pp. 27–73.

31. Cf. Isaiah 10:5: "Ah, Assyria, the rod of my anger, the staff of my fury! Against a godless nation [apostate Judah] I send him, and against the people of my wrath I command him . . ."; and Psalm 76:10: "Surely the wrath of men shall praise thee; the residue of wrath thou wilt gird upon thee."

32. Gen. 3:1, 4.

33. Exod. 3:4 *et passim.*

34. Numbers 22:28–30.

35. Matt. 6:28; cf. Luke 12:27.

36. Matt. 17:20; cf. Luke 17:6.

37. Gen. 3:1–7; cf. especially verse 5 (the serpent's invitation to become "as god").

38. Gen. 4:1–14; Cain's banishment from the land here seems to be redemptive in purpose, as if it were his attachment to the land that had led to the Lord's displeasure and the consequent murder of Abel. See Chapter VI, p. 218.

39. Cf. Gen. 11:1–9.

40. Cf. Gen. 32:24–28, 35:9–10.

41. Besides the story of his birth (from which one of the traditions regarding his name came), Gen. 25:21–26, see also the account of Jacob's relations with his brother Esau, Gen. 27–33.

42. Classical comedy should be distinguished from farce and from the "sitcoms" that dominate today's television fare. In medieval usage, reports the Oxford English Dictionary, "the term was applied to other than dramatic compositions, the 'happy ending' being the essential part of the notion." Cf. "Comedy," *The Compact Edition of the Oxford English Dictionary* (New York: Oxford University Press, 1971), Vol. I, p. 659, col. 1.

43. See Gen. 3:5.

44. For an excellent exposition of the distinction between a "cosmic" or "natural" approach to time and a historical approach, see M. Eliade, *Cosmos and History: The Myth of the Eternal Return* (New York: Harper & Brothers, Publishers, 1959); see also Reinhold Niebuhr's broader but equally brilliant analyses in *Faith and History* (New York: Charles Scribner's Sons, 1949) and *The Self and the Dramas of History* (New York: Charles Scribner's Sons, 1955).

III. Putting Christianity

on the Map

THIS CHAPTER'S TITLE may seem both presumptuous and ironic. It is indeed presumptuous to the extent that it suggests that Christianity *needs* putting on the map and that a chapter in a book could put it there. It goes without saying that such a suggestion is not the intention of the title. Nor does it intend to suggest that Christianity is a geographic phenomenon, more at home in some places than in others. Such a suggestion would be ironic indeed, in view of what was said in Chapter II about Christianity's parent faith, Judaism. There we learned that the Judaeo-Christian perspective celebrates certain events in time rather than certain sites in space. What we mean by "putting Christianity on the map," then, is not that the Christian faith is more closely tied by its nature to some places than to others, or even to one type of space (country space, say) than to another, but rather that this chapter will be devoted to fulfilling the last chapter's promise to locate Christianity within our broad outline of the world's religious families.

Our map is only metaphorical, and even within the terms of the metaphor we need to take precautions lest we oversimplify Christianity's "location" on it. Although the faith of Christians is born of history, it is in practice affected by the spaces it occupies as well as by the times. The visitor to the typical city church will therefore be impressed by the formality of its order of service and the classical, rational style of its music. The same visitor in a country or country town congregation might be struck by the informality of the service, the emotional preaching, and the rousing tempo of the singing. Both congregations are Christian in orientation: both take their bearings from the same sacred history, but they do so in ways and at tempos that reflect their spatial and cultural environments.

The diversity in Christian life and practice is as perceptible as the unity. In attending to and stressing those things which unify and typify Christian faith and behavior, we do not mean to deny this diversity. But an attempt to describe so broad and rich a diversity would take us beyond our space and purpose here. We shall therefore simply note it and shall now try to identify Christianity's essential and unifying orientation.

We have already noted that in essence Christianity is a history-based, rather than a reason-based or a nature-based, religion. This chapter will be devoted to justifying and clarifying this claim. In the first section to follow ("Christianity as a Historist Faith"), we shall seek to justify it; in the second ("Faith as Time-Consciousness and Involvement in History"), we shall seek to clarify its meaning; and in the third ("The Christian View of the Self-World Relation"), we shall attempt to spell out its implications for the art of putting a world together.

CHRISTIANITY AS A HISTORIST FAITH

Our first task is to examine Christianity's credentials as a faith born of history. Why do we classify it so, instead of as a faith begotten by nature or reason? What evidence substantiates the location of Christianity on the continent of historism rather than on the other major continents on our map of religious perspectives?

The evidence is abundant—so abundant that our use of it must be selective. We could reintroduce as evidence, for example, our entire description of the Hebrew outlook in Chapter II, for Christians look at reality through lenses prescribed and crafted largely by that outlook. Yahweh, the Lord of history, is the God of Christians as well as of Jews, and Christians, like Jews, understand themselves as reactors to Yahweh's initiatives. Christians also share with Jews the problems of maintaining identity, avoiding idolatry, and retaining responsibility. Like their Jewish precursors and contemporaries they look to the steadfast and sovereign love of God, as expressed in historical events, as their hope of salvation.

As St. Augustine argued in his epic philosophy of history, *The City of God*, the ways of God are manifest to Christian eyes not only in the histories of the old and new Israel but also in historical dramas of larger compass and of more immediate impact.[1] The relation of Christians to history is thus not one of memorization of a sacred past so much as one of confrontation by an imperious present. Though the Christian comes to the present moment armed with a remembered history and with lessons learned from that history, these can only clarify the nature of his historical responsibility; they cannot in any way shield him or her from the pressure of deciding what must be done and how to go about doing it.

The evidence that Christianity is a historist faith is thus of two sorts. There is evidence based on the testimony and the interpretations of history of predecessors in the faith and there is evidence based on the calling to participate in history which is experienced by contemporary Christians themselves. The former evidence is *extensive:* it *extends* the vision of modern Christians, providing the larger scenario or horizon within which they are to view the challenge to action which is peculiarly theirs.[2] The latter is *intensive:* it is a "burning in the bones"[3] which will not permit Christians to close their eyes or to ignore their responsibility to the historical situation to which they belong.

Most of our attention in this section will be given to the first of these types of evidence. In a sense this is the easier type of evidence to examine, for it is easier to comprehend the rather objective testimony of those who have gone before than to probe our own existential involvements or those of our contemporaries. Once we have examined this background and the philosophy of history from which Christians proceed, we shall tackle the more difficult job of characterizing the intensive engagement with history required by contemporary Christian faith.

For the sake of analysis we shall separate the *extensive* evidence that Christianity is a history-based faith into three kinds: evidence based on the Christian perception of time's form or shape, that based on crucial (revelatory) events, and that based on history's importance to the destiny of individuals. We shall deal with these types of evidence singly and serially; in the actual Christian perspective they interrelate.

Evidence From Time's Form or Shape

One of the clearest indications that Christianity is a history-based faith is to be found in the perceptions Christians have of history's shape or form. Almost from the instant at which humans began to think, they seem to have found in the forms or shapes of things significant clues to their meaning. Thus in myths which are among the first evidences of sustained human thought the first enemy to be conquered by the beneficent creator of the human circumstance is the dragon of chaos—the principle of disorder, formlessness, and confusion. And as chaos has been considered the deadliest enemy of human well-being, so its opposite, cosmos—form, order, intelligible structure—has been viewed as the indispensable ally of knowledge and progress.

In the Western tradition, form or shape indicates not only significance and intelligibility but also value. "Staying in shape" is pursued with a passion by modern Americans because the phrase is associated with the enjoyment of health, personal well-being, and the good life. Thus the very way that we describe our physical condition reflects the Western conviction that shape denotes value.

Virtually all religions and philosophies assign some shape to time, that "stuff" or duration of which history is made. This attribution of shape is perhaps a function of an intrinsic psychic mechanism by which we humans cope with the environments which crucially affect our lives. This psychic mechanism or faculty might be called a "sixth sense," a religious sense or capacity which makes possible that art of putting things together which constitutes religion.

The way a faith or philosophy views time may indicate how it puts reality together. This is one reason we paid close attention, in Chapter II, to the attitudes toward time held by the various families of religion. Now we must move from the general considerations of that chapter to a specific look at Christianity's outlook on time. We must do so because we believe that such scrutiny can provide insight into the way Christianity's vision of reality coheres.

Exhibit A in any demonstration of the Christian's perception of time's shape should perhaps be the shape, the arrangement or organization, of the Christian scriptures. The first and last books of the Holy Bible are Genesis and Revelation. Surely it is significant that the first of these deals with the beginning of cosmic and human history and that the latter deals with the end, the outcome, of these. In this arrangement of their sacred scriptures, Christianity's initiators made clear their conviction that time or history has both a beginning and an end.

If they said nothing else about history's shape, Christians would be saying a great deal by this simple act of ascribing to it a beginning and an end. This ascription indicates, at the least, that from the Christian standpoint history is not circular, for a circle has neither beginning nor end. A circle's circumference pursues itself relentlessly and endlessly, never encompassing new ground, never reaching any goal beyond itself. That Christians see history as noncircular means that they see hope for it; they see in it the promise of progress, the potential for traversing new territory and attaining transhistorical goals.

Christianity's favorite word for its message is "gospel," a word meaning "good news." The good news about history, Christians claim, is that it is not meaningless, not a merry-go-round on its way nowhere, but rather a life-gripping drama which is both rooted in and routed toward God.[4]

The beginning and end of history rest in God.[5] On that point Christians speak with a single voice. On what lies in between, their views are hardly so uniform. Although they agree that history has value, they disagree on very basic questions about the nature of its value. Some argue, for example, that history is of purely instrumental value, that it is only educational or purgatorial in character, a testing ground to prepare human beings for a life beyond.[6] Others maintain that history, as the sphere of activity of the community in which and through which God intends to establish his rule on earth, has value in itself.[7] Both of these groups are wary of historiolatry, or history worship, though on occasion each has been guilty of it.[8] But neither has been able to convince the other that its vision of history's role in the divine plan is the correct one.

Another point at dispute among Christians, where history's character and purpose are concerned, is the issue of individualism versus corporatism. Is history's objective the salvation of persons or the reconstitution of human society? Does the Kingdom of God mean primarily the rule of God over the minds and hearts of individuals or the accomplishment of the divine will in social and political spheres? Although more and more Christians are today inclined to resist radical separation of history's individual dimensions from its social aspects, many differ on the question of which is end and which is means: is the salvation of the individual merely a step toward the building of a Christ-ruled commonwealth, or is such a commonwealth to be sought chiefly as a way of developing superior individuals?

These are issues to which we shall return later.[9] Their relevance to our present question is that they indicate the seriousness with which Christians pursue history's meaning, and in so doing they illustrate the Christian conviction that history is significant. It is this conviction that has prompted Christians to seek some design or shape within history. As part of our effort to document the reality and depth of this conviction, we now must consider several of the theories or theologies which assign a significant shape to history.

Within the Christian tradition, three such theories seem especially notable. One of these is ancient, the other two of recent origin. The ancient formulation was that of Irenaeus of Lyons (A.D. 130–202). The history of humankind, according to Irenaeus, is summarized or "recapitulated" in the history of Jesus Christ.[10] Christ's history has both a unique aspect (in that he was a unique historical individual) and a universal quality (in that his history epitomizes the entire human pilgrimage).[11] Christ thus is equipped by his history to be the savior of the individual and the species alike.[12]

If, in Irenaeus's view, Christ's existence is thoroughly historical, it is no less true that he sees history as thoroughly Christ-centered. Christ is human history's center not only because he identifies with humankind's most profound historical experiences but also because he discloses history's actual meaning and embodies its ultimate purpose.[13] This history

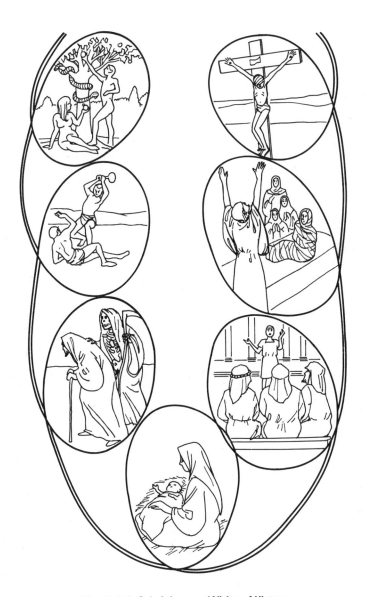

The Christic Spiral: Irenaeus' Vision of History

In one of the first attempts to think through the gospel's implications for history, St. Irenaeus (130-202) portrayed the Incarnation as history's turning point. By recapitulating the human pilgramage, Christ redeemed and sanctified the life-phases of infancy, youth, maturity, and death, reliving and countermanding the deadly works of Adam, Cain and Death itself.

is not a static circle but a dynamic, progressive spiral which dips into human life, identifying with it so as to redirect and transform[14] it. Thus Jaroslav Pelikan can write of Irenaeus' view that, for him, "the curve of man's life may follow the curve of Christ's life through death to the new life in God."[15]

For our purposes the important thing about Irenaeus' vision of Christ is that it illustrates the seriousness with which Christians take history and constitutes one of the earliest Christian attempts to grasp history's shape and find in that shape a divine purpose. History as Irenaeus perceives it is clearly redemptive. It is redemptive because the God who created it in the beginning has invaded its center and redirected it toward a transcendent end. As Pelikan's image of a horizontal spiral suggests, Irenaeus does not ignore history's ups and downs, but neither does he accept them as the final word on history. Rather, the final word is suggested by the spiral's forward motion, and by the Christ who, as the spiral's moving center and spearhead, is the dynamic source of that motion.

Irenaeus' vision of history's shape and course provides substantial evidence of the appreciation for history which characterized early Christian thought. Both his view of history and the positive shape he assigns it bespeak his appreciation for it. Nor is Irenaeus the only witness we might call on to speak in behalf of Christian antiquity. St. Luke before him and St. Augustine after him drafted formidable Christian philosophies of history. They, no less than he, saw a divine intention operating in history. They, like he, were thoroughly Christian in their perception of that intention, seeing Christ as both the hub and the horizon of history.

No less Christ-centered than these ancient analyses is an important modern analysis of history's shape, that of Oscar Cullman. Cullmann, who taught biblical theology at the University of Basel, was perhaps best known for his sustained attempt to rethink and retrace the shape of biblical history in two books: *Christ and Time* and *Salvation in History*. The general lines that biblical history follows, he suggested, are like those of an hourglass lying on its side.[16] One hemisphere of the glass (representing Old Testament history) leads up to and points toward Christ, while the other (symbolizing the New Testament era) originates in and takes its bearings from him. So Christ, as history's midpoint, gives meaning to each age, fulfilling the hope of the one and providing impetus for the other.

Cullmann's conception of history's shape lacks the dynamism of Irenaeus' progressive spiral. But both writers indicated that, in the Christian view of things, history has considerable, even sacramental, significance. Like the beginning and end of the Bible itself, these in-

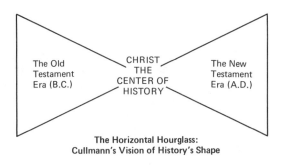

The Horizontal Hourglass:
Cullmann's Vision of History's Shape

terpretations of biblical history's shape suggest that the Christian faith is rooted in a distinctive perspective on historical events.

By far the most ambitious modern attempt to outline history's shape in Christian terms is that of the French Catholic naturalist, Teilhard de Chardin. Teilhard's historical vision stretches beyond biblical history, even beyond the human pilgrimage, to include the history of the natural cosmos or universe. For Teilhard, nature is neither history's passive backdrop or stage nor a mere bit player in its dramas. It is instead history's macrocosmic hero, even as humans are its microcosmic heroes.

The history of nature is in Teilhard's scheme an evolutionary drama in five acts: cosmogenesis, biogenesis, anthropogenesis, noogenesis, and Christogenesis. Cosmogenesis corresponds roughly to the biblical creation event; it is the coming into being, or at least the development into its present form,[17] of the natural universe. With biogenesis the cosmos took the first of a series of quantum leaps to higher stages or plateaus of development. Life emerged through biogenesis, then began the long process of evolving into ever more complex forms. Eventually, in anthropogenesis, a life form of such complexity appeared that its emergence amounts to a second quantum leap: the leap into history's human phase.

The fourth phase in Teilhard's schematization of cosmic history, noogenesis, does not appear from the physical point of view to involve a quantum leap. Noogenesis refers to the emergence of self-consciousness. Although self-consciousness did not *emerge* for quite a long time after humans' emergence, it was present as the "within" of things (that is, as their potential for self-consciousness or their potential "spirit") from the moment of cosmogenesis on. It is thus as much a thread through the process of evolution as an outcome of it. Nevertheless its *emergence* is of great importance to history, for in its emergence the "within" (spirit) of nature began to manifest itself.[18]

The manifestation of nature's "within," or spirit, reached its climax *in principle* with the appearance of Christ. In him the fifth epochal process, Christogenesis, surfaces. In his initial appearance Christ revealed the potential the universe has for becoming the body of God. The divine intention, which "super-determines"[19] the entire cosmic process, is that that process shall culminate in a Christosphere, an incorporation of the universe as a whole into the mystical body of Christ. In this sphere the promise of Paul, that God will become "all in all," will find fulfillment.[20]

Clearly for Teilhard, as for Irenaeus and Cullmann, history is an arena of significant activity. This is so because it is an arena in which God himself acts. Although the nature of this divine activity is not altogether clear (though it seems to happen largely through slow, incremental, and epoch-consuming processes), its *shape* was described by Teilhard. That shape is that of a converging or involutive coil: "Wherever we look on earth," he wrote, "the growth of the *'within'* only takes place thanks to a *doubly related involution,* the coiling up of the molecule upon itself and the coiling up of the planet upon itself."[21]

What such coiling does is create "centres" of increasing complexity in which the universe's energy becomes concentrated. Much as the sprinter's crouch makes possible a burst of speed at the start of a foot race, these coils of concentrated energy make possible advances in "interiorisation" and, ultimately, in the most dramatic of the quantum leaps, the emergence of consciousness and thought. As the total universe's "or-

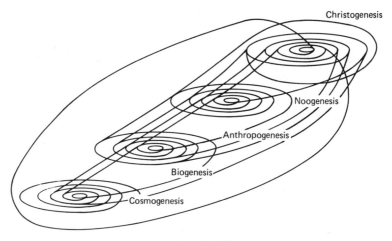

Cosmic Coilings:
Teilhard's Vision of History

In the diagram the large, all-encompassing coil represents cosmic history as a whole. Each of the smaller coils represents a stage in the evolution of that history. Note how each stage emerges from the center of its predecessor as a product of the predecessor's increasing complexity and density; note, too, how each stage reaches back to incorporate and recapitulate elements from the prior stages. History, in Teilhard's view, is a series of creative coilings, each of which recapitulates the past even as it contributes to the creation of the future.

ganic centre," Christ is its ultimate "Centre of centres," who will gather up at the horizon of history the strands of evolving energy which he inspired at history's outset, thus ushering in a kingdom of cosmic consciousness and universal love.

Teilhard's effort to educe physical or scientific evidence for his Christian vision of reality may or may not be convincing to his readers. What it certainly does do is attest to the powerful faith of one of our century's most original thinkers in the Christian interpretation of history. According to this faith, even nature is replete with the signs of divine activity and joins humans in moving history toward a divine destiny.[22] Teilhard thus joins Irenaeus, Cullmann, and the shape of the Bible itself as a witness to the historical character of the Christian faith.

Evidence from Crucial (Revelatory) Events

Oscar Cullmann's exploration of history's meaning in *Christ and Time* extends beyond the examination of time's form or shape to a consideration of certain events which in his judgment especially reveal that meaning. He sees these events as relating to and reinforcing each other. Basically they all are expressions of the covenant theme which is central to the biblical understanding of history's course and meaning.

As we suggested in Chapter II, the biblical conception of the covenant may best be described as a divine-human drama in which God is the protagonist (a term whose original Greek meaning was "first actor") and humans the antagonists ("reactors"). That the covenant is remembered chiefly through the community's recollection and reenactment in worship of certain historical *events* indicates that it is not to be conceived in static, nonhistorical terms but rather in dynamic terms of a once-lived and still lively history.

Cullmann's list of these events begins with the transhistorical or superhistorical event of creation. It then dips into history to include the emergence of humankind (Adam), the call of Abraham, the history of the prophetic movement, the climactic and portentous career of Christ, and the witness of the apostles and the Church. It looks forward, finally, to horizons both historical (the redemption of humankind) and transhistorical (the recreation of the universe).

As the accompanying chart indicates, the first four of the named events describe a progressively downward movement, a progressive betrayal by humans of the covenant commitment: creation and the emergence of humans were followed by the Fall of humankind, Abraham's call by the faithlessness of Israel, and the challenge of the prophets by deafness and defiance in their hearers. Finally, after such apostasy, the whole weight of the covenant history comes to rest on the shoulders of the sole faithful human, the Christ. In him, however, history's declining tendency is reversed, the covenant renewed and revised, and time set on an upward course. The apostles and the Church are commissioned to become the agents and proclaimers of this new day, the keepers of its new covenant. Ultimately all humanity is to be drawn into the new relationship with God that this new covenant signals, and a new heaven and a new earth are to emerge as the covenant's fulfillment.

Though Cullmann's sketch of the Bible's crucial revelatory events is just that—a sketch—and though it does not include some critically important events (for example, the Exodus, the Sinai events, the career of King David), it is nevertheless helpful as an outline of the biblical history's progression. More important to our purposes, his sketch shows clearly that the Judaeo-Christian point of view is solidly grounded in an understanding of history as a wrestling match between Yahweh, Lord of Ages, and the corporate consciences of two historic communities, Jews and Christians.

Two events illustrate particularly well the historical nature and effect of biblical faith. These events are the Exodus of Israel, usually dated about 1290 B.C. and the birth of the Christ, from which Christian historiographers date the beginning of the Christian era. The first of these (strangely omitted by Cullmann) brought Israel out of slavery into an era of new social and political possibilities. Together with the events that

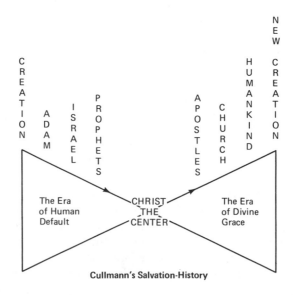

Cullmann's Salvation-History

followed it, the Exodus made Israel a viable and independent community. Its even more important and enduring result was the idea and ideal of God as a revolutionary who takes the side of the underdog, exalting the humble and humbling the exalted.

As Harvey Cox brilliantly argued in *The Secular City*, Yahweh's humbling of Pharaoh in the events of the Exodus may have done more to reshape Western political theory and practice than any other single event. For with these events, politics is in principle desacralized: kings and emperors lose all claim to divinity or divine sanction, their authority is shown to be human in origin, and their proper role becomes that of the people's servant rather than that of the unbridled monarch.

The Exodus event thus makes an enormous difference in human perceptions of history. For those who view it through the prism of this event, history is no longer the preserve of sacred dynasties but rather a stream of events in which the masses play as crucial a role as the mighty elites. Might no longer bestows divine right, and the ancient view of revolution as sacrilege is disallowed.

This portrait of God as historical revolutionary was both reinforced and enriched by the second pivotal event in biblical salvation history, the event of Christ's birth or, in theological terms, the event of Incarnation.

Incarnation—the occasion of God's self-embodiment in a person named Jesus of Nazareth—is to the Christian covenant what the Exodus was to the covenant of Israel: its inspiration and prime shaper. As in the Exodus God struck an alliance with a band of slaves, so in the Incarnation he again takes the part of the lowly, identifying himself with the last and the least among the ranks of humankind.[23] Born among animals, he lives among outcasts and dies between thieves.[24]

If St. Luke is to be trusted, no one sensed the implication of God's mighty deed of Incarnation more keenly than his partner in that deed, Mary of Nazareth. "His name is Holy," she cries after the Annunciation,

> his mercy sure from generation to generation . . . .
>   the arrogant of heart and mind he has put to rout,
> he has brought down monarchs from their thrones,
>   but the humble have been lifted high.
> The hungry he has satisfied with good things,
>   the rich sent empty away.[25]

The historical impact of what was begun in her body was not lost, in Luke's view, on Mary of Nazareth. Nor was it lost on an anonymous nineteenth-century writer who, with the advantage of considerably more hindsight, summed up this impact:

Here is a young man who was born in an obscure village, the child of a peasant woman. . . . He never wrote a book. He never held an office. . . . He never did one of the things that usually accompany greatness. He had no credentials but himself. While he was still a young man, the tide of public opinion turned against him. His friends ran away. He was turned over to his enemies. He went through the mockery of a trial. He was nailed to a cross between two thieves. While he was dying, his executioners gambled for the only piece of property he had on earth, and that was his coat. When he was dead, he was laid in a borrowed grave through the pity of a friend. Nineteen wide centuries have come and gone, and today he is the central figure of the human race and the leader of the column of progress. I am far within the mark when I say that all the armies that ever marched, and all the navies that were ever built, and all the parliaments that ever sat, and all the kings that ever reigned, put together, have not affected the life of man upon this earth as has that one solitary Life.

Eloquent interpretations of both ancient and modern vintage thus attest to the Incarnation's impact on history's course and character. But in referring to Christ's leadership of "the column of progress," our nineteenth-century interpreter contributed to a major misconstruction of Christ's meaning for history. Nineteenth-century thinkers in general thought they heard in Christ an echo of their own enthusiasm for the paramount cultural values of their day. Christ was the pioneer in history's irresistible march toward "progress," the chief patron of the idea that "every day, in every way" the human situation improves.

Such a view, however, ignores an important ingredient in the gospel portraits of Jesus. There he is portrayed not only as history's transformer but also as its judge. In him history, even sacred history, finds not only an echo but also an end. His crucifixion and resurrection indicate that, though history may be God's story, it is not God. Therefore to enshrine sacred traditions or recent progressive programs at the expense of present responsibility or future resiliency is a mistake. The hallmark of the new covenant is freedom, freedom to break with "the men of old,"[26] to "let the dead bury the dead,"[27] in short to avoid all alliances with past traditions and present practices that might impede the advance of God's rule.

No one has seen the meaning of the New Testament's view of Christ as history's end more clearly than the great German scholar, Rudolf Bultmann. For Bultmann Christ is preeminently "the eschatological event."[28] He is, in shorter, clearer words, the end[29] or conclusive event in the sacred history of Israel. In him that history comes to a close, and a new history is begun. This new history is always *frontier* history; it is, in other words, always a history of restless pilgrims who can never quite be at home in history, can never settle down into a routine or tradition but always must reside in history "as if not"[30]—that is, without becoming too attached to any of its transient forms.

Christ, as the end of history, puts an end to all history worship, all identification of historical institutions or customs with God. Life in him becomes life in "the moment" (Kierkegaard). "The moment" is a time of opportunity in which the decision may and must be made to begin anew, to live in freedom from both the pride or guilt begotten of past deeds and the anxiety or blind ambition prompted by future prospects. "If any one is in Christ," St. Paul wrote, "he is a new creation; the old has passed away; behold, the new has come."[31]

No theme is more prominent in the New Testament than this theme of a new start. "Follow me. . . . And they . . . left their nets, and followed him."[32] "Except ye be converted, and become as little children, ye shall not enter into the kingdom of heaven."[33] "Truly, . . . unless one is born anew, he cannot see the kingdom of God."[34] "Be transformed by the renewal of your mind."[35] "The old leaven of corruption is working among you. Purge it out, and then you will be bread of a new baking."[36] "Circumcision is nothing; uncircumcision is nothing; the only thing that counts is new creation!"[37]

The history that Christ ushers in, and the history Christians therefore celebrate, is that of a new age. This new age brings both a reversal of the former age's values[38] and a forgiving and transforming acceptance of those who formerly served those values. The watchword of the participants in this age was sounded long ago by St. Paul: "Forgetting what is behind me, and reaching out for that which lies ahead, I press towards the goal to win the prize which is God's call to the life above, in Christ Jesus."[39]

The Christian belief that the very course and character of history have been changed by the divine intervention through Moses (the Exodus) and through Christ (the Incarnation) is further evidence that Christianity belongs to the faiths of history rather than to those of reason and nature. History's substance, like its shape, reveals those values which to Christian eyes appear most worth serving.

Evidence Based on History's Importance to the Destiny of Individuals

The final witness in our case identifying Christianity as a faith of history is a creedal statement that, though often recited, is little understood by Christians themselves. It is the next to last phrase in the Apostles' Creed: "the resurrection of the body."

Among lay Christians, typical attitudes toward this phrase range from that of the crass literalist who identifies bodily resurrection with the resuscitation of corpses, through that of the liberal intellectual who equates it with a kind of Platonic immortality of the soul, to that of so-called secular Christians who translate it as a power to love one's neighbor which is caught like a contagion from Jesus.[40] Yet none of these attitudes or interpretations of resurrection finds any real grounding in Scripture.

The only sustained scriptural attempt to define the nature of resurrection is that of St. Paul in I Corinthians 15. This passage, regarded by scholars as the oldest resurrection account in the New Testament, makes it clear that Paul did not understand resurrection to mean any of the things just cited. Indeed, he explicitly denies the confusion of resurrection with resuscitation* and implicitly denies both the traditional liberal interpretation† and that of the secular radical.**

What did Paul mean in speaking of the resurrection? He himself approached the question of the nature of the resurrection with a reverent reserve. God alone, he seems to think, can give it a final answer ("God gives it a body as he has chosen." I Corinthians 15:38). Yet Paul's thoughtfulness and care in answering suggest that he believed that he had been granted at least some insight into the matter, and the authoritative manner in which he expressed his views indicates that in this as in other matters he expected his readers to take his views seriously.

Paul's precise phrase for the resurrection state anticipated by Christians is "spiritual body." What can this highly paradoxical phrase mean? As scholars like Bultmann, Günther Bornkamm, and J.A.T. Robinson have shown,[41] the Greek term Paul uses here, *soma,* may be obscured rather than clarified by its usual English translation, "body." Although the term does refer to the physical organism, it meant much more than that to the Greek mind and more still to the cosmopolitan rabbi, Paul.

The body was for the Greeks the *individuating principle* in human beings.[42] Physically, of course, it marked the visible boundary (Greek: *horismos*) between one individual and another. (Your rights of self-expression end, as the proverb has it, where the tip of my nose begins.) But more than that, as the self's temporal aspect it locates the self con-

---

*Cf. I Corinthians 15:44—"It is sown a physical body, it is raised a spiritual body"; and 15:50—"I tell you this, brethren; flesh and blood cannot inherit the kingdom of God, nor does the perishable inherit the imperishable."

†By his deliberate choice of the word "body" rather than the words "soul" or "spirit," terms he not only knew but actually used in other connections.

**By complete omission of any reference to it.

cretely in space and time, making the self identifiable as a product of one particular time and place rather than some other.

Although St. Paul wrote in Greek, his background was rabbinical, that is, Jewish. The Hebrew mind, unlike the Greek, thought of human beings as unitary rather than dual in character. Humans are not divisible into two parts (body and soul or spirit) but are rather indivisible beings, animated or spirited bodies. In speaking of body, then, Paul was almost certainly speaking of the entire individual or, as we would say, the "person" or "personality." That he speaks of the person primarily as "body" rather than as "spirit" or "mind," as the educated Greek would surely do, is highly significant. The educated Greek who believed in an afterlife probably subscribed to the Platonic and gnostic notion that what survives death is the intellective soul, or mind. The mind, in Greek thought, is the universal principle in humans, as contrasted with the individuating principle in them (body). The mind, in other words, is what enables the human being to participate in universal truth and in the universal mind, or God. At death, the prevailing belief had it, the individual mind that succeeds in escaping its bodily attachments can return to the universal (divine) mind and become absorbed in it, losing its individuality as it shed its body. Greek immortality was not immortality of the individual but immortality of a soul that is essentially a miniscule part of the divine spirit—a spark from the divine fire, as the Greeks sometimes put it. But it is not so with the immortality of which Paul speaks. In asserting that the resurrection life is that of the body, Paul in effect declares it to be the life of the concrete individual.

But what makes one an individual or "body"? Here the analyses of Robinson and Bornkamm are especially helpful. Robinson observes that for the Hebrew, "True individuality was seen to be grounded solely in the indivisible responsibility of each man to God,"[43] and Bornkamm notes that, for Paul, "Being present in the body . . . is meant to characterize man's involvement in time and history."[44] To be an individual or body, therefore, seems to mean not only separability from other beings but also relationship and responsibility to other beings, especially to God and to one's fellow inhabitants of time, human neighbors.

It is at just this point that Paul's teaching about the resurrection of the body intersects our idea of the historicality of Christianity. For what Paul suggests in tying resurrection to concrete, temporal individuals ("bodies") is that *history, which makes individuals what they are, does count.* Indeed, in the final analysis each of us is no more and no less than the gestalt, or pattern of intermeshing actions, habits, and relationships, that our involvement with history has made us. What we do in the body, that is, at those points at which our lives intersect history to affect it and be affected by it, has eternal consequences. Paul really said much more than meets the eye when he said to the Romans, "I beseech you . . . that you present your bodies [historical selves!] a living sacrifice, holy and acceptable unto God."[45]

As we noted earlier, the liberals of an earlier generation used to confuse Christian resurrection of the body with Platonic immortality of the soul. Another phrase of theirs, however, came considerably closer to the biblical idea. When they spoke of the "infinite worth of the individual," these liberals generally had an ethical principle in mind; but, perhaps accidentally, they expressed the object of the Christian hope very well. The individual produced by history has an eternal destiny, according to Paul, and therefore an infinite worth. What happens in history is accordingly of crucial, and thus of Christian, significance, for it makes humans the persons they are to be eternally.

Christian faith thus affirms the importance of history through its affirmation of history's premier product, the individual personality. In so doing, it affirms again its own character as a faith rooted in history.

FAITH AS TIME-CONSCIOUSNESS AND INVOLVEMENT IN HISTORY

The peculiar capacity that we human beings have for living historically is one of the most striking differences between us and the nonhuman animals. In Chapter I we observed that humans cease to be mere animals when they gain the capacity to assign values to facts. With this capacity, we also noted, the potential for religion, the art of tying together facts and values, emerges. In Chapter II, and again in this chapter, we noted that one way this tying together comes about is through a sense of time. Our consciousness of time leads us to believe that a pattern of before and after, cause and consequence, does exist in reality.[46] "Time" is a name for a peculiar sense of order which expresses the human ability to tie reality into a cohesive whole. Viewed from a certain angle, time may be seen as a "religious" sense, for it is a means by which we accomplish the essentially religious work of tying things together.

We are not arguing here, it should be noted, that our sense of time is something we invent, a product of our conscious endeavor. On the contrary, we maintain with Immanuel Kant[47] that time is a transcendental category of apperception—in plainer words, one of the mind's standard ways of organizing all it perceives. As a person cannot see without the eye, so he or she cannot tie reality together without a sense of time. And as human beings do not invent their eyes, neither do they invent the sense of time, the perceived arrangement of events in terms of before and after, past, present, and future, simultaneity and succession.

Time is a certain value or quality that we human beings invariably assign to or note in[48] all the things we perceive. It collaborates with our sense of space to set our world in order, enabling us to cope with it. Time-consciousness is thus an invariable element in the human struggle to survive and progress.

The relationship of our time-consciousness to our consciousness of space is so subtle and intricate that it has enthralled thinkers of the stature of Kant, Hegel, and Einstein. Fascinating though they are, these thinkers' complex theories about the time-space relationship must not be allowed to distract us here. But one question regarding this relationship is of great importance to this chapter's subject—the question, namely, whether the sense of time dominates the sense of space in a given religion, or vice versa. So pivotal is this question that the most profound differences between the major families of religion generally can be traced to the way they answer it.[49]

In nature religions and reason religions, the patterns of life of certain sacred spaces (country space, city space, or the "interior space" of the mind) control the conception of time.[50] In history religions, on the other hand, a sense of shared time or history makes possible the conquest of spatial adversity or limitation. As we observed in Chapter II, the Jewish people have surmounted the enormous obstacles imposed on them by spatial restriction (confinement to *shtetls* or ghettos, for example) and spatial deprivation (prohibitions from owning land, and so forth), and they have done so precisely by the power of a sense of history.

In this important respect Christianity is a true child of Judaism. Jesus reminded his disciples that winemakers never put new wine into old wineskins, lest the new burst the old. In like fashion, he suggested, the power of the new age that arrived in him was not to be contained by the provincial belief that one land alone is holy or one shrine alone the abode of God. In so teaching Jesus was not rejecting the faith of Israel but was recovering and reaffirming its genius. That genius was expressed by Solomon some nine hundred years earlier when he dedicated his temple to God: "Heaven itself, the highest heaven, cannot contain thee; how much less this house that I have built!"[51]

The God of Jews and Christians is thus a God on the loose, unfettered by sacred shrines and spaces. Time does not contain him either, but it is by its greater intangibility and transience a more fitting and flexible sacramental medium than is space.

Because of time's service as a sacrament, or a medium of divine revelation, there is a peculiar affinity between time-consciousness and what

Christians and Jews call "faith." The writer of the New Testament's
book of Hebrews brings this tie to light when he describes faith as "the
substance of things hoped for, the evidence of things not seen."[52] Faith
is here clearly tied to history, particularly history in its future mode (that
is, that history for which Christians hope). But as the words "substance"
(Greek *hypostasis*) and "evidence" (Greek *elenchos*) indicate, this faith is
not based merely on subjective hope or wishful thinking. It is based
rather on a confidence that the future has already begun, in Christ, to
break into and influence the present. The crucial clue to this in-breaking
is the resurrection of Jesus. The resurrection of Christ, claims Jürgen
Moltmann, "is. . . to be called 'historic,' not because it took place *in* the
history to which other categories of some sort provide a key,
but. . . because, by pointing the way for future events, it *makes* history
in which we can and must live."[53]

The nature of this history in which Christians "can and must live" is
to be the focus of our attention in this section. Christian faith produces
in its adherents a certain consciousness of time and a certain involvement in history. This consciousness and this involvement began in, and
still take their momentum and direction from, Christ himself. In the
preceding section we looked at some important Christian claims regarding the *extensive* (social, political, and even cosmic) effects of Christ's
career. In this section we look instead to some claims regarding its *intensive* (personal and psychological) effects.

Jesus Christ is viewed by Christians not only as faith's object (the
discloser of the divine purpose in history) but also as faith's "pioneer."[54]
He is well out ahead of believers not only as their faith's focus but as its
source and prime bearer as well. He is the producer of faith's subjective,
no less than its objective, possibility. This is the personal meaning of the
event Christians call Incarnation. On the personal, human ("subjective") level, Incarnation means "God getting under our skin," experiencing our human reality in its highest and lowest reaches.

Against all who would see the historical (social and political) and the
personal (psychological or private) as sharply separate spheres, Christianity maintains that God gets under our skin and changes the character of objective history in one and the same event. The Incarnation, that
is, has an impact on both the cosmic (world) order and the psychic
(human) order. The self, its situation, and the relationship between self
and situation all are changed by it.

In his book *The Meaning of Revelation*, H. Richard Niebuhr presents a
brilliant exposition of the difference that faith makes in a human being's
perception of history and of his or her own role in it. Faith history, he
asserts, is "lived" history as contrasted with history that is merely
"seen."[55] "Lived history" is history perceived as "the story of our lives,"

history known from the inside by those participating in its processes. "Seen history," on the other hand, is the historical process as it is viewed by objective spectators. The latter offers the broad but abstract perspective of the reporter in the press box, the former the far more intense and concrete impressions of the contestant on the field.

Implicit in Niebuhr's description of the two kinds of history is Immanuel Kant's distinction between phenomenal and noumenal realities. The world Kant called "phenomenal" equates roughly with seen history and is objectively or scientifically knowable. The reality he termed "noumenal" includes those spheres of reality that are objectively unknowable, that lie beyond the realm accessible to pure or scientific reason. Included among these spheres would be lived or "inner" history.

Noumenal reality (or what Niebuhr would call inner history) is knowable, in Kant's view, only by the will in action. What this means in simpler terms is that human beings can learn some things only by "doing"—that is, by becoming actively engaged with them, by *willing* (deciding, making up one's mind to participate in them intimately enough) to learn them. There are dimensions of reality, and of history in particular, that cannot be known by mere "seeing," the ordinary means by which pure reason knows. As the Psalmist said, "Deep calls to deep": only the deeply involved may learn the deeply significant.

"Seen history" deals with the outer and obvious surfaces of events, "lived history" with their depths, their inner meanings and motives. Niebuhr characterized the former as "the outer history of things," the latter as "the inner history of selves." In yet another telling comparison, he called seen history "the time we are in," lived history "the time in us."

The time we are in and the time in us are the same time, but the realization that historic time is in us, that it actually penetrates our bone marrow and permeates our thoughts and actions, makes a tremendous difference in our perceptions of our selves and our situations. Most importantly, when we realize that history is not just an objective phenomenon "out there" but rather is a life-engaging process which shapes who and how we are, we come to realize that at stake in history is nothing less than our humanness itself.

Among those who have reflected on "the time in us" and on the consequent close connection between our humanity and our historicity, two thinkers, Søren Kierkegaard and Martin Heidegger, stand out. In his *Concept of Dread*,[56] a trail-clearing essay in existential psychology, Kierkegaard located the cutting edge of our temporality in "dread" or "anxiety" (translations of the German *Angst*). The time in us, he argued, keeps us unsettled, makes us insecure, by simultaneously offering us freedom from the past and a dread-inducing uncertainty regarding the future. That we have a sense of time, in other words, means that we are free but insecure selves rather than totally determined things. Our sense of time is, in the argot of existentialism, the clearest indicator of our no/thing-ness, that is, of our status as selves rather than as mere things. *Things* are affected by time only from without, as, for example, rocks are eroded by natural temporal processes. *Selves,* on the other hand, are affected by time at the very core of their being. For time thrusts selves into situations in which fateful or future-determining decisions must be made.[57]

Kierkegaard's insights receive elaboration and amplification in Martin Heidegger's monumental volume, *Being and Time.*[58] The crucial element in human nature, Heidegger contends, is care (German *Sorge*). We are creatures of care largely because we are creatures of time, cast adrift amid the uncertain fluctuations of history. Care is the human way of coping with such fluctuations. We have to care, otherwise these fluctuations will drown us. We have to care, in less metaphorical words, because not to care is to lose our humanity, to close ourselves off from the demands and promise of history, in effect to lower ourselves to the status of things, insensitive to and unaffected by history.

Being human and being historical amount to the same thing, according to these existentialists. Human "inauthenticity" (Heidegger's word) or "sin" (Kierkegaard's) is a direct result of the attempt to bail out of history, out of no-thingness or selfhood into the seemingly more solid and secure status of thinghood. Such bailing out occurs when we quit "dreading" and "caring," thereby denying or repressing the time in us and abdicating that capacity to be shapers of history which makes us human.

What has all this to do with Christianity, and particularly with the Christian view of faith as involvement in history? Perhaps an answer will emerge if we note that Kierkegaard wrote as a self-conscious Christian and that Heidegger's philosophy has been described as a "secularized, philosophical version of the New Testament view of human life."[59] Both of these men were heavily in debt to the Christian understanding of history. It is from the biblical religions that they learned to view history as the arena in which the battle for human authenticity is to be won or lost. In Adam's hiding from God among the trees of the garden (Genesis 3), they could have found the perfect parable for sinful human efforts to climb into the woodwork, to abandon selfhood for thinghood in hopes of escaping the gaze of a righteous Creator. In Christ's conquest of that other tree, the cross, they could have perceived the ultimate triumph of human caring over the deadly indifference of those who, having themselves abandoned selfhood for thinghood, now treat other selves as mere things as well.

For Christians the stakes in history are high. At stake, indeed, is nothing less than the full and authentic humanness of human beings themselves. The authentic human being is the person who can care and, through caring, cope with history in such a way that the freedom and dignity (selfhood) of human beings are enhanced. Christians hold that such caring is itself impossible apart from a faith that one is cared for, that there is present in history One who cares. The basis of this faith can be found only in lived history. In the Christian view, as H. R. Niebuhr observed, "Faith cannot get to God save through historic experience as reason cannot get to nature save through sense-experience."[60]

THE CHRISTIAN VIEW OF THE SELF-WORLD RELATION

By now it should be clear that Christianity is not only a faith born of history but also a faith which inspires a particular approach to history. This approach is *extensive,* for it extends the Christian's vision of history by linking it to a transhistorical purpose and a larger historical community; it is also *intensive,* for it involves Christians in an intense struggle with the historical currents of their own situations. So faith both broadens and deepens the individual's perspective. Ideally at least, it does both simultaneously: it enables Christians to come to grips with themselves even as it enables them to put together a coherent world.

Ideally the intensive and extensive dimensions of faith are integrally related to each other. If the intensive element deepens one's sense of self and the extensive dimension broadens one's view of the world, faith as a total phenomenon should tie together the resulting sense of self and the resulting view of the world. To be sure, as long as it remains faith it cannot do this in any final or exhaustive way. Should it make the claim that it has done so, it would be claiming a finality that belongs to knowledge rather than to faith.[61] But its very character as religious faith involves it in the process of tying together self and world within a unified and life-directing vision of reality.

One of the principal points of distinction between Christian faith and other forms of faith is the peculiar way in which Christian faith defines the relationship between the self and the world. Nature religions tend to absorb the self into the world. In these religions, salvation consists of losing one's individuality in the boundless reaches and ceaseless rhythms of nature. Individual selfhood counts for little. In the words of a Hindu epigram, "Atman (the world soul within the self) and Brahman (the world soul within the universe) are one." In effect this means that individual differences must be submerged within an undifferentiated world unity.

If nature religions tend to lose the self in the world, reason religions tend to lose sight of the particularities of the world by focusing attention on universal laws within and beyond the mind. Legend has it that the very first philosopher, Thales, became so absorbed in his own thoughts that he walked into an open well. Such absorption of the world into the self does no more to legitimate individual selfhood than does the naturist's absorption of self into world. In reason religion, too, the individual self is devaluated, for the way of salvation again requires the subordination of individuating forces and inspirations to absolute and universal (in this case, rational) laws.

Only in faiths born of history does the selfhood of the individual appear to be accorded intrinsic value.[62] The self is valuable for such faiths for at least three reasons. Its value stems, first, from its status as a *product* of history. Because history is significant, the self, as a product of the interplay between organic nature and historical forces, also can be significant. Because it has the power to remember and perpetuate a valuable history, the self can gain for itself a kind of borrowed value. But human selfhood is more than history's vessel or instrument, and so its value is not simply dependent on some larger and more intrinsic value in history. Indeed, one of the major aims and results of history, in the Christian view, is the creation of selves. It could be argued as easily that history exists to create selves as that selfhood exists to preserve or perpetuate history.

The Christian conviction that history gains at least some of its value from its creation of human selves supports the Christian notion that selves are valuable. Equally great support for this notion is found in the Christian contention that selves are not only history's products but also its producers. The power that selves have to make history, to modify its course and to magnify its meaning, is important evidence, Christians believe, that the self has intrinsic value. Far from simply borrowing value from a history greater than itself, the self appears capable of *contributing* value to the historical process by investing itself, its wisdom and its energy, in that process.

The third main reason that the self is held to be of value among Christians stems from the very basic observation that the self must be of value if anything at all is to be of value. This observation is based on the realization that there is no human knowledge that is not mediated (perceived, organized, interpreted) by the self. If the self is considered to be of no value, then it cannot even be considered a reliable mediator. The denial of value to the self would amount to a denial of value to reality as a whole, or at least (and this amounts to the same thing, practically speaking) to a denial that such value can be reliably known.

The recognition that reality makes itself known to us only through the

THE CENTRAL POINT

A philosophistry

I am the Universe's Center.
No subtle sceptics can confound me;
for how can other viewpoints enter,
when all the rest is all around me?

concrete conditions of individual selfhood should produce in us a sense of dignity as well as a sense of humility. As Pascal observed,[63] the immensities of the universe may terrify the individual who surveys them, but in one remarkable way the individual is superior even to such immensities: the individual *knows* he or she can be swallowed up by them while the immensities of natural space are matched by an equally vast ignorance.

Nature's nervous system may be both infinite and intricate, but all of its complexity is meaningless, at least as far as human knowledge is concerned, unless its signals are received and deciphered by human selves. The self has the highest kind of value, if human knowledge is at all valuable, because for access to human knowledge we humans are stuck with, though preferably not on, ourselves.

The Anatomy of the Self

Because the self has great value in its own right, in the Christian view, and because it also has value as the mediator of the Christian (and indeed of every) view of reality, an understanding of the nature of the self is crucial to an understanding of the Christian perspective on reality as a whole. Because this is so, we shall attempt to provide a brief description or typesketch of the Christian perception of the self. It is important to keep in mind, however, that no general description of this sort can do justice to those qualities of individuality which are also held by Christians to be valuable.

Let us begin with a diagram or, if you will, an anatomical chart, of the self:

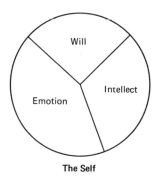

The Self

Our diagram represents the self or personality as a composite of three basic capacities or, as medieval philosophers used to say, faculties. The self can think, so it has the faculty of *intellect* (the power to think, analyze, and organize). It can act, so it has the faculty of *will* (the power to decide and act). And it can feel and perceive, so it has the faculty of *emotion* (the power to sense, sympathize, empathize).

These are the capacities that enable a self to be, and to become more completely, a self. The degree to which one has these powers, if not the simple fact that one has them, distinguishes one from those beings who do not belong to the human species. But our picture of the self would be incomplete if it referred only to these qualities. These qualities define the self to some extent simply by being resident in it. They also are definitive of the self because they afford it contact with reality beyond itself. Since there is no selfhood in a vacuum, we must look to the reality beyond the self to complete our picture of selfhood.

The Self's Situation: The "World"

As we just noted, the self is defined not simply by its parts or its powers but also by its relationships. To put the matter differently, the self is always a *situated* being, a being whose involvement with other beings situates and so defines it. Viewed in this light, each of the self's powers may be defined as a mode of relationship or a means of involvement. Through its powers of intellect, will, and emotion, the self establishes contact with realities beyond itself, and through these powers as informed by the related realities it draws the lineaments of its world.[64] Like a spider and its web, the self and its world are in a sense interwoven, mutually dependent to such an extent that an understanding of one requires an understanding of the other.

Because of the interdependence of self and world, our diagram of the self needs to be amplified. In particular, the three realms of reality known as nature, culture, and history must be brought into view. Let us amend our diagram as follows:

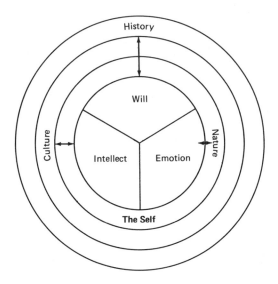

The additions to our chart try to show, first, that the self as a whole participates in each of the three spheres: nature, culture, and history. The three concentric figures representing these spheres envelop the circle representing the self, indicating that each of the spheres embraces the whole self, affecting emotion, intellect, and will. The diagram thus tries to indicate that no aspect or faculty of the self can escape the rhythms of nature, the customs and institutions of culture, and the influences of history.

Though the entire self comes under the sway of nature, culture, and history, it appears equally true that each of the self's component faculties has a counterpart among these spheres to which it stands specially related. The second thing that the diagram tries to show, therefore, is that there are special affinities between the emotions and nature, between the intellect and culture, and between the will and history. Both the small arrows on the diagram and the proximity of the associated terms indicate these affinities.

One final feature of the diagram should be noted before we explore the implications of our sketch of the self for the Christian view of reality. The two-dimensional nature of our chart requires, of course, that its concentric figures be of different sizes. But the Christian perception of reality would have required that we draw them that way in any event and that we designate the smallest of them as nature and the largest of them as history. In the Christian view, history encompasses and fulfills nature and culture, and the self that originates in nature and interacts with culture comes to fulfillment finally in history.

There is a sense in which the self is a natural being through and through. Its powers of intellect and will are grounded in nature no less than are its emotive powers. But intellect has the power to transcend nature by reproducing nature's image in thought, and will may work to disrupt and transform nature. Of the three powers, only emotion seems to be a direct expression of nature, in essential harmony with it. Generally emotion appears to be more intimately related to, or wrapped up in, nature than are intellect and will. One of the standard procedures of modern psychotherapy is to try to get the patient in touch with his or her own feelings, which are often buried from perception by habits of speech and action learned from culture and history. The theory behind such therapy is that emotions can and do express and affect the natural reality which does so much to define our being and determine our behavior.

In the nature religions, nature is of course the dominant realm of reality. Accordingly, because of the special affinity between nature and the emotions, emotion is for such religions the dominant faculty within the self. The result, as we saw in Chapter II, is a life style governed by natural rhythms as mediated through the human emotions. Intellect and will function within bounds (customs and taboos) established by an essentially emotional relationship to a reality whose limits and possibilities are defined by perceptions of nature.

In our diagram, the figure labeled "culture" envelops the one labeled "nature," indicating the view that culture transcends nature (and is thus a kind of supernature or, as we sometimes say, a second nature) even though it depends on nature. The power of human culture* to go be-

*The term "culture" here refers specifically to the world of human products as they are distributed through space in more or less permanent form. Culture is different from nature in that humans have a hand in its creation. It is different from history in that it is less transient or temporary in character and more objective than subjective in form. (History as the name of a historical record as, for example, in Gibbon's history of the Roman empire,

yond nature—to build a city, for example, where nature had provided only a field and a river—reflects the power of human selves to transcend, through thought and imagination, their primitive natural emotions. Intellect, the power to think and imagine, has an affinity to culture (the world of human artifacts) which is similar to that relating emotion and nature.

The alliance between intellect and culture is not as simple as that between emotion and nature because the intellect needs the assistance of the will in its struggle to overcome natural inertia and to produce a culture that can transcend nature. As anyone who has struggled to wake from a pleasant sleep on a balmy spring morning knows, successful defiance of the rhythms of nature requires will power; the irresolute thought "I must get up" will not get the job done. In a similar way, thought or intellectual activity by itself is not enough to overcome the powerful inertia of nature-based traditions. Intellect can dream up brave new worlds, but only when it is assisted by the considerable powers of the will can it conquer nature and bring such worlds into being.

As rationalists as far apart in time as Plato and Freud recognized, the intellect holds a position within the self which is both central and fragile. The intellect is central because it stands suspended between the emotions and the will. Plato symbolized this centrality by comparing reason to a charioteer who holds the reins of a very wild steed (symbolizing raw natural emotion) in one hand and those of a less wild but still rambunctious steed (symbolizing heroic will, or the appetite for social acclaim) in the other. It is clear that giving too much rein to either steed can get the charioteer—the intellect—into trouble. The intellect's very centrality is the source of its fragility. As Freud made clear in different terms from those of Plato, the location of the ego (the conscious, rational, "intellectual" dimension of the self) between the self's needs for emotional satisfaction and its need for social acceptance can mean its undoing. For as it becomes a rope in the tug of war between the id (seat of instinct and emotion) and the desire for social acceptance, the ego may "break" and a split self result.

As the intellect occupies a central position in the self and can succumb to either emotionalism or willfulness, so culture in the larger world is a kind of middle term which draws and depends on the resources of both nature and history. The consequence is that there are cultures which are natural in style and tone, and there are cultures which are historical.

---

belongs to culture and not to history in this definition. An example of "history," by contrast, would be the personal experience Gibbon had in writing his book or, to cite a better example, the experience of General Lee or General Meade during the Battle of Gettysburg.)

Over the past five centuries or so the cultures of the East have generally been of the former sort, and the cultures of the Occident have tended to be of the latter. But the recent triumphs of science and technology have made it increasingly difficult in this century for nature-based cultures (the cultures of most Third World nations) to withstand the pressures to forsake tradition (the preeminent conveyor of value of nature cultures) in favor of change (the usual bearer of value in history-based cultures).

On our chart, history is represented by the largest of the three concentric circles surrounding the self. This reflects the Christian view that history is the sphere in which the ultimate meaning of human existence is disclosed. Nature and culture are not devoid of meaning in this view, but their meaning can come to expression only in history. This is why the statement of the scientist that he or she can find no purpose in nature is both as unsurprising and as uninformative as the statement of the first Soviet cosmonaut that he did not "see" God in space. Purpose, meaning, and God, if knowable at all, are knowable only to selves, and selves are finally and essentially *historical* beings—that is, deciding, acting, purposeful beings. To expect a "scientific" discovery of purpose or meaning is as absurd as to expect a visual discovery of God, for science is ideally and theoretically the work of a disinterested intellect. Unless directed by a will which already believes that reality is at least possibly meaningful, the intellect will not pursue, let alone find, meaning in the world. Precisely because scientists must leave the notion of purpose behind as they enter the laboratory, they must find it impossible to discover anything resembling purpose through their experiments. An intellect not directed by the will to seek meaning shall assuredly not find it.

To say that the will is the director of the intellect or mind toward meaning or toward other human ends is to say that it is the principle of historical action in the self. History is the sphere of human intentions and actions, and intentions and actions are the work of the will. The specific meaning of the word "intention" may offer us some insight into the will's work. Funk and Wagnalls define intention as "a settled direction of the mind toward the doing of a certain act."[65] "Will" is a name for the capacity that the self has to settle the direction in which the mind or intellect is to act. Without the will, the intellect would be totally controlled by the subhuman and subhistorical powers of nature. Without the will, in other words, nature would be all-determining, "human" culture would be a product of instinct similar to the ant heap or the bee hive, and history or meaning-filled time would be nonexistent.

It is the will, the power to think and act intentionally and not just instinctually, that distinguishes humans from the other flora and fauna on earth. It is the will, in the Christian view, that makes human beings *selves* rather than mere organic offspring of the natural system. Human history is a product of the interactions of wills, of human intentions and actions. History embraces nature and culture to the extent that nature and culture determine and are determined by human purposes and deeds. But human history, as Christians perceive it, is not simply *human* history. It is also a theater of divine activity, an arena in which God's intentions and actions are expressed along with those of human beings. The power that human beings have to act intentionally, to "settle the direction of their minds," is only a reflection of God's intentional action to "settle the direction" of history as a whole. The conviction that they are involved in an historical process that is going somewhere because God has determined that it shall buoys the hopes of Christians and persuades them to act in terms of the divine intention.

History's relation to nature and culture may provide insight into Christianity's relation to other, nonhistoristic religions. As we have noted, history embraces nature and culture to the degree that the latter shape, and are shaped by, human beings, their intentions, their behavior, and the results of their behavior. In a similar way, Christianity as a history-affirming faith may embrace the history-affirming and humanity-affirming elements in nature-based and reason-based religion. Precisely because history is a more open-ended and flexible realm than either nature or culture, history-based religions must be more receptive to change, more open to the possibility of discovering the work of God in historical events and developments, than either nature religion or reason religion can be. This same flexibility and openness should enable history-based faiths like Judaism and Christianity to be receptive to the possibility that God may work in nature and culture as well.

On our map of religions, then, Christianity is most at home on the "continent" of history. But, to extend our geographical metaphor, the continent of history is not an island completely cut off from the continents of nature and reason so much as an isthmus, connecting these other continents and integrating elements from each of them into its own topography. As a faith based in history, Christianity is well equipped, in principle at least, to integrate the insights of other faiths into its own, thereby tying the facts and values comprising the self and its world into a comprehensive vision.

QUESTIONS TO GUIDE STUDY AND DISCUSSION

1. Why has the shape or form of entities been thought throughout Western history to be a good indicator of their value and meaning?

2. How does the arrangement or organization of the Bible indicate Christianity's character as a history-based faith?

3. Irenaeus based his interpretation of history on a theory regarding Christ. Cullmann erected his on a broad overview of the Bible, and Teilhard fashioned his from a synthesis of scientific and religious data. What assumptions about the nature of history do these three thinkers seem to share? In what way(s) do these assumptions reflect a Christian perspective on history held in common by the three?

4. How are the biblical events of Exodus and Incarnation especially illustrative of the Christian view of history as an arena of divine activity?

5. How does St. Paul's teaching regarding the resurrection (I Corinthians 15) disclose the Christian attitude toward history?

6. Discuss the relationship between time-consciousness and our definition of religion as the art of putting things together. This relationship (derived from Kant's analysis of the nature of time) seems to be challenged by Kierkegaard's view, discussed later, that time is a force which "keeps us unsettled, makes us insecure." Are these views of time really as incompatible as they appear to be? Why or why not?

7. Why is an understanding of the self and its relations to the world important to an understanding of faith?

8. How does the Christian view of the self and its situation differ from the perspectives on self and world of nature religion and reason religion?

9. What influence does Christianity's character as a history religion have on its capacity to relate to the religions of nature and reason?

NOTES TO CHAPTER III

1. Augustinus Aurelius, a.k.a. St. Augustine (354–430) wrote *The City of God* as a Christian response to pagan charges that Christianity had, by its pacifism and otherworldliness, subverted the Roman empire and made it susceptible to barbarian overthrow. Augustine's countercharge was that the fall of Rome was a result of God's judgment on its sordid pagan ways.

2. This is one of the several reasons that the word of the biblical book of Hebrews, that "we are surrounded by so great a cloud of witnesses" (12:1), and the words of the Apostles' Creed, "I believe . . . in the communion of saints," are important to Christians. They mean, among other things, that the vision of history with which one confronts the challenge of one's own time is not one's alone but is inherited from and shared with forerunners in the faith.

3. Jeremiah 20:9, freely rendered. Something of this same sense of compulsion is found also in the words of the prophet Amos, at Amos 3:8: "The lion has roared; who will not fear? The Lord God has spoken; who can but prophesy?"

4. That history is routed toward God is the main point of the venerable but usually misunderstood Christian doctrine of predestination. The accent in this word should lie on "destination," since the doctrine maintains primarily that God is in control of history's outcome, not of its every twist and turn. Predestination is thus not to be confused with religious or philosophic determinism, which does hold that every historical occurrence is foreordained.

5. Some would argue that the idea that God is both the beginning and the end of history contradicts the idea that history is not circular. Their reasoning is that only in a closed or circular figure can the beginning point and the end point be the same. This objection is fallacious (Christian historists would argue) in that it assumes that God, like a point on a circle's circumference, is static. It assumes that God "stays put" until time or history makes a circuit and comes back to him. This assumption reflects a nonbiblical understanding of God. In the biblical view, God does not sit still while time runs its course. To speak crassly, he runs alongside of history, or, to use a more biblical metaphor, he "goes before" it. (For example, see Exodus 13:21; Numbers 10:33–35; Deuteronomy 1:30, 33; Joshua 3:10–11.)

6. This was the view of (among others) St. Augustine, Martin Luther, and (to a slighter degree) St. Thomas Aquinas. It is the view today of many fundamentalistic and charismatic Christians.

7. Elements of this view are also found in Augustine, Luther, and (to a more considerable degree) Aquinas. It was the viewpoint of apocalyptic visionaries like Joachim of Floris (d. 1202) and of several significant Reformation sects, including the Anabaptists, the Mennonites, and (in England) the Levellers, the Fifth Monarchy Men, and the Quakers. In somewhat diluted and humanistic form, it came to be the view of the nineteenth- and twentieth-century liberals and Social Gospellers. Its most influential and creative recent exponents have been Jürgen Moltmann—cf. his *Theology of Hope*, trans. J. W. Leitch (London: SCM Press, Ltd., and New York: Harper & Row, Publishers, Inc., 1967) and Wolfhart Pannenberg, *Theology and the Kingdom of God* (Philadelphia: The Westminster Press, 1969).

8. The history worship of "instrumentalists," that is, of those who see history merely as an instrument by which God prepares people for heaven, is ironic, representing as it does a kind of contradiction of their basic position. Because instrumentalists do separate history rather radically from eternity (earth from heaven), they may end up, by inattention more than intention, submitting rather uncritically to the historical powers that be. (So Billy Graham, twentieth-century America's most celebrated instrumentalist, served several conservative presidents as a kind of chaplain without portfolio, implicitly sanctioning their governmental policies.) On the other hand, the history worship of believers in history's intrinsic value is easier to understand. Idealists of the eighteenth and nineteenth centuries, for example, virtually deified the historical process, seeing in it a redemptive force which would usher in the utopia of their dreams.

9. See Chapter X, pp. 383–85.

10. "Being a master, [Christ] also possessed the age of a master, not despising or evading any condition of humanity . . . sanctifying every age, by that period corresponding to it which belonged to himself. He therefore passed through every age, becoming an infant for infants. . . a child for children, . . . a youth for youths. So likewise he was an old man for old men." Irenaeus, in J. Pelikan, *The Shape of Death* (New York and Nashville: Abingdon Press, 1961), p. 111.

11. J. Pelikan, *The Shape of Death*, p. 102.

12. So Pelikan: "Each man can identify himself with the history and the death of Jesus Christ because Jesus Christ has identified himself with human history and human death, coming as the head of a new humanity." *The Shape of Death*, p. 102.

13. "So, 'the Word was made flesh,' in order that sin, destroyed by means of that same flesh through which it had gained the mastery and taken hold and lorded it [sic], should no longer be in us; and therefore the Lord took up the . . . incarnation, that so he might . . . overcome through Adam what had stricken us through Adam." Irenaeus, in J. Pelikan, *The Shape of Death*, p. 113.

14. Irenaeus: "Now God shall be glorified in His handiwork, fitting it so as to be conformable to, and modelled after, his own Son." In J. Pelikan, *The Shape of Death*, p. 115.

15. J. Pelikan, *The Shape of Death*, p. 115.

16. Although Cullmann does not use the term "hourglass," he does suggest that history assumes a shape describable by such a figure. Virtually all of *Christ and Time* is devoted to an account of history whose broad outlines form such a shape, but nowhere does Cullmann suggest the shape more succinctly than in *Salvation in History,* trans. S. G. Sowers (London: SCM Press, Ltd., and New York: Harper & Row, Publishers, Inc., 1967), p. 101: "The movement of New Testament salvation history which I have designated in *Christ and Time* as a line . . . leads in a progressive narrowing from mankind to the elected people of Israel, from Israel to the remnant, from the remnant to the one man, Christ. From this mid-point it then proceeds, ever-widening, to the circle of the apostles, to the first community, and from there to the Church made up of Jews and Gentiles." Used by permission.

17. Teilhard's unique angle of vision makes it difficult to discuss his thought in traditional theological terms. Indeed, during his lifetime his writings were proscribed by the Roman Catholic hierarchy because his views seemed to diverge at points from those of Roman orthodoxy. One of the points questioned in his thought was its lack of clarity regarding the traditional Christian idea of creation as *creatio ex nihilo* (creation out of nothing). For an exposition of this idea see Chapter VII.

18. At times Teilhard suggests that the birth of self-consciousness may have been the most significant event in the whole of cosmic history. "Man," he writes, "is psychically distinguished . . . by the entirely new fact that he not only knows, but knows that he knows. . . . To an observer unaware of what it signifies, the event might . . . seem to have little importance; but in fact it represents the complete resurgence of terrestrial life upon itself. In reflecting psychically upon itself Life positively made a new start. In a second turn of the spiral, tighter than the first, it embarked for a second time upon its cycle of multiplication, compression and interiorisation." *The Future of Man,* trans. Norman Denny (New York: Harper & Row Publishers, Inc., 1964), p. 307.

19. Cf. Teilhard's reference to an "over-riding super-determinism" in *The Future of Man,* p. 133. Teilhard's point in using this term would seem to be that God's governance of history does not directly determine nature's course by setting aside the laws of nature but rather utilizes those laws in the service of the divine intention.

20. I Corinthians 15:28; cf. Ephesians 1:23; Colossians 3:11. Teilhard's statements on Christ's role in the cosmic process are hard to fathom, in part because his thoughts are not at that point developed systematically and in part because his attempted synthesis of science and faith is vast in scope, complex in formulation, and at points mystical in language. Perhaps the main question to be asked is if Christogenesis is only the final phase in the cosmic history, or if it is a theological name for that history taken as a whole. In Teilhard's writings there seems to be evidence that it is in various ways both. History seems to pursue an axis between the Christ principle resident in nature's beginnings and the Christ reality regnant at nature's end.

21. *The Phenomenon of Man,* trans. B. Wall (New York: Harper & Brothers Publishers, 1959), p. 73.

22. Although nature is the initial medium of the divine activity in history, there comes a point, Teilhard maintains, when human beings and human culture assume this role. "In Man," he writes, "as though by a stroke of genius on the part of Life . . . heredity, hitherto primarily chromosomic (that is to say, carried by the genes) becomes primarily 'Noospheric'—transmitted, that is to say, by the surrounding environment." *The Future of Man,* p. 169.

23. Cf. Matthew 25:31–46.

24. Cf. Luke 2:1–20; Matthew 11:19 (Cp. Luke 7:34); and Mark 15:27 (Cp. Matthew 27:38 and Luke 23:32–33).

25. Luke 1:49b–53 (NEB). From *The New English Bible* (Hereafter "NEB"). Copyright © The Delegates of the Oxford University Press and the Syndics of the Cambridge University Press, 1961, 1970. Reprinted by permission.

26. Matthew 5:21.

27. Matthew 8:22; Luke 9:60.

28. Cf. R. Bultmann, *History and Eschatology* (Edinburgh: The University Press, 1957), pp. 151–52 *et passim*.

29. Eschatology, the branch of theology concerning the biblical anticipation of history's conclusive events, takes its name from the Greek term *eschaton*, meaning "end."

30. Cf. I Corinthians 7:29–31. For typical Bultmannian interpretations of these verses, see R. Bultmann, *Theology of the New Testament*, trans. K. Grobel (New York: Charles Scribner's Sons, 1955–57), Vol. I, pp. 182, 351–52.

31. II Corinthians 5:17.

32. Mark 1:16–20; Matthew 4:19. Cf. Luke 5:1–11 and John 1:35–42.

33. Matthew 18:3 (KJV).

34. John 3:3.

35. Romans 12:2.

36. I Corinthians 5:7 (NEB).

37. Galatians 6:15 (NEB).

38. The Christians of the first century could be described as "these . . . who have turned the world upside down." Acts 17:6.

39. Philippians 3:13–14 (NEB).

40. For this last, "secular" view, see Paul van Buren, *The Secular Meaning of the Gospel* (New York: Macmillan, Inc., 1963), pp. 132–34.

41. Cf. R. Bultmann, *Theology of the New Testament*, Vol. I, pp. 192–203; G. Bornkamm, *Paul*, trans. D.M.G. Stalker (New York: Harper & Row, Publishers, Inc., 1971), pp. 130–31; J.A.T. Robinson, *The Body: A Study in Pauline Theology* (London: SCM Press, Ltd., 1952).

42. J. A. T. Robinson, *The Body*, p. 15.

43. From *The Body: A Study in Pauline Theology*, by John A. T. Robinson. © SCM Press Ltd., 1952. Published in the U. S. A. by the Westminster Press, 1977. Used by permission.

44. G. Bornkamm, *Paul*, p. 131.

45. Romans 12:1 (KJV).

46. That the extramental reality of such a pattern is finally merely an article of faith, not a demonstrable fact, was demonstrated in the eighteenth century by the Scottish skeptic, David Hume. Cf. A *Treatise of Human Nature*. But even if time is but a "form of intuition," as Kant later argued, its residence within the mind as one of the "transcendentals" does not negate its reality but merely states its location.

47. In his *Critique of Pure Reason*. Cf. T. M. Greene, ed., *Kant: Selections* (New York: Charles Scribner's Sons, 1957), pp. 50–55.

48. The question whether time exists in "the things themselves" or only in our perception of them is one we cannot explore here. For a line of inquiry regarding it, see the two preceding notes.

49. For an instructive analysis of the key differences between space-based and time-based religions, see Paul Tillich, "The Struggle between Time and Space," *Theology of Culture* (New York: Oxford University Press, Inc., 1959), pp. 30–39, and "Historical and Non-historical Interpretations of History: A Comparison," *The Protestant Era* (Chicago: University of Chicago Press, 1957), pp. 16–31.

50. The practice of *zoning* cities and counties is an interesting modern version of the control of time by space. If one is in an industrial zone in a modern city, one can spend time only in industrial pursuits. In a residential zone one has more options, perhaps, but industrial and commercial pursuits are not normally among them. The ancient practice of designating some spaces (for example, sacred groves, temples) as sacred and others (for example, the marketplace) as secular constituted a similar attempt to control time and its uses by the zoning of space.

51. I Kings 8:27 (NEB). Note also Paul Tillich's description of Hebraism's genius in "The Struggle between Time and Space," *Theology of Culture*, p. 36: "It is unheard of in all other religions that the God of a nation is able to destroy this nation without being destroyed Himself. . . . In prophetism the glory of God is not diminished, but augmented by the split between God and nation."

52. Hebrews 11:1 (KJV).

53. J. Moltmann, *Theology of Hope*, p. 181. Emphasis in original.

54. Hebrews 12:2.

55. *The Meaning of Revelation* (New York: The Macmillan Company, 1941), pp. 59–73.

56. Trans. Walter Lowrie (Princeton, N.J.: Princeton University Press, 1957). See especially pp. 76–82.

57. Some of the existential awe with which Kierkegaard viewed this state of affairs was anticipated by Shakespeare in *Julius Caesar:*

>There is a tide in the affairs of men
>Which, taken at the flood, leads on to fortune;
>Omitted, all the voyage of their life
>Is bound in shallows and in miseries.
>(Act IV, Scene 3, Line 217)

58. Trans. J. Macquarrie and E. Robinson (New York: Harper & Brothers, Publishers, 1962). See especially Part One, Division One, VI: "Care as the Being of Dasein," pp. 225–73.

59. R. Bultmann, "New Testament and Mythology," in H. W. Bartsch, ed., *Kerygma and Myth*, trans. R. H. Fuller (New York: Harper & Brothers, Publishers, 1961), p. 24.

60. *The Meaning of Revelation*, p. 86. Copyright 1941 by Macmillan Publishing Co., Inc., renewed 1969 by Florence Niebuhr, Cynthia M. Niebuhr, and Richard R. Niebuhr.

61. This is a point we emphasize in Chapter IV, which argues that faith is always a project or a process, never a finished product. The point also is made in Chapter V, which discusses at some length the distinction between faith and knowledge.

62. Cf. Reinhold Niebuhr's spirited representation of this point of distinction between the Christian perspective and the perspectives of rationalism and naturalism, *The Nature and Destiny of Man* (New York: Charles Scribner's Sons, 1941), Vol. 1, pp. 54–92. "Without the presuppositions of Christian faith," Niebuhr argues (p. 92), "the individual is either nothing or becomes everything."

63. Blaise Pascal, *Pensées* 347, 348 in W. F. Trotter and T. M'Crie, *Pensées and The Provincial Letters* (New York: Random House Inc., 1941), p. 116.

64. Though there is a sense (as we have seen) in which the self is a product of a larger reality (which we have named history), there is also a sense in which the self constructs its own world. The world as it is produces selves, but the world as it is known is in large part a product of selves.

65. *Funk & Wagnalls New Practical Standard Dictionary of the English Language* (New York: Funk & Wagnalls Company, 1956), Vol. I, p. 696.

IV. The Christian Project

T HE CHRISTIAN FAITH is primarily a project to be lived, not an object to be studied. This is a truth often withheld from the wise and often disclosed to the simple. The Christian mother introduces her child to the faith by recounting the stories of biblical and postbiblical heroes and heroines. She knows, perhaps instinctively, that Christianity expresses itself most fully and clearly by becoming incarnate in people's life-projects.[1]

The learned priest catechizes and in so doing unfolds the mystery of complex doctrines; the theologically naive parent narrates simple stories. But in moments of holy simplicity, the priest knows no less than the parent that the Christian faith is unfulfilled unless it makes its way off the page of the sacred text and into the lives and stories of people.

Life calls to life: that is why the stories of some people's lives may be the most effective means by which to reach and affect the lives of others. But Christians and Jews rely on the stories of pioneering pilgrims and martyrs for another reason as well. The very stuff from which their faith is fashioned is life's own stuff, history, and in Jewish and Christian belief history discloses its meaning in a special way in the life-projects of certain men and women whose lives, it is believed, have been touched by history's Lord.

The fact that the Christian faith is a project conspires with the further fact that this project is nourished and sustained by the exemplary life-projects of forebears in the faith to create a problem for a book like this one. Our aim is to understand the Christian faith. But how does one understand a reality that refuses to be reduced to simple, objective terms? As every historian knows, trying to understand a historical event in a completely objective way is like trying to guess the destination of a bird in flight. Historical events elude objectification: they refuse to sur-render to even the keenest observer the indefinite number of possible

consequences they hold for the future. Much the same problem confronts us as we seek to analyze the faith project of Christians. As a
project, it is by definition never complete, never through bringing new
effects into being, never through disclosing previously unnoticed facets
of its nature.

In trying to understand the Christian faith we face not only the problem of trying to draw a bead on a moving target but also equally difficult
problems posed by human subjectivity. Before it appears in human
projects, faith originates in human subjects, and these subjects are as
baffling and perplexing as their projects. Projects, indeed, are the public
expression of subjectivity, and by their very publicness they may show
us more of themselves than they disclose of their subjective sources.
Subjectivity, on the other hand, is the sphere of interiority; it describes
the inner sphere of thought, emotion, and psychic energy in us that lies
veiled, for the most part, from public view.

Faith has both a projective (public, active) and a subjective (private,
mystical) aspect, and both of these facets make it a difficult reality to
bring into focus. Faith also has a third dimension which further compli-
cates our efforts to understand it. This dimension we may describe as
faith's *objective* aspect. Despite appearances, such a description does not
constitute a retraction of our earlier statement that faith is not an object;
what we mean to say through the term "objective" is that faith *has* an
objective. This means that faith is always faith in something: it places the
believer in a commitment to some person or value; it always seeks to
serve or glorify some being, real or ideal, beyond itself.

It is in faith's three-dimensional (projective-subjective-objective) aspect that its *religious* character becomes apparent. In Chapter I, it will be
recalled, we defined religion as the art of putting things together. It now
becomes clear that faith is the chief medium by which religion—or in any
event the Christian religion—accomplishes this tying together. *Faith is a
project that unites, or ties together, a human subject or self and that subject's
ultimate objective in life.*

In the rest of this chapter and the following chapters we shall try to
understand faith in all three of its dimensions. The key term for our
approach to faith, however, is the middle one: projective. Faith *is* a
project (the living of a life) that *expresses the values* of a subject (a human
self or community) *in the service of* an object (either the real God or a God
substitute).

The projective character of faith is made all the more central in Christianity because of this tradition's view that history is the primary
medium of divine revelation. The historical acts and projects of human
beings take on added significance when they are understood as responses to or even vehicles of God's activity. That this is the way that
Christians view them means that faith's projective aspect not only ex-

presses the human being's devotion to God but also may convey God's message to the human being. If *my* faith project expresses my love for God, it is through the faith projects of *others in history* that I may learn of God's love for me.

That faith is a project, then, means not that it is a human invention (that is, an activity you or I initiate on our own) but rather that it is a condition or state of affairs in which God and the self become related in a dynamic way. Far from viewing faith as a mere projection from the human side, most Christians follow St. Paul in understanding it as a human response prompted, even "given,"[2] by God.

Finally, faith's projective nature is of crucial importance to an understanding of the total faith phenomenon because it both discloses and explains the Christian faith's *social* dimension. The faith project of a Christian not only relates the self and God in a two-directional way, allowing the self to address God and to be addressed by him; it also links Christians to other persons. This linking comes about because projects, as we said earlier, give public expression to human subjectivity. A boy named Andrew Carnegie, we are told, used to walk past the gardened estate of a rich family in his hometown of Dunfermline, Scotland. Day after day he would peer through the locked gates of that estate to view the beauty that money had wrought. There and then he made it his project to find a means to unlock those gates and open the gardens to the children of Dunfermline. Years later, after emigrating to the United States and amassing a fortune in the steel industry, he returned to his home village to complete that project.

Andrew Carnegie's subjective desires as a child became a source of his public project as a man. Similarly, the projective character of faith impels it, sooner or later, to express itself publicly. This public expression produces what Paul Tillich called a "language of faith,"[3] and it enables the Christian perspective to be communicated (in St. Paul's phrase) "from faith to faith."[4] Its projective character gives Christian faith a way of expressing its subjective side, a way of moving toward its objective or goal, and also a way of communicating itself socially and culturally.

The social dimension of faith produces yet another problem—indeed a whole class of problems—for those trying to understand faith. The fact that faith can apparently be communicated socially leads at times to serious misconceptions regarding it and its object. Faith may, for example, be construed as merely a type of social conformity: I come to believe that I can have faith by simply accepting the beliefs about God that my fellow citizens or fellow church members accept. In this misconception *faith in* is reduced to *belief about*: total, personal commitment gives way to intellectual conformity.

A second and related misconception to which faith's social character may lead is the idea that being born into a Christian society automatically makes one a Christian. Here too faith is confused with conformity, conformity perhaps with the ideas of a cultic community, perhaps with its mores, perhaps with both. The difference between the conformity practiced here and that discussed in the preceding paragraph is simply that faith is here believed to be inherited (one's "birthright") rather than acquired on one's own initiative.

These conceptions of faith are *mis*conceptions on at least three counts: first, they distort faith by believing it to be socially communicable in a simple, straightforward way; second, they distort it by confusing it with belief (the unquestioning acceptance of an idea or set of ideas); and third, they reduce faith's public or socially expressed form from a historical project to a knowable or believable doctrinal object.

Faith is not communicable in a simple, straightforward way—for example, by simply conforming to the norms of a society (even a Christian society!)—because, as we have seen, faith is something in whose creation God (and not just society) has a hand. There is thus a considerable element of mystery in the process by which faith is transmitted. "The wind blows where it wills," Jesus said in commenting on this mystery, "and you hear the sound of it, but you do not know whence it comes or whither it goes."[5]

Faith is not the same thing as belief because it is not merely intellectual or social but profoundly personal. Its essence is personal trust rather than social agreement or intellectual assent. Its human objectives are personal integrity and responsiveness to history rather than the maintenance of correct formulas ("beliefs") or social traditions ("rituals" or "customs").

The Christian faith's character as a project to be lived out in history precludes all attempts to reduce its content to knowable or believable doctrines. Such attempts usually come about through a misunderstanding of the purposes of catechetical or doctrinal instruction. This kind of instruction can be very helpful if it clarifies or inspires faith acts or faith projects. But if it becomes an end in itself or supports the notion that faith is simply acceptance of the teachings it communicates, it will promote something other than Christian faith.

The understanding of faith as a project to be lived out in history effectively demolishes all attempts to reduce the "content" of faith to a set of pat or easy answers which can be handed down from generation to generation. As Martin Luther insisted, each person must live his or her own faith just as each must die his or her own death. I cannot "borrow" another person's faith any more than I can borrow his or her death. This means that the "answers" which I find in faith must be found the hard way—through my own personal struggle rather than through intellectual or social conformity. Each person's faith project is distinctively his or her own, even though its projective (public) character enables that person to express himself or herself to others through it.

If this is true—if faith is so personal a project—does this mean that there are no identifying marks that Christian faith projects have in common? Not at all. To argue that making faith personal is equivalent to making it idiosyncratic would be as absurd as to argue that the attribution of personality to a being would deny its humanity. There are in fact features which all Christian faith projects share. Not the least of these is that all of these projects are in some way or other responses to questions inevitably present in human life. Every human being wonders if there is purpose, meaning, value in life; every Christian faith project is a response to that question. Every human being wonders if life ends with death; every Christian faith project is a response to that question. Every human being wonders why so much in life seems unjust and unfair; every Christian faith project is a way of responding to that question. And so forth.

There are common features in Christian faith projects also because all such projects reflect that condition of relatedness which marks human life as religious. Three relationships in particular participate in the composition of a faith project: the self's relationship to God, or ultimate reality; the self's relationship to neighbors, or social reality; and the self's relationship to subhuman beings, or to natural and cultural realities.

Finally Christian faith projects have features in common because they have a common history. The shape of that history and a summary of certain crucial events in it were discussed in Chapter III. Much more must be said about them as we look more deeply in the following chapters at the qualities which make Christian faith distinctively Christian. What we must do now is describe the procedure by which we propose to approach both the universally human and the specifically historical factors which characterize this faith. As we do so we shall need to keep in focus the elusive reality that we have set out to examine. Ultimately all faith projects embrace the entire human act of living and the various acts of relating which tie this act of living together. The very diversity of faith projects is enough to make their comprehension extremely difficult. But try to comprehend them we must.

STORIES, STYLES, AND STANDARDS

Projects, as opposed to objects, are most approachable through their effects. Unlike objects, in other words, projects—the actual constellations of motives and activities which enter into faith—do not lend themselves directly to human attention. Our most direct approach to them, consequently, is through the phenomena that accompany and express them. In reference to Christian faith projects, the most important classes of such phenomena appear to be *stories, styles, standards, and modes of service.*

Stories are simultaneously the most common and the most distinctive effects of Christian faith projects. Christian faith is inescapably storied, and most of its key stories are biographical or autobiographical. This is true because, as we saw in discussing the Christian idea of resurrection in Chapter III, the Christian faith sees the individual as a being of infinite worth even as it understands him or her as a product of a definite and concrete history. This means that history itself has an intrinsic importance, for its most noble product, the human individual, is esteemed to be of great value. The historical stories (biographies and autobiographies) of individuals are thus quite significant, as they recount the progression by which human beings become such valued individuals. Stories therefore may provide extremely helpful insights as we study the nature of Christian faith projects.

Stories are especially valuable because they open doors into faith's subjective aspect which can scarcely be opened in other ways. In their stories, for example, the men and women of the Bible express their longings and confess their shortcomings, rejoice in their achievements and lament their misfortunes. They tell us, in short, about *themselves* and about the *relationships* to God and their community from which their self-image and their style of life emerge. Stories are the most personal and confessional public expressions of faith.

Another reason that many biblical stories are instructive for the student of the Christian faith is that they offer insight into faith as a lifelong pursuit. Stories like those of Abraham, David, and Paul distill the essences from faith projects which lasted lifetimes. Whether the hero of a story is mythical (Adam), legendary-historical (Abraham, Moses), or historical (Paul), the story of his career interests and inspires Christians because it offers them a summation of faith's meaning as it took particular form in him. The value of a story for the community of faith is directly proportional to this capacity it has to "share," that is, its power to help others experience the impact of its hero's faith project.

Stories are potentially very instructive, but they also can be quite treacherous. It is no accident that when Jesus told stories (he called them parables), he was frequently misunderstood or not understood at all. Stories, especially those which take the paratactic form characteristic of biblical stories,[6] may draw the reader's or hearer's attention away from the essential to the extraneous. Stories therefore demand an intensity of involvement—a hearing with an inner ear, if you will—which apparently cannot always be expected from those who hear or read them.

The Storyteller

Yet another reason that stories, especially biblical ones, can prove treacherous is that they are of mixed composition. Virtually every "historical" story in Scripture is actually a mixture of event and interpretation. This is true of many of the biblical stories because they were designed initially to serve as small sermons depicting the virtues or deploring the vices of the given story's central figure. An element of interpretation inevitably crept in as the preacher-storyteller emphasized those features of the story that best served the point.

There is a more basic reason too that these, and all, historical stories contain an element of interpretation, and that is that no human being has a God's-eye view of historical events as they happen. Every humanly told story reflects the bias, the peculiar historical prejudice—in a word, the interpretation—of its teller.

An interesting phenomenon occurs as a result of this interpretive element in stories. When I retell an oft-told story, I do it my own way, serving my own purposes and expressing my own perspective. The story becomes, in a subtle way, my own story as well as that of its initial teller and that of its hero. So stories grow incrementally and become increasingly complex. Unless their hearers are alert to this complexity, they may for yet another reason misread or misinterpret them.[7]

The process of interpreting biblical and postbiblical stories of faith projects is complicated further by the fact that these stories take many forms, including those of myth, fable, legend-history, drama, poetry, and historical narrative. Each of these forms offers its own distinctive challenge to its interpreter.

Myths, which are attempts to recount God's own actions in story form, offer the most serious challenge of all. This is so because myths squarely confront their interpreters with the problems inherent in human finitude.[8] Because human beings are finite (limited) they stand perplexed before the mystery of divine Infinity, and myths, as representations of the Infinite, cannot completely resolve such perplexity. Indeed, the finite form of the myth—that is, its stumbling attempt to say something about the infinite despite the limitations of human language—may compete with its infinite subject matter for its reader's attention. Because this finite form is more simply understandable by the interpreter's own finite mind, it may even supplant the Infinite as the focus of the interpreter's faith, thus contributing to the gravest of all sins, idolatry.*

Fables use stories of animals or other subhuman beings to depict human qualities, especially human frailties and foibles, in thinly veiled ways. The veil may be thicker than the untrained eye perceives, however, or perhaps just too thick for it to penetrate; for fables sometimes contain disguised references to historical events and contexts of which their would-be interpreter may not be aware. The famous biblical fable of Jotham, for example, is not to be read as a comment on human nature as such but rather as a response to a particular historical crisis in Israel's life. The reader who is not aware of the circumstances surrounding its original telling will almost certainly misunderstand it. The editors who gave us the story in Scripture accordingly provided along with it a note recounting the events to which the fable refers.[9]

---

*Idolatry means the displacement of the Infinite God as the object for worship by any finite thing or thought. Note that under this definition not all idolatry involves "graven images" or literal idol worship; it is possible to make an idol of a belief system or philosophy of life.

Legends differ from both myths and fables in that their heroes are always human and always historical. As we noted in Chapter II,[10] scientifically conditioned moderns tend to view the words "legend" and "myth" with suspicion, for in their perception both terms connote fantasy and unreality. Such suspicion, though understandable and even useful in a context of pure science, may have unfortunate side effects. Actually, legends and myths can convey important truths and may do so more effectively than more prosaic literary forms can. Legends have the particular merit of offering the historian a window, however small, into the minds of those who produce them. Although they do not provide literal accuracy, they do supply insight into the history from which they spring.

Only the naïve reader will be fooled into interpreting legends literally, but even for the skilled interpreter they may pose a challenge. Because the persons whose memory they honor are historical figures and because they are usually persons of genius and charisma, the separation of the factual core from the honorific accretions in legends can be difficult. This is even truer for many of the legendary figures of scripture because these figures are often described in ways which are not only realistic but even unflattering. So Abraham lies about his wife Sarah to save his own skin, David's lust for Bathsheba leads him to conspire in the murder of her husband, and Simon Peter quails in cowardice before the accusing gaze of the high priest's housemaid.[11] Many biblical stories are laced with a realism unrivalled in ancient literature, and their interpreter must wonder if a similar realism might not underlie those aspects of them which glorify their heroes.

The Bible also has its *drama* and *poetry*. At points these are recognizable as such, but on occasion (for example, in the books of Job and Jonah) they are accompanied or "bracketed"[12] by a prose narrative form which may lead the unwary reader to miss their more profound points by becoming enmeshed in a prosaic literalism.

In important respects drama and poetry, like legend and myth, are particularly suitable vehicles for the message that the Bible and other religious texts seek to convey. Far from disqualifying them, the nonliteral character of these forms equips them to express religious truths more effectively than more prosaic forms can. For one thing, their nonliteral character forewarns the reader that the message presented through these forms is not reducible to, or relatable through, ordinary human language. Drama conveys to its reader that very real sense of confrontation by a reality beyond oneself which frequently accompanies religious experiences, and poetry captivates the mind with images which can lead it beyond its ordinary perceptions and toward that same reality. But if taken literally, both of these forms lose their power to lead the reader toward a condition of deeper religious engagement.

Legend, myth, drama, and poetry are commonly and abundantly present in the scriptures of the world's major religions. But no other book of scripture gives to *historical narrative* the degree of prominence accorded it by the Bible. Such prominence follows naturally from the fact that the faiths of the Bible, Judaism and Christianity, are history-based faiths. Among the major self-conscious religions they stand virtually alone in seeing history as an arena of meaning and potential. They express their positive estimate of history by recounting certain historical stories that seem to them to support that estimate.

The Bible contains much historical narrative, but it would be a mistake to assume that it is simply a history book or that its interest in history is that of the modern historian. The modern historian proceeds from an entirely different set of premises than did the chroniclers who gave us the historical portions of the Bible. Modern historians are concerned primarily with "what actually happened"[13]—in other words, with what H. R. Niebuhr called "external" or "seen" history. Biblical historians, on the other hand, seek to discover and convey an "internal" history, one both they and their community have "lived." Modern historians write, as it were, as objective spectators whereas the biblical historians write as people who participate, either firsthand or by faith, in the history they record.

The objectives of modern and biblical historians are different. Although modern students of history have no illusions that they can reach their goal of complete objectivity, they nevertheless work strenuously to discover the truth about their subject. Like pure scientists, they must subordinate all other aims to those of accurate description and explanation. This is not the case with biblical historians. In their narratives they are not concerned primarily with historical accuracy but rather with history as a vehicle of divine revelation. They are as much theologians or preachers as historians.

The recognition of these important distinctions between the objectives and approaches of the modern and the biblical historians can and should steer today's reader of the Bible away from the misunderstandings fostered by a naïve literalism. More important, this recognition can point readers to levels of insight unattainable by such literalism, for it constantly reminds them that what the stories of scripture offer are not objective data per se but *projective* data—that is, descriptions of human faith projects which their own writers understand as responses to God's own projection of himself into history.

Christians respond to God's projects in history in ways that lead to the telling of stories. Although these stories assume many diverse forms, they are marked by certain common features which combine to express a distinctively Christian (or Judaeo-Christian) *style*. One may deduce from this that a style is in some ways a sociocultural counterpart and by-product of the living out of stories. In Chapter II we examined a life style common to Jews and Christians—the style of the shaper. In the outline developed there this style was greatly oversimplified, but the outline nevertheless helped us distinguish the Judaeo-Christian perspective from those of other major religions. It is thus apparent that styles may be quite useful in understanding religious phenomena.

Styles are expressed in many ways, not only in stories but also in music, art, social mores, political give and take, and modes of work, worship, and play. These activities suggest by their variety that a style is not so much a matter of what gets done as of *how* it gets done. The common element in the style of most Western (Euro-American) Christians is a streak of practicality and activism; Eastern (Greco-Russian) Christians by contrast tend to be contemplative and mystical. But in their *how* the concerns of Christians of East and West tend to converge. Both exalt activity, the committed exercise of the will, though the Eastern Christian typically believes contemplation to be activity's higher form whereas the Westerner tends to consider public activity the higher form. Both Easterner and Westerner are shapers, but the Easterner is primarily concerned to shape and discipline his or her inner life while the Westerner seeks to reshape the external world.

The surface differences between the styles of Christians of East and West give way to an underlying unity. Both value human individuality as it is expressed through the will; both see this individuality as a major product of history, and both proclaim the good news that, through Christ, the major obstacles to its fulfillment have been overcome in principle. Though their immediate aims and the consequent styles differ superficially, there is an essential harmony between them.

Styles of Christian living and thinking in both East and West offer additional sources of insight into the nature of the Christian faith project. Moreover, because styles are sociocultural in character, they tend to produce yet another important source through which faith can be understood. When styles become established in a given culture they produce in the popular mind an expectation of their own continuation. Conformity to a traditional style comes to be expected within that culture. Another way of saying this is that styles become *standards*. Standards are the guidelines, conscious or unconscious, of expected behavior within a society. Once a style becomes established (usually subconsciously) as the accepted way of behaving, it in effect becomes a behavioral standard: the *is* becomes the *ought*. It appears that those whose styles produce standards seldom understand the significance of what they have done. The owl of Minerva, noted the philosopher Hegel, takes flight at dusk. His point was that societies and individuals grow wise only as they grow old, and, sadly, only as they grow too weak to put their wisdom to maximum use.[14] A large part of the reason for this apparent law of history may be that we seldom appreciate the value of a thing until we stand in danger of losing it. No one has a clearer idea of the value of life than the person who is terminally ill. Only when something begins to slip away from us does our distance from it become great enough for us to see it clearly and assess its value accurately. Standards thus come most clearly into view only when their existence is threatened by newly emerging styles.[15]

New and vigorously pursued styles come into being amid the ecstasy and excitement of moments of fresh discovery.[16] Standards, on the other hand, as clearly perceived definitions of a culture's expectations, get stated only when that culture has matured sufficiently to know its own mind. So it may be said that standards epitomize and codify styles by transforming them into objective form.[17]

A process of idealization frequently accompanies this transformation of styles into standards. Perfection comes easier in ideas than in deed or fact. When societies, groups, or persons look back on the "good old days," distance lends enchantment to the view, and a similar idealization occurs with the projection of future utopias. Standards, as idealizations, tend to gain a more exalted status than prevailing styles even as they are used by some to justify and defend those styles. When we consider standards as a source of insight into faith projects, we are in effect considering styles that have come to govern cultures or individuals as their written or unwritten, conscious or unconscious, norms. In the Christian scriptures such norms are stated in terms of what theologians call "the Law." The Law recounts what people must do for God just as the Gospel recounts what God does for people. Viewed in its broadest terms, the Christian faith project is a Gospel-inspired and a Law-guided project. It is God's project to the extent that it reflects and expresses the "good news" (= Gospel) of God's actions in humankind's behalf; it is the faithful individual's project to the extent that it reflects the Law's word regarding what humans must do in response to God's initiatives. St. Paul expressed this quality of divine-human collaboration in faith projects when he wrote, "If we live by [take our life and strength from] the Spirit, let us also walk by [take our standards of conduct from] the Spirit."[18]

Standards abound within the Bible. Important explicit standards are found in the law of Moses, in the preachings of the prophets and of Jesus, and in the precepts of the apostles. As practical guides regarding the Christian life these standards are invaluable. But adhering to them does involve perils. That fact was probably uppermost in Paul's mind when he urged Christians to "walk by the Spirit." Elsewhere he wrote: "The letter of the law [that is, a standard taken literally] kills but the

Spirit gives life."[19] Again he (or a disciple of his)[20] warned his fellow Christians to beware of those who "have the form of godliness [conform outwardly to the standards of godly living] but lack the power thereof."[21] Christians came to believe quite early that the same standards that, properly used, make good and faithful servants may, if improperly used, become evil and inhumane masters. One must be wary, therefore, of identifying any concrete standard, or set of standards, as the hallmark of Christian existence.

Standards, like stories and styles, are generally autobiographical in origin. A culture's *story*, or history, summarizes the significance (or at least its historian's perception of the significance) of its entire life span; a culture's *style* expresses the values which govern the actions of daily living within that culture; and a culture's *standards* objectify these values in a frequently unattained but potentially attainable ideal. Thus, upon careful analysis, it appears that stories, styles, and standards may be viewed as the public expressions or consequences of the three aspects of faith projects discussed earlier in this chapter, namely, its subjective, projective, and objective aspects. People tell us about themselves, their *subjectivity*, chiefly through their stories; people act out or *project* these stories in their styles of behavior; and people state the *objectives* or ideal ends of their projects in their standards.

Story, style, and standard have a way, in life itself, of flowing in and out of each other. Stories reflect the styles and standards of their age and of their heroes, whereas styles and standards emanate from the actual lives which provide the substance of stories. This dynamic interplay reflects a corresponding interplay which constantly goes on among faith's subjective, projective, and objective elements.

In his novel *The Inheritors*,[22] William Golding retells the story of a primeval people. What is striking to the person steeped in biblical tradition and stories is the way in which Golding's novel weaves together motifs from biblical and other religious sources. Equally striking is the way he combines the story, styles, and standards of the primeval culture he describes into a seamless tapestry which wraps itself around the reader and conveys an almost tactile experience of the world described. Because it has these qualities, *The Inheritors* may serve as a vehicle for illustrating the interrelationships we have noted among stories, styles, and standards and the correponding interplay among faith's three elements. As we perceive these interrelationships and develop a sensibility for such interplay, we may become better equipped to interpret these faith phenomena and thereby to approach the faith projects which underlie and inspire them.

The Inheritors is the story of a Neanderthal man named Lok and his tribe. Golding draws us into their lives as the seasons are changing and as Lok's tribe makes its annual pilgrimage to the mountain shrine of Oa, the tribe's earth goddess. Oa is the mother of all living beings, and in the view of Lok and his people she has endowed the earth itself, and all things in it, with life. So Lok lives in a world in which all is alive: logs swim, rocks run, and trees talk. Lok and his people are very much enmeshed in their world's natural rhythms. Their senses are keenly attuned to nature's least move, though their thoughts are ill-formed pictures and their speech a series of turbid syllables, grunts, and gestures.

Lok's people fare well until they are challenged territorially by a strange new people, a technically advanced tribe who have learned to navigate the river which cuts Lok's world in two. Awed by this people's prowess and stunned by the realization that they themselves are not the earth's sole inhabitants, Lok's people are eventually overwhelmed and assimilated by the more advanced and aggressive tribe of interlopers (a Cro-Magnon people, it appears), who thereby become the literal inheritors of the earth.

This simple plot—summarized here in terms a modern historian might use in relating a *seen history*—becomes through Golding's art an account of *lived* history. The novel's message is conveyed as much through its style as through its substance. Golding tells the story as Lok himself, given literary powers, might have told it. The pace of the narrative is Lok's own plodding pace, the dim light in which the shape and significance of events are perceived and described is that of Lok's befuddled mind, and the remarkable sensitivity to the subtlest nuances of nature's moods and movements is also Lok's own.

With this observation we reach the first important point Golding's novel can help us illustrate: had it been told in a *style* other than Lok's own, Lok's story would not have been Lok's story. The key features of the story's substance might have been there, but had Lok's own style not framed them the reader would have lost touch with both the integrity and the intention of the story. A major rule for interpreting such stories therefore would appear to be: *Stay as alert and as sensitive to the story's style as to its substance,* for its style says much about its teller's standpoint and style, and perhaps about those of its hero or heroine as well.

To apply this rule to the task of interpreting Golding's novel, for example, we first would have to identify his story's literary genre. We might conclude that *The Inheritors* is best described as an artfully constructed myth—not a folk myth, it should be noted, despite its artful attempts to emulate folk myths.* Having determined this we then would

---

*A folk myth would originate as a kind of campfire tale and would evolve into a composition of an entire community rather than of a single imagination.

have to note that (1) a slavish literalism would be inappropriate to an interpretation of the novel, since the author would undoubtedly have chosen a more straightforward literary form had he desired to be taken literally; and (2) rational approaches to interpretation must be used only with the greatest deftness and with the greatest regard for the novel's artistic integrity, for the rational ("scientific") approach is completely out of accord with the way Lok's world is put together and with the corresponding mythical form that Golding adopts.

Awareness of the mythical or "mosaic" form which supplies the novel's integrity will make its reader alert to a quality in *The Inheritors* common in myths, namely, their capacity to speak to the reader on more than one level of understanding. The story of Lok may thus be read as a poignant (lived-history) description of the demise of one man and his people, as a philosophic treatise on the primeval attitude toward nature, or as a mythopoetic account of human evolution. This many-faced quality in myths leads to a second rule of thumb for the interpretation of such stories: when reading them, one should *be prepared to be surprised*, since much more meaning resides in them than initially meets the eye.

In his classic study of Western literature, *Mimesis*, Erich Auerbach commented that biblical stories in particular are, in his phrase, "fraught with background."[23] In contrast with the Greek myths of antiquity, to which Auerbach compares them, the myths and legends of the Bible usually leave much to their reader's imagination. The Homeric myths are typical of Greek thought, Auerbach found, in that their heroes appear never to have an unspoken thought or an unstated motive. Action and thought alike are brought to the surface and made clear to the reader by the poet. Homer thus offers his reader a virtual God's-eye view of the dramatic conflicts he recounts. By contrast, biblical narratives leave much unexplained. A divine call comes to Abraham to leave his father's house, or to sacrifice his son, Isaac, and no reason or explanation is given. The righteous Job is tormented, and God refuses to respond to his angry and defiant "Why?" Jesus must go to Jerusalem to suffer and die, and not even his most intimate companions understand his motives. Paul is stoned, shipwrecked, ostracized, tormented by some grievous thorn in the flesh, but his pleas for light on the meaning of his sufferings are answered only in the most general way.[24]

One wonders at this: if the Bible is indeed "God's word," as Christians claim, why is God's word so much less clear, so much more clouded and murky in meaning, than pagan myths like those of Homer? Why, indeed, does it not offer us a more authentic version of the God's-eye view of reality afforded by these pagan narratives?

A complete answer to these questions would be complex, for many features of the Judaeo-Christian perspective would contribute to its formulation—among them this perspective's declaration of the transcendence or "hiddenness" of God and its belief that meaning lies within and not beyond the ambiguities of history. Certainly any answer must also include reference to the Judaeo-Christian understanding of faith. Faith, as we noted in beginning this chapter, is a project to be lived, not an object to be grasped intellectually. Another way of saying this —a way we shall examine more fully in the next chapter—is that in the Christian view God is to be met and known by a relating that is more than reasoning. The mysterious, many-faced stories of the Bible are the literary outgrowth of this conviction. They are, we have noted, the stories of faith projects lived out by the initiators and formulators of the Judaeo-Christian tradition, those pioneers who first put together the biblical perspective or world view. If these stories operate on several levels, it is because the lives and faith of the tradition's pioneers were multi-dimensional. To some extent this multi-dimensionality traces to the individuality and the particular historical circumstances of particular writers or protagonists. But in large measure such multi-dimensionality is common to all of the stories because it is common to the acts of faith which produced them. These acts of faith consistently express the faith act's three dimensions of subjective (profoundly personal) involvement, projective (active, public) expression, and objective (goal-directed or God-directed) orientation. Any effort to understand the stories of such faith acts which hopes to be successful must have these same qualities. To put the matter briefly, *only those engaged in projects are fully prepared to understand projects.*

With this observation we reach our final rule of thumb for the interpretation of stories, styles, and standards, namely, that *one who would understand faith must be prepared to retrace, at least in imagination, the way of the faithful as that way is marked out by their stories and other legacies.* The recognition of this principle may account for the peculiar style that Golding used to recount Lok's story, and it may also explain the paratactic (reader-involving) style of many of the biblical narratives. In both cases the style draws the reader into the situation depicted in the story. The degree to which the reader actually participates, by imagination, in the situation determines the degree to which he or she may fathom its reality and meaning. Golding's descriptions of Lok, for example—of his enchanted entanglement in nature, his childlike verve when, half-famished, he stumbles on a doe killed by hyenas, his confusion before the challenge and threat posed by the new people—all introduce the reader to Lok's subjectivity, his dim and stunted sense of himself. Similarly the novelist's depiction of his Neanderthal hero's acts and demeanor leads his reader into Lok's "project," his real but weak and increasingly ineffectual attempts to cope with a world whose fast-changing face he cannot comprehend. Finally, Golding's allusions to the cultural standards by which Lok and his tribe live—their reluctance to kill animals and to eat meat, for example—tell the reader much about this people's objectives in life: the survival of, and harmony among, all living beings.

As we have already suggested, the style with which Golding spins his tale is not unlike the style one frequently encounters in the biblical narratives. These narratives, too, have the power to engage their reader in the reenactment of their heroes' life projects, and they do this by enabling the reader to recite and relive the stories, standards, and styles which gave those projects both their original existential meaning and much of their eventual literary form.

MODES OF SERVICE

The stories, styles, and standards of faith's biblical pioneers inspire and inform the faith careers of today's Christians. But these careers are not just mirrors of ancient practice. They have, indeed, their own special contributions to make to the enrichment of the Christian heritage. Although these contributions cannot be simply or neatly catalogued, they appear to come about, for the most part, through Christian engagement in certain modes of service.

The major modes of Christian service are three: service through worship, service through reflection on and the sharing of the Word, and service through work. In what follows we shall seek to show how these relate to and express faith's character.

Service through worship is the most basic expression of the Christian faith project. Worship is faith's first product, indeed its very essence. Although the Old Testament's first commandment implicitly demands worship and the New Testament's first law explicitly requires it,[25] worship is not a mere response to legal requirements but ideally is a spontaneous expression of faith. As such, it issues from a spirit of gratitude and praise which originates in a sense of God's reality and presence and in the recognition that life itself, the courage to go on living, and life's meaning and fulfillment all are gifts from him.

The form and meaning of Christian worship and of the other modes of Christian service will be discussed more fully in Chapter IX. Our aim here is simply to show how worship relates to and expresses faith. As we have already suggested, their relationship is one of virtual identity. Worship, like faith, expresses the human relationship to God and to his creation. Again like faith, worship has three aspects: its subjective aspect, or spirit, is thorough devotion or purity of heart; its projective aspect, or form of expression, is self-surrender or sacrifice; and its objective aspect, or aim, is a life committed to the glory of God.

The basis of worship is a sense of one's relationship to God. That relationship is fundamentally one of dependence or, to use the more technical theological term, one of contingency. Psalm 100 gives eloquent voice to a conviction that arises from this sensed relationship: "Know ye that the Lord, he is God; it is he that hath made us, and not we ourselves."

The realization that we do not give ourselves being dawns on us only rarely, perhaps, but its rarity in no way diminishes its truth. In moments of encounter with what Paul Tillich termed the abyss of being[26]—that is, in moments when we recognize our own capacity to evaporate into nonbeing—our impulse to worship is quickened and intensified.

Christian worship celebrates not only God's gift of existence but also his gift of a good world. The creation story found in Genesis, chapter 1, was probably composed originally as a liturgy* for use in the Jewish worship services conducted in the temple of Jerusalem.[27] The most common refrain in that liturgy occurs at the end of each day's creation achievement (the second day excepted), at which point we are told that upon looking over his day's work, "God saw that it was good." In this word of world affirmation, Judaeo-Christian worship sounds another important note which distinguishes it from the worship of other traditions. In a way and to an extent uniquely its own, Judaeo-Christian worship expresses the faith that this world and human life in this world are essentially good.

It is from these basic convictions of human dependence and life's goodness that the worshipper's spirit of gratitude arises. In worship the Christian acknowledges that the life and the world which come from God still belong to God. In its subjective aspect, therefore, worship expresses faith's awareness that the realities God has given must be returned, totally and single-mindedly, to him. The subjective condition for which the worshipper strives is accordingly one of complete devotion or purity of intention, for only through such single-minded devotion can worship's project of total self-surrender and its objective of divine glorification be attained.

What we have described is worship's ideal or authentic form. Unfortunately, faith's form may be distorted in worship no less than in stories, styles, and standards. A particularly pernicious distortion occurs, for example, when Christian service through worship is reduced to simple

---

*A liturgy, from the Greek *leitourgia*, is literally a form of service rendered in public. In the ancient world the word could refer to public rites performed for the state as well as to the worship of deities. In the Judaeo-Christian context it refers generally to the forms and rituals of public services of worship.

identity with the routines of the Sunday worship service. Although that service can assuredly be the vehicle of genuine worship, it also can be perverted by the egotism of preachers, the esoterica of priests, and/or the complacent self-satisfaction of the would-be worshippers. The Sunday service provides ample evidence that worship, like the faith it expresses, can be distorted and that such distortion can affect any or all of worship's three dimensions.

In its subjective dimension worship is particularly vulnerable to distortion by *emotionalism*. Authentic worship contains emotive moments, but ideally such moments should direct the worshipper's attention beyond himself or herself by ushering him or her into the presence of Another. As we saw in Chapter I, the words "emotive" and "emotional" suggest in their etymology just such a moving-out, just such an opening and entering of new dimensions of reality. Unfortunately worship's moving experiences may be so powerful that they call attention, and may even attract devotion, to themselves. Most of us know people who believe that the aim of religion, and accordingly that of worship, is to produce in them good feelings or cathartic emotions. The real success of the Christian worship service is to be measured not by the quantity or quality of emotion it can educe but rather by the degree to which the emotion it evokes is directed toward and governed by the worshipped Other.

If worship founders subjectively when an emotional effect displaces an authentic relatedness as its focus, its public expression or projective dimension suffers when it becomes too closely identified with the performance of certain rites or rituals. When it reaches extreme proportions such an identification produces a sterile *formalism*. The worship acts of such a formalism are as empty of real significance as are the artfully induced attitudes of religious emotionalism. Faith's focus is distorted in the one case by an excess of form, in the other by an excess of feeling.

Emotionalism and formalism dilute worship's capacity to embody faith effectively, but the most egregious distortion of worship is the distortion of its objective aspect. When worship's true aim or objective is lost, its very integrity and authenticity are destroyed. Worship's true aim, we have noted, is the glorification of God; whenever some other aim—perhaps self-satisfaction or institutional advancement—displaces its authentic aim, worship becomes false worship or idolatry, that is, devotion to an object unworthy of devotion.

Worship is one way, indeed the primary way, faith expresses itself in the lives of Christians. It is an essential outgrowth of faith, but it is highly volatile, subject to distortion in all three of its aspects.

A second mode of service which betokens and evokes faith is *the service of the Word*. If worship is faith's primary product, the Word is in a sense its source as well as one of its products. The Word of the gospel produces faith even as faith produces the power to understand and proclaim the Word of the gospel.

The service of the Word takes two forms: preaching or *kerygma* and prayerful reflection or *theologia*. Preaching or *kerygma* (a prominent New Testament word meaning "proclamation" or "message") is the way the Word is shared; reflection or *theologia* (a Greek term literally meaning "study of God") is the way it is applied to one's own life and the life of one's community.

In most people's minds the service of the Word is primarily associated with the professional offices of preacher and theologian, but the sharing of the Word and reflection on the Word are duties not only of ministers, priests, and academic theologians but rather of all Christians. This idea was expressed vigorously by Martin Luther's concept of the universal priesthood of believers. In formulating this concept Luther did not intend to suggest that every Christian is his or her own priest but rather that each Christian is called to be his or her neighbor's priest. Sharing the Word of God's sustaining and saving acts in creation and in Christ was in Luther's view the duty of every Christian. Reflecting on the Word in prayerful contemplation also is a duty of all.

Faith itself mandates these duties. Faith's very practice dictates a profound subjective involvement in the Word. As Luther put it, "The whole life and substance of the Church exist in the Word."[28] This is true because faith, both as it occurs in the believing individual and as it occurs in the believing community, or Church, is a direct product of the Word. As God said in the Creation "Let there be light" and there was light, so God says "Let there be faith" or "Let there be the Church" and faith or the Church comes into being.

Perhaps it is impossible to improve on this poetic or mystical way of describing faith's origin and its subjective impact. It may be helpful, though, to examine more attentively the kinds of subjective human experiences toward which the terms "Word" and "faith" point. We all have had moments of special insight when realities we had never brought together in our minds suddenly came together to tell us something new—perhaps even life-changing—about ourselves or our situations. Such moments may be triggered by experiences of trauma or crisis,[29] or they may result from our engagement with some creative project or some creative person or persons,[30] or again they may happen under relatively routine circumstances.[31] In any event these experiences are analogous to what Christians mean by the experience of "hearing the Word by faith." When the Word is really heard, it is as though a new world, a changed situation, is brought to light. Realities which may have seemed at cross-purposes with each other suddenly come together to compose a message, sometimes positive, sometimes negative.

It is such a word, such a new and renewing perspective, that Christians are called on to share with each other and with the world through reflection and proclamation. Nor should the words "called on" be taken to indicate that such reflection and such proclamation are optional extras or mere additions to faith. Faith's dependence on the Word means that faith participates in the Word's imperious nature and that it accordingly not only unleashes but also actively impels proclamation and reflection as two of its major projects.

The imperious nature of the faith-received Word is amply and starkly illustrated in the lives and careers of the Bible's reluctant prophets. Almost without exception the great prophets or preachers of scripture, from Moses on, were brought into the service of the Word against their will. At the burning bush Moses hems, haws, and stammers before acceding to the Lord's demand that he declare the Word to Pharaoh.[32] Elijah, tired and frightened, flees to the wilderness lest the imperious Word get him into still deeper trouble with Queen Jezebel.[33] Jonah flees even faster and farther, "to Tarshish, away from the presence of the Lord,"[34] when he is commissioned to preach to the hated Ninevites. Jeremiah, perhaps the most reluctant prophet of all, speaks of the Word of the Lord as a fire in his bones which he must speak even against his will, lest it consume and devour him.[35] Amos sums up the common prophetic attitude, intimating that he too is under orders: "When the Lord speaks, who can but prophesy?"[36]

The sharing of and reflection on the Word are inevitable, indeed inescapable, projects of faith. Like all such projects their ultimate aim, or objective aspect, is to draw human beings into responsible relationships with God—into authentic faith. Unfortunately, however, the service of the Word, like the service of worship, may become misdirected and distorted. If its subjective aspect becomes dominant, it may produce personality cults or preacher-worship,[37] or in its theological form a privatism or misguided spiritualism.[38] On the other hand, if its projective or public aspect dominates, it may eventuate in a clerical or doctrinal authoritarianism,* and in its objective dimension it is susceptible to being reduced to an arid biblicism or bibliolatry.†

The third major mode of service through which faith expresses itself

---

*Clerical authoritarianism is a perversion of the legitimate authority of the clergy in which fellow churchpersons, and on occasion even nonchurchpersons, are deprived of their autonomy by the exercise of ecclesiastical or quasiecclesiastical powers. (Cf., for example, the interdict imposed on Henry IV of Germany by Pope Gregory VII in the year 1076). Doctrinal authoritarianism uses doctrines or church teachings to effect a similar dominance.

†*Biblicism* may take a number of forms but in virtually every case it involves an unthinking acceptance of teachings that are, or purport to be, biblical. *Bibliolatry* is an extreme form of biblicism which literally means "the worship of the Bible."

CIRCUMSCRIPTURE

As Pastor X steps out of bed
  he slips a neat disguise on:
that halo round his priestly head
  is really his horizon.

is that of *work* or *works*. In Protestant circles this mode finds expression particularly in the concept of vocation: ordinary secular work, many Protestants believe, is as much a calling from God and as much an opportunity to serve the neighbor as is church-related work. For their part Catholics believe in doing good works, not only because they believe, with Protestants, that faith acts by works of love but also because they hold good works to be meritorious in God's eyes and to contribute to the attainment of salvation itself.

Protestants and Catholics agree that good works inevitably accompany authentic faith. The New Testament epistle of James speaks for all Christians in maintaining that "Faith without works is dead."[39] Genuine faith always manifests itself in works of love toward God and one's neighbor. The order here is of crucial importance: faith must exist in the believing subject before true love or authentic concern can be projected toward God and the neighbor. On this point Catholics and Protestants alike look to one of Jesus' teachings for instruction. A tree, said Jesus, cannot bring forth good fruit unless the tree itself is good.[40] Faith must set the springs of human action right before the action itself can be right.

Up to this point, then, Catholics and Protestants agree. The greatest of the Catholic philosophers, St. Thomas Aquinas, advocated the principle *agere sequitur esse*—"doing follows being." A leading Protestant philosopher, Immanuel Kant, asserted similarly that the one truly good thing is a will which is good enough to produce good actions. "Good works depend on good faith" is a common Christian axiom. But beyond this point Catholic orthodoxy and mainstream or Reformation Protestantism[41] part ways. Catholicism sees works as not only products of faith but also as builders of a stronger and more worthy faith, whereas Protestants hold that works can never improve faith but can only express it.

Faith is perfected, Catholics believe, and salvation effected, in two stages. First, God gives believers, through the sacraments of the Church, an *empowering* grace. This grace strengthens that rudimentary faith that brought the believer to the sacraments in the first place. In so doing it makes faith sufficiently strong to produce good works. Such good works in turn make their doer worthy to receive God's *accepting* grace or favor.

In the Roman Catholic view, then, good works are faith's projects in two senses: first as its products and then as its perfecters or strengtheners. Mainstream Protestants, on the other hand, see works as faith's products but not as its perfecters, for in their view faith is itself a work of God to whose perfection works of human beings can contribute nothing.

From what has been said to this point it is obvious that, despite the differences between these two points of view, works are an important expression of faith for Catholic and Protestant Christians alike. It follows that they may offer us important clues to faith's meaning. Therefore yet another avenue we shall want to explore as we study Christian faith is that of service through works.

The sphere of Christian action is not limited to deeds performed under narrow titles like "good works" or "charitable actions." As we noted earlier, many Protestants perceive ordinary "secular" work as a vocation or calling from God. In part this perception issues from an attempt by Protestants to pursue the larger implications of biblical monotheism. If there is only one God worthy of the name, then it would be absurd to act as if this God rules one's behavior in sacred matters while another God or "principle" controls one's conduct in so-called secular spheres. Since God cannot be divided or considered indifferent to one area of life while concerned about another, one's service to him cannot consist merely of overtly "religious" actions.

This understanding of ordinary work as a religious vocation or divine calling has obvious implications for the nature of faith. If God cannot be divided, neither is faith in him divisible. If he cannot be served in one area and ignored in another, neither can faith in him be turned off as one moves from a so-called sacred to a so-called secular sphere. "No one can serve two masters," said Jesus, "for either he will hate the one and love the other, or he will be devoted to the one and despise the other. You cannot serve God and mammon."[42] Faith, or loyalty to the ultimate, is indivisible.

The manner and nature of a human being's work or occupation can tell us much about his or her faith. This mode of service, too, provides us an opening into faith's nature and meaning. But as we approach faith through its expression in works or in vocational endeavors we must use fully as much caution as when we approach it by the other means we have examined. From the Christian standpoint no deed or career filled with deeds can be classified simply as good, or as a work of authentic faith, unless it expresses a good will or intention. A good will is, from this standpoint, one which is informed by a desire to glorify God and do good to his children. As a good will produces good faith, so an evil or corrupt will produces bad faith. The problem is that the works of good faith and those of bad faith are sometimes hard to distinguish from each other.

In Christian mythology this difficulty of distinguishing good works from bad is dramatized in the idea that the Devil sometimes appears as an angel of light. Christians know from their own painful struggles to be rightly motivated that things are not always what they seem. The temptation to do things for one's own glory instead of for God's appears to lie behind Jesus' teachings that the giving of alms and the saying of prayers ought not to be done in public.[43] Works which appear noble on their face may be ignoble in intention.

Perhaps the most perverse distortion of faith's impulse to do good works is the reduction of that impulse to one of blind obedience to authority or unquestioning conformity to moral and cultic laws. This distortion is doubly destructive, for it robs the doer of the work of his or her creative moral sensibilities even as it promotes an ill-grounded pride or self-righteousness. Whereas authentic faith does not stifle human autonomy but instead fulfills it, bad faith or wrongly directed faith may replace such autonomy with the delusion of self-sufficiency.

If works that appear good are not always in fact good, neither can one accept without question the Protestant view that doing a secular job well amounts to performing a Christian duty. Here again the question of intention is crucial. People frequently perform their secular duties well for very selfish reasons. Although a secular vocation may very well be, or become, a Christian vocation, it is not necessarily such. Even if the person engaged in a given occupation is nominally a Christian, and even if he or she believes, by way of some theory of enlightened self-interest, that despite a selfish or impure motive what he or she does must help the neighbor, the matter of intention remains crucial. From a Christian point of view, the goodness of works ultimately depends on the goodness or authenticity of the faith that produces them. Authentic faith's intention consistently places the glory of God and the neighbor's well-being ahead of selfish desires and aspirations.

Service through work and through works is still another avenue to be explored as we seek to understand faith. Like the other modes of Christian service and like stories, styles, and standards, this mode of service does not speak as directly and unequivocally of the meaning of faith as we might wish. But in company with the other phenomena of faith, it may assist us considerably as we pursue the meaning of the Christian project.

TIES THAT BIND:
THE CHRISTIAN VISION PROJECTED (A PREVIEW)

In Part One we have thus far identified religion as the art of putting a world together, and we have defined Christian faith as an essentially historical project by which Christians seek to construct such a universe of meaning. We have thereby suggested that faith is simultaneously formative and dynamic: it *forms* a world view even as it *projects* a life style. The dynamism in a living, historical faith makes such a faith's world view an organic, growing project rather than a static, unchanging object. The phenomena (stories, styles, standards) of faith are accordingly products of a rich history of change, a history that in fact is never complete but grows and changes with each faithful act of service performed by the contemporary Christian individual or community.

Though it is indeed changeable and variegated, Christian faith nevertheless has certain constant features which characterize it as a total enterprise. These features make up what we may call *the common Christian vision* or, in more technical language, *the basic Christian myth*. Most of the rest of this book will be devoted to describing this vision/myth. In preparation for that larger task, we shall present in the remaining pages of this chapter a preview or preliminary outline of the Christian vision's major features. Just as the worker of a jigsaw puzzle finds the picture on the boxtop immensely helpful as a frame of reference within which to locate various pieces of the puzzle, so we may find an overview of the ground we are to cover in later chapters very helpful as we seek to fit together in Part Two those concepts and precepts which Christians use to tie their world together. It perhaps does not need repeating that these concepts and precepts usually function subconsiously. As in astronomy it is not apparent what keeps the sun and the earth suspended at a certain distance from each other, nor what keeps these two heavenly bodies in certain ratios of relation to other planets and stars, so the faith concepts that unite values and facts lie beyond and behind ordinary perception.

These concepts are not so much objects of knowledge as assumptions which condition and shape knowledge. They are not the apparent working out of actions as much as their less than apparent motives. They are, in brief, the unspoken assumptions that bind the inner world of personal values and meanings to the outer world of natural and historical facts. They are "religious" in the literal sense, for they tie bits and pieces of reality into a cohesive whole and provide a basis for dynamic and constructive living.

In Part Two we shall frequently refer to this unitary vision of reality as "the Christian perspective" or "the Christian myth." The literal meaning of the term "perspective" provides a particularly apt insight into the nature and function of this vision. Derived from the Latin root *speco*, "to see," and the prefix *per*, "through," the word "perspective" literally describes something one sees through. Like the eyeglasses ("spectacles") some of us wear, a perspective literally determines and conditions everything its holder sees. Because it is what the holder sees with rather than the object he or she sees, it lies beyond the ordinary field of vision. Its power to influence what is known and done is not diminished but is increased by the quiet and unobtrusive way in which it operates. It is in effect an invisible presence, shaping, modifying, and motivating every perception and decision of the self. It is accordingly far more powerful than any of the ordinary ideas or "facts" that the mind consciously "knows." Ordinary ideas or facts may give the mind a grasp of particular things or theories; a perspective gives it the entire frame of reference or matrix of meanings which makes individual things and theories valuable and useful to the self. Though it is of course modifiable by such things and theories, the perspective's force ordinarily is not reduced by such modifications. Indeed, such changes generally strengthen rather than diminish the hold of a perspective on the self, much as a change in one's eyeglass prescription enhances one's power of vision.

The perspective afforded by faith provides the Christian with the meaning world within which he or she resides. The importance of Christian stories, styles, standards, and modes of service is that they express elements or aspects of this meaning world. These elements combine to form a multi-faceted mosaic, various facets of which catch more light than others at certain points in Christian history and at certain points in the faith pilgrimages of individual Christians and Christian communities.

The following numbered paragraphs list, briefly and with minimal comment, the more important of these facets.

1. The most basic element in the Christian vision is the conviction that **reality is rooted and grounded in love.** This means

THOUGHTS AND THINGS

I concentrate on
  the concentric rings
produced by my pen
  in the ink.
The thing that distinguishes
  thoughts from things
is that thoughts are harder
  to think.

From Grooks 3 *by Piet Hein. Copyright 1970 by the author.*
Used by permission of Mr. Hein.

that God, the source of reality, is supremely personal as well as supremely powerful. The notion that personal good will is responsible for everything that is is probably the most audacious of all Christian claims. It is also the most crucial of such claims, for unless it is true all other Christian convictions are baseless, and the entire Christian world view collapses.

2. **Love is the principle or source of unity.** It belongs to the nature of love to unite or unify. To say that God is love is to say that the divine will for reality is unity. **God does not create a multiverse** (many self-sufficient realities) **but a universe** (one reality with many interdependent parts).

3. **Love is the principle or source of goodness.** To say that God is love is to say that God wills the goodness of creation. "And God saw everything that he had made, and behold, it was very good."[44] That God wills the good means primarily that he wills that his creatures *be* good rather than that they *have* or *enjoy* good.

4. **Love is both the source and the purpose of freedom.** To say that God is love is to say that God wills to love and that he wills to receive love from the creatures made in his likeness. Love cannot be compelled. Its very reality depends on its being freely given. Therefore God must endow that being from whom he expects love with a capacity to be free. So God's love makes human beings free, and freedom makes it possible for people to love.

5. As love is the source and purpose of human freedom, so **human freedom is the source and purpose of the distinction between moral goodness and moral evil.** Human freedom is morality's source or basis. Without this conviction, all the structures of moral accountability and social justice would be baseless, for if offenders against the laws of morality and society are not free, by what right are they held morally responsible for their actions? Human freedom is also morality's purpose or aim: only in the making of authentic moral decisions can freedom become real. Had God made humans amoral he could not have made them free, and had he made them unfree he could not have made them moral.

6. **Human freedom is the principle or source of all moral evil.** Moral evil has no independent standing in the world. It is instead a result of the human distortion or perversion of the divinely given order of things. In the original divine order all was good. Evil comes into being, and remains in being, because human beings worship lesser goods (themselves and/or other creatures) instead of the supreme Good—the *Summum Bonum,* or God.

7. Because evil is a distorted relationship or a perverse mode of relating rather than an entity of independent standing, **the conquest of evil requires the introduction or reintroduction into the world of the authentic mode of relating which was God's original intention** in creation. This mode of relating was and is reestablished in *the Incarnation of God in the man Jesus of Nazareth.* Jesus the Christ not only embodies and exemplifies this authentic mode of relating but also makes it accessible to the human community and the human individuals who are evil's perpetrators and victims.

8. **The new relationship to God established in and by Jesus the Christ is mediated to contemporary human beings by the Holy Spirit,** who works primarily and normatively through a description of the new relationship as it was disclosed in the character and career of Jesus himself. The Holy Spirit is the Christian name for that principle of unifying love which resides in and unifies God himself, and as such the Spirit is also the divine force who units God to human beings and human beings to each other in and through Jesus the Christ.

9. **The primary theater of God's saving and reuniting ("reconciling") activity is human history.** Through a particular historical community (Israel), God made known his intention that the human race should become covenanters and co-workers with him as he seeks to make history the sphere of authentic relationships. Through a particular historical individual (Jesus of Nazareth) he worked to establish a New Co-

venant and a New Israel through which that intention could be realized.

10. **The Christian Church is the New Israel.** As such it is the chief (but not necessarily the only) historical agent used by God the Holy Spirit to establish the new mode of relating that he desires to promote within the world. The proper name for this new relating is *love*—unifying, goodness-inducing, liberating love. The last word for Christians is the same as the first: the divine objective in salvation is one with the divine objective in creation—the inculcation and triumph of love.

The Christian faith is a project, an open-ended and hard-to-define process that commits the total self to the pursuit of certain objectives. But, precisely because it has such objectives, Christian faith is not a blind project. It is rather a project launched on the basis of a certain perspective, a certain view of reality. Though it may be dim in the Christian project's initial stages, that perspective may grow clearer as the project's aims are faithfully pursued.

QUESTIONS TO GUIDE STUDY AND DISCUSSION

1. What is the difference between a "project" and an "object"? Why is the Christian faith more aptly called a project than an object?

2. Name and distinguish the three dimensions, or aspects, of the Christian faith project. What does an understanding of each of these dimensions contribute to an understanding of faith as a whole?

3. What universally human and definitively religious factors do Christian faith projects have in common?

4. Why are biblical and other Christian stories especially helpful as vehicles through which the Christian faith can be understood? In what ways are styles and standards helpful to the same end?

5. How are stories, styles, and standards related to each other? How does the interplay among them reflect the interplay among faith's subjective, projective, and objective aspects?

6. How may William Golding's novel, *The Inheritors*, illustrate the close relationships among stories, styles, and standards and between these three in concert and the effective depiction of a faith perspective?

7. How are faith and worship related? What can worship teach us about faith?

8. How are faith and the Word related? What can this relationship and the resulting service of the Word teach us about faith?

9. How are faith and work(s) related? What can this relationship teach us about faith?

10. What perils and problems attend the various attempts to understand faith through stories, styles, standards, and modes of service discussed in this chapter?

11. What do personal perspectives contribute to our perceptions of the world, other people, and ultimate reality?

12. Be prepared to discuss the major elements in the Christian perspective.

NOTES TO CHAPTER IV

1. The terms "life-project" and "faith project" will be used in this chapter to indicate the dynamic and always unfinished character of human life and faith. The word "project" derives from words meaning "to throw forward" or "to throw forth." When applied to life and faith, it suggests that these activities propel one into spheres of reality beyond oneself—a condition which Martin Heidegger called "being-toward." See Martin Heidegger, *Being and Time*, trans. J. Macquarrie and E. Robinson (New York: Harper & Row, Publishers, 1962), pp. 184–85, 243 *et passim*.

2. Ephesians 2:8: "For by grace are you saved through faith, and that not of yourselves: it is the gift of God." (KJV)

3. *Dynamics of Faith* (New York: Harper & Brothers, Publishers, 1958), p. 45.

4. Romans 1:17 (KJV).

5. John 3:8. The mysterious workings of the Holy Spirit, to whose activity Jesus' metaphor "the wind" refers, have been used by some to promote the idea of predestination. Why, they argue, do some members of a group who hear the gospel accept it, while others do not? Obviously the social conditions—which are objectively the same in both cases—cannot explain these differences in response. The difference can best be explained, predestinarians argue, by the election of the Holy Spirit, whose choosing opens some persons to the hearing of the Word and leaves others spiritually deaf.

6. See Chapter I, pp. 15–17.

7. One way in which biblical scholars have sought to circumvent this particular danger is through an approach to scripture called form criticism. Form critics seek, by analyzing the form of biblical narratives, to determine how these stories grew or otherwise changed as they went through successive retellings and copyings.

8. Even so astute an analyst as Paul Tillich did not take adequate account of these problems when he wrote, too loosely, that "from the objective side one must say that faith is true if its *content* is the really ultimate" (*Dynamics of Faith*, p. 96, emphasis added). The word "content" denotes containment, but neither myths nor faith can *contain* God. They can at best (as Tillich recognized elsewhere) be "grasped" by him or "participate" in him.

9. Judges 9:7–21.

10. See footnote, p. 47.

11. Genesis 12:10–20, 20:1–18; II Samuel 11:1–27; Mark 14:66–72 (= Matthew 26:69–75, Luke 22:56–62).

12. The long dramatic poem which provides the heart of the Book of Job is thus surrounded, in the version that has come down to us, by a narrative introduction and a narrative conclusion which may lead one to interpret the book with a degree of historical literalism which has little to do with and may even detract from the work's main theological point.

13.   These words translate the famous phrase *wie es eigentlich war,* coined by Leopold von Ranke (1795–1886), a German historian who led the movement to make historical research an exact science.

14.   So Hegel: " . . . it is only when actuality is mature that the ideal first appears over against the real. . . . When philosophy paints its grey in grey, then has a shape of life grown old. By philosophy's grey in grey it cannot be rejuvenated but only understood. The owl of Minerva spreads its wings only with the falling of the dusk." *The Philosophy of Right,* trans. T. M. Knox, *Great Books of the Western World,* ed. R. M. Hutchins (Chicago: Encyclopedia Britannica, Inc., 1952), Vol. 46, p. 7. Used by permission of Oxford University Press.

One is reminded here of a celebrated remark sometimes attributed to George Bernard Shaw: "Youth is such a glorious thing; what a shame it is wasted on children."

15.   The ascendancy of the style of the swinger during the 1960s, for example, made clear how heavy a hold the styles of square and shaper had on the cultural consciousness of Americans at that time.

16.   A case in point would be the era of the Protestant Reformation. Out of the new perspective afforded by the Reformers and by the discovery of the New World and the invention of the printing press, a new psychological perspective and an attendant new style emerged. See Max Weber, *The Protestant Ethic and the Spirit of Capitalism,* trans. Talcott Parsons (New York: Charles Scribner's Sons, 1958).

17.   "Religion is embedded in behavior and institutions before it is consciously codified, and the alteration of social and economic policies always entails religious change." Harvey Cox, *The Secular City,* rev. ed. (New York: Macmillan, Inc., 1966), copyright © Harvey Cox 1965, 1966.

18.   Galatians 5:25.

19.   II Corinthians 3:6, freely rendered.

20.   Many scholars believe that St. Paul himself did not write the second letter to Timothy, which contains the "warning" we cite here. The scholars who believe this generally believe, though, that the letter is a product of a person who knew Paul's mind well and sought to apply his theology to a later situation.

21.   II Timothy 3:5, freely rendered.

22.   *The Inheritors* (New York: Harcourt Brace Jovanovich, Inc., 1962).

23.   "In the story of Isaac [Genesis 22], it is not only God's intervention at the beginning and the end, but even the factual and psychological elements which come between, that are mysterious, merely touched upon, fraught with background; and therefore they require subtle investigation and interpretation. . . . Since so much in the story is dark and incomplete, and since the reader knows that God is a hidden God, his efforts to interpret it constantly find something new to feed upon." *Mimesis: The Representation of Reality in Western Literature,* trans. W. R. Trask (Princeton, N.J.: Princeton University Press, 1953; paperback 1968), p. 15. Copyright 1953 by Princeton University Press. Reprinted by permission of Princeton University Press.

24.   Genesis 12:1–5, 22:1–14; Job 38:1–40:2; Luke 18:31–34; II Corinthians 12:7–9.

25.   Exodus 20:3–6 and Mark 12:30 (=Matthew 22:37).

26.   *Systematic Theology,* Vol. I, pp. 110, 113, *et passim.*

27.   Cf. B. W. Anderson, *Understanding the Old Testament,* 3rd. ed. (Englewood Cliffs, N.J.: Prentice-Hall, Inc., 1975), p. 426.

28.   "Tota vita et substantia ecclesiae est in verbo Dei." D. Martin Luthers Werke, Vol. 7, Kritische Gesamtausgabe (Weimar, 1883–   ), p. 721, in W. Pauck, *The Heritage of the Reformation* (Glencoe, Ill.: The Free Press, 1961), p. 34.

29.   Blaise Pascal (1623–1662), inventor of the barometer and developer of Pascal's law of hydraulics, underwent such an experience in 1654, when runaway horses almost took his carriage with them into the river Seine. Soon therafter, according to Saxe Commins, Pascal "all but embraced the monastic life" and sustained a mystical experience which compelled him "to abandon his pursuit of science until just before his death." Saxe Commins, "Introduction," B. Pascal, *Pensées and the Provincial Letters*, trans. W. F. Trotter and Thomas M'Crie (New York: Random House, Inc., 1941), p. xii. Copyright Random House Inc. Used by permission.

30. One of the more striking features of the gospel accounts is found in their descriptions of Jesus' encounters with demoniacs or (as we might say today) psychotics. These distraught people, it appears, were among the first to recognize Jesus as a person of extraordinary powers (Cf. Mark 1:21–24=Luke 4:31–34). Their capacity to do this provides ancient documentation for today's growing recognition that mentally ill persons have basically the same experiences as "normal" persons do but experience these to a highly exaggerated degree because they are extraordinarily sensitive. The demoniacs' exaggerated reaction to Jesus indicates also, perhaps, that he forced them to see themselves and their predicament in an entirely new and threatening light.

31. For example, the Rev. Donald J. Welch, chaplain of Wofford College, disclosed in a sermon that his thinking about birth control changed profoundly when it occurred to him that he was a sixth child.

32. Exodus 3:11, 13, 4:1, 10.

33. I Kings 19:1–14.

34. Jonah 1:1–3.

35. Jeremiah 20:7–9.

36. Amos 3:8, freely rendered.

37. Such cults and preacher-centered cliques have plagued the Church from its earliest days; for Paul's response to an instance of this, see I Corinthians 1:10–27, 2:1–5.

38. Cf. Thomas Luckmann, *The Invisible Religion* (New York: Macmillan, Inc., 1967), especially pp. 97–99, 115–17.

39. James 2:26b (KJV).

40. Matthew 7:17–18, 12:33.

41. One should be extremely wary when speaking of Protestants as a group or class of Christians. Protestants are notorious advocates of freedom and inveterate (at times obnoxious) practitioners of it. It is therefore almost impossible to find a position to which absolutely all Protestants would adhere. We resort here, therefore, to speaking of "Reformation or mainstream Protestants," by which we generally mean the adherents of the principal traditions and communions established during the Protestant Reformation—Lutheranism, Calvinism (the Presbyterian and Reformed Churches), and Anglicanism.

42. Matthew 6:24 (=Luke 16:13).

43. Matthew 6: 1, 5–6.

44. Genesis 1:31a.

part two

FAITH
AND
THE
WORD

V. Faith and Knowing:
The Word as Relation

THE CHRISTIAN FAITH can be understood thoroughly only by a relating that surpasses reasoning. Christian *beliefs* lend themselves to rational analysis—to memorization, explication, and other forms of intellectual data-processing. Christian *faith* is another matter; it is, as we have seen, a project to be lived out, not an object whose meaning can be exhaustively reflected in thought. The way to a full understanding of faith is consequently a way of vital relationship, not a matter of simple reflection.

Reasoning or reflection is itself, of course, a form of relating. It is the means by which the mind relates itself to things. The relating by which faith's meaning is approached must assuredly include reasoning. By itself, however, reasoning will not suffice as a way of grasping faith's nature and meaning. Beyond the *intellectual* relating which can be established by reason, a comprehensive understanding of faith requires a *vital* relating—a relating which involves the would-be knower's *life* as well as his or her *thoughts*.

If a vital, reason-inclusive relating is the only way that Christian faith can be fully understood, this is primarily because this faith is itself such a relating. The old Greek principle of knowledge, "Like knows like," applies to the knowledge of faith as to the knowledge of other matters. In explaining this principle, Aristotle taught that we can *know* a thing only by *being* that thing in an intellectual way. It was his conviction, to speak metaphorically, that the mind must wrap itself around the entity to be understood and so allow that entity to imprint a replica of itself on the mind's eye. Every act of knowing is thus a change of mind: it is a matter of letting the mind become like—assume the form of—the thing to be known. In Teilhard de Chardin's vivid figure, "Object and subject marry and mutually transform each other in the act of knowledge."[1]

When the Christian faith is the thing to be known, the task of letting the mind assume the form of the thing it wishes to know is extraordinar-ily difficult. Establishing a relationship to a passive object may be a relatively simple matter; establishing one with an active project is much harder. This is especially true when that project is not merely an in-tellectual one but a vital one like faith. To return to the metaphor used in describing Aristotle's views, how can the mind "wrap itself around" such a project? How can it become a vital or existential thing in an *intellectual* way?

Perhaps the extent of this problem can be made clearer through a brief experiment in thought. Suppose we close our eyes for a few moments and try to form a mental image of life. Then suppose we consider the thoughts that have flashed through our minds in pursuit of this elusive subject, asking ourselves "Do these images really reflect, in an adequate way, what we mean by 'living'?" It is likely that the images by which our minds have tried to capture life consist chiefly of moving pictures—pictures of a child pumping on a swing, a halfback breaking through the line for a broken-field run, grass rustling in the breeze, and the like. We associate life most closely, it seems, with moving and acting beings. But no single image or collage of images seems to encompass or "wrap itself around" life itself. We can take life's pulse, perhaps, but we cannot take its picture.

The reason for our mind's incapacity to picture life may be located in two simple, related facts: (1) life produces thought; (2) unaided thought cannot produce life. Jesus seems to have recognized the second of these when he asked rhetorically, "Is there a man of you who by anxious thought can add a foot to his height?"[2] The implication of his question is that, no matter how effective thought may be in affecting the *quality* of human life, it cannot on its own affect the *reality* of life or its most elemental conditions (mortality, physical stature, limitation in time and space). If we ask why this is so, the obvious answer seems to be: Because life produces thought, and not vice versa.

As the offspring of life, the mind or power to reason is in a position of dependence on life which deprives it of the power to know or com-prehend life in any direct or objective sense. The terms of an analogy we used in Chapter III may help us again here. It is fairly obvious that the eye is the organ by which we see and that our seeing is dependent on our having eyes. Yet we do not see the eye with which we see. As it seems quite impossible for an eye to see itself, so it appears equally impossible for life (at least finite life), which supplies the very power by which we know, to know itself in a direct or objective way.

This dilemma is a serious one. Our ordinary powers of reasoning run up against their own boundaries as we encounter vital or existential realities and conditions such as faith. As a result, we are forced to confess that, if faith is understandable at all, it is understandable only when we engage it on a deeper level than that of abstract thought. St. Augustine appears to have recognized this centuries ago; in his famous dictum *Credo ut intelligam* ("I believe in order to understand") he clearly indicated that in his view an existential commitment of the will must precede clarity in the mind.

The realization that intellectual insight may depend on personal or existential commitment forces us to admit that, do what we will with ink and paper, idea or image, we cannot convey to the reader a complete or thorough understanding of faith's nature and meaning. What we can do, at best, is to examine and interpret the public face of faith—the sorts of phenomena (stories, styles, and so on) that, as we saw in Chapter IV, seem constantly to accompany faith and express it. To attend to these phenomena and to the impact they have on human beings must be our main objective in this chapter and in those to follow.

Throughout these chapters we generally shall use one catch-all term for these faith phenomena. That term is "the Word." This is basically the same "Word" discussed in Chapter IV under the rubric of "the service of the Word." As we pointed out there, faith and the Word are in notable ways inseparable and interdependent. Christians believe that the Word, when it becomes God's Word rather than that of human speakers or actors, begets faith in its hearer, and that faith in turn produces the receptivity necessary to hear the Word's deeper tones and nuances. Word and faith are thus the two poles of that existential relationship we have called the faith project. "The Word" refers generally to those public expressions of the faith relation which we have called "projective," while "faith," when not used as a shorter name for the faith project as a whole, refers to the faith project's private or subjective dimensions.

In this chapter and the next we shall examine how the Word communicates itself to men and women of faith. Communication occurs, of course, only when there is a receiver as well as a sender, a hearer as well as a speaker, a reader as well as a writer. Accordingly, the Word is a real word, that is, an effective communication, only when it is received by faith in its hearer; so again we are constrained to note the inseparability of Word and faith.

When Word and faith come together, Christians believe, communication occurs. This is no ordinary communication: it is rather a communication of the most crucial sort, one between God and human beings. But what is the nature of this communication? In what form does it express itself, by what criteria is it authenticated, and through what medium or media is it conveyed? Finally, what is communicated through it? If in fact its main result is faith, how does this result differ from that ordinary result of communication, conceptual knowledge? These are questions that must be answered if we are to clarify faith's nature and significance. In this chapter we shall focus on the first and last questions cited above: What is the nature of the communication that produces faith, and how does the faith it produces differ from knowledge? The next chapter will discuss faith's origin in revelation and a debate among Christians regarding revelation's scope, form, means of authentication, and media. Subsequent chapters will deal with revelation's content and its implications for life.

TWO WELL-EXPLORED ROUTES:
REVELATION AND REASON

Through most of Christian history two responses have been made to our question regarding the nature of divine-human communication. The first response is that God communicates with human beings exclusively through *revelation*—that is, only on his own initiative and only through his own choice of means. The second is that the communication established by revelation may be supplemented or supported to some extent by the exercise of human *reason*.

Within the context of Christian theology, *revelation* means basically the activity by which God discloses himself to human beings. *Reason,* as understood in this same context, is that exercise of their minds by which humans seek to discover God, or something about God, on their own initiative. Virtually all Christians agree that God is knowable to some extent through revelation, but they disagree sharply on the question whether he is knowable through reason.

The way of revelation, which we may call the way of disclosure or the way downward from God to humans, contrasts with the way of reason, which its supporters might characterize as the way of discovery or the way upward from humans to God. Revelation begins in God and moves toward the world; reason is a human power employed to move toward God. The two seem to be in fundamental contrast if not in direct opposition. But are they in fact opposites? What is the precise relationship between them?

Final or "correct" answers to these questions should not be expected here, or anywhere else in theology. Theologians learn very early in their careers that, for reasons we have already discussed,[3] "correct" theological answers are an impossible quantity to deliver. The existential truths with which theology deals lie beyond final intellectual formulation. Early in Christian history, therefore, theologians recognized that they must deal in consensual, as opposed to absolutely correct, answers. Accordingly, when important theological issues came into dispute, it became a standard procedure for Christian leaders and thinkers to assemble in regional or ecumenical councils and to seek, by consensus, to resolve the dispute.[4]

Unfortunately no such council was ever held to decide the fundamental question that we have raised regarding revelation's relation to reason. Theologians and churches consequently tend to group themselves around several different answers. A brief résumé of three of the more important answers must suffice here.

The first answer stresses the differences between revelation and reason. God is God, this answer goes, and is therefore infinite, but humans are human and therefore finite. The finite can never approach, much less attain, the infinite. The only way that the infinite God can be known to finite beings is by miraculous means—by the bestowal on the finite of a capacity that it does not have normally or naturally. Revelation is not merely the exclusive way God can be known but also a supernatural or miraculous way: revelation and reason operate on entirely separate wave lengths, and the ways of reason are simply unavailing as routes to a knowledge of the ultimate.[5]

The second major answer to the revelation-reason question is that of those who see the two as continuous and complementary. St. Thomas Aquinas, for example, taught that reason can take us a certain distance toward the knowledge of God even though revelation is necessary to the attainment of a "saving" or existential knowledge of him. Sometimes called the two-story theory, this understanding of the relationship between reason and revelation leads to the separation of theology into two branches: *natural theology*, which is based on what reason can tell us about God, and *revealed theology*, which contains higher or second-level truths about him knowable only through revelation.

A third approach to the question of revelation's relation to reason combines elements from the first two. Like the first viewpoint it maintains that unaided reason cannot confer any acquaintance with God; but at the same time it insists, as does the second viewpoint, that revelation and reason are capable of cooperation. It differs from the first viewpoint by insisting that it is precisely human rationality that makes humans the prime recipients of revelation, and from the second school of thought in holding that reason is able to speak authentically of God only when aided and preceded by revelation. Paul Tillich, a leading contemporary spokesman for this position, held that ordinary reason cannot make God known to us but that ecstatic reason, or reason assisted and transformed by revelation, is the subjective medium God uses to disclose himself.

This list of three major approaches to the revelation-reason question certainly does not exhaust the number of possible approaches. To deal with the problem justly would require the writing of several more books.

Fortunately, that larger task has already been attempted,[6] and our brief outline of the major approaches to the question must suffice here as an introduction to it. You should note, however, so that you will know the standpoint from which the following discussions are written, that the writer's own viewpoint accords most closely with the third response described.

TWO REJECTED PATHS: GNOSTICISM AND AGNOSTICISM

Later in this chapter we shall look more extensively at some efforts to approach God through reason, and in the next chapter we shall examine some ways in which theologians understand revelation. Before we do either a somewhat more basic question should be answered: Why is theology, the reflective attempt to sort out how and what we know of God, necessary?

In answering this question we stumble upon a curious fact: history appears to indicate that theology was initially as much a creature of the enemies of Christian faith as of its friends. The impulse to theologize, it seems, did not come entirely naturally to the early Christians; it developed in them in large part as a result of their encounters with two dangerous and potentially destructive forces.[7] One of these forces took the form of direct attacks upon their faith by pagan philosophers. The other, more insidious because more subtle, resulted from the Church's very success; because of Christianity's rapid growth, many previously pagan people became nominal Christians, bringing pagan ideas into the Church with them. There developed, as a result, a considerable tension between these ideas and key Christian concepts. In order to sustain authentic faith against both pagan philosophies without and alien attitudes within, the Church developed theology, that activity of reflection by which Christians seek to distinguish divine revelation from human speculation.

As history has sadly demonstrated again and again, theology is by no means an automatic antidote to the problems which beset and threaten the integrity of Christian faith. Sometimes the cure seems worse than the disease. Martin Luther, for example, spoke frequently of the *carcer theologicus,* or "theological jail," in which some theologians seek to confine the divine Spirit. But for good or ill, theology is the only means the Church has so far been able to devise to defend faith's integrity and to settle disputes over faith's meaning. And so the Church has perennially insisted that the only corrective for bad theology is better theology.

Where our specific question of revelation's relation to reason is concerned, theology has been historically necessary because of threats to faith from two quarters. To one of these threats theologians give the name "gnosticism;" the other, virtually opposite impulse they call "agnosticism." In what follows we shall first establish preliminary definitions for these terms and then amplify these definitions by more extended and separate essays on each of the threats to faith so named and defined.

Gnosticism and Agnosticism: Preliminary Definitions

The obvious similarity of sound and spelling which links the words "gnosticism" and "agnosticism" bespeaks their common basis in the Greek term "gnosis" (pronounced "knów-sis"), meaning "knowledge." Both terms pertain to knowing. More precisely, each term denotes a certain human attitude toward knowing and a corollary attitude toward the larger problem of faith and knowledge (or revelation and reason) with which we are concerned in this chapter.

The historical origins of the attitude or perspective called *gnosticism* ("naħ-sti-sism") are not clear. Scholars still have not resolved, for example, the historical question of whether gnosticism originally was a post-Christian or a pre-Christian movement. What interests us here, however, is not the question of history but the question of meaning,* particularly the question of gnosticism's meaning as a threat to Christian faith. To that question, fortunately, history seems to speak far more clearly. Historically, the initial Christian experience of gnosticism was that of a very ancient and very seductive heresy. But, as we shall see, its branding as a heresy did not by any means remove the gnostic movement or spirit as a perennial and pernicious rival to authentic Christianity. Though that original form of it which purported to stem from revelation no longer poses a grave danger to the faith of Christians, several later and subtler versions, most of which claim to be based in reason, are even yet among the Christian faith's greatest rivals.

In describing gnosticism, then, it is necessary to distinguish an ancient revelation-based version of it from several modern, reason-based versions. In the ancient forms, whose adherents claimed to know God on the basis of an exclusive revelation, gnosticism was a self-conscious religion, replete with gods, revealed myths, and cultic rituals. Most disciples of the modern versions, on the other hand, pride themselves that their knowledge is based on reason, disdain the trappings of reli-

---

*This constitutes a major distinction between a *phenomenological* approach to a subject, such as that undertaken in this book, and an *historical* approach. The former is concerned primarily with the questions "what" and "why" and sets aside the question "when" except in cases where the answer to that question provides answers to the what and why questions.

gion, and in some cases even proclaim themselves atheistic. But, in the phrase of a distinguished German historian,[8] these versions too function in practice as "ersatz religions," providing as they do the perspective from which many moderns tie reality together.

The trait that enables scholars to assign a common name to both the revelationist and the rationalist brands of gnosticism is their common infatuation with, indeed their virtual worship of, knowledge. Gnostics of both types believe that human fulfillment or salvation comes about through knowing. For the revelationist gnostic, saving knowledge is a result of a divinely given revelation; for the rationalist gnostic, fulfillment comes through the enlightenment afforded by reason; but in both cases a knowledge or *gnosis* of God or ultimate reality is considered not only possible for human beings but essential to their full conformity with that reality's nature and purpose. Gnosticism is thus built on two definitive ideas: first, the idea that profound and accurate knowledge of God or ultimate reality is possible, and second, the idea that such a knowledge is necesary to salvation or human fulfillment.

If knowledge is savior for the gnostics, it is equally true that they view ignorance as humanity's greatest enemy. The original revelationist gnostics described the difference between knowing and not knowing in the most vigorous and vivid contrasts with which they were familiar—contrasts between light and darkness, matter and spirit, visible and invisible, God and anti-God. The rational gnostics of later times, while less extravagant in their descriptions of this difference, still see ignorance as the enemy that must be banished before human beings can realize true humanity, and they all but deify reason as this enemy's conqueror.

Rational and revelational gnostics appeal to the same basic impulse in human beings—the inveterate desire to be "in the know." The two forms of gnosticism claim to have discovered, or to have had disclosed to them, mysteries or ideas that unlock and make accessible the secrets of reality itself. Whether these secrets consist in mystical passwords, as in revelationist gnosticism, or in a dialectic believed to govern the secular order, as in some of the rationalist versions, they in any case are believed to provide the key to salvation or fulfillment.

Further discussion of gnosticism's diverse forms and of the ways it threatens faith must wait until our next section. Our purpose here—to develop a preliminary definition of the gnostic perspective which applies to all of its forms—may be considered accomplished. Gnosticism, we may conclude, is a perspective which offers human beings a knowledge of reality's inmost secrets and promises its adherents that through such knowledge they may achieve that special status in the order of things for which they yearn.

Agnosticism is in some respects a natural and healthy response to gnosticism. The term "agnostic" means literally a "nonknower" and describes those who pride themselves on their honesty and on their skeptical approach to questions of truth. Agnostics accordingly entertain strong doubts about gnostic claims to possess ultimate truth. Doubting Thomas is the patron saint of the agnostics, as it were, and they are loath to affirm any truth claim that has not met stringent tests that they themselves establish.

In an important respect, then, agnosticism is the implacable antagonist of gnosticism: it strongly doubts and tends to attack gnostic claims that true knowledge of ultimate matters is possible for human beings. But in another and perhaps more crucial respect, agnosticism and gnosticism are kindred attitudes: *both exalt knowledge as the value that promises fulfillment to human beings.* If agnostics deny that the ultimate or infinite can be or is known, they do so because of their devotion to the ideal of authentic knowledge or truth. It is precisely because of their commitment to the integrity of the knowing process and its product that they refuse to relax their strict standards when confronted by religious truth claims in general and gnostic claims in particular. Agnosticism's devotion to true knowledge is thus as thoroughgoing as that of any gnostic. It differs with gnosticism not on the matter of the ultimate human goal—for both see knowledge (or "truth") as the goal to be sought if humans are to find fulfillment—but only on the questions of the nature of that goal and of the degree to which, and the methods by which, it can be reached.

Both gnosticism and agnosticism view knowledge as the avenue to the fulfilled life, and it is this common view which makes both problematic from the standpoint of Christian faith. Though it does not disparage knowledge, much less consider it valueless, Christian faith does not regard it as the route to salvation. In lifting knowledge to that level, gnosticism and agnosticism place knowledge in a position which Christian faith cannot accord it. The result is that the highest value of Christian faith (which as we shall see is a form of selfless love) must inevitably clash with that attitude of complete devotion to peculiar conceptions of knowledge which dominates the gnostic and agnostic approaches to life. Before we discuss further the Christian critique of these approaches we need to examine the approaches themselves more closely, looking particularly at the ways they react to and affect Christian faith.

Revelationist and Rationalist Gnosticism

The origins of revelationist gnosticism are hazy. For a long time scholars believed it to be simply an heretical offshoot of early Christianity. Later researches have indicated the likelihood of a pre-Christian gnosticism, a finding that suggests that the gnostic attitude was more cosmopolitan than was once believed. For our purposes, however, it will suffice to consider only those branches of the gnostic movement which, as heresies, posed a threat to the faith of the early Church.

The earliest Christian references to the gnostic threat are found in the letters of St. Paul. Sections[9] of Paul's First Letter to the Corinthians seem quite preoccupied with this threat. In I Corinthians 8, for example, Paul wrote—in a formula that exposes the heart of the issue between Christian faith and gnosticism—that " 'Knowledge' puffs up, but love builds up." Again, in I Corinthians 13, he insisted that "if I have prophetic powers, and understand all mysteries and all knowledge . . . , but have not love, I am nothing." In such assertions Paul obviously was trying to counter in Corinth an attitude in which knowledge threatened to displace love as the hallmark of Christian existence. This attitude is what later came to be designated as the gnostic attitude.

Gnosticism soon grew to be far more than an internal attitude or disposition. A leading modern authority on gnosticism, Hans Jonas, writes that "the powerful Gnostic impulse to elaborate its basic vision into grandly constructed, quasi-rational systems of thought . . . makes Gnosticism a landmark in the history of the speculative system as such."[10] The incipient gnostic attitude soon became, in other words, a complete, articulate, and systematic philosophy regarding the divine, the human, and the secular spheres of reality.

The shaping principle of this gnostic philosophy was an all-pervading *dualism.* The gnostic vision split reality[11] in two: the divine became two, a god of matter and a god of spirit; the world became two, a material universe transcended by a spiritual; and each potentially gnostic human being became two, a material body superimposed on an immortal mind or spirit.

The ancient gnostics believed that this duality or twoness in things produced life's most fundamental problem. Essentially that problem was one of *alienation,* for in the gnostic view the material and the spiritual have become intermixed in human beings, and the human spirit has become estranged, by its entrapment in flesh, from its true habitat in the realm of pure spirit. The most basic problem besetting humans is this split within themselves. Deep within their spirits there resides a strong craving for reunification with the spiritual realm from which they have somehow become separated. In practical terms their problem is to overcome the distance between their present material condition and that spiritual station for which they yearn.

How is this problem to be solved, this distance to be overcome? The answer, the gnostics insisted, lies in knowledge. The spirit must first come to know its own history: how it was created or fashioned by the god of pure spirit; how it was intended for a destiny in that god's domain; but also how it fell from that domain into a state of bondage to flesh. Beyond this, it must come to know the way out of this present sorry condition: a way that consists essentially in release from the flesh through initiation into the revealed secrets of the gnostic sect.

The precise secrets on which gnostics relied for their escape from bodied existence were so supernatural as to defy definition. This fact should not surprise us, for after all these secrets were, in the gnostic view, revealed truths, not rational ones. But, though we cannot exhaust the meaning of these secrets by rational means, we can at least clarify the context in which they operated and thereby ascertain their function. That context was cosmic or universal in scope, and to understand it we must examine the gnostic perception of the universe as a whole.

The universe in which the gnostic lived was multi-layered. Its many layers had resulted from the various ways in which, and the various degrees to which, matter and spirit had become intermixed through the course of cosmic history. The universe was arranged in a series of concentric and tiered spheres which had the earth as its base and center and a purely spiritual heaven at its apex. The higher one went in the hierarchy of spheres, the closer one came to this heavenly realm; the lower one descended, the nearer one drew to the dreary lifelessness of despirited matter. Cosmic reality was thus something like a ladder; if the human spirit could make its way up the ladder, beyond earth and the other spheres of dense materiality and through intermediate spheres of increasing immateriality, it could eventually achieve its goal of reunion with fellow spirits in the domain of pure spirit. This was what "knowledge"—the revelation of gnostic secrets—could enable one to do. The secrets learned through gnostic rites of initiation[12] would serve as mystical-magical passwords by which one might climb the cosmic ladder, gaining entry to each intermediate sphere in turn, until finally one attained the desired reunification.

We have described the basic elements in the classical gnostic schema: two gods, material and spiritual, producing two worlds, material and spiritual; a meeting and mixing of these two worlds in human existence and in intermediate cosmic realms; and a human struggle to regain, through knowledge, that spiritual station believed to be the human spirit's point of origin and proper destiny. But up to this point in our examination of gnosticism nothing distinctively Christian has surfaced. How then, one may ask, did gnosticism become sufficiently affiliated with Christianity to become labeled a Christian heresy?

There is a historical answer to that question and a logical or philosophic answer. We can give the historical answer only in broad terms, for there are simply not sufficient historical data to determine precisely how gnosticism took on a Christian tint, or vice versa. It does appear that gnosticism initially approached Christianity as a philosophy friendly to it rather than as a religious rival or philosophic antagonist. In all likelihood, then, the two became wedded not as a result of intellectual jousting between rival perspectives but rather through the incorporation into the Church, through nominal conversion, of pagan "seekers" or philosophers. Perhaps these lovers of wisdom saw in Christianity a vehicle by which their gnostic speculations might gain a wider influence. More likely, they sincerely believed that Christianity expressed historically and institutionally the values formulated in their speculations. Through their presence and activity in the Church, in any event, Christian and gnostic ideas became wedded in a single comprehensive vision. That vision was possible because the gnostics saw a considerable degree of logical and philosophic compatibility between their ideals and those of Christianity.

What did Christianity have to contribute to this vision? Its primary contribution, it appears, was Christ himself. That early Christian gnostics appreciated and accepted Christ in a way peculiarly their own seems clear from a passage in Paul's First Letter to the Corinthians which makes no sense at all unless one understands it as a response to a gnostic interpretation of Christ. In this passage, found in chapter 12, Paul writes that "no one speaking by the Spirit of God ever says 'Jesus be cursed!' and no one can say 'Jesus is Lord!' except by the Holy Spirit."[13] Why should anyone in a Christian congregation like that at Corinth have to be warned not to curse Jesus? The answer lies in a curious element in the view of Christ held by a gnostic faction within that congregation. The revelationist gnostics believed, as we have seen, that matter is inferior to spirit, and indeed that matter is, as the source of human alienation, the principle of evil itself. The Corinthian gnostics, it appears, carried this matter-spirit dualism into their interpretation of Christ himself. "Jesus" seems to have been their name for the material element in the Christ figure, while "Christ" was the name they gave to his spiritual nature. If Christ was to be the Savior from evil, the gnostics "knew," he could not be its victim, and so the materiality or "Jesus" in him had to be vanquished or "cursed."

Later gnostics carried this Corinthian interpretation of Christ still further, to the point of denying that the material element in Christ was even real. Many gnostics thus gained for themselves a second name—"Docetist," deriving from the Greek verb *dokein*, "to seem"—because they insisted that Jesus only *seemed* to have a body, that his body was in fact a mere apparition or phantasm used by the god of spirit as a medium through which to submit his saving knowledge to matter-bound humans. Had the Christ actually become flesh, these docetic gnostics argued, he would have been ineffectual as an exemplar of that sinlessness, or liberation from materiality, afforded by his teachings.

It is in this gnostic vision of Christ that we encounter most clearly that alteration of the Christian perspective which led as early as the second century to the denunciation of gnosticism as a heresy.[14] Even earlier than that, much Christian literature, including several of the writings of Paul and John,[15] appears to have been deliberately and directly designed to counter this vision. And no wonder: the gnostic Christology threatened to undermine the most central and basic of all the Christian concepts—that God so loved the *world*, the created material order, that he himself became flesh and dwelt within it.

Early revelationist gnosticism thus placed in peril the most fundamental of Christian ideas, the idea of Incarnation or of divine involvement in history. Its own inherent logic dictated this outcome, for given its deprecation of the material world it could not allow that world to be the scene of a worthwhile history, much less an object of divine redemption.

Christians rejected gnosticism not only because it imperiled the gospel of Incarnation but also because it posed a threat to three other conceptions by which Christians tie things together. The first of these was the doctrine of divine unity. Christians, like Jews, are inveterate monotheists: the one God is for them the sole ultimate explanation for all that is. The revelationist gnostics, eager perhaps to absolve their god of spirit (and their own spiritual selves!) from the authorship of evil, needed and posited a second god—a god who, as the maker of material reality, could bear the blame for the pains and sufferings of material existence. Such a violation of the monotheistic ideal could of course not be tolerated by the Church.

Another Christian principle subverted by the gnostic speculations was faith in the goodness of creation. Both during and after his creation, the God of Genesis 1 surveys all he has made and declares it good. Material things are given the stamp of his approval no less than spiritual things. To the extent that gnosticism sought to undermine this affirmation of the goodness of creation as a whole, it branded itself heretical on still another count.

Finally, revelationist gnosticism was rejected by the Church because it denied the goodness of the human body itself. If God deemed the body, that is, the human individual,[16] worthy of resurrection, worthy of being his temple,[17] and worthy to incarnate his own Word or Logos,[18] how could its essential goodness be denied? Yet the gnostics did in fact deny the body's goodness and in so doing questioned the validity of crucial Christian tenets. On this count too the gnostic threat had to be confronted and countered by the Church.

Early Christianity's list of charges against gnosticism was a long one, and we have not exhausted all of its elements here.[19] Perhaps we have cited enough, however, to make it clear that ancient revelationist gnosticism threatened to transform Christianity into just another pagan, polytheistic faith. At the heart of this threat, as its mainspring, was the attempt to transform faith itself from a relationship to reality based on love to a relationship based on and virtually equivalent to knowledge. The Christian controversy with gnosticism illustrates clearly why Christians from the very earliest times have had to deal with the problem confronting us in this chapter: the problem of the relationship, and of the differences, between faith and knowing.

The long struggle of the Church with revelationist gnosticism cannot be traced here. We can only note that, theoretically and formally, the movement was vanquished long ago by vigorous assaults on it led by theologians like Irenaeus[20] and Tertullian.[21] In practice revelationist gnosticism remains alive in a somewhat subdued and modified form even today—in the contentions, for example, of some fundamentalists that the *knowledge* of certain revealed doctrines (for example, the Virgin Birth, the inerrancy of Scripture, and the physical resurrection of Jesus) is essential for salvation. In making salvation a matter of knowing certain truths which purportedly lie beyond the range of rational inquiry, such fundamentalists fall into the attitude of ancient gnosticism even as they reject its dualism and its ditheism. They, like the original revelationist gnostics, tend to transform Christianity from a faith based on existential love to one based on speculative constructions and scriptural interpretations which are presumed to be both infallible and necessary to salvation.

The gnostic spirit is alive in today's world not only in certain Christian quarters but also on a much broader front. In virtually every political campaign a favorite theme of candidates is that education is the key to solving the vast social, political, and economic problems that plague humanity. Two ideas seem to lie behind this political prescription: first, the idea that the acquisition of knowledge is a good in itself, and second, the idea that knowledge is a practical panacea for the world's ills. Both of these ideas, and especially the second, are eminently challengeable. But, given modern history, it is understandable that we tend to place a great deal of faith in them. For, as Eric Voegelin has shown in a most convincing way,[22] modern Western history has been the playground or laboratory of several powerful varieties of secular gnosticism. Though the diversity among these various gnostic forces has been quite impressive, they have in common the strong gnostic assumption that knowledge can and will save those who are fortunate enough to possess it.

What distinguishes these modern and secular versions of gnosticism from the ancient and the fundamentalist versions is that the modern forms purport to be based on reason rather than on revelation. The rationality of their premises is perhaps questionable, but without notable exception the intention of these versions is to be as rigorously rational as possible. This means that, however diverse they may be in some respects, such modern gnosticisms share certain assumptions and attitudes.

The most important common assumption of the rational gnostics is that human reason is infinitely elastic and that it can accordingly enfold, explore, and explain the nature of reality as a whole. Only if we understand this assumption can we understand the conviction of a Karl Marx (to name one rational gnostic) that the outcome of history is predictable or the equal certitude of an Auguste Comte (to name another) that certain laws of society operate as rigorously in social processes as do the laws of nature in natural ones. Marx "knew" that history must eventuate in classless communism because he "knew," through the use of his reason, the dialectic or mechanism which precasts history's direction and destiny. Comte "knew" that laws of society must determine cultural development because he "knew," through the incisiveness of a similarly powerful mind, that the behavior of all beings, including human beings, is ultimately explicable in rational, therefore lawful, terms.

Their powerful faith in the mind's capacity to know tends to produce in the rationalist gnostics an attitude of scorn and skepticism toward the myths and mysticism of traditional religion. Myth is in their view a product of unrestrained emotion and untrained imagination, two forces in the human psyche which are the mortal enemies of rationality. So myth must be transcended, even as its two parents in the psyche must be tamed, by the operations and ideas of a purified reason.

Traditional religion is virtually equated, in rational gnostic thinking, with superstition. The tenets of Christianity and other traditional faiths are considered the products of a prescientific era in which the human mind was governed by ignorance and emotion. Natural science and the other children of reason have worked to break the fetters which tradition and fear had imposed on the mind. This liberation of human consciousness signaled the arrival of a new age in which religions that claim revelation as their basis have been superseded, relegated to the status of museum exhibits.

For rationalist as for revelationist gnosticism, ignorance is the primary enemy. This is so because ignorance is perceived as the chief source and major support of all evil. Tyrannical institutions could not have held the human mind in tutelage through the long centuries of the ancient and medieval eras without the aid of an unalleviated illiteracy among the masses and of a worse, because arrogant, ignorance among their leaders. Only with the advent of the so-called "modern" era, made modern by the incursion and advancement of rational enlightenment, has it become possible to combat evil in an organized and effective way.

The man who unleashed the spirit of rationalist gnosticism in the world was a seventeenth-century Frenchman named René Descartes. A brilliant scientist and mathematician, Descartes resolved as his primary principle that the mind should be its own master. This meant in practice that the mind should accept nothing as true that it could not verify by its own powers, using its own criteria. Descartes, true to these convictions, set out to doubt everything that the mind itself had not taught him. This led him to a systematic dismantling of the entire world picture he had inherited from the authorities of university and Church.

Though Descartes set loose the genie of rational gnosticism in Western culture, he himself did not succumb completely to that genie's charms. He still lived, after all, in a context in which churchly authority carried great weight; and he took pains, after carrying out his dissolution of the medieval world view, to reconstruct it along lines acceptable to the hierarchs of French Catholicism.

If Descartes failed to follow his initial gnostic impulse to its logical conclusion, one of his disciples, Benedict de Spinoza, was not so timid. To begin with, Spinoza was Jewish and so (unlike Descartes) he owed the Christian establishment no fealty. Beyond this he was a person extraordinarily devoted to the life of the mind, willing to pay the price of penury and loss of reputation which was required in his time to protect the mind's integrity.

It appears that the problem which motivated Spinoza's thought was that ancient riddle which Parmenides and Plato made the central one for all of philosophy—namely, the problem of the One and the Many. Spinoza, it seems, sought to approach this problem as if it were a matter of simple arithmetic. He attempted, to state the matter briefly, to find the common denominator that underlies and defines the innumerable phenomena comprising the universe. This denominator, he concluded, may be called "substance," a term whose original Latin form designates a reality that "stands under" other realities as their foundation or underlying principle. The traditional name of this substance, said Spinoza, is God. But God should not be viewed as a reality separable from other realities. Rather he is the logical source and form of reality as a whole, the giant First Premise of a cosmic syllogism whose elaboration comprises the history of the universe. Or, to change the metaphor from logical to organic terms, God is the genetic structure of the entire cosmos, a "blueprint in embryo" which supplies the form and dictates the result of cosmic evolution. As the acorn contains and foreshadows the oak, so the divine substance or God contains, foreshadows, and foreordains the entire universe.

Spinoza's synthesis of insights from mathematics, logic, natural science, and theology is of monumental proportions. It is small wonder that a man caught up in such a vision should believe himself to have stumbled upon the key to reality's closest secrets. The German poet Novalis' description of Spinoza as "a God-intoxicated man" suggests quite aptly the euphoric sense of discovery that may well have flooded his mind as it savored its own achievement. Spinoza himself spoke of his vision as an apprehension of the world *sub specie aeternitatis*—"under the form of eternity," or as God himself might see it.

To see things as God sees them is heady stuff. But it is the stuff of which gnostics, whether revelationist or rationalist, are made. Gnostics, let us remember, aspire most of all to be knowers. Their motivating ambition is to plumb the depths of what is and to foresee what is to be. Spinoza surely stands high within the ranks of those who harbored this ambition and moved to act on it. What distinguishes Spinoza from his predecessors in the history of gnosticism is that he claimed to have explored reality's depths and to have uncovered its secrets using reason alone, without the aid of revelation.

The mere discovery of knowledge, even knowledge that is cosmic in scope, does not a gnostic make. Gnosticism, as we have noted, is defined by two ideas: its exaltation of (and claim to have) knowledge and its conviction that knowledge is the source of salvation. So by itself Spinoza's pursuit of, and claim to have attained, knowledge would not qualify him as a full-fledged gnostic. That he exalted knowledge is clear, but if he had failed to see in it a savior from human ills and deficiencies he still should have lacked one of the identifying traits of the true gnostic.

Spinoza was in fact no mere pursuer of knowledge for knowledge's sake. He was an eminently practical thinker—so much so that he named the work in which he published his magnificent synthesis *Ethics*, the name for that branch of philosophy which deals with practical issues. It appears from this work that he believed that knowledge is to be praised not only for its beauty and truth but also for its practical power to save and fulfill humanity. Knowledge has this power because through it alone are human beings enabled to cope, in a genuinely human way, with their situation within the order of reality. Basically, that situation is one that has been divinely foreordained. Human existence, indeed cosmic existence as a whole, is in Spinoza's theory a logically predetermined outgrowth of the nature of divine substance. That substance, as we have seen, is a kind of genetic blueprint for the entire universe, and cosmic history consists of a mere unfolding of this blueprint. The notion that human beings are free, in some kind of detached or absolute sense, is an illusion. What freedom there is for human beings consists, first, in their knowledge that they are not really free at all in the actual or ontic sense (a freedom from illusion), and, second, in their knowledge that their sole power to modify their station in reality resides in the power to make their cooperation with Substance's determining processes a conscious rather than a blind cooperation (a freedom to affirm reality as a divine process).

Spinoza thus sees human fulfillment as an aspect of or an element in cosmic fulfillment. Salvation comes about through collaboration with a cosmic process whose course has been foreordained. Human freedom does not exist in reality (or ontically, as a philosopher might say) but only in the knowing mind (epistemically). The way to fulfillment is the way of knowledge because freedom is to be found in the life of the mind, or in knowledge, alone.

The impact of Spinoza's gnostic vision on Western patterns of thought and action is immeasurable. Perhaps his most significant contribution to these patterns lay in the marvelous way his philosophy captured and expressed the spirit of the new science which was just coming into its own in his time. At that juncture in its history science was just discovering that paradoxical method by which it was to become the dominant force in modern Western thought, the method of conquest through submission. Scientists were learning, in other words, that nature can be controlled only through the knowledge of, and then submission to, its own way.[23] The human power to control hinges therefore on the human capacity to submit to cosmic or natural control. Astounding as it seems, this insight, which became the main principle of the new empirical sciences, was intuited by Spinoza long before those sciences could prove its truth.

A search for the sources of Spinoza's intuitions would take us back both to his Jewish heritage and to his philosophic mentors among Greek, Arabic, and medieval European philosophers.[24] Our concern, however, is not with Spinoza's thought per se but with so-called rational gnosticism as a formidable modern rival to Christian faith. Accordingly, the direction we must take from Spinoza leads not into his past but along the trail of rational-gnostic thought which proceeds from him toward our own time. This means that the next landmark system we must discuss is that of a thinker deeply impressed by Spinoza, yet deeply dissatisfied with his conclusions.

This thinker's name was Georg Wilhelm Friedrich Hegel. German in nationality and Lutheran by religious heritage, Hegel lived through roughly the last third of the eighteenth century and the first third of the nineteenth. Perhaps no thinker in the history of philosophy has shown greater dedication to the pursuit of knowledge and to reflection on the means to knowledge than Hegel did. In these activities he appears to have found a strong source of inspiration and support in the system of Spinoza. With Spinoza he insisted that the whole of reality is knowable by human reason. But he believed Spinoza's own reasonings to be too simple and static to do justice to the complexities of reality, and he was particularly dissatisfied with his great predecessor's views on divine and human freedom.

In Spinoza's world system even God is not free but determined by his own nature. A God who is not free is, to Hegel's way of thinking, not God. In his own system, therefore, he replaces Spinoza's understanding of God as impersonal Substance with an understanding of him as a living, active Subject or Mind. The significance of this substitution may elude us unless we look deeper, for the contrast between the words "substance" and "subject" is not as pronounced in English as in the Latin terms from which the English words derive. Since the original Latin meanings stand behind the major distinction between Hegel's theology and that of Spinoza, it will be well to note them here. Whereas the Latin term for substance incorporates the static verb "to stand," the verb embodied in the Latin word for subject is an active one, meaning "to throw." In replacing the idea of God as Substance with that of God as Subject, therefore, Hegel makes it clear that his God does not simply *stand under* the universe, as had Spinoza's; instead he *throws* himself out of his primordial form and into objective form in nature. Nature as a whole is thus the incarnation of the divine Mind or (to use Hegel's favored term) the divine Idea (German *Begriff*). Cosmic history in its entirety is a continuing process of creation and contradiction in which this Idea struggles to fashion a somewhat recalcitrant Nature (its own "body") in its own image.

This brief sketch of Hegel's key concept, like that given earlier of Spinoza's, involves a massive oversimplification. In Hegel's case the degree to which we must simplify is both more severe and more inevitable, for his views were highly fluid and complex.[25] Thought, Hegel believed, must emulate life. All of reality is alive, and the static, syllogistic thought patterns of traditional logic do not offer adequate inroads into reality's depths. Hegel therefore called for, and tried to develop himself, a new logic which would be more adequate as a vehicle for exploring these depths. This logic, he believed, must not outlaw contradiction, as classical logic had done.* It instead must recognize and incorporate it, for contradiction is an obvious feature of life. Life abounds with illustrations of this fact. This morning for breakfast, for example, I ate cereal: oat and wheat plants died so that I might live. If

---

*The basic principle of classical or Aristotelian logic was that two contradictory statements cannot be simultaneously true. Although Hegel recognized the usefulness of this logic for carrying out certain formal exercises in thought, he believed that it failed woefully as a means of understanding the real, contradiction-laden world.

you had bacon and eggs for breakfast, a pig was killed and an embryo was aborted so that your life processes might continue. Life cannot go on, Hegel recognized, without relying on its own contradiction: death. Life and death must somehow be allies as well as antagonists, if either (at least either as we know it) is to persist. And as with life so with reality in its entirety: it moves forward, coheres, grows, develops through contradictions inherent within itself.[26] A logic that would cope with (that is, help us *know*) this contradiction-laden universe must have within it the power to incorporate and understand such contradiction. Hegel set out to develop such a logic.[27]

The greatest contradiction of which logic must take account, Hegel found, is that between God and the World or, in even more fundamental terms, that between Being and Nothing. The confluence and contradiction between Being and Nothing produce the actual world of Becoming. In theological terms, the world of Becoming is a world in which God the Subject projects himself into objective form (into what we call nature) and then seeks, through the processes of history (processes of "Becoming"), to impose that form on the entire universe. This struggle to remake the world in the divine image is neither automatic nor easy. The combat reflects a split not only *between* God and the world but one *within* God himself. It could not be otherwise; for if God is alive, and if life is a dynamic process marked by confluence and contradiction, then God too must wrestle with internal contradictions.

Although the confluence and contradiction that characterize reality are universal as well as constant and continuing, divine as well as human, they are far from pointless. Against Spinoza, who denied not only ontic freedom but also actual purpose in the universal process, Hegel insisted that this process is purposive. The purpose toward which it moves is the attainment of infinite freedom through the maximization of knowledge. The maximum knowledge is of course that of God himself, and the infinite freedom toward which history moves via knowledge is his also. At cosmic history's outset neither freedom nor knowledge, even as each resides in God, has attained to its maximum potential. Universal history is a struggle by God to free himself from all limits through the acquisition of perfect knowledge.[28]

Two analogies may help us comprehend Hegel's thinking. The first compares Hegel's conceptual scheme to Thomas Edison's efforts to invent an incandescent light bulb. Edison presumably proceeded from an idea or purpose: to bring light out of darkness. If he were to accomplish this purpose in the objective, physical realm, he had to embody his idea somehow within a synthesis of physical forces and elements (capturing an electrical charge in a filament of metal or, as in Edison's first successful case, a piece of treated string). His idea thus must be thrown out of his mind into a laboratory setting and, through a process of trial and error, come to embody itself in material reality. Similarly, Hegel's God throws his Purpose or Idea into the "laboratory" of nature and, through a process of trial and error (the cosmic history of the confluence and contradiction of Being in contact and combat with Nothing), seeks to embody it there in increasingly perfect form.

God is in Hegel's view a kind of divine Inventor, working feverishly in his laboratory to perfect his creative concept. This analogy needs to be supplemented by another, however, if we are to understand the ultimate objective of the divine creativity. This second simile compares God to a sculptor and creation or nature to clay or some other semipliant, semiresistant medium. Like the divine Scientist we just described, our divine Sculptor seeks to make his medium express his purpose or idea. But in this analogy the artisan does not seek simply to fashion an object independent of himself but rather to make the external reality a bearer of his own image—indeed, a virtual extension of himself. His aim in so doing is to hold up a mirror of himself, so that he can perceive himself in objective form. So, too, with Hegel's God: his long-range objective in history is to fashion all reality in his own likeness, so that in perceiving himself in it he may come to a complete self-consciousness or self-knowledge and in the process accomplish a self-control and a world control which constitute unlimited freedom.

The ultimate objective of universal history is thus the fulfillment of divine freedom, the conquest and reshaping of finite Nature by infinite Spirit. The agent that God uses in moving toward this objective is human consciousness or knowledge. Hegel elevates human knowledge to sublime status, holding it to be the medium not only of human fulfillment but also of the accomplishment of history's divine intention. In Hegel's view humans not only think God's thoughts *after* him but also in some sense think them *for* him.

Earlier we saw that Spinoza somehow intuited and articulated the chief principle of the new science of nature which began to take hold in his century. In similar fashion we now may note that Hegel anticipated and stated a principle which underlay a new perception of history which came to dominate Western thought during the nineteenth and twentieth centuries. That principle, almost as paradoxical as Spinoza's, was that of progress through conflict. On the cultural level the main antagonists in this conflict were humankind and nature; if the principle of the new science was nature's conquest through submission to its laws, the principle of the new industrialization was nature's exploitation through technological cunning and ingenuity. The new industrial technology, in other words, used the new science not only to turn nature's laws to humankind's benefit but also to turn its resources into riches for venturesome capitalists. Hegel and other Idealists undergirded this development philosophically by teaching that nature was in important respects the enemy of both God and the human spirit.

In seeing in nature a kind of stone to be resculpted by the divine and human spirit, Hegel and his cohorts did not quite attain the degree of contempt for things material which had characterized ancient gnostic thought, but they did show certain affinities with that movement by making the natural order a mere foil and tool for human ambitions. The person who can think God's thoughts both after and for him can become, without much ado, the person who identifies his or her own purposes with God's. It is but a short step from this identification to the arrogant conviction that everything in nature that does not bear the image of divine and human reason must be whipped into line, organized and rearranged until it conforms to the purposes of that reason. Hegel's views could well be used to sanction lines of thought and practice which led to nature's exploitation and, eventually, to today's ecological crisis.

The ecological effects of Hegel's teachings and of the teachings of his fellow Idealists illustrate a point made forcefully by John Maynard Keynes:

> The ideas of economists and political philosophers, both when they are right and when they are wrong, are more powerful than is commonly understood. Indeed the world is ruled by little else. Practical men, who believe themselves to be quite exempt from any intellectual influences, are usually the slaves of some defunct economist.[29]

Thinkers, then, may cast long shadows. None has cast a longer one over the nineteenth and twentieth centuries than Hegel. We shall try to indicate the length of that shadow somewhat more fully, but before we do so we need to consider briefly the reactions of Christians of Hegel's own time to his thought.

Hegel, unlike Spinoza, was a Christian. For a time his thought, whose main lines he himself viewed as a rational elaboration and clarification of the Christian revelation, gained a large following among Christian intellectuals. But gradually the Christian community as a whole, alerted by the writings of Søren Kierkegaard and others, came to see in Hegel's philosophy the neo-gnosticism it in fact is. Though he did incorporate the doctrines of Christ and of the Trinity into his system—seeing Christ as the Revealer of the divine Mind's universal presence and the Trinity as the form of the interaction between God and the world—his ideas that God the Creator is not infinitely free from eternity and that the Christ is not unique in his divinity were crucial modifications of the classical Christian perspective. More serious still, his concentration on knowledge and freedom as supreme values tended to be made at the expense of the divine agape, or love.

From the Christian standpoint, Hegel's system, like those of Spinoza and the revelationist gnostics, fails as an account of the relationship that God has established between himself and the world. Although the God of Christians is involved in history, the divine tracks are not so easily traceable by dialectical detectives as Hegel presumed they were. As Luther and Kierkegaard both insisted, God did not become any the less God in entering history. That means that if he became knowable by his incursion into time, he became knowable as who he is—that is, as the Incomprehensible, the Uncontrollable, the Unpredictable One. The fundamental error of rationalist gnosticism, Hegel's variety included, is that it reduces God to terms that humans can understand. In other words, it refuses to "let God be God." This is the more regrettable because Hegel proved to be so eloquent and persuasive a proponent of a view which amounts to a Christian heresy. On the political front—the area in which his influence was most notable—historians and pundits have blamed or credited him for inspiring movements as diverse and antithetical as communism and fascism. In fact his claims regarding the powers of the mind to uncover the secrets of reality have been used by advocates of both of these movements to justify their totalitarian pretensions.

Because of Hegel's broad political influence, we may well conclude our discussion of rationalist gnosticism by noting and elaborating the connection between his viewpoint and that of a formulator of the twentieth century's most successful political ideology, Karl Marx. Marx adopted Hegel's method, then turned it against Hegel's premises. Hegel, he argued, had set reality on its head; he, Marx, would set it on its feet again. The truth is, said Marx, that God does not create nature, as Hegel and Christianity maintain. Instead nature (particularly human nature) creates God. God is but a projection of human wishes, which in turn are born of human needs. Meet human needs in some other fashion, Marx insisted, and the need for God (and therefore God himself) will disappear.

Marx's prescription for meeting human needs through social ownership of the means of production is so generally familiar that it need not detain us here. What is of interest to us, instead, is the remarkable confidence Marx had in that prescription. It is a confidence born of gnostic certitude. Marx *knew* that his prescription was correct. He knew because he had convinced himself that, in Hegel's dialectic, and in his own inversion of that dialectic, he had discovered the key by which the pattern and direction of history could be discerned and predicted.

TYPE	ULTIMATE REALITY	BASIC DUALISM (GOOD VS. EVIL)	SOURCE(S) OF EVIL	NATURE OF EVIL	SAVING PRINCIPLE	MEANS TO SALVATION	AIMS OF SALVATION	FEATURES TO WHICH CHRISTIANS OBJECT
REVELATIONIST	God of Spirit	Spirit vs. Matter	God of Matter and Matter Itself	Bondage to Material Order	Revealed Gnosis (Knowledge of soul's history and destiny, secret passwords)	The Gnostic Teacher and Initiatory Rites	Liberation of Spirit	1. Ditheism 2. Dualism
RATIONALIST								
1. Spinoza	Divine Substance	Knowledge vs. Ignorance	Illusion	Ignorance	Rational Enlightenment	Conquest by Submission	Freedom from Ignorance	Denial of Freedom (Divine and Human)
2. Hegel	Divine Subject	Spirit vs. Nature	Natural Recalcitrance	Limited Knowledge and Freedom	Divine Dialectic at Work in History	Progress Through Conflict	Self-Awareness and Self-Control, Human and Divine	"Domesticates" God and "Deciphers" His Ways
3. Marx	Matter	Have-nots vs. Haves	Private Ownership of Means of Production	Alienation of Producer from Product and Resulting Economic Inequity	Dialectical Determinism vs. Class Struggle	An Alerted and United Proletariat	Classless Utopia	1. Atheism 2. Naive View of Human Nature

Varieties of Gnosticism

Marx, like Hegel and Spinoza, believed not only that he *had* knowledge but also that the knowledge he had could and must save humanity. The *Communist Manifesto* is the master product of that conviction. As the workers of the world come to *know* that they have nothing to lose but their chains, and as they come to *know* that the objective forces of economic history will favor their freedom from oppression, they will in fact unite to bring in a new order of justice and equality. The gnostic spirit of supreme confidence in knowledge thus informed and motivated the atheistic Marx no less than it had a God-intoxicated Spinoza and a Christian Hegel.[30]

To our roster of rationalist gnostics we might add a number of other illustrious names: Comte, Friedrich Nietzsche, and Sigmund Freud, to note but a few. But perhaps the breadth, variety of form, and pervasiveness of the gnostic influence have been sufficiently elaborated by the attention we have given to the three pioneers whose perspectives we have sketched. Our purpose in describing their positions has been to convey some sense of the nature and magnitude of the threat that the gnostic attitude poses for the Christian faith in general and for its modern practice in particular. That attitude, as we have seen, underlies and pervades much of the faith in science, much of the impulse for industrialization, and much of the confidence of Marxist materialism which shape the modern scene. It is an attitude with which the Christian faith must continue to reckon, for through its many offspring as well as in its own right it constitutes a formidable alternative to the Christian perspective. We now shall outline a Christian response to this alternative.

The Problem with "Knowing":
A Christian Response to Gnosticism

The history of Christian heresies makes for fascinating reading. In important respects this history offers us an account of Christianity's relationships with the world, especially the world as it describes itself in its major philosophies and ideologies. As a faith born of history and as a faith that consequently holds history to be important, Christianity has to come to grips with the world and the world's descriptions of itself. Because of this concern for history and its products, the Christian faith has to flirt constantly with heresy.

Heresies are, in a manner of speaking, the illegitimate children of liaisons between Christian faith and non-Christian attitudes and perspectives. The revelationist gnosticism of antiquity was a product of the wedding of Christian ideas with those of Greek philosophy and Oriental mysticism, while Spinoza's rationalist system[31] similarly involved a compounding of biblical with Aristotelian and Arabic motifs. This hybrid quality in heresies contributes greatly to their power to subvert and destroy authentic faith. Because they wear the garb of Christian ideas, heretical values and attitudes may exercise a far greater power to attract and seduce than they could on their own. The large followings attracted from within the Church by major Christian heresies[32] are sufficient witness to their potency.

A phrase we just used—"heretical values and attitudes"—requires further comment if we are to understand the main issue between heresies (for example, gnosticism) and Christian faith. At bottom the choice between the Christian perspective and heretical perspectives is a choice between values or, theologically, between differing ideas of God and of his relationship to human beings. Whenever Christians address the question of heresy, in other words, they deal with more than abstract questions of logical validity or intellectual cogency; they deal, basically, with the very practical question of the Value that is to rule their lives. Though the formulation of the issues may seem abstract and the debates about them even abstruse, the issues in the classical struggles against heresy have always been issues affecting life, never merely issues of thought.

From the Christian point of view the highest value or objective for which humans can strive is the accomplishment of the will of God. What is the will of God? What values best express this will? What value tops the list of those that express this will? Christians call themselves Christians—name themselves after Christ—because they see in Jesus the Christ the supreme expression of the divine will. But what values are expressed in Christ's career, crucifixion, and resurrection? More specifically, what *supreme* value is expressed?

Even the casual reader of the Gospels and Letters of the New Testament is likely to be struck by the attention they give to one particular value. The reader's eye seldom scans a page which does not yield some reference, by direct expression, implication, or illustration, to this value. No other value is mentioned with such frequency, fervor, and eloquence. It is the governing subject of the New Testament's two supreme laws,[33] its four most sublime poems,[34] its three most moving parables,[35] and its central protagonist's unique life. It is the value of love, thoroughgoing, unqualified, other-directed, self-giving love.

The will of God, Christians believe, is love. This will—this love—is communicated through an occurrence called revelation, or "the Word of God." This Word is no mere word, no mere sound or exchange of information. Rather it is a word of relation, an event which actively relates human beings to God's will and purpose and to each other. The proper name for this relation also is love. It is love that, in the Christian view, begets faith—that faith which we described earlier as an existential, a personal and not merely a rational, relationship.

When these qualities of the Christian perspective are understood, it becomes much easier to see the basis from which Christians proceed as they respond to gnosticism. Gnosticism has many good qualities: it takes life seriously, it seeks human fulfillment, and it pursues and offers human beings a coherent and consistent philosophy of life. But gnosticism's definitions of life, of fulfillment, and of universal reality reduce those magnitudes to the size of the human mind, even to the size of some particular human mind: a Spinoza's, or a Marx's, or a Hegel's. In so doing gnostic systematizers tend to oversimplify the basic human problem, locating that problem outside of people in ignorance-producing externals like matter or body (as did the ancient gnostics) or private property (as did Marx). They are thus deceived into believing that the solution to the human problem can be had through the increase of knowledge, which means the increase of the human power to conquer the external environment, whether by mystical initiation (the original gnostics), submission (Spinoza), or ingenuity (Hegel and Marx).

Christians believe that the human problem runs far deeper than this and that definitions of life and reality accordingly must be much harder to find. The source of humans' basic problem is not an alien environment or entity. It rather lies in humans themselves, in their inability to relate to and to cope with themselves, their environment, and their ultimate questions. Such an inability is not correctible by the mere ingestion of knowledge; it is an existential inability that will yield only to an existential solution. The source of that solution, Christians think, is a Conditioner of existence, a Straightener of life-warping relationships, whose nature is love.

From the Christian standpoint, the problem with knowing is not really a problem with knowing as such but one with a certain attitude toward knowing. In exalting knowledge to the role of savior, the gnostics purport to remold and recast faith into a form of knowledge. They believe that in so doing they are expanding faith's role in and importance to the lives of human beings by elevating it to an activity of mind that can offer human beings greater certainty and greater control over their own destinies. As viewed from the Christian standpoint, however, they shrink faith's dimensions from those of an existential conditioner affecting all of life to those of a condition of mind that reduces reality to those of its pieces which the mind (particularly the mind of the gnostic guru) can enfold and explain. Christians believe, accordingly, that the net effect of the gnostics' "knowing" is not authentic knowledge at all but a massive self-delusion in which humans, nature, and God himself are reduced to the figments of a philosophic or speculative system.[36]

But who are Christians to make such a judgment? Are they not guilty of the very thing, the very pretension, self-delusion, and pride of knowledge with which they charge the gnostics? Must they not presume to *have* authentic knowledge in order to deny that the gnostics have it? Christian faith, too, appears to make a certain truth claim, and from the standpoint of this claim it appears to reject other claims. On what basis does its truth claim rest, and how are we to know (if indeed we can know) that its approach to the entire truth or knowledge question is viable? These are questions posed for the Christian faith by gnosticism's opposite number, agnosticism. And they are questions we must now consider.

Thoroughgoing and Limited Agnosticism

In turning to do battle with gnosticism, Christianity exposes its flank, as we have just noted, to an attack from agnosticism. As a result it has to fight on two fronts simultaneously. Can it avoid becoming a "house divided" as it does this? Does it have the resources to remain internally consistent as it copes with the threat posed by the "knowers" on the one hand and that posed by the "nonknowers" on the other? These are questions which our discussion in the following pages must consider. But first we must consider more closely the agnostic attitude as such.

Theoretically, agnosticism may take two forms; in practice, it may take but one. Because the purely theoretical form cannot be maintained as a responsible position, we shall deal with it only long enough to show why this is the case. Most of our attention in this section will be devoted to the only form of agnosticism that constitutes (in its own view anyway) a practicable alternative to Christian faith.

In purely theoretical terms it seems possible to conceive of a form of agnosticism or not-knowing which is *thoroughgoing* or *complete*. An agnostic of this persuasion would deny that anything at all is or can be known. But such a conception falls under the weight of its own affirmation. If it were true that nothing can be known, it would clearly be impossible for anyone to know or discover this truth. The theory of thoroughgoing agnosticism is thus impossible to maintain, simply because it contradicts itself. To affirm the truth of the statement "Truth cannot be known" is simultaneously to deny its truth: if the statement itself is known to be true then at least one truth can be known.

A thoroughgoing agnosticism is therefore impossible to maintain even in theory, for the very affirmation of the concept's truth ("It is true that...") contradicts the concept's content ("... truth cannot be known"). Only the second form of agnosticism, which we shall call its *limited* form, can make any claim to viability.

WEAKNESS THROUGH STRENGTH

Fanatics
may defend
a point of view
so strongly
as to prove
it can't be true.

From Grooks 4 *by Piet Hein. Copyright 1972 by ASPILA SA.*
Used by permission of Mr. Hein.

Limited agnosticism takes its name from the fact that it carefully limits its claims regarding the possibility or impossibility of knowledge, thereby avoiding the logical trap into which thoroughgoing agnosticism stumbles. Though there are in fact several possible varieties of limited agnosticism, all of them are duly cautious in their statements regarding the accessibility of truth.

There is an agnostic element in both rationalism and empiricism, the two major viewpoints into which philosophic approaches to the problem of knowledge fall. Rationalism, which teaches that human thought or reason offers the only assured route to truth, generally doubts knowledge claims based on mere sense experience. In direct contrast, empiricism, which holds that sense experience is the only valid road to knowledge, doubts the claims of rationalists and revelationists that truth is to be had through supersensible or extrasensory means. Each position affirms the possibility of knowledge via its own preferred route while denying the reliability of the other position's approach. Each practices a form of limited agnosticism, allowing the validity of some approaches to knowledge and disallowing that of others.

The forms of limited agnosticism vary not only in kind or type but also in the extent to which they believe the mind's power to know is limited. In other words, some forms of limited agnosticism restrict knowledge more than others do. Some agnostics (particularly some of the empiricist type—for example, the logical positivists) doubt the knowability, and the status in objective reality, of *values* of any sort. *Facts* are knowable, they argue; but values, which they tend to view as products of human emotion, are not. This is the case, in their view, because facts can be proved true by sense experience, whereas values cannot.

Other agnostics—usually of the rationalist type (for example, Plato and those in his tradition)—keep their doubts under tighter rein. Values can be known to exist subjectively, they would contend, and can with some validity be believed to exist objectively. But in the view of some of these rationalists (for example, Immanuel Kant), serious questions must be raised about the knowability of beings or values that purportedly transcend both sense experience and the categories of the mind (space, time, cause, and the like). Since Jews and Christians claim that God is such a transcendent being, these agnostics would strongly doubt, if indeed they did not rule out, this God's knowability.

Limited agnostics thus range from those who rule out any knowledge beyond that demonstrable to the senses to those who allow validity to sense-transcending value experiences but deny it to beings like God who transcend the mind's own categories. They include as well the most modest agnostics of all, those tolerant souls who do not deny that God may be knowable and who refuse to attack the position of those who claim to know him but nevertheless insist that they themselves have no experience which conveys or validates such knowledge.

Agnostic claims vary in both form and scope. Their essential feature is in any case doubt. It would appear, therefore, that doubt is the common quality in agnosticism that must be confronted and countered by faith. In a certain sense this is true. But as we suggested earlier in this chapter, the more potent foe of faith among those which wear the guise of agnosticism may be an attitude other than doubt. Accordingly, as we formulate the Christian response to agnosticism, we must ask not only how intelligent Christians regard doubt but also how they view the deeper attitude of reverence for knowledge which produces agnostic doubt.

The Problem with "Not-Knowing": A Christian Response to Agnosticism

The Christian response to agnosticism must begin with words of affirmation and appreciation. In important respects Christian faith and agnosticism occupy common ground. Both are nongnostic, and they stand together in their opposition to gnostic attitudes. Moreover, both

TYPE	OBJECT(S) DOUBTED*	REASON(S) FOR DOUBTING	CRITERIA FOR KNOWING	"KNOWABLES"	HIGHEST VALUE(S)	FEATURE TO WHICH CHRISTIANS OBJECT
RATIONALIST						
1. Classical Idealism	Sensory Data	Variability of Sense-Data as Circumstances Change	Immutability, Noncontradiction	Eternal Ideas and Values	The "Good" (Universal Goodness)	Depreciates Historical or Temporal Experience
2. Critical Transcendentalism	Transcendent Realities	Unverifiable in Principle because They are Neither Sense Objects Nor Conditions of Sense Knowledge	Logical Necessity and Sense Verification	Transcendential Categories and Sense Objects	The "Right" (Unconditional Duty) and The "Rational"	Defines "Knowing" Too Narrowly
EMPIRICIST						
1. Scientific Empiricism	The Existence of Nonverifiable Entities	Unverifiability by Sensory Observation	Observability and Predictable Repeatability	Sense Objects	The "True" (Verifiable Fact)	Ignores the Individual and Unique in Favor of the Universal and Repeatable
2. Social Utilitarianism	Absolute Values	Conviction That Values are Mere Social Conventions	Social Agreement	Social Conventions	"The Greatest Good for the Greatest Number"	Tends to Sacrifice Individual Rights to the "Public Good"
3. Economic Pragmatism	Unproductive Theories	Theories Fail to Satisfy Economic Needs	"It Works"	Practical Results	Efficiency and Productivity	Tends to Define and Value Persons in Too Simple Terms of Economic Achievement
4. Materialism	Immaterial Entities	Unverifiability by Senses	"It Pays"	Material Objects	Acquisition of Material Wealth	Ranks Things Above Persons
5. Hedonism	Values Beyond The Self	They Fail to Produce Pleasure	"It Satisfies"	Sense Experiences	Enjoyment of Pleasure	Its Essential Selfishness

Varieties of Agnosticism

*It should be noted that not all advocates of the viewpoints listed doubt the reality of these objects. The chart describes *agnostic versions* of the various perspectives, not the perspectives themselves.

allow room in human thought and existence for honest doubt. Was it not after all a Christian poet who wrote in the nineteenth century that "There lives more faith in honest doubt... than in half the creeds"?[37] And was it not an eminent Christian thinker who declared in the twentieth century that "serious doubt is confirmation of faith"?[38] A quality which distinguishes Christian faith from gnostic "knowledge" is a certain humility born of the recognition that faith itself is not knowledge so much as a rich mixture of conviction and doubt.

Christianity and agnosticism join forces to combat gnosticism. They come together, too, to oppose human presumption, pretension, and absolutism, all of which they view as forms of a false and ill-based spirit of certitude. Theirs is nonetheless a strange alliance, for they are united more in what they stand against than in what they stand for. The most formidable modern expressions of the agnostic spirit stand for scientific integrity, pragmatic efficiency, and materialistic satisfaction. Practically speaking, these values function as the criteria by which most contemporary agnostics would assess truth claims. And they are indeed considerable values, even from the Christian standpoint. Why, then, do Christians disagree with the agnostic decision to make them the chief standards for determining the truthfulness of knowledge claims?

Basically, Christians disagree with agnostics not because of what the latter affirm but because of what they deny and because of the actual and potential effects of their denial on life and the pursuit of truth. Virtually all agnostics, at least of the contemporary sort,[39] deny that they know God, and many of them deny that a being like the Judaeo-Christian God can be known at all. If the term "knowledge" is reserved purely for the sort of knowledge that the scientist can have of physical objects, even Christians would agree that God cannot be "known." But knowledge surely has a broader meaning than this. We know (have an acquaintance with) not only physical things but also persons and events, ideas and values, none of which can be reduced to the quantitative or sensory terms by which physical objects are knowable. To be sure, the exactness and degree of certainty we achieve in knowing these entities do not match the precision and certainty attainable by the scientific method. But the practical evidence favoring the validity of such knowing is generally convincing enough to lead us to make many, if not most, of our decisions and plans on the assumption that it is valid. Therefore, before we insist that the knowability of persons, values, and so forth must be denied because they fail to conform to scientific canons, we need at least to compare the effects of such a denial of their knowability with these effects of faith in it.

As a way of getting at the possible effects of such a denial, suppose we adopt for a moment the standpoint of a very rigorous agnostic, one who believes that knowledge consists exclusively of scientifically verifiable information. For such a person, it appears, any knowledge we can gain about persons, values, or the like, must be established under laboratory conditions—that is, through efforts to deal with them in a laboratory setting, using laboratory protocol. But, practically speaking, this would seem to entail making the whole of ordinary life into a sustained scientific experiment in which every person encountered and every conversation and occurrence of daily life become specimens for scientific scrutiny. Laboratory conditions and controls would perforce be imposed on all experiences and human relationships, and our observer would of necessity be very controlled and computative in all that he or she did.

Most of us would probably find the product of such an approach to life quite laughable. We can imagine our mad scientist ultimately wiring his or her companions and associates in much the same way hospital technicians wire up heart attack victims in the cardiac care units of modern hospitals. Moreover, as Jonathan Swift suggested in satires written in the eighteenth century,[40] the mere effort to process and analyze the flood of data secured from his or her cosmic laboratory would probably immobilize the "scientist."

Our illustration is admittedly a terrible caricature of the agnostic position. Responsible agnostics would quite justly be incensed by such highhanded treatment. But unfair though it is when applied to actual cases, our illustration nevertheless makes a point: If, as we said earlier, it is impossible to develop a *theory* of agnosticism which is thoroughgoing, it is equally impossible to *practice* agnosticism in a thoroughgoing way. To restrict the human approach to knowledge to scientific methodologies or to sense experiences may be theoretically possible, and to stay exclusively with these methodologies *in certain areas of activity* may even be practically possible, but to live an entire life on the basis of such methods and the knowledge they produce would constitute an exercise in absurdity.*

Our absurd illustration, then, does not apply to actual cases. But this is true only because in actual cases agnostics do not completely practice what they preach. In practical matters agnostics—even those who seek scientific rigor—frequently proceed as if knowledge gained by nonscientific and nonsensory means were fully as legitimate as scientific and sense-based knowledge. From the Christian standpoint the realization that agnostics proceed thus is not at all surprising. Agnostics are as-

---

*Suppose a suitor, for example, were to woo his beloved only on the basis of scientifically demonstrable data. As evidence of his feelings for her, he might then present her with electroencephalographs instead of long-stemmed roses. On the basis of what is *known*, albeit unscientifically, about courtship, we have little difficulty imagining how far such a courtship would proceed.

suredly human beings, and human beings are, as Christians perceive them, always *valuing* beings. Agnostics can deny the Judaeo-Christian God, therefore, only because they "know" and revere some other god, some other supreme value. At the basis of their denial is not a not-knowing at all but a knowing, an acquaintance with life and reality from which they derive a certain scale or hierarchy of values. Those values may be partially a product of sensory or scientific processes, but they are based to a considerable and more significant extent on processes of experience, thought, and judgment which cannot be tested by scientific or sensory means.[41]

Once this state of affairs is realized, it becomes apparent that the nature of the dispute between agnosticism and Christianity must be redefined. Agnostics' derivation of their values through a broad acquaintance with life is strikingly similar to Christians' derivation of those values that form and motivate their faith. Agnostics, in other words, have a faith of their own, and the issue between their viewpoint and that of Christians is at bottom not one between faith and doubt but one between rival faiths and rival doubts. The meaningfulness of any conversation between Christians and agnostics hinges on the recognition of this point by both sides. Agnostics represent not only a certain doubt but also a certain faith (a faith, for example, in the scientific process as the final court of appeal in theoretical matters, and a corresponding faith in perceivable results in practical matters). Christians represent not only a certain faith but also a certain doubt (a doubt, for example, that the scientific process can get at those realities which are most important in human life and a further doubt that perceivable results can be the acid test of the validity of a life commitment).

In the final analysis, the choice between Christian faith and agnosticism is not a choice between faith and no faith but a choice between one faith and another. The intelligent questions thus become: Which faith is the more adequate? Which makes more sense of reality as humans generally experience it? Which provides a sounder basis for human efforts to find fulfillment, to be open and teachable before experience, and to live responsibly, ethically, and creatively?

No simple or comprehensive answer to these questions is possible here. Even a sustained analysis of the main approaches to answers is not feasible. What we can do at best is to outline the approach such an answer might take. The following chapters will elaborate the basis from which the Christian apologist could proceed to address the agnostic.

A viable Christian strategy for responding to agnosticism might begin with the recognition that agnostics must be addressed on the level of their premises rather than on that of their formal arguments. The agnostics' premises, like human premises generally, may be presumed to derive from their experiences and their interpretation of those experiences.

Christians might well ask agnostics if they have not had the experience of contingency, an experience which conveys a sense that one does not give oneself existence, that existence is rather a product of realities and conditions beyond one's own powers to create and control.[42] They might ask agnostics, too, if they have not experienced love—not only the love of others in their behalf or their own love for others but also the love that seems to be implied by the supportive nature of reality (as evinced in the gift of life itself, for example).[43]

Because the experiences of contingency and love are irreducible to concepts, they are not communicable through arguments or logical discourse. All such discourse can do is point persons beyond itself to experiences, engagements with and by reality which transcend logical form. But can the impotence of conceptual reasoning and formal language honestly be said to make these experiences less real or reliable?

To this point some agnostics at least—namely those humanistic agnostics who recognize the interdependence of finite beings and who have been grasped by certain value commitments—could doubtlessly appreciate the observations of Christian apologists. To those who have followed and concurred in their analysis to this point, apologists may put their final, pivotal question: Can the transrational experiences of dependence and of being loved honestly be considered self-explanatory?

In support of the Christian answer to this question (which would of course be "no"), Christians may invoke the ancient metaphysical principle *ex nihilo nihil fit*—"out of nothing is nothing made" or "nothing comes from nothing." Somehow, they could argue, the nature of reality must be such that the experiences of dependence and love are possible. Such experiences seem to be what Abraham Maslow has called "peak experiences," highly illuminating and fulfilling experiences. Can such enriching experiences derive from a reality which lacks the capacity to produce them? Can more come from less? Could such deep personal realizations ever have emerged from a universe in which personhood was not a first principle, an incipient reality from the outset? Could such incipient personhood have emerged from something less than Personhood, mind from something less than Mind, spirit from something less than Spirit?

In pressing upon agnostics their own interpretation of reality, Christians must remain aware that that interpretation does not constitute an exhaustive demonstration or an indubitable explanation of reality's nature. But without abandoning such an awareness Christians may well argue that their reading of reality is the more ethically viable and existentially valid of the alternatives. The agnostic attempt to behave ethically despite doubts that ethical values are grounded in ultimate reality seems more heroic than rational. Rational behavior is presumably that behavior which accords closely with the way things actually are, and to argue that the way things actually are is ultimately unknowable seems to undercut the very possibility of a rational ethic. By way of contrast, the Christian faith contends that the ways things actually are has been disclosed, that the intention of things as they are is the perfection of humankind and of the world, and that to act ethically is to express and not to defy this intention rooted in the nature of things.

Though it would surely be supercilious for Christians to claim any degree of ethical superiority to agnostics—or, for that matter, to gnostics or devotees of other faiths—Christians may at least question the claim of some ethical agnostics that they have taken the higher, more rational road by renouncing "faith" in the name of "reason." The reason that agnostics employ and serve may be more restricted in focus—that is, may be applied to and defined by a narrower range of experience— than that reason employed by Christians in the service of their faith, but such restriction does not necessarily make it more rational. Indeed, the commitment of agnostics to the service of ethical ideals whose status in reality is in their view dubious seems to require a leap of faith whose rationality is questionable. One of the classical criteria of rationality is consistency—the coherence of one's life style with one's world view. To the degree that the ethic and life style of Christians adhere closely to their world view, their behavior is, by this criterion anyway, rational. And to the degree that ethical agnostics act on a basis not grounded in their world view, their behavior is by the same measure irrational.

But let us suppose, for the sake of argument, that the agnostics claim that their ethic is grounded in a world view, albeit a world view that does not include faith in God. In such an event, the Christian apologist must attempt to determine the nature of the particular agnostic's world view and engage its holder in the terms of that view.

From the Christian standpoint, it would appear that agnostics have to develop their world view in one of two directions. They may try to suspend judgment on the God question altogether, denying that they know an ultimate Value and that in practice they serve one. Or they may deny that they know an ultimate Value, yet acknowledge that they live their lives in the service of something that they conceive to be of supreme importance.

As we have already suggested by means of our "caricature" of the committed agnostic, agnostics who seek not only to deny a knowledge of God but to withhold service from any value whose reality they cannot prove will likely end in a state of moral paralysis. Such agnostics will in effect become vegetables. Not only will they find nothing toward which to direct their efforts, but they will also (like vegetables in general) be at the mercy of the most potent forces and pressures in their environment.

The second direction in which agnostics might move seems more viable. But those who deny knowledge of an ultimate Value even as they serve some ultimate concern have to face not only a charge of inconsistency but also another basic decision about direction. They must decide, in effect, whether the value to which they give themselves (by "faith," obviously, and not by "knowledge") is purely temporal and finite or whether it is enduring and at least potentially infinite. If they decide that the value they serve is temporal and finite, they must face the rationally embarrassing question: Why is one temporal and finite value superior to the myriad of other temporal and finite values which have been denied ultimacy by this decision? On the other hand, if they decide that the value they serve is superior to finite values because of its power to endure, they are in effect affirming a faith in a transtemporal being who (in being transtemporal) resembles the God with whom they claim to be unacquainted. If this direction is chosen, indeed, the only remaining point at issue between the agnostic's position and the Christian's position has to do with the nature of such a transtemporal being.

If and when agnostics have come to recognize that the issue between their stance and that of Christians has to do with the *nature* of the ultimate rather than its existence, Christian apologists may ask them to examine the implications of the experiences of receiving life and receiving love for the question of ultimacy's nature. Christians maintain that the openness of human beings to reality, the readiness of people to learn, must be large enough to allow them to sit humbly before such experiences and learn from them. Christians contend that when such learning does take place, the experiences of being loved and loving provide our most adequate clues to the question of reality's meaning and nature.

Reprinted by permission of Newspaper Enterprise Association (NEA).

These are the main lines that a Christian response to agnosticism might take. The lines of debate suggested here by no means exhaust the directions in which such a debate might go. Much would depend on the positions taken and the responses made by particular agnostics. Christians ought to be able at all events to affirm the positive values of intellectual honesty and technical proficiency which motivate most agnostics. What they question in the agnostic approach to reality is not that approach's values but its ordering of these values so as to depreciate or exclude from consideration values which Christians consider even more important than those exalted by agnosticism. From the Christian standpoint, agnostics, in defining knowledge in a way that keeps the mind from adequately attending to the phenomenon of love, not only misread reality but also, ironically, tend to underestimate the mind's capacity to know. The likely result is not that enrichment of knowledge which agnostics fervently seek but an arbitrary restriction of the potential sources of knowledge to certain types of experience.

With this observation—that agnostics pursue knowledge in such a way as to restrict its pursuit—we are brought back, full circle, to the question with which our discussion of agnosticism began: Can Christian faith combat gnosticism and agnosticism simultaneously without becoming a house divided against itself? Can it cope with the knowers on one side and the nonknowers on the other without forfeiting its own integrity? The answer of thoughtful Christians would be yes. They would say that the Christian criticism of agnosticism and that of gnosticism are in the last analysis the same criticism. Agnostics no less than gnostics tend to reduce reality to terms their own minds can explain and manage. This is true because both gnostics and agnostics make the mind's experience of knowledge, rather than the total self's experience of love, the supreme clue to reality's nature and meaning. Gnostics serve a knowledge which is to them very *real* and which they already have attained; agnostics serve instead an *ideal* of knowledge and certain methods of getting at it. Both consider knowledge the main means of access to reality. Against both Christians maintain that reality releases its meaning primarily through a faith born of the experience of love.

FAITH AND KNOWING:
A SUMMATIVE POSTSCRIPT

In his famous study of human modes of communication, Marshall McLuhan observed that "We *live* mythically but continue to think fragmentarily and on single planes."[44] This observation expresses concisely and provocatively the major point of our description of faith and of its relation to knowledge. As we discussed gnosticism and agnosticism in the course of this chapter, we noted that these approaches to reality tend to reduce the real to the thinkable or the sensible. In doing this they illustrate a predicament in which we all are caught: the predicament McLuhan describes as "thinking fragmentarily."

Gnosticism and agnosticism illustrate this common predicament. In the Christian view, however, they err not in evincing it but rather in absolutizing it. They err, that is, not in thinking fragmentarily but in representing their fragmentary thoughts or their "single planes" of thought as adequate approaches to a universe which cannot be adequately comprehended by such approaches but in fact can only be "lived mythically."

An attempt to understand the precise meaning of McLuhan's contention that we live mythically cannot be ventured here. A Christian perception of reality can embrace his words, whether or not it can accept his precise intention in them. For the thoughtful Christian, "living mythically" implies living meaningfully, and that in turn means living in terms of a vast and intricate network of relationships whose basis is God, whose name is the universe, whose duration is cosmic history, whose meaning is the integrating and sustaining love disclosed in Christ, and whose beneficiaries include Christians themselves and all of their creaturely companions.

To be sure, Christians are aware that they, too, usually attend to this universe of relationships very fragmentarily, one or two relationships at a time. In the course of their lifetimes, some relationships assume far more importance than others. Even in their relationships with other people, they see only fragments of their larger histories. If they are sales persons, they deal with people usually as customers; if they are mail carriers, other people are in effect their addresses; and if they are teachers, others become primarily minds in process of development. So their relationships are often not only fragmentary but also narrow and functional. Christians remain Christians only as they strive to realize that their momentary involvements and passing preoccupations take their meaning and purpose from a far fuller, far richer frame of reference—the one described in the Christian myth. That myth places them, even as they go about menial daily tasks, within the larger purposes of God and the long and significant panorama of creation history.

The difference between Christians and gnostics or agnostics is that the former are made constantly aware that they live mythically precisely through their awareness that they think and know fragmentarily. Like blind persons whose other senses are made more acute because of their handicap, Christians are led by their limitations into a strong sense of their dependence on and symbiosis with what Eric Voegelin termed the "bonds of reality."[45] Using their fragments of knowledge, Christians seek to understand as best they can their faith and its myth. At the same time, the myth from which they take their life's meaning makes them restless and dissatisfied with what they know. Thus their faith leads them to seek knowledge even as it alerts them to the inadequacies of all knowledge.

In thus enabling persons to "live mythically," faith demonstrates that it is more than a mode of knowing. It is essentially a mode of being alive, a life-posture that expresses itself in a life style and in the stories, standards, and deeds of service that depict, exalt, and exemplify that life style.[46] Still, faith includes a mode of knowing, some of whose findings we shall discuss in later chapters. Before proceeding to such a discussion, however, let us summarize some of the implications of what we have said in the first five chapters for faith's mode of knowing.

Whatever else it is, faith's mode of knowing is a *religious* way of knowing. In Chapter I we defined religion as the art of putting a world together. The knowing of faith, like the religious approach to reality it expresses, is primarily *synthetic* or *relational*. It sees the things of the world primarily in their togetherness rather than in their apartness, in their relatedness rather than in their separateness.[47] Its essential vision of a world harmony motivates the religious mind to make sustained and earnest efforts to heal the world's brokenness, wherever it is found.

Though the religious perception of the world is relational and synthetic in essence and intention, in form it is *paratactic* and *mosaic*. Another way of saying this is that the religious "vision" is not "visual." St. Paul contrasted walking by faith with walking by sight.[48] That contrast has often been taken to mean that walking by faith is like stumbling down a dark alley, whereas walking by sight means proceeding with a sure and steady gait down a well-lit path. To an extent this does seem to have been Paul's meaning.[49] But there is another angle from which the distinction between faith knowledge and sight knowledge can be viewed, an angle that places faith in a more positive light. In this view, sight knowledge is knowledge from a distance, a theoretical knowledge, while faith knowledge is participatory or experiential knowledge.[50]

The word "paratactic," as we saw in Chapter I, describes a language that demands that the hearer *get involved* or *participate* in what is being communicated. The price of the authentic religious vision or synthesis is a willingness to become involved, to participate. Faith is the Christian name for such participation. The participation which comes with faith is the glue that holds things together in faith knowledge. To say that the Christian revelation is paratactic is to say that it requires personal involvement on the part of its recipients. Without such involvement, the message or vision goes uncomprehended, is in fact nonsense. As the bearer of love (the power to sense one's relation to ultimate Reality), revelation grasps its recipient and thereby conveys the power of comprehension, the power to put things together into a comprehensive synthesis.

The synthesis which results from the Christian revelation, that synthesis which is equivalent to "faith knowledge" or to what we have elsewhere called "the Christian myth," is a *mosaic* synthesis. A mosaic is essentially an artistic construction that brings pieces of material which by themselves convey no message, bear no meaning, into relation with other pieces which are also "speechless" or meaningless, in such a way that the composite result forms a significant whole. In a typical mosaic (a stained-glass window, for example), the lines or seams between the composing pieces remain visible. But the viewer loses sight of the brokenness represented by these lines and seams as he or she is caught up in the powerful unity of the mosaic as a whole.

The religious approach to reality, and the faith-knowledge which derives from that approach, are strongly relational: the parts take their meaning from their relation to the whole. The faith relation is not abstract, not shallow or distancing, as if the religious person were like the owner of an erector set who fashions things to suit his or her desires. It is relational instead in a self-involving way in which one is fashioned as one fashions. The paratactic character of revelation draws the whole self into the revelation's force field, informing and transforming the self in the process. To the extent that the result of such involvement can be called "knowledge," it is the extremely personal or existential knowledge of a participant rather than the abstract or theoretical knowledge of a spectator.[51]

The participatory knowledge of Christians, as we saw in Chapter III, is *history-based* knowledge rather than nature-based or reason-based knowledge. In Chapter II, and again at the end of Chapter III, we looked at the diverse ways in which religious approaches to reality can put the world together. Nature-based religion ties the world together chiefly by emotion, by swinging-with the largely subconscious rhythms of the natural world. Reason-based religion proceeds more coolly, with an aloofness regarding nature that reflects an awareness of the mental powers which distinguish human beings from simpler natural beings. In reason religion a sense of proportion (ratio) displaces emotion as the principle through which reality is perceived and tied together. The mark that distinguishes history-based religion, on the other hand, is its appreciation for time. Time is the main integrating principle of historists, the means by which they tie the stuff of life together. Time itself is both integrated and impregnated with meaning by the conviction that God himself makes time the arena of his purposive (creative and redemptive) activity.

Faith-knowing that is historical is thus no more *relational* (that is, religious) than faith-knowing based on nature or on reason. It is distinguished from these, instead, by its perception of certain relationships (covenants) established in time as life's definitive relationships. Such time-based relationships are necessarily open ended: history is not a snake chasing its own tail but a bird in flight whose destination is real though not immediately perceptible. The God of Jews and of Christians is thus a God on the move, a Being who pursues his purposes actively, vigorously, and historically. Accordingly, as we saw in Chapter IV, the relation to such a God can never be a static, immobile relation which can be made the object of direct perception. The faith relation rather must be the continuing project of historical subjects who join an "historical" God in pursuit of divinely defined objectives. In historical faith-knowledge, an historically revealed, time-mediated, future-directed intention displaces the emotion of nature religion and the sense of proportion of reason religion as the governing and life-integrating principle.

The chief media through which historical (Christian) faith-knowledge is communicated are, as we also saw in Chapter IV, stories, styles, standards, and modes of service. These media, however, are only that:

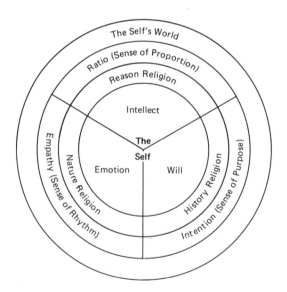

Religious Modes of Knowing as Ways of "Putting Together" the World

The way in which the self is religious — i.e., puts its world together — hinges largely on which of the self's power of relating (emotion, intellect, will) and modes of relating (empathy, ratio, intention) controls the others.

media. They cannot claim to be the *source* either of faith or of the knowledge resulting from faith. As we have learned in this chapter, Christian theology gives faith's source the name "revelation." We must turn in the next chapter to a more definitive discussion of revelation.

QUESTIONS FOR STUDY AND DISCUSSION

1. Why is faith best described as an existential, as opposed to an intellectual, way of relating to reality? What problems does its existential character present to those who attempt to understand it?

2. Compare and contrast reason and revelation as ways by which human beings try to know God.

3. Why do theologians find it impossible to offer "correct" answers to questions pertaining to the relation between God and humans and the relation between reason and revelation?

4. Describe and compare the three major ways theologians have viewed the relationship between revelation and reason.

5. What are the main functions of theology? What historical circumstances influenced the emergence of theology? Why is the theological "cure" sometimes as much of a problem as the disease it is designed to counter?

6. Define gnosticism. To what impulse in human beings does it appeal? How does revelationist gnosticism differ from rationalist gnosticism? What qualities do the two forms share? What attitudes and/or movements indicate the continuing influence each form exercises in today's church and world?

7. Describe the nature of heresy. What factors in the nature of Christianity contribute to the emergence of heresies? Why are heresies especially powerful as rivals to orthodox Christianity? What is the nature of the basic issue between Christianity and heresy?

8. Why do Christians reject gnosticism as an approach to reality?

9. Define agnosticism. Distinguish thoroughgoing agnosticism from limited agnosticism. Why is the former impossible to maintain? What positive attitude or value underlies the doubt common to all forms of limited agnosticism?

10. Characterize the Christian attitude toward agnosticism. What qualities can Christians appreciate in agnosticism? Why do they reject the agnostic approach to knowledge questions? If you were (are) an agnostic, how would (do) you answer the Christian critique of agnosticism?

11. Summarize and criticize this chapter's discussion of the way Christians perceive the relation between faith and knowledge.

NOTES TO CHAPTER V

1. *The Phenomenon of Man,* trans. B. Wall (New York: Harper & Brothers, Publishers 1959), p. 32.

2. Matthew 6:27 (NEB).

3. Such reasons include the elusiveness of faith projects and the thought-transcending quality of existence, not to mention divine infinity.

4. The most significant of these were the seven ecumenical councils, which met to consider matters of great moment to the unity of the entire Church, regardless of region. These councils, which were convened as needed between 325 and 787, took their name, "ecumenical," from a Greek term meaning "from the whole inhabited earth." That phrase exaggerates their scope somewhat, but they were attended by bishops and bishops' representatives from most of the provinces and major dioceses of the Roman Empire. The most important councils were the first, the Council of Nicea, which met in 325 and affirmed the full divinity of Christ, and the Council of Chalcedon (451), which reaffirmed the full divinity but decreed that Christ was simultaneously and paradoxically fully human.

5. The most consistent and vigorous champion of this point of view in the twentieth century has been Karl Barth. See especially his book *The Word of God and the Word of Man,* trans. Douglas Horton (New York: Harper & Brothers, Publishers, 1957).

6. Especially distinguished by their lucidity and incisiveness are John Baillie, *Our Knowledge of God* (New York: Charles Scribner's Sons, 1959); Emil Brunner, *Revelation and Reason,* trans. O. Wyon (Philadelphia: The Westminster Press, 1946); and Ragnar Bring, *How God Speaks to Us* (Philadelphia: Muhlenburg Press, 1962). For a very comprehensive and effective presentation of the second standpoint described, a standpoint that has long dominated Roman Catholic thought, see Jacques Maritain, *The Degrees of Knowledge,* trans. B. Wall and M. R. Adamson (London: Centenary Press, 1937).

7. Fr. Aloys Grillmeier describes the situation as the Church entered the second century thus: "Men were conscious that the *mysterium* [God's revelation in Christ] was something beyond words. We will further find that the church grasped the totality of the picture of Christ more in a kind of spiritual intuition than in words and formulas. . . . The church measured newly emerging doctrines as much by her intuition as by her formula and made from them new fixed forms for her proclamation.

"The incentive for this came less from within than from without, not least from the church's encounter with the pagan world and its philosophy. The need to construct a *théologie savante* emerged from this encounter with pagan philosophy." *Christ in Christian Tradition,* Volume One: *From the Apostolic Age to Chalcedon (451)* (2nd, rev. ed.), trans. J. Bowden (Atlanta: John Knox Press, 1975), p. 36. Copyright, A. R. Mowbray Ltd.

8. Eric Voegelin. See the second essay in his *Science, Politics, and Gnosticism,* trans. W. J. Fitzpatrick (South Bend, Ind.: Gateway Editions, Ltd., 1968), pp. 81–114.

9. These "sections" actually may have comprised separate letters. Most scholars believe that a number of shorter letters were combined to form the Corinthian correspondence as we have it today. For a discussion of this composition theory and of attempts to relate it to questions regarding gnosticism in the Church of the first century, see W. Schmithals, *Gnosticism in Corinth,* trans. J. E. Steely (Nashville, Tenn.: Abingdon Press, 1971).

10. From "Gnosticism," by Hans Jonas. Reprinted with permission of the publisher from *The Encyclopedia of Philosophy,* Paul Edwards, Editor, Volume III, page 336. Copyright © 1967 by Crowell Collier and Macmillan, Inc.

11. The word "reality" is here used in the ordinary, as opposed to the peculiarly gnostic, sense. For the revelationist gnostic, as for Platonism, the spiritual sphere alone is genuinely real; the material sphere only *seems* real.

12. Students whose fathers are Masons may find it interesting to know that an idea akin to the Masonic idea of "degrees of initiation" was an important element in the thinking of some of the gnostic sectaries. Gnostics believed that the more degrees of initiation that one had experienced, the better one would "know" reality and the further one would have progressed along the way of salvation.

13. I Corinthians 12:3. The interpretation here made is heavily indebted to W. Schmithals, *Gnosticism in Corinth*, pp. 124–30.

14. The most famous ancient synthesis of gnostic with Christian ideas was that of Marcion of Sinope (100?–160?) whose views were condemned as heretical around 140. Cf. Hans Lietzmann, *A History of the Early Church*, trans. B. L. Woolf (Cleveland: World Publishing Co., 1961), Vol. I, pp. 249–50.

15. See especially I Corinthians 8, 12–14; Colossians; and portions of the Gospel of John and of the three Letters of John.

16. See Chapter III, pp. 73–76.

17. I Corinthians 3:16.

18. John 1:14; Colossians 2:9.

19. Among those that we have omitted from our list, surely the most important charge against gnosticism was that it rejected the Old Testament or, even worse, recast the sacred history recounted there as a history inspired and dominated by the Prince of this World (the Devil or the God of matter).

20. See Chapter III, pp. 64–65.

21. Tertullian (160?–230?), a Carthaginian priest who was initially trained to be a lawyer, was the first great Latin theologian. Of a practical bent, he was put off by the speculations of the gnostics and wrote treatises attacking both Marcionism and Valentinianism, another major gnostic sect.

22. See Voegelin's essay, "Ersatz Religion," in *Science, Politics, and Gnosticism*, pp. 81–114.

23. Failure to recognize this principle of science mars the otherwise insightful view of the relationship between biblical faith and science which one finds in Harvey Cox's *The Secular City* (New York: Macmillian, Inc., rev. ed., 1966) and in Lynn White, Jr.'s famous essay, "The Historic Roots of our Ecologic Crisis," *Science*, 155, no. 3767 (March 10, 1967), 1203–1207. Positively speaking, science is much more akin in perspective to Islamic determinism as represented by philosophers like Avicenna and Averroes than it is to the biblical perspective. The biblical idea of human dominion over nature was not interpreted scientifically by ancient and medieval Christian thinkers, but rather religiously. In other words, the idea was viewed as pointing to human dignity and to kinship with God, rather than toward scientific subjugation of nature. Only after the advent of science and only in view of its many remarkable conquests of nature has it become apparent that Genesis 1:26–27 can also be read as a kind of Magna Carta of science. Even among those to whom that recognition appears valid, the differences between a Magna Carta, which gives science its rights, and a Novum Organon, which outlines its method, must be remembered.

24. H. A. Wolfson, *The Philosophy of Spinoza* (New York: Meridian Books, 1958), Vols. I and II, *passim*.

25. Such fluidity and complexity are unavoidable elements, Hegel believed, in any attempt to render an account of reality's true nature. For, he wrote, "Truth is . . . the bacchanalian revel, where not a member is sober." Cf. the preface to Hegel's *Phenomenology of Mind*, trans. J. B. Baillie (New York: Harper & Row Publishers, Inc., 1967), p. 105.

26. One of Hegel's own illustrations of this is both more complex and more comprehensive than is our illustration about breakfast habits. Note especially that his illustration is designed to show how a certain collaboration between subjective forces (the desire to build a house) and objective realities (physical substances like iron and wood and natural elements like wind and rain) leads to the checking (contradiction) of one by the other: "The building of a house is, in the first instance, a subjective aim and design. On the other hand, we have, as means, the several substances required for the work—iron, wood, stones. The elements are made use of in working up this material: fire to melt the iron, wind to blow the fire, water to set wheels in motion, in order to cut the wood, etc. The result is that the wind, which has helped to build the house, is shut out by the house; so also are the violence of rains and floods, and the destructive powers of fire, so far as the house is made fireproof. The stones and beams obey the law of gravity, press downward, and so high walls are carried up. Thus elements are made use of to co-operate for a product, by which their operation is limited. Thus the passions of men are gratified; they develop themselves and their aims in accordance with their natural tendencies and build up the edifice of human society; thus fortifying a position for right and order *against themselves.*" The Philosophy of History, trans. J. Sibree, *Great Books of the Western World,* ed. R. M. Hutchins (Chicago: Encyclopedia Britannica, Inc., 1952), Vol. 46, p. 165. Emphasis in original.

27.   The word "develop" should be taken literally here. Hegel did not "invent" the so-called "Hegelian" dialectic, as is popularly assumed, but instead extended the application of a logical system devised by F.W.J. Schelling and others. The most familiar feature of this system is its replacement of the classical syllogistic triad of major premise–minor premise–(deduced) conclusion with a triadic movement from a thesis (initial idea or force) to a situation of conflict between this thesis and an antithesis (counteridea or counterforce) to a resolution of the conflict in a synthesis (comprehensive idea) which transcends (*aufhebt*) both the thesis and the antithesis even as it takes up (*aufhebt!*) elements from both.

28.   The implication here, that God is not perfect in knowledge and freedom from eternity, is a clear departure from the classical Christian conception of God. But Hegel's views do have some affinities with the implications of certain biblical statements; for example, the statement in Genesis 6 that "the Lord was sorry that he had made man" seems to imply that God did not foresee or foreknow that his experiment in creating humans would turn sour.

29.   John Maynard Keynes, *The General Theory of Employment, Interest, and Money* (London: Macmillan & Co., Ltd., 1936), p. 383. Used by permission of Macmillan, London and Basingstoke, and Harcourt Brace Jovanovich, New York.

30.   The essentially gnostic character of Marx's position may also be seen in two other features of his thought: (1) his contention that true knowledge or philosophy always issues in action, and (2) his conviction that, after the revolution and the rise to power of the proletariat, the state would wither away—presumably because *knowledge* of what is right would suffice to guarantee observance of what is right. In (1), knowledge seems to be credited with ethical power, in (2), with redemptive power.

31.   Since Spinoza was not a Christian, his system does not qualify technically as a Christian heresy (a main law of heresy being that it can only be committed by an insider). It is significant, however, that Spinoza was expelled from the synagogue as a very young man because of his departures from and doubts about rabbinic orthodoxy. Thus, though his system is not technically a Christian heresy, it does illustrate quite effectively the general nature of heresy.

32.   At one time or another in Christian history three major heresies have attracted particularly large followings. The three were Gnosticism, Arianism, and Pelagianism. Gnosticism was particularly popular within the Church during the second and third centuries. Arianism, a fourth-century movement named for Arius, an Alexandrian presbyter, may well have held the loyalty of a majority of the world's Christians during parts of that century; eventually, however, the Arian idea that Christ was but the first-born among creatures rather than "very God of very God" fell into disfavor. Pelagianism, also a product of the fourth century, took its name from the British monk, Pelagius, who quarreled with Augustine's orthodox notion that all human beings are victims of original sin.

Though it has had no "golden age," as did Gnosticism and Arianism, Pelagianism has almost always had a good number of adherents within the Christian fold.

33. Mark 12:30–31; cf. Matthew 22:37–40 and Luke 10:27.

34. John 1:1–18; Romans 3:28–29; I Corinthians 13; and Philippians 2:6–11.

35. Matthew 25:31–46; Luke 10:30–37; Luke 15:11–32.

36. No one has put the problem here into clearer focus than did Immanuel Kant, whose view is summarized by Richard Kroner as follows: "As finite beings we can never reach wisdom; the highest thing we can accomplish is love of wisdom, i.e., philo-sophy. If finite and limited beings seek the infinite and unlimited, the result can only be that the infinite and unlimited will be forced into a finite and limited mold." *Kant's Weltanschauung,* trans. J. E. Smith (Chicago: University of Chicago Press, 1956), p. 48.

37. Alfred Lord Tennyson, "In Memoriam," part XCVI, stanza 3, from J. D. Morrison, ed., *Masterpieces of Religious Verse* (New York: Harper & Row, Publishers, 1948), p. 387.

38. Paul Tillich, *Dynamics of Faith* (New York: Harper & Brothers, Publishers, 1958), p. 22.

39. The more restrained agnosticism of Plato and the Platonists generally entertained greater doubt about the information transmitted by the senses than about the conviction that God existed. See pp. 41, 157–58.

40. Paul Turner, ed., *Gulliver's Travels* (New York: Oxford University Press, 1971), pt. III, chaps. 2–4.

41. Teilhard de Chardin wrote: "During the last fifty years or so, the investigations of science have proved beyond all doubt that there is no fact which exists in pure isolation, but that every experience, however objective it may seem, inevitably becomes enveloped in a complex of assumptions as soon as the scientist attempts to explain it. But while this aura of subjective interpretation may remain imperceptible when the field of vision is limited, it is bound to become practically dominant as soon as the field of vision extends to the whole." *The Phenomenon of Man,* p. 30.

42. Such an experience obviously inspires a quatrain in Edwin Arlington Robinson's poem, "King Jasper":
> I don't say what God is, but it's a name
>> That somehow answers us when we are driven
> To feel and think how little we have to do
>> With what we are.

Reprinted with permission of Macmillan Publishing Co, Inc., from *Collected Poems,* by Edwin Arlington Robinson, p. 1472. Copyright 1935 by Macmillan Publishing Co., Inc., renewed 1963 by Macmillan Publishing Co., Inc.

43. For an incisive and comprehensive discussion of this idea of a cosmically distributed love, a love engrained in the nature of things, see M. D'Arcy, *The Mind and Heart of Love* (New York: Meridian Books, 1962).

44. *Understanding Media* (New York: McGraw-Hill Book Company, 1964), p. 25.

45. *Science, Politics, and Gnosticism,* p. 67.

46. The difference between faith, as an activity of the whole person, and knowledge, as an activity of the mind alone, is suggested quite effectively by Bernard Lonergan: "The whole person with all his powers tends towards a goal that is proportionate to man. In contrast, the scientist, or the speculative thinker, tends towards a goal that is not that of the whole man, but only of his intellect. . . . Bearing this distinction in mind, it is not hard to see that what corresponds to the gospels is undifferentiated consciousness, whereas what corresponds to dogma is differentiated consciousness. For the gospels are addressed to the whole person, on all levels of operation. The dogmas, on the contrary, demand a subject who can focus attention on the aspect of truth alone, so that other powers are under the sway of intellect, or else are somehow stilled." From *The Way to Nicea: The Dialectical Development of Trinitarian Theology* by Bernard Lonergan (Philadelphia: The

Westminster Press, n.d.), p. 3. This translation © copyright 1976 by Bernard Lonergan and Conn O'Donovan is a translation of pages 17–122, *Pars Dogmatica*, of *De Deo Trino*, Rome, Gregorian University Press, 1964. Published in the U.S.A. by the Westminster Press. Used by permission.

47.   Here some of Collingwood's words, cited in Chapter I (note 13) may well be recalled: "The whole of life, regarded as a whole, is the sphere of religion, and... the same whole, regarded as made up of details, is the sphere of science."

48.   II Corinthians 5:7.

49.   Cf. I Corinthians 13:12.

50.   For a brief but insightful discussion of the contrast between these two ways of knowing, see William Barrett, *Irrational Man* (Garden City, N.Y.: Doubleday & Co., Inc., 1958), pp. 69–91. See also R. G. Collingwood, *Faith and Reason*, ed. L. Rubinoff (Chicago: Quadrangle Books, Inc., 1968), pp. 108–47, and above, pp. 14–24, 78–81.

51.   St. Paul could declare, in the court of King Agrippa, that "I was not disobedient to the heavenly vision" (Acts 26:19); and a disciple of Paul could compare the life of faith with fighting the good fight and finishing a race (II Timothy 4:7).

VI. Faith and Relating:
The Word as Revelation

W E HAVE SO FAR DETERMINED that the Christian faith functions as a relationship which ties reality together for people called Christians. This relationship is dynamic and life impelling, and so we have called it projective. It embraces and affects existence, and so we have called it existential. It is highly personal, life enriching, and behavior transforming, and so we call it love. It provides believers with a frame of reference which integrates their fragmentary perspectives and in the process prevents them from idolizing them, and so we call it mythical. It thereby transcends and transforms ordinary knowing, and so we trace its roots to a transrational experience called revelation.

What we have learned so far can teach us at least a few things about this faith-inducing experience which Christians have named revelation. We know from the data just recited that revelation is a relation-establishing experience. We know that it is a history-changing, life-molding experience. We know that it transcends thought but also affects thought. Still, much about revelation remains a mystery. This chapter will examine this mystery. When we have concluded much still will remain mysterious, for revelation as Christians understand it is essentially a Word beyond words, an Act irreducible to concepts, a divine Project perceivable only in its effects, never in itself. But we may hope to deepen and extend our perception of those effects and to find in them some traces of their source and of its nature.

It is the relation-establishing and relation-modifying character of revelation that is of most interest to us in this chapter. Human beings are born related. This fact underlay our claim in Chapter I that human beings are inescapably or "essentially" religious. A relation, or a whole network of relations, was established for each of us at birth or, more literally, at conception. In some ways this initial relatedness may itself be revelatory, revealing much about our lives.[1] But the Christian faith teaches that our circumstances are such[2] that this revelation, or this innate "religiousness," does not suffice to keep us in right relation to things. Another mode of relationship must be established, a new birth must occur, if our lives are to be fulfilled in accord with God's intention. It is the nature of this second birth, this reorientation of life through a different style of relating, which gives Christian revelation its distinctive quality and which therefore must guide our thinking about it.

A large part of our agenda in this chapter is inherited from Chapter V. There we noted that revelation is a kind of communication that begets faith, and we went on to discuss the relationship and the distinctions between faith and knowledge. At the same time we deferred consideration of certain questions on the form, media, and criteria of revelation to this chapter.

Our deferred questions were: In what form does revelation express itself? By what criteria is it authenticated? Through what medium or media is it conveyed? To these we shall add a number of other questions and subquestions as the chapter progresses. Both our main questions and our subquestions will be directed toward the objective suggested in this chapter's title, understanding faith as an act of relating which determines and directs the lives of Christians.

THE MEANING OF REVELATION

Most of the world's major self-conscious religions claim to have originated in experiences of revelation or enlightenment. The commissioning of Moses, the enlightenment of the Buddha, the call of Mohammed, and the baptism of Jesus each in its own way launched or revitalized a major religious perspective. Each of these events was revelatory- extraordinary, reason-transcending, relation-establishing, horizon-expanding. Each accordingly set its recipient on a new course, a course whose impact modified the course of human history and of countless human individuals and communities.

Revelation in the Judaeo-Christian tradition is distinctive in that it not only affects history but also uses history as its principal medium. The Christian revelation occurs through historical events. Certain historic occurrences are viewed by Christians as normative happenings in which the nature and meaning of revelation are most clearly disclosed. In Chapter III we discussed several of these normative or paradigmatic events. Chief among these—the norm of norms, as it were—is the event of Incarnation. As we shall see later, this event must be the touchstone or the compass point from which we take our bearings as we seek to understand the character, the intention, and even the Bible as the chief medium, of the Christian revelation.

The most basic question about revelation may well be the very rude one, Who needs it? Why, in other words, is it necessary to speak of revelation at all? What dimension of human experience does the term "revelation" name? Do all human beings undergo revelatory experiences, or is revelation a kind of snakebite remedy that church folk try to foist on other people? What does the word "revelation" *mean*, or refer to, anyway?

Much of what was said in Chapter V bears on these questions. Revelation, we learned there, is an experience of our fundamental relatedness to the other beings on whom we depend and to and for whom we are responsible. We called it a relation-establishing experience also because it raises our condition of relatedness to a higher level of intensity, so that what had been a preconscious condition of relatedness becomes established in consciousness. Relationships to which we were blind we now see. In our blindness we were oblivious to our dependence on and responsibility for other beings; now we are acutely, perhaps joyfully, perhaps painfully, aware of these. More than mere knowledge is communicated through this awareness: it transmutes—raises to a higher power, as it were—our state of relatedness; it ushers us into a different universe of meaning and thereby transforms our ways of interacting with the universe of being.

The dimension of human experience to which revelation points is this primordial dimension in which we perceive our essential participation in a web of relationships: natural relationships which make us *what* we are, social and cultural relationships which make us *how* we are, and psychological and theological relationships which teach us *who* and *why* we are.

One implication of this broad understanding of revelation is that the term need not be reserved for exclusively Christian experiences. Some Christian theologians (notably, today, the followers of Karl Barth) do discount and even disallow the notion that non-Christians may experience authentic revelation. Other Christians hold that, although all authentic revelation is *mediated* by Christ, not all of it has the image and message of the incarnate Christ as its content, and its reception is not confined to those who call themselves Christians.[3] Revelation is in this view a possibility for all human beings, for in its elemental form it simply raises to consciousness and to a state of significance the common condition of relatedness which marks creaturely existence as such.[4]

When defined in this way—and this is the way we choose to define it for the purposes of the discussions that follow—the idea of revelation is not a creature of the Christian imagination but rather a term that describes a class of human experiences. The occurrence of these experiences is not directly or simply predictable, but their character and function are at least in some measure describable. Their function is to reveal something about the nature of reality, and so they are aptly called revelatory. Their character is experiential, that is, prerational. Far from being the mind's creatures, in other words, they are its illuminators and shapers.

In ordinary English speech we sometimes use a phrase that may help clarify the relationship between revelation and reason. Sprinkled through conversations and discussions one occasionally hears the brief remark "It occurs to me. . . . " When its user is not just using the phrase as a convention, he or she would seem to be saying something like "The thought just appeared on my mental horizon that. . . . " The appearance of the thought in such a case is an unexplained given; the speaker may confess that he or she has no awareness of whence it came: it simply propelled itself into consciousness as a way of bringing some or all aspects of the conversation into focus.

Such intrapsychic experiences may or may not be revelatory in the technical theological sense. They may or may not, that is, be revelations of or from God. But theologically revelatory events appear to occur in much the same fashion. Such events are horizon-expanding, pushing back the darkness and confusion that surround the self's perceptions; they are integrating, tying together aspects of reality that previously appeared to be unrelated; and they are consequently reorienting, for they change the direction of their recipient's attitudes and actions.

THE SCOPE OF REVELATION:
THE REASON-REVELATION QUESTION REVISITED

The definition we have just given revelation is largely functional. It describes revelation in terms of certain functions (illumination, integration, reorientation) that the revelatory event accomplishes. But these appear to be functions that reason, too, can be observed to perform, at least in certain respects and to a certain extent. Our functional definition of revelation thus pushes us back to a reconsideration of the frontier between reason and revelation.

Let us begin our reconsideration with a brief review of what we learned about the relationship between reason and revelation in Chapter V. First, we determined there that revelation *transcends* reason. It occurs to the total self, not to the mind alone, and it originates in a reality or realities beyond, though not unrelated to, the self. Second, revelation *transforms* reason. The transformation of the total self that revelation effects means necessarily the transformation of the mind as well. In producing new identities or new persons, revelation simultaneously produces new perspectives. Third, revelation *empowers* reason. It does not close doors to the questing mind but opens them. In its affirmation of reality's essential goodness, it inspires a confidence that reality is worth studying, and in its disclosure of human dependence and its call for responsible human dominion over the natural order it produces an awareness that such study is crucial to total human fulfillment.

To these conclusions gleaned from our earlier reflections, we may now add one that approaches the revelation-reason question from reason's side. Revelation, as far as we can tell, happens exclusively to rational beings. Some have taken this to imply that reason's presence is a necessary presupposition or prerequisite to the occurrence of revelation. But because we cannot experience reality as it occurs to prerational or subrational beings (animals or rocks, for example), this is an untestable proposition. Moreover, some theologians are loath to place limits on the revelatory powers of a God who, in the words of John the Baptist, "is able from these stones to raise up children to Abraham."[5] It seems the wiser course, therefore, to stop with the simpler observation that reason appears to be the organ revelation uses to raise faith, or the basic condition of human relatedness, from a preconscious, virtually instinctual level to a conscious and intentional one.

Some theologians would charge, however, that to restrict reason's religious function to that of a servant of revelation is to demean that rational capacity from which human beings draw much of their dignity. This charge comes especially from the champions of *natural theology.* Natural theology is a branch of the theological enterprise which pursues a knowledge of God by "natural" means, that is, without the "supernatural" assistance of revelation. The natural theologians are convinced that the natural powers of reason can lead human beings to a certain knowledge of God and that they can do this entirely without the aid of revelation. Our consideration of the frontier area between reason and revelation must therefore include a consideration of the arguments by which natural theologians purport to prove God's reality.

The Reach of Reason:
The "Proofs" of Natural Theology

> Canst thou by searching find our God?
> Canst thou find out the Almighty unto perfection?
> It is high as heaven:
> What canst thou do?

> Deeper than Sheol:
> What canst thou know?
> (Job 11: 7–8)[6]

These words from Job's counselor express the reservations many religious people feel as they sense the awesomeness of God. To them it is as though the earth trembles at the mention of the divine name. Can human reason, that frail reed blown so easily about in the winds of opinion, reach and relate to this awesome Being? To some devout souls the thought itself seems blasphemous. Yet equally devout minds have insisted that it can be done, that reason working on its own can put us in touch with God.

Christians differ, then, in their answers to the question of whether reason can discover God. Whence comes this sharp division within the ranks of the faithful? Those who look for its source in differing perceptions of God are likely to be disappointed. Christians who hold that God is somehow knowable by reason hold no less exalted a view of him than those who believe that he transcends reason's reach. Indeed, most of those who believe in reason's power to reach God restrict themselves to the claim that the mind can prove God's existence and/or postulate certain divine attributes, and they assert that it cannot discover the deity's essence—those qualities of being which make the deity who or what he is.* Revelation, they insist, is still necessary for a comprehension of God's nature, will, and purpose.

The advocates of a reason-based knowledge of God would be properly indignant if they were charged with deliberately belittling God in order to demonstrate his accessibility to finite reason. They would insist that their regard for the divine majesty is in no way diminished by their esteem for the powers of reason. They might argue that the real problem between them and their opponents stems not from irreverence toward God on their side but rather from an inadequate estimate of reason's powers by their opponents.

The real issue in the debate regarding natural theology thus appears to arise from different understandings of the nature and scope of reason rather than from different attitudes toward the sublimity or majesty of God. In one of his many instructive analyses, Paul Tillich distinguished three definitions of reason which have won support from various segments of the Western intellectual community.[7] Since these definitions have a direct bearing on the positions of the various parties to the debate

---

*This restriction in the claim made for reason is what generally distinguishes natural theologians from rationalist gnostics. Spinoza and Hegel, for example, believed reason capable of exploring the nature or essence of God.

on natural theology's "proofs," it will be worth our while to survey them here.

Ancient and medieval thought were controlled largely by a perspective which viewed reason as a *structure* informing the nature of reality as a whole. Reason is a force, in this view, not only in the minds of individuals but also in the world at large: it keeps the stars in their courses, makes the tides flow and ebb in predictable ways, and governs the many other operations of the natural order. It is just because reason is *out there* in the great world or macrocosm that it is possible for me to understand that great world by the reason which resides in my mind. My mind indeed is so informed by that rational structure that informs the larger world that I may call the mind a world in miniature, or a microcosm. Because the world within is so much like the world without (the macrocosm), it can become that world in an intellectual way—that is, it can reflect or *know* it.[8]

Tillich cites other definitions of reason, but before we turn to them we should note that an entire class of the natural theologians' arguments for the existence of God rests on the definition of reason as a structure. After we have examined the other definitions of reason, we shall describe these arguments, which as a class are generally given the name "cosmological."

A second definition of reason that has found advocates in Western culture, according to Tillich, identifies reason with reality's *depth dimension*. Reason here is understood in spiritual rather than structural terms. It is an infinite, dynamic principle which underlies the finite structures of that world which meets the eye (the "world of appearances," as Platonists liked to call it). Reason expresses its essence, therefore, not in static concepts or ideas but in the dynamic *operations* of the mind. This means that true reason is by definition restless reason; its métier is the question rather than the answer, the surging excitement of searching rather than the staid serenity of a satisfied mind.

This understanding of reason as spirit, like that of reason as structure, does not restrict reason to the processes and products of human minds. Reason is present in all that is, and the mind can know realities beyond itself because in encountering these it encounters a rationality very like its own. The classical idea that like knows like (colloquialized as "It takes one to know one") is satisfied by this conception of reason no less than by the understanding of it as a structure.

One of the beliefs of the ancient Stoics may help us grasp this conception of reason as a highly dynamic process in both the mind and the world. In some forms of ancient chemistry, all things were conceived to be composed of four basic elements: earth, water, air, and fire. Of these, fire was considered the most potent, for in the presence of fire some types of "earth" (solid matter like ice or coal, for example) could be reduced to water or air (smoke), and water could be converted to air (steam). This marvelous power fire has to transform the other elements is accompanied by an equally marvelous volatility and unpredictability, qualities which appear to have established fire's reputation as the subtlest of the material elements. Perhaps for this reason the Stoics, who were thoroughgoing materialists, believed that they had found in fire a material element subtle enough to make up the World Soul or divine Mind which in their view enveloped and permeated the universe. In any event, we know that they referred to the World Soul as a Universal Fire.

The significance of the Stoic viewpoint for our discussion of reason is that the Stoics equated this Universal Fire with cosmic Reason, or (to use their Greek term) the *Logos*. Moreover, they defined human reason as a *scintilla divinitatis*, or spark from this divine fire. The reason in the human soul is thus akin to the reason of the World Soul. Because of this kinship the human mind can know (become in a rational way) the depths of the world.

To the extent that their reference to reason as fire suggests that reason is a dynamic, reality-transforming power, the Stoics were typical of those in the Western tradition who define reason as reality's depth dimension. They represented this tradition also in their belief that the fiery depths of the human mind can illumine the mind sufficiently to enable it to take in the truth about the larger world.

For those who perceive reason as the depth dimension of the soul and the universe, one of the traditional arguments for God's existence has particular appeal. Though this argument has been stated in various ways, it usually bears the name "ontological." The perception of reason as depth dimension also underlies another, more recently developed argument: Immanuel Kant's argument from moral experience. Later we shall examine these arguments, but first we must consider briefly the third understanding of reason discerned by Tillich.

This third understanding of reason stands in sharp contrast to the first two. Whereas the first two define reason as a universal force, the third understanding defines it purely in terms of the capacities and operations of the human mind. This means that reason is conceived as a mere *tool*, a means that human beings use to organize and control their natural and cultural environments. The natural environment per se is considered either to lack rational structure and purpose or to be a realm of mystery whose inner qualities, whether rational or irrational, lie beyond the mind's reach.

The classic exposition of this understanding of reason is that of Immanuel Kant. In Kant's view ordinary rational thought cannot take us into the realm of "the things themselves." Whether reality has a rational nature or not is undiscoverable. Although it appears that Kant himself wanted to believe that it has such a nature, he stressed that the only rational principles of which we can be certain are those of our own minds. The operation of these inner rational principles always stands between us and external reality. How can we tell, therefore, whether the rational structure we see in a studied object is put there by the thing itself or by our own intervening minds? That our minds contribute some degree of rationality seems clear; that the thing studied contributes any can only be a matter of conjecture.

Kant and others understand reason as a tool by which the human mind organizes its experiences. For those who so conceive reason, the natural theologian's arguments for the existence of God can never have the weight of proof. This is true for a very simple reason: If the mind cannot demonstrate that reason itself exists beyond the human intellect, how can it prove that anything else, including God, exists beyond the mind? Existence, as we noted earlier,[9] is a matter that seems to elude thought. The mind may know of its own rationality from the proximity and self-evidence of its own operations. But the existence and essential nature of reality beyond the mind are not immediately accessible to it. Those who define reason as a tool are therefore unconvinced by the claim of natural theology that reason can reach God.

Estimates of the efficacy of natural theology's "proofs" vary in direct proportion to evaluations of reason's power and scope. Even among themselves natural theologians differ in their definitions of reason's nature, and accordingly some of them prefer the arguments based on the perception of reason as structure whereas others favor the arguments originating from a view of it as reality's depth dimension or spirit. As we consider the arguments themselves, we may find it instructive to note how the various arguments correlate with the various appraisals of reason that we have just described.

Those natural theologians who understand reason as a universal *structure* tend, as we have noted, to prefer arguments for God's existence that are called *cosmological*. A brief analysis of the word "cosmological" may serve to show why. "Cosmology" may be translated literally as "structure (or logic) of the world-order."* The cosmological arguments are aptly named, for they begin by assuming that a certain rational structure or logic pervades the universe or world order as a whole.

Ultimately each of the cosmological arguments rests on two kinds of evidence: evidence that they all share as members of the cosmological class of arguments and evidence distinctive to each argument consid-

---

*The Greek word *kosmos*, from which "cosmos" comes, is the exact opposite of the Greek term which translates and transliterates as *chaos*.

ered in its own right. Since the latter kind of evidence proves little unless the former evidence is persuasive, let us look first at the evidence for the arguments as a group.

The evidence is essentially practical. It goes something like this: All of us live our daily lives as though they are significant. We conduct our affairs in terms of what is generally called common sense. As long as we view matters in common-sense terms, it does not occur to us to doubt that life is worth living. The natural universe provides us with life itself and with the necessities to continue living: sunshine for light and warmth, oxygen to breathe, food to eat, water to drink, and the biological apparatus to convert these externals into nutriments. Does common sense[10] not make it obvious, when all of this is taken into account, that life is no accident, that it is an integral part and product of a well-ordered and rationally intelligible system? Can we not speak with justice of a *cosmos*, of a rationally structured world order? And if we find signs of order and rationality throughout reality, may we not logically infer that some ordering power, some Cosmic Mind, has arranged things in such an ordered way?

This line of thought or "reading of the evidence" underlies all of the so-called cosmological arguments for God's existence. They are called cosmological because without fail they presuppose the view that the world is a *cosmos*, a rational, well-ordered totality, all of whose parts point to an underlying unity of the whole and beyond that to an original Unifier or God.

This, then, is the basic perspective from which the cosmological arguments proceed: the universe is a cosmos or ordered system whose existence and essential features are best explained by the hypothesis that a divine Arranger, or God, exists. Indeed, this statement of the cosmological perspective all but states the most broadly based of the five traditional cosmological arguments—the so-called *teleological* argument. Although some natural theologians place the teleological argument in a class by itself, it is in one respect the cosmological argument par excellence, because it is the only one of the arguments which typically begins with an observed aspect of the entire cosmos rather than with one or another of the cosmos's operations or parts. Taking its name from the Greek word *telos*, meaning "end" or "purpose," this argument begins from the observation that the operations of natural entities and of the entire natural system seem to be marked by certain aims or designs. For example—to attend again to a kind of evidence mentioned just a bit ago—nature seems to be designed to produce and sustain life. The convergence of the forces which had to converge and cooperate to accomplish the emergence of life seems far too complex to be explained by chance or accident. It appears far more likely and logical that such a convergence resulted from a *design* or *purpose* inherent in the operations of nature. But if nature is purposive, if it has order, design, *telos*, does this not bespeak the presence within and/or beyond it of an Orderer, Designer, Purposer? It does indeed, according to the teleological argument, and this Orderer, Designer, Purposer is God.[11]

Unlike the teleological argument, the other cosmological arguments proceed not from an interpretive survey of the entire natural system but rather from particular experiences in human life. They move on to generalizations about the universal structure to which these particular experiences seem to point, and from these generalizations they conclude to the existence of God. The particular starting point in each case is some relatively common human experience. A recognition of this quality of commonness or ordinariness in the experiences on which the arguments are based is important, for such a recognition demonstrates that these arguments are not mere contrivances of abstract philosophy but the results of common-sense reflection on the experiences of ordinary people.

The first ordinary experience from which natural theology proceeds to develop a "proof" is that of motion. As I write these words, my fingers move a pen. My fingers would not move the pen unless they were themselves moved. Neural impulses, set in motion by ideas, which are in turn set in motion by purposes and other stimuli, cause the fingers to move the pen. As with this motion, so with all motion: it occurs only through the activity of a mover, indeed of a whole series of movers. Since every series must have a basis or beginning, all motion must be traceable ultimately to the activity of some first, Unmoved or Self-moved Mover who inspires the universal process of motion. And this First Mover is God.

Another cosmological argument rests on a larger class of experiences to which the experience of motions and movers belongs. The experiences in this class are called *causes* and *effects*. If I become ill, I visit a doctor on the assumption that something is causing my illness and that the doctor can help me determine not only what is causing it but also how to cause its remission. The influenza from which he tells me I suffer is an effect of a virus or bacterium. From the effect I (or the doctor) must infer a cause. The cause itself is an effect of other causes. Beneath the entire series of causes, as its ground, is a Self-caused Cause, who is God.

The third ordinary experience that the natural theologians find quite significant is the activity of grading things. School teachers have a lot of company when it comes to grading things. Hardly a decision is made in our lives that is not based on conscious or unconscious processes by which we grade things: Given X, Y is better than Z; or given today's gas prices and my bank account, the subcompact is better than the gas guzzler. The experience of gradation, by which we determine degrees of good, better, best (or of bad, worse, worst), is one to which all of us become accustomed. If we reflect on this experience, we will recognize that we are able to take part in it only because we are mentally equipped with certain powers of discrimination. These powers enable us to evaluate not only things but even the standards by which the evaluations themselves are made. We therefore are able to refine our standards, indeed to refine them again and again, in a way that suggests that we have an inner or transcendental acquaintance with a Standard of goodness which makes us constantly dissatisfied with all imperfect standards. This perfect Standard to which our valuing minds or consciences point is God; if he does not exist, then the entire valuing process by which we order our lives is without basis—unfounded in objective reality.

The experience on which the final cosmological argument is based is not as commonplace as those on which the other arguments in this group rest. The experience may be triggered in any of a variety of ways, but in the typical human being's life it occurs only rarely. Perhaps it happens on the highway, when a potentially tragic accident is narrowly averted and our lives are spared. Or perhaps it occurs on a battlefield, where others die but I do not. Whatever the form of the experience, it serves to make me aware of my own *contingency*, my own inability to give or guarantee myself existence. Moreover, when I look about at other earthly realities—realities on which or whom my own existence depends in various ways—I become conscious that they, too, are contingent: dependent on an entire life-care system (ultimately the universal ecosystem!) whose present operation they did not produce and whose continued functioning they cannot guarantee.

My eyes may turn, then, to the life-care system as a whole. But if I examine it carefully enough, I am startled by the realization that it too, viewed both in its parts and in its entirety, bears the marks of contingency, limited duration, entropy. Can a contingent reality, a contingent system that is by definition dependent and caused, give itself reality? Can it, in other words, be uncaused or self-caused? To think thus—that the contingently caused can simultaneously be the uncaused or self-caused—is to think non-sense. Reason itself, that sense that outlaws non-sense, thus demands that there be some noncontingent Being, some Being who has to be if anything at all is to be. And this Being, called by the cosmologists Necessary Being, is God.

If the first in our list of arguments, the teleological, is the most broadly based of the cosmological arguments, this last argument in our list, the argument from contingency, best captures the spirit, the main point, of the cosmological arguments as a class. That point, briefly, is that God or a Necessary Being must exist if the world is to make sense. The choice between God and no God is for the proponents of the cosmological arguments a choice between order and confusion, rationality and irrationality, cosmos and chaos. Unless a self-caused Intelligence exists, the universe is ultimately a realm of contingency, accident, and chance. Reasonable people must seek to demonstrate God's existence because the reliability of reason itself is at stake in the question of divine existence. Is reason anchored in the nature of Ultimate Being, or is it only a bit of froth on the surface of universal reality? Reason exists, the cosmologists insist, and it is the rational structure's own existence that provides the best evidence for God's existence; but at the same time it is God's existence, and it alone, that finally can guarantee reason's long-term value and validity, for it is only God's existence as the Sovereign Intelligence of the universe which can assure us that reason is grounded in reality.

A second type or class of arguments for God's existence bears the general name *ontological*. As we noted earlier, the arguments in this class assume that reason is a dynamic principle or spirit which underlies, informs, and permeates reality. Reason as spirit is reason as process rather than as static structure. The ontological argument therefore begins with the *operations* of the mind rather than with its observations or conclusions. Recognizing this can help us avoid the most fundamental and persistent of the misconceptions surrounding this argument. After we have given a brief account of the argument itself, we shall respond to some of these misconceptions in an attempt to clarify the basic point of the argument.

Though the ontological argument seems to be implicit in the structure of Plato's thought, it received its classic Christian form from St. Anselm of Canterbury in the eleventh century. St. Anselm began by assuming that the human mind can conceive an idea of Perfection or Perfect Being. He then defined the content of this idea as "that being than which none greater can be conceived." But, he went on, if it is possible to conceive a being that has all perfections *except* existence and also possible to conceive a being that has all perfections *including* existence, which of these beings best accords with the definition of Perfection as "that than which none greater can be conceived"? Obviously the being whose concept includes existence corresponds more accurately to Perfection as so defined. Thus the very concept of Perfection or God implies that Perfection or God exists.

The standard rejoinder to Anselm's argument—a rejoinder which goes back to his contemporary and fellow monk, Gaunilo, and one which has been reiterated frequently since—is that existence can be neither deduced nor produced from a concept. Gaunilo argued, for example, that he could conjure up in his mind the concept of a perfect island, but in no imaginable way could he, by mere thinking, demonstrate or effect the existence of such an island.

St. Anselm's reply, still unsurpassed for its trenchancy if not for its clarity, was that Gaunilo had made a very fundamental mistake. He had sought to understand the concept of Perfect Being or God, a unique concept in that it is the concept of the one Being whose nonexistence cannot be thought without thinking a contradiction, as if it were an ordinary product of the mind. Fantasies about perfect islands do not imply the existence of such islands, to be sure, but this is simply because the concept of an island can never be the concept of a Necessary Being. God or Perfect Being, on the other hand, is by definition a Necessary Being: his nonexistence would contradict the very idea of him.

In order to clarify Anselm's point, let us trace its logic in several steps:

A. God is by definition a Perfect Being. If one thinks something less than Perfect Being, one is not thinking God, for God is "that than which none greater can be conceived," and since the concept of a Perfect Being is obviously greater than that of a less than perfect being, one must equate God with Perfect Being.

B. Perfect Being is Necessary Being, or Being that has to exist, because that Being which has all perfections including existence is obviously greater than the being that has all perfections except existence.

C. Those who think (have a correct concept of) God must either admit that God's existence is proved by the thought itself, or else they must make the contradictory claim that "A being who by definition must exist does not exist."

D. Contradictory statements are *ipso facto* false.

E. Therefore the statement (concept) "God exists" must be admitted to be true (since the second option in C is impossible for rational beings to choose because of D, the first option in C must be rationally preferred).

The crucial turn in Anselm's argument is at step D. He in fact did not express the idea in D explicitly and openly. The idea in this point is clearly implied, however, in his contention that only a fool (an irrational, self-contradictory person) could say in his heart, "There is no God."[12]

The crucial assumption in Anselm's argument is that contradiction is a sign of falsehood and that, conversely, noncontradiction is a sign of truth. This is an assumption which most modern philosophers do not share. Lack of contradiction may establish a proposition's logical validity, these philosophers maintain, but it cannot establish its factual accuracy. To establish the latter one must use the five senses as well as the mind. Therefore, since the existence of God is not verifiable by the senses (for the obvious reason that the God concept is a concept of a being beyond the reach of the senses), the divine existence is not verifiable or provable at all.

Although he would have admitted that the concept of God defines a Being who eludes the senses, Anselm's response to these modern philosophers might be very like his answer to Gaunilo. He might accuse these philosophers, as he accused Gaunilo, of reducing the concept of God to the status of an ordinary concept. Ordinary concepts are the mind's products, not its conditioners. They are *logical* concepts, the products of a human logic. But, as the name given his argument indicates, Anselm was talking about an *ontological* concept. The word "ontological" combines the Greek terms meaning "being" (*ontos*) and "logic" (*logos*). The idea of God is not a product of the human mind, but an idea given by the logic or nature of being itself, and therefore the denial of its implications is a contradiction of reality as well as of logic.

An interesting quality permeates Anselm's discussion of his mind's search for God in the *Proslogium*, the work in which he sets out the ontological argument. That quality could be described as one of perplexity; he seems restless and dissatisfied because of his mind's inability to deal with God's reality. And the ironic thing is that most of his statements of perplexity and dissatisfaction regarding his mind's impotence *follow* his statement of the ontological argument. It appears that, despite what one would think that he would regard to be a singular and wondrous feat by his mind—namely, the proof that God exists—he was in no mood at all to congratulate his mind on its accomplishment. The reason for this lack of a self-congratulatory air is probably quite simple: Anselm did not believe that this "proof" was his mind's own accomplishment. His mind has simply been an instrument of the Mind of Reality: it simply gained a glimpse of the logic of being itself and has seen that a Necessary Being makes itself known through the operations of the human mind. [13]

Anselm's argument for the existence of God depends, then, upon a glimpse into the ordinary mind's depth dimension. But this means that his argument is not so much an argument as an analysis of a mystical insight into the mind's depths. Those depths disclose to the restless mind of Anselm an idea ablaze with all perfections. In the light of this horizon-illuminating idea he can only be dissatisfied with his own mind's incapacity to take it all in. But the one thing he cannot do is shake off the certainty that what he has perceived is real, and he is impelled by his sense of its reality into an effort to demonstrate its reality logically.

Ultimately, then, Anselm's "proof" is an ontological assertion in logi-

TYPE	CHIEF PROPONENT(S)	PERCEIVES REASON AS:	DIRECTION OF ARGUMENT	SPECIAL FEATURES	MAIN WEAKNESS
COSMOLOGICAL					
1. Teleological	Thomas Aquinas Wm. Paley	Cosmic Structure	From Perceived Design to Designing Intelligence	When based on cosmic order, it is the most broadly based of the cosmological arguments	Based on selective reading of the evidence (ignores evidences of disorder and entropy in nature)
2. Motion	Aristotle, Aquinas	"	From Motion to Movers to Prime Mover	More specific version of argument from effects to cause	Begins with questionable assumption that an infinite regress is impossible
3. Causation	Aquinas	"	From Effects to Causes to First Cause		"
4. Gradation	Augustine, Aquinas	"	From Grading to Standards to Perfection		"
5. Contingency	Aquinas	"	From Contingent Being to Necessary Being	Best expresses spirit of cosmological arguments	May demonstrate that some being is necessary for anything to be (a circular argument) but can identify this being with "God" only by a leap of faith
ONTOLOGICAL	Anselm, Descartes, Hegel	Spirit, or Depth Dimension of Mind	From Concept of Perfection to Perfection's Necessary Existence	Best viewed, perhaps, as an affirmation of an insight rather than a logical argument	May demonstrate that a highest conceivable being exists but can equate this being with "God" only by faith
MORAL	Immanuel Kant	Spirit, or Practical Reason (Conscience)	From Unconditional Sense of Duty (Categorical Imperative) to Unconditioned Conditioner of Conscience	Not a proof or argument so much as a hypothetical affirmation	Argument confesses its own limits by admitting its hypothetical character

Arguments for God's Existence

cal guise rather than a strictly logical argument. In effect he counsels us to look within and decide whether what we behold in the operations of our own mind can be understood reasonably (that is, within the terms of the law of noncontradiction) as anything other than an immediate expression of God's reality. The statement "God does not exist" must be false, in his view, not because it involves a *logical* contradiction (though it does that, too) but because it expresses an *ontological* contradiction: it denies the Reality manifest in the depths of rationality itself.

The same kind of insight into reason's depths appears to underlie a recasting of Anselm's ontological assertion which can be found in Immanuel Kant's idea of a categorical imperative. Kant had grave doubts, as we have seen,[14] about the powers of the theoretical mind. On the basis of these doubts, he was himself a critic of the logical form of Anselm's proof. But in introducing the notion of the categorical imperative, it seems clear that he revives, in different terms and on moral rather than on intellectual grounds, the spirit of Anselm's argument.

The categorical imperative is Kant's name for an unconditional sense of duty with which he believes human beings are endowed. This imperative breaks into our awareness most clearly when we ourselves do something that, as we say later, "nobody in his right mind would do." Perhaps we dash into a burning building to try to save a total stranger, or we jump into a swimming pool to save a neighbor's child even though we ourselves cannot swim. Whatever the form of the deed, its spirit is one of total disregard for all those ordinary considerations of self-regard and self-interest that usually control our behavior. What we do may later cause us to shake our heads or tremble within, but in the moment of crisis our response is spontaneous, uncalculating, as though we are impelled by a force from beyond and empowered by a strength not our own.

Such moments of spontaneous and selfless activity express in a dramatic way a moral sense which seems to be constantly at work in us. The fact that this sense erupts into selfless behavior in moments of crisis indicates its unconditional character—in other words, that it is the bearer of a demand about which we have no choice and on which we act regardless of the cost. When the mind reflects on it, this sense of unconditional obligation conveys, in Kant's words, *"the recognition of our duties as divine commands."*[15] But the sense of being divinely commanded bears with it as an immediate correlate an awareness of the reality of a divine Commander, just as Anselm's sense of the depths of his mind conferred an awareness of infinite Mind. Thus Kant can write that "the concept of God and the (practical) conviction of His Being originate from the fundamental ideas of morality."[16]

Kant's argument, like Anselm's, seems to depend on a sense of divine reality rather than on an unassisted logic. As God was an Infinite Spirit who conditioned and lent credence to the operations of Anselm's intellect, so in Kant's case God appeared as an Unconditioned Conditioner of the human conscience. Both the Anselmian intellect and the Kantian conscience are the instruments of a spiritual dimension of reality which transcends ordinary (Kant would say "theoretical") reason.[17]

In grounding their assertions of God's existence in insights into the depths of rationality, Anselm and Kant were outstanding representatives of that tradition that understands reason as reality's depth dimension. On one crucial point, however, the attitudes of these thinkers toward their assertions of divine reality differed dramatically from each other. Kant, unlike Anselm, denies that any argument for God's existence can have the force of a proof.[18] The best we can do, Kant insists, is *affirm* or *postulate* God's reality for practical, ethical reasons. Reason's depth dimension may drive us toward such an affirmation, but that depth dimension is itself beyond the reach of the ordinary, tool-like reason by which we "prove" things (that is, establish their probability to a point beyond reasonable doubt).

The philosophy of Kant bears within itself, then, the marks of two of the conceptions of reason that we have discussed. Ordinary scientific or "theoretical" reason is a tool which resides exclusively within the human mind, but ethical or "practical" reason expresses what Kant called the noumenal sphere and what we have called (following Tillich) reality's depth dimension. Kant's marvelously fecund thought embraces and appreciates elements drawn from both the perspectives of those who define reason in a way favorable to natural theology and the perspectives of those who define it in a way inimical to such theology. Kant's philosophy thus poses within its own composition the question "Are natural theology's claims for its 'proofs' valid?" And it is to this question that we must now turn.

The "Proofs" Evaluated:
Certificates of Reality or Creeds in Disguise?

Natural theologians attach great significance to the arguments for God's existence because so much hinges, in their view, on the success or lack of success of these arguments. These theologians believe that the person who desires to live within the rules of rationality needs the assurance that these rules have a basis in reality. Unless reality is ultimately the domain of an Absolute Intelligence which grounds and explains the evidences of intelligence that reside in human reason and in the regularities of nature, this assurance is unfounded.

On its face this rationale for the importance of the proofs seems fairly compelling. But philosophical critics of the arguments counter that natural theologians overstate the proofs' significance. After all, atheists live in the same universe as theists do, and most atheists seem to function quite rationally and effectively—that is, with a sufficient sense that reason is reliable—without affirming Absolute Intelligence. Moreover, these skeptics observe, why should we believe that some mysterious being called God is a more sufficient guarantor of reason's reliability than is a being which is much closer to hand and much more easily known—Nature, or the Universe?[19]

These two approaches summarize, inadequately to be sure, but not altogether inaccurately, the range of attitudes that Western philosophers have adopted toward the proofs. The attitudes of Christians toward them differ somewhat, both in type and in nature, from the attitudes of philosophers. Since the attitudes of Christians (or at least of thoughtful Christians) are more germane to the concerns of this book than are the attitudes of philosophers, we now need to pay special attention to them.

Generally it appears that the proofs elicit one or another of three types of response from Christians who consider them. Some Christians are convinced that the arguments do prove the existence of God; some hold that they are complete failures as proofs; and a third group concludes that the arguments prove something but that what they prove to exist is not God.

The arguments strike some Christians as virtual certificates of God's reality. If asked why the proofs have this effect on them, the more philosophic souls among these Christians might echo the views expressed in the first paragraph of this section. But many Christians who are not philosophically or intellectually oriented also find the arguments compelling. Because they affirm a sense of cosmic order, both the cosmological arguments and Kant's argument from moral experience tend to validate the Christian moral sense, and this of course makes these arguments appealing to Christians who are especially concerned about ethical behavior. In similar fashion the teleological argument, or argument from design, offers those Christians who yearn for aesthetic and artistic forms of fulfillment both a passive aesthetic satisfaction and a valuable psychological support for their creative endeavors. The awareness afforded by this proof undergirds the sense that efforts to be intelligently creative are harmonious with the nature of reality.[20]

Those Christians who find the arguments unconvincing frequently point out that the so-called proofs originate from a faith stance and that they therefore prove only that their proponents *believe* that God exists. The arguments fall victim, in this view, to the logical fallacy called *petitio principii* or "begging the question." In other words, they begin by assuming the truth of the thesis they set out to prove. The cosmological arguments begin with the assumptions (founded only in faith) that an infinite series of movers (or causes, or gradations) is impossible and that there must therefore be a first, self-subsistent Mover (or Cause, or Standard of Perfection) in every series. The only things the logical form of the argument adds to these beliefs are a degree of clarity and the equation of the ultimate element in each series with God. The arguments thus amount to little more than creeds in disguise: they dress out in logical garb ideas which originate in the faith of their proponents.

Another group of Christian critics of the arguments is willing to grant that they prove something but not that they prove what their formulators intended to prove. At the least, these critics concede, these arguments demonstrate that the human mind can function rationally, and at the most they may be construed as showing that the universe itself is rational and supports rational endeavor. But the claim that the arguments

MAKING SENSE

Life makes sense
and who could doubt it,
if we have
no doubt about it.

From Grooks *by Piet Hein. Copyright 1966 by the author.*
Used by permission of Mr. Hein.

prove the existence of God is not substantiated either logically or empirically by the arguments. Far from being logically or empirically proved, this claim amounts to little more than an invitation from natural theologians to join them in their belief that the logical order or principle demonstrated in their arguments is worthy of being identified with the awesome God of the Christian scriptures. But does the pallid abstraction which the arguments purport to prove really resemble the Mighty One of the Bible? Is the Christian not better advised to follow Pascal in worshipping the "God of Abraham, Isaac, and Jacob, and not the God of the philosophers"?[21]

Whether one considers the arguments successful or not, simple honesty would seem to demand that they be recognized as serious efforts to make sense of reality and to support the authority of reason. But honesty should also require the natural theologian to recognize that human approaches to the question of God's reality can never be based totally on reason. Because so much more than reason is at stake in the God ques-

tion, because the worthwhileness of human existence itself is at stake, the question and its answer must ultimately be transrational or existential. The relation to reality of the total self must therefore be the focus of any approach to the question of God's existence. For this reason natural theology must be understood, finally, as an attempt to understand an existential or transrational relationship by rational or cognitive means. The problems it encounters in doing this illustrate the dilemma faced by theology in general. The relationship to God which underlies theology impels it to say something, but that relationship does not lie "out in the open" where the mind of the theologian (or any other human mind) can get at it.

Natural theology faces one problem, however, with which revelation-based theology does not have to cope. That problem stems from its claim that reason, *even when unaided by revelation,* offers an adequate instrument for probing, at least to some degree, the sphere of the supernatural. The irony in this claim is that it is itself based on faith. The natural theologian seems to be telling us that, if we will have faith in reason, then we can have certainty about God. But a reason in which we can only have faith seems to be a grander or at least a profounder and more mysterious phenomenon than a God about whom we can have certainty. Natural theologians thus appear to be caught in a dilemma. Either they must confess the God of their proofs to be but a pale product of finite logic, a confession that they refuse to make,[22] or they must exalt reason to a status which seems more divine in some respects than the God whose existence it proves. Ultimately, then, natural theology raises as many questions as it answers. Its answer to the question of God's existence raises the question of reason's adequacy, and its answer to the question of reason's adequacy raises grave doubts about the stature of the God whose existence reason purportedly proves. The fact that natural theology's answers seem in every case to contain the seeds of new questions leads one to wonder whether there can be any genuine answer to the question of God's reality which does not rely on transrational authority. The question of transrational authority is, in Christian terminology, the question of revelation. Our consideration of natural theology and of the powers and limits of reason drives us inevitably to a fuller consideration of the nature and form of revelation.

THE QUESTION OF REVELATION'S NATURE AND FORM

Christians who hold that revelation is the sole basis for a knowledge of God sometimes summarize their position in an epigram: "By God alone can God be known." This statement at first might appear to suggest that human beings can have no acquaintance with God at all. But that is not the point of the epigram's users. Rather they mean to suggest that, when God does become known to human beings, he does so through means he himself provides rather than through means at their disposal. This means that, though reason itself may be divinely adopted as a medium of revelation, only God's use of reason, and no human use of it, can make God known.

The theological name for such divine self-disclosure is "revelation." On the basis of our earlier, functional definition of revelation, as a relation-establishing, horizon-expanding, experience-illuminating event, we now must discuss qualities peculiar to Christian revelation. On this as on most other significant theological questions, we encounter a lively discussion among thoughtful Christians. Participants in this discussion fall generally into three groups: (1) those who believe that the Christian revelation consists of objective truths communicable in oral or written propositions; (2) those who conceive of it as a subjective, self-illuminating experience best (but never totally) communicated in meditative and confessional monologues or poetry; and (3) those who understand it as a form of intersubjective or interpersonal communion best (but not totally) expressed in stories, sermons, and social deeds.

Diverse though they are—and we must consider their diversity at length later—these definitions of revelation are united in affirming that revelation transcends and transforms (or reorients) reason. Reason is not vitiated or weakened by such a reorientation; instead its powers are enhanced and extended. The range of relationships with which it has to deal now includes the relationship to God as well as relationships to finite beings. Indeed, revelation pushes the mind's horizons not only farther out, toward Transcendence, but also deeper in, toward dimensions of the self that are opened up by the new-found relation to God. Reason is not weakened but strengthened and challenged by revelation.

Having noted an important point at which Christian conceptions of revelation converge, we must now consider the main points at which these conceptions differ from each other.

Revelation as Objective, Propositional Truth

Those who hold that revelation consists of statable truths about the nature of reality consider it highly important that revelation have the force of an objective authority. Revelation can be distinguished from those frail and questionable children of reason, opinion and speculation, only if it is objectively true. If it is objectively true, it can be described and expressed, like other objects, in objective language. Its essence can therefore be captured, and in fact has been captured, in the sentences of scripture, creed, and dogma.

The chief proponents of this point of view include, as we might suppose, both Roman Catholic infallibilists and Protestant fundamentalists. Roman infallibilists are most closely identified with the doctrine of the infallibility of the pope, but this doctrine is actually a simple extension of the more fundamental Roman Catholic concept of an objective and infallible revelation. The initial revelation that Jesus was the Christ, a revelation granted exclusively to and through the disciple Simon Bar-jonah, provided the basis for Jesus' renaming of Simon as Peter, "the rock" on which the Church should be built. With this renaming, Roman Catholics believe, the institution of the papacy came into being.[23] The reality and the objective authority of the papal office thus rest on the objective validity of the revelation to Simon and his consequent renaming. The same values that necessitate that the initial revelation to Simon be adjudged valid make it equally imperative that sufficient authority be vested in Peter's successors, the popes, through whom revelation continues to occur. Those values are the unity, durability, authority, and redemptive power—in brief, the Petrine or rocklike dependability—of the Church.

Similar arguments support the views on revelation of Protestant fundamentalists. The objective authority they argue for is not that of the pope but that of the Bible. They, like the Roman infallibilists, hold that revelation must be infallible and objectively statable if its authority and power to save are not to be thrown into question. This is true, they insist, because the objective character of the revelation contained in scripture is the sole buffer separating God's Word, which can save, from human words, which cannot.

From the standpoint of the objectivists, the most important quality at stake in the debate over revelation's nature and form is revelation's God-givenness. If revelation is not objectively true, it becomes impossible to distinguish it from human opinion, and this means that Christians have no real assurance that their faith is grounded in reality. But mystics and spiritualists, who seek assurance no less than do the objectivists, believe that the objectivist route toward assurance is a dead end. They observe that the attempt to establish the objective truth of revelation can be undertaken only by one of two methods: one may seek to establish such objectivity by reason, or one may do so by referring to some transrational experience. If one chooses to proceed by reason, the reason one must use is human, that is, personal and subjective, reason; and so one ends up seeking to establish the *objective* truth of revelation by *subjective* means, a manifest impossiblity. On the other hand, if one chooses to invoke transrational experience (for example, faith), one must somehow establish the objectivity of that experience before using it to establish the objectivity of the truth it reveals; and so the objectivist winds up with *two* phenomena whose objectivity must be proved, instead of one, and is forced to use subjective reason in trying to demonstrate the objectivity of both.

Revelation as Subjective Insight and Assurance

If the case for revelation's objectivity cannot be objectively made, is the subjective route to assurance any more valid? Yes, argues the subjectivist, because the subjective approach to assurance depends not on the establishment of revelation's objective truth but rather on an immediate and powerful awareness of a subjective event by which the self is liberated and illumined. This event—it is the event of revelation itself—is self-substantiating. Accordingly, it does not need the crutches of objective argument or of institutional authority; the assurance it confers is immediate, direct, self-evident, and manifest in the changed lives of its recipients.

Christian mystics or subjectivists insist no less than objectivists that the revelation they experience is God-given. The evidence they cite for this, however, cannot be expressed by propositional or textual means. The media more appropriate to its expression are the strongly subjective media of music, poetry, fervent personal confession, and sacrificial deeds. Some of Christendom's most moving hymns, much of its great devotional literature, and many of its most exemplary lives have been products of the mystical and the spiritualist (pietist and pentecostal) traditions. But the fact that these highly personal media are the only means by which subjectivism can express itself indicates that this perspective, too, has its Achilles heel.

The basic problem with subjectivism was indicated in our discussion of the major concern of the objectivists. Essentially it is the problem of an objective uncertainty which may produce a loss of social cohesion. Granted, revelation as a subjective event may confer on its recipient a certain *subjective* assurance. But such subjective certainty may have socially destructive effects. Suppose, for example, that all of the Christians in a congregation decided to seek God purely in personal, subjective terms, and having found him, spoke of him only in highly personal, musical, charismatic, and/or poetic ways. Soon there would be no common ground to which all could repair; as each went his or her separate way, the sense of a common concern would languish and perhaps die. With this development the Church as a community of shared values would cease to exist.

This weakness in subjectivism is criticized not only by objectivists but also by those who define revelation in interpersonal or intersubjective terms. This latter group views the problem of subjectivism as a mere symptom of a deeper problem which plagues subjectivism and objectivism alike. Both of these groups, argue the interpersonalists, are victims of an inordinate concern for assurance. Because of that concern they focus on the question of revelation's form and authority without paying sufficient attention to revelation's source and content. Objectivists assign so much weight to revelation's God-givenness that they all but raise the gift—namely, the media (scriptures and institutions) through which revelation occurs—to the level of the Giver. The authority of revelation and the assurance conferred by it thus upstage its Source as the focus of much objectivist concern. In similar fashion, some subjectivists make the experiential aspect of revelation a virtual end in itself; instead of raising the seeker's eyes to its own Source, the spiritual experience tends to capture and hold the spiritualist's attention, thereby offering a sense of self-assurance but also diverting attention from the divine other.

Equally regrettable, argues the interpersonalist, is the tendency of subjectivists and objectivists to divorce the question of revelation's form and authority from the question of its content. The source of this tendency is clearly that same overweening concern for assurance. In reality, the interpersonalists maintain, the *content* of revelation is as disturbing as it is assuring. Instead of letting sleeping dogmas lie, it may arouse and upset their proponents. Revelation's chief results—love, humility, a new freedom, a passion for justice—seldom harmonize with simple assurance or authoritative institutions and texts.

Revelation as Interpersonal Communion

From the standpoint of the interpersonalist, neither the objectivist perspective nor the subjectivist offers an adequate understanding of revelation. Interpersonalists hold that revelation must be understood essentially as a social and socializing phenomenon. Revelation, in other words, occurs chiefly in and through communities, and it works to create and enhance the spirit of community.[24] Revelation is interpersonal in the literal sense: it occurs *between* persons and not simply *to* persons. By bringing my vision of reality into touch with the visions of others, it enlarges and corrects my vision, and it may modify theirs as well.

No doubt it was this conception of revelation which underlay and inspired Martin Luther's idea of a universal priesthood of believers. As we have noted before,[25] the idea of universal priesthood should not be translated "every person his own priest" but instead "every person his neighbor's priest." Luther pushed this notion to the point of claiming that every Christian could and should become a "little Christ" to his or her neighbor. Implicit in this claim is the conviction that all Christians can, through their conversation and actions, be mediators of divine revelation. If this conviction becomes paramount in one's approach to the revelation issue, then personal encounters and relationships become revelatory media which are at least as important as the sacred texts and the mystical experiences by which revelation is also conveyed. Indeed, viewed in the light of this conviction, sacred texts and mystical happenings themselves assume a different significance. The sacred text—the Bible primarily—comes to be seen as the work of an historical community and as a record of the revelations which created, inspired, and sustained that community. Mystical experiences are seen to depend on images learned in communities and to be of value mainly because they provide new energy for life in the community.[26]

Some of the proponents of the interpersonal form of revelation hold that revelation may occur not only through encounters within the historical community or Church and not only through mystical encounters with God conceived as a person, but also through a communion with God established through natural beings. In this context, the word "person" assumes a broader and older meaning. In ancient Latin, the word *persona* meant not a discrete human individual ("person") but a *mask* worn by an actor in dramatic productions. Through the simple device of changing *personae* or masks, a single actor could play several parts in the course of a drama. Some of the Christians who think of revelation as interpersonal ascribe to God this practice of changing *personae*, of assuming different masks, natural as well as human and historical, in revealing himself to people of his choice. The classical biblical example of such revelation was the commissioning of Moses, during which the *persona* or mask employed was a bush that burned without being consumed.[27] Martin Luther, among others, believed that God can and does use natural creatures as masks and that he may even speak through them to lesser mortals than Moses.[28]

Interpersonalists, as we have seen, can muster a rather formidable argument against both subjectivism and objectivism. As they seek a way past the perils and problems of these other positions, however, they are repaid in kind from both sides. The assault on interpersonalism from the subjective flank makes essentially the same point as that from the objective: the interpersonal or intersubjective perspective on revelation undercuts Christian assurance. Revelation as the interpersonalist conceives it is not self-authorizing, as it is for the objectivist, nor self-substantiating, as it is for the subjectivist, but self-correcting. The Christian interpersonalist, in other words, is never convinced that God has said his last word. New revelation may correct and complement prior revelation. Revelation is a dynamic, continuing process rather than a finished propositional product or a remembered and treasured mystical experience. Humility and openness to new experience thus replace authority and assurance as the chief qualities conveyed by revelatory events.

Interpersonalists are frank to admit the truth of the charges made against them by fellow Christians of the other perspectives. For those Christians who hold personal assurance or institutional authority to be the primary aim of revelation, the intersubjective understanding of revelation is bound to have less appeal than the subjective or objective approaches do. But to those who perceive revelation as a purveyor of love, humility, and freedom rather than as a conveyor of assurance, the interpersonalist perspective seems to afford the most adequate approach to an understanding of revelation's nature and form.

To summarize: Though Christians generally agree that revelation transcends, transforms, and empowers reason, and that in so doing it reorients the entire self, they disagree on the question of revelation's exact nature and form. Some Christians, whom we have called *objectivists*, conceive revelation's nature as that of truths about objective (human, cosmic, and divine) reality. Because it has an objective nature, revelation may in this view take objective, propositional form in the creeds and scriptures of Christendom. But not all Christians agree that

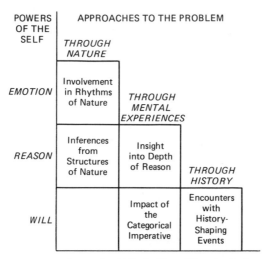

Approaches to the Problem of Knowing God

revelation is objectifiable. Some, designated here as *subjectivists,* define revelation's nature in terms of its effects on their personal lives. Because revelation is so personal, they hold, it is inexpressible in abstract, objective statements. Only the very personal language of music, poetry, and confession seem capable of expressing it. Finally, yet a third Christian viewpoint, described here as that of the *interpersonalists,* conceives revelation as a kind of social phenomenon, an event through which one enters into communion with Another and is bound in relationship with a congregation of others. Here the chief medium of revelation is neither a body of written propositions nor the testimony of believers but rather fellowship among the members of a caring community.

A person unfamiliar with the Christian tradition might be tempted to try to correlate one or another of these viewpoints with particular Christian denominations. Such efforts are bound to fail. None of the concepts of revelation discussed commands the allegiance of all the communicants of any single denomination. In fact even individual Christians may understand revelation as a combination of elements from two or all three of the conceptions described. The preference for one understanding as opposed to the others is in most instances a matter of emphasis rather than of exclusion.

THE BIBLE AND THE WORD OF GOD:
THE QUESTION OF REVELATION'S MEDIUM AND NORM

Christians, as we have just seen, are far from unanimous in their conceptions of revelation's nature and form. On one matter, however, they generally agree: the primary and/or normative medium of revelation is the Holy Bible. We turn now to the question of the Bible's role in revelation.

Though usually bound in a single volume, the Bible is not a single book but a small library of books. The Jewish Bible, which comprises that portion of the Christian Bible generally called the Old Testament, contains by Christian reckoning some thirty-nine books, five of which were traditionally called books of the Law or Teaching (Hebrew *Torah*), twenty-one of which were dubbed books of the Former and Latter Prophets (*Nebi'im*), and thirteen of which comprise a section called the Writings (*Kethubim*). The entire thirty-nine were officially sanctioned as the Jewish canon* by a council of rabbis which met at Jamnia, in western

---

*The word "canon" literally means a "rule," "standard," or "criterion." It derives from the Greek word *kanon*, which referred to a type of reed used in antiquity as a measuring rod. Holy Scripture is designated a "canon" presumably because it contains those writings by which the validity of all other religious documents is to be measured.

Palestine, about A.D. 90. One aim of the rabbis was to distinguish works that could be considered authoritative in Judaism from works composed by first-century writers who belonged to a Jewish sect which preached that Jesus of Nazareth was the Messiah for whom many Jews had long hoped.

Some of the writings rejected by the rabbis at Jamnia form the nucleus of the Christian New Testament. Eventually twenty-seven separate works became recognized as of sufficient value to merit inclusion in this body of specifically Christian writings. Protestants add these twenty-seven New Testament writings to the thirty-nine approved by the Council of Jamnia and consider the resulting total of sixty-six books sacred scripture. To these the Roman and Greek Orthodox churches add some of the so-called books of the Apocrypha,[29] books that were part of a pre-Jamnian Greek rendering of the Jewish scriptures but that were refused sanction by the rabbis at Jamnia because they were not written in Hebrew or because their antiquity was questionable.

Though it may be surprising to learn that Christians do not agree even on the number of books in the Bible, that fact in itself does not divide the Christian fold as much as the fact that they also do not agree on the significance of the total compilation and its contents. The Bible is a remarkably diverse volume, and its inner diversity provides a basis, or at least a large number of pretexts,[30] for diversity and disagreement among Christians. Even so, many of the deeper and broader differences among the faithful are prompted not so much by the diverse *contents* of Scripture as by divergent *attitudes* and *approaches* to it. These attitudes and approaches reflect and express both general theological perspectives and particular conceptions of revelation. Here we shall consider three complexes of attitude and approach which stem from the three conceptions of revelation's nature and form discussed in the preceding section.

In general these variations in attitude and approach may be explained fairly simply as diverse answers to a single question. The question itself arises from the common Christian affirmation that Scripture is made the vehicle of revelation by the agency of the Holy Spirit. John Calvin spoke of the Spirit's role in revelation as the "the internal witness of the Holy Spirit" (*internum testimonium spiritus sancti*). Scripture speaks the Word of God to its reader, Calvin asserted, because it serves as the medium of God's revealing power or Spirit. But here a thorny and divisive problem arises: Granted that the internal witness of the Spirit is essential to the occurrence of revelation, to what is the Spirit's witness internal? Did the Spirit work mainly in the *writing* of Scripture, leaving us a text that is objectively inerrant, valid, and understandable by all who approach it with reverence? Or did he work primarily in the *minds and hearts* of Scripture's authors, so that our reception of revelation depends on aligning our minds with the minds of these authors? Or, again, does the Spirit work primarily neither in the text itself nor in the mind of the reader but rather in the *interactions* between text and reader? For those who answer "yes" to the first of these questions, it is true to say that the Bible *is* in some literal sense the Word of God. For those who deny the first but affirm the second, it is more correct to say that the Bible *contains* the Word of God or at least the words of human beings about the Word of God. For those who reserve their "yes" for the third question, it is better to say that the Bible *becomes*, under certain circumstances, the Word of God.

Christians are agreed, then, that Scripture conveys revelation through the internal witness of God's Spirit. They disagree in answering the question, "To what is the witness of the Spirit internal?" Their answers to this question follow the general lines just suggested. This means in effect that for some the Holy Spirit's witness is to be found largely in the *text* of Scripture; for others, it is to be found in the human experiences that the text reports, experiences that must be recovered and reenacted in the mind or *spirit* of the interpreter; and still others believe that the Spirit works mainly in the *dialogue* between the text and the reader as they encounter each other. For brevity's sake we shall refer to the first of these views as the *textualist* view, to the second as the *spiritualist* view, and to the third as the view of the *dialogist*.

The Bible IS the Word of God (Textualism)

Many devout Christians equate the Bible with the Word of God in a direct and absolute way. In the view of these believers, the Bible is a result of direct and deliberate divine activity. The general name for this divine activity is *inspiration*.

Inspiration means that the human writers of Scripture were chosen by God to write the Holy Scriptures, inspired (told what to say) by him as they wrote them, and kept from error in all they wrote. The end product of such inspiration is a sacred and inerrant text, a body of errorless propositions—in sum, the Holy Bible.

Because it focuses on the text, virtually equating it with the witness of the Spirit (and therefore with the Word of God), this position may be called *textualism*. All textualists share at least two beliefs: that God is directly responsible for the writing of the Bible and that the Bible is consequently free of significant error.

Textualists are unanimous in ascribing responsibility for the Bible to divine inspiration, but they disagree among themselves on the nature and extent of biblical inerrancy. Some textualists insist that the Bible is *literally* without error—that, in the original manuscripts at least, even the spelling and the grammar of the text were flawless. Such textualists could well be called *literalists*. Other textualists prefer the view that Scripture is inerrant in content though not in letter or form. It is their view that whenever the Bible refers to history, it is historically accurate, that whenever it speaks theologically it is theologically correct, and that whenever it contains an apodictic ethical decree, that decree is to be obeyed by the faithful without hesitation. Despite their high esteem for Scripture's historical, ethical, and theological content, however, they do not hold that the grammar and spelling of the text are inerrant.

The view that the Bible is errorless in content, though not necessarily in form, represents a version of textualism sometimes called *plenarism*. Plenarism comes from the Latin word *plenum*, meaning "full" or "complete." Though they do not agree with the literalists that the Bible is errorless even in its grammar and spelling, plenarists do maintain that it is completely or fully inspired, sufficiently inspired to be thoroughly reliable. Though the grammar and spelling (the text's "literal" features) may contain minor errors, even in these there can be no errors that would affect or alter the divinely intended meaning.

Textualists of both types approach the Bible in terms of an understanding of revelation as propositional truth. Textualists believe that revelation conveys objective truths about reality and that accordingly revelation's content may be stated in objective, propositional form (therefore in written texts). The textualist view of the Bible thus accords closely with the objectivist view of revelation.

The Bible CONTAINS the Word of God (Spiritualism)

Christians who define revelation in subjective rather than in objective terms tend to associate the Bible and the Word of God in less direct fashion than do textualists. As we have seen, subjectivists understand revelation as a very personal experience in which God speaks directly to the heart of the believer. But if revelation occurs in so direct and inward a fashion, what need is there for a revelatory medium like the Bible? Why can God's Spirit not "bear witness with our spirits"[31] without relying on external media such as Scripture?

The answer of many subjectivists is that God can in fact do so. Scripture is of value, they believe, not because God has to use it, but because it provides an account of the spiritual experiences of significant men and women at crucial points in the past. The Bible is basically a book of testimony: it contains the witness of ancient persons and groups concerning events which transformed their lives and influenced subsequent history. The lively and vibrant accounts of such events can quicken the spirit of today's reader, sensitizing and preparing it for divine illumination.

From the subjectivist viewpoint, the inspiration that produced the Bible is not the quasi-mechanical inspiration of the objectivists/ textualists. God's Spirit moved in the hearts of the Bible's writers, to be sure, but it did not override or negate their humanity. They remained very human and very fallible beings as they wrote, and what they wrote reflects their humanity, and even their fallibility, even as it bears the marks of divine inspiration. The value of their works does not hinge on some presumed infallibility but rather on the divine profundity and the human passion of the experiences that the works describe and interpret.[32]

For those who view the Bible in this light, revelation's principal effect is on the human spirit, and the writing of the texts which later comprised the Bible was only a secondary and subordinate result of this effect. Christians of this persuasion are thus better called *spiritualists* than textualists. Unlike textualists, spiritualists tend to view the Bible as an important but not as an essential or indispensable medium between God and human beings. God can speak to human beings directly, but what he says and does through such speaking is essentially harmonious with what he said and did in the lives of the people who composed the Bible.

The question of Scripture's status and role in the transmission of revelation has been a source of considerable disagreement among spiritualists. More conservative spiritualists see in the great spiritual experiences recounted in Scripture a normative quality by which contemporary experiences of revelation should be measured. Others of a more liberal bent view the events reported in Scripture as simple examples of experiences which are accessible to all human beings equally. All spiritualists agree, however, that the arena in which revelation occurs is the human heart or spirit. The Bible's chief role in revelation is that of a stimulus that enlivens the spirits of its readers and prepares them for an experience comparable to those that Scripture describes. As long as the biblical text remains an objective, independent account of events in the lives of other people, it remains ineffectual. Only as biblical experiences come to life in the conscience and imagination of the reader are they valuable. Angelus Silesius, a famous German spiritualist and hymnwriter, wrote:

> Though Christ a thousand times
> In Bethlehem be born,
> If He's not born in thee
> Thy soul is still forlorn.

> The cross on Golgotha
> Will never save thy soul,
> The cross in thine own heart
> Alone can make thee whole.[33]

In the view of most spiritualists, the agent by which the biblical text comes to life in the spirit of the reader is the Holy Spirit. But on the question of the Spirit's mode of working, spiritualists are far from unanimous. This question, in fact, separates spiritualists into two types: *mystics* and *rationalists*. Though both of these groups define the arena of the Spirit's activity as the human spirit, they conceive of the human spirit in different terms. Mystics regard spirit as a human dimension or capacity which transcends reason, whereas rationalists regard it as a virtual synonym for reason. Mystics believe that the Holy Spirit is more likely to work in that person who has cultivated certain transcendental capacities through a life style stressing prayer, meditation, and self-denial. Rationalists, on the other hand, believe that the biblical text is more likely to come alive when the mind uses all the resources at its command in an effort to understand it; accordingly, rationalists believe it important to study the biblical text as history and literature no less than as theology. Though the illumination of the inner person is the first aim of both the mystic and the rationalist, the ways of seeking such illumination are remarkably different. This difference in approach stems from a very fundamental difference in their conceptions of the human spirit itself.

The Bible BECOMES the Word of God (Dialogism)

The third major Christian perspective on the Bible has had a long informal history, but its actual formulation has been a relatively recent development. Indeed, though textualism and spiritualism have had self-conscious advocates for centuries, *dialogism* (as we choose to call it) has received clear definition only in the twentieth century.[34]

In large measure this third view of the Bible emerged because of dissatisfaction with the older alternatives. Textualists, according to the dialogists, sacrifice intellectual honesty on the altars of piety, frequently substituting praise of the Bible and contrived rationalizations regarding its problem passages for honest and open biblical study. Spiritualists, on the other hand, may promote intellectual rigidity and/or private piety at the expense of theological integrity, for they tend to reduce the Bible's message to terms which reinforce either the rational predilections or the spiritual prejudices of modern readers.

Because of the problems they perceive in textualism and spiritualism, dialogists hold that the Bible must be approached neither as an infallible objective authority nor as a mere record of ancient human experiences but rather as a kind of partner in dialogue. That the Bible is a *partner* means that it is to be approached with respect but not with fawning reverence or worship. To approach it in the latter way, as textualists tend to do, is to confuse God's medium with God himself, and such confusion entangles one in the sin of bibliolatry, or worship of the Bible. On the other hand, that the Bible is a partner *in dialogue* means that it is far more than just another book. To approach it as a mere human record of random spiritual experiences (as rationalistic spiritualists sometimes do) or as an echo or confirmation of typical mystical experiences (as mystics sometimes do) is to foster a view that God's Word is a mere amplification of human words (a form of idolatry as pernicious as bibliolatry).

The dialogist approaches the Bible as a product of a unique history. The particularity of the history that produced the Bible constantly reminds the dialogist of the independence of the biblical revelation. In recognition of this independence, the reader of Scripture must be prepared to be interpreted as well as to interpret. Indeed, genuine interpretation is possible, in the dialogist's view, only by virtue of a "circle of interpretation" in which the reader's questions regarding the text may be corrected by the text. If, for example, readers put to the creation accounts in Genesis 1 and 2 the scientific question of how the earth was made, they will find that honest listening to the text requires a change of questions. These accounts, like virtually all biblical narratives, are not directly concerned with the scientific questions "how" and "what" but rather with the religious questions "who," "whence," "why," and "whither."

The concern of the dialogist for the integrity of the text is balanced by an equal concern for the integrity of the reader. The dialogist would paraphrase one of Jesus' statements[35] to make it read "Scripture was made for man, not man for Scripture." The genius of the Bible is precisely its ability to respond to the deepest human questions. The reader may therefore approach the Bible boldly, putting to it hard questions which a timid piety might inhibit. The Bible can be addressed with tough, existential questions, questions born of doubt and despair no less than those born of faith, precisely because it was composed by persons beset by such questions.

The main questions to which Scripture speaks are thus existential questions—questions about the source, meaning, and destiny of human life. Scripture therefore should be approached with these questions in mind. When this is done, dialogists believe, the stories in the Bible can become personal responses to one's deepest concerns; they can become, in Kierkegaard's phrase, letters with the reader's own name on them. When this happens, it may even be hoped that Scripture will become personal in the profoundest possible sense: that it will become a *persona*, or mask, of God himself.

The dialogical view of Scripture is partly the product and partly the producer of the interpersonal view of revelation. The chicken-and-egg relationship between dialogism and interpersonalism stems from their common conviction that what gets revealed through scriptural revelation is neither a body of doctrines nor a new self-concept but rather a divine Person who enters into communion with human beings. The dialogue in this communion is inseparable from the conversation continuing throughout history among Scripture's producers, compilers, and interpreters. In the last analysis, the dialogue that Scripture makes possible is not simply one between God and individuals but one between God and a certain historical and ecumenical community, the Church.

St. Paul once compared the Church to the body of Christ.[36] As the various members of the human body (hands, feet, eyes, and ears) are interdependent, he argued, so members of Christ's body, the Church, must rely on each other for an understanding of divine revelation. Though such mutual reliance is crucial to the Church's well-being, it is even more crucial that the Church as Christ's body be ruled by Christ's mind.[37] The norm of revelation is thus Christ—not the Christ of any single interpreter but the Christ of the whole Christian community. This point, interpersonalists believe, is of critical importance to a Christian understanding of revelation. Because each Christian is a member of Christ's body, they observe, he or she has something to contribute to the body as well as something to learn from it. In contributing his or her personal insight, each Christian helps form the mind of Christ; through what he or she learns, on the other hand, each person's insight stands to be corrected by that mind as it resides in the larger community. Scripture's role in this process of mutual contribution and correction stems from its power to bring ancient and authoritative voices into the dialogue, among them those of Abraham, Moses, Jesus, and Paul. But more than that, when the Holy Spirit acts to make it a divine *persona*, Scripture contributes the eternal voice of God as well. For dialogists, it is accurate to say that the Bible, as discussed and interpreted within the Church, *becomes* the Word of God whenever God chooses to speak, and to form or enhance a community, through it.

The Word, the Spirit, and Revelation's Norm

Through his epic tale *The Odyssey*, the poet Homer bequeathed Western literature one of its most enduring images—that of Scylla and Charybdis. On his way home from Troy after engineering the Greeks' conquest of that city, Odysseus, the tale's hero, confronts a whole series of challenges that are easily the equals of Troy's forbidding walls. None of these challenges is more formidable, however, than that posed by the twin perils of Scylla and Charybdis. Scylla was a sea monster who sat on a rocky cliff, leering angrily at ships as they approached. The threat Scylla posed was greatly heightened by the presence, across the narrow straits between the Italian and Sicilian coasts, of Charybdis, a sister monster who inhabited a treacherous whirlpool. To make their way home, Odysseus and his doughty band of sailors had to steer their ship through the narrow channel between Scylla on the one side and Charybdis on the other.

The leaders of the early Christian movement faced a challenge very much like that confronting Odysseus. On one side of them stood a kind of Scylla, a monster of the rock—the rock of Scripture, of Judaic tradition, of ancient doctrine. On the other side stood a sort of Charybdis, a menace within a whirlpool—the whirlpool of religious experience, of emotion, spiritual ecstasy, and enthusiasm. The Christian counterparts of Scylla and Charybdis, in other words, were two camps within Christianity itself. The Scylla camp stood on the rock of Christ, the rock of God's revelation of himself in history, the rock of the "written code" or Scripture. The Charybdis camp swirled about in the whirlpool of the Spirit; it depended on prayer and on immediate and direct revelation from God.

It is notable, and many Christians would consider it normative, that the leaders of the early Church, particularly St. Paul, perceived great peril both in the Scylla of doctrinaire scripturalism and in the Charybdis of emotional spiritualism. St. Paul ran into people from both sides. He ran into people from the Scylla side who were always quoting Scripture to him. To these, who took their stand chiefly on the written word, Paul wrote that "the written code kills, but the Spirit gives life."[38] What good, he asked, is Scripture without the Spirit which enlivens it? Paul also knew people from the Charybdis camp—people caught up in the Spirit, people claiming to have a hotline into the throne room of God, people who claimed they had received special knowledge or other special gifts from the Holy Spirit. To such people as these Paul stated emphatically that "no other foundation can any one lay than that which is laid, which is Jesus Christ."[39] The Christian, he insisted, cannot bypass God's gift in Jesus Christ; even and especially when visited by the Spirit, the Christian cannot claim to have some revelation which supersedes or disagrees with the revelation manifest in the historic career of Jesus of Nazareth.

St. Paul steered clear of both Scylla and Charybdis. He was not of a mind to leave the wreckage of Christianity on either. He seems to have believed that the only safe course between the bedrock of revelation received in Christ and the whirlpool-like revelations of the Holy Spirit is the course identifying the two. Thus his declaration: "the Lord [= Christ] *is* the Spirit."[40]

It is significant that Paul here does not equate the Spirit with the written code as such but rather with the One to whom he believes the written code bears witness. To the extent that textualists tend to equate the witness of the Spirit with the written code or text, they appear to have missed Paul's point. In Paul's view, study of Scripture is not an end in itself but a means to an end. To the degree that textualists make the biblical message its own end, they become rather like the driver of a car who pulls up under a road sign which says "Chicago—500 miles" and announces "How nice to be in Chicago!"[41]

If it is true that Paul does not equate the witness of the Spirit with the Bible, it is equally true that he does not separate the Spirit's work in the present from his historic work in Christ. To the extent that spiritualists make such a separation, they are like foolhardy travelers who head into territory unknown to them without consulting either maps or roadsigns.

The Christian, then, must neither confuse the Bible with the Bible's God nor dispense with the Bible in favor of some immediate revelation. The Christian must rather view the Bible as a kind of John the Baptist, who announced as he stood in the presence of Christ that "He must increase . . . I must decrease."[42] The purpose of the Bible is to point beyond itself to Another. To coin an ungainly term, its purpose is not to make people "Biblians," disciples of the Bible, but to make them Christians.

The Bible's Christ-ian bent has definite implications for the way Christians should read it. The Christian reader might well note, first, the attitude and approach Jesus himself employed with regard to Scripture. Jesus' attitude toward the Scriptures seems to have combined genuine reverence for these, the traditions of his fathers,[43] with an equally sincere sense of his own authority to interpret, revise, and even rescind[44] Scripture in the light of the inbreaking Kingdom of God. In this attitude today's Christian can find a sanction for both serious immersion in the life-enriching lore of Scripture and a Christian liberty from pedestrian literalism.

What is most surprising about Jesus' use of Scripture is the relative rarity with which he refers to it. In the Gospel of Mark, which is generally viewed by scholars as the oldest of the four canonical gospels, Jesus refers directly and unequivocally to Scripture only twenty or so times.[45] The originality and independence of his teachings led the gospel writers to note that those who heard him "were astonished at his teaching, for

he taught them as one who had authority, and not as their scribes."[46] The radical significance of this observation is likely to be missed unless one recalls who the scribes were. As the copiers and interpreters of Scripture, they were the chief conservators of Jewish tradition. If they did not teach as people "who had authority," that was because in their eyes only the texts and traditions of Scripture itself "had authority." In claiming authority for his own teaching and in asserting his freedom to reinterpret and go beyond scriptural traditions, Jesus departed drastically from the customary scribal approaches to questions of interpretation. The emphasis in his preaching and teaching was on events in the present, rather than (as in scribal teaching) on events and dicta of the past. The coming of the Kingdom of God in his own lifetime and through his own ministry made necessary a new and radically different approach to scriptural traditions, one that spoke not so much of what God *did* in earlier times as of what God *is doing* or *will do* in the present and the imminent future.

In Jesus' teaching one encounters a dramatic reversal of the traditional scribal attitude. The scribes sought by their teaching to exalt and assert the authority of Scripture. Jesus, conversely, sought by his use of Scripture to exalt and express the authority of his own teaching. Thus when he came home to Nazareth shortly after his baptism, he chose to base his sermon to the home folk on a text from Isaiah which points not to its own authority but to his:

> The Spirit of the Lord is upon me,
> because he has anointed me to preach good news to the poor.
> He has sent me to proclaim release to the captives
> and recovering of sight to the blind,
> to set at liberty those who are oppressed,
> to proclaim the acceptable year of the Lord.

This text, from Isaiah 61, probably referred in its initial context to the calling and tasks of Israel as a covenant people. Jesus, however, appears to use it as a description of his own calling, his own mandate from God. "Today," he says, as if in reference to his own return home, "this scripture has been fulfilled in your hearing."[47]

That Scripture should need fulfilling in something beyond Scripture was an idea not likely to appeal to the traditional scribal mind. Within the framework of that mentality Scripture was essentially a teaching to be obeyed, not a promise to be fulfilled. For centuries God had spoken through his prophets; now (believed the scribes) he speaks mainly through Scripture—through channels, so to speak. That he should raise up a new Prophet, one to whom Scripture witnesses as well as one who

would fulfill Scripture, was for scribal traditionalists hardly a likely occurrence.

Yet here is Jesus, not only claiming the anointment of God (that is, to
be a Prophet) but also proclaiming himself the true heir of God's charge
to Israel. It is as though he sees the entire history of his people, tran-
scribed in their scrolls, arranging itself so as to point beyond itself toward
his own mandate and mission.

It thus appears that Scripture had validity, in Jesus' view, but only
a provisional or promissory validity. Its validity was that of a signpost,
rather than that of the destination to which the signpost points. The
error of the scribes was that they had confused the signpost with the
destination, the sign with the thing signified. The Bible, or Torah, had
become for many of them its own Christ, its own Messiah, and so when
another Messiah appears they are confounded. If Jesus is unhappy with
them, it is because they go on vainly, trying to contain the new wine of
the Messiah's new age in the old wineskins of familiar traditions.[48]

If Jesus' own use of Scripture is a crucial guide to the Christian use of
it, another extremely helpful guideline regarding Scripture and its use is
suggested by the Church's ultimate resolution of the question of Jesus'
identity. At the Council of Chalcedon in 451, the Church declared definitively that Jesus the Christ was simultaneously fully man and fully
God. This extremely paradoxical formula preserved the Church's perception of two truths which came to be viewed as indispensable to an
understanding of salvation. The first was that, since salvation consists
in being with God, Christ could offer salvation only if he conferred the
full presence of God, only if he made that presence real in and through
his own person. Christ thus had to be fully divine if he were to be the
bringer of salvation. But—and this was the second crucial reality which
needed affirming—salvation also depended on the *accessibility* of God,
on his reality within human experience itself. If Christ is Savior, therefore, he must not only be God but also God present to and resident in
human experience—God in human form.

The Church's declaration that Christ was God in human form, God
getting under our skin, implies clearly, then, the Christian belief that
salvation must be both divinely initiated and humanly accessible. If this
belief is carried over to the Christian attitude toward the Bible, it means
that the Bible, like the Christ it represents, is to be viewed as simultaneously human and divine. In itself the Bible is fully human, a work of
human minds and hands and a work subject to all the ills and error to
which flesh is heir. But in its intention the Bible is fully divine, for its
intention is the realization of a relationship between God and human
beings which became possible in the coming of Christ.

The main implication of this view of the Bible for our discussion of
revelation is that the Bible is the primary medium of revelation but not

its primary norm. The Bible itself teaches that normative revelation is to be found not in Scripture per se but in him to whom Scripture bears witness, namely, that Word who was in the beginning with God and was God. Revelation's norm, then, is that relationship between God and humans exemplified in the life and teaching of the "Word made flesh" in Jesus the Christ.

REVELATION AS THE REALIZATION OF A RELATIONSHIP

The intention of the biblical message, as we just noted, is the realization of a relationship between God and humans. The biblical word for this relationship is *covenant* (Hebrew *běrith*). The Bible in its entirety may be interpreted as a record of God's efforts to fulfill a divine-human covenant and of the corresponding human efforts to understand and live in terms of this covenant. But the purpose of this record is not simply historical. The Bible's purpose is not merely to preserve a history of the covenant but to keep the covenant itself alive.

If the covenant is to be kept alive, the divine-human relationship must be realized again and again. Such realization is both the aim and the meaning of revelation. "Revelation," wrote Paul Tillich, "is a *realization*, not a communication."[49]

The ambiguity of the word "realization" makes it a peculiarly appropriate word for describing revelation's role in establishing the divine-human relationship or covenant. "Realization" can mean both "making real" and "coming to know." Revelation as Christians perceive it entails both. Revelation's first function is to confer the knowledge of a state of affairs which, according to Christian belief, God has made an objective reality. But when revelation makes that state of affairs *known* to its recipients, it also makes it *actual* for them, so that it (the new state of affairs) now becomes an active force in the decisions and deeds that shape the recipients' future. Thus, though revelation does not produce their relationship to God in a primary way, it does make that relationship an empowering reality which conditions their knowing and doing.

When revelation affects the self, it affects the self as a *whole*. Revelation does confer new "knowledge" of a certain kind, but it is perhaps more significant that revelation confers a new posture toward all knowledge. Similarly, though revelation may change one's behavior in certain particulars, it changes, more significantly, the intentions and ends that prompt and shape all of one's behavior. As perceived in its effects, therefore, revelation is not a fact or value which we can bring into focus but a realignment of relationships which brings all facts and values into clearer focus.

Two biblical stories, one from the Old Testament and one from the

New, provide especially graphic depictions of how revelation realigns relationships. The Old Testament story is that of Cain and Abel. As in many biblical stories, the focus of the story is on how people are defined by crucial relationships. According to Genesis 4, Cain and Abel are related not only to each other and to their parents, but also to God and to Mother Nature. Their relationship to God shows up in their offering of sacrifices. Their relationship to nature is mentioned far more subtly, with the quick comment that "Abel was a keeper of sheep, and Cain a tiller of the ground."[50] But that quick comment and the variant relationships to nature it betokens are crucial to an understanding of the story. From the standpoint of the Israelite writers of the story, God favors the life style of the shepherd above that of the "tiller of the ground," or farmer.[51] He does so, in the Israelite view, because the farmer becomes so closely tied to a piece of ground (his farm) that his relationship to nature threatens to displace that to God. In contrast to the shepherd, who is footloose and able to follow the divine beckoning with less hesitation, the farmer is tempted to invest too much of himself in the ground beneath him and too little in the God beyond him.

Cain's behavior is a prime exhibit in the Israelite case against the life style of the farmer. Cain's ties to Mother Earth become so strong that they undermine not only his relationship to Father God but also that to Brother Abel. Alienated from God, Cain murders Abel. The perversion of the relationship to God (suggests the story) destroys the relationship to fellow humans.

That is not the sole, or even the chief, lesson of the story. More important than the actions of Cain is the response of God. The story makes it plain that the divine response is not simply punitive in purpose but also redemptive. Cain's punishment is to be "cursed from the ground" and to become "a fugitive and a wanderer on the earth," and his lament is that "My punishment is greater than I can bear. Behold, thou hast driven me this day away from the ground...."[52] His "punishment" thus is to have the tie to earth, which has kept him from God, broken.

God's revelation of himself to Cain requires Cain to start over, to establish a new identity with a new determining relationship at its center. In letting Mother Earth control him, Cain has built his life around a relationship which is personally unfulfilling and socially destructive. In requiring Cain to break that relationship, the divine revelation sets in motion a realignment of relationships which has Cain's salvation as its aim.

Our story from the New Testament also makes the point that revelation involves the realigning of life-shaping relationships. In his story of Jesus' encounter with a man named Nicodemus, the writer of the Gos-

pel of John conveys the impression that Nicodemus, a respected citizen of Jerusalem, very much wants to protect his reputation[53] as he establishes a relationship with this street-corner rabbi, this preacher without a church, Jesus of Nazareth. Though his image in the community may be threatened by his visit, Nicodemus is so drawn to Jesus that he must take the risk. "You are a teacher come from God," he says to Jesus, "for no one can do these signs that you do, unless God is with him."[54]

Jesus' initial response to Nicodemus could only have heightened the latter's sense that Jesus posed a threat to his accustomed way of life. Ignoring the flattering cast of Nicodemus' opening remark, Jesus answers bluntly: "Truly, I say to you, unless one is born anew, he cannot see the kingdom of God."[55] So stark and unexpected are these words that Nicodemus seems to be forced back into himself, back into his own sense of superior status. We can all but hear him whistle under his breath, then ask himself, "Where'd this fellow go to school? What kind of biology course can he have taken! He's never heard about the birds and the bees!" But to Jesus himself he makes only the shocked rejoinder, straight from his notes in Zoology 101: "Can a man be born when he is old? Can he enter his mother's womb a second time, and be born?"[56]

In Nicodemus' reaction to Jesus, John's gospel may offer us as clear and effective a picture as we can have of the initial impact of a revelatory experience. Nicodemus first perceives the revelation embodied in Jesus' statement as an impudent and infuriating claim, a claim violating the bounds of common sense and ordinary judgment. If taken seriously such a claim could only prove subversive, could only undermine the canons of normality which control most of our lives. Rebirth indeed! What need can there be for rebirth in lives controlled by reputation and reason?

The initial impact of revelation is that of a threat, that of an audacious and apparently insidious claim that our lives require reorientation, reconstruction—in a word, rebirth. In this particular case, Jesus seems to be asserting that Nicodemus has put his world together on false foundations, that he is counting on his first birth, his Jewishness, his citizenship among the chosen people, to satisfy God. Or perhaps, beyond that, Nicodemus is depending on his achievements, his establishment of a reputation as a "ruler of the Jews,"[57] to win God's favor. But, avers Jesus, neither set of relationships, neither blood relationships nor hard-won social and political ties, can bring one into the Kingdom of God. For, in Jesus' words, "that which is born of the flesh is flesh, and that which is born of the Spirit is Spirit."[58] To be born of the Spirit, to be reborn and thus belong to God's Kingdom, requires a drastic realignment of personal priorities, an elevation of the relationship with God to a status higher than all natural and social relationships. The

realization of a relation to God means the *realignment* of all other relationships.

So central to the Christian faith is the idea that revelation means
rebirth, a realignment of the relationships from which one lives, that a
number of the churches of Christendom have tried to institutionalize it.
Within Roman Catholicism and a number of the branches of Protestantism, to undergo baptism is to undergo a rebirth, a rite of passage
from the human family into God's family. In this rite the baptized person is even given a second name, a "Christian" name, which signifies
that he or she lives henceforth not only from earthly relationships but
also (and most basically) from the relationship with God disclosed in
Christ.

In a number of ways, baptism is a peculiarly good symbol, or
analogue, for revelation. It is like revelation, first, because it is a transrational experience: the whole person is immersed, literally or figuratively,
in the baptismal waters. It is like it also because, as a sacrament which
cleanses from sin, it breaks relationships which hinder life and makes
possible a new and renewing relationship with God. But in no way is
baptism more important as an analogue to revelation than in the way it
enables the Christian to participate symbolically in the dying and rising
of Christ. As St. Paul teaches in Romans 6, the Christian immersion into
the waters of baptism is an entrance into the death of Christ, and the
rising from the waters is a veritable participation in his resurrection.
Baptism thus reminds the Christian that the normative revelation of the
covenant between God and humans, the normative expression of the
way persons should relate to God, is found in Christ. It is in the New
Testament portrait of Jesus as the Christ, that Jesus with whom the
believer dies and rises in the waters of baptism, that Christians find the
most adequate definition of revelation. It is in and through that portrait
that they find disclosed, and that they experience personally, God's
realization of a new relationship with the world.

A SUMMARY AND CONCLUDING CRITIQUE

In this chapter we have outlined a spectrum of possible conceptions of
revelation. Given the divine omnipotence, God might well choose to
reveal himself through nature, through reason, through supernatural,
transrational, and transhistorical (mystical) experience, or through
supernatural and transrational (historical and social) experience. The
argument that God reveals himself in and through nature accords well
with the cosmological arguments of the natural theologians. The argument that he reveals himself through reason agrees not only with

natural theology's ontological and moral (Kantian) arguments but also with the views on revelation of the rational spiritualists. The argument that revelation occurs through superrational and superhistorical modes of experience harmonizes equally closely with mystical spiritualism. Finally, the argument that revelation occurs chiefly in historical and social contexts has special affinities with interpersonalism.

In attempting to do justice to each of these perspectives on revelation, we have tried to describe each "from the inside." We have attempted to depict each in terms that its own adherents could accept. But we have also attempted to criticize each of the perspectives from the standpoint of one or more of its rival perspectives. A summary review of that critical process seems unnecessary here. It may be more helpful, instead, to designate the perspective that this writer deems to be most adequate and to enumerate the reasons for his choice. Such a procedure should bring into clearer focus our discussion of the *content* and *effects* of revelation in subsequent chapters.

The understanding of revelation as a form of interpersonal experience seems to the writer to be the most adequate of those we have surveyed. Whatever else it means, revelation must mean an event in which God encounters and addresses human beings. Such encountering and addressing embraces and transforms the whole person, not just the person's natural powers (energy, emotions, appetites) or rational aptitudes (power to think and to dream) or social capacities (power to plan, decide, communicate). Whatever else it does, revelation must reconstruct or realign the total self's relationship to its world. To the degree that the interpersonal conception of revelation expresses revelation's power to do this more adequately than do the alternatives, it seems to offer the best description of revelation's nature. For three basic reasons it does seem to express this power more adequately.

The first reason is that the interpersonal concept depicts revelation as essentially *personal*. Revelation through nature addresses its recipients on the level of a subpersonal emotionalism (as in religions born of nature) or on that of a superpersonal, cosmically attuned, nature-determined intellect (as in the nature gnosticism of Spinoza or the cosmological version of natural theology). Analogously, revelation by supernatural means (for example, through the infallibly inspired texts of the textualists) sacrifices personal autonomy on the altars of impersonal authority. On the other hand, revelation through reason addresses the intellectual faculty as it participates in the superpersonal Mind of God (as in the reason religion of Plato and the ontological branch of natural theology). In a similar vein spiritualism requires the loss of integral personhood in the interest of a superhistorical union with God. On all of these fronts revelation is conceived as addressing only part of the person, in the interest of rescuing that part and uniting it with superpersonal (impersonal!) forces.

When conceived rationalistically and naturalistically, then, revelation is understood as preferring some part of the person to other parts, and the result is a rending of the self in the interest of a union of the preferred part with an impersonal reality (mind or nature) beyond the self. In similar fashion, when revelation is conceived in supernatural (textualist) or mystical (spiritual) terms it requires an almost total abandonment of ordinary personal life in pursuit of a thoroughly transcendental experience. Only when revelation means interpersonal communion does it affirm the entire human personality. On this understanding, no dimension of personhood must be denied or suppressed to make way for revelation. The concrete individual as a whole is accorded the status of a valued being.

The interpersonal conception of revelation seems the most adequate of the alternatives, second, because it is more *comprehensively relational.* It enables the self to establish a more comprehensive relationship to reality. Or, to put the matter less abstractly, it enables the self to live in a bigger world. One of the marks of distinction of Judaeo-Christian faith is its world-affirming quality. The tone is set in the book of Genesis: "And God saw everything that he had made, and behold, it was very good."[59] It is continued in the New Testament: "God so loved the world. . . ."[60] That view of revelation would seem most adequate that would allow everything in God's world to enjoy to the full its standing as a being God loves. In focusing attention on nature, reason, or transrational spirit as the media for revelation, the nonpersonal approaches to revelation tend to ignore or devalue those aspects of reality that are not accessible through the preferred medium. A revelation that occurs to total persons, on the other hand, accords value to each of the dimensions of the person's being and to the dimensions of reality to which these correspond.

The third reason that revelation is best understood as an interpersonal process is that this understanding reflects most adequately two features of biblical revelation. The first of these is that the Bible consistently portrays God as a person. Whether one argues that the biblical portrait of God is anthropomorphic or that the biblical understanding of humanity is theomorphic,[61] it is true in any event that God and human beings alike are portrayed throughout Scripture as persons. If God's revelation is in fact an act of *self*-disclosure and if God's selfhood is in some sense personal, it is essential that the revelatory act be personal. And, if revelation is an act of disclosure to *people,* it is essential that it be *inter*personal.

The sphere of interpersonal relations is the sphere of *history.* As we

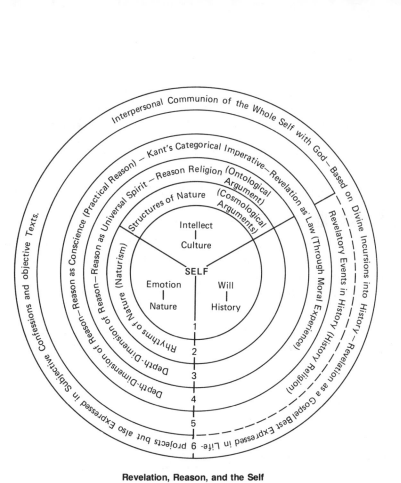

Revelation, Reason, and the Self

The innermost circle (1) represents the three-dimensional self (see Chapter III). Circle 2 represents the natural world in which the self lives, and the approaches to the God-question this world offers through emotion (see Chapter II) and intellect (see the discussion of the cosmological arguments above, this chapter). Circles 3 and 4 describe the world of the mind, which broadens and deepens the self's quest for ultimate meaning (see the ontological affirmations of Anselm and Kant discussed above, this chapter), while circles 5 and 6 represent historical and personal dimensions of experience which, as bearers of the Christian revelation, realign life's defining relationships.

have emphasized again and again, a second peculiarity of biblical revelation is its historicality. History is the medium of revelation and the primary recipient of its effects. If history is indeed the sphere of interpersonal transactions, it seems necessary that a revelation that is understood as historical also be understood as interpersonal.

The recognition that revelation is historical does not mean that it cannot employ nature or reason or transcendental experience as its media. Such modes of revelation can be meaningful, though they must be viewed as partial and therefore as subject to supplementation and correction by the revelation of the personal God and of the larger, historical world made accessible to the total person through interpersonal revelation.

QUESTIONS FOR STUDY AND DISCUSSION

1.   To what dimension of human experience does revelation point?

2.   What does it mean to say that revelation is "horizon-expanding"? that it is "integrating"? that it is "reorienting"? (In discussing these functions of revelation, avoid mere repetition of the terms used in the chapter. Try to relate them to experiences that you yourself have had and to translate their meaning into your own words.)

3.   Revelation, we noted in this chapter, transcends, transforms, and empowers reason. What are the main practical effects of such changes in reason?

4.   Discuss the three traditional views of reason enumerated by Tillich. How does one's approach to the arguments for God's existence relate to how one understands reason?

5.   Outline the five cosmological arguments for the existence of God. Describe the basic perspective from which all of these arguments proceed. Do you find the arguments convincing? Why or why not?

6.   Write a brief, clear statement of Anselm's ontological argument. Show how Kant's argument from the categorical imperative parallels Anselm's argument and how it modifies it. Do you find these arguments convincing? Why or why not?

7.   To what features do the arguments for God's existence owe their continuing philosophic, ethical, and aesthetic appeal? On what grounds is their claim to be proofs subject to doubt?

8.   Characterize the views of revelation of the objectivists, subjectivists, and interpersonalists. How do these views correlate with the major approaches that Christians have taken to the question of the Bible's relation to the Word of God?

9.   Why did St. Paul seek to steer the Church away from textualism, on the one hand, and spiritualism, on the other?

10.   What is the "norm" of Christian revelation? How are Christian views on revelation and the Bible affected by such a definition of the norm?

11. How do the stories of Cain and Nicodemus illustrate the description of revelation as the realization of a relationship?

12. On what grounds may it be argued that the interpersonal understanding of revelation is the most adequate understanding? What counter-arguments in favor of other ways of conceiving revelation can you think of?

NOTES TO CHAPTER VI

1. See Chapter VII, pp. 237–46, 260–67.

2. See Chapter VIII, pp. 278–87.

3. The view of Christ as a cosmic principle (*logos*) present in all human minds is a very ancient one. Such a principle, according to John 1:1–3, is the presupposition and means of creation; it is also the basis and source of a universal revelation ("the true light, which lightens every man who comes into the world" John 1:9, freely rendered).

4. In his excellent study of faith entitled *Faith and Community* (New York: Harper & Brothers, Publishers, 1959), Clyde Holbrook described this initial, common relatedness as a kind of "primal faith." Cf. Holbrook, pp. 13–25.

5. Matthew 3:9.

6. The translation is that of *The Modern Reader's Bible*, ed. R. G. Moulton (New York: The Macmillan Company, 1895).

7. *Systematic Theology*, Vol. I, pp. 71–105. Note that Tillich begins his analysis by referring to only two concepts of reason (technical and ontological, or structural) but later amplifies it by discussing the depth of reason, or ecstatic reason.

8. Cf. Chapter V, p. 129.

9. See Chapter V, p. 130.

10. The appeal to common sense—or better perhaps, *a* common sense—is one of the oldest features of natural theology. Some of the ancient Stoics all but made the common belief of the multitudes in the existence of God (the *consensus gentium*, as they called it) a separate argument for his existence. Cf., for example, Cicero, *De natura deorum*, Book I.

11. St. Thomas Aquinas (1225–1274), who compiled the five cosmological arguments and became their greatest champion, concluded each with the simple but classic phrase "and this [that is, the Being whose existence had been "proved" by the argument] is God."

12. St. Anselm, "Proslogium," in *St. Anselm: Basic Writings*, trans. S. N. Deane (LaSalle, Ill.: Open Court Publishing Company, 1951), pp. 7–10.

13. To cite a key passage: "Hast thou found what thou didst seek, my soul? Thou didst seek God. Thou hast found him to be . . . a being than which nothing better can be conceived. . . . But, if thou hast found him, why is it that thou dost not feel thou hast found him? Why, O Lord, our God, does not my soul feel thee, if it hath found thee? Or, has it not found him whom it found to be light and truth? For how did it understand this, except by seeing light and truth? Or could it understand anything at all of thee, except through thy light and thy truth?

"Hence, if it has seen light and truth, it has seen thee. . . . It strains to see thee more . . . but it sees that it cannot see farther, because of its own darkness.

"Why is this, Lord, why is this? Is the eye of the soul darkened by its infirmity, or dazzled by thy glory? Surely it is both darkened in itself, and dazzled by thee. Doubtless it is both obscured by its own insignificance, and overwhelmed by thy infinity. Truly, it is both contracted by its own narrowness and overcome by thy greatness.

"For how great is that light from which shines every truth that gives light to the rational mind? How great is that truth in which is everything that is true, and outside which is only nothingness and the false?" *St. Anselm,* pp. 20–22.

14. See pp. 184–85.

15. *Critique of Judgment,* trans. J. H. Bernard (New York: Hafner Publishing Co., 1951), p. 334. Emphasis in original.

16. *Critique of Judgment,* p. 335.

17. When Kant gave his great work on the philosophy of religion the title *Religion within the Limits of Reason Alone,* he was not limiting religion as much as might at first appear to be the case. He did, to be sure, restrict religion largely to ethical dimensions, but ethics in his view is rooted not in reason as the tool that organizes nature (the "pure theoretical reason" of his vocabulary) but in reason as an agent of, if not an element in, the divine Spirit (reason as "conscience," the "pure practical reason") which expresses itself most purely as the categorical imperative.

18. Kant was in fact a leading critic of the Anselmian "proof." Cf. his *Critique of Pure Reason,* trans. J. M. D. Meiklejohn (Chicago: Encyclopaedia Britannica, Inc., 1952), *Great Books of the Western World,* ed. R. M. Hutchins, Vol. 42, pp. 179–82.

19. Questions of this sort express the spirit of a logical principle sometimes called the principle of Occam's (or Ockham's) Razor. Named for the great British logician William of Occam (1285–1349?), the principle holds that the best explanation of an occurrence is the *simplest sufficient* explanation of it. Those who use the principle against the proofs for God's existence regard the God of the proofs as an unnecessary principle of explanation which adds nothing to our knowledge of the world. At least as an explanation of nature, they argue, the God concept is a bit of metaphysical clutter that needs to be excised by application of the Razor.

20. Long before the Christian era, this sense appears to have developed among Pythagorean and Dionysian musicians. The later phrase "music of the spheres," which was eventually incorporated into Christian hymnody, puts into words the sense that the cosmos as a whole is a virtual work of art. Cf. F. Nietzsche, *The Birth of Tragedy from the Spirit of Music,* trans. W. Kaufmann (Garden City, N.Y.: Doubleday & Co., Inc., 1956), especially pp. 36–42, 97–102. It is not a long distance, surely, from Nietzsche's claim in this book that "only as an esthetic product can the world be justified to all eternity" (p. 42) to the claim of the teleological argument that the world is the work of an artistic or designing Intelligence.

21. This phrase was found on a piece of paper that Pascal had sewn inside his jacket, a paper on which he had recorded his thoughts about a conversion experience he had had on November 23, 1654. For the thoughts in their entirety and a helpful discussion of their significance, see David E. Roberts, *Existentialism and Religious Belief,* ed. Roger Hazelton (New York: Oxford University Press, Inc., 1959), pp. 20–22.

22. See p. 182.

23. After Jesus declared Simon the Rock and, further, that "On this rock I will build my Church" (Matthew 16:18), Simon Peter went on (Catholic tradition has it) to become the first Bishop of Rome. Through the laying on of hands (an ancient rite akin to the later rite of ordination), he transmitted the special authority that Christ had given him to successive bishops of Rome, the popes.

24. This is a conception of revelation which St. Paul himself seems to have favored. In I Corinthians 14 he wrote: "Now, brethren, if I come to you speaking in tongues, how shall I benefit you unless I bring you some revelation or knowledge or prophecy or teaching? If even lifeless instruments, such as the flute or the harp, do not give distinct notes, how will any one know what is played? . . . So with yourselves; if you in a tongue utter speech that is not intelligible, how will any one know what is said? . . . There are doubtless many different languages in the world, and none is without meaning; but if I do not know the meaning of the language, I shall be a foreigner to the speaker and the speaker a foreigner to me. So with yourselves; since you are eager for manifestations of the Spirit, strive to excel in building up the church." Revelations, or manifestations of the Spirit, Paul here indicates, demonstrate their potency and authenticity by their power to overcome alienation and build community.

25.   See Chapter IV, p. 114.

26.   The biblical stories of Moses, Elijah, and Isaiah provide models for understanding apparently private, mystical experiences in intersubjective terms. Moses was by himself, true, when he met God in the bu ning bush. But he still remembered the plight of his people in Egypt, and he was commissioned by God to do something about that plight. A "private" experience thus led to community involvement. In like fashion, Elijah, who actually had fled from his community responsibilities, was turned back in their direction by his private encounter with God at Mt. Horeb (I Kings 19). And in the story of Isaiah's call (Isaiah 6:1–8), the prophet meets God in what appears to be splendid isolation, yet both his confession of sin (Woe is me! for I am a man of unclean lips, and I dwell in the midst of a people of unclean lips) and his response to God's calling itself (Here am I; send me) indicate a sense of solidarity with his people.

27.   Exodus 3:2–3.

28.   Luther's term for the masks of God was *larvae Dei*. A version of the term *larva* (mask) is used today as a name for the early, "disguised" forms of natural creatures like the butterfly.

29.   The entire Apocrypha (literally "hidden works") contains some fourteen books; of these seven are in the Roman Catholic canon and six (all of the Catholic group except *Baruch*) are in the Orthodox canon.

30.   Cf. H. R. Niebuhr, *The Social Sources of Denominationalism* (New York: Henry Holt & Co., Inc., 1929). Niebuhr demonstrated that many of the theological and scriptural reasons cited in support of the divisions among Christians are rationalizations for divisions rooted in ethnic and sociopolitical differences.

31.   Cf. Romans 8:16.

32.   No one stated this point of view more eloquently than did the eminent New Testament scholar, C. H. Dodd. "God is the Author not of the Bible," Dodd wrote, "but of the life in which the authors of the Bible partake, and of which they tell in such imperfect human words as they could command. . . . In this sense we find a religious authority in the Bible—the authority of experts in the knowledge of God, masters in the art of living. . . . Whatever else we may have to say of their 'inspiration,' it is clear that it is something intensely personal in themselves. It is not their words that are inspired. . . . it is the men who are inspired." *The Authority of the Bible* (New York and London: Harper & Brothers, Publishers, 1929), pp. 16, 24, 30.

33.   "In Thine Own Heart," from J. D. Morrison, ed., *Masterpieces of Religious Verse* (New York: Harper & Row, Publishers, 1948), p. 148.

34.   Textualism was articulated vigorously as early as the late second century by Tertullian (160–230?). Mystical spiritualism has an equally long heritage, traceable back at least to the second-century heretic, Montanus; and rational spiritualism goes back in principle to Origen of Alexandria (184–254?) and the early Christian gnostics. Though there were certain impulses toward dialogism in the conciliar movement of the Middle Ages and in the Protestant (especially the Lutheran) Reformation, that position has found articulate champions chiefly in this century, especially in the work of such "dialectical" or "neo-orthodox" theologians as Karl Barth, Emil Brunner, and the two Niebuhrs, Reinhold and Richard.

35.   Cf. Mark 2:27.

36.   I Corinthians 12:12–31.

37.   Cf. Philippians 2:1–11.

38.   II Corinthians 3:6.

39. I Corinthians 3:11.

40. II Corinthians 3:17. Emphasis added.

41. I am indebted to my teacher, the late Carl Michalson, for this illustration.

42. John 3:30.

43. Though no official canon existed in Jesus' day, a considerable number of writings were held to be of sacred authority among his people. The most conservative Jewish party, or "denomination," that of the Sadducees, held only the five books of Moses (our Genesis, Exodus, Leviticus, Numbers, and Deuteronomy) to be of sacred authority. The Pharisees, with whom Jesus was more closely aligned despite their representation in some of the gospel accounts as his chief enemies, believed that a number of other writings—the works of the great literary prophets, for example—were also authoritative. In both cases, the antiquity of the writings and their reliability as records of the patriarchal and prophetic traditions were the chief elements in their claim to sacred standing.

44. For interpretations in which Jesus revised Scripture as generally interpreted, see the Sermon on the Mount, Matthew 5:21–48. For reports of occasions on which he virtually rescinded the prevailing interpretation, see the accounts of his disputes with the Sabbatarians in Mark 2:23–3:6 and John 5:1–18.

45. Some of these references are direct or free quotations—for example, Mark 11:17 (=Isaiah 56:7; Jeremiah 7:11), 15:34 (=Psalm 22:1). But most are simply allusions—for example, Mark 2:25–26 alludes to I Samuel 21:1–6 and 10:6 to Genesis 1:27 and 5:2. For their part, Matthew and Luke appear to have had access to versions of Jesus' teachings Mark did not use. Their references to the Old Testament (especially Matthew's) are accordingly more numerous. It is precisely in Matthew, however, that Jesus most clearly sets his authority against "those of old" (Matthew 5:21, 33), and it is in Luke (4:17–21) that he uses Scripture to emphasize the divine authorization of his own message.

46. Matthew 7:28b–29. On the tasks and attitudes of the scribes and the issues between Jesus and the religious authorities, see J. Bowker, *Jesus and the Pharisees* (Cambridge: Cambridge University Press, 1973), especially pp. 21–22, 44–45; and E. W. Saunders, *Jesus in the Gospels* (Englewood Cliffs, N.J.: Prentice-Hall, Inc., 1967), pp. 83–84.

47. Cf. Luke 4:18–21.

48. Cf. Matthew 9:17.

49. "Revelation and the Philosophy of Religion," in J. Pelikan, ed., *Twentieth Century Theology in the Making*, Vol. II, trans. R. A. Wilson (New York: Harper & Row, Publishers Inc., 1971), p. 50.

50. Genesis 4:2.

51. This is the implication of the close association of verse 2 ("Now Abel was a keeper of sheep, . . . ") with verse 3 through 5a: " . . . Cain brought to the Lord an offering of the fruit of the ground, and Abel brought of the firstlings of his flock. . . . And the Lord had regard for Abel and his offering, but for Cain and his offering he had no regard."

52. Genesis 4:11–14a.

53. This is the likely point of the Gospel's statement that Nicodemus came to Jesus "by night." These words may have a second, allegorical meaning as well. The writer might have been suggesting that when Nicodemus first approached Jesus, he was spiritually in the dark. Cf. John 3: 2–12.

54. John 3:2.

55. John 3:3.

56. John 3:4.

57. John 3:1.

58. John 3:6.

59. Genesis 1:31.

60.   John 3:16.

61.   "Anthropomorphism" is a term describing the biblical and general religious practice of referring to God in human terms, as if he could be spoken of as though he were in the form (Greek *morphé*) of a human being (Greek *anthropos*). "Theomorphism," on the other hand, is a view that human beings, as bearers of God's image, have the form (*morphé*) of God.

VII. Faith and Being:
The Word as Creation

T HE CHRISTIAN FAITH affects human life both creatively and critically. It is creative because it relates human beings to the creative powers inherent in reality. It is critical because the new creation wrought by these powers judges forces of cultural inertia, human indifference, and human insolence which would impede or forestall such creation.

In Chapter VIII we shall examine the critical function of faith. In anticipation of that discussion, we note here simply that faith's critical function is a by-product of its creative function. Faith criticizes mainly because criticism of the old necessarily accompanies creation of the new: the old wineskins of custom and tradition cannot contain the new wine of God's continuing creation.[1]

Faith's creative function thus precedes and underlies its critical function. Though we shall treat these functions in separate contexts—the creative in this chapter, the critical in the next—it is important to keep in mind their practical inseparability. If creation is the ground or basis of criticism, this means that the final aim of criticism or judgment is not destructive but creative. The purpose of the divine judgment against Cain, as we noted a few pages back, was not to destroy Cain but to create a new relationship between him and God. Similarly, when the Christian community expresses its faith by criticizing a practice or an institution, it does so, ideally, in the name of a "yes" and not in the name of a "no." The "no" it says to the practice or institution is incidental to the essential "yes" it says to the creative processes that the judged practice or institution is guilty of denying. Creation, not criticism, is the essential aim of faith.

Creation is faith's essential aim, in the Christian view, because it is God's initial and continued work. The statement "In the beginning, God created" is rivaled in Christian literature only by statements like "The Word became flesh" and "God was in Christ reconciling the world unto himself." Since the latter statements depend on the former for much of their meaning, we must try to understand the faith in creation expressed in Genesis before we can hope to understand the promise of redemption expressed in the Gospel.[2] Faith is the mediator of creative and redemptive powers concurrently.

With our discussion of creation, we begin actually to put together the Christian view of the world (or of "reality"). The Christian idea of creation constitutes the background and the broad and somewhat formal framework within which any Christian portrait of reality must be drawn. To press somewhat further our analogy between the religious view of the world and the work of an artist, we may say that the Christian understanding of creation does for the Christian idea of salvation or redemption what the background in a painting does for the painting's foreground theme: it serves to provide the terms of reference, the sense of scale and proportion, which make the foreground comprehensible.[3]

If understanding creation is necessary to understand redemption, it is also true that creation's full meaning becomes clear only in the light of redemption. Just as artists do not sketch in the background of their paintings until they have a working vision of the theme that will occupy the foreground, so Christians do not conceive of creation as an abstract objective occurrence but as an event bearing on their own lives, an event intimately connected with personal and communal experiences of salvation and fulfillment. A full understanding of creation thus depends on a full participation in the salvation history, or human search for fulfillment, within which the perception of creation occurs. Even the original biblical accounts of creation were products of such a history. As the eminent Old Testament scholar Gerhard von Rad notes,

> Faith in creation is neither the position nor the goal of the declarations in Gen., chs. 1 and 2. Rather, the position of both the Yahwist and the Priestly document [the two primitive sources of the Genesis creation stories] is basically faith in salvation and election.... Israel looked back in faith from her own election to the creation of the world.[4]

Despite the initial and essential connectedness of creation and salvation, there has been a recurrent tendency in the history of the Judaeo-Christian tradition to separate the two. A story in the fifth chapter of the Gospel of John recounts Jesus' reaction to one such attempt to divorce salvation from creation. One Sabbath day, the story has it, Jesus healed a man who had been a victim of a paralyzing illness for some thirty-eight years. Instead of rejoicing that a human being had been saved from a life of misery, the religious authorities in Jerusalem were upset because in performing the healing Jesus had violated the traditional laws prohibiting work on the Sabbath. Those laws, the defenders of the Sabbath believed,, went back to the very creation of the world when, as Genesis 2:2–3 reports, God himself rested on the seventh ("Sabbath") day.

Two things are especially noteworthy in the reaction of the Sabbatarians, or Sabbath party, to Jesus' healing of the paralytic. The first is their distorted scale of priorities: they had elevated the observance of religious rules or laws to a place of such importance that even the meeting of critical human needs had to give way to such observance. The second is the theological basis of this distortion in the separation of the idea of creation from the reality of salvation. Divine creation was for the Sabbatarians, as John pictures them, a remote event that had come to an end when God rested on the Sabbath day. It was more important in their eyes to commemorate the completion of creation and to imitate the divine rest than to act creatively and redemptively in the face of human need.

It is significant that in his response to the callous legalism of the Sabbatarians Jesus did not attack their behavior but rather their behavior's theological basis. "My Father is working still," he told them, "and I am working": even on the Sabbath day, when you say God himself rests, I insist that he continues to work, and that he demands that I work, to meet human needs.

If John's portrait of him is at all correct, it is clear that for Jesus creation was not a six-day process which ended long ago and culminated in a sustained Sabbath rest for God as well as for humankind. Creation is instead a continuing process in which God works to heal and restore, and so to finish and fulfill, his cosmic project. Creation cannot be divorced from salvation, from that process by which the broken are made whole and the sick are made well.

The understanding of creation as an event or experience in human life and as an event which has a direct bearing on human salvation and fulfillment is thus basic to the subject in Christian terms. In the next two sections ("What Creation Does Not Mean" and "What Creation Means"), we shall explore some of the implications of such an understanding.

WHAT CREATION DOES NOT MEAN

Several fundamental misconceptions have plagued Christian thinking about creation through the centuries. The most significant misconception, just noted, separates God's intention and action in creation from his intention and action in undertaking the redemption of the world. The extreme version or *reductio ad absurdum* of such efforts at separation was the ancient gnostic system, which ascribed the creation of the material order to one God, redemption from the material order to another. There have been less extreme forms of the misconception as well. Perhaps the most recurrent and obvious form, popular among certain Christian sects and within monastic and pietist movements, has been the notion that sex and salvation are archenemies, that one cannot devote one's whole heart to the pursuit of salvation without abstaining from the creative work of propagating the race.

Part of the trouble Christians have had in relating sex to salvation was inherited from St. Paul, who believed that "the form of this world is passing away,"[5] that is, that the end of history was almost at hand and that earthly involvements, including the sexual kind, might prevent the Christian from becoming adequately prepared for the arrival of God's approaching kingdom. St. Paul himself, then, was responsible to some degree for the tendency to set the saving work by which God would end history in tension with, if not in opposition to, the creating work by which God began history and the procreating work by which humans participate in God's continuous creation.

A second and stronger source of the recurrent tension between salvation and sex in traditional Christian thinking is Platonic dualism. As we have seen,[6] Plato taught that human beings are rational animals, rational minds encased in animal bodies. The body is in this view extraneous to and in some ways the enemy of the mind. Salvation is the release of the soul or mind from the body,[7] which is inferior because it does not originate from divine creation directly but from prime matter, a basic substance or "stuff" God used (according to Plato's theory)[8] to "create" the world. So pervasive was this dualistic view of selfhood and salvation that it strongly affected the popular Christianity of the ancient and medieval periods, and it continues to affect it in many quarters today. Instead of being viewed as the creations and as the good gifts of God, sex and the other bodily appetites were (and are) portrayed as the inventions of the Devil and as major obstacles to salvation.

Such radical separation of sex from salvation is thoroughly inconsistent with the Judaeo-Christian idea of creation. Unlike Plato, who conceived of creation as a manufacturing process in which God simply refashioned a raw material or "prime matter" already (and eternally) on hand, Christians believe that God creates the universe "from nothing" (*ex nihilo*). There is thus no second source, no principle coeternal with God, behind the universe, and so there is no metaphysical dualism on which to base a mind-body dualism. Both mind and body are creatures of God; therefore both are essentially good and both are capable of working together in harmony toward the fulfillment of creation's intention.

The Christian doctrine of creation from nothing (*creatio ex nihilo*) effectively undercuts all efforts to deny the ultimate and essential unity of reality. When Genesis says that "God saw everything that he had made, and behold, it was very good," it does not exclude from the divine vision or the divine approval either the body in general or sex in particular. Indeed, the same Genesis account makes it clear that sex is not the enemy of creation but the means to its continuation. "Be fruitful and multiply, and fill the earth and subdue it," says God to the creatures, male and female, who have been fashioned especially in his creative image.[9]

Although sex is not only perfectly compatible with creation but is also a virtual means to it, these very facts make possible a third source of tension between sex and salvation. Because sex *is* so creative and because it is so good, it may displace God himself as the object of human loyalties. The gift of sex is the gift of a certain God-likeness, for in *procreation* human beings participate most fully in *creation*, God's own primary work. The physical ecstasy that accompanies the act of procreation is a fitting symbol of the metaphysical heights to which the act lifts those who engage in it. Expressing as it does a kind of divine power, the sex act simultaneously elevates and intoxicates. It becomes all too easy, under such circumstances, to forget that sex makes one a creator only by proxy rather than a creator per se. The God-like power of sex and the God-like authority that parents have over their children can lead people to forget their dependence on a Creator and Authority beyond themselves.

The only proper grounds on which Christians can perceive sex as an enemy to salvation come about when sex is no longer simply sex, no longer simply an instrument by which God continues his creation and shares the joy of creating, but an idol, a life-determining value which has displaced God. When sex becomes such an idol, it becomes an obstacle not only to salvation but also to the intention, if not to the act, of creation. The purpose or intention of creation is the coming into being of the Kingdom of God, and the purpose of salvation is the rehabilitation of rebellious creatures so that they might live in that Kingdom. The two purposes are essentially harmonious; nothing in creation (including sex) stands *necessarily* in the way of either, but everything in creation (including sex) *can*, if it becomes an idol, obstruct both. Because of their essential harmony, nothing can obstruct the purpose of creation without obstructing that of salvation, and vice versa. In intention, creation and salvation are inseparable.

The misconception which divorces creation from salvation is sometimes a cause and sometimes a result of other misconceptions. Two other misconceptions that have accompanied this one as its cause or result have been persistent and widespread enough in Christian history to warrant attention here.

Creation Does Not Mean Just a Primordial Event by which the World Got Started

People of the past who lived in prescientific times or in nonscientific cultures may be excused, perhaps, for having read the creation stories in Genesis as literal accounts of the world's physical beginnings. In a scientific age and culture, however, such an interpretation is untenable. The notion of a "firmament" or solid vault which separates the oceanic waters from the "waters above"[10] is clearly a piece of primitive, prescientific cosmology, and it is surely a throwback to a premodern form of science to think that light could have existed in any scientific (physical) sense before the sun and the stars were created.*

The intentions of those who would make the Genesis account conform with modern science may be good, but their grasp of the implications of both faith and science is weak, their reasoning is consequently contorted, and their efforts must therefore fail. From the standpoint of an understanding of faith, the most regrettable thing about such efforts is that they are so unnecessary and that they serve to distract from, rather than to enhance, the essential meaning of creation. In defining creation as an event in the primordial past that happened in a certain way (the way described in Genesis 1 and 2), these interpreters confuse faith in creation with belief in the correctness of a theory of the world's origins when such faith actually means openness to the continuing creation of God in the here and now.

Creation Does Not Mean a Completed or Closed System

If conservative Christians tend to think of creation as an originating event or process, completed in the long ago, liberal Christians tend to identify it too simply with the relatively self-sufficient natural order which resulted from such an originating process. Such identification found its most extreme expression in the thought of a number of eighteenth-century Christian intellectuals known as *Deists*. The Deists

---

* Compare Genesis 1:3–5, which speaks of the creation of light and darkness, day and night on the first day of creation, with 1:14–18, which tells of the creation of the sun, moon, and stars on the fourth day.

promoted an image of God as an inventive Genius who fashioned the universe as a kind of cosmic clock which he then wound up and left to run on its own. There is no need for continued divine involvement in the cosmic process, from their point of view, because the natural order is so ingeniously constructed.

The mainspring in the cosmic clock of the Deists is the human mind. God has effectively retired from the world scene, but intelligence is still present in the form of human minds, which have been empowered by creation[11] to take command of the processes of nature and history in God's stead. Such a view accents human dignity and responsibility, but in so doing it sacrifices other important values in the Christian idea of creation. In particular, it tends to promote a conception of reality as a closed system devoid of all values except those conceived or favored at any given moment by the minds of individuals. Because the minds of individuals tend to promote the self-interest of those individuals at the expense of the interests of others, the ironic result may be diminution in practice of that sense of human responsibility for the well-being of creation as a whole which Deism (and liberalism generally) champions in principle.

Liberals and Deists, like conservative Christians, miss the mark chiefly by magnifying a piece of the Christian story of creation into the whole story. Conservatives are correct in affirming that creation means that all things have their ultimate basis in God's creative work. They are incorrect only in insisting that the creative process must be understood as having been completed in six days, or six ages, or according to some other quasi-scientific rendering of the Genesis account.[12] Liberals, similarly, are correct in maintaining that creation confers dignity on human beings. They are incorrect, however, when they define such dignity in terms of a human self-sufficiency and when they consider creation a completed process and its result a closed, God-abandoned system. Conservatives and liberals alike tend to view the divine act of creation exclusively as an event in which the universe originated and to lose sight of the evidences that it is an unending process. Because (in their belief) creation is a completed process, any continuing involvement that God has in the world must be for purposes of salvation rather than for those of continuing creation. For some conservative Christians such involvement apparently occurs only through miraculous disruptions of normal natural processes; the processes that resulted from creation must be violated so that salvation can be made effective. For some liberal Christians, on the other hand, for whom the processes resulting from creation are virtually inviolable, salvation must be a matter of human self-help rather than of direct divine involvement in natural or human affairs. Conservatives generally speak of salvation, therefore, as a divine miracle, whereas liberals tend to speak of it as a matter of human morality.

Both, because of their restricted and inadequate conceptions of creation, mistakenly separate the means and purposes of salvation from those of the creative process.[13]

WHAT CREATION MEANS

If, as we have argued, faith in creation expresses a vital personal relationship rather than belief in a theory, and if the intention of this relationship is inseparable from that of the Christian experience of salvation, what are the implications of these facts for an understanding of creation? The theses developed in the following paragraphs will seek to spell out the more important of these implications. As the theses are developed, two criteria must be satisfied. First, the understanding of creation they express must be in accord with that expressed in the Bible, especially that expressed in Genesis 1-2 and in Jesus' teachings;[14] and second, the understanding of creation that they express must illumine human experience.

THE MIRACLE OF SPRING

We glibly talk
of nature's laws
but do things have
a natural cause?

Black earth turned into
yellow crocus
is undiluted
hocus-pocus.

From Grooks *by Piet Hein. Copyright 1966 by the author.*
Used by permission of Mr. Hein.

Creation Means the Gift of Existence
and the Conferral of Order

Two ideas dominate the conception of creation presented in the first two chapters of the Book of Genesis. The first is that creation is God's gift of existence to everything that in fact exists. The second is that through creation God not only brings reality into being but also orders its operation, thereby producing *cosmos* or world order out of *chaos* or lawless disarray and assigning value to the result.

"In the beginning God created the heavens and the earth." The scope of creation, announced the writer of Genesis, is universal. It embraces everything—"the heavens and the earth." As Gerhard von Rad stated, "God, in the freedom of his will, creatively established for 'heaven and earth,' i.e., for absolutely everything, a beginning of its subsequent existence."[15]

If creation is universal in its scope, according to Genesis, it is absolute in its depth. This means that creation is not, in its primary sense at least, a kind of divine manufacturing process in which God works over a raw material which was there all along. Instead creation is an act based on one Source alone—the infinite power of God. Creation is, as Christians perceive it, a creation *by* God *from* nothing, or (in the time-honored Latin formula) *creatio ex nihilo*.[16]

Creation means principally the gift of existence—not just the existence of those persons who happen to appreciate the gift, but the existence of everything, including those other beings (for example, air and water) on whose existence the human mode of existing depends. Besides raw existence, creation confers an order which makes possible the emergence and sustenance of particular kinds or modes of existence. The Genesis account alludes to the relation between creating and ordering in a number of significant ways. First, the writer of the account observes that "the earth" (the first concrete product of creation mentioned in the account) was initially "without form [in disorder] and void [empty]." There thus seems to be an essential connection, in the view of the writer, between universal formlessness, or lack of order, and universal emptiness. Without the imposition of order, the existence of actual, concrete beings who fill up the "void" would be impossible.

The second connection that the writer of the Genesis account makes between creation and order builds on and is at the same time the reverse side of the first. In verses 3 through 10 of Genesis 1, God's acts are all acts of separation, of sorting out, of bringing concrete beings into existence by ordering, setting limits on and thus segmenting, the undifferentiated "deep."[17] The formless and empty deep, whose formlessness is symbolized by its watery nature,[18] is the first of all creatures; the name given this creature is simply "the earth," and it is the vessel of raw, homogeneous, indeterminate existence. Verses 3 through 10 thus portray God in the act of launching a second phase or aspect[19] of creation which presupposes the reality of raw existence, or of the deep. This aspect of creation involves the fashioning of *particular* concrete beings through a process of parting the waters[20] of primeval "earth" and sorting out light from darkness, the waters below from the waters above, and the dry ground ("Earth") from the seas. Here, as in the rest of Genesis 1 (and also in Genesis 2), God seems not to be creating out of nothing so much as by the ordering or transformation of a primordial raw material.

The gift of existence and the conferral of order are thus intimately related elements or moments in the creative process. In its most radical and most distinctively Judaeo-Christian sense, the word "creation" means the granting or awarding of being itself, the radical beginning and the thoroughgoing dependence on God of everything that is real. In a secondary though closely related sense, creation also means the ordering of all that is. As the divine gift of existence is necessary if there is to be "something and not nothing,"[21] the divine gift of order is necessary if a world like the one we know is to exist. The world we know is not a cauldron of undifferentiated energy or of raw existence but a world of distinct and ordered objects—of shoes and ships and sealing wax, of cabbages and kings.

If our analysis of the Genesis creation story is correct, then one other fact about the story seems to follow naturally: the writer of the story was trying to make sense of the world as it actually is. The story, in other words, is an account of an actual human experience of the world. The account is not "scientific" in the modern sense. Neither the methods that produced it nor the results it records are scientific. In the terms of its own purpose it would be a poorer, not a richer, story if it were scientific. For its purpose is not to determine what makes the universe tick but rather to explore the human meaning of the universal process by which things and persons come to be. The basic human meaning, the story makes clear, is that both the existence and the order of the world are gifts to be received gratefully, to be appreciated continually, and to be used for the glory of their Giver and the well-being of the Giver's creatures.[22]

Creation Means Continuous Preservation and the Emergence of the New

In the story of the healing of the paralytic related earlier, Jesus implies that divine creation never ends, that the six days of Genesis 1 are not to be taken literally. God does not rest even on the Sabbath but "is working still." This idea of continuous creation has never died out among thoughtful and informed Christians, but on the popular level and among Deistic intellectuals it has had to compete with the more simple Sabbatarian notion of a dramatic and completed divine deed. Recent developments in science, however, have increased the prospects that the idea of continuous creation can receive a wider hearing.

In recent decades scientists and cosmologists have discovered and emphasized that nature, too, has a history. Much of the significance of Charles Darwin's theories on evolution lay in their recognition that nature is not static and unchanging but is constantly bringing new states of reality into being. Textualistic Christians saw in Darwin's contentions an attack on their own idea of creation. They correctly perceived that a creative process which is still evolving is sharply inconsistent with a creation that ended in six days.

As we have seen, however, the idea of creation in six days is not necessarily the Christian perception of the subject. The Jesus of John's Gospel seems to have disagreed openly and flagrantly with the doctrine of a completed creation. Moreover, a form of the idea of evolution is at least as old, in Christian thought, as St. Augustine,[23] who himself borrowed the idea from the Stoics. Augustine's idea that creation is not a finished product but a continuous process became common coin in the Middle Ages.[24] What the ancient and medieval theologians lacked was not the desire to see in history the emergence of God's new creation but rather a picture of the world (a cosmology) that would assist them in seeing the world this way.[25] In a real sense Darwin, with Hegel and others, made such a world picture possible.[26] If nature is not unchanging but changing, not static but historical, not cyclical but evolving, creation is most aptly perceived neither as a completed process nor as a closed system. It instead would appear to be a process that contains the potential both for its own remaking and for the emergence of the new. The ancient idea of continuous creation (*creatio continua*) is far more compatible with such a picture of nature than it was with the static world picture of antiquity and the Middle Ages.

Considered as a whole, creation may be defined as a process by which old reality is preserved, more or less in its own image, while new reality emerges. Creation thus combines conservative with progressive impulses. It *re*-news, to be sure, more obviously than it *makes* news.[27] But the fact that it produces the new at all seems theologically significant. This fact means that creation is not a dead or closed process. The ushering in of new realities within the natural sphere is a fitting symbol or sacrament of God's intention for the larger historical sphere which embraces the natural.

Creation Means Absolute or Total Dependence on God

When Christians speak of creation in the broadest sense, they refer not only to the universe as a continuing process or to the total natural order but also to a dimension of human experience. We have spoken of this dimension in other contexts[28] as the experience of contingency or of the "iffyness" of existence. The experience may be described in more positive terms as the emergence of an awareness that both life and the conditions which make life possible are gifts.

Within the context of faith, the experience of contingency produces a new attitude toward ordinary life. When analyzed, this attitude is seen to include three basic convictions:

1. Life would be impossible without sustaining relationships.
2. Practical human life—that is, those activities through which human beings seek to learn what is true, to do what is good, and to create what is functional, beautiful, or otherwise satisfying—would be impossible without confidence that the relationships on which life depends are trustworthy and conducive to the success of such activities.
3. The relationships on which life and practical activity depend are genuinely trustworthy only if they relate one to a Reality or Being who is both powerful enough to sustain life and life's conditions and moral enough to warrant the confidence that practical activity is worthwhile.[29]

The awareness of contingency (or of "createdness," to use a more theological term) introduces one first to a fundamental relatedness on which one's existence depends. A sense of such relatedness makes one aware that he or she is responsible neither for life nor for the conditions within the larger world that confer life. As mental health depends on staying in touch with reality, so, more basically, finite existence depends on elemental ties to what is real. The complexity of the human organism is such that the ties necessary to sustain it are virtually innumerable.[30] Whatever their number, the pertinent and significant fact is that taken together these ties place human beings in what we called earlier a *religious* condition—a condition of being bound up in and quite dependent on realities beyond themselves.

We are contingent not only in our sheer physical existence. Our practical endeavors also depend on sustaining relationships. The relationships that sustain moral, intellectual, and aesthetic endeavor must tie us not only to reality ("facts") but also to morality ("values"). Apart from the double conviction that (1) the value called truth exists and (2) humans are related to reality in such a way that this value is accessible to discovery, the pursuit of truth would be folly. But even devout atheists do not live as though they believed that the pursuit of truth is folly. Nor do they act as if the pursuit of other values—the good, the functional, the beautiful—were folly. The common, though unspoken, assumption behind practical human activity is that such activity is worth one's time and effort.[31] Unless the values pursued in such activities actually exist, however, this assumption is fallacious, and the total human enterprise is Lord Macbeth's "tale told by an idiot, . . . signifying nothing."

Creation as understood through the experience of contingency is a power which sustains human creativity as well as human life and the conditions that confer human life. But human creativity, as we have just seen, depends on moral conviction, a confidence in the reality of values, as much as on physical energy. The universe can provide a sufficient basis for creative (purpose- or value-pursuing) activity only if the fabric of the universe, the Force that holds the universe together, is itself moral.

In developing their idea of creation, then, Christians might well turn the tables on the atheist or the agnostic. Your actions, they could tell the creative nonbeliever, speak so loudly that we cannot take your creed or anticreed seriously. Your actions show that the universe is not only physically but morally sustaining. Can a universe not moral in nature account for the presence within it of moral beings? Can there be qualities in the flower which are neither in the seed nor in the environment that nurtured the seed nor in the potential results of the interaction between seed and environment?

To argue that the universe is moral is to argue that it is in some sense *personal*. Personal beings alone are capable of pursuing moral purposes and projecting moral values. The natural universe, to be sure, can be viewed as void of moral value—but only if the creative activity of human beings is considered either extranatural, an illusion, or a mere freak of nature. If such activity is any of these things, however, its pursuit by a "naturalist" seems illogical, unrational, and arbitrary. Why then do so-called naturalists (or amoralists) engage in such activity? Surely they can do so only by abandoning their own first principles. Their actions, indeed, betray a certain existential loyalty to entirely different first principles. In pursuing truth, they evince a certain faith in the objective reality of the values of truth and of nature's trustworthiness.

Although the arbitrary character of amoral naturalism does not prove the validity of the Christian faith in creation, it does show that that faith is based on an interpretation of human experience which is at least as viable as (and probably more rational than) that of its main contemporary rival. No more adequate account of human creativity can be found, the Christian argues, than that implied in the conviction that such activity is grounded in and supported by an ultimate reality whose own nature is creative. The name of that reality, whose power is directed by a morality grounded in personhood, is God.

In actual Christian living, faith in creation produces not only a basis for creative and moral activity but also a basis for a more comprehensive attitude toward life. Life is after all more, much more, than acting; it is receiving, enjoying, suffering, feeling, sharing, and so forth. Faith in creation sets all these elements, too, into a context of meaning. That I am created means that I owe the very possibility of these experiences to the Giver of life. It means that I am renewed in each new moment, that in every instant I receive the breath of life and the opportunity to share the experiences of that instant. Faith in creation, then, is not an abstraction from ordinary experience but an enriched understanding of such experience. Creation is a "gift that keeps on giving" because it expresses the dependence of the self, of the self's power to act, and of the self's world of experiences on a Giver who never stops giving.

Creation Means the Essential All-Rightness of the World

A recurrent theme runs through the sublime account of creation contained in the first chapter of Genesis: "And God saw that it was good." The affirmation of the theme reaches its crest in the chapter's concluding verse: "And God saw everything that he had made, and behold, it was very good." Thus the universe as a whole is proclaimed good by its Creator.

The declaration that everything in the universe is good is one of the two distinguishing marks of the Judaeo-Christian concept of creation. The other is the concept's more basic claim that everything in the universe is created, that is, dependent on God for its very being. Plato and other dualists of the ancient world conceived of creation as a reshaping of eternally existent materials. In this view God gives the world its essence or form but not its existence, not its raw potentiality for form. The universe is thus dependent on God for its essence but not for its existence. From the Judaeo-Christian standpoint, on the other hand, the universe is contingent through and through. Nothing *is* unless God wills it to be.

God gives the world not only its essence and its existence, according to the Bible, but also its value. Here, too, the distinction between the biblical view and rival views is crucial and epoch-making. The grounding of all value in God, and of all creaturely value in the creating Word of God, means at least three things: (1) that the universe is ultimately and essentially moral; (2) that creatures are intrinsically, not just functionally, valuable; (3) that life within the created, material universe is significant and important (value-laden).

The view that the universe is ultimately and essentially moral has been widely and fiercely contested. In the preceding section, we noted that naturalistic amoralists dispute and reject this view. But we also noted that, although the Christian claim that the universe is moral cannot be logically or empirically demonstrated, it seems as viable a claim as the amoralist alternative. But what practical difference does this claim make? What are its implications for the practical conduct of life?

The most obvious effect of this claim is an optimism about life in general and about moral and creative forms of endeavor in particular. The French existentialist Albert Camus once observed that there is finally only one issue worthy of human consideration: the issue of suicide. Life is either worth living, or it is not. Under ordinary circumstances, it hardly occurs to us to question the worth of continued existence. We live in the implicit faith that life is valuable. Such faith is strongly affirmed by the Christian idea of creation. One of the twentieth century's most remarkable Christians, Albert Schweitzer, made this affirmation the keynote of his entire philosophy. He argued that at the heart of the Christian faith, indeed at the heart of being human, there must reside a profound and all-comprehending reverence for life.[32]

If the Christian faith in the value of creation affirms life as such, it affirms with equal emphasis the struggle to live morally and creatively. The Book of Genesis, too, contains a gospel, for it bears the good news that human beings live in an environment which is neither inimical nor indifferent to moral endeavor but is rather both stable and morally supportive. To live morally is to go with the grain of reality, and not against it.

The conviction that creation has intrinsic value encourages not only moral endeavor but other forms of creative endeavor as well. As we have noted before, the account of creation in Genesis is not a scientific account. Even so, there is a sense in which that account comprises a kind of Magna Carta for science. Its declaration that God is not identical with nature but is rather nature's transcendent Creator implies that the investigation and control of nature will not involve the scientist in acts of sacrilege. Although it might appear from the modern secular standpoint to constitute a relatively minor concession to scientific freedom, such a "desacralization of nature"[33] has actually been of historic importance. Its effect has been to open the way for science's many triumphs in the West even as that way has remained blocked in the East by nature-based religions.[34]

If its demotion of nature from the status of a god has done a great deal to promote the scientific spirit in the world, its idea of human dominion has also made the creation faith of Christians a powerful stimulus for that spirit. The account in Genesis of the Creator's decision that human beings should "have dominion" over lesser creatures[35] amounts to a virtual mandate that the human creature become a scientist. That mandate is reinforced by the implication of the account that nature or the created order is worth studying. That implication is obviously present in the central conviction of the Genesis story that the natural order, bearing as it does the stamp of a good Creator, is moral and reliable.

The Genesis story affirms not only the goodness of creation as a whole but also the inherent goodness of the many creatures within the whole. It is not only on the sixth day, when all is complete, that God looks over his work approvingly. On earlier days,[36] too, "God saw that it was good." The creatures and their operations, both singly and together, are embraced by the Creator's approval. The practical significance of such approval is momentous. In effect it means that the ultimate Determiner of value is God alone and that all human definitions of value are subject to question; and second, it means that the basic value of each of God's creatures is not functional but intrinsic.

The assertion that God is the final Determiner of all values has great practical significance because it undermines the claim to absoluteness of all earthly beings and institutions. Against the claim of King George III that the British monarch ruled by divine right, that is, with absolute authority, Thomas Jefferson appealed to the Judaeo-Christian conviction, based on the faith in creation, that all persons are created equal and that, because they are invested by the Creator with "certain unalienable rights," no earthly ruler can presume to devalue or disenfranchise them. The Christian affirmation that creatures derive their value from God thus stands as a bulwark against efforts to deny human dignity and worth.

The conviction that creatures receive their value from God has ecological as well as political implications. The kingdom of nature, too, resists tyranny. So balanced are its operations that the subjugation of some elements in the ecosystem by other elements may well place the entire system in peril. The notion that God's conferral of the right to dominion on human beings is a license to exploit nature is refuted not only ecologically, by the penalties nature imposes on its exploiters, but also theologically, by the Creator's impartation of value to all creatures. Dominion is not a license to rape and pillage but a commission to preserve and enhance the values already present in creation.

The divine basis of the values inherent in creatures supports both political freedom and a certain ecological equity. It also works to safeguard the rights of persons to a degree of economic independence. There are in fact those who attach a certain value to persons but fail to understand that persons are valuable not just because of the energies they have to expend or the economic function they can serve. Moral functionalists or utilitarians tend to undercut the significance of the individual, perhaps unintentionally, by their willingness to sacrifice individual equity wherever such a sacrifice is necessary to promote "the greatest social good." An even more potent threat to the idea of the inherent sacredness of creatures is present in the collective and corporation mentalities of the modern economic systems of the Soviet Union and the United States. These systems, like the utilitarian philosophy, tend to assign value to persons largely in terms of the socially useful or economically profitable functions they can render. Against all such systems and philosophies the gospel of creation declares that human beings, indeed all creatures, are valuable in and for themselves; their value is intrinsic and "unalienable," the Christian faith holds, because it is God-given, and what God gives no earthly power can legitimately deny.

Yet another claim inherent in the biblical conception of creation is that life within the material universe is significant and important. Both of the biblical faiths, Judaism and Christianity, are distinguishable from most of the world's other self-conscious religions by their "materialism." "God saw *everything* he had made," the text has it, "and behold, it was good." "Everything" clearly includes matter, the body, and the bodily appetites, including sex. There is no warrant in the biblical idea of creation for that hatred of material goods which some take to be the hallmark of religion. Material goods are essentially just that: goods. They, too, have been invested by the Creator with value. If they are dangerous to human well-being, it is because they are valuable, not because they are worthless or evil. The same goodness that makes them expressions of divine grace can make them occasions for human sin, for such goodness grants them the power to draw persons away from the goodness of God and toward the idolization of material wealth. In any case material beings are good, and that means that they are to be wisely enjoyed and used, not despised or raised in other ways to a controlling place in one's thoughts.

To sum up: the Word by which God creates the world is at the same time a Word by which he affirms it. Both the world order as a whole and the particular creatures who make it up are beings of value. Even material beings, despised by some of the world's faiths, are held by the creation faith of Christians to be beings of value. Everything created takes its value from God, and this fact has profound implications for the political, ecological, and economic dimensions of human life.

CREATION AS A PAINFUL PROCESS
(THE PROBLEM OF EVIL)

The obvious question that emerges from the Christian claim that creation is essentially and totally good is "Where, then, did evil come from?" We shall discuss the moral dimension of evil, known theologically as

"sin," in the next chapter. Here we shall deal with that dimension only as it relates to the larger problem of general or "natural" evil.

The most basic point that traditional Christian thought makes regarding evil is that evil is a parasitical perversion of goodness. Evil is simultaneously a parasite on, and a perversion of, the good. Let us begin our discussion of evil by examining the meaning and significance of these claims.

A parasite is by definition a being that exists at the expense of a host being (a being on whom it depends for the conditions of its own being). In a real sense, given what has been said about creation to this point, all created beings are parasitical, for they depend on a power beyond themselves, a Creator, for their existence. But when Christians say that evil is parasitical, they mean that it is parasitical in a markedly different sense. For evil, in the Christian view, is *not* a created being. It is not, in other words, attributable to the direct creative activity of God. If God looked on *everything* he had made and saw that it was good, quite clearly he saw *nothing* among the things he had made that was evil. Whence, then, came evil?

Evil came about, according to Christian thought, through a disordering, or perversion, of goods. Whether one attributes the origin of evil to a rebellion among the angels, as did a long mythological tradition which reached its climax in Milton's *Paradise Lost,* or to a disobedient Mother of humankind, as did the Book of Genesis, the act that introduced evil was in any case motivated by a desire to secure a certain good (a universe-controlling power in the case of the angel Satan, a life-controlling wisdom in the case of Eve). Evil thus originates in the decision to value one's relation to some created good more highly than one's relation to God.

The displacement of God by the good, of the Giver by one of the gifts, is the source and the essence of evil's most serious and radical form, so-called "moral" evil. If this is what evil means, it is obvious that it does not exist on its own but only as a distortion or disordering of goods. The existence of evil is totally dependent on the existence and the false adulation of created goods. It is in this sense that Christians consider evil to be parasitical.

There is another type of evil, however, which seems to elude this explanation. Perhaps moral evil is adequately explained as a phenomenon which results from the misuse of human freedom, from the human decision to worship the creature instead of the Creator. But the so-called *natural* evils—evils that result from natural calamities like earthquakes and outbreaks of disease—clearly cannot be explained in this way. Is the Christian faith not wrong, then, in absolving God and his creation from responsibility for evil?

The accusatory tone of this question is not entirely groundless. Indeed, the biblical Book of Job puts the question with great force, and the decision to include Job within the sacred canon indicates that Jews and Christians see some validity in the question. Though space does not permit a thorough discussion of the many religious and philosophical arguments by which Western thinkers have sought to answer it, we may at least survey some of the more significant of those arguments. At the outset of our survey, however, it must be noted that none of the attempts at an answer is entirely satisfactory.

The first answer to the questions "Why does evil exist?" and "Is God responsible for its existence?" may be called an *ontological* answer. According to this answer, developed by the philosopher Leibniz among others, natural evil and human suffering are necessary to the creation of the best of possible worlds. The world is a giant organism, and it is necessary at times that its parts suffer in the interest of the health of the whole. Dreadful storms may kill persons, animals, and plants even as they provide nitrogen for the soil and thereby make it possible to feed and give life to many. The needs of the natural order as a whole must supersede the needs of its parts.

The *aesthetic* answer to the problem of evil is a somewhat cynical variation of the ontological one. God is portrayed here either as something of a hedonist who organized the universe to entertain himself and uses his creatures as pawns in a cosmic stageplay[37] or chess game, or as an artist who, to make his picture complete, must use the darker colors and shadows of death and suffering as well as the brighter tints of life and joy. Evil is the shadow side of good, the tragic element in the divine handiwork.

The *teleological* answer is yet another version of the ontological one. Here, as in the ontological and the aesthetic answers, the well-being of creation's parts must be subjugated to the interests of the whole. There is an overriding cosmic purpose (*telos*)—perhaps the establishment of the rule of God or the maximization of divine freedom (Hegel[38])—that makes it necessary that some of the parts of the cosmic whole should suffer, languish, and even die.

Yet another approach to the problem of evil may be called the *meontological* approach. The word "meontological" comes from the Greek words *me* ("not" or "non-") and *on* ("being"). Meontological theories differ from ontological ones in that, where ontological theories seek to explain the nature or structure of *being*, meontological theories focus attention on *nonbeing*. Nonbeing may seem a strange subject for study unless and until one realizes that *me on* does not mean absolute nonbeing or sheer nothingness (the Greeks had another term, *ouk on*, for that) but rather *relative* nonbeing, a relatively diminished or unrealized state of being to which we refer with words like "possibility" and "potentiality."

Meontology is the study of possibility and potentiality as contrasted with the study of fulfilled being or actuality (a form of study called ontology). In reflecting on possibility, meontologists generally notice and stress the presence of two elements within it. Possibility *exists* (is actual) in one sense, and so it is a form of being (that is, potential being—as, for example, a block of granite has the potential for being a statue or a tombstone). Yet it does *not* exist in one sense, because it remains only potential, unfulfilled, and unactualized (as the medical student is *not* a doctor even though he or she has the potential to become one).

In applying these insights to the problem of evil, meontologists may (and do) proceed in either of two directions. They either stress the meontic (unfulfilled, incomplete) character of the world, or they maintain that there is a meontic quality in God. Since they offer two distinct answers to the problem of evil, let us look separately at these versions of meontology.

The meontologists who view evil as a result of the meontic character of the world may hold that evil is either an illusion (a result of an incomplete human vision of the world—that is, of a meontic or incomplete knowledge), as the Christian Scientists do; or that it is a product of the world's meontic (incomplete) nature, to be overcome through progressive and continuous creation. The latter form of the argument is the more genuinely meontological. Evil here is not simply a corollary of human ignorance, as Christian Science teaches, but is an inescapable consequence of the incompleteness of things.

Some meontologists look beyond the incompleteness of the world for an answer to the problem of evil. Evil, they maintain, derives from a much more fundamental incompleteness or unfulfilled potential in God. This incompleteness may be defined in a variety of ways. Some (for example, E. S. Brightman, A. N. Whitehead) even dare to call it a finitude or essential limitation in God. Others (for example, Paul Tillich, N. Berdyaev) think of it as a boundless but unfulfilled potentiality. For our purposes it is enough to notice that this condition within God can produce evil in either of two ways. According to the first way, evil is purely and simply a surd in creation which is unavoidable because of a degree of divine powerlessness or incompleteness. To the philosopher Voltaire, who once asserted that in the light of evil God is either good and not God (that is, not all-powerful) or else he is God (all-powerful) and not good, meontologists of this type would reply that God is good but not all-powerful. To note one of the lesser limitations (deficiencies of power) from which God conceivably suffers, meontologists may argue that God cannot create a universe of beings who are his own equals (infinite, uncreated). God is necessarily limited, then, to the options of creating a world of more limited, contingent beings or of not creating a world at all. But limitation and contingency carry with them the potential, and the likely actuality, of evil, for wherever limits exist one may readily expect to suffer the pain of running up against those limits. A limitation on knowledge, for example, means ignorance, and if ignorance itself is not evil, it at least leaves one highly vulnerable to evil as it places one in situations of danger that knowledge could help one avoid.

The second way in which the meontic limitation in God may be conceived to contribute to evil is through a kind of divine self-limitation. The boundless potential in God which Tillich calls a "creative abyss" indicates the possibility of conceiving of God's nature as that of a self-limiting limitlessness. Out of the infinite potentiality within himself, in other words, God must choose which of the potential worlds to actualize. The universe he has chosen to actualize stands before us, all around us, in us. That universe, it appears, is one to which God has granted semi-independence. The degree of independence that it enjoys would not be possible, however, without a further act of divine self-limitation, directed in this instance toward the created world instead of toward the abyss of divine potentiality within God himself. The world's semi-independence is not an unmixed blessing. It makes possible, to be sure, a certain creaturely freedom, but it makes equally possible the two inevitable counterparts of such freedom—the power to do evil and the risk of suffering it.

An answer to the problem of evil akin in some respects to this last form of the meontological answer is sometimes called the *moral* answer. This answer may indeed correlate with the meontological answer but goes beyond it to hold that God allows evil in the world for a definite moral purpose. In this view God allows the world to be semi-independent in order that it may be a sphere of human responsibility within which human creatures may become fully moral beings. Within such a sphere, however, evil is inevitable. Without it human freedom would be impossible, moral choices could not be made, moral character could not evolve, and God would have no way of testing, molding, and perfecting a moral universe.[39]

Still another answer to the problem of evil may be called the *romantic* answer. In his novel *Emile,* the great French romantic Jean-Jacques Rousseau developed this answer with simple and imperious certainty:

> Enquire no longer then, who is the author of evil. Behold him in yourself. There exists no other evil in nature than what you either do or suffer, and you are equally the author of both.... Take

TYPE	EXPLANATORY PRINCIPLE(S)	MAIN POINT(S) OF VULNERABILITY
ONTOLOGICAL	Some beings must suffer for the good of reality as a whole	The principle itself is unfair—an expression of evil rather than an explanation of it
AESTHETIC	Evil is necessary to the supreme good of cosmic beauty or divine satisfaction	Seems to conceive of God in amoral, and even sadistic, terms
TELEOLOGICAL	Evil is the means to a noble end such as the divine glory or enhanced divine power and freedom	Justifies means by ends; portrays God in amoral terms
MORAL	Evil is the inevitable "flip side" of good, whose management and conquest are necessary to a moral universe and/or the development of moral agents	The idea of "inevitable" evil suggests a certain impotence in God (see the meontological explanation below)
MEONTOLOGICAL	Evil results from limitations in the nature of reality—from a certain powerlessness or a raw, unformed power in God; from human ignorance and/or impotence; and/or from callous indifference in nature	In some of its forms, this answer denies the divine omnipotence; in others, it throws divine righteousness and love into question
ROMANTIC	Evil is no more than the human corruption of an innocent natural order or the tragic result of an accident or aberration in human history (e.g., the advent of private property)	Oversimplifies evil's nature, sometimes overemphasizing humankind's role in causing it, sometimes overestimating the human power to overcome it

Theodicies, or Explanations of Evil

away . . . everything that is the work of man, and all that remains is good.[40]

Although its emphasis on human responsibility is both biblical and Christian, this answer oversimplifies the nature of that responsiblity. Human beings are clearly implicated, Christians believe, in both the origins and the continuing reality of evil. Christians also believe that the *potential* for evil resides in the goodness, and the consequent seductive power, of the natural order. Rousseau's drawing of a sharp line between human guilt and natural innocence thus seems to thoughtful Christians to offer too simple an answer to a complex problem. In similar fashion, neo-romantic answers like that of Karl Marx, who held that evil is mainly a product of the human institution of private property, fail to recognize that such human institutions must have some ground or basis in human and/or cosmic nature.

The variety and range of the several answers to the problem which we have surveyed leave little room for doubt about the power of the problem of evil to fascinate and perplex thoughtful people. From a biblical or Christian perspective serious questions can be raised about any of these answers. Since considerations of space and purpose make a lengthy critique impractical here, let us conclude our discussion of the problem of evil by outlining an answer to the problem drawn from biblical and traditional Christian sources.

The basic biblical insight regarding evil has already been stated: evil emerges as a by-product from and remains a parasite on goodness. The good that we know and experience as human freedom presupposes the possibility of moral evil. So Eve stands poised in the garden of creation between a God who is *supremely* good and a creature (the tree of the knowledge of good and evil) that is *relatively* good. Evil comes into existence when she prefers the relatively good to the supremely good.

The Adam and Eve story makes it clear also that evil is experiential, not theoretical. The theoretical possibility of evil is not itself evil. As long as the fruit of the tree goes untasted, the knowledge of evil is a mere possibility, not an actuality. But so, too, is the knowledge of good. Adam and Eve may have been the *beneficiaries* of good before their involvement in evil, but they were hardly the *appreciators* of good. The appreciation or "knowledge" (conscious awareness) of the good depends on an acquaintance with evil. The moral answer to the problem of evil seems correct, from the Christian point of view, to the extent that it holds that the presence of evil is somehow necessary to the reality (realization in human consciousness) of a moral universe.

The presence of the tree of the knowledge of good and evil in the garden of creation may well be the biblical writer's way of suggesting that God creates the *possibility* of evil. One wonders, indeed, if the very declaration of the Creator that all of the creatures are good does not suggest the possibility of a fall into evil by those creatures. Be that as it may, the fall, or the actualization of evil, is not the Creator's doing but the creature's. The human will, induced or seduced by the beauty and value inherent in the larger created order, introduces evil into the world as an actual human experience.

The Genesis myth thus implicates both humankind (personified in Eve) and the natural order (exemplified in the tree of knowledge and the seductive serpent) in the primal crime which brings evil into being. Primary responsibility undoubtedly rests with the one responsible creature: the human one. But it is significant, too, that the myth implicates nature in the process by which evil comes to be. To some extent this merely reflects the ancient Hebrew antipathy for the nature worship of the Baal cults. That antipathy itself seems to have been grounded, as we saw in our analysis of the Cain story in Chapter VI, in a conviction that nature may become God's powerful rival for human affections. The very goodness and beauty of nature, not to mention its power to affect the human condition, make it a seducer whose wiles bear watching.

The implication of natural as well as human creatures in the reality of evil is stressed by the Genesis myth not only in its references to evil's origins but also in its attention to evil's consequences. Confronted by God with her crime, Eve passes the blame along to the serpent. Not only is a permanent enmity thereafter established between the woman and the serpent,[41] but God also takes Eve's accusation seriously enough to place a curse upon the serpent.[42] The co-responsibility of humans and nature for the emergence of evil seems divinely confirmed. Adam, too, though a somewhat tardy accessory to the crime, finds himself estranged from nature: "Cursed is the ground because of you; in toil you shall eat of it all the days of your life; thorns and thistles it shall bring forth to you.... In the sweat of your face you shall eat bread...."[43] His decision to prefer the allure of nature to the command of God means, further, that his destiny is now more intimately linked to that of mortal nature than to that of the immortal God: "You are dust, and to dust you shall return."[44]

The fall of humanity is thus portrayed in Genesis 3 as a fall having cosmic repercussions. The whole world, natural as well as human, is changed by it. Cain's love for the ground from which he is banished (in Genesis 4) simply proves him a true child of the primal parents. The attachment to the creature, when it rivals and displaces the attachment to the Creator, is the root of all evil. The human creature is the more responsible partner in the primal sin, but the natural creature is a necessary accomplice who becomes as well an inevitable co-victim.

For all its insight, the Genesis myth does not entirely dispel the mystery surrounding the problem of evil. Its provocative suggestion that moral evil and natural evil are not so separable as they at first appear raises as many problems as it answers. From a humane standpoint, for example, it appears absurd to suggest that natural catastrophes victimize people as a way of punishing them for their sins. But the myth's suggestion that there may be natural retribution for the pride and greed that lead humans to dethrone God and to abuse and exploit nature sounds remarkably similar to the warnings of today's ecologists that the ecosystem is all of a piece and that the fate of humankind and the fate of the natural system are inextricably linked.

There is one other point at which the link-up that Genesis establishes between moral evil and natural evil seems instructive. In his Letter to the Romans St. Paul wrote:

> The creation waits with eager longing for the revealing of the sons of God; for the creation was subjected to futility, not of its own will but by the will of him who subjected it in hope; because the creation itself will be set free from its bondage to decay and obtain the glorious liberty of the children of God. We know that the whole creation has been groaning together until now; and not only the creation, but we ourselves ... groan inwardly....[45]

In attributing human characteristics ("longing," "groaning,") to nature, Paul reflects the ancient practice of thinking of nature as a giant organism or Cosmic Animal.[46] His ascription of these qualities has another significance as well. Nature, he suggests, is incomplete, unfulfilled, meontic. More than that, nature evinces a certain restlessness, a dissatisfaction as it were, with the "bondage" which characterizes its present state; it "longs" to evolve into a higher, freer, more fulfilled form of being.

Paul thus joins the writer of Genesis in tying the state of nature closely to that of humankind. United in their bondage to evil, nature and humanity are also united in their longing for redemption. Their joint struggle with evil is bearable because they feel the power within themselves of a continuing creation, a new and renewing creation, an evolution toward "the glorious liberty of the children of God." Although the link between moral and natural evil cannot be demonstrated theoretically, Paul suggests that it does make sense of some of our experiences and that it does lend a cosmic significance to the struggle against evil.

If Genesis 3 offers Scripture's deepest insights into the origins of evil, the stories of Job and Jesus offer its deepest glimpses into the potential significance of suffering. In the matter of the beginnings of evil, the views of the author of Job appear to parallel quite closely the views found in Genesis. There can be little question that Job's author identifies God as evil's ultimate source, but the way the book establishes the identification is quite significant. The book begins with a conversation between God and one of his angels. The angel's name—"Satan"—is more of a title than a personal name, for it defines the angel's role within the heavenly court. "Satan" means "the tempter," or "the adversary,"

and Job's author quickly indicates that the task of the angel who bears that name is to put God's human children to the test. By bringing a third figure (Satan) into the picture between God and Job, the writer expresses a conviction that God *allows*, but does not directly *impose*, natural evil and suffering. When Satan asks permission to torment Job, permission is granted. The author of Job thus boldly charges God with complicity in the perpetration of natural evil.

If God is Satan's accomplice in afflicting Job, it is not for some ignoble reason, such as sadism or his own amusement, that he joins in. In his initial conversation with Satan, the Lord points to Job as an outstanding example of human righteousness. It is to test the mettle of that righteousness, and perhaps also to refine it and perfect it, that Satan is licensed to afflict Job with evil.

When seen within its own historical context, the story of Job must be viewed as a rebuttal to a very simplistic theory of good and evil which was popular among the people of Judah from the late seventh century B.C. on. Known as the Deuteronomic philosophy, the theory developed as a result of an effort by the temple priests in Jerusalem to recall the Judahites to lives of moral rectitude which would be pleasing in God's sight. To encourage such uprightness, the priests fostered the belief that God would materially reward the righteous and that he would punish the unrighteous by imposing all kinds of physical and emotional hardships on them. As a protest against this simple moral calculus, the author of Job wrote his great play. Perhaps he had seen how the moralizing of the Deuteronomists had compounded the sufferings of the innocent. Such moralizing added the mental anguish of guilt to the physical agony of pain or the emotional burden of grief. But it was not simply because such moralizing was inhumane that the writer of Job opposed it. He opposed it too, it appears, because it was based on a false, Pollyanna theology. Its God was a kind of Goody Twoshoes, a prim and proper headmaster who cared more about rules than about the well-being of his creatures. Against such an overly moral God, the reality of the mystery of God must be reasserted and reinstated. That God is righteous is not to be doubted, and that he cares about human righteousness is also not to be doubted. But that the divine caring may take strange and mysterious forms is also one of the plainer facts of human existence.

If the perception of the human situation in Job is correct, it is clear that the problem of evil will never yield to simple moral or theoretical solutions. Indeed, in Job's responses to his Deuteronomic counselors, the writer indicates at least implicitly that one of the greater sins in life may be the sin of offering people curt and simple theoretical solutions to profound and painful existential problems. An entirely different approach to such problems seems necessary. The Deuteronomic

Job Sorely Afflicted

approach—do good and prosper, do evil and suffer—inevitably makes
the suffering of evil an occasion of alienation from God. When such
simple moralism prevails, the sufferer of evil is besieged not only by the
immediate suffering at hand but also by self-doubt and a depressing
guilt. Job argues that there may be another, and better, way to perceive
evil: perhaps evil is better understood as an occasion for union with God
than as a time of alienation from him. Consider that inhabitant of Uz,
whose name was Job. Here was a man whom the Lord God himself
declared "a blameless and upright man, who fears God and turns away

from evil."[47] Yet so righteous a person as this was afflicted and tormented by a great company of evils. Had he been a Deuteronomic person, Job's misfortunes would surely have undone him. But against his counselors and "comforters," who were indeed Deuteronomic persons, he steadfastly maintained that his sufferings had no basis in his sins.[48] Despite, indeed amid, the afflictions wrought by grief, pain, and his preachy companions, he found a new strength, a new sense of God's necessary presence. From his ash heap and out of his anguish we hear him declare of God that, "Though he slay me, yet will I trust in him."[49]

The Book of Job celebrates not only the dauntless faith of its hero but also a certain insight into the nature of God. The boldness with which Job addresses God and the volume and vigor of his complaint against God are quite remarkable. The language Job uses in laying out his grievance is closer to that of a street brawl than to that of the Sunday morning prayer service. The truly remarkable thing is that, despite its dependence on the vernacular, Job's complaint does not go unheard. The divine response is equally vigorous, to be sure, and it gives as good as it gets. But it confirms not only the infinite superiority of God the Judge to Job the plaintiff but also the willingness of the Almighty to confer with his afflicted creature.

The essential message of the Book of Job thus seems to be threefold:

1. Evil and suffering are not always signs of overt or covert immorality.
2. Though God does not directly impose evil, he may allow it for purposes of his own.
3. The divine purposes for allowing evil, though ultimately mysterious, may include the testing of human righteousness and the enhancing of human faith through the realization that evil may be a source of union with, rather than a source of alienation from, God.

To a remarkable degree the career of Jesus gave historical, flesh-and-bone expression to the essential attitude toward evil found in the Book of Job. The sorrowful prayer of Jesus in the Garden of Gethsemane on the night before his death echoes, in a New Testament setting, the affirmation of Job: "Though he slay me, yet will I trust in him." In his prayer Jesus stares into the depths of the agony and death which await him, and St. Luke reports that "his sweat became like great drops of blood falling down upon the ground."[50] But despite the anguish of that moment, he gives himself over to the awful prospect: "My Father, if it be possible, let this cup pass from me; nevertheless, not as I will, but as thou wilt."[51]

Though it reflects in a notable way the spirit of Job, Jesus' attitude toward evil seems to have been more directly inspired by several passages in the Book of Isaiah. A poem from the pen of the so-called Second Isaiah seems to have been especially meaningful to him. It reads in part:

> He was despised and rejected by men;
>   a man of sorrows, and acquainted with grief;
> and as one from whom men hide their faces
>   he was despised, and we esteemed him not.
> Surely he has borne our griefs
>   and carried our sorrows;
> Yet we esteemed him stricken,
>   smitten by God and afflicted.
> But he was wounded for our transgressions,
>   . . . upon him was the chastisement that made us whole,
> and with his stripes we are healed.
>
> He was oppressed, and he was afflicted,
>   yet he opened not his mouth;
> like a lamb that is led to the slaughter,
>   and like a sheep that before its
>   shearers is dumb
> so he opened not his mouth.[52]

This segment from one of the poignant Servant Songs, as they are called, speaks of the mission of a messianic figure who bears witness to the covenant-love of God through suffering. Second Isaiah—actually an anonymous sixth-century prophet who is given this name because his writings are found in the Book of Isaiah—is believed by scholars to have been one of the Judean exiles in Babylon. It is quite possible that the messianic figure he depicts in his poem is an idealized personification of the community of exiles to which he belonged. He may have been exhorting his fellow exiles to recall the covenant-promise to Abraham, that the Israelites who descended from Abraham would be a light to the nations. The evil condition of exile, which has caused great pain to Abraham's children—caused them, indeed, to be "despised and rejected by men"—may in fact be a means by which they can fulfill the covenant-promise which God had made to their revered ancestor.[53] The occasion of their suffering, in other words, could by the power of God be transformed into an occasion for sharing the light of God among the foreign peoples with whom their state of exile forced them to live.

For the Second Isaiah, then, suffering is much more than a condition to be endured and lamented. When placed in the context of the covenant faith of Israel, suffering can become an opportunity for witnessing to the love of God for the world. It was this understanding of suffering, it appears, that shaped Jesus' conception of his mission. His entire career reflects his commitment to proclaim the reconciling, healing love of God. Such love, he seems to conclude, means that God must become involved in the sufferings of his people no less than in their sacred celebrations. The people who are well, after all, have no need of a physician,[54] and so we find Jesus forsaking the havens of the respectable and the upright and consorting with sinners, ne'er do wells, lepers, insane folk (demoniacs), and other victims of social ostracism.

The haunts of evil doers and sufferers thus become, through Jesus' ministry, the sanctuaries of God. As Sherman Johnson observed, a new element enters the faith of Israel in the message of the Nazarene, for he declares that God is no longer willing to wait for sinners to seek him out but has instead elected to seek them out.[55] Evil and suffering are no longer simply to be shunned as the accursed lot of godless souls; they are instead to become the occasions for declaring the unlimited love of a seeking God.

It is in the light of their acquaintance with such a seeking God that many Christians claim that the ultimate word regarding suffering and evil is a cry from a cross: "My God, my God, why hast thou forsaken me?"[56] This cry, uttered by Jesus just before he died, signifies for many Christians the descent of God himself into the awfullest of human conditions, the condition of knowing oneself abandoned by life's creative Source. This act of divine self-abandonment is momentous not only in itself but also because it completes the act of incarnation by which, through the life and death of Christ, God identifies himself with all aspects of the human reality. In experiencing to the dregs the reality of human suffering, and in going beyond the pain and bitterness of suffering into death itself, God has in Christ displayed the infinite depths of his love for creation. If the gruesome reality and the awful loneliness of death on a cross are events in God's own experience, then how shall one escape the range or the reach of that experience? Evil remains real, to be sure, and its sting remains potent, but, as St. Paul asserted triumphantly in Romans 8,

> Who shall separate us from the love of Christ?
> Shall tribulation, or distress, or persecution,
> or famine, or nakedness, or peril, or sword? . . .
> No, in all these things we are more than conquerors
> through him who loved us . . . .
> For I am sure that neither death, nor life,
> nor angels, nor principalities,
> nor things present, nor things to come,
> nor powers, nor height, nor depth,

nor anything else in all creation,
will be able to separate us from the
love of God in Christ Jesus our Lord.[57]

In summary, we may note that the divinely initiated and divinely perpetuated creative process is, in the Christian view, a process plagued by natural as well as by moral evil. Creation is accordingly a painful process. But what is the significance of this fact? What does it say about God, about the human environment, or about the human creature itself? Christians maintain that the ultimate purposes of the pain—the evil, the suffering—in the universe lie hidden in the mystery of God. But they find insights in Genesis and in Job, in Jesus and in Paul, which suggest that the pains of creation are essentially growing pains rather than pains of death and decay. Evil is not the final word on the universe. The same God who allows the possible knowledge of it in Genesis and the application of it to a righteous man in Job experiences the human knowledge and the human reality of it in Jesus. On the cross, the pain that seems an inevitable aspect of the creative process is experienced in the extreme by the Creator himself. It becomes clear that the painful aspect of creation is well within the purposes of a God who claims as his own both the doers and the sufferers of evil. In the end as in the beginning the Creator may look on all creation, and behold, it will be good.

CREATION'S HUMAN DIMENSION

The problem of evil makes it clear that the relationship between the human creature and the rest of the created order is a complex one. If creation is a painful process, both the process and the pain are essential elements in it. The struggle to make sense of the process and of the pain leads Christians to the conviction that both must be purposive—must, that is, be aspects or elements of the divine intention for the created *plenum*. The possibility of pain is the presupposition of sentient life just as the natural process is the presupposition of any kind of life at all. Pain and its counterpart, pleasure, along with the reality of a process of natural change, were essential to the eventual evolution of creation's human dimension.

The human creature is an outgrowth of a natural process as well as of the divine intention. If the stories in Genesis provide creation's why— creation occurs to produce a creature sufficiently similar to God to commune with him and to lead creation in freely adoring and serving him— the story of evolution provides creation's how—creation occurs through the interaction of creatures and their cosmic environment. The human creature, indeed in a sense every creature, depends on the creative

WHY DO THE CHIMPS LOOK WORRIED?

Anthropomorphological grook

When the Apes became Mankind
just a few were left behind.
Some are still around.
Grey, neurotic, anxious, lined, —
can it be that they've divined
whither they are bound?

From Grooks 4 *by Piet Hein. Copyright 1972 by ASPILA SA.*
Used by permission of the author.

natural process and on its own responses to that process as well as on
God. As a result there is an intriguing and powerful ambivalence in the
human situation. Humans, like all other creatures, are sustained by
three realities: their Creator, their own natural composition, and external nature. But humans, like none of the other creatures, can *realize* their
dependence on these realities. It is the power to realize its state of
relatedness that makes the human creature the *religious* creature (*homo
religiosus*). The human creature is unique not because it is defined by its
relationships but because it can know that it is so defined.

To know oneself defined by certain relationships is the most elemental form of religious experience. It is not, as we have emphasized, a
cognitive or theoretical type of knowing. It is instead a visceral or gut-
level knowing, experienced in a sense even by the infant whose squawls
for his or her mother's attentions disclose a deep dependence on help
from beyond.

As human beings we are defined by our relationships. In this we are
distinguished from other creatures only by our ability to realize that we

are so defined and by our ability to act on that realization. The portrait of the human situation in the first four chapters of Genesis is an ancient and archetypal result of such a realization. The genius of the stories contained in these chapters resides to a large extent in their power to illuminate the implications for human life of the human creature's simultaneous dependence on God, on its own resources of mind and will, and on nature. In the remaining pages of this chapter, we shall examine several of these implications.

The Genesis stories make four main points about the human condition, two of which we shall examine in this chapter and two of which we shall return to in Chapter VIII. The four points are:

1. Being human means being a creature.
2. Being human means being a very special creature.
3. Being human means being a rebellious creature.
4. Human beings are beings for whom God continues to care, despite their rebellion.

To be human means first simply to be a creature. We have discussed what it means to be a creature off and on throughout this chapter, so it may suffice here simply to summarize and analyze some of our earlier observations.

To be a creature means, most basically, to lack self-sufficiency. It means to be contingent, depending on beings beyond oneself for the power of one's existence. It means, therefore, that one's very reality depends on certain sustaining relationships.

Creaturehood also means limitation. The most fundamental limit on the creature is the limit suggested by contingency, namely, the limit on its very power to be. This most fundamental limit is graphically represented in human experience by the threat of death. Death makes it plain, plainer than anything else can make it, that creatures are limited. But there are other limits on the reality of creatures as well. They are limited by time: they cannot relive or recover the past, and they cannot thoroughly anticipate or control the future. They are limited by space: they cannot be in more than one place at once. They are limited in durability or stamina: they cannot last forever. They are limited in strength: they cannot exert total control over their environment or even over their immanent condition (the creature born blind, for example, cannot give itself sight). As for human creatures, the humanity which makes their list of powers longer also makes their list of limitations longer. Their power of choice is limited: they cannot have their cake and eat it too. Their skill and insight are limited: the inmost intricacies of both nature and the human psyche elude them. Their wisdom and moral capacity are limited, and so their longings for peace, justice, and equity go unsatisfied.

Creaturehood means, finally, a certain relativity and relationality. Creatures are dependent for their being not only on their Creator but also on each other. Human beings call their closest kin, those on whom they are most intimately dependent for both survival and identity, their relatives. There is a sense, however, in which all creatures are relatives. Only rarely does a human being appear who discerns the full meaning of this fact, as St. Francis of Assisi did in the thirteenth century. As his hymns to Brother Sun and Sister Moon and his sermons to his little sisters the birds and to his fierce friend, the wolf of Gubbio, attest,[58] St. Francis already knew a truth that has been verified by the science of our own century: the truth that all creatures are relative because all are in fact relatives, members of a single creation family.

The accounts in Genesis express the view that creatures are not only relative, the work of a single creative Mind in whom they all stand related, but also relational, that is, related in definitive ways to God and to nature. The focus of the Genesis accounts is on the human creature. Human beings are in reality *very special creatures* because the relationships that define them are of a special sort. These relationships are three: the relationship of humans to the God beyond them; their relationship to the neighbor beside them; and their relationship to the natural world beneath and within them.

The special relationship of the human creature to the transcendent Creator is the major source of human uniqueness. In Genesis and in subsequent theology, that relationship is expressed graphically in the declaration that humans are made in the image of God (*imago Dei*). The doctrine of the image of God states that human creatures are so closely related to God that they bear the divine likeness.

The biblical idea that humans bear the divine image has been interpreted in Christian thought by means of three basic ideas. These ideas are:

1. The image of God in humankind attests to the glory of God as that glory is reflected in creation.

2. The image of God is a kind of brand which marks the human creature as God's highly valued property.

3. In the *imago Dei* human beings receive from God a certain property or trait which distinguishes them from all other creatures by granting them an especially intimate relationship with the Creator.

In expounding the doctrine of the image of God, some theologians have emphasized that it is the source of human dignity. It is very possible that in the thinking of the writers of Genesis the emphasis lay completely elsewhere. They may have viewed the divine image in humans as a disclosure of the glory of God rather than as a glorification of humanity. In Psalm 8, which is a poetic rewriting of the major themes of Genesis 1, reference is made to the idea of the image of God ("What is man . . . ? . . . thou has made him little less than God, and dost crown him with glory and honor"). Yet the allusions to the "glory and honor" of humans are surrounded on either side by the ascriptions, "O Lord, our Lord, how excellent is thy name in all the earth!" and the psalmist confesses a sense of thankful wonder that lowly humans have been honored ("visited") by so majestic a being as God.

If the image of God confers a certain dignity on human beings, then, it seems to be a borrowed dignity, a dignity arising not from anything humans have done or can do but from their special election by the Creator to be the recipient of his likeness. It thus seems clear that the biblical idea of the image of God is principally *a theological* idea, not an anthropological one: *it says something about the grace and goodness of God before it say anything about the special status of humankind.* It makes it clear who is Creator and who is creature, which is the image and which the reality.

The biblical emphasis on the primacy of God leads some to compare the image of God in humans to the image of an object in a mirror. The reflection of the object is not a permanent property of the mirror. If the object were removed from its place before the mirror, or if the mirror were turned so that it no longer faced the object, the mirror would no longer bear the image of the object. So it is, some would argue,[59] with the image of God. When the human creature turns away from the Creator through disobedience, it forfeits the divine image. The image is not an ineradicable property of human nature. The source of the image lies beyond human control; it lies in the smile of God upon his creature, and that smile can be reflected only when the creature is authentically related to the Creator in faith and obedience. Whatever else it means, then, the image of God does not mean that God or even the likeness of God is a permanent property that the human creature can claim, like a proud owner, to "possess."

The second thing that the image of God means for the relationship between God and humankind is that *human beings are God's highly valued property.* In its human dimension the relationship between God and creation is only incidentally a relation which limits the proud claims of the creature. It is principally a positive relation which discloses that God has a special interest in human beings. If God endows all creatures with value, it is no less true that he regards his last and most complex creature as a being of special value. The human creature alone has been made "little less than God" and crowned "with glory and honor."

Theologians who view the image of God mainly as a source of human dignity and worth sometimes compare it with the image engraved on a coin. The engraving on a coin presumably has two main functions. First, it identifies the coin's ultimate owners and sponsors—as, for example, the engraving on the nickel in my hand tells me that the nickel's ultimate owners and backers are the government and people of the United States. But, beyond this, the engraving on the coin also indicates the value, or worth, of the coin. It does this not only by its engraved numbers but also by its identification of the coin's backers. If the coin's makers and backers lack the intention or the power to stand behind the coin's stated value, then the stated value is not a fair sign of true value.

To compare the image of God in humans to the engraved images on a nation's coinage is to say in effect that the value of the human creature is doubly assured. Not only does the divine image declare the high value of its bearers, but it also declares that the guarantor of this value is none other than the God of the universe. Backed by One whose resources are infinite, human beings themselves may well be called beings of infinite value.[60] Indeed, so deeply engraved in the fiber of their being is this value, that even the dishonorable acts by which they defile or deface the image express the power the image confers. The very abuse of the image attests to its reality and to the continuing place that humans have in the esteem of God.

Though the understanding of the *imago Dei* as analogous to a coin differs in some respects from the understanding that compares it to an image in a mirror, the two comparisons are quite compatible in their essential affirmations. Taken together, they teach us that, although the human creature is God's valued property, God is assuredly not the human creature's property.

The third main element in the Christian idea of the image of God is the idea that *the special relationship granted to humans by the conferral of the image distinguishes them from all lesser creatures.* Genesis 1 makes this point in two ways—first, by making the creation of humankind the virtual capstone of creation, the culminating event of the sixth day; and second, through the substantive point of God's creative pronouncement: "Let us make man in our image, after our likeness; and let them have dominion over the fish of the sea, and over the birds of the air, and . . . over all the earth. . . . "[61] The human creature's likeness to God thus says something about its relation to the other creatures as well as about its relation to the Creator. The relationship of humans to the rest of creation ("nature," if you will) is defined by the image as a relationship of "dominion."

Human beings are like God because, like God, they enjoy a certain lordship or rule or dominion over nature.

The image of God makes the human relationship to nature special even as it expresses a special relationship to God. At the outset of this discussion of the human creature, we noted that that creature depends for its being on not one but two realities beyond itself. The concept of human dominion clarifies the character of this state of double dependency. Whereas the relationship to God is almost totally one of dependence, the human relationship to nature is mutual and reciprocal. Human beings are controlled considerably by nature, but they also exercise a considerable degree of control over nature. If you are sitting in a heated or air conditioned building as you read these words, then the artificial weather in your immediate environment is sufficient evidence to show that human beings have a certain dominion over nature. In advanced industrial societies the evidence of such dominion or control seems almost boundless—sometimes nauseatingly so.

The claim that humans bear the image of God helps substantiate the larger claim that the human creature, like all creatures, is defined relationally. The idea of the *imago Dei* points us to two relationships which are especially definitive of the common human situation: a relationship

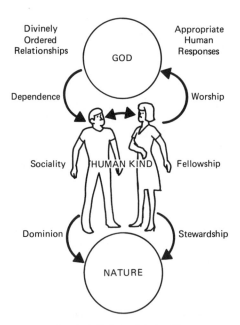

Creation's Defining Relationships

of dependence on, but likeness to, the Creator; and a relationship of dependence on, but dominion over, the lesser creatures. There is, however, yet a third relationship, which also defines the human lot. It is the relationship to fellow humans, to a social order which transcends the natural order.

The very same passage in Genesis that speaks of our likeness to God speaks also of our innate and inescapable sociality. "Let us make man in our image, after our likeness; and let them have dominion ... over all the earth. ... So God created man in his own image, in the image of God he created him, *male and female he created them.* ... "[62] Then, as if it is a part of the same general charge to humans to take charge, to have dominion, there follows a command *to the couple:* "Be fruitful and multiply, and fill the earth and subdue it. ... "[63] The sociality of humans, in other words, and their sexuality as well, are means by which they enter still further into the divine likeness. Their sociality and sexuality not only compound the power they have to take charge of the garden of creation but also provide them the means of procreation and cultural sustenance by which they can reflect the likeness and participate in the creative work of the Creator himself.

Human creatures are triply relational. Made in the image of God, they are intimately related to their Creator, and they are called to express this relationship by participating in the divine dominion and in the divine creativity. Set apart from the lesser creatures by this same image, they are bound nevertheless to recognize their dependence on, as well as their responsibility for, the natural world. United by creation in an indissoluble sociality, they are empowered by that union to play the vital role assigned them in the creative process.

QUESTIONS FOR STUDY AND DISCUSSION

1.   How does faith's critical function relate to its creative function?

2.   Why and how are creation and redemption closely related in Christian thought?

3.   On the basis of this chapter's discussion of creation, sex, and redemption, write a brief summary of the Christian view of sex. Be sure to include in your summary misconceptions and unhealthy attitudes regarding sex which have plagued Christian thought at times, and be sure, too, to indicate whether or not these misconceptions and attitudes are inevitable implications of the Christian standpoint.

4.   To what major misconceptions has the Christian idea of creation been subject historically? Whence came these misconceptions?

5. What basic convictions are affirmed by the Christian affirmation of creation? What practical effects can such convictions have on the living of life?

6. If the whole created order is essentially good, as Christians maintain, whence comes evil? Discuss the various ways in which Christian thinkers have sought to reconcile the existence of evil with faith in the goodness of God and of his creation.

7. What are the implications for the problem of evil of Genesis 1–4, the Servant Songs of Second Isaiah, and the stories of Job and Jesus?

8. What does the affirmation that "human beings are creatures" say about the human condition?

9. What are Christians saying about human life when they declare that the human creature is "made in the image of God"?

10. Summarize as well as you can the significance of the idea of creation for the Christian understanding of the human situation.

NOTES TO CHAPTER VII

1. Cf. Matthew 9:17.

2. The inseparability of the message of the Gospel from the message of Genesis has been emphasized to great effect by Karl Barth, *Church Dogmatics*, vol. III, pts. 1–3, trans. Harold Knight and others (Edinburgh: T. & T. Clark, 1958), especially Articles 40, 41, 43–48; by Emil Brunner, *The Christian Doctrine of Creation and Redemption*, trans. O. Wyon (Philadelphia: The Westminster Press, 1952); and by Regin Prenter, *Spiritus Creator*, trans. J. M. Jensen (Philadelphia: Fortress Press, 1953).

3. "The doctrine of creation is the one on which the doctrines of the Christ, of salvation and fulfilment, depend. Without it, Christianity would have ceased to exist as an independent movement." Paul Tillich, *Biblical Religion and the Search for Ultimate Reality* (Chicago: University of Chicago Press, 1955), p. 35.

4. *Genesis: A Commentary*, trans. J. H. Marks (Philadelphia: The Westminster Press, 1961), p. 44. "Election" here refers to Israel's sense of having been chosen, or elected, by God to be the covenant people.

5. I Corinthians 7:31.

6. See Chapter II, pp. 44–45.

7. The language of "saving souls," so popular in the medieval period and among some evangelical groups today, is more Platonic than biblical. The record of the earliest Christian preaching speaks, significantly, not of saving *souls* but of saving *selves*. Cf. Acts 2:40.

8. See his *Timaeus*, trans. Benjamin Jowett, *Great Books of the Western World* (Chicago: Encyclopedia Britannica, Inc., 1952), Vol. 7, pp. 447–52.

9. Cf. Genesis 1:27–31.

10. Genesis 1:6–7.

11. This Deistic principle underlay Thomas Jefferson's famous dictum in the Declaration of Independence that "All men are created equal, and . . . endowed by their Creator with certain unalienable rights." Jefferson, himself a Deist, believed that God had empowered human beings to govern themselves; therefore, the best government is that government that interferes least with the individual's control of his or her own affairs.

12. For discussions of the attempts by conservative and fundamentalist Christians to retain the sixfold structure (and thus the presumed scientific accuracy) of the creation story in Genesis, see P. Stoner, *Science Speaks* (Chicago: Moody Press, 1952); and H. J. Morris, *Scientific Creationism* (San Diego: Creation Life Publishers, 1976), especially pp. 221-30.

13. E. L. Mascall makes an observation that pertains to the world view of all (whether conservatives or Deists) who conceive the world as the work of a divine Machinist: "Even a Newtonian universe cannot escape from its Creator, but he can only intervene by overruling his own laws; there is no place for his intervention *within* them." Cf. Mascall's excellent treatment of *Christian Theology and Natural Science* (Hamden, Conn.: Archon Books, 1965), p. 185. Emphasis in original. Copyright Longman Group Ltd., Harlow, Essex, England.

14. See pp. 231-32, for a discussion of a very pertinent contribution to the subject by Jesus' teachings. Other hints of his view of creation and of nature may be found in his teachings in Matthew 6:25-33, 7:16-18, 13:31-32, and in John 15:1-8.

15. *Genesis*, p. 46.

16. Though this idea of creation from nothing is not stated explicitly in the Genesis account, it is implicit both in the traditional absolute rendering of the account's opening phrase ("In the beginning," with no "of" attached to tie God's creation to the beginning of a particular thing, as opposed to everything) and the Hebrew verb rendered "create" (*bara'*). On the preferability of the traditional absolute rendering to other possible renderings of the account's opening phrase, see von Rad, *Genesis*, p. 46, and C. A. Simpson, *The Interpreter's Bible*, ed. G. A. Buttrick (New York: Abington-Cokesbury Press, 1952), Vol. I, pp. 466-67. For the meaning of *bara'*, see von Rad, p. 47: "It is correct to say that the verb *bara'*, 'create,' contains the idea both of complete effortlessness and *creatio ex nihilo*, since it is never connected with any statement of the material."

17. Genesis 1:2. "The deep" (Hebrew $t^e hom$) is very likely a reference to a fathomless "sea of chaos" (von Rad, *Genesis*, p. 47). Its implied identification with the earth in a formless state, together with the earth's identification (in verse 1) as a divine creature, makes it clear that the Hebrew $t^e hom$, despite its etymological affinities with the Babylonian *Tiamat*, is not, like *Tiamat*, a principle coeternal with God.

18. Cf. Genesis 1:3. One of the most obvious traits of water, of course, is that it takes its form not from itself but from its container. It is thus an apt symbol for a formless "something."

19. "Aspect" is perhaps the better word, when the story is considered in terms of later Christian reflection. Whereas "phase" implies that there is a *chronological* order in God's initial creative activity, traditional Christian thought has emphasized that the ascription of a chronology to that activity is inappropriate. That the "days" of Genesis 1 were not chronological or temporal days is apparent from the fact that, in the creation story itself, the sun, in terms of whose course temporal days are measured, was not created until the fourth day. Cf. F. Copleston, *A History of Philosophy, Volume II: Medieval Philosophy* (Westminster, Md.: The Newman Press, 1950), p. 76.

20. May the writers, who wrote long after the events of the Exodus and of the conquest of Canaan, have had in mind two events in Israel's salvation history—namely, the parting of the Red Sea (Exodus 14:21-31) and the parting of the Jordan (Joshua 3:14-17)?

21. The most basic of all metaphysical questions, according to Martin Heidegger, is "Why is there something and not nothing?" This is the fundamental question that faith in creation seeks to answer. Cf. Heidegger, "What is Metaphysics?" trans. R. F. C. Hull and A. Crick, in *Existence and Being*, ed. W. Brock (Chicago: Henry Regnery Company, 1949), pp. 325-61, especially p. 349.

22. In the Christian view, the glory of the Giver and the well-being of his creatures are intimately related. According to St. Thomas Aquinas, says Frederick Copleston, "God's glory, the manifestation of His goodness, is ... not something separate from the good of creatures, for creatures attain their end, do the best for themselves, by manifesting the divine goodness." *A History of Philosophy, Volume II: Medieval Philosophy,* p. 366. Some three centuries after St. Thomas's time, Martin Luther sounded much the same theme: "God, who alone is true and righteous and powerful in himself, wants to be such also outside himself, namely, in us, in order that he may thus be glorified (for this is the glory of any good that is in any one that it must pour itself out beyond itself among others). ..." From *Lectures on Romans.* The Library of Christian Classics, vol. XV, newly translated and edited by Wilhelm Pauck, copyright © MCMLVI, W. L. Jenkins, p. 79. Used by permission of the Westminster Press.

23. For a brief but incisive outline of Augustine's concept of the evolution of the Stoics' "seminal reasons" (*rationes seminales* [Lat.] or *logoi spermatikoi* [Greek]), and of his reasons for developing such a concept, see Copleston, *A History of Philosophy,* Vol. II, pp. 76–77.

24. A clear and forceful exposition of this idea is found in the *Summa Theologiae* of St. Thomas Aquinas, Part I, Question 104, Article 1, Reply to Objection 4: "God does not maintain things in existence by any new action but by the continuation of the act whereby he bestows *esse* [=existence]; an act subject neither to change nor time." T. C. O'Brien, trans., *Summa Theologiae* (New York: McGraw-Hill Book Company, and London: Eyre and Spottiswoode, 1975), Vol. XIV, p. 43. Copyright Blackfriars 1975. O. Zöckler characterized the more general medieval view thus: "The scholastics designated the conservation of the world as a continuance of creation. ... The creation, the preservation, and the governance of the world are an inseparable group of activities." "Creation and Preservation," *The New Schaff-Herzog Encyclopedia of Religious Knowledge,* ed. S. M. M. Johnson (New York and London: Funk & Wagnalls Book Publishing Company, 1909), Vol. III, p. 303.

25. Because the world picture they inherited from the Greeks and antiquity generally was that of a vertical, two-story universe, with heaven occupying the top story and earth the bottom, the new could emerge not as new *natural* beings but only as *supernatural* beings newly introduced to time. This is the significance, for the present context, of the miracle of transubstantiation in the Eucharist or Lord's Supper: the bread and wine became new not historically (in terms of their temporal, natural appearance) but supernaturally (making available the supernatural benefits of Christ's exalted body and blood). Regarding the shift from medieval naturalism to modern historism, see E. L. Fackenheim, *The Religious Dimension in Hegel's Thought* (Bloomington: Indiana University Press, 1967), pp. 10–12; F. Gogarten, *Demythologizing and History,* trans. N. H. Smith (London: Camelot Press, 1955), pp. 21–33; and (also by F. Gogarten) *The Reality of Faith,* trans. C. Michalson and others (Philadelphia: The Westminster Press, 1959), pp. 9–27, especially p. 23: "To medieval man ... the real was what is, was, and has always been. ... to modern man ... the real is what is yet to be, what will come into being through him. ..." Copyright © W. L. Jenkins MCMLIX. Used by permission of the Westminster Press.

26. See R. G. Collingwood, *The Idea of Nature* (New York: Oxford University Press, Inc., 1960), pp. 121–77.

27. When nature is left to itself (without human attempts at crossbreeding or hybridization), the evolution of species and of more complex and multi-functional variations within species is an extremely slow process. Cf. R. J. Nogar, *The Wisdom of Evolution* (New York: New American Library, 1966), pp. 45–68.

28. See Chapter V, pp. 163–65 and Chapter VI, pp. 188–89.

29. Restated in theological shorthand, these convictions are: (1) God must exist if anything is to exist; (2) God or ultimate Reality must be trustworthy if creative human endeavor is to be worthwhile; and (3) God must be both powerful enough to keep the universe in being and moral enough to sustain human trust.

30. These ties are not only physical but psychological. Cf. Viktor Frankl, *Man's Search for Meaning: An Introduction to Logotherapy,* trans. Ilse Lasch (Boston: Beacon Press, 1963); and *The Doctor and the Soul,* trans. R. Wilson and C. Wilson (New York: Alfred A. Knopf, Inc., 1955).

31. As Schubert M. Ogden remarks in his thoughtful essay, "The Reality of God," "Even the suicide who intentionally takes his own life implicitly affirms the ultimate meaning of his tragic choice." *The Reality of God and Other Essays* (New York: Harper & Row, Publishers, Inc., 1963), p. 36.

32. For an excellent selection of Schweitzer's statements on reverence for life, see Charles R. Joy, ed., *Albert Schweitzer: An Anthology* (Boston: Beacon Press, 1947), pp. 259–82; for some of the ethical implications of Schweitzer's attitude, cf. A. Schweitzer, "The Ethics of Reverence for Life," *Christendom*, Vol. I, no. 2, (Winter 1936), 225–39.

33. The phrase is Harvey Cox's. For his discussion of the idea behind the phrase, see *The Secular City*, rev. ed. (New York: The Macmillan Company, 1966), pp. 19–22.

34. See Chapter I, pp. 21–23.

35. Genesis 1:26–27. Cf. pp. 265–67.

36. Only on the second day is the word of divine approbation missing. Although the reason for its omission is not definitely known, C. A. Simpson reasons that "If its omission is intentional on the part of the author, it is probably due to the fact that the business of bringing the waters to order was not yet completed" at the end of the second day. See *The Interpreter's Bible*, Vol. I, p. 472.

37. For a particularly vivid description of such a divinely staged drama, see the imagined conversation between Mephistopheles and Dr. Faustus with which Bertrand Russell opened his essay, "A Free Man's Worship," in *Mysticism and Logic and Other Essays* (London: George Allen & Unwin, Ltd., 1917), pp. 46–47.

38. Besides the discussion of Hegel's views in Chapter V, see G. W. F. Hegel, *The Philosophy of History*, trans. J. Sibree, *Great Books of the Western World*, ed. R. M. Hutchins (Chicago: Encyclopaedia Britannica, Inc., 1952), Vol. 46, pp. 160–78 *et passim*.

39. The moral answer to the problem of evil can be classified as a subtype of the teleological answer; God allows evil, according to the moral answer, for a specific purpose or *telos:* the development of a moral universe. (The moral answer was favored by St. Augustine, who argued in *The City of God* that God allows evil in order to test and refine the saints whom he has chosen to replenish the heavenly ranks vacated by the fallen angels.)

40. Trans. O. Schreiner, cited by Crane Brinton, ed., *The Portable Age of Reason Reader* (New York: The Viking Press, 1956), p. 375. Reprinted by permission of Viking Penguin, Inc.

41. Genesis 3:15.

42. Genesis 3:14.

43. Genesis 3:17–19a.

44. Genesis 3:19b.

45. Romans 8:19–22.

46. Cf. R. G. Collingwood, *The Idea of Nature*, pp. 3–4, 31–32.

47. Job. 1:8.

48. The artistry with which Job is kept from sounding arrogant and self-righteous as he answers his accusers is impressive. Cf. especially Job 6:24, 7:20, 9:1–3, and 19:4–6.

49. Job 13:15 (KJV).

50. Luke 22:44.

51. Matthew 26:39; cf. Mark 14:36 and Luke 22:42.

52. Isaiah 53:3–5,7; cf. Mark 10:33–34, 14:61, 15:5; Matthew 8:17, 26:63, 27:12–14; and Luke 18:31–33 and 23:9.

53. In this connection, see especially Isaiah 49:1–7 and 51:1–6.

54. Matthew 9:12 (=Mark 2:17, Luke 5:31).

55. *Jesus in His Homeland* (New York: Charles Scribner's Sons, 1957), p. 166.

56.   Matthew 27:46 (=Mark 15:34).

57.   Romans 8:35, 37–39.

58.   Cf. Hugh Martin, ed., *The Practice of the Presence of God and Selections from the Little Flowers of St. Francis* (London: SCM Press, 1956).

59.   The best-known champion of this position was the late Karl Barth, who held that apart from God's intervention in Christ there is absolutely no contact point (*Anknüp-fungspunkt*) or analogy between God and the human creature. Cf. Barth's famous debate with Emil Brunner on this question in P. Fraenkel, trans., *Natural Theology* (London: Centenary Press, 1946).

60.   Such a theology underlay the high view of the human individual in classical liberalism and Deism.

61.   Genesis 1:26.

62.   Genesis 1:26–27. Emphasis added.

63.   Genesis 1:28a.

VIII.   Faith and Becoming:

The Word as Redemption

C HRISTIANITY HAS DONE many remarkable things with Christ. It has made him the object of its worship, the central article in its creeds, the hero of its hymns, and the dominant figure in its art. It has enshrined and represented him in every sort of medium from stained glass to grocer's bread and grape juice.[1] Yet, for all of this, it has never completely understood him. Though his identity and career are the two fundaments of Christian faith, though they give it both its name and its distinctive character, that faith does not fully comprehend them. In struggling to define the identity of Jesus in the fourth and fifth centuries, the Church was forced to resort to paradox: he is "at once complete in Godhead and complete in manhood, truly God and truly man . . . ; the characteristics of each nature being preserved and coming together to form one person and subsistence."[2]

On their face these formulas do not make much sense. How can a person be simultaneously completely divine and completely human? Yet the formulas do express the definitive or "orthodox" understanding of Christ within Christendom. What, then, are we to make of them? Were their formulators simply playing with words? Were they engaged in priestly pettifoggery or verbal hocus-pocus? To ask such questions is to ask for the motives behind, as well as the meanings within, the formulations. These motives and meanings are accessible, however, only to those who are willing to enter into the uncertainties, the doubts, and the debates, as well as the faith, of the formulators themselves. This done, it eventually becomes clear that the fundamental question which produced those doubts and debates was not "Who is Christ?" but rather "Why did Christ come?" or "What did he come to do?"[3] It was the resolution of these questions that led to the description of Christ's identity, not vice versa.

In their answer to the question "Why did Christ come?" Christians have generally been united: Christ came to save or redeem humankind, and perhaps beyond that the entire cosmos,[4] from the effects of sin. But ironically the general agreement among Christians on that question has led to greater virulence in their disputes about the nature of redemption, the extent of the need for it, and the way Christ wrought it. Because the issue of redemption is so important, many believers hold that questions about it are worth fighting over. Many of the denominations and reform movements within contemporary Christianity have resulted from just such fighting.

The long history of division and debate regarding redemption's nature, extent, and form cannot occupy us here.[5] We must concentrate instead on the precipitating questions—Why did Christ come? What did he come to do? Who was he anyway?—and on a rationale for, and a résumé of, the eventual answers of mainstream Christianity to these questions.

REDEMPTION'S SETTING AND PURPOSE: CREATION AND THE CREATOR'S IMAGE

It is no accident that in its earlier historical stages the Christian debate about salvation or redemption was a debate about creation. Whether or not it is true, as Chesterton averred,[6] that the essence of every picture is the frame, it is assuredly true that the existence of any picture depends on a frame. Apart from delimiting boundaries of a physical or mental sort, no object or arrangement among objects comes into focus for human viewers.[7] The Christian understanding of redemption depends, as we have observed before, on the broader and more basic understanding of the world which is given in the concept of creation. When the unity and goodness of the created order were questioned by ancient gnosticism, concern for the reality of salvation as well as for the integrity of creation compelled the Church to respond.

Creation is the necessary backdrop to salvation because it defines the terms of the salvation drama. Goodness and evil receive their definition from creation's nature and purpose. Since salvation by anyone's definition must foster what is good and combat what is evil, the understanding of good and evil implied in the concept of creation inevitably defines the aims of salvation. Indeed, one may go so far as to say that the ultimate aims of salvation are one with those of creation.[8]

In the view of the Creator, one may reasonably presume, whatever agrees with the purpose of divine creation is good and whatever thwarts or resists the accomplishment of that purpose is evil. This conception of good and evil is in thorough accord with that developed in our discussion of the problem of evil in Chapter VII. There we saw that good resides in creatures through their origin in God, and that evil is a perversion or distortion of the created order. Good is a primary reality, evil a parasitical perversion of that reality. As a distortion of the created order, evil obviously defies the divine purpose in creation. In this section we shall define creation's purpose as clearly as possible, in the awareness that God's work of redemption in Christ seeks to fulfill that purpose by overcoming the evil that obstructs it.

In concrete, biblical terms, the purpose of creation is the establishment of the Kingdom of God. The Kingdom of God is, quite simply, the rule of God over the universe. But if the Kingdom of God is something as simple as the rule of God, why is its establishment problematic? Is God not the Creator of the universe? Can the maker of a thing not make it so that he can control or rule it? The obvious answer of Christians to each of the last two questions is yes. If that is so, why is the establishment of the rule of God not automatic? Why, in other words, is God's continued involvement in the world, as its Redeemer, necessary?

The answer lies in the peculiar character of the world that God created and in the consequent peculiar meaning of the phrase "rule of God." The world God created is not an automaton. It is rather a world, as it were, with a mind of its own. Dependent on God for its existence, it is nevertheless separate from God in essence. The establishment of the rule of God is consequently not a matter of mechanical or logical necessity but entails instead a dramatic bid for the loyalty and love of semi-independent and relatively free beings. The rule of God is thus personal rather than mechanical or technical in nature.

That the world is made for persons, for the maturation and fulfillment of persons, is clearly affirmed in the Genesis accounts of creation. As we saw in Chapter VII, the human creature, the one creature who is a person in the sense of an autonomous being, is the capstone of creation. Fashioned in the divine likeness, the human creature alone is given authority to rule ("have dominion over") nature. God thus shares with men and women a very significant divine power: the power to be a shaper, to modify and regulate nature, to "make history." This power, this gift from the Creator, is the basic ingredient of human autonomy.

Though human autonomy is one of the gifts of creation, it is not the ultimate aim of creation. That aim, we have noted, is the establishment of the rule of God. What, then, is the nature of the relationship between the gift of creation—human autonomy—and the aim of creation—the rule of God? Must that relationship not be problematic at best? Can human beings be genuinely *free* if God rules their lives? Can God actually *rule* free beings?

The answer to these questions requires a deeper analysis of the nature of human freedom or autonomy. Human beings must be free, Christians believe, if they are to be persons as distinguished from things. But it is equally true that freedom must be personal if it is to be freedom. The essence of freedom, in other words, is an ability in one person to respond to the call of other persons. Freedom is essentially a personal ability to respond to persons. It is a power to be accountable, a power to answer *by* one's actions as well as *for* one's actions. It is, to use a word coined earlier, a certain response-ability.

When freedom is defined this way, the biblical concepts of the image of God and of the rule of God take on a different significance. To the degree that the image of God means personal freedom, it also must mean the ability to respond to the call of God and to the appeals of other persons. To the degree that the rule of God is the rule of free beings by a Being who is supremely free, it must be a rule based not on raw power but on personal or interpersonal communion. The remaining paragraphs of this section will be devoted to an elaboration and correlation of these concepts of the image of God and the rule of God. Together, as we shall see, these concepts define God's purpose in creation and redemption.

The image of God is the likeness of God. The human creature is like God because it receives from God certain powers that resemble God's own powers. Besides the power to control nature, shape the environment, and make history, the human creature also receives power to live a life which is responsive to the spirit of creative love abroad in the world. The most important resemblance between God and humans is precisely this power to love as God loves. In creation God not only creates raw natural power but also unleashes the sublime personal power of love. For the sake of such love, indeed, God restrains and restricts his fearful power. Accordingly, though the powers of nature are immense and awesome, they are still reduced to relative insignificance in the presence of persons. What shall it profit a man, Jesus asked, if he gain the whole world and lose his own soul?[9] Such a man would have struck a poor bargain: in gaining much he would have lost all. In a similar vein, Pascal remarked:

> If the universe were to crush him, man would still be more noble than that which killed him, because he knows that he dies and the advantage which the universe has over him; the universe knows nothing of this.... By space the universe encompasses and swallows me up like an atom; by thought I comprehend the world.[10]

The image of God in humans does not consist of brute strength or raw natural power but of the power to be a person, a thinking, feeling, deciding, acting being who, like the Creator and through these capacities, can comprehend nature and respond to other persons.

A proper understanding of God's image thus depends on a proper regard for the distinction between personal power and natural power. Similarly, a true understanding of the rule of God depends on the recognition that God himself is more properly compared to a personal being than to a natural being. To recognize this is to recognize that the anthropomorphic or personal language used to describe God in Scripture is not incidental or accidental to the Subject it describes. The language is personal because God is personal. The ultimate expression of the Word or essence of God occurs, in the Christian view, when that Word incarnates itself in a person. In commenting on this act of Incarnation, Paul Tillich wrote:

> The Word appears *as* a person and only secondarily in the words of a person. The Word, the principle of divine self-manifestation, appearing as a person, is the fulfilment of biblical personalism.... God is so personal that we see what he is only in a personal life. God can become man, because man is person and because God is personal.[11]

The rule of God is not the rule of a blind power or of a sighted but uncaring tyrant but of a being who is profoundly and thoroughly personal. The rule of God and the image of God—in other words, the Kingdom of God and the freedom of humans—are quite compatible, for the personal freedom of humans is a major intention of the personal rule of the Creator.

Though the setting in which redemption occurs is one of vast and awe-inspiring proportions, it is also a setting in which the personal dimension outweighs the natural in importance. The natural dimension is by no means to be despised because of this. The conviction of Teilhard de Chardin that the natural universe has a built-in bias toward personhood is surely far closer to the Judaeo-Christian perception of things than is the view of some medieval ascetics that nature is the implacable enemy of the soul. The God who makes persons on the sixth day is the same God who makes nature during the first five. Persons and natural beings are best understood as compatriots in the cosmic drama, a fact symbolized in the Genesis story of Eden by the active involvement, with Eve, of the serpent.

The setting of the drama of redemption is thus the created order as a whole; the main actors in the drama are the Creator and the human creature; and the action which transpires between the actors is personal. The image of God in humans makes them personal, addressable beings who enjoy the freedom to respond to divine initiatives in history along with the capacity to participate in the creative processes of nature. The rule of God over the created order does not deny but instead affirms the autonomy and worth of persons.

What are the implications of this understanding of the Creator and of creation for the events of redemption? What does such an understanding contribute toward an answer to the question "Why did Christ come?" The implications are important, and their contribution to our answer is significant. If, as we have assumed, the aims of creation and the aims of redemption are ultimately the same, we may recognize in the light of the concept of creation that Christ came in order to establish a new covenant, a new relationship between the divine Person and human persons, a relationship through which the rule of God breaks into history so as to confer a new autonomy and a new dignity on the human creature. In creation God brings creatures into being. In Christ he grants to human beings, beyond the gift of being, a certain "power to become"[12]—the power to become his children as well as his creatures, free coparticipants in the cosmic drama as well as recipients of the gift of life.

REDEMPTION'S NECESSITY:
THE SIN OF THE CREATURE AND THE JUDGMENT OF THE CREATOR

The image of God in human beings assigns them a peculiar position within reality. On the one hand, the image relates them to God as personal beings fashioned in the divine likeness. On the other, it relates them to nature by conferring on them both the authority and the power to control the natural order. The image thus places the human creature in an ambiguous and ambivalent situation, poised between the Creator beyond itself and the lesser creatures beneath itself. The image, then, simultaneously signifies a certain dependence and a certain dignity: a dependence on the Creator and a dignity that distinguishes humans from less gifted creatures.

The Garden of Eden stories in Genesis 2 and 3 portray the peculiarity of the human situation in a remarkably vivid and effective way. In the first of the stories, God creates Adam by breathing life into the dust of the ground. Human nature itself, the story thus suggests, is a curious compound of the earthly and the heavenly. The divine principle is the supreme and governing principle, but the tug of the earthly element remains strong even in the lordliest of creatures. Though Adam and Eve are assigned to be lords of the garden, "to till it and keep it,"[13] they nevertheless are very much at home in the garden, and the kinship between the human creature and lesser creatures is so strong that the

Creator can entertain the thought of finding a partner for Adam among the lower animals.[14]

The human creature is thus situated in a distinctive position, somewhere between the Creator and the nonhuman creatures, and it is this situation which supplies the occasion for sin.

As most of the biblical authors conceive of it, sin originates in a highly personal action, an act of rebellion (Hebrew *pesha*) against the Creator and the law of creation. Only a creature constituted as the human creature is constituted has the capacity to sin, for sin as rebellion means the flaunting of the divine will by a creature with a will of its own. In conferring freedom on the human creature, the image of God ironically makes possible the defiance of God.

A walk through Eden with Eve may serve to dramatize this point. Let us imagine ourselves companions of the queen of the creatures as she takes her first stroll through the garden of paradise. Perhaps Eve's ears still ring with the acclaim of her Creator who, pleased with his latest achievement, has commissioned the human couple to rule the garden. If that is true, the echo of the Creator's voice soon has a rival for her attention. She encounters a serpent, a creature whose lowliness seems to accent her own lordliness. The contrast between the lowly creature and the lordly one is so great that through its very lowliness the serpent seems to speak: "Hey-ho, Eve! You're a pretty important character around this place. Hasn't God made you ruler of the garden? Hasn't he given you his own lordly image? Why, compared with lowly creatures like me, you could even pass for God! Did God really set any limits on this marvelous lordship of yours? Surely, if he did, he couldn't have meant it! Why should he make you so glorious a being if he didn't mean for your glory to rival his?"[15]

So Eve hears the serpent. She hears it, and she finds it quite convincing, for its voice seems simply another echo of the voice of God. Has God not indeed commanded her to rule the garden? Has her Creator not assigned her to this lordly station among the creatures? The serpent's word is but a reinforcement of the divine Word! She must indeed take charge, must indeed behave in lordly fashion.

Eve hears the word of the serpent, and she finds it quite believable because it seems to echo the word from God. But the echo hides a distortion. The echo sets the freedom of the creature, which the Creator intends to be fulfilled through the rule of God, in opposition to the rule of God. In defiance of the Creator's command, Eve eats the forbidden fruit from the tree of the knowledge of good and evil. She takes her understanding of good and evil from a creature instead of from the Creator and thus throws off the rule of God in favor of rule by the creature.

The story of Eve may be illuminated, perhaps, by comparing it to another story. In one of his celebrated fables, Aesop described a little dog who wanders contentedly down a country road with a bone in his teeth. Eventually he comes to a small roadside pond. From the road bank he looks into the pond, and there he sees another dog looking back at him, also with a bone in his teeth. Instinctively, he decides that that bone, too, should be his, and so he plunges into the water, and in snapping at the watery image drops his bone to the bottom of the pond.

Aesop's point is easily seen. His little dog was deceived, and in confusing an image with a reality pursued the image and lost touch with the reality. Much the same thing happens to Eve: in beholding within herself the image of God, she confuses that image with the reality of God and in worshipping the image loses touch with the reality. Her sense of dignity overpowers her sense of dependence, and so she asserts her independence of divine authority.

The story of Adam and Eve is, as we have noted before,[16] a highly symbolic story—a *myth* in the theological, as opposed to the popular, sense.[17] This means that it should not be taken literally, as though it were an objective historical account of the life of the first human couple, but that it should instead be understood as a description of the common human situation. The story itself suggests this through the names it assigns its hero and heroine. "Adam" is a Hebrew word meaning "man" in the sense of "humankind," whereas "Eve" is a Hebrew noun meaning "life." The story of Adam and Eve thus may be viewed as a story which discloses something about the whole of humankind and the nature of human life. If this is true, the story of Adam and Eve is the Bible's way of telling your story and my story. What the writer of the Eden story suggests is that you and I, too, are implicated in Eve's act of rebellion—that her sin is a sin of which we all are guilty.

Because of its universality, this special sin which Genesis attributes to the Mother of humanity was designated in older theologies by a special name: *original sin*. A more accurate name for it, perhaps, would be the *originating* sin, the *condition* of sin from which all sinful *acts* originate.

In Scripture the original or originating sin has a definite, concrete name. It is called *idolatry*, for it amounts to a displacement of God by a false god, an idol. In Eve's case (and that means in every case), the idol, the graven image, is the image of God itself. *The universal and originating human sin is the displacement of the reality of God by the image of God in oneself.* In every case idolatry amounts finally to self-worship, a state of self-centeredness in which all other creatures and the Creator himself become satellites of the great god Self.

It is the Christian view that we all are caught in webs of self-worship. We have dethroned God and set in his place our own lordly likeness to him. Or so matters would appear. But in reality something even worse has happened. Though we *think* we have exalted the lordly image of God, we have in fact lost that image. Instead of receiving our definition of ourselves from the God beyond us, we have received it from the lesser creatures, the serpents and other lowly creatures beneath us. Instead of obtaining our understanding of good and evil from the transcendent Creator, we look for it in finite beings. Instead of seeking our own good in the One who is supremely good, the *Summum Bonum*, we seek it in the transient goods of the created order. Instead of asking God, "What is man? Who am I? What is good?" we ask serpents, trees, and other lesser creatures, preferring their flattering, pride-inducing answers to the truth. In doing this we ironically surrender our dominion over such creatures and become their dupes, their bondslaves, owners possessed by our own possessions. We forfeit the image of the Creator in favor of an image of superior self-sufficiency projected on us by fellow creatures, and in the process we become the slaves of the creatures who so define us. Though our *sense* of dependence has given way to a sense of self-sufficiency, in actual *fact* we are more dependent than ever.

Sin originates, then, in self-worship. The self that worships itself is ironically less worthy of respect than the self that worships God, for it receives its self-image not from a Creator who empowers and liberates by conferring actual dominion but from creatures who demean and enslave by conferring delusions of unlimited dominion. A powerful and terrible irony thus victimizes sinners. In exalting themselves at the expense of the Creator, they in fact demean themselves by becoming the slaves and dupes of sycophantic creatures. The creature who would not be ruled by God is ruled by fellow creatures. The order of creation is thus reversed. The divine intention was that God should rule humankind and that humans should, within divinely imposed limits, rule nature. But within the regime of sin, nature rules humankind, who in turn, through acts of deluded self-adulation, rules God out of existence.

To illustrate this point, let us take another walk through the garden of creation, this time not with or as Eve but instead with or as a modern scientist. As we approach creation scientifically, we must inevitably be impressed by the power that science has given us to understand and control the natural order. The technologies that science has enabled us to develop accentuate our power to control the lesser creatures. As a result, the temptation is strong to let our very sense of control control us. The submissiveness of the creatures that we control may persuade us that we are indeed lords of all we survey. And so we may join in the paean of Swinburne: "Glory to man in the highest, for man is the master of things!"

Nature, as subtle as any serpent, may by the very subtle device of its own submission gain control over human consciousness. When this happens we become no longer simply scientists but philosophic naturalists, persons for whom the only significant, life-determining relationship is the relation to nature. We come to see that nature submits to us more fully and efficiently when we submit to its laws, and through such submission we devise technologies of self-advancement which give us an even more exalted image of human powers. Eventually our naturalism may become so thoroughgoing that we may say with Laplace: "God? We have no need of that hypothesis!"[18]

If such philosophic naturalism illustrates most clearly the reversal of creation's intended order, that could well be because the naturalist is more honest, or perhaps simply more self-aware, than the rest of us are. In the Christian view, every human being, whether a professing naturalist or not, is controlled to some extent by the distorted self-image that results from letting the word from below, rather than the Word from beyond, define life's meaning. The human creature is still very much a relational being, even within the regime of sin. The tie to nature has simply displaced the tie to God as the governing relationship.

The distortion of the created order wrought by sin touches every dimension of that order. This is clearly a part of the message of Genesis 3. Eve's defiance of God spread like a contagion to Adam, and Adam returned the compliment by blaming the entire problem on Eve.[19] Rebellion against God thus quickly becomes perfidy toward fellow humans. For her part, Eve, despite her adherence to the serpent's counsel, placed the blame for her disobedience entirely on the tempter.[20] Like the modern lawbreaker who blames his or her criminal behavior on nature (hereditary conditioning) or environment (social or economic conditioning), Eve points an accusing finger at her circumstances. Responsibility lay outside herself, in powers over which she had no (!) control. The irony is again apparent: the creature given authority to control the whole operation is the creature who pleads no control!

The severing of the relation to God thus has an immediate impact on the relations to neighbor and to nature. Their relationship to God in ruins, Eve and Adam flee from the divine presence, hiding themselves (the story says) among the trees of the garden. It is as though they envy the subhuman creatures their immunity to prosecution by the divine Judge-advocate. And so, as the Lord comes through the garden, calling out "Where are you?"[21] we can all but hear a tragicomic answer from Eve and Adam: "Nobody here, Lord; nobody but us trees!" If we can but bury ourselves deeply enough in nature, they seem to reason, no longer need we answer for what we do or who we become; nature must become our mask, a giant fig leaf which can hide our nakedness, our vulnerability, our guilt, from the judging gaze of the Creator.

Thus would the sole creature who is able to respond to the Creator's

Used courtesy of Rick L. Miller

The Damnation of Adam and Eve

initiatives forfeit that very power to respond, if he or she could but avoid the consequences of the act of rebellion. Yet (to add another irony to our list) that forfeiture itself is one of the worst of the rebellion's consequences. Sin injures not only nature and neighbor but also the human rebel. As the neighbor and nature lose their integrity, as they become mere routes of escape or disguises artfully employed to release the self from responsibility, the self too loses its integrity, sacrificing the very control over nature that attests its resemblance to God.

The effects of the sinner's rebellion are thus severe. Though relationships still define the self, the governing relationship is now the relation to nature rather than that to the Creator. The rebel's whole way of relating to reality is diseased and distorted by the radical act of idolatry. The rebel still seeks the good—but he or she now sets the good in opposition to the Source of good, the creature against the Creator. The evil fostered by such creaturely rebellion is most fundamentally a misalignment or disordering of relationships. It is not a thing but a way of dealing with things; it is not a what but a *how*.

Despite sin's distortion of life's defining relationships, human beings are no less religious because they are sinners. In popular thought, religion and sin are frequently thought to be contradictory. From the Christian standpoint, a very different view of these terms is possible. Human creatures are religious, whether or not they are sinners, for religion is a name for the bare *fact* of human relatedness, whereas sin is a name for the condition or the state of health of such relatedness. The real human problem, from the biblical point of view, is not atheism or irreligion but polytheism or idolatry. Practically speaking, atheism and irreligion are impossibilities. No human creature can remain human without worshipping and serving some value of supreme importance to him or her, and so no human can be a *practicing* atheist. Similarly, no human creature can remain human without living in terms of relationships organized and governed by a supreme Value, and so no human can be completely without religion. The question is not whether humans are to be atheists as opposed to believers, or unrelated atoms as opposed to parts of a larger whole, but rather whether they will be governed by the relation to God or by the relation to false gods.

That the gods humans worship are many is a fact beyond dispute. On Christian premises a case can be made that the number of gods extant at a given moment is roughly equal to the number of people alive at that moment. If such an estimate of the number of the gods misses the mark, it probably does so on the low side. Humans are, as Voltaire observed, incurably religious, and their minds are, as another Frenchman named Calvin observed, factories of idols. That humans are endowed by their

Creator with an irrepressible power to create is nowhere more obvious than in their amazing capacity to manufacture deities.

The existence of so huge a pantheon of deified ideas and idols attests not only to the almost infinite inventiveness of the human psyche but also to a nearly infinite restlessness in the psyche which inspires such inventiveness. On the subjective level (that is, within the domain of the self per se), sinners are persistent monotheists; they persist in serving one God—the self. But such worship fails to satisfy the deeper longings of the self;[22] deep-seated doubts cast a shadow on the self's vaunted sense of sufficiency. So the sinner turns outward, seeking some assistant deity, some God who can function as a "co-pilot"[23] to the high god Self. The rebel's subjective monotheism thus contains within itself the seeds of an objective polytheism, for the deficiencies in the self's exalted but erroneous image of itself eventually force it to look to the objective world for fellow gods who might conceivably bolster its own flagging fortunes.

In the Christian view, the restlessness of the psyche reveals not only the incapacity of the self (and of all things finite) to serve as a god but also another very important fact, that the "dethroned" God is not dead. The human being who lives as if God is no more, or as if he had never been, suffers from a great delusion. "The *fool*," asserted the psalmist, "says in his heart, 'There is no God!' "[24] From the Judaeo-Christian point of view, only a fool, one who is thoroughly fooled, could make such an assertion. The human "heart"—mind, soul, spirit, personality —is in fact so constituted that anyone who is alert to what is going on within the daily quest for satisfactions (and within the just as daily dissatisfaction with attained satisfactions) must be aware that the quest itself is impelled by an infinite Reality.

Here we need to recall that the human quest for redemption, for healing and wholeness, takes place in the context of creation. Creation,

THE BORN LOSER   By Art Sansom

Reprinted by permission of Newspaper Enterprise Association (NEA).

as we noted in the last chapter, has critical side effects. The creation of the new comprises an implicit critique of the old, and, beyond this, God's creation works as a constant critique of all human creations.[25] God the Creator is simultaneously God the Judge. The glory and beauty of divine creation stand in awful contrast to even the most noble products of human creativity. It is precisely such glory, such beauty and creative perfection, resident within the noblest of God's creatures, the human one, that inspires that creature's quest for the Perfect and the Infinite and leaves him or her dissatisfied with all lesser realities.

Within creation, then, there resides a certain "hunger and thirst after righteousness."[26] The self, like all creatures, is a good being but not a self-sufficient one. Despite its pretensions to moral and even divine grandeur, and despite its delusions that it deserves the worship of fellow creatures, it is thoroughly dependent on the Creator for both its being and its goodness. Its persistent dissatisfaction with the states of being and goodness to which it attains is a constant signal of its dependency. Such dissatisfaction constantly indicates that the divine intention in creation is still alive and that it stands in judgment on the actuality of human attainment.

Divine judgment is in fact the first element in the transaction of redemption. The aim of divine judgment, as we noted in Chapter VII, is not punitive but redemptive. In his *Confessions*, St. Augustine penned a prayer which stands with the Lord's Prayer, the prayer in Gethsemane, and the prayer of St. Francis as one of the peaks of Christian devotion. Perhaps no single sentence in Christian literature describes the continuity of intention and action which unites divine creation, divine judgment, and divine redemption more effectively than the single line of Augustine's prayer: "Thou has made us, O Lord, for Thyself, and our hearts are restless until they find rest in Thee." In its opening phrase ("Thou has made us, O Lord"), the prayer acknowledges both the act and the Source of creation. In its next phrase ("for Thyself"), it recognizes that creation is not a pointless divine activity but a purposive process which must end, as it began, in the Creator. With the phrase "our hearts are restless," the saint confesses a sense that creation is no mere event in the past but rather is a living and judging reality in the present: living to the degree that God and his purpose remain alive in our restless hearts, judging to the extent that restlessness reflects the great distance between the intention of creation and the state of creatures within the regime of sin. Finally, with the words "they find rest in Thee," the prayer gives voice to the redemptive force and aim of the divinely implanted restlessness.

Though God's acts of creation, judgment, and redemption may be perceived as separate, they must at the same time be perceived as synchronous. The intention first expressed in creation remains alive as a judging restlessness within the souls of creatures, and this same intention is to be completed and perfected through the reunion with ("rest in") God effected by redemption. Throughout the process—at the beginning in the making, in the middle in the making restless, and at the end in the finding of rest—the same prime Actor is alive and active, working all in all. We must now attempt to learn something of the will and ways of that Actor.

REDEMPTION'S SOURCE:
THE GOD WHO IS ALIVE

The statement "God is alive" is for Christians far more than a truism. It is by no means to be equated with the simple statement "God exists." The fact is that a great many beings *exist* who are not alive, and it is very possible to conceive of God as a being who exists but who lacks the qualities by which most of us would distinguish living from nonliving beings.

As we noted in Chapter V, "life" is a highly elusive quality. Within the common-sense world of ordinary, observable objects, life is generally associated with certain powers to act in transitive and/or intransitive ways. When a being acts in ways that affect other beings—as, for example, when I hit a baseball—that being exhibits a power to act transitively. On the other hand, when a being acts in ways that seem to affect only itself—as, for example, when I perform the mental act of deciding to abstain from a bedtime snack—that being is said to act intransitively. At the very least, living beings must possess the intransitive power to perform the act of living.[27] The more complex and sophisticated the living being is, the more powers of intransitive and transitive action it will presumably enjoy.

God "Lives":
The Gospel versus Greek Conceptions of God

If living means, as it appears to mean, the possession of certain powers of action, it would seem to follow that God, who is by definition the possessor of all powers (that is, the sole all-powerful being), would be the most alive of all beings. That, indeed, is how Jews and Christians think of God. But certainly it is not the only conceivable way to think of God. Classical Greek thought, particularly, had an entirely different way of conceiving of God. In the view of classical Greek rationalism, the Judaeo-Christian conception of God as a living being who acts tran-

sitively bordered on blasphemy. Indeed, even within the ancient
Church the debates regarding Christ's work and identity received much
of their momentum from pagan critics of the gospel who held that the
Church's claims regarding Christ belittled and insulted God. The idea
that God had incarnated himself in an humble Nazarene was particularly objectionable, in the view of such critics. Under the influence of
Plato and Aristotle, sophisticated pagan thinkers had long since carried
out a program of demythologizing* through which God had come to be
viewed as a cosmic Mind quite separate from the physical order. The
Christian claim that in Christ God had acted transitively, invading the
physical universe and even assuming a personal, physical form, could
only be viewed by such thinkers as a retrograde step, a step back into
the era of pre-Socratic superstition. The God of Pure Thought of the
philosophers was far too sublime a being to become entangled in
the dark and dour affairs of earthly life. Such entanglement was entirely
excluded, in some Greek theories, by the absolute independence and
consequent indifference of the deity. The God of Aristotle, for example,
was so completely self-sufficient that he (or better, it) was totally self-
enclosed and self-absorbed, neither needing nor establishing relations
with beings beyond itself.

The theory behind the Greek idea of God was eminently logical.
In its Aristotelian version the theory followed deductively from the
philosopher's theory of natural motion. Aristotle explained motion as a
child of imperfection. Natural beings (and that means all beings except
God) move because they are imperfect. Their movement constitutes an
attempt to perfect or fulfill those powers which define them. The acorn,
for example, has the power to become an oak tree, and all of the motions
that originate from the acorn's inherent nature move it toward becoming
an oak tree. Once it has reached its "perfection" (completeness or maturity), its native motion or growth ceases, only to be replicated by the
acorns which are the oak's offspring.

Although the motion of entities on earth (for example, acorns) seems
to go and stop, stop and go, the motion of celestial or heavenly bodies
appears to occur in smooth and unceasing cycles.[28] What, Aristotle
asked, is the source or cause of such celestial motion? The heavenly
beings, too, to the degree that they move, must be imperfect, incomplete, and in need of fulfillment. But in what could the fulfillment of

---

*The term "demythologizing" has been made famous in this century by the efforts of
Rudolf Bultmann and the so-called Bultmannian school of biblical interpretation to "de-
mythologize" the biblical message. The theology of the Bible, Bultmann argues, must be
rescued from its archaic and outmoded mythical trappings. It appears that Socrates and
Plato sought to do for the Greek traditions of their day much the same thing Bultmann has
attempted to do with respect to the biblical traditions.

beings of the magnitude of planets and stars consist? Only in a perfection equivalent to that of God! And since such total perfection lies beyond the reach of all natural (material, merely "potential") realities, celestial motion and physical motion in general are constant, continuous, eternal, reflecting the perennial imperfection of the physical order.

If cosmic motion is eternal, it is obvious that God is not distinguished from the world, in Aristotle's view, by being eternal. What, then, is the difference between God and the world? The difference is that God resides beyond the sphere of change and motion altogether, in a state of pure and perfect actuality. Because God is perfectly actualized, the divine being has need of nothing beyond itself. There is thus no hunger for fulfillment in the divine nature, nothing that could move the divine reality beyond itself. God sits in isolated splendor, far beyond the world and outside its reach. Though the divine Being serves as a kind of magnet, an unmoved Mind whose perfection inspires the physical cosmos to move in a vain attempt to match such perfection, on its side that all-attracting magnet cannot even take cognizance of the physical universe or of any of the things in it; for if it *knew* such realities, they could in becoming known contribute something to it which it had previously lacked, and since Perfection by definition lacks nothing, such a contribution is out of the question.

The God of Aristotle was an impersonal or transpersonal being, as unconcerned with earthly affairs as it was unaffected by them; and though the Platonic and Stoic traditions did not stress the divine transcendence in so radical and total a way, they too conceived of God as a sublime, impersonal being whose nature was determined by a certain *apathia,* or indifference, toward the world. To Platonists and Stoics, then, as well as to Aristotelians, the Christian notion that God is alive and that he cares enough about the world to become involved in it could only smack of "foolishness."[29] So with fierce taunts a second-century Platonist named Celsus could attack the Christian idea of Incarnation as a reversion to a mythological mode of thought which belonged to an earlier, infantile stage of human culture. God could rightly be believed to have become incarnate, Celsus argued, only if he had changed his nature (an impossibility, since all change is alien to the divine nature), or if he had perpetrated a fraud (appearing to become human when in fact he had not). The latter case would be as impossible as the former, for God was by definition righteous and truthful as well as unchanging.

The Christian claim that God was in Christ, working to redeem creation, thus evoked strong opposition from Greek and Roman intellectuals of the pre-Constantinian period. For the most part such opposition was inspired not by atheism but by a desire to defend the dignity, the exalted standing, the very perfection of God. God was far too sublime a being to have become entangled in the fortunes of a Nazarene peasant, the pagan intellectuals argued, and the contention that God suffered on a cross in the person of that peasant was particularly blasphemous. If God acts at all, his acts are self-contained acts of pure thought. To say that God is alive, that he performs transitive actions or suffers from them, is to desecrate the divine name.

The responses of Christians to such attacks were conspicuously varied. In general, the responses were of three types: responses in which Christians virtually capitulated to their critics, in effect conceding the correctness of pagan critiques; responses in which Christians compromised or sought a middle ground which would obviate the criticisms or placate the critics; and responses in which Christians counterattacked, reasserting with vigor the intellectual scandal that God had been incarnated and crucified in Christ.

The length of our discussion of the modes of Christian response to pagan philosophy on this question must be disproportionate to the significance of the subject. The debate over Christ's meaning and significance ran hot and cold through the better part of four centuries, and massive tomes have been devoted to analyzing it.[30] The fact that the Church itself contained capitulators, compromisers, and counterattackers meant that the debate frequently became a veritable civil war among Christians as well as a pitched battle against paganism. Ultimately, a certain spirit of compromise brought that war to its conclusion. Although most of the main values defended by the counterattackers were retained under the terms of the conclusive compromises,[31] the thought-forms of Greek philosophy also left their imprint on the resulting definition of the gospel.

The Greek conception of God won its most thorough victory in the thought of a presbyter from Alexandria named Arius (260?–326). Arius adamantly insisted that his theology was not a capitulation to paganism but instead a legitimate use of the categories of classical Greek thought to expound biblical themes. Ultimately, however, the larger Church concluded that the interpretive categories that Arius employed had worked to transform the scriptural themes. What he believed to be a healthy compromise between the gospel and Greek philosophy came to be viewed by the majority of the Church's leaders as an heretical capitulation to pagan ways of thinking.

Arius' primary concern was for the unity of God. Under the influence of Platonic thought-forms, he reasoned that Christ could not be "of the same substance" with God, for then God would not be One but Two. Though Christ may be called "divine," therefore, he may be called "God" only in a secondary or metaphorical sense. Christ was in fact a very exalted being, the first-born of all the creatures. But he was not to

be equated with God, as though he were cosubstantial with the Father, for to say this would be to admit that God was mutable and divisible— that, like organic, corporeal beings, God could act transitively and change form.

Though God sent Christ to earth, in Arius' theology, God himself remained aloof, transcendent, and uninvolved in the created cosmos. This meant that salvation was not a direct work of God but an indirect one. God effected salvation by long distance, as it were. Instead of coming himself to confer redemption, he sent a messenger, the first and best of all the creatures, the Logos or Christ. The immediate, incarnate Savior was thus not God but an archangelic being, the Archangel of archangels, whom Christians call Christ.

These implications of Arius' theory for the doctrine of salvation disturbed some of the leaders of the fourth-century Church greatly. More upset than anyone else was Arius' fellow Alexandrian, Athanasius (298?–373). Arius was guilty of a number of heresies, Athanasius believed, but his arch-heresy lay in his fallacious understanding of salvation. In effect Arius' theology robbed Christians of the very reality of salvation, for salvation consists essentially in a union with God which began in the union of Jehovah with the man Jesus. In denying that an actual union between God and humanity existed in Jesus the Christ, Arius has gutted the gospel of its main theme and has deprived the Christian of the reality and the actual accessibility of salvation.

For these reasons and other, more technical ones, Athanasius led a fierce counterattack against Arianism. Though dressed out in the rather static philosophic vocabulary of the day, his attack amounted to a vigorous reassertion of the biblical idea that God is alive, that he has acted and continues to act transitively, involving himself in the lives and the concerns of his creatures. The God of the Greeks, a God boxed up in heaven or confined by the transcendence of his being, must give place to the God of the gospel, the God who so loved the world that he came to live in it and to make possible the gift of a "new supernatural life"[32] for human beings.

Despite the ferocity of his counterattack on Arianism, Athanasius too was greatly influenced by Greek philosophy. Though his christology or definition of Christ was essentially biblical, its reliance on traditional Greek terms and thought-forms meant that it too lost some of the force of the biblical picture of Jesus. Against the *substance* of Arianism, Athanasius launched a counterattack, but, somewhat ironically, he used the vocabulary and thought-forms of Arius and the Platonists to do so. The result was that, though he insisted that the real God (and not a lesser, angelic being) was in Christ, the God who so united himself with the man Jesus is sometimes represented as being the immutable and relatively inert God of the Greeks. To us there appears to be an obvious paradox, if not an outright contradiction, in this. To speak of God "coming" or "becoming incarnate" is clearly to attribute transitive action to him. How he could engage in such action and remain immutable is a mystery. Obviously, the Greek clothing in which Athanasius dressed the gospel did not fit its wearer very well. Athanasius can thus be numbered among the compromisers with pagan Greek thought in certain respects, even though in other respects he was a leader of the counterattack on capitulators to such thought.

After dominating the thoughts and debates of Christian leaders for the better part of a century, the controversy between the Arians and the Athanasians ended in victory for the party of Athanasius.[33] The victory preserved both the biblical and the Greek philosophical aspects of Athanasius' position. It was therefore not a total victory for the biblical view of God, for it retained the Greek concern for divine immutability. But it did, at the very least, reaffirm the Judaeo-Christian idea that God can and does intervene in vital ways in the history of his creation.

The Concept of the Trinity
as an Affirmation That God Lives

Though the creeds adopted at the Councils of Nicea and Constantinople[34] were composed chiefly in order to affirm the Athanasian concept of the full divinity of Christ, both creeds affirmed as well the Christian faith in the other persons of the Trinity. The notion of the Trinity has been viewed by many unlettered Christians, as well as by many literate critics of Christianity, as an unintelligible exercise in mystical mathematics. Some of the more abstruse and speculative debates among the Church's ancient fathers tended to justify such a view. But the thrust of the Athanasian concern to defend the tri-unity (three-in-oneness) of God against the simple unity of Arius should alert us to the real motive behind Trinitarianism. It is God's three-in-oneness which makes it possible to say that God is alive. Although the mathematical terms do seem abstract and sterile, the intention of the terms is just the opposite: to point to a concrete and real vitality within the Godhead itself. As St. Augustine observed in his treatise *On the Trinity*,[35] the reality of love requires that there be a lover and a beloved as well as the action of loving. Similarly, the being of every vital, transitive reality requires the existence of a subject to do the acting, an object to receive it, and an action to transmit it. Since one could hardly hold that God is inherently and essentially alive without holding that the divine reality is vital and transitive, it follows that the God who is genuinely alive must possess subjective, objective, and transitive powers. This does not mean that such a God is any the less a unity; it simply means that he is a *living* unity.

The doctrine of the Trinity originated, then, not as an attempt to mystify or dazzle the unlettered but rather as an attempt to affirm that God is one, that God is alive, and that he is both simultaneously. God the Subject (in traditional terminology, the Father) can make himself the Object (the Son) of his own knowing and acting (God in Action, or Spirit). To declare that God has these powers is to say that the divine being is best compared not just to living beings but to those particular living beings, namely persons, who possess the powers of self-transcendence and self-expression.

The doctrine of the Trinity thus affirms the personality as well as the vitality of God. The classical Latin formulation of the doctrine—*una substantia in tres personae* (one substance or underlying reality in three persons)—contained an implicit but incomplete allusion to the divine personhood. As we have seen,[36] the Latin word *persona* refers to a mask worn, or a role played, by a stage actor. To speak of God as one substance in three persons is to suggest that he is a single Actor who plays three roles—a creating role, a redeeming role, and a revealing and reconciling role—in the cosmic drama. God is personal, on this view, by virtue of his actions, that is, as an actor, a player of roles or wearer of personae, is personal. But the classical doctrine of the Trinity implies that he could not be personal in this sense, indeed that he could not act at all, if he were not personal in essence, that is, if he did not possess the essential power that distinguishes persons from other beings: the power to transcend oneself, to go outside oneself and act transitively toward oneself or other beings. The affirmation of an *economic* Trinity, as the Church fathers called it—the affirmation that God's actions toward the world are essentially *three* deeds (creation, redemption, and reconciliation) which express *one* intention—seems to require the affirmation of an *immanent* Trinity, that is, that God is a single being who is able to express himself (not only to the world but also to himself) in three ways: as Subject, as Object, and as the Action uniting Subject and Object.

The God of Christians, then, is the trinitarian God becuase he is a God who is alive. The conviction that God is alive is not automatically attained, perhaps, on the basis of revelation. But it seems to be clearly implied in the Christian revelation. Revelation discloses that God acts in history. The conviction that God is alive stems from a question prompted by the divine acts in history: What kind of being must God be in order to act in history? It appears that he must be, at the very least, a being who has the power to act transitively, to break out of himself and into the human situation. To say this is to say that God must be alive and that he must be alive as persons are alive.

Biblical Affirmations That God Is Alive

There are several ways that the biblical witness affirms that God lives. One of the most impressive forms of this affirmation appears in the Bible's chief name for God, Yahweh. As we saw in Chapter II, Yahweh is actually a verb, not a noun. But Yahweh is not just a verb; it is an active, transitive, vigorous verb meaning "He causes to happen." How marvelously the name fits the being it describes! That Being, too, according to the biblical witness, is highly active, astoundingly transitive, a Being who, by action or permission, causes to happen everything that happens. In both its name for God and its description of him the Bible suggests that he is a vital and active Subject, a Being who lives and acts.

Another way in which the Scriptures affirm that God is alive is by the anthropomorphic or "human" terms it uses in its portrait of Yahweh. Yahweh is depicted as the possessor and employer of a personal will, as a Being who, like the human creature who is made in his image, has the power to make up and/or change his mind and then to act on the decisions so made. The God of the Bible is preeminently a God defined by will, by freedom, energy, and purpose, rather than one who sits in sublime isolation and savors his own thoughts. Yahweh is accordingly a deity who is more likely to be met in life than to be proved by logic. Like the human person, the divine Person eludes all efforts to capture his essence in a logical formula. Formulas like the trinitarian one are best viewed, therefore, not as exercises in logic (though they are indeed the products of a certain logic) but as pointers to a personal vitality in God which has been disclosed in history and described in Scripture.

Surely the most audacious and startling way in which the Bible affirms that God lives is to be found in its declaration that he embodied himself in a human being. "The Word was God. . . . And the Word became flesh and dwelt among us. . . ."[37] "God was in Christ reconciling the world to himself."[38] "God shows his love for us in that while we were yet sinners Christ died for us."[39] In these and other affirmations, the New Testament proclaims not only that God lives but also that he expresses himself in a profoundly personal way. As we have seen, it was the Christian claim that such an act of divine self-expression had taken place which led to the fierce debates from which the doctrine of the Trinity evolved. How can the God of Gods be simultaneously the sublime Lord of the universe and a provincial peasant destined to die a criminal's death? What strange God is this, who can so defy the most noble and logical definitions of deity that human minds have been able to contrive? Whatever else he is, such a God is thoroughly and personally alive.

Both the Bible and the doctrine of the Trinity go beyond the affirmations that God is alive and that he is personal to declare that he acts in certain characteristic ways. Though the acts of God are described in numerous ways in Scripture, all of his acts may be encompassed, according to trinitarian thought, in three broad forms of intentional action. Whatever the particular form of a divine act toward the world, it will in this view inevitably express either the intention to create and rule, the intention to redeem, or the intention to reconcile and reunite. When God acts to create or rule he is perceived, in trinitarian terms, as God the Father; when he acts to redeem, he is perceived as God the Son; and when he acts to reconcile and reunite estranged parties, he is perceived as God the Spirit.

In later sections of this chapter and the next, we shall examine the redemptive work of the Son and the reconciling activity of the Spirit. The rest of this section will be devoted to an analysis of the Judaeo-Christian conception of God as Father.

God the Father:
Creator, Ruler, Provider, Source of Redemption

Neither the biblical writers nor the Christian Church hold a patent for the application of the metaphor "Father" to God. The practice of calling the deity "Father" is not uncommon in other religions and other holy books.[40] The metaphor is particularly apt, however, as a way of describing two main qualities in the Christian understanding of God. By definition a father possesses certain creative powers; the existence of his children attests to that. Accordingly, in the trinitarian formulas the metaphor "Father" conveys the idea that God is creative. But, as civil society's laws requiring child support make clear, a father's creative responsibility does not end with the birth of his children. Parents are responsible for giving the world not only children but also responsible adults. Increasing recognition of this responsibility has led in recent years to a considerable expansion of the meaning of the word "parenting"; in many circles the term now refers to the difficult work of helping one's children grow up no less than to the prior (and in some ways easier) work of giving birth to them.

A father or parent is not only a creative person but also a person faced with the task of helping children grow into mature and responsible adults. Similarly, the divine Parent accepts the responsibility of helping his creatures obtain what St. Paul calls "the glorious liberty of the children of God."[41]

These rather obvious observations about the analogy between divine and human parenthood fail to state adequately the actual historical significance of the idea of God as Father as that idea is developed in the Bible. God is called Father in both the Old and the New Testaments. In the Old Testament, the term does not refer to God's role as Creator as much as to his role as a quasi-parental authority. There is a good reason for this. The Hebrews were leery of father-creators because the Baal gods of their pagan foes were such creators. In Baalism creation was believed to result from acts of sexual intercourse between Father Baal and Mother Anath.[42] The two biblical creation stories, by contrast, describe creation as a product of God's word (in the case of Genesis 1) or of his "manual" labor (Genesis 2). In neither story is there any suggestion of a sexual liaison between the Creator and some other divine or demi-divine being. Though some of the Old Testament writers assume that there are grounds for referring to God as "Father," none of them links such fatherhood closely to the idea of creation.

A more likely motive for the ascription of the term "Father" to God in the Old Testament was a conviction among the Hebrews that God treated his creatures in a rather austere patriarchal fashion. In the Hebrew patriarchy, the father was the absolute lord of the family. Yahweh was believed, similarly, to be the absolute Lord of Israel and of creation. As such he was both more powerful and more mobile than the land lords (Baalim) of the Baal cultists were. His authority extended not only to the regulation of nature's routine operations[43] but also to the governance of history. Indeed, Yahweh uses his power over nature to accent and augment his Lordship over history. His wondrous feats frequently involve the use of natural powers (and the miraculous suspension or suppression of natural powers!) as ways of accomplishing historical ends. Although occasional miracle stories and stories of natural wonders seem to stand by themselves, unrelated to historical purposes,[44] more typical are the miracles and wonders of historical import: the births to barren women which keep the Abrahamic history going, the dreams and wondrous interpretive powers of Joseph which saved the house of Jacob during lean years, the call of Moses at the burning bush which prefaced the turnaround of Israel's fortunes, the plagues visited on Pharaoh to force the emancipation of the Hebrew children, the miraculous crossing of the Red sea, the manna and quail in the wilderness which again ensured Israel's survival, the collapse of the walls of Jericho, and so on.[45]

Yahweh is preeminently the Lord of history, but he is a Lord of history who uses the powers of nature to accomplish his objectives in and for history. It is as Lord of history, too, that Yahweh discloses yet another aspect of the divine fatherhood. Though he is frequently portrayed as a stern, patriarchal Judge, sending the flood on the generation of Noah, the curse of many tongues on the builders of the Tower of Babel, and fire and brimstone down upon Sodom and Gomorrah,[46] Yahweh's Lordship or Fatherhood is essentially that of a benevolent Redeemer and Provider.[47]

One of the key Old Testament passages in which the idea of divine parenthood appears is a passage that relates not to God's role as Lord but to his role as liberator or redeemer. In Hosea 11:1, the prophet quotes God: "When Israel was a child, I loved him, and out of Egypt I called my son." Though the Gospel of Matthew later interpreted this passage messianically, as a prediction applicable to Jesus,[48] the passage refers mainly, no doubt, to the historic liberation (calling out) of Israel from Egypt in the Exodus event. Thus, even though the Old Testament view of God is that of a simple monotheism rather than that of a developed trinitarianism, God nevertheless is portrayed, even within the Old Testament, as a Redeemer or Liberator. In the Old Testament context, however, a context within which the concept of the Trinity had not yet emerged, the redemptive as well as the lordly work was attributed to God as father.

As we saw in Chapter VII and again in the first section of the present chapter, Christians believe that God's work as Redeemer cannot be understood apart from his work as Creator. Creation and redemption have the same essential aim: the establishment of the rule, or Lordship, of God. The Old Testament affirms this unity of intention no less than the New Testament does. The Old Testament name for the redeemed community, Israel, can be translated "May God rule,"and the first and supreme commandment in the old (Sinai) covenant asserts God's lordship over all the creatures who might seek divine status.[49] God the Father is primarily God the Lord, but he establishes his Lordship through both creative and redemptive forms of activity.

The New Testament reinforces the Old Testament idea of the Lordship of the divine father. Thus, after addressing God as Father in its opening phrase, the Lord's Prayer offers as its first petition the plea "Thy kingdom =[rule, lordship] come."[50] But even as it reinforces the concept of divine fatherhood inherited from the old covenant, the New Testament witness enriches and deepens that concept. Jesus' favorite word for God is "Father," and when he utters it his tone is not that of a scared child but that of a trusting and expectant son. In Jesus' descriptions of him, God is a benevolent and evenhanded creator and provider who "makes his sun rise on the evil and on the good, and sends rain on the just and on the unjust."[51] As Father, God goes the second mile: "he is kind to the ungrateful and the selfish."[52] As Father, he rewards the humble, hearing the secret prayers of his children and knowing what they need before they ask him.[53] As Father, he tenders his favor toward those who neither sow nor reap: the birds of the air, the lilies of the field, and the trusting human soul.[54] He pours out "good things to those who ask him"[55] and proclaims his Word through people who face tribulation without anxiety.[56] He knows when a sparrow falls, and numbers the hairs on the heads of human creatures, who are of more value than many sparrows.[57] He reveals things to and through the humble, things that are withheld from the proud.[58] Above all he is faithful to the One he has chosen to be his Son, taking counsel from him.[59] Yet for all this there is an element of firmness and determination in his character. He tenders his grace ungrudgingly but still in the expectation that what he sows will return to him thirty, sixty, and a hundredfold.[60] Those he adopts as his children are expected to do his will,[61] and lip service will not serve as a substitute for obedience.[62]

Jesus identifies God not only as the Father of all creatures but also, in a special way, as his own Father. The Gospel of John emphasizes again and again the special Father-Son relationship between Jesus and God. "I and the Father are one," says John's Jesus, and "No one comes to the Father but by me."[63] He has been sent into the world by the Father, and it is by the Father's authority that he sends others.[64] In all, John's Gospel refers to God as Father more than a hundred times, and in the vast majority of cases the term designates his special relationship to the Son. In the other gospels, too, though less frequently, the theme of special Sonship recurs. The idea is presented directly, in the synoptic gospels, in the stories of Jesus' birth,[65] baptism,[66] and crucifixion.[67] It is also represented, though indirectly, in the concept of the Virgin Birth found in Matthew and in Luke.[68] Finally, it is given express trinitarian form in the so-called Great Commission recorded in Matthew 28:19-20.

One need not proceed beyond the gospels to find in the New Testament an amazing quantity of material on the theme of divine fatherhood. The references to the theme in Paul's letters, which were written before the gospels, and in the other New Testament literature, virtually all of which was written after the gospels, are both numerous enough and evenly distributed enough[69] to make it clear that the concept came to define early Christian thinking about God in an extremely pervasive way.

When compared to that of the Old Testament, the New Testament treatment of the theme of divine fatherhood redraws the portrait of God in more personal and less patriarchal terms. God remains Lord of all, but because he is now known as "the God and Father of our Lord Jesus Christ" he is no longer a distant and dreadful being but one who has drawn near, getting under the human skin and making human selves his temples.[70] The true spirit of God the Father has thus been disclosed in God the Son, and that spirit is seen to be the spirit of a total, self-giving love. Such divine love is not sentimental or spineless. On the contrary, it judges even as it saves, afflicting the consciences of the affluent who fail to show love even as it comforts those who need love. This is the message of the greatest single word picture of God the Father that Jesus offers us. In his parable of the prodigal son,[71] the love of the rejoicing father who greets his errant child with forgiveness and favor stands as a scathing judgment on the lovelessness of the prodigal's elder brother. But though it judges severely the lack of love which characterizes so much human behavior, love's judgment no less than its benefits are aimed at redemption, a liberation from lovelessness which comprises the "glorious liberty of the children of God." The same God who is the Source and Ruler of the world thus is revealed in and by Christ to be the Source of the world's redemption.

REDEMPTION'S REALIZATION:
JESUS THE CHRIST

"Redemption" is a term with many meanings. Literally, it means "to buy back" or "to set free." Historically, it refers to the ancient practice of ransoming slaves, purchasing their freedom by paying their master's price. In the modern American marketplace the term has been demeaned and trivialized by its association with trading-stamp exchanges. The word deserves a better fate. It is a noble word as well as an ancient one, and historically theologians have viewed it as the one term which expresses most adequately the nature of the saving deed by which God seeks to put his world in order and to reestablish his rule. Although these theologians recognize that the effects of that deed are transmitted to various people in various ways and that it therefore means different things to different percipients, they nevertheless believe it possible to identify certain common qualities that mark the deed as redemptive. These common qualities in the redemptive event will be the focus of our discussion in this section.

The Christian understanding of the word "redemption" goes back to the ancient practice of redeeming or emancipating slaves. All human beings, Christians believe, are caught in a kind of slavery. To state the matter briefly, they are slaves to themselves: slaves to the sin, the original or originating sin, of self-worship. The nature of such slavery was discussed earlier in this chapter, in the section entitled "Redemption's Necessity." As we observed there, sin is basically a condition or state of being rather than an activity; it is a disorientation, a distortion or misordering of relationships which throws life out of kilter, out of accord with the divine intention. The result is that sin's victims live and act on the basis of distorted perceptions, from relationships to reality that dethrone the Creator and deify the creature.

When orthodox Christians like St. Augustine or Martin Luther refer to sin as slavery, it is important to realize that they are not using the term "slavery" in a figurative sense. In their view sin is quite literally a form of slavery. As such it is not to be compared to a bad habit that one could break by an act of will as much as to the states of addictive dependency one encounters in alcoholics or victims of other drugs. As groups like Alcoholics Anonymous have stressed, alcoholics are literally slaves to their need for alcohol. The belief that they can overcome their dependency through their own strength of will is a destructive delusion. A dependency is just that: a reliance on something or someone else to do something you cannot do alone—to do what you depend on them to do! A dependency therefore will not yield to even the firmest determination to become independent, to go it alone. A dependency will yield only to another dependency, a supportive relationship only to another supportive relationship. Just as a badly broken leg leaves one with only two options—the option of not walking at all or that of depending on something other than the bad leg for support in walking—so an addictive dependency leaves one with only the option of progressive self-destruction or that of the discovery and substitution of a healthier form of dependency.

The Christian identification of sin with slavery follows not only from the realization that humans are essentially dependent beings but also from insight into the nature of sin itself. If sin is self-centeredness, it follows that the only escape from sin must be a release or liberation from the self-centered condition. Efforts to save oneself or to liberate oneself can serve only to keep the self at the center of one's thoughts and actions. Instead of releasing one from self-centeredness, therefore, efforts to save oneself—even when these efforts are of the most devout or religious sort—simply illustrate, and may aggravate, the problem.

Sin as self-centeredness has the human creature in its grip, and self-initiated efforts to break its grip only tighten it by keeping the self in the position of life's central concern. Efforts at self-redemption produce a kind of vicious cycle, illustrating St. Augustine's description of the sinner's condition as that of a "heart curved in upon itself" (*cor incurvatum in se*). The self chases after (or as the Old Testament says "goes awhoring after") many gods, worshipping now at one altar, now at another in a way which reflects its doubts about its own adequacy as a deity. But its dependencies on other creatures prove no more satisfying or sustaining than its dependency on itself, for these beings share the creaturely inadequacies of the self.[72]

When confronted by such an appraisal of the human condition, many persons, especially those of an optimistic bent, are inclined to react with dismay. Surely Christians sell people short when they portray them as such inveterate and helpless sinners. Surely it is possible to escape the circle of self-concern if one makes up one's mind to do so. Surely people do good things for other people every day, with no thought of reward or of benefit for themselves.

Orthodox Christians might begin their response to such criticism of their views by making a distinction. The Christian declaration that people are self-centered does not mean that people cannot, or do not, do good things for other people. It does not mean, either, that such things cannot be done without thought of reward. It *does* mean, however, that the self's own interests are conscious or unconscious factors in the decision to perform such deeds. And it does assuredly mean that the circle of self-concern cannot be escaped by an unassisted act of will.

From the orthodox Christian standpoint, it is not at all surprising that persons caught in the circle of self-concern should resent, and react strongly to, unflattering appraisals of the human condition. It is possible, to be sure, to regard such reactions as refutations of the Christian analysis, but it is equally possible to view them as evidence for the accuracy of that analysis. Christians of the Augustinian persuasion hold that sin always travels in the company of self-deception. The fig leaf always has been, and remains, one of the powerful symbols of the Adam and Eve (that is, the human) story. The devices people use to hide from God may also shield their own eyes from unpleasant truths. Apart from the gospel, indeed, human beings are generally victimized by a double deceit. First they are deceived about themselves, and second about their deceit. In their own judgment the words of the serpent to Eve have come true: they have indeed become "as gods." So in every playground fight, each child involved in the scrap asserts the rightness of his or her own cause and lays the blame for the whole affair on the other scrapper(s). Similarly, in every political battle, my party or political champion has the right of it, and those who see matters differently are either unenlightened or deliberately acting from self-interest. In wars and other international conflicts, acts of barbarity are justified in the name of the righteousness of one's cause or the cause of one's nation. The combatants in any of these types of conflict somehow manage to transfer whatever evil imbues their cause to the cause of their foes and to claim all righteousness for their own motives. That they do so is to be expected, in the Christian view, for subconsciously they (or their party or nation) are virtual gods, and gods are invariably in the right and their foes in the wrong.

There are good reasons why no court of law allows the defendant to judge his or her own case, and equally good reasons why no court in which justice is served allows the plaintiff or the prosecutor to double as judge. We are all incurable self-justifiers. Reasons can always be found to justify our actions, even when those actions are seen to be vile or bestial when fairly and objectively appraised.

Acts of self-justification are so commonplace that St. Paul found the term "justification" a very helpful one as he attempted to define redemption's necessity and its meaning. As Paul defines the terms, the sin

that makes redemption necessary shows up most clearly in human attempts at *self-justification,* while God's action in Christ, which makes redemption possible, may best be understood as another, entirely different form of justification, which the apostle calls *justification by grace through faith.*

The sin of self-justification shows up more clearly in what Paul called "boasting."[73] "Boasting" (Greek *kauchaomai*) is mainly an attitude and only secondarily an action. As an attitude, it permeates everything the sinful person does. When it appears in its blatant and recognizable form, in the behavior, let us say, of the egotist or the braggart, the boasting attitude is almost universally condemned as boorish and contemptible. But the very reason we may not like to see such blatant displays of the condition may be that the display shows us too much of ourselves. In putting down braggarts and boors, indeed, we may well be asserting a more subtle form of the very egotism we condemn in them.

A far more common way of expressing the attitude of boasting or self-justification is that of simple *rationalization.* If I cheat on my tax return, that is all right: I can put the money to better use than the army of incompetent government bureaucrats ever could. If I produce sloppy goods, that is acceptable: if my boss wants me to do my best work, he or she should pay me what I'm worth. If I submit as my own work a copy of a term paper from the fraternity files, that is all to the good: it will allow me to study more important subjects, help me get good grades, get me into medical school, and enable me to become a physician who can make a real contribution to society. And so the story goes. Honorable motives are adduced for the most dishonorable and dishonest kinds of actions. In our own eyes we are justified in manufacturing the motives no less than in performing the actions, for in our own eyes we are "as gods," defining good and evil for ourselves and acting righteously, as gods always do.

Another way in which the attitude of self-justification rules our lives is to be found in that ancient and much practiced art known colloquially as "passing the buck." According to the Eden stories, the practice goes back to the parents of humankind: Adam launched the tradition by blaming Eve for his act of disobedience, and Eve kept it alive by pointing to the serpent. Cain took his cue from both parents, blaming his rejection by God on his brother and later disclaiming all responsibility for the brother's whereabouts and well-being.[74] The behavior of all of these primordial figures is a typification of human habits of behavior in general.

In developing his description of sin as self-justification, St. Paul does not exempt himself from the ranks of the self-justifiers. Instead he uses his own life story as an exhibit of the power and effects of self-

THE HELPING HAND

Good-neighbor grook

We perceive that we must
do our bit, on the score
of community labors;
so we each sweep the dust
from in front of our door
to in front of our neighbor's.

justification. He then goes on to argue that there is another form of justification which is far more powerful and effective, which in fact redeems people from the need for self-justification by releasing them from the self-centeredness which prompts it.

Paul tells his story most succinctly in the third chapter of his Letter to the Philippians:

> ³... we [Christian disciples] are the true circumcision, who worship God in spirit, and glory in Jesus Christ, and put no confidence in the flesh. ⁴Though I myself have reason for confidence in the flesh also. If any other man thinks he has reason for confidence in the flesh, I have more: ⁵circumcised on the eighth day, of the people of Israel, of the tribe of Benjamin, a Hebrew born of Hebrews; as to the law of Pharisee, ⁶as to zeal a persecutor of the church, as to righteousness under the law blameless. ⁷But whatever gain I had, I counted as loss for the sake of Christ. ⁸Indeed I count everything as loss because of the surpassing worth of knowing Christ Jesus my Lord. For his sake I have suffered the loss of all

things, and count them as refuse, in order that I may gain Christ [9]and be found in him, not having a righteousness of my own, based on law, but that which is through faith in Christ, the righteousness from God that depends on faith. . . .

So run Paul's credentials, his personal list of things about which he might boast, about which he once in fact had boasted. Behind all his boasting, as he makes plain in verses 5, 6, and 9, was his special relationship to what he calls "the law." The law to which he refers here was the law of Moses as interpreted in the Pharisaic tradition. This law, Paul assures us elsewhere,[75] was a gift from God and as such was holy and just and good; yet, he says (speaking metaphorically, of course) "the very commandment which promised life proved to be death to me."[76]

How could this have happened? How could a good thing like the law have proved Paul's undoing? It proved his undoing because it became for him the prime instrument in his attempts at self-justification. The law, he had come to believe, was a way by which he might prove himself just or righteous before God. If he could but keep the law—and he says in Philippians 3:6 that he had in fact kept it so well that he was "blameless"—then he might enter into the court of the divine Judge with a sure defense against every possible charge that could be raised against him; through the law, in other words, and more precisely through the keeping of the law, he could justify himself, even before God.

Paul tells us, then, that he had kept the law. He was "as to righteousness under the law, blameless." But then he says a strange thing: "But whatever gain I had, I counted as loss for the sake of Christ." In coming to know Christ, Paul has attained some new insight, some new understanding regarding his situation. The glorious law, on which he had long depended for his good self-estimate, had been cast overboard as so much "refuse" or "rubbish" (J. B. Phillips' translation) because of this insight. The futility of all attempts at self-justification had somehow become apparent to him through the new understanding of God given him by Christ.

Paul's new insight seems to have been two-pronged. First, it appears that he came to see *himself* in an entirely different light. He now saw that his avid adherence to the law had indeed made him "good," but that it had made him good for totally wrong reasons and with totally wrong results. He had sought goodness so that he might boast of it, so that he might justify himself before God through it, so that he might enjoy superiority to the lesser breeds without the law, so that he might with a clear conscience bring harm to heretics like the Christians whom he had zealously persecuted before his conversion. But, he had discovered, in the end his goodness had produced in him effects totally contrary to those he had sought: a pride extending to arrogance, a zealous hatred for those he perceived as enemies of the law, and even a sense of estrangement from God.

Paul thus came to recognize that the law had been to him what the serpent had been to Eve. He had taken his definition of himself from the law much as Eve had taken hers from the serpent, and like Eve he had become "as God" in his own eyes. The law had led him to believe that acts of self-justification were not only possible but were actually required by God. Though he kept the law, after keeping it he seemed to himself farther removed from God than ever. The pride, the boasting, which his relation to the law had produced, had not united him with God but had in fact estranged him from God.

Thus the first thing that Paul learned from his encounter with Christ was *to see himself in a totally different way.* He learned what it means to discover that one has spent one's life walking in the tracks of Adam. The sin of Eve and Adam was the sin of exalting themselves to the rank of gods. They had committed their sin by valuing the Creator's gifts more highly than the Creator himself. Paul learned through his encounter with Christ that he had been guilty of the same sin, that both God's good gift of the law and the high self-image he could achieve through keeping the law had become more important to him than God himself.

The second thing Paul gained through his relation to Christ was *a new understanding of God.* The God of the law was essentially God the Lawgiver, God the Judge, an austere being who relates himself to humans only from a distance and through the intermediate institution of the law. If such a God can be thought of as a Father at all, he is the kind of Father before whom one must constantly prove one's sonship. Paul may have felt before him much like a child who rises with the dawn of each day, works frantically throughout the day to earn his parents' favor, and is finally driven to the extremity of bringing out the family Bible, finding the family genealogy in its pages, and presenting it to his parents with the desperate cry, "See Mother! see Father! I am your child! I am your child!"

If such an aloof and fearful deity was the God of Paul the Pharisee, the God of Paul the apostle of Christ was an altogether different being. To the Romans Paul wrote:

What then shall we say to this? If God is for us, who is against us? He who did not spare his own Son but gave him up for us all, will he not also give us all things with him? Who shall bring any charge against God's elect? It is God who justifies; who is to condemn? . . . I am sure that neither death, nor life, nor angels, nor principalities, nor things present, nor things to come, nor powers, nor height, nor depth, nor anything else in all creation, will be able to separate us from the love of God in Christ Jesus our Lord."[77]

"It is God who justifies." With those five words, the entire conception of God of Paul the Pharisee is overturned! God is no longer distant and aloof. In Christ he has drawn near. He has intervened in his creation to set his creatures free, that they may enjoy "the glorious liberty of the children of God."[78] Efforts at self-justification are no longer necessary. The divine Judge's verdict has been rendered, and it proves to be the verdict of a loving and forgiving Father rather than that of a jealous Lawgiver.

Paul's new understanding of God and his new perception of himself set him on an entirely different course from the one he had previously pursued. His attempts at self-justification were abandoned, and the focus of his life was now on what God had done rather than on his own accomplishments. If he boasted at all now, his boasting had to be in praise of God's accomplishment rather than his own.[79] Justification, he makes clear, is not something humans achieve through keeping the law but rather something God gives with the gift of faith.[80]

In developing his newly attained concept of justification by faith, St. Paul made clear the difference between efforts at salvation through the law and the gift of salvation through the gospel. As we saw in Chapter IV, the law is a disclosure of what God expects the human creature to do for him, whereas the gospel is a report of what God does for humankind. Salvation by the law (if it were possible) would amount to salvation by one's own efforts, one's own meritorious deeds or good works. Such salvation is in fact not possible. It is not possible because salvation requires a redemption or liberation from self-centeredness, and the self that seeks to save itself by keeping the law remains very much in the grip of self-concern.

If genuine salvation from self-concern is to occur, it must occur through self-forgetfulness, a refocusing of one's concern away from oneself and upon something or someone else. This is why, according to the Christian faith, salvation can only come from beyond the self, never from within it. This is also why the gospel of Jesus Christ is such good news. For the gospel declares that, in Jesus the Christ, God acted to give human life a new focus, to destroy the human dependency on the great god Self, and to restore the life-giving relationship to God the Creator.

The two pivotal figures in St. Paul's theology of sin and salvation are Adam and Christ. The two are pivotal because they express the two ways in which human beings may relate to reality. The way Adam related to reality, Paul says, is the way of death. The way Christ related to it is the way to life. But what is the essential, practical difference between the two ways?

Practically speaking, the way of Adam is the way of self-exaltation. As our earlier analysis of Genesis 3 indicated, the parents of humanity confused the image of God in themselves with the reality of God and, turning to worship their own powers, turned away from the Creator. The way of Adam thus became the way of idolatry, of self-worship or self-exaltation. This way, St. Paul indicated, can lead only to death, for it entails dependence on a god who cannot save and cuts one off from the God who is life's source. Yet it is the way of the whole human family,[81] when that family is left to its own devices. The history of the children of Adam is a sad epic in which idolatry, inhumanity to fellow humans, and the rape and pillaging of nature have been prevalent.

With the coming of Jesus the Christ, however, the human creature is offered a new chance, a chance to begin again, to strike a new covenant with the God of creation, and to live and act on an entirely different basis. Because this is so, St. Paul can refer to Christ as a new Adam, a "last Adam."[82] Christ is the new Adam because he offers humankind a new beginning. The new beginning is one of great promise, "for as in Adam all die, so also in Christ shall all be made alive."[83] By forsaking the path of Adam for that of Christ, the human creature may depart the way of death for the way to life. Even the way to life entails a certain kind of death—a dying to sin and to self—but in Christ death becomes a door to life rather than a final destination.[84]

The way of Christ is, according to the gospel, the way to life. But in actual practice how can one adopt the way of Christ as one's own? What does taking the way of Christ actually mean? What difference does it make in the way one lives? Once again St. Paul is our most helpful guide. In Philippians 2, just one chapter before he reports what had been involved in his own adoption of Christ's way, he describes the way to life as Christ himself walked it:

> Have this mind among yourselves, which you have in Christ Jesus, 6who, though he was in the form of God, did not count equality with God a thing to be grasped, 7but emptied himself . . . being born in the likeness of men. 8And being found in human form he humbled himself and became obedient unto death, even death on a cross. 9Therefore God has highly exalted him and bestowed on him the name which is above every name, 10that at the name of Jesus every knee should bow, in heaven and on earth and under the earth, 11and every tongue confess that Jesus Christ is Lord, to the glory of God the Father.

Scholarly commentators generally agree that this description of the way of Christ was not just Paul's description but rather that of a hymn used in the worship services of early Christian congregations. If this is so, the description may be viewed as a creedal statement of sorts. As a statement familiar to and used by a number of congregations, it would carry even more weight as an indicator of early Christian ideas than it would as an original creation of the apostle. In any event, it is a remarkable summation of the shape and significance of Christ's career as that career is described elsewhere in the New Testament. Whoever the hymnwriter was, it is hard to believe that he was not directly contrasting the life style of Jesus Christ with the dramatically opposed life style of Adam and the rest of humankind. Let us examine the hymnwriter's picture of Christ in the light of these possibilities.

Note first that the writer portrays Christ as by nature an exalted being, not only "in the form of God" but even sharing "equality with God" (verse 6). Yet, for a reason not explained in the hymn but amply elaborated elsewhere[85] by Paul and other New Testament writers, the one who was equal with God "did not count equality with God a thing to be grasped, but emptied himself" of his divine powers, assuming not only "the likeness of men" but even the lowly "form of a servant" (verse 7).

The hymn's message would be startling enough, and its claim audacious enough, if it stopped here. Enough has already been said to evoke shouts of "Blasphemy!" from Greek intellectuals. But the hymnwriter went on, far enough to scandalize Jewish messianists as well. If the news that one had come from God would not surprise messianic traditionalists, and if the application of the title "servant" to the Coming One would not be totally beyond their ken, the idea that God's Messiah or Christ could become "obedient unto death, even death on a cross" would place an almost insurmountable obstacle in their way. "Cursed be every one who hangs on a tree,"[86] went the Jewish proverb, and the notion that God's Anointed (*Mashiah* or Messiah) could suffer such a curse was, from the standpoint of traditional Jewish messianism, arrant sacrilege.

Paul surely knew that in endorsing a portrait of Christ like that in the Philippian hymn he would raise the hackles of devout Jews and philosophical Greeks, for elsewhere he declares that "we preach Christ crucified, a stumbling block to Jews and folly to Gentiles."[87] Yet he apparently believes that he cannot portray Christ otherwise, for his encounter with Christ has convinced him that

God chose what is foolish in the world to shame the wise, . . . what is weak in the world to shame the strong, . . . what is low and despised in the world, even things that are not, to bring to nothing things that are, *so that no human being might boast in the presence of God.* [88]

As we found from the apostle's confession in Philippians 3, [89] Christ had forced Paul himself, as a proud Pharisee, to give up all his reasons for boasting. Similarly, that human wisdom (of the Greeks) and those human traditions (of the messianists) that would place God in a strait-jacket were expressions of the way of Adam which would simply have to yield before the way of Christ.

The most striking thing about Paul's hymnic portrait of Christ may be its assault on the sensibilities of philosophers and messianists. But a more positive and significant thing about it is the way in which it con-trasts the pattern of God's action in Christ with the actions of human beings as they are depicted in the Adam myth. In both direction and destination the two patterns are diametrically opposed. Their opposition may be demonstrated best, perhaps, by means of diagrams.

Diagrammed, the pattern of Christ's action as portrayed in Philip-pians 2 would look something like this:

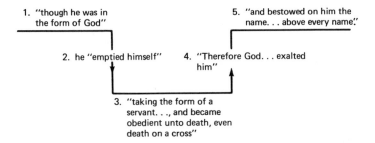

1. "though he was in the form of God"

5. "and bestowed on him the name. . . above every name."

2. he "emptied himself"

4. "Therefore God. . . exalted him"

3. "taking the form of a servant. . ., and became obedient unto death, even death on a cross"

Similarly diagrammed, the story of Adam in Genesis 3 would take a markedly different shape:

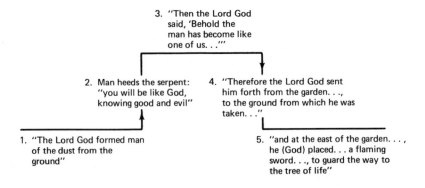

3. "Then the Lord God said, 'Behold the man has become like one of us. . .'"

2. Man heeds the serpent: "you will be like God, knowing good and evil"

4. "Therefore the Lord God sent him forth from the garden. . ., to the ground from which he was taken. . ."

1. "The Lord God formed man of the dust from the ground"

5. "and at the east of the garden. . . , he (God) placed. . . a flaming sword. . ., to guard the way to the tree of life"

So portrayed, the contrast between the self-giving way of Christ and the self-exalting way of Adam could not be clearer. The way of Adam begins as the way upward but ends as the way of death. The way of Christ begins as a downward way but leads to life. That Paul believes both ways remain alive as options becomes quite clear when a diagram is made of the apostle's record of his own pilgrimage in Philippians 3:

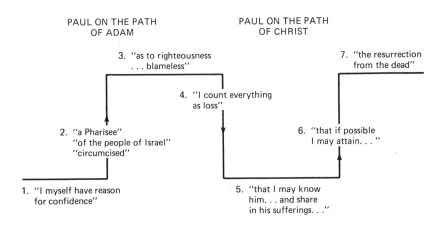

In Paul's own life, it is clear, the way of Christ had come to have enormous significance. His encounter with Christ stopped him in his tracks, set him on a different course, and radically altered his life style. As Christ had done before him, he forsook the company of the smug saints for that of outcasts and sufferers. His question was no longer "How can I become righteous?" but "How can I show people that God loves them, that he accepts them in spite of their sin and that he is with them in the middle of their suffering?" His answer to that question was to tell them of Christ, who had not counted equality with God a thing to be clung to but had humbled himself, bringing God himself into the haunts of servants and sinners and sufferers.

His new-found knowledge of Christ was of enormous personal significance to Paul: it had drastically altered his life style. But this knowledge was also of enormous cosmic significance: it had affected the apostle's *world view* as well as his style of life. This is true because, as the new Adam, Christ changed the history of humankind no less than he changed the career of Paul of Tarsus. Indeed, the personal effects of Christ's achievement are only entrances into its cosmic effects: "When anyone is united to Christ, there is a new world; the old order has gone, and a new order has already begun."[90] The course of history, directed toward death in Adam, has in Christ been redirected toward life. In incarnating and establishing the new covenant Christ has brought humankind the possibility of a new life, a new history, and a new way of putting the world together. In more concrete terms, he came to mend the relationship to God which was broken (and *is* broken) by the decision to worship God's human image rather than God himself. The breaking of that relationship led, and still leads, to the loss of the power to act responsibly in the face of the challenges set before humans by the God of history, challenges that are made more complicated by irresponsible human behavior. Apart from the new covenant established in Christ, humans will continue to emulate Adam, now defying God, now hiding from him, now claiming to be history's absolute masters, now burying themselves in nature to escape history's demands altogether. But in Christ the Adamic impulse has been countered. Redemption—freedom from the consuming sin of self-concern—has been realized.

At the beginning of this chapter, we noted that the big question about Christ in the life of the early (pre-Constantinian) Church was not "Who was he?" but rather "Why did he come?" or "What did he come to do?" The outlines of the early Church's answer to that question have now emerged. Christ came primarily, if Paul and the New Testament generally are to be believed, to bear the good news that God has not abandoned his creation, despite the rebellion of the creature. In Christ God instead moved to reestablish his rule by breaking into the circle of human self-concern and exposing the worship of self and of the self's satellite deities as the deceivers and destroyers they are. But Christ did more, far more, according to the New Testament witnesses. He revealed the reality of God even as he exposed the unreality of the pretender gods. He revealed God's reality, indeed, by incarnating that reality, by embodying God in his own person.

Redemption does not end with liberation from the tyranny of self-concern. Jesus once noted that those released from demonic powers would only be worse off if their release from one demonic force led to their enslavement by seven others.[91] Redemption is both incomplete and ineffectual unless it replaces the false way of relating which would destroy life with an authentic way which gives life. Authentic redemption must therefore lead to what theologians call *reconciliation*, the restoration of the life-giving relationship of the Creator to his creatures.

The efficacy and completeness of redemption depend, then, on its power to bring humans and God together again in a life-renewing way. What begins in redemption must end in reconciliation. Salvation as a total event must perform the negative work of judging the sinner and conquering sin, but it must also perform the positive work of reuniting the freed and forgiven creature with the Creator. Salvation must include not only a Word from on high, a judging Word from the Holy One before whom sinful beings must quake and repent, but also a Word drawn near, an incarnate Word in whom God and the human creature are reunited. This was the insight which led Athanasius to defend so vigorously the view that Christ was fully divine. If it is not really God who approaches us in Christ, he reasoned, then Christ cannot bring us genuine salvation. But Christ was in fact, as the birth narratives in Matthew's gospel declared, "Emmanuel," which means "God with us,"[92] and because that is true the gospel of salvation is true.

Though Athanasius began with the question "What did Christ come to do?" he seems to have discovered that the answer to that question leads to another, "Did Christ in fact have the power to do what he came to do?" and that in turn to another, "Who was Christ anyway?" If Christ came to confer salvation and if salvation means a renewed relationship to God, then Christ must have the power to usher us into the presence of God himself. If that is true, the One the human creature faces in Jesus of Nazareth must be none other than the Lord of Israel, the God of all the world.

After Athanasius had won the battle for the divinity of Christ, the Gospel of Incarnation had to survive two other major challenges to its integrity. In the early Church there were thinkers who, in agreeing with Athanasius that Christ was fully divine, tended to minimize or ignore his humanity.[93] There also were thinkers who, though they affirmed both the humanity and the divinity of Christ, failed to affirm an actual or "personal" union between his divine nature and his human nature.[94] Once again the stiffness and abstruseness of the terms used in the controversies over such questions tend to throw us off the trail of the questions' significance. Far more was at stake, however, than the intellectual vanity of the theologians involved. If Christ's full divinity was essential to his power to redeem, his full humanity was equally essential to his power to reconcile. Unless the one reunited with God in Christ was actually human, then God would remain as remote as ever from the human situation, and the human creature would remain estranged from the Creator. God and sinners would remain unreconciled.

The full humanity of Christ is thus as important to the Gospel of Incarnation as the full divinity. That is why the Council of Chalcedon (451) adopted that paradoxical formula quoted in part at the beginning of this chapter:

> We all with one accord teach men to acknowledge one and the same Son, our Lord Jesus Christ, at once complete in Godhead and complete in manhood, truly God and truly man... of one substance with the Father as regards his Godhead, and at the same time of one substance with us as regards his manhood....

Only as Christ was divine was he able to redeem, but only as he became human did redemption become actual and complete in the event of God's reunion with, or reconciliation to, the human creature.

The Chalcedonian fathers affirmed both the full humanity and the full divinity of Christ. But they did not stop there. They went on to affirm as well an intimate union between Christ's human nature and his divine nature, "the characteristics of each nature being preserved and coming together to form one person and subsistence, not as parted or separated into two persons, but one and the same Son."[95] Here, too, the fathers seem to have been moved by the requirements of the gospel. Their language is stilted and stiff, to be sure, but properly heard it is language which announces the good news of reconciliation. That good news is that God and humans are not only present in Christ but that they have actually been reunited in him, that the relationship established between the Creator and the creature in him is fast and real and enduring. In Christ God not only touched the borders of human existence as a tangent touches a circle; he instead cut through to the heart of the circle, establishing a profound, personal unity with humankind.

REDEMPTION AND BECOMING

The title of this chapter relates both faith and redemption to the idea of becoming. We are now prepared to see that redemption is the link between two kinds of becoming. Redemption presupposes and depends on a certain *divine* becoming, and it precedes and makes possible a certain *human* becoming.

The prologue to the Gospel according to St. John contains one of the earliest Christian announcements of the divine becoming: "In the beginning was the Word, and the Word was with God, and the Word was God. . . . And the Word became flesh and dwelt among us, full of grace and truth."[96] The same prologue promises also a human becoming: " . . . to all who received him [the Word become flesh] . . . he gave power to become children of God."[97] In the preceding section we discussed at some length the nature of the divine becoming. In this concluding section we shall deal briefly with the relation between God's becoming human in Christ and the consequent power of human creatures to become children of God.

As we saw earlier in the chapter, the classical Greek idea of God was incompatible with any notion that God might change or "become." God, in the Greek view, resides in a realm quite beyond that of change and mortality. If God had to "become" anything, that would betray a very ungodlike imperfection, for it would indicate that God needed to become something he (or it) was not.

In order to gain a hearing and win followers among the Greek intellectual class, the leaders of the early Church made important, almost calamitous, concessions to the Greek idea of God. Among the points conceded or given up was the idea—the very biblical idea—that God changes, that he can become different in response to different occasions. The biblical idea of God was thus seriously affected, if not altogether replaced, by the Greek idea.

Even so, there remained alive in the Church, as we saw in the cases of Athanasius and the Chalcedonian fathers, a strong concern that the event of salvation be properly proclaimed. The result was that extraordinary tension we noted between the language the Fathers used and the content the language was designed to convey. The language is the cool, formal language of classical Greek thought, but the ideas come out of the heat of biblical history. The two, language and ideas, tend to cancel each other out. But if the formal philosophical packaging is stripped away, the intention of the formulations can be seen again to agree with the intention of the biblical gospel. We are thus enabled to see that the biblical gospel is the gospel of a God who changes, acts, moves, *becomes*.

The idea that God changes, becoming different from what he had been, is particularly strong in the Old Testament. In Genesis 6:6 and I Samuel 15:35, God changes his mind about previous acts or decisions: "And the Lord was sorry that he had made man." "And the Lord repented that he had made Saul king over Israel." In Exodus 32:14, II Samuel 24:16, I Chronicles 21:15, and Jeremiah 26:18, Yahweh changes his attitude toward and his intention regarding his people: "And the Lord repented of the evil which he thought to do to his people" (Exodus 32:14). Again in Amos 7:3,6, God becomes more forbearing because of the prophet's entreaties. In these and other ways,[98] the Old Testament portrays God as a dynamic, changing being.

If the New Testament is not as explicit in its references to God as a being who changes and becomes, it is very possibly because it simply takes for granted the Old Testament conception of God. That the God of the New Testament is a dynamic, living, unpredictable being is clear, in any event, from Jesus' teachings regarding him. According to those teachings, God is full of surprises, as unpredictable as a thief in the night[99] or as a wind that "blows where it wills."[100] Rational, human standards of reward and punishment do not govern such a God.[101] Though his intention remains constant, the attitudes and responses of human beings may lead him to change his tactics.[102]

In the New Testament one act of divine change or becoming overshadows all others. The act itself is reported in John 1 and Philippians 2, its result in Colossians 2: "The Word became flesh, and dwelt among us." "Christ Jesus . . . did not count equality with God a thing to be grasped, but emptied himself." As in the Incarnation he became empty, so as the risen Lord he has become full: "God has highly exalted him" and "in him the whole fulness of deity dwells bodily."[103]

Jesus himself summarized the whole meaning and intent of the divine becoming in a single word: Father. God wills above all to be the Father, the benevolent Creator and Ruler of everything that is. The stern and forbidding Patriarch who dominates the message of the Old Testament has in the New Testament stepped out of the shadows to relate himself personally and paternally to his people. As Father, he expresses his character and will through the gift of a Son, a person in whose life is disclosed "what man means when he says 'God' and what God means when he says 'man,'" (H. F. Rall).

But if God becomes Father he does not do so pointlessly or purposelessly. He does so, indeed, with the express purpose that human beings may become his children. The entire aim of redemption is the transformation of those who have been (in Paul's words) "slaves to the elemental spirits of the universe"[104] into children of a living Father. So St. Paul sums up the meaning of the Christ event:

> But when the time had fully come, God sent forth his Son, born of woman, born under the law, to redeem those who were under the law, so that we might receive adoption as sons. And because you are sons, God has sent the Spirit of his Son into our hearts, crying "Abba! Father!" So through God you are no longer a slave but a son. . . .[105]

Even as the process of redemption involves a divine becoming, then, so its result involves a human becoming. Whether one thinks of the mode of human becoming as that of rebirth,[106] that of new creation,[107] or that of adoption,[108] such becoming eventuates in any case in "the glorious liberty of the children of God."[109] In the next two chapters we shall focus on the nature of that liberty and on the renewed and renewing relationships to God, neighbor, and nature which make it possible.

QUESTIONS FOR STUDY AND DISCUSSION

1. What particular understanding of human freedom is associated with the Christian idea of the Kingdom, or rule, of God?

2. What is the basic nature of humanity, according to the story of Adam and Eve? How does that story serve to illumine the general human situation?

3. What does it mean to say that sin is the distorting of crucial or definitive relationships? Using the Adam and Eve story, show how the relationships to God, neighbor, and nature are affected by human self-worship.

4. How does the prayer of St. Augustine ("Thou has made us, O Lord, for Thyself, and our hearts are restless until they find rest in Thee") express the essential unity of divine creation, divine judgment, and divine redemption?

5. How does the conviction that God is alive distinguish the biblical conception of God from that of classical Greek philosophy? To what extent and in what way did the settlement of the ancient controversy over Christ's divinity amount to a compromise between the biblical view and the philosophic?

6. How does the doctrine of the Trinity express the idea that God is alive?

7. In what ways does the Bible portray God as an active, living being?

8. What does it mean, within the Judaeo-Christian context, to call God "Father"?

9. Define the term "redemption." Why is this term a particularly apt name for what Christians mean by "salvation"?

10. What did St. Paul mean by "justification"? by "boasting"? How does his summary of his own life story in Philippians 3 help us understand his struggle for justification and his attitude toward boasting? What understanding of salvation or redemption comes through in this summary?

11. Compare the way of Adam with the way of Christ. Show how the contrasts between these ways can help us make sense of Paul's summary of his own history in Philippians 3.

12. Why is the full humanity of Christ as important to the Christian conception of redemption as the full divinity? Why is the complete personal union of the divinity and the humanity also important, if salvation is to be properly understood?

13. Why is the idea of a divine "becoming" essential to the gospel of redemption? What kind of human becoming does this divine becoming make possible?

NOTES TO CHAPTER VIII

1. A number of Protestant communions celebrate the sacrament of the Lord's Supper using ordinary bakery bread and grape juice as the elements instead of the traditional wafers and wine.

2. The Definition of Chalcedon (451). Cited in Henry Bettenson, ed., *Documents of the Christian Church*, 2nd ed. (New York and London: Oxford University Press, Inc., 1963), pp. 72–73. Copyright Oxford University Press 1963. Used by permission of Oxford University Press.

3. I am indebted for this insight, as for many others, to Reinhold Seeberg's *Textbook of the History of Doctrines*, trans. C. E. Hay (Grand Rapids, Mich.: Baker Book House, 1958). Cf. his discussion of the Trinitarian controversies (vol. I, pp. 201–243) and especially his introductory statement (p. 201): "We shall utterly fail to understand the conflicts of the period before us [the pre-Nicene period], if we shall interpret them as merely a result of the metaphysical tendency of Grecian thought. On the contrary, beneath these controversies lay most thoroughly practical and religious motives.... Christ must be conceived of as in nature and character capable of bestowing the divine life upon men."

4. Cf. Allan Galloway, *The Cosmic Christ* (New York: Harper & Brothers, Publishers, 1951).

5. As the continued existence of competing movements and denominations attests, this history is by no means over. For a classic study of its early and in many ways definitive stages, see A. Grillmeier, *Christ in Christian Tradition, Volume One: From the Apostolic Age to Chalcedon (451)*, 2nd, rev. ed., trans. J. Bowden (Atlanta: John Knox Press, 1975). For an extremely useful typology describing the positions of the major parties to the debate, see H. R. Niebuhr, *Christ and Culture* (New York: Harper & Brothers, Publishers, 1941).

6. G. K. Chesterton, *Orthodoxy* (Westport, Conn.: Greenwood Press, 1974), p. 71.

7. Cf. T. S. Kuhn, *The Structure of Scientific Revolutions* (Chicago: University of Chicago Press, 1962), pp. 23–42, 77–91 *et passim*.

8. See Chapter VII, pp. 231–32.

9. Matthew 16:26.

10. Blaise Pascal, *Pensées* 347–48, in *Pensées and the Provincial Letters*, trans. W. F. Trotter and Thomas M'Crie (New York: Random House, Inc., 1941), p. 116. Copyright © E. P. Dutton & Company.

11. *Biblical Religion and the Search for Ultimate Reality* (Chicago: The University of Chicago Press, 1955), p. 38. Copyright © The University of Chicago Press, 1955. Used by permission.

12. John 1:12.

13. Genesis 2:15.

14. Genesis 2:18–20.

15. Cf. Genesis 3:1–7, especially the serpent's promise (verse 5), " 'you will be like God, knowing good and evil.' "

16. See Chapter II, footnote on p. 54.

17. For a definition of myth in the theological sense, see Chapter I, footnote on pp. 9–10.

18. There is considerable truth in Laplace's remark, as Dietrich Bonhoeffer and others have pointed out, as long as one remains within the context of theoretical science. In the classical Christian view, however, the human need for God is not theoretical and cannot in any case be reduced to a need to fill in the blanks within a theory or picture of nature. Cf. E. L. Fackenheim, *God's Presence in History* (New York: Harper & Row, Publishers, Inc., 1970), chap. II.

19. Genesis 3:6b, 12.

20. Genesis 3:13.

21. Genesis 3:9.

22. One is reminded of Groucho Marx's oft-quoted remark that he would not belong to a country club that would have him in it; a similar ambivalence may plague the sinner who has the misfortune of becoming self-conscious about his or her self-worship.

23. One wonders if those who adorn their cars with bumper stickers reading "God is my co-pilot" are fully aware of what that claim implies. A co-pilot is, in every system of air command, the subordinate of the pilot!

24. Psalms 14:1, 53:1. Emphasis added.

25. An awareness of this fact may inform Jesus' response to a questioner who addressed him as "Good Master": "Why do you call me good? No one is good but God alone." (Mark 10:17–18)

26. Matthew 5:6 (KJV).

27. Zoologists could well argue, of course, that even the basic act of living is a transitive act, since it depends on the ingestion, consumption, and excretion of nutrients. For our purposes, however, it is sufficient to stick with the traditional categories of common-sense observation and the common language.

28. Among the ancients, the unceasing circular or cyclical movements of the celestial bodies (sun, moon, planets, stars) were taken as evidence of the superiority, the more manifest immortality, of these bodies. All earthly beings die, and the cycles of earthly life (life, death, rebirth or reincarnation) are spasmodic and irregular. The heavenly bodies move in constant circuits which illustrate their higher standing among the hierarchies of being.

29. Cf. I Corinthians 1:22–24: "For Jews demand signs and Greeks seek wisdom, but we preach Christ crucified, a stumbling block to Jews and folly to Gentiles, but to those who are called, both Jews and Greeks, Christ the power of God and the wisdom of God."

30. Probably the best and most comprehensive of these to date is that of A. Grillmeier, *Christ in Christian Tradition, Volume One: From the Apostolic Age to Chalcedon (451)*. Other excellent studies are to be found in J. N. D. Kelly, *Early Christian Doctrines*, 2nd ed., Parts II and III (New York: Harper & Brothers, Publishers, 1960), and H. A. Wolfson, *The Philosophy of the Church Fathers, Volume I: Faith, Trinity, Incarnation*, Parts Two and Three (Cambridge, Mass.: Harvard University Press, 1956).

31. The main documents that set forth the terms of the conclusive compromises are the Creed of Nicaea, the later so-called "Nicene" Creed, and the Definition of Chalcedon. See H. Bettenson, ed., *Documents of the Christian Church*, pp. 36, 37, 72–73.

32. The phrase is Reinhold Seeberg's. See his *Textbook of the History of Doctrines*, Vol. I, p. 206.

33. The victory actually came in stages. Though the controversy appeared to be resolved by the condemnation of Arius at the Council of Nicea in 325, the political machinations of the Emperor Constantine and of leading churchmen led to the resurgence of the Arian view in the decades between Nicea and the Council of Constantinople, which reaffirmed the Athanasian-Nicene position in 381. Cf. Bettenson, *Documents of the Christian Church*, pp. 35-37, 54-62.

34. Cf. Bettenson, *Documents*, pp. 36-37.

35. See *On the Trinity*, in P. Schaff, ed. *A Select Library of Nicene and Post-Nicene Fathers of the Christian Church*, First Series (Buffalo, N. Y.: Christian Literature Company, 1886–88), vol. III, Book IX *et passim*.

36. See Chapter VI, p. 202.

37. John 1:1, 14.

38. II Corinthians 5:19.

39. Romans 5:8.

40. Cf., for examples, A. C. Bouquet, *Sacred Books of the World* (Baltimore: Penguin Books, 1954), pp. 29–31, 215–16, 243.

41. Romans 8:21.

42. See Chapter II, pp. 34–35.

43. That it did extend to such routine operations is clearly implied in the divine promise given in the covenant with Noah: "While the earth remains, seedtime and harvest, cold and heat, summer and winter, day and night, shall not cease." Genesis 8:22.

44. To this category, for example, belong a number of the miracles reported in the cycles of stories relating to Elijah the prophet and his successor, Elisha. Cf. I Kings 17 and II Kings 2:6–14, 19–25, 4:1–7, 25b–37.

45. Cf. Genesis 17:15–21, 18:1–15, 21:1–7, 25:21, 29:31, 30:22–24, 37–50; Exodus 3:1–4:23, 7:14–12:32, 13:17–14:31, 16:1–35; Joshua 5:10–6:20.

46. Cf. Genesis 6:5–17, 11:1–9, 18:20–19:28.

47. The Old Testament portrait of God as a provider was without doubt a main source of the later Christian synonym for God, Providence. For instances of God's providential care for Israel, see note 45.

48. Matthew 2:15.

49. Cf. Exodus 20:3–4.

50. Matthew 6:10; cp. Luke 11:2.

51. Matthew 5:45.

52. Luke 6:35.

53. Matthew 6:5–8.

54. Matthew 6:25–34.

55. Matthew 7:11.

56. Matthew 10:19–20; cp. Mark 13:11 and Luke 12:11–12.

57. Matthew 10:29–31; cp. Luke 12:6–7 and 21:18.

58. Matthew 11:25–26; cp. Luke 10:21.

59. Matthew 10:32–33; cp. Luke 12:8–9.

60. Matthew 13:1–9, 18–23; cp. Mark 4:1–20 and Luke 8:4–15.

61. Matthew 12:46–50; cp. Mark 3:31–35 and Luke 8:19–21.

62. Matthew 7:21–23; cp. Luke 6:46.

63. John 10:30, 14:6.

64. John 17:18, 20:21.

65. Matthew 2:15; Luke 1:32,34.

66. Matthew 3:17; Mark 1:11; Luke 3:22.

67. Matthew 27:54; Mark 15:39.

68. Matthew 1:18–23; Luke 1:26–38.

69. *Cruden's Complete Concordance,* which is by no means exhaustive, lists sixty-five references, scattered through eighteen separate writings.

70. Cf. I Corinthians 3:16, 6:19; cp. Romans 8:9 and II Corinthians 6:16.

71. Luke 15:11–32.

72. For a choice piece of Old Testament sarcasm bearing on this point, see Isaiah 44:9–20.

73. Cf. I. Corinthians 1:26–31; Romans 3:27–4:2.

74. Cf. Genesis 4:8–9.

75. Romans 7:12.

76. Romans 7:10.

77. Romans 8:31–34a, 38–39.

78. Romans 8:21.

79. Ephesians 2:8–10.

80. Romans 1:17, 3:21–26.

81. Cf. Romans 3:9–18.

82. I Corinthians 15:45.

83. I Corinthians 15:22.

84. Cf. Romans 6:3–11 and I Corinthians 15:54–57.

85. Cf., for example, Romans 8:28; John 3:16; Matthew 1:21.

86. Galatians 3:13, citing Deuteronomy 21:23.

87. I Corinthians 1:23.

88. I Corinthians 1:27–29. Emphasis added.

89. See pp. 304–6.

90. II Corinthians 5:17 (NEB).

91. Matthew 12:43–45; Luke 11:24–26.

92. Matthew 1:23, citing Isaiah 7:14.

93. Chief among these thinkers was Apollinarius of Laodicea (310?–390?), a friend of Athanasius from whom the *Apollinarian heresy*, which taught that Christ did not have a human mind or soul, took its name.

94. This view, opposition to which led Apollinarius (see note 93) to his heretical position, later became associated primarily with Nestorius, fifth-century patriarch of Constantinople whose views of the independence of the divine and human natures in Christ were condemned as heretical by the Council of Chalcedon (451).

95. H. Bettenson, ed. *Documents of the Christian Church*, p. 73. Used by permission of the Oxford University Press.

96. John 1:1, 14.

97. John 1:12.

98. Foremost among these, as we noted in Chapter II and earlier in this chapter, is the use of a verb rather than a noun to name God. See pp. 50–51 and 294.

99. Matthew 24:42–44; I Thessalonians 5:2.

100. John 3:8.

101. Cf. Matthew 5:43–48, 20:1–16.

102. See p. 299.

103. Cf. John 1:14; Philippians 2:5–6; Colossians 2:9.

104. Galatians 4:3.

105. Galatians 4:4–7.

106. John 3:3–8.

107. Cf. II Corinthians 5:17; Galatians 6:15.

108. Cf. Romans 8:14–23; Galatians 4:5.

109. Romans 8:21.

IX.   Faith and Community:

The Word as Reconciliation

THE CHRISTIAN PORTRAIT of the human situation is now taking shape. Christians tie their view of the world together with certain ideas or convictions. They perceive, first, that the human creature is a being who is defined by certain relationships. They come to believe that the relationship which should define humans above all others is the relationship to God, a relationship expressed in the terms "rule of God" (which expresses human dependence on God) and "image of God" (which expresses human likeness to God and the human dominion over nature). They also become convinced that the relationship by which humans prefer to define themselves is not the relation to the Creator but that to creaturely reality. So strong is this preference that human creatures forsake the Creator, worshipping the image of God in themselves and losing touch with the divine Reality.

Left to their own devices, the human creatures' plight would be quite hopeless. But the Christian gospel is that God has not left people alone in their plight. In Christ God acted decisively to reestablish his rule over creation. In relating himself to the man Jesus of Nazareth, earth's Creator acted to become earth's Redeemer, to break the false ties that had given the lesser creatures dominion over the human creature. The pattern of relating established in Adam—a pattern of *apparent* self-exaltation which proves on examination to be a pattern of *actual* self-enslavement—has in Christ been reversed. "For as in Adam all die, so also in Christ shall all be made alive."[1]

All who follow Christ shall be made alive because in Christ the life style of self-exaltation which cuts the creature off from God has been supplanted by a life style of self-giving which relates the creature anew to the self-giving Creator. "For whoever would save his life will lose it," Jesus taught, "and whoever loses his life for my sake and the gospel's will save it."[2] Life is thus to be found in being given away. The supreme model for such self-giving is the Lord Christ himself, who "though he was in the form of God, did not count equality with God a thing to be grasped, but emptied himself, taking the form of a servant. . . . And being found in human form he humbled himself and became obedient unto death, even death on a cross."

The human situation has thus been drastically altered by two epoch-making events in the history of the race. Through the event of Adam and the event of Christ, two entirely opposed ways of relating to reality have become options for human beings. In the first, humans may attempt to assert their independence of the Creator, to go it alone, defining good and evil for themselves and determining their own destinies. But this way, the Christian faith holds, is a snare and a delusion. Persons who would make themselves God forfeit that freedom to respond which can make them persons. They become in effect the dupes and bondslaves of their own highly deceiving sense of control.

The second way of relating to reality which history has disclosed was revealed supremely in the career of Jesus of Nazareth. The life and life style of Jesus make it clear that human fulfillment and freedom are not to be found in frantic or determined efforts to control history's outcome but rather in an openness to the leadership of history's Lord. "Unless one is born anew," Jesus said—unless one is prepared to start over, to make a new beginning, to surrender the way of Adam for a new way—"he cannot see the kingdom of God."[3] Again, "unless you turn and become like children"—not childish, but childlike, open and responsive to what God is doing in history—"you will never enter the kingdom of heaven."[4]

The way of Adam and the way of Christ: ultimately all human options reduce to these two. The evidence that the way of Adam is a live (and lived) option is abundant. In the everyday competitive scramble it becomes all too clear that humans are very much in the grip of the cycle of self-concern which originates in the usually subconscious decision to be one's own god. But what of the second option? Is it a real, a viable option? Is it possible for human beings to find life by giving it away? The Christian faith makes just such a claim. Let us explore further what that claim means.

REDEMPTION'S APPROPRIATION:
THE HOLY SPIRIT

Christians hold that the way of Christ is a live option for contemporary human life because the Spirit of Christ remains alive in the world. The way in which Christ's Spirit works is a profound mystery; *that* it works is for Christians an equally profound certainty. The wind blows where it will, and one knows neither its whence nor its whither, but that it blows is a lived and enlivening experience.

The ways of the Spirit are mysterious, in the Christian view, largely because the Spirit himself is a figure of mystery. Such mystery is no accident but instead a straightforward expression of the Spirit's nature. Indeed the very word "Spirit" is primarily a name for the mystery, the indefinability, the inscrutable transcendence, of God. Because God is infinite Spirit, it is absurd to think that finite images, whether physical or mental,[5] can describe him. Because he is infinite Spirit, it is equally absurd to think that a finite world can offer one a hiding place from him.[6] Spirit expresses the boundlessness both of the divine person and of the divine presence.

There is another reason that the Spirit remains a figure of mystery within the biblical descriptions of his workings. As described in Scripture, the Spirit is as modest as he is mysterious. Much of the mystery surrounding him is traceable to his modest habit of glorifying the Father and the Son while he himself remains in the background. Throughout Scripture the term "Spirit" rarely appears without the accompanying phrases "of God," "of the Lord," or "of Christ." It thus appears that the Spirit prefers to work as a supporter, reinforcer, and revealer of God's acts in creation and in Christ rather than independently. Like the operator of the stage lights in a dramatic production, the Spirit does not claim the stage for himself but illumines it for other Actors.

The Spirit first becomes known, then, as the Illuminator, the Revealer of God. As the stage lights collaborate with a script to introduce the persons and the plot of a drama to an audience, so, as we saw in Chapter VI, the Spirit enlivens the Word of Scripture to usher God and an understanding of God's will into human lives. Like the director of lighting in a stage play, the Spirit calls no attention to himself but is nonetheless indispensable to the drama.

The drama in which the Spirit plays so vital a role is no ordinary one. It is, as Christians perceive it, earth's most important drama, the drama of redemption. The work of the Spirit is absolutely crucial, Christians believe, because through it human beings are enabled to come on stage, as it were—to enter directly and personally into the divine-human drama through which God works to liberate human beings, fulfill their lives, and establish his rule among them.

During the experimental decade of the 1960s, many theater-goers were given an opportunity they had never had before, the opportunity of taking part in the plays of eminent playwrights. The audience-participation plays of Jean Genet and others sought to convert spectators into participants. In a real sense, such playwrights were stealing a page from the book of the Holy Spirit. It is the Spirit, Christ taught,[7] who will lead the redemptive drama's spectator-participants "into the truth." If it is not the work of the Spirit to take the limelight for himself, neither is it the Spirit's work to present an objective spectacle in which the Father and the Son occupy a stage remote from the concerns of ordinary life. The Spirit brings God and the human creature on stage together, as it were, and in so doing engages them in history's most significant drama, that of redemption.

In our earlier discussion of the Trinity,[8] we noted a quality in the Spirit which equips it particularly well for the work of stagesetting we have just described. Within the Trinity itself, we observed, the Spirit is the transitive and unitive principle. The name "Holy Spirit" refers first to a *transitive* capacity in God, a capacity by which he transcends or goes beyond himself to make himself his own object. Because of this capacity we may speak of God as "alive." So in speaking of God the Holy Spirit, we speak mainly of the divine "life" or "vitality." But beyond this transitive capacity, the term "Holy Spirit" also names a certain uniting or reuniting power in God. In an illustration of this power which we borrowed from St. Augustine in Chapter VIII, we compared it to the love that goes between, and so unites, a lover and a beloved. The Spirit refers, then, not only to a power to live which enables God to transcend himself but also to a holy self-love which enables him to remain the same being through all the changes that his power of self-transcendence makes possible. As we stated in Chapter VIII, God remains a unity though he is forever a *living*, a changing and developing, unity.

Spirit, then, names those capacities in God that enable him to remain himself even as he transcends himself: to live without doing violence to his self-unifying love, and to love, or remain self-consistent, without surrendering his freedom to live, to change, to develop. It is precisely these capacities that both enable and motivate God to take the initiative in the dramas of creation and redemption. Because God is Spirit, he lives; and because he lives, he can transcend himself, can reach out to fashion a world and to participate in the world he fashions. Unlike the aloof and sterile god of Aristotle, God the Spirit is God the Actor, the Shaper, the Lord of nature and of history. He is, in short, the God of creation. But because God is Spirit he also loves, and because he loves he remains true to himself and to his intention of love, even when his own actions and those of his creatures change the context and conditions within which love must be expressed. Precisely when those conditions and that context seem most opposed to love, precisely when the creature's hatred flies in the face of love and seems to cancel love's effects, precisely there must love prevail if redemption is to take place. Unlike the vengeful gods of Olympus, then, God the Spirit must be

Lord not only of creation but also of his own emotions and of his own enemies. He must be a God whose love forbids hatred within himself and overcomes hatred within his creatures; in short, he must be a God who acts to redeem and reclaim sinners.

This, according to the Christian perspective, is precisely what God the Spirit has done. "God's love has been poured into our hearts through the Holy Spirit which has been given to us," wrote St. Paul; "God shows his love for us in that while we were yet sinners Christ died for us."[9] Through the Spirit, that divine love which was expressed supremely on the cross "has been poured into our hearts." The result is that (again to quote Paul) "the law of the Spirit of life in Christ Jesus has set me free from the law of sin and death."[10] This means that the Spirit's human recipients have been drawn into a relationship with God analogous to that of the man Jesus, so that they too can be called "children of God":

> For all who are led by the Spirit of God are sons of God. . . . When we cry "Abba! Father!" it is the Spirit himself bearing witness with our spirit that we are children of God, and if children, then heirs, heirs of God and fellow heirs with Christ, provided we suffer with him in order that we may also be glorified with him.[11]

Paul thus portrays the Spirit as the chief agent of a divine work which he elsewhere (in the fourth chapter of his Letter to the Galatians) describes as "adoption":

> [4]But when the time had fully come, God sent forth his Son, born of woman, born under the law, [5]to redeem those who were under the law, so that we might receive adoption as sons. [6]And because you are sons, God has sent the Spirit of his Son into our hearts, crying "Abba! Father!" [7]So through God you are no longer a slave but a son, and if a son then an heir.

Thus that same Spirit who will be viewed in later theology as One who unites the divine Father and the *divine* Son is portrayed in theology's earliest formulas (those of Paul) as One who unites the divine Father and his *human* children. But the fact that God could "send forth" his Son (verse 4) and the fact that "the Spirit of his Son" could also be "sent" (verse 6) indicated to later Trinitarian theologians that, already in Paul's thought (by implication at least), the unity between God and humans depends on a prior unity, and a co-operation, between "God," "his Son," and the "Spirit of his Son."

The Spirit, as the principle of God's self-transcending life and of his self-uniting love, thus becomes the means by which he expresses his life and love within the history of humankind. The God who came on the human scene in his Son remains on the human scene in the "Spirit of his Son." Through the Son God incarnated himself in Jesus of Nazareth; through the Spirit he extends the effects of that incarnation into the lives of other human beings. The redemption that became *real* in Christ must be *realized* in other humans through the reconciling ministry of the Spirit.[12]

The Holy Spirit is known primarily through his effects, or as St. Paul called them, his "gifts."[13] The Spirit's gifts are in the first place existential or personal. They affect human existence and the human personality directly, radically redirecting them. These profound, personal changes effect equally profound and practical changes of an ethical, social, and historical sort. The rest of this chapter and all of the next will deal with these practical effects.

REDEMPTION'S EXISTENTIAL EFFECTS: LIBERATION AND RECONCILIATION

When defined in terms of his work among human beings, the Holy Spirit, as we have noted, is the Christian name for Christ's continued presence. As Wolfhart Pannenberg observed, "the Spirit guarantees the participation of the believers in the living Jesus Christ."[14] The Spirit not only brings Christ to the Christian; he also affords the Christian the power to participate in the redeemed life Christ offers. But in what does such a redeemed life consist? How does the life of the redeemed differ from that of the unredeemed? Until these questions are answered, the whole question of Christianity's practical import for human life remains in doubt, for unless redemption changes the way people live and think, it is of no practical effect.

In the Christian view, redemption does indeed change how people think and live. In conferring his gifts of creation and redemption, the Holy Spirit confers on human beings powers similar to those he expresses in the being of God—the powers to live and to love. The power to live makes Christians aware of their participation in God's life-giving creation; it also makes them capable of living life freely and responsibly. The power to live is thus a power which *liberates*, sets free, makes response-able. The power to love breaks the hold that sin has on human affections. Sin's grip is broken as the lives of persons become God-centered and neighbor-focused instead of self-centered and self-focused. The power to love is thus a power that *reconciles*, straightening and restoring the relationships to God, nature, and the neighbor which sin has twisted and perverted.

The Spirit's Liberating Work

The Spirit's gift of the power of life has special meaning for human beings. Human life is by definition a life in freedom: as we noted earlier, the distinction between human selves and subhuman things inheres in the capacity of the former to participate actively in defining their own histories. Christians are convinced that this power human beings have to define themselves is itself a gift of God. "Man *is* what he is in the sight of God," St. Francis of Assisi is reputed to have said, "no more and no less." Whatever powers of self-definition the human creature enjoys are believed by Christians to derive from God's ultimate power to define all things. The free action of the divine Spirit is the presupposition of that authentic freedom by which human beings can shape their own lives.

The close tie between human freedom and the free action of God is made more vividly apparent when the reality of sin is taken into account. Sin, we have noted, is a form of slavery. Sin's human victims are caught in the grip of a vicious self-concern. The more intently they struggle to break that grip, the greater their concern for themselves becomes. Human efforts to break the hold of sin are bound, therefore, to be ineffectual. Only a reorientation of life, away from self and toward Another, can restore the human capacity to participate freely and healthily in history. Such a reorientation is properly called redemption, precisely because it does redeem or emancipate the self from its bondage to itself.

In freeing the self from its infatuation with itself, the Spirit also frees it from other life-depleting dependencies. As an evangelical tradition stretching from Paul through Augustine to Luther and John Wesley has consistently emphasized, the Spirit's gift of redemption means not only freedom from sin and self, but also freedom from the law, from death, and from what we today would call "popular opinion." Because it releases the self from inordinate self-concern, the liberating Spirit releases it from the need for the law as a way of self-salvation, from the fear that death will destroy the self that is the center of one's concern, and from that anxiety about one's standing in the community which also stems from self-concern.

FREEDOM FROM THE TYRANNY OF THE LAW   Redemption liberates from *the law.* "The law" here does not mean the civil or criminal law of the state, of course, but rather the behavior codes that various religions have devised as ways of pleasing God. In themselves such codes are the products of worthy human efforts to understand and define the will of God, and as such they may be (as St. Paul said) "holy and just and good." But when these codes are drawn into the orbit of sinful self-concern, they become transformed from ways of pleasing God into devices for saving and serving the self. Under such conditions the exercises of religion itself become the instruments of sin and self-delusion. The displacement of God by the self is nowhere more thoroughgoing and tragic than when one's own efforts to do good are a source of the displacement. To the degree that the observance of the law promotes notions of self-acquired righteousness, thus reinforcing the slavery of self-worship, it becomes one of the demonic forces which Martin Luther dubbed "tyrants" because of their power to deprive people of authentic freedom.

Authentic freedom from the law is not a freedom to disregard God's will or to ignore codes that express it but rather a freedom to keep the law for the right, as opposed to the wrong, reasons. The example that Christians cite in this connection, as in so many others, is that of Jesus himself. Throughout his career he opposed what Christians have called "legalism" (the idea that keeping the law is meritorious in itself) even while he advocated, with equal vigor, a thoroughgoing obedience to the divine commandments. That legalism which makes law-observance an occasion for self-glorying or for formal but insincere rite-keeping was a favorite object of Jesus' righteous anger. "You hypocrites!" he said to the legalists; "Well did Isaiah prophesy of you, when he said: 'This people honors me with their lips, but their heart is far from me; in vain do they worship me, teaching as doctrines the precepts of men.'"[15]

On the question of the keeping of the law, Jesus' cardinal principle is expressed in his summary of the law:

> You shall love the Lord your God with all your heart, and with all your soul, and with all your mind. This is the great and first commandment. And a second is like it, You shall love your neighbor as yourself. On these two commandments depend all the law and the prophets.[16]

This summary makes it clear that the proper aims of law-observance are to glorify God and to enrich human life. Far from being a way of saving oneself, the law provides a way by which one may lose oneself in the service of God and others.

Jesus was quite aware, however, that the law undergoes a transformation when it is drawn into the orbit of self-concern. Within that context the law may well become an occasion for, and a means to, self-promotion. Thus, in his parable of the Pharisee and the tax collector,[17] Jesus portrays the upright, law-observing Pharisee as a person who employs his own obedience to the law as a kind of perch from which he can boast before God and belittle his neighbor. Similarly, against those who pride themselves on their observance of the written law's minutiae, he protests that such pride blinds them to the law's proper ends, "justice and mercy and faith."[18]

If pride is a main product of the law's misuse, it is equally true, according to Jesus, that the law properly used can foster a healthy humility. "When you have done all that is commanded you," he told his disciples, "say, 'We are unworthy servants; we have only done what was our duty.'"[19] The humility of the tax collector, sinner though he is, is to be preferred to a blind, pharisaic pride. The God Jesus represents is not to be compared to a bookkeeper who records good deeds in one column and evil in another but to a father who rejoices more in the return of a humble and penitent sinner than in the diligent but grudging labors of the sinner's proud brother.[20]

For Jesus the law is important as an expression of what God expects of his human children, but it will not do to take it as a description of the divine disposition or of the path to salvation. Far from acting legalistically, God "makes his sun rise on the evil and on the good, and sends rain on the just and on the unjust."[21] He is like the owner of a vineyard who pays persons who worked but a single hour as much as those who toiled through the heat of the day.[22] God's ways fly in the face of that calculating rationality by which legalists compute righteousness. God's ways are the ways of the gospel rather than the ways of the law, and in launching his Kingdom he makes it possible for human beings, too, to live from the gospel rather than from the law:

> You have heard that it was said, "An eye for an eye and a tooth for a tooth." But I say to you, Do not resist one who is evil. But if any one strikes you on the right cheek, turn to him the other also . . . and if any one forces you to go one mile, go with him two miles. . . . Love your enemies and pray for those who persecute you, so that you may be sons of your Father who is in heaven. . . . For if you love those who love you, what reward have you? Do not even the tax collectors do the same? . . . You, therefore, must be perfect [that is, all-comprehending in your love], as your heavenly Father is perfect.[23]

The implications of Jesus' teachings regarding the law are elaborated and extended in the teachings of St. Paul. With an even greater emphasis than that of Jesus, if that is possible, Paul stresses the contrast between the way of the gospel and the way of the law. There is a real sense, he taught, in which the law is entirely transcended through the power of the Spirit. As Jesus had earlier implied,[24] the law is transcended not by being abrogated but by being fulfilled. Paul is in complete agreement with Jesus that the full intent of the law is satisfied when authentic love is expressed; thus with consummate directness the Apostle writes that "love is the fulfilling of the law."[25]

Because love fulfills the law, both the complexion and the composition of the law are changed. The law has a different complexion, a different appearance, to Christian eyes because it is no longer viewed as the source of salvation. It has a different composition, or content, because all of the ifs, ands, and buts of the legal tradition have been superseded by the simple commandment to love. That commandment expresses the law's essential intention, its spirit as opposed to its letter;[26] and, as Jesus had taught in his conflict with the Sabbatarians,[27] it is the law's intention, rather than its wording, which must be obeyed if the law is to be fulfilled.

Paul's radically new understanding of the law's intention means that the law's very form is changed. The law is now not a written code so much as "the law of the Spirit of life in Christ Jesus."[28] In more down to earth terms, this means that the law, that is, what God expects of human beings,[29] is a spirit of helpfulness in people's dealings with their neighbors. The form of the law—in other words, the ways in which one may be required to act in order to be helpful to the neighbor—is as wide as the world is wide. The acid test regarding the law is not *what* one does but *why* one does it. "All things are lawful," Paul writes, "but not all things are helpful. 'All things are lawful,' but not all things build up. Let no one seek his own good, but the good of his neighbor."[30] And again, elsewhere: "You were called to freedom, brethren; only do not use your freedom as an opportunity for the flesh, but through love be servants of one another. For the whole law is fulfilled in one word, 'You shall love your neighbor as yourself.'"[31]

The first effect of the Spirit's redemptive work is thus freedom from the law. But freedom *from* one understanding of the law is freedom *for* another understanding of it. The law's *intention* becomes primary in the believer's thinking, and it becomes plain that the law's intention is not to provide a way to save oneself but rather a way to serve one's neighbor. Salvation or redemption is the free gift of God. Efforts to save oneself, by the law or by any other means, are not only futile but unnecessary. At the same time, the gospel of redemption delivers one from the obsession with self which both sin and frantic efforts to escape from sin promote. Freed from such obsessive self-concern, persons can act in terms of the law's true intention—for the good of others.

FREEDOM FROM THE TERROR OF DEATH   The same freedom from self-concern which frees one from the tyranny of the law also liberates from inordinate anxiety about death. The Christian attitude toward death is complex, and not all Christian analyses of death agree on its significance. Some theologians view physical death itself as a form of punishment for sin. Others see death as a natural and normal consequence of organic life. Though the resulting debate has theological significance, it is not sufficiently relevant to our discussion of redemption to warrant investigation here. Whether one considers death a form of divine punishment or not, the human fear of death is real. In his book *The Denial of Death*,[32] Ernest Becker makes a strong case for the idea that the fear of death controls our lives in ways that usually go unperceived. The general human reaction to this fear is to hide from it or, as Becker suggests, to deny the reality of its source. Even our funeral customs are in large measure efforts to cover over, to hide from, death.[33] The cosmetic corpse lies pulseless in its coffin and our comments are "How natural he looks!" or "How peaceful!", never "How Dead!"

Our human flight from death is reflected also in the attitude of many persons in American culture toward aging. As viewed by many Americans old age is a veritable curse, to be postponed by devices ranging from the white lie on one's birthday to the scalpel of the plastic surgeon, but to be postponed at any cost. In Confucian China the elderly enjoyed a dignity begotten of filial and societal reverence for their age. In modern America, old people are often consigned by familial and societal indifference to the sterile environment of nursing homes, where they simply wait to die. They become victims of our culture's headlong flight from death.

But why? Why are we so afraid of death and of that aging process which must culminate in death? The answer the Christian faith offers is that death tells us more about ourselves than we want to know. Death tells us, and aging as the advance guard of death tells us, that we are not God. Do what we will to hide from death, to secure ourselves against it, death breaks in to announce that we are mortal, fragile, dependent creatures. It strips away our illusions of security and heightens our sense of self-concern. It may thereby move us in either of two directions: the direction of even more frantic efforts to secure ourselves against the inevitable, or that of trust in a Reality greater than death.

In antiquity death probably was far more terrifying than it is today. The remedies and painkillers of modern medicine were not available, and the slightest illness brought with it a certain fear for one's life. Then as now, but with an intensity proportional to their chronic danger, human beings sought to assuage death's power with funeral rituals and myths of immortality. But at least one ancient thinker looked beyond such palliatives to search for the source of death's terror. "O Death, where is thy sting?" he wrote, and then, answering himself, "The sting of death is sin."[34]

That ancient thinker was St. Paul, and his words comprise the decisive Christian interpretation of the religious problem of death. Death's terror, Paul claimed, is not a natural consequence of having to die but instead is a result of that inordinate self-concern whose name is sin. No greater threat can confront such self-concern than the threat of having to face the truth. Because death destroys all those ruses by which humans convince themselves that they are worthy of their own self-worship, it must at all costs be held at bay. As Pascal declared,

> Man wishes to be happy, and only wishes to be happy, and cannot wish not to be so. But how will he set about it? To be happy he would have to make himself immortal; but, not being able to do so, it has occurred to him to prevent himself from thinking of death.[35]

There is, however, another way, an alternative besides that of hiding from death. The Christian faith asserts that in Christ death has been confronted and conquered. In the same passage in which he identified sin to be death's sting, St. Paul stated that, for the Christian, "death is swallowed up in victory. . . . Thanks be to God, who gives us the victory through our Lord Jesus Christ."[36]

Christ overcomes death, in the Christian view, not by overpowering it from "outside," as it were, but by going through it. Through the centuries Christ's own death has served as the supreme example of what medieval Christians called the *ars moriendi*, the art of dying. The same Lord who showed Christians how to live showed them how to die.[37]

Christ's death, exemplary as it is as an instance of human death, has been assigned in Christian lore a far greater significance than other human deaths. The impact of his death was so deeply felt by his disciples, early and late, that several mythological interpretations evolved as a result of ancient and medieval efforts to understand it. In one interpretation, whose dualistic assumptions are questionable on the grounds of Christian monotheism, Christ's death was a kind of ransom paid by God to the Devil in exchange for the release of spiritually dead souls. In another view, less dualistic but equally dubious for what it says about God, Christ's death was a payment not to the Devil but to God himself, so that, the requirements of the divine justice having been satisfied, God could justly release sinners from death and judgment. In yet another, even more ancient interpretation, Christ is the Christian counterpart of the Jewish lamb of the Passover, for his sacrificial death symbolizes and effects the release of God's people from the state of bondage to sin and death much as the slaying of the Paschal lamb symbolized the sparing of Israel's first-born from the angel of death.[38]

Whatever their other merits or demerits, such attempts to assess and interpret the meaning of Christ's death have at least one merit in common, according to the Christian belief. That merit inheres in their common contention that salvation from death and from the sting of death originates in God and consists finally of becoming reunited with God. As we saw in Chapter VIII, salvation's essential result is the uniting of the human creature with the Creator. The theories of Christ's death, though diverse in other particulars, reflect that understanding of salvation in their common name—"theories of atonement." That name expresses the theories' common interest and their common idea, for the word "atonement" denotes a certain "at-one-ment," a process by which God and humankind, heretofore estranged, become "at one" with each other. Whatever else Christ's death means, all of the Christian theories of atonement agree that it signifies an event through which the new covenant between God and humans, a covenant established when God became human in the act of Incarnation, became accessible to humankind as a whole.

The general Christian answer to the problem of death is thus to be found in a general Christian affirmation regarding the death of Christ. In Christ, the life-giving Creator incarnates himself in his creation. In Christ's death, the same Creator takes on himself the full impact of the forces of destruction which dominate and direct the history of sinful humanity. In Christ's resurrection, the death knell of death itself is sounded, as death's tyranny over humans and its demonic opposition to God are overcome. In Christ's Spirit, he whose death released him to the ages makes the reunion with the life-giving Creator a reality for the believer in the here and now.

The Christian attitude toward death is best conveyed, perhaps, in story form. Death's meaning, like that of life, has a way of evading abstract definition. The concreteness of stories can sometimes draw us closer to the meaning of both realities. In what he described as "an artless tale," Professor John Baillie recounted an incident in the life of a devoutly Christian doctor that says more about the common Christian perception of death than many a scholarly tome does. Asked by a dying patient what, if anything, lay beyond death,

> The doctor [Baillie wrote] fumbled for an answer. But ere he could speak, there was heard a scratching at the door; and his answer was given him. "Do you hear that?" he asked his patient. "That is my dog. I left him downstairs, but he grew impatient and has come up and hears my voice. He has no notion what is inside that door, but he knows I am here. Now is it not the same with you? You do not know what lies beyond the Door, but you know your Master is there."[39]

FREEDOM FROM "WHAT THE NEIGHBORS THINK"   The redemptive Spirit liberates not only from the tyranny of the law and the terror of death but also from the deeply engrained habits of self-concern which control everyday life. As Søren Kierkegaard and Martin Heidegger argued, the most pernicious of these habits is that of following the crowd or, to use Heidegger's name for it, "the they."[40] The great hosts who comprise the social order known as "Christendom" are, in Kierkegaard's view, the most insidious foes of authentic Christianity.[41] These hosts and their leaders have stretched Christ's narrow gate which leads to life into that broad and easy way which leads to destruction.[42] In the general life of "Christendom," the gospel itself has somehow been subverted and transformed by self-concern.

The human penchant for recasting the gospel in more palatable and popular terms is described nowhere more vividly than in Fyodor Dostoyevsky's portrait, in *The Brothers Karamazov*, of Christ's encounter with the Grand Inquisitor. Ivan Karamazov, who tells the story in the novel, sets it in sixteenth-century Seville, "in the most terrible time of the Inquisition." The Lord Christ himself has returned, according to Ivan's tale, to visit one of the great cities of Christendom. As he walks among the people of the city, astounding and arousing them, he is intercepted and arrested by the minions of the Grand Inquisitor, whose task it is to detect and suppress all heretical departures from the Church's dictates. Ivan continues:

The guards lead their prisoner to the close, gloomy vaulted prison in the ancient palace of the Holy Inquisition and shut Him in it. The day passes. . . . In the pitch darkness the iron door of the prison is suddenly opened and the Grand Inquisitor himself comes in with a light in his hand. . . . He goes up slowly, sets the light on the table and speaks.

"Is it Thou? Thou? . . . Why, then, art Thou come to hinder us? . . . For fifteen centuries we have been wrestling with Thy freedom, but now it is ended and over for good. . . . Today, people are more persuaded than ever that they have perfect freedom, yet they have brought their freedom to us and laid it humbly at our feet. But that has been our doing. Was this what Thou didst? Was this Thy freedom? . . . Thou didst reject the only way by which men might be made happy. But, fortunately, departing Thou didst hand on the work to us . . . Nothing has ever been more insupportable for a man and a human society than freedom. . . . But what happened? Instead of taking men's freedom from them, Thou didst make it greater than ever! Didst Thou forget that man prefers peace, and even death, to freedom of choice in the knowledge of good and evil? Nothing is more seductive for man than his freedom of conscience, but nothing is a greater cause of suffering. And behold, instead of giving a firm foundation for setting the conscience of man at rest for ever, Thou didst choose all that is exceptional, vague and enigmatic. . . . Instead of taking possession of men's freedom, Thou didst increase it, and burdened the spiritual kingdom of mankind with its sufferings for ever. . . . We have corrected Thy work. . . . And men rejoiced that they were again led like sheep, and that the terrible gift that had brought them such suffering was, at last, lifted from their hearts. Were we right teaching them this? Speak! Did we not love mankind, so meekly acknowledging their feebleness, lovingly lightening their burden, and permitting their weak nature even sin with our sanction? Why hast Thou come now to hinder us? . . . Tomorrow, Thou shalt see that obedient flock who at a sign from me will hasten to heap up the hot cinders about the pile on which I shall burn Thee for coming to hinder us."[43]

If Dostoyevsky's story grips us, it does so as much because of its truth as because of its art. The real villain of the piece, from the Christian standpoint, is not the Inquisitor as much as the sin that controls both the Inquisitor and his flock. The self-concern which enables the Inquisitor to rule is not his own concern for himself but the concern of his subjects for themselves. Sin is a social, and not simply an individual, illness. When John Wesley contended against his sister that "the voice of the people is the voice of God," her rejoinder was, "Yes. I can hear the people now, crying 'Crucify him!' " The point of Dostoyevsky's parable appears to be that Christ is ever and anon the victim of the crowd.

In an age when scarcely any major venture is launched without first consulting a public opinion poll, Dostoyevsky's point hardly needs further illustration. The tendency to let current fashions and fads dictate one's attitudes and actions is familiar to virtually every member of today's media-dominated societies. What the neighbors think may have become less important as people have become more urban and cosmopolitan in their attitudes, but the role of fashion setters within various cultures and countercultures has been magnified by the rise of the mass media. Physically, Americans may be more mobile today than ever before, and culturally they may have more options, but spiritually or attitudinally they are often the victims of media-created yearnings and commercially or politically inspired appeals to the fear that they may fall behind the Joneses.

The power of the mass media, like that of the Grand Inquisitor, is not self-generated power. It is instead a power generated by the acts of surrender through which self-preoccupied humans have forfeited their autonomy for a presumed security or a present self-gratification. As the Grand Inquisitor argued and as Kierkegaard and Heidegger demonstrated, freedom can be a terrifying reality. To be oneself has never been easy, and to be oneself in a day when Norman Brown[44] and other gurus of East and West are declaiming selfhood itself to be the main source of evil can be especially difficult. The heart of the difficulty lies within freedom's own nature. True freedom, as Christians understand it, is not only the freedom to be oneself but also the freedom to transcend one's self-concern. This is why Jesus could teach that only those who can lose themselves (that is, their self-concern) will be able to find themselves (that is, the freedom to live their own lives without obsessive concern about the opinions of others).[45]

The power to lose oneself is not, however, a power that the self-focused person (the sinner) has at his or her command. As we have remarked before, even one's efforts to escape self-concern are motivated by self-concern. Efforts at self-salvation illustrate the problem of sin instead of solving it. Nor, on Christian grounds, are efforts to escape the self altogether, through mystical exercises, authentic remedies. The abolition of the self and the autonomy of the self are not the same thing, and the gospel advocates the latter, not the former. Authentic freedom or autonomy does not seek a historyless Nirvana but values instead that unique individuality which is history's main product.

If the power to be one's authentic self comes neither from strenuous self-assertion nor from mystical self-abandonment, whence does it come? It comes, states the gospel, as the free gift of God. In reestablishing the relationship to the life-giving Creator, the redemptive Spirit makes real once again the power of human creatures to exercise dominion over their situation. The Word which liberates from self-concern liberates also from the opinions of others which are so important to the concerned self. Others' opinions are not totally devalued; indeed, they are properly valued for the first time, for they are now perceived in their own terms rather than as threats to or saviors of the self. No longer does the self need them to confirm its self-esteem. The one judgment that counts—that of the divine Judge himself—has been pronounced in the gospel of God's accepting love, and such a judgment brings with it freedom from the idea that human judgments, whether one's own or one's neighbor's, are of ultimate value.

Faith renders one free not only from the law and death but also from false dependence on the views of others. But in all three areas it confers a freedom *for* as well as a freedom *from*. Freed from the law, the self is free for a new way of expressing love for God and care for the neighbor. Freed from death, it is free for trust in a Reality greater than death, a

God who in Christ tasted death and conquered it. Freed from the judgments of other selves, it is free to take charge of its situation and to express its authentic selfhood.

The Spirit's Reconciling Work

In discussing the Spirit's liberating work, we have dealt almost exclusively with the impact of redemption on the individual. Faith and freedom, which are the Spirit's primary gifts, are given in the first instance to individuals. Faith must in fact originate in individuals. This is true even though biblical faith can well be described as the faith of a community. Every human faith that is to avoid becoming a form of fanatical eccentricity must eventually establish a set of community values and maintain itself through community traditions. But this does not mean that faith's absolute origins lie in community life. The faith of Israel was and is assuredly the faith of a community, a social faith. Despite its eventual communitarian nature, however, the faith of Israel began with an individual named Abraham, was reborn in an individual named Jacob, and was revived and recast yet again by an individual named Moses. Any faith worthy of human practice must originate in the courage and commitment of individuals. The depth of faith's original courage may be enriched by the variety of expressions faith finds in a community. But every community of faith must have its Abrahams and Jacobs, its patriarchs and pioneers.

Martin Luther was right when he said that one must believe for oneself no less than one must die for oneself. Even so, if faith ended with the individual, that would soon be the end of faith. There is a second impulse within faith besides the power to be oneself. God's liberating Spirit is simultaneously God's reconciling Spirit, and the power he gives one to live contains within itself the power to love. Accordingly, to be oneself does not mean to be *for* oneself, self-enclosed. The power to control one's situation is simultaneously the power to care about the situations of others.

Liberation is thus linked closely to reconciliation. The freedom to be oneself, free from self-concern, is the freedom to be for others. Dietrich Bonhoeffer, a German Christian who became a martyr for his faith as a result of his opposition to the Hitler regime in the 1930s and 1940s, saw in Jesus himself the supreme example of such freedom for others.[46] As the "Man-for-others" (Bonhoeffer's phrase), Jesus unleashed an infectious freedom which enables his followers to subordinate their own concerns to the needs of others. According to Paul Van Buren, one of a group of Christian "secularists" who take many of their cues from

Bonhoeffer, the meaning of Christ's resurrection is that Jesus' freedom to love survived his death and became a possibility for the rest of us.[47] The adequacy of such an interpretation of the Resurrection is questionable; the interpretation seems to confuse the Resurrection's reality with its effects. But as a description of the Resurrection's effects, the interpretation has merit. The phrase "freedom to love" is an extremely apt summary of salvation's essential practical effects. The freedom God gives through Christ and the Spirit is always freedom to love. The Spirit who liberates is the Spirit who reconciles.

Reconciliation means the restoration of a relationship. Christian reconciliation, indeed, means the restoration of all of the primary relationships that define authentic humanity: the relationship to God, the relationship to oneself (identity and self-transcendence), and the relationship to other finite beings (nature and the neighbor). In concrete human experience these relationships are not separable; an authentic relationship to God carries with it the authentication of the relationships to self, neighbor, and nature just as (as we saw in Chapter VIII) a distortion of the God-relationship carries with it a distortion of all these relationships.

Reconciliation's effects come to light in the changed attitudes and life styles of the persons whose defining relationships have been restored by it. Reconciliation with God produces trust, gratitude, and humility, attitudes which seek expression in worship. Reconciliation with oneself produces attitudes of openness, confidence, and self-acceptance which result in a prayerful thoughtfulness and a desire to share the good news of one's new-found freedom. Reconciliation with nature and with the neighbor produce a new appreciation of God's creation and a renewed concern for one's neighbor which result in a life of caring service. The three main modes of Christian service defined in Chapter IV—the service of worship, of the Word, and of work—are thus expressions of reconciliation's three primary effects. We must now discuss these modes more extensively as the defining marks of the community of reconciliation, the Church.

REDEMPTION'S ECCLESIASTICAL EFFECTS:
THE CHURCH AS CORPORATION, AS SECT, AS COMMUNITY

The Christian Church, like the Christian individual, lives in a certain tension between the Word of God and the world of human affairs. Both the Word and the world have a part in defining the Church. Another way of saying this is that the Church has both a theological nature (for it expresses an intention of God) and a sociological nature (for it inevitably expresses, too, the peculiarities of the folk who comprise its membership). Our interest here is mainly in the Church's theological nature. For good or ill, however, human sociology (the way people think about their lives in society without reference to God) has a way of influencing human theology. Every theology contains some sociology just as every church contains human viewpoints that have not been deliberately defined by reference to God's nature and purpose. In reading what follows, therefore, it will be important to realize that none of the conceptions of Christian community which we discuss is God's conception. Instead, each conception represents an honest attempt by Christians to apply their devout but limited understanding of God's will to the problems of community life.

The Church as Corporation (A Constitutional Community)

Some theologians hold that God has protected his Church from human distortion by constituting it as a corporation. A corporation is by definition a legal entity, as opposed to a natural or social one. To say that the Church is a corporation is to say that it is not defined by its human members but by the legal identity and authority conferred on it by God. Just as a human corporation is designed to "secure a succession of members without changing the identity of the body,"[48] so the Church as a divine corporation remains the same regardless of the character of its human constituency. In practical terms, this means that even the failure

FRANK AND ERNEST   by **Bob Thaves**

Reprinted by permission of Newspaper Enterprise Asociation (NEA).

SOONER OR LATER ALL OF HISTORY'S MAJOR, SELF-CONSCIOUS RELIGIONS HAVE BEEN FORCED TO MAKE THE TRANSITION FROM INSPIRATIONAL TO INSTITUTIONAL FORMS.

or apostasy of its leaders or members cannot destroy the Church's capacity to function as God's agent in the world.

The largest and most self-consistent practitioner of the corporate understanding of the Church is the Roman Catholic church. Other major Christian bodies who define themselves in corporate terms are the Anglican, Eastern Orthodox, Lutheran, Methodist, and Presbyterian churches. There are significant disagreements among these communions, and between each of them and Roman Catholicism, regarding the nature of the divine incorporation. Here we shall discuss the corporate idea of the Church in terms as self-consistent as possible, and our general model will accordingly be Roman Catholicism.

The *intention* of the definition of the Church as a corporation has already been stated. When defined in corporate terms, the Church is and remains a transcendent, divinely authorized institution whose essential functions are unaffected and uninfluenced by human failings and foibles.

The *origins* of the corporation concept are believed by its exponents to reside in the redemptive activity, authority, and explicit commandments of Christ himself. Roman Catholics believe that by his redemptive activity Christ made available to the human community, through the Church, a boundless treasury of merit. According to St. Anselm,[49] whose theory of atonement underlies the Roman view of the Church as a dispenser of meritorious righteousness, Christ not only canceled the human debt to God by his sinless life but went beyond that to establish, through his sacrificial death, an infinite store of righteousness. But even before his death, according to the Roman view, Christ made sure that the benefits of his death would be properly administered and lawfully distributed. Through his divine authority he conferred upon his twelve closest followers, the Apostles, the authority to rule his Church; and he chose one of their number, Simon whom he surnamed Peter, to be his primary spokesman, the Church's corporate head. "You are Peter," he told Simon. In Greek Peter means a "rock," and Jesus went on to disclose to Simon that "On this rock I will build my Church."[50]

The authority of Christ thus became the authority of Peter, according to Roman belief. Peter later became the first bishop of Rome and passed his authority, through the rite known as apostolic succession, to successive bishops of Rome. The Church is thus founded on, and must be organized around, the authority of the Roman pontiff, or pope. But Christ did not leave the pope and his apostolic cohorts, the other bishops, without guidance for their governance of the Church. He not only commissioned them to administer the benefits of his redemptive work[51] but also guided them by his express commandments and other teachings as recorded in the gospels. He further promised them that the Holy Spirit would come to guide them "into all truth."[52] The Church's leaders are therefore impressively empowered to be Christ's representatives on earth.*

The Roman view of the Church as a corporation is grounded in the idea of the authority of the bishops in general and of the Roman bishop in particular.† It took centuries, however, for the Church to clarify the relationship of the Roman pontiff's authority to that of bishops generally. Over the centuries two schools of thought evolved regarding this issue, and the struggle between them did not reach a conclusion until the nineteenth century. One of these may be called the "Roman" school, the other the "Catholic."

The Catholic school regarded the bishop of Rome as *primus inter pares,* "first among equals." In this view the Roman pontiff enjoys greater dignity and prestige than his peers but no greater formal authority. Final authority in the Church is vested not in the pope but in the collective judgment of the body of bishops throughout the Church as a whole. When differences of judgment among the bishops become great enough to constitute a threat to the authority or unity of the Church universal, such differences are to be resolved by the decisions of ecumenical councils, assemblages of bishops from across Christendom. In these gatherings the issues are to be debated and their resolution sought under the tutelage of God's reconciling Spirit.

Such a view of the powers of the episcopacy and of the papacy may well be called "Catholic" because it defines the authority of Christ as residing in the catholic, or universal, Church. Each bishop, including the bishop of Rome, is a point on a circle equidistant with all other points from the circle's center, Jesus Christ. Collectively, the bishops represent the mind of Christ. Individually, within his own diocese, each bishop is the supreme authority, subject legally only to the decisions of ecumenical councils.

Opposition to the Catholic interpretation of the Church's authority emerged quite early in the life of the church. The situation in the fourth century is reflected, for example, in St. Augustine's advice to a lay Christian in *On Christian Doctrine:*

> In the matter of canonical Scriptures he [the believer] should follow the authority of the greater number of catholic Churches. . . . He

---

*The pope himself is thus called "the vicar of Christ." The word "vicar" means a "substitute" or "stand-in." (Compare the word "vicarious.") According to Catholic teaching, the pope is in effect Christ's "stand-in" on earth.

†This theory of church government is called "episcopal," from the Greek word for bishop, *episcopos.*

will observe this rule . . . that he will prefer those accepted by all catholic Churches to those which some do not accept; among those which are not accepted by all, he should prefer those which are accepted by the largest number of important Churches to those held by a few minor Churches of less authority. If he discovers that some are maintained by the larger number of Churches, others by the Churches of weightiest authority, although this condition is not likely, he should hold them to be of equal value.[53]

In its portrait of a Christian suspended between two equally weighty authorities, Augustine's advice may have been more amusing than reassuring. He did remark, of course, that such a standoff between the many churches and the more authoritative churches is not likely to occur. But the fact that he could envision it at all indicates that, by the fourth century at least, a second view had arisen to challenge the Catholic idea that all bishops and bishoprics were of equal authority. Augustine simply assumed that there were "Churches of weightiest authority" whose bishops were to be accorded greater deference than other bishops.

The logical (and historical!) culmination of the idea that some bishops have more authority than others may be designated as the Roman (as opposed to the Catholic) view of episcopal authority. Adherents of this view hold that the occupant of the Roman bishopric is not only vested with more authority than his fellow bishops as individuals have but even with more than the rest of the bishops acting collectively. Thus, in a decision that finally secured the victory of the Roman over the Catholic school, the First Vatican Council, meeting in 1870, decreed that it is illegitimate "to appeal from the judgments of the Roman Pontiff to an Oecumenical Council, as to an authority higher than that of the Roman Pontiff."[54]

Even within the Roman view, the authority of the pope stands under certain constraints. For example, Pius IX, the pope who convened the First Vatican Council, interpreted that Council's decision in favor of papal infallibility to mean that the pope's decrees are infallible—hence, beyond debate—only in matters of faith and morals and only when his pronouncements are made *ex cathedra,** that is, deliberately and officially (in the form of a "dogma") from the chair of Peter. Though many devout Catholics consider every general papal pronouncement infallible,[55] such assessments clearly derive more from personal piety than

---

*The Latin word *cathedra*, meaning "chair," is the root of the word "cathedral." A cathedral is a church that contains the "chair" or seat of authority for a diocese or archdiocese. It is, in other words, the church of a bishop. When a bishop speaks *ex cathedra* ("from the chair"), his pronouncement carries the weight of apostolic authority.

from official church doctrine. Explicit use of the *ex cathedra* form has been extremely rare since 1871.[56]

Though the circular or distributive ("Catholic") view of episcopal authority eventually succumbed to the pyramidal, hierarchical ("Roman") view, the resulting concentration of power in Rome was by no means total. In practical, daily matters, the power of the corporate Church is wielded on the diocesan level by the bishop, on the parish level by the priests (the *rector* and his assistants, the *curates*), and in monasteries and convents by *abbots* and *abbesses*. These persons (with the exception of the last) are, by virtue of their ordination, members of the Church's magisterium—its priesthood or teaching order. The magisterial body to which they belong may be diagrammed as a pyramid:

The magisterium thus defined is responsible for the ongoing life of the corporate Church. That life expresses itself essentially in those three modes of service which we named and defined in Chapter IV: worship, study and witness (the service of the Word), and work.

The *worship* of the corporate Church is generally *formal* and highly *liturgical*.[57] For several centuries prior to the Second Vatican Council (1962-65), the Roman Catholic liturgy was virtually uniform; the same Latin text was employed in virtually every Catholic service, with variant elements (the Scripture readings for the day, for example) dictated by a standard lectionary. Since that council, liturgical practices have been both vernacularized and liberalized in the interest of greater congregational participation. Even so, the typical Catholic service, like that of other corporate churches, avoids extemporaneity and informality in favor of prescribed and traditional forms of praise and prayer.

A second mark of the corporate church's service of worship is *objectivity*. The aim of worship in corporate churches is to direct the attention of the worshippers away from themselves and their own subjective concerns toward the one worthy object of worship, God. Any sentiments or emotions that the worshipper may experience are quite incidental to the purpose and success of worship. The glorification of God, not the satisfaction of the worshipper, is the essential aim of worship, though of course the ideal state is attained when the sole desire which the worshipper seeks to satisfy is the desire that God be glorified. As an expression of the Spirit's work of reconciliation, corporatists believe, worship should lead the worshipper out of himself or herself and into genuine communion with God.

The service of *the Word* in corporate churches is officially if not exclusively the task of the Church's priests. In a strictly corporate church like the Roman Catholic, the priest alone (except in the most extreme instances)[58] is authorized to declare the saving Word through his teaching and the sacraments. Though this authority stems directly from the priest's ordination, the Church takes great care to see that the authority is not abused. It does so, first, by requiring an extensive education of all candidates for the priesthood and, second, by stressing that the primary and saving expressions of the Word are to be found more certainly in the universal forms of the sacraments than in the individual interpretations made in priestly sermons.

Corporatists view the sacraments as the principal expressions of the divine Word because they conceive the sacraments essentially as works of God. In administering the sacraments the priest is simply an instrument of the divine commandment and an effecter of the divine promise. If he is in fact a *magister* or master over his flock, that is not because he is a superior human specimen but solely because God has entrusted to the priestly office, of which he is the occupant, the "keys of the Kingdom"—the powers to make the sacraments effective through words of institution and of absolution.*

The first sacramental Word is baptism. Nowhere is the sacramental understanding of the Word more clearly evident than in the baptismal theory and practice of the corporate churches. Without exception these churches practice infant baptism. The complete inability of the infant to do anything to merit that forgiveness of original sin which is conferred in baptism is the clearest possible illustration that the gifts of God—in this case, the forgiveness of sin—are totally free expressions of divine love. The sacrament of infant baptism is thus a direct expression of the gospel that God loves human beings before they love him. The fact that in corporate churches the sacrament also confers a new, "Christian" name makes the gospel of reconciliation all the clearer: as the child receives the new name, he or she is received into the family of God. Hereafter the child bears not only the name of his or her parents but also a God-given name which identifies him or her as a Christian. The sin of

---

*The words of *institution* are those words of the priest by which the sacramental occasion becomes a genuine act of God. They are the words in the Eucharist (for example) by which the bread and wine are transformed (or *transubstantiated*) into the body and blood of Christ. The words of *absolution* are the words (*Te absolvo*) by which guilt for sin is remitted in the sacrament of penace.

alienation from the Creator has been overcome through the fulfillment, in the sacrament, of the promise of reconciliation.

Besides baptism the only other expression of the Word accorded the status of a sacrament by all of the corporate churches is the Eucharist or Lord's Supper. According to the general corporate view, the aims of the Eucharist are three: to proclaim and offer deliverance from the sins of the believer's past life; to proclaim and effect a present communion with Christ, who is really present in the bread broken and the wine poured; and to celebrate in advance the feast of Christ's coming Kingdom. The Eucharist thus presents a threefold gospel and offers an occasion to give thanks not only for the effect of Christ's sacrificial death (that is, for forgiveness) but also for his continued presence and his promised Kingdom.

Roman Catholics accord five other church practices sacramental status along with baptism and the Eucharist. *Confirmation* is a sacrament that completes baptism, ushering those who were baptized as infants into the life of the church as fully instructed and self-aware communicants. *Penance* has been called a "second baptism," for it evolved as a

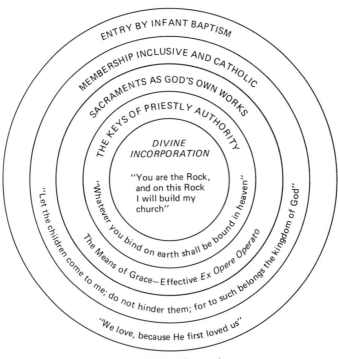

The Church as Corporation

means by which persons who had committed mortal sins after baptism might, through confession, be absolved of guilt for such sins.[59] *Extreme unction* is a sacrament which completes penance much as confirmation completes baptism.[60] Known popularly as the "last rites," it entails the anointment of the dying person with holy oil. Such anointment is believed to purge the soul of unexpiated sins and to strengthen it for the crisis of death.

To these *evangelical* or *gospel* sacraments, which may be so described because they are actual works of God[61] which convey grace and so confer salvation, the Roman communion adds two further *empowering* sacraments: marriage and ordination. *Marriage* effects and empowers the union of a man and a woman who wish to become husband and wife: so powerful is God's work in joining them that their union is all but indissoluble, and divorce[62] is out of the question. *Ordination* is a kind of supernatural marriage, uniting the ordinand to Holy Mother Church and empowering him to administer the evangelical sacraments. In ordination as in marriage the union effected is lifelong and indissoluble; the rite confers on its recipient an indelible character (*character indelebilis*) which cannot be eradicated by any human action.

The *Eastern Orthodox* church joins the Roman Catholic in recognizing these seven sacraments. Its main theological difference from Rome appears in its greater stress on the sacraments as instruments of regeneration or "deification." Through participation in the sacraments, Eastern churchmen believe, communicants receive a "new being" in the likeness of God. The main effect of the sacraments is thus a restoration of the *imago Dei*, not, as in the Roman church, a restoration of moral righteousness. The Roman doctrine of a sacramentally distributed treasury of merit is accordingly not an element in the sacramental theology of the Eastern church. Instead, the Orthodox faith stresses the power of the sacraments to confer immortality. So from very ancient times the elements of the Eucharist were described in the East as a "medicine of immortality" (*pharmakon athanasias*). [63]

The Eastern church differs from the Roman not only with respect to sacramental theology but also in certain sacramental practices. In the East baptism (even of infants) is generally by threefold immersion (honoring each of the three persons of the Godhead); confirmation may be administered by priests and not just by bishops; and the cup as well as the loaf is offered to the laity in the Eucharist. Whereas the Roman church holds that the actual ministers in the sacrament of marriage are not priests but rather the couple saying the vows,[64] the Orthodox view is that the sacrament is effected only in the blessing of the presiding priest. The Eastern church also departs from Rome by holding that marriages are dissoluble by divorce.

In a number of *Protestant* churches of the corporate sort, the minister's Sunday sermon is accorded virtually equal footing with the sacraments as a way of serving the Word.[65] The reasons for such an emphasis
on the sermon's importance are partly historical and partly theological.
Historically, the Protestant Reformation was directed mainly toward
correcting the abuses of the medieval sacramental system. More fundamentally, the Reform was an attempt to correct what the Reformers
perceived to be a fallacious sacramental theology. The Reformers were
particularly opposed to the notion that the sacraments offered access to a
mystical treasury of merits whose key was in the hands of the Church's
priests. Salvation, they contended, is a free gift of God which may be
mediated orally, by a simple proclamation of the Gospel, as well as
sacramentally.

Though the Reformers refused to recognize five of the Roman
church's sacraments (confirmation, penance, ordination, marriage, and
extreme unction) as authentic sacraments, it could be argued that they
accorded sacramental status, informally and implicitly at least, to two
practices that had not traditionally enjoyed such standing. The first was
the sermon; the second was the study of the Scriptures. Both, the early
Protestants believed, could become instruments of the Holy Spirit and
the means to reconciling grace. When they did in fact become the instruments of God's working, they were in effect saving sacraments and
means to communion with God himself.

Though the major Protestant Reformers did protest what Rome and
the scholastic theologians of the time had made of the corporate Church,
they were in no way inclined to deny the validity of the corporate
conception of the Church as such. In their view, the most important
distinction between the Church and other human communities was that
the Church had been divinely incorporated to be the bearer and proclaimer of the Word. The major error of Rome, they believed, lay in its
teaching that the Church could define the Word. Their own leading
conviction was that quite the reverse was true: the Word defines the
Church. Accordingly, in place of the Roman *magisterium* (or "mastery")
of the Word, they instituted in the Church a *ministerium* (or "ministry")
of the Word. The authority of the priest or minister does not reside in
some supernatural power which comes to inhabit him or her at ordination; it resides instead in the authority to interpret and proclaim a Word
which, when acted on by a supernatural power quite independent of the
minister (namely, the Holy Spirit), has saving effects. The magister may
grant or withold the Word—may bind as well as loose. The minister can
neither grant nor withhold the Word; he or she can only be its servant,
its vessel, whenever the Spirit makes this possible.[66]

The corporate understanding of *service through works* is scarcely less diverse than that of the service of the Word. The main lines of the diversity, sketched already in Chapter IV, are those separating Protestant from Catholic corporationists. Once again the theological basis of the distinction relates to the question whether a mystical treasury of merits exists and to the even more basic question whether Christians can do works of merit which contribute not only to their own salvation but also (when they are so-called works of supererogation)* to the salvation of others. Catholic Christians believe that such a treasury does exist and that the works of the saints and other devout Christians can and do contribute to it. The human works of Christ and the saints become the means of the divine work of salvation as priests, acting in God's behalf, distribute to the faithful the excess merit acquired through these works. Protestant Christians, adopting a totally different approach, view the whole idea of merit and of meritorious human works as a denial of the sufficiency of the gospel. The gospel declares that only one good work can save, and the doer of that good work is God himself, who in Christ did all that was necessary to redeem humankind. The notion that human work can have saving merit is in Protestant eyes a reversion to the idea of salvation by works of the law, an idea that St. Paul and other New Testament writers appear to have rejected.

Because of their distaste for the idea of meritorious works, the leaders of the Protestant Reformation (Luther and Calvin in particular) rethought and recast the entire conception of works. In their view, efforts to do good are not only not to be despised but are in fact demanded of the Christian. But such works are directed toward a different end than that of the accumulation of merit. They must be directed to the glory of God and to the temporal well-being of the neighbor (the latter's eternal well-being being entirely dependent on the work of God).[67]

The Reformation conception of work led to a further refinement of the idea of the Christian *ministerium* or ministry. Medieval Catholics had separated Christians into two types—the ordinary laity, who were required only to obey the Ten Commandments, and the seekers of perfection, who sought to obey Christ's "counsels of perfection" in the Sermon on the Mount through lives of poverty, chastity, and obedience. Similarly, though for entirely different reasons, Reformation Protestants conceived of two types of ministry—that of the laity, who were called to be "little Christs" (Luther) to their neighbor through faithful pursuit of their worldly vocations, and that of the clergy, whose works were different in character but directed no less to the good of the neighbor.

In general, Eastern Orthodoxy stands closer to Protestantism than to

---

*Works of supererogation are "second-mile" works performed by Christ, the saints, and other devout souls (for example, monks) for the sake of others.

Roman Catholicism on the question of works. The Roman doctrine of meritorious and supererogatory works has no counterpart in Orthodox thought. The daily morning prayer of Orthodox Christians echoes the evangelical emphasis of the Reformers:

> O my Saviour, by Thy grace deliver me; for if it were Thy will to save me according to my works, that would be neither grace nor gift but only a burden. . . . Do not ask me from my own strength for the works which should justify me, but let my faith be all-sufficient, let it answer for me, let it make me a partaker of Thine eternal glory.[68]

To summarize: corporatists stand united in their view of the Church as a divinely constituted legal entity whose existence and effectiveness are in all cases independent of its human constituents and of their sins, large and small. They generally agree, too, that the purpose of worship is to praise and glorify God, and they tend therefore to look askance at informal and extemporaneous worship practices. In their service of the Word and their service through works, on the other hand, corporatists disagree markedly in both theory and practice. Despite such disagreements, however, they remain corporatists in their emphasis on the efficacy of the Word without regard to the character of its human mediators and on God as the primary, if not the sole, agent in the redemptive process.

The Church as Sect (A Congregational Community)

Since the age of Constantine, at least, the great majority of Christians have belonged to churches that have defined themselves in terms of the corporate model. The idea of community is governed in that model by the idea of law, of constituted order and authority. The community is therefore, in some degree at least, authority-focused, pyramidal, hierarchical. The theological basis for this structure is the belief that the Church's reason for being is the reconciliation of the human community to God. The other dimensions of reconciliation, to self and to neighbor and nature, are subsidiary to the restoration of a right relationship to the Lord of creation. The Church must therefore, through its hierarchical structure, its theological emphasis on the divine initiative, and even its architecture,[69] direct the attention of human beings upward toward God.

Long before the time of Constantine another conception of the Church was alive among Christians. According to this conception, the Church is called to transcend the world not only in law but also in practice. Reconciliation to God and reconciliation to self and neighbor must be simultaneous and coinherent. It would not do to combine the proclamation of a divinely perfect institution, a Church "without spot or wrinkle,"[70] with tolerance toward or acceptance of human imperfection. The holiness of God and the holiness of the Church must be fully reflected in the holy living of Christians. The Church must therefore strive to be a society of the perfect, an outpost of the coming Kingdom, a spring of living water in a dry and thirsty land. Those who adhere to this ideal and contribute to its accomplishment are to be accepted and appreciated within the society of the saved; those who default on the ideal or betray it must be confronted and, if need be, excised.[71]

Even in the heyday of Christendom, that era known as the high Middle Ages (the twelfth and thirteenth centuries) when the corporate church was unrivaled in its power, the vision of the Church as the society of the perfect remained alive. In general, the corporate church dealt humanely and wisely with those who were captured by such a vision. Instead of stifling the impulse to seek perfection, the constitutional community amended its constitution, as it were, so that it might charter the impulse and channel it into forms that would threaten neither the power of the ecclesiastical corporation nor the unity of Christendom. As a result the broad church's life was enriched and somewhat purified by the birth and burgeoning of several monastic and mendicant orders,[72] into which seekers of perfection could be directed and organized and within which they could be subtly controlled.

Some visionaries were less subject to constraint than others, however, and some ecclesiastical authorities were less tolerant of dissent and dissimilarity than others. Occasionally, too, the visionaries and the authorities were so separated by political and geographical circumstances that no accommodation of one by the other could be arranged. To some extent all three of these factors entered into the estrangement that developed in the late Middle Ages between the corporate church and puritanical groups like the Albigensians and Waldenses of Southern France. Ultimately the only winner (physically speaking) in the resulting conflict had to be the corporate church, which held virtually all of the reins of power. Since the victors wrote the histories of such struggles, the losers forever after were tagged with the unflattering name "sectarians" or "sectaries."

Despite its original pejorative cast and its consequent ugly flavor, the word "sect" is a fairly descriptive name for the community envisioned by the Waldensians and other Cathari. "Sect" is a shortened form of the past participle of the Latin verb "secare," which means "to cut." The sectaries of the Middle Ages sought in effect to cut themselves off from the world and from the corrupt corporate body of Christendom. They sought to do this, as we have seen, in the name of a higher ideal, the ideal of a society of Christians perfectly devoted to God and to that austere life which would make the saints ready for the coming Kingdom. The name "sect" is an apt description for such a society because it expresses the chief distinction between it and the corporate church. That distinction is the *exclusiveness* of the sectarian church.

The word "exclude" means to "shut out." The church that seeks to shut out the world's imperfections must cut itself off from the world. Such a church must be a sect, cut off by its very intention from the larger human community. Whereas the corporate church is *inclusive*, stretching out its arms to the entire human community and seeking to sanctify or transform the secular order, the sectarian church is *exclusive*, calling on its members to abandon the secular order.

This definitive difference between the sectarian and the corporate conceptions of the Church is reflected in the ways in which entry into the church community is accomplished in the two contexts. In the corporate churches, entry is ordinarily by *infant* baptism, which as we have seen expresses the gospel that God accepts people before they can accept him. In sectarian churches, on the other hand, entry is by *believers'* baptism, an initiatory rite through which the new convert publically professes his or her faith and the intention to devote himself or herself to the quest for perfection. In the eyes of many sectarians, infant baptism is a main source of that lack of spiritual commitment which marks the lives of many members of the corporate churches.

Another definitive difference between the sectarian church and the corporate church is found in the sectarian's preference for congregational as opposed to hierarchical forms of church government. The sect church is essentially a *congregational* rather than a *constitutional* community. Each sectarian congregation is self-governing. The Holy Spirit is believed to work through congregational debates and decisions rather than through long-established hierarchical channels. Particularly in first-generation sects, which are usually filled with a sense of discovery, the life of the congregation is marked by spontaneity and excitement. Sectarians believe that the presence of the Holy Spirit is the source of their new-found enthusiasm and joy.[73]

Because the congregation is the seat of authority in the sectarian church and because it is also the embodiment of a grand vision, a high value is placed on congregational integrity. Entry is solely by believers' (in effect, adult) baptism because admission to the congregation is reserved for those who are fully aware of what the community is about and are fully and voluntarily committed to the search for perfection in which it is engaged. Moreover, strict sects do not just restrict entry; they also impose on their members a strict moral regimen and may expel members who have not proved loyal to the community and its goals.[74]

Worship within the sectarian church is generally more flexible and informal than the worship of corporate communions. Self-involvement and self-expression are common elements in sectarian worship. If there is a certain abhorrence of what is sometimes called the cold and barren formality of highly liturgical services, it is because such liturgical forms seem to many sectarians quite incapable of touching the heart and moving the will of the believer. Sectarian worship emphasizes spontaneity and extemporaneity in the belief that the Holy Spirit can move more freely and fully in less formal services.

Though it is no less God-focused than corporate worship, the worship of the sectarian community proceeds from a different understanding of God and of his ways than does that of the corporate church. Sectarians believe that as long as God remains an object, distant from the worshipper, worship avails little. Only when God is recognized to be a Reality in my subjective experience, a Being closer to me than breathing and nearer than hands and feet, can he be the God who gave himself for me and other people in Jesus Christ. The meaning of the Incarnation, according to sectarian belief, is that God is no longer just in heaven, transcendent and removed from human experience, but that he has become present in the lives of all who truly believe. Worship is a festive affair, a celebration of God's presence in the midst of his congregation. Such a celebration emphasizes the believer's assurance of his or her own salvation as much as it does the adoration of God.

Within the sectarian context *the Word* takes on a much more subjective and much less sacramental hue. Historically speaking, perhaps the most self-consistent sectarian group has been the Society of Friends, popularly known as the Quakers. The Quakers, like many of their predecessors in the so-called left-wing Reformation of the sixteenth century, believed that Luther and Calvin and the other prime movers in the Reformation had simply replaced a sacramental form of tyranny with a scriptural form. As the Church of Rome had identified the Word too closely with the power of the hierarchy and the sacraments of which the priests were custodians, so the Reformers had identified it too simply with the Scriptures. The Reformers had thus replaced one sacramental or mediatorial form of the Word, one tyrant over consciences, with another. So, said the Quakers and other left-wing Reformers, the Protestant Reformation needs completing. The Word of God must again become recognized as the Word *of God*, and it accordingly must not be simply equated with the word of the Church or the word of Scripture.

If the sacraments and scriptures are not to be regarded as the primary source of the Word, where is one to look? One must look, according to George Fox and his fellow Quakers, within oneself. One must attune oneself, by patient and attentive waiting, to hear what Fox called the "inner Word," the Word of God's Spirit directly to and through the conscience.

If it can be said that sectarians in general throw open the windows of the Church in order to be open to the Spirit, it appears from what has just been said that the most self-consistent or extreme sectarians are prepared to take down the institutional church's very walls in the interest of such openness. This in effect is what Fox's completion of the Reformation accomplished among the Quakers. All external and institutional aids to the service of the Word—professional ministers, liturgy, music, visual symbols, even "steeple houses" (church buildings) themselves—were entirely rejected. The conscience of the individual believer and the consensus of the spiritual society became the sole means through which the Spirit proclaims the Word. The logic of congregationalism thus reached extreme expression. In the Friends society "Church" means nothing less and nothing more than a congregation of people, sitting silently in each other's presence until the Spirit speaks through their consciences and through the consensus of the group or "sense of the meeting."

Not all sectarians follow the Quakers in such a rigorous application of the congregational principle to the theology of the Word. The Quakers, indeed, constitute a tiny minority among those congregational groups that organize their lives on sectarian principles. Most sect churches (including some Quaker congregations) retain a high regard for the scriptural form of the Word, and some are even dominated by proponents of biblical infallibility. Almost without exception, however, sectarians have a low—a symbolic or ordinantial, rather than a "realistic"—view of the sacraments. The sacraments, in other words, are not viewed as sacraments in the sense given that word by corporatists. Corporatists, whether Catholic or Protestant, perceive the sacraments as vehicles of saving grace, as real instruments and expressions of the gospel. God himself is at work in the sacraments, in the view of corporate churchmen. Sect churchmen, on the other hand, perceive the sacraments as human works in response to specific commandments of Christ. Sacraments are expressions of a faith already present in the soul, not means to the birth of faith. Infants are therefore not to be baptized, for they are incapable of a decision of faith; and when adults undergo baptism, they do so as a way of professing a faith already received, rather than as a way of acquiring faith.

In the sectarian view, the sacraments are a product of God's law rather than of the gospel. Christians observe the sacraments because the Lord Christ instructed them to. The sacraments are not avenues to

Christian discipleship but expressions of it. Through observance of the sacraments the congregation demonstrates its obedience to its Lord. Christ expressly commanded his followers to observe only two sacraments, baptism and the Lord's Supper, and so the church fulfills its sacramental obligation when these are faithfully shared.

Although most sect churches do not go to the extremes of the Quakers in their definition of the Word, one element in the Quaker definition is found in virtually all sectarian conceptions. The Quakers hold that any human being, even the most common and uneducated, may be chosen by God to speak the Word. Here again *congregationalism* is taken seriously. No single person, not even the ordained clergyman with his Th.D. or D.D., holds a patent on the Word. The sectarian concept of the ministry is thus decidedly different from that of the corporate churches. When the Church is understood as a corporation, the clergy are like corporate officers who differ in *rank* from ordinary church members. The minister of a sect church, on the other hand, is simply a lay person whose vocation or "calling" differs from those of other churchfolk. This means that, theoretically, the sectarian minister is distinguished from his or her flock solely by *function*, not by rank. In practice, of course, many ministers of sect churches make up for their lack of formal or official authority by personal talent and diligence. Their influence is greatly enhanced, too, by the privilege they enjoy of occupying the pulpit Sunday after Sunday. But in principle they remain the subordinates, the functionaries, of the congregation.[75]

The importance of *service through works* is a frequent and recurrent note in sectarian thought. At the time of the Protestant Reformation, sectarian forces attacked the immorality of the established church with far greater vigor than did Luther, Calvin, and the other corporatist Reformers. As we said at the outset of our discussion of sectarianism, sectarian visionaries have since ancient times dreamt of a Church that could transcend the world in practice as well as in law. Such a dream can be fulfilled, sectarians believe, only through works, through the actual practice of that "higher righteousness"[76] which Jesus defined in the Sermon on the Mount. Whereas corporatists are willing to accept moral diversity in the interest of institutional unity, sect-Christians stress the moral integrity of the congregation even if that makes for the multiplication of institutional entities (denominations and/or congregations).

During the Middle Ages, the "new law" given in the Sermon on the Mount was regarded as binding only on those Christians who wished to perfect their own devotion to God and to contribute to the Church's treasury of merit through works of supererogation. The austere demands of the Sermon were therefore given the name "counsels of perfection" or "evangelical counsels" and were by these names distinguished from the Ten Commandments, whose observance was required of all Christians. In practice the chief keepers of the counsels of perfection were the mendicant friars and the more conventional monks and nuns who took the vows of chastity, poverty, and obedience. In effect, through its monastic movements the church promoted a two-level Christianity. On the first level lived ordinary Christians who, though redeemed by Christ, were not required to keep the new law of Christ but only the old law of Moses. On the second level resided the seekers of perfection, who gave themselves unreservedly to the task of obeying every precept in Christ's manual of discipleship.

Throughout the medieval period there were sporadic protests against such a sorting out of Christians into separate "classes." Only after the success of the Protestant Reformation were sectarian groups sufficiently freed from the shadow of corporatist power to attempt, over a sustained period of time, to implement the ideal of a Christian democracy. When such an attempt did become feasible, good works were a crucial element in it. Generally speaking, however, the aim of such works was not (as in Catholicism) the accrual of saving merit but rather the achievement of true equality, justice, and a spirit of Christian benevolence within the life of the congregation.

Within the sectarian concept of the Christian community, service through works remains an important expression of the reality and authenticity of faith. Works demonstrate salvation, though they do not effect it. Sectarians stress, therefore, the necessity of going beyond justification (the divine forgiveness of sin) to pursue *sanctification*—the living of a life of "scriptural holiness" as John Wesley (a corporatist with sectarian leanings) called it. Such a pursuit is essential not only to the attainment of individual spiritual fulfillment but also to the creation of a society of the perfect.

In summary, the sectarian vision of the Church is that of an integral, intentional, and disciplined body, a body composed of believers who achieve an almost organic unity by their high standards of admission to membership, their rigorous expectations of each other, their common experience of the Spirit in worship, their abnegation of all claims to worldly or ecclesiastical rank, and their scrupulous efforts to attain moral purity through compliance with the law of Christ.

The Church as a Covenant Community:
Toward a More Ideal Ideal

In traditional Christian parlance, corporate churches are sometimes referred to as "high" churches and sectarian congregations as "low" churches. The terms are descriptive rather than pejorative. They refer

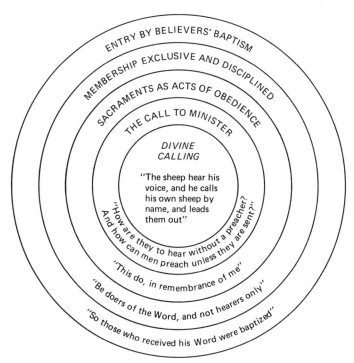

The Church as Congregation

popularly to the degree of formality featured in the worship services of a given church, though they are more correctly used to indicate whether a church has a "high" view of the Eucharist (a view of the bread and wine as vehicles of the actual presence of Christ) or a "low" view of it (a view of the elements as simply symbols of Christ's presence and sacrifice). Because corporate churches generally emphasize formality of worship and the Real Presence of Christ in the Eucharist, they are on both counts high churches. Similarly, because sectarian worship is informal and observes the Lord's Supper as a symbolic representation of Christ's presence, sect churches are appropriately called low churches.

In actual practice, it is simpler to classify Christian groups as high and low than to classify them as "pure-corporate" and "pure-sectarian." As one moves from the congregational to the denominational level among Christian groupings and as one adds more terms of comparison in comparing groups, it becomes progressively more difficult to determine the precise position of particular groups on the spectrum between the pure-corporate and the pure-sectarian types. Even relatively self-consistent groups such as Catholicism and the Society of Friends are marked by diversity. Quakers of the American West and Midwest, for example, incorporate a number of the institutional aids of conventional Protestantism (churches, ministers, and so forth) into their congregational pursuits, whereas those of the Northeast generally retain the traditional informality. And, as we have seen, Catholicism brings the sectarian principle under the roof of the corporate conception by the chartering of monastic groups populated by perfection seekers.

Particularly difficult to classify in terms of the corporate and sectarian ideals are the churches of British and American origin: Anglicanism, the Baptist churches, Congregationalism, Methodism, and Presbyterianism. The pragmatic Anglo-American temperament has done a great deal to moderate the dogmatic and liturgical views of these churches, so that scarcely a one of them can in practice be classified as pure-sectarian or pure-corporatist. Though Anglicanism stands closest among these groups to the corporate ideal, the presence and power of the vestry in American Anglican churches moderates the power of the church's hierarchy considerably in the direction of congregationalism. The formation of associations and bureaucracies of clergy folk in Congregationalist and Baptist circles moves these churches away from congregationalism and toward constitutionalism.

Among the churches of British-American background named, the Methodist and Presbyterian churches come closest to being "broad churches," or churches that strike a balance between the corporatist and the sectarian ideals. Presbyterianism is perhaps the most carefully worked out and finely balanced compromise between sectarian and corporate principles ever effected within Christendom. In the resulting "constitutional congregationalism" or "ecclesiastical republicanism," both the authority of the clergy and the prerogatives of the laity are carefully defined and protected. American Methodism, although it does not come nearly as close to finding a *theoretical* or constitutional middle way as does the Presbyterian church, embraces in both its polity and its constituency such diverse elements that it is ruled in fact by neither a corporate nor a sectarian vision but by a mediating pragmatism. Its name, Methodism, may thus be the best clue to its essential orientation: it is more concerned with methods, with pragmatic and effective ways of getting things done, than with either laws or sectarian visions.

The churches of the middle way are of interest to us here not so much in themselves but because they point us to both a fact and a possibility. The *fact* is that strict, practical adherence to either the corporate definition or the sectarian vision of the Church is rare. As we have seen, the most self-consistent practitioners of the two viewpoints are on the corporatist side Roman Catholicism (which, however, constitutionalizes

ENTRY BY BELIEVERS' BAPTISM

MEMBERSHIP EXCLUSIVE AND DISCIPLINED

SACRAMENTS AS ACTS OF OBEDIENCE

THE CALL TO MINISTER

DIVINE
CALLING

"The sheep hear his voice, and he calls his own sheep by name, and leads them out"

"How are they to hear without a preacher? And how can men preach unless they are sent?"

"This do, in remembrance of me"

"Be doers of the Word, and not hearers only"

"So those who received his Word were baptized"

The Church as Congregation

popularly to the degree of formality featured in the worship services of a given church, though they are more correctly used to indicate whether a church has a "high" view of the Eucharist (a view of the bread and wine as vehicles of the actual presence of Christ) or a "low" view of it (a view of the elements as simply symbols of Christ's presence and sacrifice). Because corporate churches generally emphasize formality of worship and the Real Presence of Christ in the Eucharist, they are on both counts high churches. Similarly, because sectarian worship is informal and observes the Lord's Supper as a symbolic representation of Christ's presence, sect churches are appropriately called low churches.

In actual practice, it is simpler to classify Christian groups as high and low than to classify them as "pure-corporate" and "pure-sectarian." As one moves from the congregational to the denominational level among Christian groupings and as one adds more terms of comparison in comparing groups, it becomes progressively more difficult to determine the precise position of particular groups on the spectrum between the pure-corporate and the pure-sectarian types. Even relatively self-consistent groups such as Catholicism and the Society of Friends are marked by diversity. Quakers of the American West and Midwest, for example, incorporate a number of the institutional aids of conventional Protestantism (churches, ministers, and so forth) into their congregational pursuits, whereas those of the Northeast generally retain the traditional informality. And, as we have seen, Catholicism brings the sectarian principle under the roof of the corporate conception by the chartering of monastic groups populated by perfection seekers.

Particularly difficult to classify in terms of the corporate and sectarian ideals are the churches of British and American origin: Anglicanism, the Baptist churches, Congregationalism, Methodism, and Presbyterianism. The pragmatic Anglo-American temperament has done a great deal to moderate the dogmatic and liturgical views of these churches, so that scarcely a one of them can in practice be classified as pure-sectarian or pure-corporatist. Though Anglicanism stands closest among these groups to the corporate ideal, the presence and power of the vestry in American Anglican churches moderates the power of the church's hierarchy considerably in the direction of congregationalism. The formation of associations and bureaucracies of clergy folk in Congregationalist and Baptist circles moves these churches away from congregationalism and toward constitutionalism.

Among the churches of British-American background named, the Methodist and Presbyterian churches come closest to being "broad churches," or churches that strike a balance between the corporatist and the sectarian ideals. Presbyterianism is perhaps the most carefully worked out and finely balanced compromise between sectarian and corporate principles ever effected within Christendom. In the resulting "constitutional congregationalism" or "ecclesiastical republicanism," both the authority of the clergy and the prerogatives of the laity are carefully defined and protected. American Methodism, although it does not come nearly as close to finding a *theoretical* or constitutional middle way as does the Presbyterian church, embraces in both its polity and its constituency such diverse elements that it is ruled in fact by neither a corporate nor a sectarian vision but by a mediating pragmatism. Its name, Methodism, may thus be the best clue to its essential orientation: it is more concerned with methods, with pragmatic and effective ways of getting things done, than with either laws or sectarian visions.

The churches of the middle way are of interest to us here not so much in themselves but because they point us to both a fact and a possibility. The *fact* is that strict, practical adherence to either the corporate definition or the sectarian vision of the Church is rare. As we have seen, the most self-consistent practitioners of the two viewpoints are on the corporatist side Roman Catholicism (which, however, constitutionalizes sectarianism in its monastic orders) and on the sectarian side the Quaker movement (which, perhaps because of its self-consistency, has never grown to be a large, conventional church). It would appear, then, that the pure types of church life are destined either to grow impure or to grow scarcely at all.

Both the rarity and the fate of pure types indicate something which is of definite importance to us as analysts and could be of potential importance to practical church people. The analytic lesson (as we have seen before[77]) is that types are of value only for purposes of comparison, not for purposes of complete description. The potential lesson for the Church of the future is that both the Church's own history and the complexity of the human situation seem to favor a certain hybridization in the Church's life. As botanists have been able to make remarkable improvements in plant strains by methods of crossbreeding, so the Church may grow stronger by combining the best elements from the corporate and the sectarian conceptions of church life.

In his First Letter to the Corinthians, St. Paul suggests just such a course by pointing the Church in the direction of both the organic unity so desired by sectarians and the official or ministerial diversity championed by the corporatists:

> Now there are varieties of gifts, but the same Spirit; and there are varieties of service, but the same Lord; and there are varieties of working, but it is the same God who inspires them all in every one. . . . For just as the body is one and has many members, and all the members of the body, though many, are one body, so it is with Christ. For by one Spirit we were all baptized into one body—Jews or Greeks, slaves or free—and all were made to drink of one Spirit.
>
> For the body does not consist of one member but of many. If the foot should say, "Because I am not a hand, I do not belong to the body," that would not make it any less a part of the body. And if the ear should say, "Because I am not an eye, I do not belong to the body," that would not make it any less a part of the body. If the whole body were an eye, where would be the hearing? If the whole body were an ear, where would be the sense of smell? But as it is, God arranged the organs in the body, each one of them, as he chose. If all were a single organ, where would the body be? As it is, there are many parts, yet one body. The eye cannot say to the hand, "I have no need of you," nor again the head to the feet, "I have no need of you." . . . But God has so adjusted the body, giving the greater honor to the inferior part, that there may be no discord in the body, but that the members may have the same care for one another. . . . Now you are the body of Christ and individu-

ally members of it. And God has appointed in the church first apostles, second prophets, third teachers, then workers of miracles, then healers, helpers, administrators, speakers in various kinds of tongues. Are all apostles? Are all prophets? Are all teachers? Do all work miracles? Do all possess gifts of healing? Do all speak with tongues? Do all interpret? But earnestly desire the higher gifts.[78]

St. Paul, it appears, envisioned a Church that would combine the strengths of unity with those of diversity. The same God, he maintained, gives both. Ultimately the Church's strength lies neither in being constitutional nor in being congregational but rather in being God's people, knit together by his redemptive and reconciling Spirit. The key word in defining such a people is neither "constitution" nor "congregation" but rather "covenant," that new relationship with the Creator which has come about through his union with the man Jesus. As Paul suggests in Philippians 2, the Church can really be the body of Christ only when it has the mind of Christ, who being in the form of God did not cling to his position of power but chose a way of humble service, a way of self-emptying and incarnation which ended on a cross. The Church of such a Lord must be a servant Church, following the God of the covenant into a world of oppressive institutions and despairing human beings and into the act of surrendering power and status for the sake of such a world. When a vision of the Church as servant prevails, the Church's redemptive and reconciling functions will be viewed as of greater consequence than either the constitutional or congregational form, and the Church will be free to adopt whatever forms the service of those functions may require within a given historical context.

QUESTIONS FOR STUDY AND DISCUSSION

1. What powers within the Godhead does the Christian conception of the Spirit affirm?

2. How does redemption affect the Christian's attitude toward, and use of, the divinely given law?

3. What common concern lies behind the various theories that Christians have developed to explain the significance of Christ's death? What is the significance of that death for human death in general, in the Christian view?

4. How does redemption liberate the Christian from undue concern about the opinions of others?

5. What does "reconciliation" mean within the Christian context? How are the self's basic relationships to God, itself, nature, and the neighbor affected by reconciliation?

6. How is the Church defined when it is understood in terms of the corporation model? What values does the corporate model serve and express?

7. How does the "Roman" view of the authority of the corporate Church differ from the "Catholic" view, within Roman Catholicism? What values are paramount in each of the two views?

8. On what major point does the Eastern Orthodox view of the sacraments differ from the Roman Catholic view?

9. How do Roman Catholic and corporate-Protestant views regarding the standing and role of clergy persons differ from each other? Show how the contrast between these views reflects equally contrasting views of the relationship between the Church and the Word of God.

10. How does the sectarian or congregational concept of the Church differ from the corporate concept? What values or vision of the will of God does the sectarian concept seek to serve?

11. Compare and contrast the corporate and sectarian conceptions of the sacraments, noting particularly how these conceptions differ on such issues as the basic reasons for observing the sacraments and the function of baptism as an initiation into the Church's life.

12. Criticize the corporate and sectarian ideals of Church life from the standpoint of the "more ideal ideal" of the Church as a covenant community.

NOTES TO CHAPTER IX

1. I Corinthians 15:22.

2. Mark 8:35; cp. Matthew 10:39, 16:25; and Luke 9:24, 17:33.

3. John 3:3.

4. Matthew 18:3; cp. Mark 10:15 and Luke 18:17.

5. The Old Testament disallows not only the identification of physical images or idols with God (cf. Exodus 20:4–5) but also the identification of human ideas with him (cf. Isaiah 55:8: "For my thoughts are not your thoughts, neither are your ways my ways, says the Lord").

6. The Psalmist wrote, "Whither shall I go from thy Spirit? Or whither shall I flee from thy presence? If I ascend to heaven, thou art there! If I make my bed in Sheol, thou art there!" (Psalm 139: 7-8)

7. John 16:13.

8. See Chapter VIII, pp. 292–94.

9. Romans 5:5,8.

10. Romans 8:2.

11. Romans 8:14, 15b–17.

12. "In the Spirit 'the resurrected Lord' manifests himself 'with his resurrection power, which is more than mere power of ecstasy and of miracle, which reaches for the world and leads in the new creation. The Spirit incorporates men into the worldwide body of Christ.... '" From *Jesus—God and Man*, by Wolfhart Pannenberg. Copyright MCMLXVIII, The Westminster Press, p. 172, citing E. Kaesemann's article "Heiliger Geist" in *Die Religion in Geschichte und Gegenwart*, 3rd ed., ed. K. Galling (Tübingen: J. C. B. Mohr [Paul Siebeck], 1957), Vol. II, p. 1274. Used by permission of The Westminster Press.

13. Cf. I Corinthians 12:1–11.

14. From *Jesus—God and Man*, by Wolfhart Pannenberg, copyright MCMLXVIII, The Westminster Press, p. 172. Used by permission.

15. Matthew 15:7–9, quoting Isaiah 29:13.

16. Matthew 22:37 (cp. Mark 12:30, Luke 10:27).

17. Cf. Luke 18:9–14.

18. Cf. Matthew 23:23; cp. Luke 11:42.

19. Luke 17:10.

20. Cf. Luke 15:11–32.

21. Matthew 5:45.

22. Cf. Matthew 20:1–16.

23. Matthew 5:38–39, 41, 44b–45a, 46, 48.

24. In the gospel accounts of Jesus' teaching, the idea that the law must be fulfilled (an idea emphasized in Matthew's gospel, especially in 5:17–18) is balanced by the idea, present in Luke and in John, that the law has been transcended by the gospel of grace (see especially Luke 16:16—"The law and the prophets were until John [the Baptist]; since then the good news of the kingdom of God is preached," and John 1:17—"For the law was given through Moses; grace and truth came through Jesus Christ"; but see also the echo of Matthew's emphasis in Luke 16:17).

25. Romans 13:10; cp. Galatians 5:14.

26. Cf. II Corinthians 3:6.

27. Cf. Mark 2:23–28; cp. Matthew 12:1–8 and Luke 6:1–5.

28. Romans 8:2.

29. See Chapter IV, p. 106.

30. I Corinthians 10:23–24.

31. Galatians 5:13–14.

32. New York: The Free Press, 1973.

33. Cf. Jessica Mitford, *The American Way of Death* (New York: Simon & Schuster, Inc., 1963).

34. I Corinthians 15:55b–56a.

35. Blaise Pascal, *Pensée* 169 in *Pensées and the Provincial Letters*, trans. W. F. Trotter and T. M'Crie (New York: Random House, Inc., 1941), p. 60.

36. I Corinthians 15:54b, 57.

37. Thoughtful Christians as a rule hold Christ's example to be valuable as a general pattern for life and death rather than as a precise and detailed prescription for these. Historically, Christians have found works like Jeremy Taylor's *Holy Living* (1650) and *Holy*

Dying (1651) more helpful than books (such as Charles M. Sheldon's *In His Steps,* [1899]) which represent Christ's life as a kind of roadmap rather than as a spiritual compass.

38. Cf. Exodus 12:21-28. For a fuller exposition of the major efforts by Christians to understand the religious significance of Christ's death, see G. Aulén, *Christus Victor,* trans. A. G. Hebert (London: S.P.C.K., 1931).

39. *And the Life Everlasting* (New York: Charles Scribner's Sons, 1933), pp. 237-38.

40. *Being and Time,* trans. J. Macquarrie and E. Robinson (New York: Harper & Brothers, Publishers, 1962), pp. 163-68 *et passim.*

41. Cf. S. Kierkegaard, *Attack Upon Christendom,* trans. Walter Lowrie (Princeton, N.J.: Princeton University Press, 1944) and *The Present Age,* trans. Alexander Dru (New York: Harper & Row, Publishers, Inc., 1962).

42. Cf. Matthew 7:13-14.

43. F. Dostoyevsky, *The Brothers Karamazov,* trans. Constance Garnett (New York: Random House, Inc., 1950), pp. 295-99, 302, 305, 309.

44. See N. O. Brown, *Love's Body* (New York: Random House, Inc., 1966), pp. 80-108.

45. Mark 8:35; cp. Matthew 10:39, 16:25; Luke 9:24, 17:33.

46. Cf. D. Bonhoeffer, *Letters and Papers from Prison,* enlarged ed., trans. R. Fuller and others (New York: Macmillan, Inc., 1975), pp. 164-65.

47. See *The Secular Meaning of the Gospel* (New York: Macmillan, Inc., 1968), pp. 126-134; and above, Chapter III, p. 74.

48. *Funk & Wagnalls New Practical Standard Dictionary of the English Language* (New York: Funk & Wagnalls Company, 1956), Vol. I, p. 302.

49. See his treatment of the atonement, "Cur Deus Homo?", in S. N. Deane, ed. and trans., *St. Anselm: Basic Writings* (LaSalle, Ill.: Open Court Publishing Company, 1951), pp. 171-288.

50. Matthew 16:18.

51. An authority granted through Christ's authorization of Peter and the other apostles to "bind and loose"; see Matthew 16:19, 18:18; John 20:23.

52. John 16:13.

53. *On Christian Doctrine,* trans. D. W. Robertson, Jr. (Indianapolis: The Bobbs-Merrill Co., Inc., 1958), p. 41. Copyright 1958, The Liberal Arts Press, Inc.

54. Philip Schaff, *The Creeds of Christendom, Volume II: The Creeds of the Greek and Latin Churches* (New York: Harper & Brothers, Publishers, 1889), p. 265.

55. Cf. John P. Dolan, *Catholicism: An Historical Survey* Woodbury, N.Y.: Barron's Educational Series, Inc., 1968), p. 187.

56. There has in fact been only one theological exercise of that power since Vatican I: the declaration by Pius XII in 1950 of the Bodily Assumption of the Virgin Mary into heaven.

57. A church's "liturgy" consists of the prescribed rites used in its worship. See Chapter IV, footnote on p. 112.

58. In certain emergency situations—as, for example, when a profession of faith is made by a person facing imminent death—the sacrament of baptism may be administered (if a priest is not available) by lay persons. For a more general exception to the rule of priestly administration, see the Roman views on marriage cited on p. 347.

59. Emperor Constantine, tradition has it, refused baptism until the time of his death. A reluctance to receive baptism was common among the ancients because of the general belief that the commission of a mortal sin after baptism was unforgivable and would therefore consign one to everlasting punishment. Through its institution of the sacrament of penance, the Church in effect offered sinners a second chance and relieved their fears concerning early baptism.

60.   W. Niesel, *The Gospel and the Churches: A Comparison of Catholicism, Orthodoxy, and Protestantism*, trans. D. Lewis (Philadelphia: The Westminster Press), p. 89.

61.   The gospel, as we saw in Chapter VIII, assumes that God is One who acts. In Catholic doctrine the sacraments are God's chosen modes of action. Catholics take God's promise to act through the sacraments so seriously that they declare that the sacraments are effective *ex opere operato*, or "by the work worked." This means that the efficacy of the sacraments does not depend in any way on the condition (moral worthiness, consciousness, and the like) of the officiant or recipient. Their efficacy depends instead on the promised faithfulness of a God who cannot fail.

62.   "The question of divorce can only arise on the basis of the *privilegium Paulinum* (I Cor. 7:12–15), or in the case of a marriage that has been entered into but not yet consummated. Apart from that the Roman Church will accept a separation of the married couple from bed and board, but not a divorce." From *The Gospel and the Churches*, by Wilhelm Niesel, p. 93. Translation by David Lewis, copyright 1962, Oliver & Boyd Ltd. Published in the U.S.A. 1962, The Westminster Press. Used by permission.

63.   A phrase apparently coined by Ignatius of Antioch (d. 111). Cf. J. N. D. Kelly, *Early Christian Doctrines*, 2nd ed. (New York: Harper & Row, Publishers, Inc., 1960), pp. 197–98.

64.   The priest does serve, of course, as the celebrant of the nuptial mass which accompanies the exchange of vows, and the marriage is not really effective in the eyes of the Church unless the vows are said in the presence of a priest. Cf. W. Niesel, *The Gospel and the Churches*, p. 94.

65.   This is especially true of the Lutheran, Presbyterian, and Methodist churches. The high regard that Protestants have for the preached Word traces to Martin Luther himself. Cf. Regin Prenter, *Spiritus Creator*, trans. J. M. Jensen (Philadelphia: Muhlenberg Press, 1953), who speaks (p. 143) of Luther's "sacramentalization of the message."

66.   Niesel states this Protestant viewpoint very effectively: "The Church's Lord is present by the agency of His Spirit. He is never there as a thing, an object which we can control. On the contrary, He comes to us with sovereign freedom where and when He wills." *The Gospel and the Churches*, p. 14. Used by permission.

67.   Cf. Gustav Wingren, *Luther on Vocation*, trans. C. C. Rasmussen (Philadelphia: Muhlenberg Press, 1957).

68.   Metropolitan Seraphim, *Die Ostkirche* (Stuttgart: 1950), pp. 59–60. Cited in W. Niesel, *The Gospel and the Churches*, p. 142. Used by permission.

69.   So the great Gothic cathedrals erected during the Middle Ages expressed the upward striving of the human spirit through their pointed arches, flying buttresses, and soaring towers and steeples.

70.   Cf. Ephesians 5:27.

71.   The first clear-cut attempt to implement the ideal of the Church as a society of the perfect is reported in the Acts of the Apostles. When members of the Church failed to conform to the expectations of the community, the consequences could be dire. Cf. the story of Ananias and his wife, Acts 5:1–11.

72.   Chief among these were the Dominicans, an order of mendicant and itinerant preachers founded by St. Dominic (1170–1221), and the Franciscans, an order of mendicants founded by St. Francis of Assisi (1182–1226).

73.   Their establishment-oriented critics do not agree. Among corporate churchmen, the English term "enthusiast" and its German equivalent *Schwärmer* were once treated as virtual synonyms for "fanatic" and "anarchist."

74.   On the use of the so-called *ban* (banishment from the congregation), see F. H. Littell, *The Anabaptist View of the Church* (Boston: Starr King Press, 1958), pp. 86–95.

75.   The clearest official indication of this subordination lies in the powers of the local congregation to ordain ministers and to call and dismiss its pastors.

76.   Cf. Matthew 5:20, 43–48; and R. A. Spivey and D. M. Smith, Jr., *Anatomy of the New Testament* (New York: Macmillan, Inc., 1969), pp. 104–111.

77.   See Chapter II, pp. 30–31, 55.

78.   I Corinthians 12:4–6, 12–21, 24b–25, 27–31.

X. Faith and Caring:

The Word as Promise

THE CHRISTIAN CHURCH, like the Christian individual, is defined by two restored relationships: a relationship to God the Creator and one to a renewed creation. But the restoring of these relationships does not complete the work of redemption. As St. Paul observes in his letter to the Roman Christians, even the renewed creation "has been groaning in travail together until now; and not only the creation, but we ourselves, who have the first fruits of the Spirit, groan inwardly as we wait for... the redemption of our bodies."[1] The redemptive process begun in Christ and evinced in "the first fruits of the Spirit" is incomplete; Christians and creation alike have tasted enough of it to desire it earnestly, or "groan" for it. But they still await its promised completion.

Paul's reference to the redemption "of our bodies" indicates that the redemption Christians await is not merely an otherworldly affair. As we saw in Chapter III, Christianity is marked as a faith of history by its high evaluation of life in the body. "The body" is shorthand for the historical self, the self that participates physically as well as mentally in, and is at least in part defined by, the affairs of history. Instead of being a value-less or evil container of the soul, the body represents a life-involvement which is the object of redemption.

The importance of the historical self within the Christian frame of reference indicates that Christianity is an eminently practical, down-to-earth religion. Christian faith does not lift people out of the world but instead changes their approach to the conditions and challenges that the world presents. In this chapter we shall try to define the difference Christian faith makes in the practical lives of its adherents. Two concepts—that of the love (or caring) of God and that of the rule (or Kingdom) of God—will guide us as we do so.

REDEMPTION'S ETHICAL EFFECTS:
THE WAYS OF LAW, LIBERTY, AND LOVE

Faith changes not only what and how one believes and not only how and to whom one belongs but also the way one decides and acts. The self's restored relationships to God, neighbor, and nature become the bases for its ethical decisions and actions. The principal effect of these restored relationships is a new-found freedom to love. God's redemptive love for the self makes possible the self's love for God and the neighbor.

Though Christians agree that redemption sets persons free to do the loving thing, they disagree on what the loving thing is. Some contend that the meaning and requirements of love have been set forth most adequately in the divine gift of the law. Others claim that the way of true love is the way of Christian liberty. Still others hold that love is defined principally by attending to the specific needs of other persons as those needs are expressed in concrete situations. In this section we shall analyze these three ways of defining love and conclude with a comment on the larger ethical perspective from which each of these definitions proceeds.

The Way of the Law

The way of the law, as Joseph Fletcher found,[2] makes of love a program rather than a norm. The advocates of this way seem to assume that God has put forth in the law a rather complete definition of what love means. To love God, and to love others as God commands, means following the law's direction in one's dealings with God and others.

There is some theological merit in this view, and some ethical merit. The theological merit may outweigh the ethical. The idea of the law as the most adequate definition of love serves to remind Christians of their faith's claim that the root of all ethics is theological—that God, in other words, is the ultimate definer of good and evil. Advocates of the way of the law accordingly never tire of saying that the abandonment of the sure ground of God's revealed law can lead one only into a quagmire of relativism and human rationalization. If one follows the law without question, one can at least be certain that one's mind is not playing ethical tricks, that one is not in fact pursuing a self-serving line of action for morally dubious reasons.

The theological merit of the legal viewpoint—that is, the merit inherent in its insistence that God's will is the ultimate standard of right and wrong, good and evil—converges with the ethical merit in the legalists' argument that ethical decisions should proceed from a clearly defined perspective with clearly ordered priorities. Thus (their argument may continue) Jesus established both a theological and an ethical scale of priorities when he gave the commandment to love God precedence over the command to love the neighbor. In ordering the commandments as he did, he made it clear that the love of God is of higher value than the love of the neighbor. The basis of the *ethical* priority of love for God is the *theological* (or ontological) priority of God himself. God should be loved first, in plainer words, because God *is* first, both in the order of being and in the order of importance. As important as he is, the neighbor is not indispensable to the universe. Only one Being is, and it is only appropriate to accord that Being his ethical as well as his religious due. Indeed ethical behavior in accord with God's will is, on Judaeo-Christian principles, the highest expression of religious devotion.

The law provides the Christian with an ordered theological and ethical perspective from which to proceed in making decisions and acting. It has the further ethical merit of being a condensation of much of the ethical experience and wisdom of the past. Perhaps it is true, as James Russell Lowell opined, that "Time makes ancient good uncouth," but the only way to find out is to have access to definitions of the ancient good. The law, at least, provides such access.

Beyond its theological and ethical merits, the way of the law affords believers a degree of psychological assurance which can be of great practical value. Because they do not have to wonder about the motives for their actions—they are, after all, acting as God's law dictates and not on the basis of their own preferences—law-guided Christians can act singlemindedly and with confidence. Moreover, because prompt and confident action is essential to the success of many ethical endeavors, their chances of being ethically effective are considerably increased.

The way of the law, finally, has the merit of being a strong expression of Christians' faith in the future. The way of the law is an example of what Kant called *deontological* ethics. Deontological ethics advocate action on the basis of a sense of duty, without regard for the consequences. Such ethics express a strong faith in the future or, more accurately, in God's benevolent control of the future. In actions based on law, one acts and leaves the consequences to God.

Overall the way of the law offers Christians a sense of order and of assurance, a clearly defined set of priorities, enhanced prospects of success, an opportunity to express their trust in God, and perhaps even a definition of what God means by love. These are valuable resources to have in hand when setting about the task of loving God and his world. But the way of the law has drawbacks as well. Its first drawback is that it is by no means always clear what the law commands us to do. Because of such a lack of clarity, a vast interpretive and casuistic* literature has arisen over the centuries. Conflict among the interpreters and casuists regarding the law's meaning may undermine that confidence with which believers might otherwise act on the law. Lost in a maze of interpretations and counterinterpretations, believers in the law are hardly better off than those antilegalists who (according to the law's advocates) sink in the quagmire of relativism.

A further problem for the way of the law is that there seem to be more ethical situations than there are laws to deal with them. What does the law of Scripture have to say, after all, about genetic experimentation, the ethics of organ transplants, cryogenics, or space exploration? Even if one grants that it does have something *indirect* to say about these subjects, there remains the formidable task of finding the implications of the legal perspective regarding them.

Perhaps the gravest danger posed by the way of the law, however, is that that way may disguise, or even offer an escape from, the real ethical issues of the day by convincing Christians that their ethical responsibilities have been met by keeping certain ecclesiastically sponsored laws. So, for example, slave owners in the ante-bellum South could be convinced that they had fulfilled their Christian duty by providing places of worship for the slaves. Similarly, today's suburban realtors, persuaded that they have fulfilled their Christian obligation by attending and supporting the Church, may find nothing incongruous in their unwillingness to show houses in certain neighborhoods to members of minority groups.

The Way of Liberty

The most outspoken enemies of the way of the law are the advocates of the way of liberty. The aim of Christian love, they argue, is identical to the aim of the divine love expressed in the gospel. The aim of the gospel is to confer "the glorious liberty of the children of God." In conferring this liberty, God in effect puts an end to the age of the law. Redeemed persons are no longer slaves, defined by a legal relationship to God as their master and judge; they now are "heirs" related to God in a profoundly personal way. The difference between an heir and a slave is that the heir is a free agent, an inheritor of a divinely granted freedom. The heir therefore acts from inner motives rather than from outer con-

---

*Casuistry, the noun from which "casuistic" comes, is the art of applying general statements of moral law or principle to specific cases.

straints. The law, though helpful in a slave economy, is of little value within a context of freedom.

The ethics of liberty values liberty both as an end and as a means. Liberty is of value not only in itself but also as the ground or basis of love. Love cannot be coerced but must be freely given. Love is therefore possible only between or within free beings.[3] God's motive for granting human beings freedom cannot be perceived with certainty, but the most plausible of the possible motives that theologians have been able to conceive is that the Creator prefers the freely given love of sons and daughters to the unwilling compliance of slaves.

Liberty is of value not only as a means to love but also as a means to wider and fuller liberty. There is considerable truth in the adage that "Free people make people free." The exercise of liberty is essential both to its continued existence among those who enjoy it and to its communication to others. St. Paul appears to have recognized this as he counseled the Christians of Galatia: "For freedom Christ has set us free; stand fast therefore, and do not submit to a yoke of slavery."[4]

Liberty's chief value, in the Christian view, consists not in what it can do—not even in what it can do to promote love and further liberty—but rather in what it is. Liberty *is* an aim of creation and a mark of human maturity. It is in fact the quality in human beings that makes them God-like and that confers on them value and dignity. The name for "liberty" in the Genesis creation story is "dominion." Dominion or liberty is, according to that story, a gift of God. It is, therefore, a hallmark of authentic existence, a clear sign of God's intention for the human creature. Accordingly, the most valuable ethical contribution that any human being can make to another may consist of acts that facilitate or enhance the other's God-given freedom.

That liberty is a principal Christian value is beyond dispute. That the

FRANK AND ERNEST   by Bob Thaves

Reprinted by permission of Newspaper Enterprise Association (NEA).

way of liberty is the most adequate ethical course open to Christians is hotly disputed. If the way of liberty is conceived, as it has sometimes been,* as an ethical course directly opposed to the way of the law, the heat of the dispute approaches the boiling point. Let us look briefly at some of the heat-generating issues in this dispute.

The main problem with the way of the law, according to the libertarians,† is to be found in what it says about, and in what it consequently does to, people. In depriving people of their ethical autonomy, it treats them as though they were automatons, God's puppets, rather than free beings. Human creativity and initiative are stifled, and the ethical imagination is placed on a leash. The damage thus done to the practitioners of ethics is only compounded by the damage done to those who might benefit from ethical deeds. Distracted and stultified by the law, those who wish to do good fail to perceive the true needs of others and consequently overlook opportunities to render service.

If the way of the law tends to blind its adherents to human needs as they are, the way of liberty (according to the law's defenders) leaves one unable to distinguish between the law of God and the will of the human agent. "Ethical imagination" and "creativity" may accordingly become cover words for self-serving rationalizations. Liberty may then degenerate into its perverse extreme, license, producing in the process a hardy and sinful pride.

The lines are clearly drawn between the way of the law and that of liberty. Theologically speaking, the basic issue is whether reconciliation with God must be the route to reconciliation with self and neighbor (as the law party maintains) or whether, instead, reconciliation with one's authentic, autonomous self is the avenue to reconciliation with God and neighbor (as the liberty party insists). In focusing attention on the problem of staying rightly related to God, the law party tends to lose sight of concrete ethical situations in the world. In concentrating on their powers of free choice, on the other hand, libertarians run the danger of confusing their own imaginings and desires with the will of God.

The debate between the way of liberty and the way of law thus reaches something of an impasse. It would appear that one must surrender either one's assurance regarding the will of God or one's liberty of action. Perhaps, however, there is a third and (as St. Paul declared) "more excellent" way. That possibility must now be explored.

---

*Such a conception is particularly identified with the so-called *antinomians*, persons within the primitive Church who appear to have taken Paul's preaching of freedom from the law as a license to do as they pleased. Paul addresses the antinomian view in general terms in Romans 6.

†The term is here used in a general, rather than in the modern-political sense.

The Way of Love

The war between legalism and libertarianism runs hot and cold throughout the pages of the New Testament. It is present preeminently in Jesus' battle with the Pharisees and the Sabbatarians[5] and in Paul's conflicts with the so-called legalizers and with proto-gnostic antinomians.[6] It fell to Paul, more than anyone else, to hammer out the implications of the gospel regarding the question. As the apostle and pastor who had to construct the main bridge between the traditional Jewish wing of the Church, which became the law party, and his own Gentile converts, who were generally advocates of liberty, Paul had to look for a course that could simultaneously express the will of God and preserve the unity of the Church. With astounding patience and perseverance and with almost unerring insight, he appears to have done just that. As a result he eventually transformed the war *between* legalism and libertarianism into a war *against* both of them, for he saw that either "ism," if followed full course, would lead to the fragmentation of the Church.

The war is shrewdly fought. Paul uses the weapons of the party of liberty against the legalists, then turns about and directs the legalists' firepower against the libertarians. His whole aim in so proceeding is the victory of his own (and what he believed to be the gospel's) "more excellent way," the way of love.

Paul agrees with the party of the law that the will of God must be found and fulfilled outside the self. The self in its "natural" or ordinary (ungraced) condition is a slave to sin,[7] incapable of doing good even when it comprehends what the good is.[8] The self in its "free" or graced state remains vulnerable to sin precisely because of its recovered liberty. To rely on oneself or on one's own judgment is to remain caught in what Paul called, variously, "the desires of the flesh"[9] or the "wisdom of this age."[10] Such a state of bondage is a state of folly, not of wisdom:

> Let no one deceive himself. If any one among you thinks that he is wise in this age, let him become a fool that he may become wise. For the wisdom of this world is folly with God. For it is written, "He catches the wise in their craftiness," and again, "The Lord knows that the thoughts of the wise are futile." So let no one boast of men.[11]

If God's will transcends the self's power and "wisdom," human reliance on the law or "written code" must be doubly condemned, for as humans use the law it not only reinforces and becomes part of the "wisdom of this age" but it also confirms and strengthens the human bondage to such "wisdom." Although libertarians may be *vulnerable* to the confusion of their own will with God's and may become its *victims* when they actually equate the two, members of the law party are *already* the victims of such a confusion—though in their case it is not their own wills that they confuse with God's but rather the will of Moses.[12]

The way of liberty and the way of law thus become dead ends, in Paul's view, if and when they become ends—definers or definitions of God's will—in themselves. Both law and liberty are capable of being redeemed, however, when they become harnessed to a third principle: *love.*

"Love," Paul wrote, "is the fulfilling of the law."[13] And again: "For the whole law is fulfilled in one word, 'You shall love your neighbor as yourself.'"[14] The commandment to love *reveals* the law's intention; the practice of love *fulfills* that intention. Unfortunately, the advocates of the law have become devoted to its *form* (the "written code") as a way of serving their own intention (principally the intention of self-salvation). By redirecting human attention away from self to the neighbor, love brings the law's intention to light again and makes its fulfillment possible.

In disclosing the law's intention, the commandment to love points the self beyond both the form of the law and the self's own "wisdom" to the neighbor. At this point Paul's teachings regarding the law and love are helpfully supplemented by those of Jesus, who attended to the question of the neighbor's identity and significance more closely than did Paul. In the parable of the last judgment, Jesus identifies the neighbor as any person in need: those who are hungry and thirsty, strangers, sick folk, prisoners. Beyond that he makes the unprecedented judgment that such persons are the veritable incarnations of the righteous Judge himself: "And the King will answer them, 'Truly, I say to you, as you did it to one of the least of these my brethren, you did it to me.'"[15]

In Jesus' view, then, love appears to be defined by the concrete needs of the neighbor rather than by the law or by the consciences of free agents. So, in the parable of the good Samaritan, two devotees of the law, a priest and a Levite, preoccupied perhaps by their meditations on the Torah, fail to see and/or meet the needs of the man who had fallen among thieves. "Which of these three ... proved neighbor," asked Jesus, "to the man who fell among the robbers?"[16] In view of the context, which shows the parable to be an interpretation of his own familiar summary of the law, Jesus' question might be read, "Which of these three actually fulfilled the law's intention?" Clearly the intended answer is, not those schooled in the law (the priest and the Levite) and not those who used their liberty to pass by on the other side (the same worthies), but rather the person who saw, felt, and met the fallen neighbor's need (the despised Samaritan).

Liberty no less than law needs love for its fulfillment. Paul, after counseling the Galatians to stand fast in their new freedom, continues: "For you were called to freedom, brethren; only do not use your freedom as an opportunity for the flesh, but through love be servants of one another."[17] And then, as if he wants to suggest that love is the linchpin that makes liberty and law yokefellows, he adds that line quoted earlier, "For the whole law is fulfilled in one word, 'You shall love your neighbor as yourself.'"[18]

The problem of Christian liberty came to a head for Paul in issues raised by the presence in the Corinthian congregation (and perhaps in other young churches as well) of so-called "weaker brethren." The weaker brethren included those new Christians who still believed in pagan idols and in the efficacy of pagan rituals. The main question these brethren posed was whether it was sinful for Christians to eat the meat of animals that had been offered sacrificially (perhaps as part of the butchering process) to idols. The main lines of Paul's answer to the question are found in I Corinthians 8:

> Hence, as to the eating of food offered to idols, we know that "an idol has no real existence," and that "there is no God but one." ... However, not all possess this knowledge, But some, through being hitherto accustomed to idols, eat food as really offered to an idol; and their conscience, being weak, is defiled. Food will not commend us to God. We are no worse off if we do not eat, and no better off if we do. Only take care lest this liberty of yours somehow become a stumbling block to the weak. ... If food is a cause of my brother's falling, I will never eat meat, lest I cause my brother to fall.[19]

It was not enough, in Paul's view, for new Christians to learn that animal sacrifices were ineffective; it was far more important that they learn that sacrifices for their sisters and brothers are crucial to both the authentication of their liberty and the fulfillment of the law's intention. Christian freedom is best defined, as we noted in Chapter VIII, as a power to respond to persons. Paul himself enjoined such responsiveness by his own example:

> For though I am free from all men, I have made myself a slave to all. ... To the Jews I became as a Jew, in order to win Jews; to those under the law I became as one under the law—though not being myself under the law—that I might win those under the law. To those outside the law I became as one outside the law ... that I might win those outside the law. To the weak I became weak, that I might win the weak. I have become all things to all men, that I might by all means save some.[20]

Paul's total attitude toward the law, liberty, and love and his assertion of their interrelatedness are summarized in yet another word from his Corinthian correspondence: " 'All things are lawful,' but not all things are helpful. 'All things are lawful,' but not all things build up. Let no one seek his own good, but the good of his neighbor."[21] The law is good and is to be followed, he implies, when it is recognizable as a law of helpfulness. Liberty is good and is to be enjoyed, but not at the expense of the neighbor. Indeed because of Christian liberty, as Martin Luther later said, "A Christian is a perfectly free lord of all, subject to none." But because of the still-effective law of love, as Luther said in the next breath, "A Christian is a perfectly dutiful servant of all, subject to all."[22]

To sum up: It would appear that the discord that has sometimes separated Christians into legalists, libertarians, and personalists is already overcome in principle within the New Testament writings of Paul and the sovereign example of Jesus' way of dealing with people. Christians who ignore the Apostle's teachings and the Lord's example are much more likely to run aground on the reefs of legalism or to drown in the whirlpools of a purposeless liberty than are those who carefully attend to those teachings and that example. The balanced and judicious approach of Jesus and Paul to questions of law and liberty is approximated in an adage well known among church folk: "In essentials let there be unity; in non-essentials, liberty; in all things, charity."

REDEMPTION'S ESCHATOLOGICAL EFFECTS: CARING AND HOPING

The English word that most adequately translates the New Testament idea of neighbor love is the word "care." Neighbor love is not a matter of affection or sentiment; it does not necessarily involve feeling good about one's neighbor or enjoying his or her company. Nor is neighbor love a cooperative venture, a transaction or exchange of goods based on common interests or self-interest, and so my love for the neighbor cannot be contingent on what I may or do expect in return from the neighbor. If either of these meanings defined neighbor love, it hardly could include the love of enemies, those hard-to-live-with souls for whom one can feel no affection and from whom one can expect little but trouble. Yet it appears, from the story of the Good Samaritan and other hints, that Christ clearly intended to include one's enemies among one's neighbors.[23] But how can one love one's enemies? One can love one's enemies, in the Christian sense, by *caring* about them. One can recognize them as fellow children of God and as persons of such value to

Christ that he died for them. One can respect their legitimate rights and aspirations. Most important, one can seek their well-being.

The roots of such Christian caring are three: the reality and revelation of a God who cares, the essential solidarity of the human race, and the temporality of human existence. In the following paragraphs we shall examine these roots in an effort to determine their influence on caring itself and on the ultimate object of Christian caring, the Kingdom of God.

The declaration that God cares stands at the very heart of the gospel. The New Testament word for God's caring love is *agape*. *Agape* is best defined by noting the characteristics that distinguish it from two other types of love represented in the Greek words *eros* and *philia*. *Eros* is the root of the English word "erotic" and has strong romantic and sexual connotations. In antiquity, however, its meaning was considerably broader than our general understanding of "erotic" would suggest. The ancient Greeks could mean by *eros* any love born of desire or appetite. The recognition that there are higher, intellectual appetites as well as the more common physical ones led the Greeks to employ *eros* in several contexts.

Philia best translates into English, perhaps, as "liking." It is an affection based on common interests and companionship. Whereas *eros* illustrates the principle "unlikes, or opposites, attract," *philia* illustrates the adage "like knows (and likes!) like."

The essential difference between *agape* and these other types of love is to be found in *agape's* inclusive, nondiscriminatory, and unconditional character. Both *eros* and *philia* exclude certain potential objects of love in favor of others. In order to do so, both discriminate, observing differences among the potential objects and choosing their actual objects on the basis of those observations. *Agape*, on the other hand, is all-comprehending. It does not even distinguish friends from enemies or righteous folk from sinners. Its clearest biblical definitions are found in Matthew 5:43–48 and Romans 5:8:

> You have heard that it was said, "You shall love your neighbor and hate your enemy." But I say to you, Love [*agapate*] your enemies and pray for those who persecute you, so that you may be sons of your Father who is in heaven; for he makes his sun rise on the evil and on the good, and sends rain on the just and on the unjust. For if you love those who love you, what reward have you? . . . Do not even the Gentiles do the same? You, therefore, must be perfect, as your heavenly Father is perfect.

> But God shows his love [*agape*] for us in that while we were yet sinners Christ died for us.

Agape is thus a love with no strings attached, a love without conditions. It is the basis in God of what the New Testament calls grace (Greek *charis*) or unmerited divine favor. *Agape's* sole source and cause lie in the nature of God, for only a being who is not conditioned and governed by needs, limits, and preferences can love without regard to merit or some other standard of discrimination. Whenever agapeic love is expressed by humans (as in situations in which strangers give their lives for other strangers[24]), Christians generally attribute such expressions to the complete immersion of the will of the doer within the will of God.

The expression of pure *agape* by human beings is thus rare. *Agape's* expression requires a type of sacrificial selflessness that human beings are seldom given to. The supreme expression of such selflessness can be seen in the death and demeanor of Jesus on the cross. A death made uniquely selfless by its motives is made the more so by its manner. He who commanded his disciples to love their enemies here exemplifies such love with a prayer for his killers: "Father, forgive them; for they know not what they do."[25]

With respect to the showing of *agape*, Christians are not on a par with their Lord but are judged by him. Though they may not attain to his complete selflessness, genuine Christians must strive, in Martin Luther's term, to become "little Christs" to their neighbors. Their love can seldom become pure *agape*, but it can and must strive to be "agapeic," agape-conditioned. The commandments of the Johannine Jesus, "Love one another as I have loved you"[26] and of the Matthaean Jesus, "Be perfect [that is, all-comprehending in your love] as your heavenly Father is perfect,"[27] state the aims of daily Christian practice.

Christian caring is a product not only of the divine *agape* but also of the solidarity of the human family. Throughout Scripture, humanity is conceived and discussed in *corporate* terms. The individual is understood not as an integral, self-sufficient unit, nor as an abstraction or legal fiction, but as a responsible being who is defined by his or her relationships to, and historical actions within, the human community.[28] The human race is in a real sense all of a piece. The acts of one affect all; the state of all affects the one. The consequence is that no one can be human without *caring*.[29] Caring is the means by which one is psychologically incorporated into the human condition. The human being cares for others not simply because he or she chooses to but because his or her psychic security is bound up in the fate of others.[30] Such caring lies for the most part beneath the surface of the mind, perhaps driven there by the psyche because of the unpleasant effects it produces when it breaks into consciousness.

Caring results from the way the human creature is constituted as well as from the revealed presence of a God who cares. And there is another element too in the constitution of human beings which conspires with their racial solidarity to make them care. That element is their essential *temporality*. Human beings are time-bound beings. Time is the stuff of their lives. Three score and ten, in the words of a mountaineer, "ain't much, but it's all we got." Because it is all we have, we *care* about it. Our care for time is a familiar form of our care for ourselves.

Time compounds our care by running out. Deadlines come—and death, the ultimate deadline, comes. In both cases time runs out. Our lives are not only temporal but temporary. Short-term deadlines make our opportunities temporary, and by its constant presence as a possibility death reminds us that the whole enterprise of living is temporary. The possibility that our opportunities will be wasted or that our lives will end before we find fulfillment deepens the care we have for ourselves and our neighbors.

Hope is a child of such caring. Time has a way of eroding and undermining human possibilities and achievements, and these effects of time collaborate with human ambition and pride to produce a condition of intense care. It is from such intense caring that hope is born.

As a child of caring, hope is a kind of caring. It is a caring about the future, a caring which is expectant and eager as it faces the future. There is, in the Christian view, an authentic version of hopeful caring and an inauthentic version. Inauthentic hope is cheap hope. It is hope born of irresponsibility (the something-for-nothing syndrome) rather than of responsibility. It may be accompanied by desperation or by a boastful, ill-grounded, and therefore presumptuous confidence. The caring in such hope is selfish caring. Authentic hope, by contrast, is hope for personal and community fulfillment *as the God who cares defines such fulfillment.* The divine caring (*agape*) is the criterion for authentic human caring. God sanctions as authentic the hope that prays "Thy kingdom come, thy will be done," and "Nevertheless, not as I will, but as thou wilt."[31]

Authentic Christian hope is thus oriented toward the Kingdom, the rule, of God. In authentic Christian hope, caring of the human sort (for example, caring about the future) has been transformed and redirected by caring of the divine sort. Like *agape*, the Christian hope is all-encompassing; it is the hope of Paul, "that God may be all in all."[32] It is thus no narrow hope, no small hope tailored to the desires[33] or speculations[34] of particular individuals. It is hope for the world as a whole, and it is a hope which orients the world as a whole toward the future. Filled by such hope, St. Paul wrote: "The creation waits with eager longing for the revealing of the sons of God."[35]

As a "waiting with eager longing," Christian hope is simultaneously passionate and patient. It patiently waits as it passionately longs. Its passion means that its waiting is not an idle, inactive, while-away-the-time waiting. Its patience means that its longing is not a presumptuous, fretful longing.

The early Church was a hope-dominated community. The main object of the Church's hope was an early establishment of that Kingdom of God which had been promised and expected in the Old Testament[36] and proclaimed by Christ himself.[37] Christ's own disciples seem to have misunderstood the nature of this Kingdom, and only in the light of the resurrection were they able to see the meaning of many of his teachings regarding it. Moreover, even after the resurrection they seem to have harbored misconceptions regarding the manner and timing of the Kingdom's coming. Universally present in their talk of the Kingdom, however, is a spirit of committed and confident expectancy grounded in a sense of God's presence within the existing Christian community.

The Kingdom Here and Hereafter

As the early Church matured, so did its conception of the Kingdom of God. With the passage of time, the Church's conception of the Kingdom's nature became clearer, or at least more definite, while its ideas regarding the manner and timing of the Kingdom's coming became less definite. This process of maturation—or, in any event, of change—is reflected in Scripture. As one moves from the earliest New Testament writings (the letters of Paul and the Gospel of Mark) to later writings (Luke/Acts, for example, and the Gospel of John), the conception of the Kingdom and of its manner of coming changes markedly. In this section we shall outline some of these changes and try to explain their significance.

THE NATURE OF THE KINGDOM   From the outset both Jesus' disciples and his enemies failed to understand the radically new conception of the Kingdom he proclaimed. Jesus himself, it appears, had arrived at that conception only through a sustained season of temptation and struggle. After his baptism by John the Baptist, he retired (or was "led" or "driven" by the Spirit[38]) to a place in the wilderness, where he wrestled mightily with several contending conceptions of the messianic kingship. Each of these conceptions may well have represented a view of the Messiah and his Kingdom which had a following among Jesus' contemporaries. Each, in any event, seems to allude to one or more Old Testament figures who could have been viewed by segments of the populace as prototypes or forerunners of the expected Messiah.

In both of the biblical accounts of Jesus' temptations (Matthew's and

Luke's), Jesus' first temptation is to turn stones into bread. The way to win people's hearts, the Tempter suggested, was through their stomachs. Loyalty to the coming Messiah could be won by gorging the appetites of the famished poor. The form of this temptation recalls an incident in the life of Elijah the prophet, whose promised return[39] was a vivid element in the popular expectation of a Messiah.[40] Elijah too had spent forty days in the wilderness, beset by temptation, but he had been sustained through it all by miraculous bread baked on hot stones.[41] Jesus' reliance on God rather than on the bread of miracles for sustenance may indicate that one greater than Elijah has come and that even the pattern of ministry of the greatest of the prophets will not suffice as a model for the Messiah's ministry.*

If Matthew's ordering of the temptations is followed, Jesus' second temptation took the form of an invitation to usher in the messianic Kingdom by means of a dramatic sign which would clearly demonstrate his divine vocation. Transported by the Tempter to the pinnacle of the Temple, he was urged to throw himself down, "for it is written, 'He will give his angels charge of you,' and 'On their hands they will bear you up, lest you strike your foot against a stone.'"[42] The words here are from Psalm 91:11-12, and their quotation by the Tempter may have had considerable force with Jesus because of their association in the popular mind with the Messiah. Israel's recent history had been so marked by historical reversals and misfortunes that some despairing Israelites had begun to look beyond the horizon of history for the appearance of a savior. The superhistorical king described by Daniel 7:13 as "one like unto a son of man" would not in fact be a son of man, it appears, but a kind of archangelic being who would come "in the glory of his Father with all his holy angels."[43] Though this conception of God's future agent of salvation seems to have made a strong impression on Jesus,[44] he nevertheless refused to model his own immediate ministry on it. Compassion and suffering, rather than spectacular exhibitions of angelic power, will be the hallmarks of his career.

The third temptation (again by Matthew's reckoning) was perhaps the most powerful to which Jesus was subjected. Removed to "a very high mountain," Jesus was shown "all the kingdoms of the world and the glory of them."[45] The temptation was to make himself political lord of the kingdoms of earth by striking an alliance with the Tempter and

---

*It is possible that the prototype with whom Jesus was tempted to compare himself was Moses instead of (or perhaps along with) Elijah. Moses spent forty days and forty nights on the mountain with God when he received the law. He also provided a type of miraculous bread (manna) to the Hebrew children during their forty-year sojourn in the wilderness. Cf. Exodus 24:18 and 16:1-35.

using the world's ways instead of God's. Such a temptation could have gathered force in Jesus' thinking on any or all of three fronts. First, it appealed to the universal human desire for power and recognition. Surely the fully human Jesus of Christian orthodoxy must have felt the pull of that desire.[46] Beyond that, however, Jesus was steeped in the lore of Jewish tradition. The terms of that tradition indicated that God's Messiah would be a descendant of King David who would reestablish, extend, and make permanent the glory that had been Israel's during the Davidic era (ca. 1000–960 B.C.). Israel would become a light to the nations, as God had promised Abraham, through the ascension to power of a Son of David.

The very blood in Jesus' veins lent force to this temptation. As a person of Davidic ancestry, he surely not only knew the tradition on which the temptation was based but also would have had a hard time resisting its allure. That allure could only have become stronger as he considered yet a third factor in this temptation: it promised to satisfy not only the universal human longing for power and recognition and not only the yearnings of national and familial tradition but also the clamor of the populace for political deliverance from, and vengeance on, their Roman oppressors.

Despite its human, traditional, and popular appeal, Jesus withstood this temptation too. To cater to self-interest is not to conquer it. To yield to Israel's patriotic self-concern would not be to make it a light to the nations but to lead it to confuse the divine glory to which it was to bear witness with national glory. Jesus will do nothing to contribute to such confusion. The worship of the world's glory must give place to the service of God's glory: "Begone, Satan!" (he tells the Tempter) "for it is written, 'You shall worship the Lord your God and him only shall you serve.' ''[47]

The Kingdom of God and an earthly kingdom for God's Christ are thus incompatible. They may best be viewed as incompatible, not because God is indifferent (as some might surmise) to the political situations in which his children live, but for just the opposite reason. Those political situations are, or at least can be, exercises in human autonomy—laboratories, as it were, in which experiments in human maturation are conducted. Such exercises and experiments are fully within the compass of God's will for creation and are by no means in competition with either the divine glory or the divine rule. What is needed for the disclosure of God's glory and the attainment of God's aims is not a divine despot who overrules or eradicates human governments but instead the reorientation of those governments toward the ends of human freedom and freely given obedience to the purposes of God. Such reorientation can occur when the governors and the governed are liberated from sinful self-concern and reconciled with their human neighbors both within and beyond their national borders. Jesus set his course, therefore, not toward political power for himself or his nation but rather toward works of liberation which would make possible political maturity for the human community. "The Son of Man," he will later say, "came . . . to give his life as a ransom"—a means to freedom—"for many."[48]

Jesus' struggles in the wilderness enabled him to fashion a new and revolutionary conception of the Kingdom of God. The Kingdom of God is, to be sure, a realm in which God is king. But God the king does not will to rule unwilling subjects. He would be king, instead, of persons who offer him their fealty freely, gladly, joyously. What he offers people through Jesus is not the security of a divinely guaranteed dictatorship but the chance to participate in a divine dream—the dream of a creation in which self-interest no longer governs human affairs, in which instead the peoples of earth "shall beat their swords into plowshares, and their spears into pruning hooks" and "nation shall not lift up sword against nation, neither shall they learn war any more."[49]

Whatever else it is, it seems clear that the Kingdom Jesus envisions is to be earthly as well as heavenly, temporal as well as eternal. According to John's Gospel, Jesus announces to Pilate that his Kingdom is not of this world[50] and (as we have just seen) this Kingdom is certainly not to be equated with a divine dictatorship. These facts should not be taken to mean, however, that God's Kingdom as Jesus defines it is completely otherworldly. When examined carefully even the wording of the statement to Pilate does not support such an interpretation. To be *of* the world means one thing, to be present and at work *in* the world means something else entirely. To say that the Kingdom is not of the world—that is, that its origins and chief Sponsor lie beyond the world—does not preclude its being *in* the world. Indeed, in the model prayer Jesus gives his disciples, he prays "Thy kingdom come, thy will be done, *on earth* as it is in heaven." And he declares in other contexts that the Kingdom has begun to arrive on the earthly scene through his own ministry: "The kingdom of God is at hand."[51] "The kingdom . . . is in the midst of you."[52] "If it is by the finger of God that I cast out demons, then the kingdom of God has come upon you."[53]

Two questions about the precise nature of the Kingdom's earthly effects have occasionally divided the Christian community. The first is: Is the Kingdom of God a purely subjective reality, residing in the minds of people, or is it in some sense an objective, political reality manifest in some political or ecclesiastical institution? The second, kindred query is: Does the Kingdom effect only the salvation of individuals, or does it bring about social salvation as well?

Jesus himself gave no clear or definitive answer to either of these questions. Nor has the Church arrived at a definitive or universal answer. Jesus' teachings do suggest, however, that the questions may be posed too simply—that they may in fact offer false alternatives.

With respect to the first question, it seems clear that Jesus did not understand the Kingdom in purely subjective ("spiritual") terms; nor, it appears, did he foresee or sanction in advance the later tendencies among churchmen to equate the Kingdom with the Church; even less would he have countenanced the ambitions of later kings and emperors to identify the throne of God with their own thrones. The Kingdom is not purely subjective because it must rule people's actions as well as their thoughts and words.[54] On the other hand, it is not to be equated

with any earthly institution or regime precisely because it is the Kingdom of *God*—that God who does not allow humans to identify him with
anything in heaven above, in the earth beneath, or in the waters under
the earth.[55]

If the Kingdom is not subjective, breaking as it does out of thought
and prayer into action, and if it is not objective, or identifiable with any
earthly object, what positive description may one apply to it? Perhaps
the most apt positive term for it is the one we used in Chapter IV to
describe faith. The Kingdom, like faith in the Kingdom, is projective,
dynamic, on the way, in the making, not an object but a project. When
this is recognized, a step is taken toward answering the second of our
two questions as well. If the Kingdom is seen as a project of God in the
world, this second question too may be seen as posing a set of false
alternatives. If God is king (that is, sovereign ruler of his creation), all of
life must account to him. His plans and projects for and within the world
must be comprehensive—must embrace, in other words, the social no
less than the individual aspects of life. Love for the neighbor, as Jesus
put it in the second of his great commandments, is *like* love for God.
One cannot love God on the vertical plane without loving "the least of
these, my brethren" on the horizontal plane;[56] indeed God may be said
to come disguised in the persons of those neighbors who stand in need.
Salvation may first take root within the individual heart, but it must bear
fruit in both personal and political relations to one's fellows in society.

St. Paul amplifies Jesus' teachings on the nature and scope of God's
rule by his view that the event of salvation or Christ event has implications for the human race as a whole. "As in Adam all die, so also in
Christ shall all be made alive."[57] Paul's use of the future tense in this
statement is important: in his eyes, the effects of Christ's work are not
yet complete. The promised scope of Christ's work ("All" shall be made
alive) is also important: Christ is a latter-day Adam, a new beginning for
the race. Though Paul does not often use the word "kingdom" for the
new situation,[58] there can be little doubt that God's new day has saving
effects in the entire human community (indeed for the whole creation[59]),
not just in and for occasional individuals. The present incomplete work
of Christ will one day be complete. In the climactic phrase of Handel's
Messiah, "The kingdom of this world will become the kingdom of our
Lord and of his Christ."[60]

Salvation is corporate as well as individual. It brings into being a new
"body" of humankind, a "body of Christ" whose vanguard is the
Church. Christ speaks of the care he expects his disciples to have for
the world—a care which extends even to their enemies. Paul announces
the appearance of such care in the care of some members of Christ's
body for other members.[61] Clearly both the Savior and the Apostle ex-

The Harrowing of Hell

pect that the fullness of God's rule will bring with it a restoration of the entire creation as well as a reconciliation of individuals to the Creator.

THE MANNER AND TIMING OF THE KINGDOM'S COMING   One of the most enduring theological debates of the twentieth century has centered on the two questions: Did Jesus *expect* the Kingdom of God to come in his lifetime? and Did Jesus *believe* the Kingdom had come in his lifetime? Although these questions do not have to be viewed as mutually exclusive,[62] the participants in the dispute regarding them have generally acted as though the answers to them did exclude each other. One school of thought, whose position was set forth in Albert Schweitzer's *The Quest of the Historical Jesus*,[63] proceeds as though only the first question is worthy of attention. According to Schweitzer and his school, Jesus fully expected the Kingdom to come in his own lifetime; that expectation, however, went unfulfilled, and much of the theology of the early Church was devoted to trying to explain away Jesus' mistake.[64]

A second school of thought, although somewhat less dogmatic in its conclusions, tends nevertheless to overstate the case that Jesus' preaching was basically about the Kingdom's presence in and through his ministry rather than about his expectation of the coming Kingdom of a messianic Son of Man.[65] Both points of view find sufficient warrant in Scripture to make the respective cases promoted by their champions plausible. But the fact that both points of view *do* have basis in Scripture should give us pause whenever we are tempted to designate either point of view as the correct Christian doctrine. The statements of Jesus in the synoptic gospels appear to indicate that he expected a Kingdom of judgment and majesty to come in the future and that he believed that a Kingdom of saving efficacy had already come, via his own ministry, in the present. The best explanation of these diverse, though not necessarily divergent, ideas is perhaps a conception of the coming Kingdom as a project stretching from beginnings in the ministry of Jesus to a climactic conclusion in the rule of the coming Son of Man. Such a conception accords rather closely, it appears, with the theology of the Gospel of St. Luke, who conceives the age since Christ's death and resurrection as the age of the Church, an age in which the good news of the already begun but incomplete rule of God is to be proclaimed from Jerusalem to Judea to Samaria, and thence to the farthest parts of the earth.[66]

Luke's view of the coming Kingdom stands in a kind of middle position, it appears, between the views of Mark, whose gospel speaks of the Kingdom and the return of Christ mostly in the future tense, and the views of John's Gospel, which stresses the idea that Christians need not become anxious about Christ's return in the future because he is present in the here and now.[67] All three of the synoptic evangelists (Matthew, Mark, and Luke) represent Jesus as teaching that "no one knows" the time of the Kingdom's coming—"not even the angels in heaven, nor the Son, but only the Father."[68] But Luke adds to this warning against speculation a promise from the risen Christ: "But you shall receive power when the Holy Spirit has come upon you." Thus, it appears, Luke replaces the idea of a quick return of Christ (and a quick arrival of the fullness of the Kingdom!) with that of the gift of the Holy Spirit. He then goes on to recount how the Spirit descended on the assembled disciples in Jerusalem during the festival of Pentecost.[69] Until the Kingdom arrives in power, Luke apparently believed, the community of believers must stay busy establishing outposts of the Kingdom throughout the world. Believers have been adequately empowered to do this by the coming of the Holy Spirit.

In Luke's writing, then, the attitude of breathless expectancy regarding the Kingdom's coming gives place to a posture of joyous, Spirit-filled activity within the world. It is not enough for Christians to wait expectantly for God to establish the Kingdom. God has already acted to initiate his rule, and the faithful must now respond to his gifts of Christ and the Spirit by making these gifts known throughout the empire. The acts of God which Luke recounts in his gospel are thus appropriately followed by the Acts of the Apostles, the apt name of the sequel to his gospel.

The writer of the Gospel of John completes the movement begun by Luke. For this writer as for Luke, the matter of central importance is not the manner and timing of the Kingdom's future arrival but rather the situation of the community of faith in the here and now. "Kingdom" is not a prominent term in John's vocabulary. His attention is not on God's future rule but on Christ's present Lordship in and over the Church by faith. Emphasis is placed in his gospel on the past and present tenses rather than the future tense: "To all who received him . . . he *gave* power to become children of God"; "I *am* the resurrection and the life."[70] Judgment day is not a matter of the future but is here, now: "This *is* the judgment, that the light has come into the world, and men loved darkness rather than light because their deeds were evil."[71] And if people do not have to wait for judgment, neither must they wait for salvation: "This *is* eternal life, that they may know thee the only true God, and Jesus Christ whom thou hast sent"; "He who believes in him is not condemned; he who does not believe is condemned already."[72]

Thus, in the twenty-five or so years that separated the writing of Mark's Gospel from that of John,* Christian thinking regarding the return of Christ and the completion of the Kingdom underwent a pronounced shift. In Luke's view and again in John's, Christ has returned to the Church under the aliases of the Spirit (Luke) and of the present Lord of the Church (John). His spiritual return makes his more perceivable return in power a matter of less urgency. The Kingdom which was launched through his earthly ministry is now to be continued and extended through the acts of his apostles and the great deeds of the community of faith. So John's Jesus can promise his disciples, "he who believes in me will also do the works that I do; and greater works than these will he do."[73]

---

*The writing of Mark's Gospel is generally dated about A.D. 65, that of John's Gospel about A.D. 90. Luke is thought to have been written between these, around A.D. 85.

The maturation of the Church's view of the Kingdom's nature was accompanied by a parallel development in its view of the manner and time of the Kingdom's completion. Any objective historian must conclude that these changes in the Church's beliefs stemmed, at least in part, from a fairly keen disappointment that Christ did not immediately return in the power of his Kingdom. But many Christians would insist that, no matter how the lesson was learned, the important thing was the learning of it. Somehow or other, the Church had to learn that the Kingdom of God must be both defined and given by God and that no amount of human speculation or endeavor could bring it to pass.[74] That God's ways are past finding out does not mean that God has no ways. Christians must seek to deal with what the Lord of history gives them through history, and by faith they can do so in the confidence of Lowell that

> Though the cause of evil prosper,
>   Yet 'tis truth alone is strong;
> Though her portion be the scaffold,
>   And upon the throne be wrong;
> Yet that scaffold sways the future,
>   And behind the dim unknown
> Standeth God within the shadow
>   Keeping watch above his own.[75]

THE CHRISTIAN'S DESTINY:
NOT-SO-FINAL THOUGHTS ON FINAL THINGS

The general belief among New Testament Christians that the Kingdom of God would assume an earthly shape should not be perceived as an effort by them to limit the scope of this Kingdom to earthly dimensions. Clearly Jesus' first-generation disciples understood the Kingdom that was to come (and that was in the process of coming) as already extant in "heaven." The precise meaning they assigned to the term "heaven" eludes us. Though it is probable that they conceived of it in spatial terms, as a place somewhere beyond the clouds, that aspect of their concept does not seem to express its essence. The fact that the terms "Kingdom of heaven" and "Kingdom of God" can be used interchangeably in the New Testament suggests that "heaven" is a virtual synonym for "God"—that it is, in other words, primarily a theological and only incidentally a geographical or "cosmographical" concept. If this is the case, then the term could be defined, perhaps, as the state of being in the full presence of God.

The Christian hope centers, certainly, on the goal of entering ever more fully into God's presence. Basic to this hope is the idea that life can be enhanced and enriched only by becoming more closely and completely related to the Source of life. The ultimate object of Christian hope must therefore be nothing less than God himself. To hope in God is to have hope for oneself. But such hope for oneself must not be allowed to become narrow, selfish, other-excluding hope. Count Tolstoy somewhere tells of how an old Russian woman died and arrived at the gates of heaven, only to be denied admission because the keeper of the gates could find in her life story scarcely a trace of charity. Finally, after much looking, the keeper did stumble on one act of kindness: she had, on one occasion, given an onion to a beggar at her door. With that discovery, the keeper, imbued with true Christian hope, handed the *babushka* one end of the onion and held on to the other. He then lowered her by means of the onion into the pit of hell. As she dangled in suspense between hell and heaven, the occupants of the pit saw in her a way to salvation. They began to grab at her feet and legs and to try to reach and wrestle away the onion. With that she began to scream and to kick, shouting, "No, no! Stay back! It's my onion!" whereupon the onion broke, and she fell headlong into the pit. So she who would not honor the hopes of others ended herself in hopeless oblivion.

The Christian hope, then, is not an exclusive or presumptuous hope. It is a hope that does not separate people but relates them, unites them one to another. It is a hope, indeed, that could lead one to sacrifice one's own future for that of others. Writing in the power of such a hope, St. Paul can declare that "I could wish that I myself were accursed and cut off from Christ for the sake of my brethren, my kinsmen by race."[76] Clearly there is more here than the pragmatic self-interest of a Benjamin Franklin ("We must all hang together, or assuredly we shall all hang separately"); there resounds in St. Paul's comment, and in the Christian hope generally, the sort of "second mile" caring for others which Jesus preached.[77]

Hope is a vigorously real and life-shaping force in the consciousness of Christians. It is the other side of that intense caring that we described earlier, and like that caring it expresses a relation to a God who cares, to the human family God cares for, and to the future God will give. Hope as caring-about-the-future must always be tempered, in the Christian context, by caring about God and caring about others. Hope is nevertheless distinguished from simple caring because it does express an attitude in which the future is eagerly anticipated. Hope is a caring which has been modified by confidence. To rephrase a somewhat hackneyed but still descriptive aphorism, the Christian is convinced that, whatever the future holds, God holds the future.

It is far easier to describe the immediate psychological effects of the Christian hope than to describe its ultimate eschatological results. Hope gives Christians a strong sense of destiny, a deep belief that history is headed somewhere, and an accompanying conviction that they must respond to the initiatives of history's divine Director. The same hope strongly motivates Christians in times of optimism and strongly sustains them in times of gloom. It supplies a quiet assurance that no moment of time exhausts the potential of God's future but that each moment can make one more ready for that future and lead one more fully into the presence of God.

The chief eschatological result toward which Christian hope looks is variously described in Scripture as "everlasting life," "eternal life," and "immortality." All of these terms are nebulous, but they do refer, it seems obvious, to some form of life beyond death. Their life with God, Christians believe, will be both continued and enriched beyond the grave.

Several considerations have led twentieth-century theologians to speak only reluctantly of the question of the Christian's ultimate destiny. The first consideration follows from the nature of the subject. If there is an afterlife, it is well named: it will occur only *after* (that is, beyond) the experiences of the present life. That means that theologians, indeed human beings in general, have no experience on which to base a discussion of the topic. One of the counsels of Ludwig Wittgenstein thus applies: "Whereof one cannot speak, thereof one must be silent."[78]

A second reason that theologians are reluctant to talk about a life beyond the present one is ethical in character. Discussion of the subject may easily degenerate into an expression of, or an appeal to, that self-concern which plagues human experience. Perhaps the most pernicious of all the forms of selfishness is the "sacred" selfishness that converts religious faith itself into a means to self-exaltation. Jesus warned his disciples that those who sought to save their lives would lose them. Yet many of his latter-day disciples have ignored the point of his teaching and have turned Christian faith itself into a means of self-elevation. So, like the charlatans who took their medicine shows through the old West, some modern "evangelists" use the mass media and/or their pulpits to "peddle" Christian faith as a panacea for this life's ills and as a stock medicine guaranteed to confer eternal bliss. Precisely because such preachers dwell at length on the wonders of heaven and the horrors of hell, persons who are better informed by the gospel should be wary of doing so.

From the time of St. Paul on, one of the barriers that theologians have sought to erect against the perversion of the idea of heaven is the doctrine of election or predestination. The original aim of this doctrine was to proclaim that God alone is God and that it is his judgment of us and

ETERNITY AND THE CLOCK

A homage to finity

Eternity's one of those mental blocks –
    the concept is inconceivable.
The clock concedes it in ticks and tocks,
    belittled, belabored, believable.

Each passing moment is seized and chewed
    with argument incontestable.
Premasticated, like baby food,
    eternity is digestible.

From Grooks 3 *by Piet Hein. Copyright 1970 by the author.*

Used by permission of Mr. Hein.

not our judgment of ourselves that determines our destiny. Heaven—
the fullness of his presence—is God's alone to give, not ours to earn or
deserve. Moreover, when he gives his presence, God does not confirm
self-concern but liberates from it. In effecting such a liberation, God's
electing or predestining love as revealed in Christ should free one from
anxiety about one's eventual fate. So John Calvin, the theologian who
emphasized more than any other the idea of predestination, taught, as
a logical corollary of that idea, that the proof of authentic faith is the
believer's willingness to go to hell for the glory of God. Persons redeemed by Christ should be so consumed by the glory and goodness of
God, Calvin believed, that they are prepared to leave the question of
their destiny entirely in the hands of such a God. Speculation regarding
their destiny or that of other people amounts to an impertinent en-
croachment on the prerogatives of the divine Judge. Discussions of

heaven and hell are thus to be discouraged, for they contribute neither to the increase of authentic faith nor to the glorification of God.

The final reason that many theologians are loath to speak of the afterlife is that it places the emphasis of faith in the wrong place. Though my eternal destiny is bound up in God, my faith in God must not hinge on the question of my eternal destiny, or on "what's in it for me," but rather on the nature of God himself. In the Christian view God alone is worthy of faith and worship. To convert faith and worship into vehicles for reaching my own objectives (even so "noble" an objective as life in heaven) is to pervert them theologically as well as ethically. The ethical perversion is apparent, as we noted, in the essential selfishness of such faith and worship. The theological perversion occurs because such faith represents a warped sense of reality—a displacement of God's will by my own wishes and a consequent distortion of the truth about reality.

A Union general noted for his high opinion of himself once sought to impress Abraham Lincoln with his derring-do by beginning a letter to the commander in chief with the pretentious return address, "Headquarters in the saddle." On opening the letter, Lincoln studied the words with amusement, then remarked: "Isn't that just like General So-and-so? He's got his headquarters where his hindquarters ought to be." The problem with theologies which assign priority to the afterlife is much like the problem of Lincoln's general. Such theologies put last things first and in the process twist and distort the proper order of reality.

If last things cannot properly be treated first, perhaps some attention to them here, at the very end of our book, would be appropriate. We cannot, to be sure, fathom the depths or describe the features of any presumed world beyond the present one. It may be possible, however, to glean from the Christian tradition certain elemental teachings about death and about the gospel's promise that there is life beyond it.

We noted in Chapter III that there is a profound difference between the Christian concept of "resurrection of the body" and the classical pre-Platonic and Platonic concept of "immortality of the soul." We may now note that the two concepts are distinguishable by more than one definitive difference.

The difference noted in Chapter III had to do with the emphasis that the Christian concept places on the historical self or individual. Most doctrines of the immortality of the soul begin with the idea that the human animal is a two-part being whose bodily part is mortal and whose mental or vital ("soul") part is immortal. At death the mortal body simply disintegrates and the immortal soul returns to a spiritual realm where it is absorbed into a cosmic Mind or World Soul. Individuality, which derives from the soul's transitory association with a body and with the body's temporal activities, is shucked off and left behind. In the Christian view, on the other hand, body and soul are indivisible; they are two names, indeed, for a single, integral being. This being, moreover, is a concrete historical individual who carries his or her history-derived individuality into the hereafter.

Another basic difference between the Christian view of final things and the views of classical or Platonic religion lies in their respective views of death. For the Platonist death is actually only a half-death. The body dies, to be sure, but the soul does not. Death may indeed be an occasion of elation for the soul, for it frees the soul from its bondage to the body. If the soul has been properly prepared (e-ducated[79]), its escape from the entanglements of the physical order may be total and lasting. If, however, its affinities for the body remain strong, it will be reincarnated. For the Christian, death is quite a different story. It is total: no "part" or "piece" of the human self survives it. The individual personality in its entirety dies.

This distinction between the Christian view of death and the classical view is less important in itself than it is as an indicator of another, more essential difference between the two perspectives. The fact that in the classical scheme the soul is unphased by death, that it has the power to survive death without aid from beyond itself, indicates that the soul is, in some respects, on a par with God; for example, it is immortal, unaffected by death. On the other hand, the Christian conviction that death is total and that nothing in the human personality survives it means that the human creature is thoroughly finite and that any pretense to divine status on the part of human beings is a serious departure from the truth. The classical view of the self may properly be called *theandric*, whereas the Christian view is more aptly described as *theocentric*. The word *theandric* combines the Greek words for God (*theos*) and man (*aner* or *andros*). In a theandric view of the human situation, the distinction between God and humans is obscured if not entirely eliminated. The word *theocentric*, on the other hand, means "God-centered." According to the God-centered perspective of Christians, there is no legitimate basis for the tendency of human beings to identify themselves with God. Death provides ultimate and adequate proof that a great gulf separates human existence from divine.

As Christians perceive it, death makes it clear that humans are not divine. But though it demonstrates the inherent fallacy in all simple equations of human with divine reality, death does not have the last word even about human reality. When brought into the presence of God, the same death which proves all creatures finite is itself disclosed to be finite. God does not die, though in the person of Jesus of Nazareth he experiences full-strength the sting of death. God does not die; instead, in the presence of God, death dies. And this dying of death, which was supremely manifested in the resurrection of Jesus the Christ, is the ground of the Christian hope for a resurrection of the body or historical personality.

The Christian hope is thus based altogether on God's power to conquer death. The God who is the Source of life is greater than death. He who gives life to begin with and who renews it in every new moment by his continuous creation is able to confer it again when and as he will. The Christian faith in resurrection is in the last analysis simply an expression, and an extension by hope, of the Christian faith in God.

In this chapter—to sum up—we have discovered that Christian hope and love, like Christian faith, are rooted and grounded in God. From the Christian point of view, God alone is literally capable of putting a world together. He has conferred that capability, to a limited degree, upon the creature made in his likeness. Yet a creature, even a creature so endowed, can construct a world only by faith, not by sight. Through faith, enough of a relationship to God may be gained to give some glimpse of the divine view of things. By hope that view may even reach beyond the confines of the immediate present into the promised future. Finally, however, faith and hope alike rest on an historic experience which does more than all else to confer coherence and meaning on the rest of life's experiences. That experience is the revelation of God's love through Jesus the Christ. From the standpoint of that experience, no finer summary of the Christian perspective can be found than that simple sentence from the pen of the apostle Paul: "So faith, hope, love abide, these three; but the greatest of these is love."

QUESTIONS FOR STUDY AND DISCUSSION

1. Compare and contrast the attempts of the ways of law, liberty, and love to define what love means.

2. What is the theological merit of the way of the law? What is its ethical merit? What are its drawbacks and disadvantages?

3. Describe the merits and the perils of the way of liberty.

4. Show how both liberty and law require love for their fulfillment, according to Paul.

5. Compare and contrast *eros, philia,* and *agape* as modes of love. Which of these represents the Christian ideal? Why?

6. Discuss the relationship between caring and hoping, as Christians perceive them.

7. Describe Jesus' conception of the Kingdom of God. How do the stories of his temptation pertain to his formulation of that conception? How does his conception differ from other views of the Kingdom which were current and popular during his lifetime?

8. Trace the development of early Christian views on the manner and timing of the Kingdom's coming. How did St. Luke modify the earliest views on the subject? How did the author of the Gospel of John modify these views?

9. What is the likely theological meaning of the term "heaven"? Does this meaning change your understanding of heaven? Why or why not?

10. Why is it difficult—and perhaps unwise—to deal exhaustively or even thoroughly with questions of heaven and hell and other "last things"?

11. How does the Christian conception of death and the life beyond death differ from the pagan-classical idea of the immortality of the soul? What is the main point of the Christian conception?

12. In the light of this chapter and of our book as a whole, what new meaning, if any, do you find in St. Paul's statement: "... faith, hope, love abide, these three; but the greatest of these is love"?

NOTES TO CHAPTER X

1. Romans 8:22–23.

2. *Situation Ethics: The New Morality* (Philadelphia: The Westminster Press, 1966), p. 19.

3. That love exists *within* as well as between free beings is an implication of the doctrine of the Trinity. Charles Williams wrote of the opponents of that doctrine that "they deny love to God except by means of his creation. But the Church has not believed that there lack in Him any of love's experiences." *The Descent of the Dove* (London: Faber & Faber, Ltd., 1939), p. 40.

4. Galatians 5:1.

5. Cf., for example, Mark 2:23–28; Matthew 12:1–14; Luke 6:1–11.

6. The *locus classicus* reflecting Paul's debate with the legalizers or "Judaizers" is the Letter to the Galatians, especially 1:6–5:12. His counsels against the antinomians (see footnote on p. 371) are found not only in Romans 6 but also in Galatians 5:13–25, I Corinthians 6:12–20 *et passim*.

7. Galatians 4:3, 8–9; cf. also Romans 1:18–24, 5:15–23.

8. Romans 7:13–25.

9. Galatians 5:17; cf. also Romans 8:5–8.

10. I Corinthians 2:6.

11. I Corinthians 3:18–21a.

12. Cf. Romans 10:1–9 and II Corinthians 3:4–16. In the latter passage, note particularly that Paul can speak of the law of Moses in very harsh terms indeed—as the "dispensation of death" (3:7) and the "dispensation of condemnation" (3:9).

13. Romans 13:10.

14. Galatians 5:14.

15. Matthew 25:40.

16. Luke 10:36.

17. Galatians 5:13.

18. Galatians 5:14.

19. I Corinthians 8:4, 7–9, 13.

20. I Corinthians 9:19–20, 22.

21. I Corinthians 10:23–24.

22. "The Freedom of a Christian," trans. W. A. Lambert, rev. Harold J. Grimm, in *Three Treatises* (Philadelphia: Muhlenberg Press, now Fortress Press, rev. ed. © 1970), p. 277.

23. Cf., besides the story of the Good Samaritan, in which the "enemy" of the fallen man is the one who shows love toward him, Jesus' praise, in his first sermon at Nazareth, for the merciful acts of Elisha and Elijah toward persons who were traditional enemies of Israel (Luke 4:25–27).

24. See the discussion of Kant's categorical imperative in Chapter VI, pp. 192–93.

25. Luke 23:34.

26. John 15:12.

27. Matthew 5:48.

28. See Chapter III, pp. 74–76.

29. See M. Heidegger, *Being and Time,* trans. J. Macquarrie and E. Robinson (New York: Harper & Brothers, Publishers, 1962), pp. 225–73.

30. The familiarity of the oft-quoted words of John Donne in no way lessens their truth: "No man is an island, entire of itself; every man is a piece of the continent, a part of the main; if a clod be washed away by the sea, Europe is the less . . . : any man's death diminishes me, because I am involved in mankind; and therefore never send to know for whom the bell tolls; it tolls for thee." *Devotions* (1624).

31. Matthew 6:10; Matthew 26:39 (cp. Mark 14:36, Luke 22:42).

32. I Corinthians 15:28 (KJV).

33. Matthew 20:20–23; cp. Mark 10:35–40.

34. Matthew 24:3–5, 23–28 (cp. Luke 17:20–24); Matthew 24:36 (cp. Mark 13:32; Acts 1:7).

35. Romans 8:19.

36. Cf. John Bright, *The Kingdom of God* (Nashville, Tenn.: Abingdon-Cokesbury Press, 1953), chaps. 1–6.

37. Cf. his very first preaching (Mark 1:14–15) and much of his subsequent preaching and teaching (Matthew 6:33, 9:35, 13:1–51, *et passim*).

38. Matthew (4:1) and Luke (4:1) use the milder verb "led," whereas Mark (1:12) indicates he was driven.

39. Cf. Malachi 4:5.

40. Cf. Matthew 17:9–13; cp. Mark 9:9–13.

41. I Kings 19:1–8.

42. Matthew 4:6; cp. Luke 4:10.

43. Mark 8:38; cp. Mark 13:26–27 and Matthew 16:27–28.

44. Cf. his frequent use of the term "Son of Man" with reference to himself—for example, Mark 2:10; Matthew 8:20, 16:13, 17:12, 20:28.

45. Matthew 4:8; cp. Luke 4:5.

46. This was clearly recognized as early as the time of the theologian who wrote the Letter to the Hebrews. Cf. Hebrews 2:14–18, 4:15.

47. Matthew 4:10; cp. Luke 4:8.

48. Mark 10:45 (=Matthew 20:28).

49. Isaiah 2:4.

50. John 18:36.

51. Mark 1:15; cp. Matthew 4:17.

52. Luke 17:21.

53. Luke 11:20; cp. Matthew 12:28.

54. So Jesus: "Not every one who says to me, 'Lord, Lord,' shall enter the kingdom of heaven, but he who does the will of my Father. . . ." (Matthew 7:21; cp. Luke 6:46).

55. Cf. Exodus 20:4.

56. Matthew 25:31–46; see also I John 4:20; "If any one says, 'I love God,' and hates his brother, he is a liar; for he who does not love his brother whom he has seen, cannot love God whom he has not seen."

57. I Corinthians 15:22.

58. For notable exceptions, see Romans 14:17 and I Thessalonians 2:12.

59. Cf. Romans 8:19–23.

60. Cp. Revelation 11:15.

61. Cf. Corinthians 12:12–26.

62. To cite a possible combination of the ideas, Jesus might at an early point in his career have *expected* the kingdom to come and at a later point have *believed* that it had in fact come, at least in some sense.

63. Trans. W. Montgomery (New York: Macmillan, Inc., 1966).

64. Cf. Martin Werner, *The Formation of Christian Dogma,* trans. S. G. F. Brandon (New York: Harper & Brothers, Publishers, 1957).

65. This school of thought, whose doctrine is sometimes called "realized eschatology," was championed most effectively by the great British scholar, C. H. Dodd. Cf. his books *The Coming of Christ* (Cambridge: Cambridge University Press, 1958) and *The Parables of the Kingdom* (New York: Charles Scribner's Sons, 1961). In the thought of Rudolf Bultmann an existentialist variety of this view appears; cf. his books *History and Eschatology* (Edinburgh: The University Press, 1955) and *Jesus Christ and Mythology* (New York: Charles Scribner's Sons, 1958).

66. Acts 1:8. For an incisive and stimulating discussion of Luke's theology of history and eschatology, see Hans Conzelmann, *The Theology of St. Luke,* trans. G. Buswell (London: Faber & Faber, Ltd., 1960).

67. Cf. Hans Schwarz, *On the Way to the Future* (Minneapolis: Augsburg Publishing House, 1972), pp. 61–66.

68. Mark 13:32; cp. Matthew 24:36 and Acts 1:7.

69. Acts 2:1–4.

70. John 1:12 and 11:25. Emphasis added.

71. John 3:19. Emphasis added.

72. John 17:3 (emphasis added) and 3:18a.

73. John 14:12.

74. So St. Paul, speaking of the mystery of God's saving work of election, observed that "it depends not upon man's will or exertion, but upon God's mercy." (Romans 9:16).

75. The fourth stanza of the hymnic condensation of "The Present Crisis," by James Russell Lowell. Quoted as found in *The Book of Hymns* (Nashville, Tenn.: United Methodist Publishing House, 1966).

76. Romans 9:3.

77. Cf. Matthew 5:38–41.

78. *Tractatus Logico-Philosophicus*, trans C. K. Ogden (London: Routledge & Kegan Paul, Ltd. and New Jersey: The Humanities Press, 1958), p. 27 (preface) and p. 189 (7).

79. See Chapter II, pp. 44–45.

Epilogue

STUDYING RELIGION is not the same thing as being religious.
One may study the world in which avowedly religious people live—the world of fact and value their faith puts together—without living in that world oneself. There are emotive and volitional elements which go into the making of that world, and which inform the religious person's understanding of it, and these will always escape the grasp of academic study. An academic or intellectual survey of religion inevitably tends to reduce religious meanings to their intellectual or cognizable content. While an awareness of this tendency should not reduce one's appreciation for the study of religion in the least, it should make one wary of identifying the results of such study with the whole truth about the faith under consideration.

In this study we have barely scratched the surface of the meaning Christian faith has for its adherents. But if our study has offered you a glimpse into the faith's central concerns and if it has whetted your interest in the impact that religion in general and Christianity in particular have on your world, and so on your life, it will have been worth the writing.

Selected Bibliography

ADAM, KARL, *The Spirit of Catholicism* (rev. ed.), trans. J. McCann. Garden City, N.Y.: Image Books, 1954.

ALTIZER, T. J. J., *The Gospel of Christian Atheism*. Philadelphia: The Westminster Press, 1966.

ALVES, RUBEM, *Tomorrow's Child: Imagination, Creativity, and the Rebirth of Culture*. New York: Harper & Row Publishers, Inc., 1972.

ANDERSON, B. W., *Creation versus Chaos: The Reinterpretation of Mythical Symbolism in the Bible*. New York: Association Press, 1967.

———, *Rediscovering the Bible*. New York: Association Press, 1951.

———, *Understanding the Old Testament* (3rd ed.). Englewood Cliffs, N.J.: Prentice-Hall, Inc., 1975.

AUERBACH, ERICH, *Mimesis: The Representation of Reality in Western Literature*, trans. W. R. Trask. Princeton, N.J.: Princeton University Press, 1953.

AULÉN, GUSTAV, *Christus Victor*, trans. A. G. Hebert. London: SPCK, 1931.

BAILLIE, DONALD M. *God Was in Christ*. New York: Charles Scribner's Sons, 1948.

BAILLIE, JOHN, *And the Life Everlasting*. New York: Charles Scribner's Sons, 1933.

———, *The Idea of Revelation in Recent Thought*. New York: Columbia University Press, 1956.

———, *Our Knowledge of God*. New York: Charles Scribner's Sons, 1959.

BAINTON, ROLAND H., *Christendom: A Short History of Christianity and Its Impact on Western Civilization*. 2 vols. New York: Harper & Brothers Publishers, 1964, 1966.

BARBOUR, IAN, *Issues in Science and Religion*. New York: Harper and Row Publishers, Inc., 1971.

BARRETT, C. K., *From First Adam to Last*. New York: Charles Scribner's Sons, 1962.

BARRETT, WILLIAM, *Irrational Man*. Garden City, N.Y.: Doubleday & Co., Inc., 1958.

BARTH, KARL, *Christ and Adam*, trans. T. A. Smail. New York: Harper & Brothers Publishers, 1957.

————, *Church Dogmatics. Volume I: The Doctrine of the Word of God.* 2 pts., trans. G. T. Thomson and H. Knight. Edinburgh: T. & T. Clark, 1936.

————, *Church Dogmatics, Volume III: The Doctrine of Creation,* 4 pts., trans. G. W. Bromiley and others. Edinburgh: T. & T. Clark, 1958, 1961.

————, *The Humanity of God,* trans. J. N. Thomas and T. N. Wieser. Richmond, Va.: John Knox Press, 1960.

————, *The Word of God and the Word of Man,* trans. Douglas Horton. New York: Harper & Brothers, Publishers, 1957.

BECKER, CARL, *The Heavenly City of the Eighteenth Century Philosophers.* New Haven, Conn.: Yale University Press, 1932.

BECKER, ERNEST, *The Denial of Death.* New York: The Free Press, 1973.

BERDYAEV, NICOLAS, *Freedom and the Spirit,* trans. O. F. Clarke. New York: Charles Scribner's Sons, 1935.

BERNE, ERIC, *Games People Play.* New York: Grove Press, Inc., 1967.

BOMAN, THORLIEF, *Hebrew Thought Compared with Greek,* trans. J. L. Moreau. Philadelphia: The Westminster Press, 1960.

BONHOEFFER, DIETRICH, *The Communion of Saints,* trans. W. Collins and Sons Ltd., London. New York: Harper & Row Publishers, Inc., 1963.

————, *The Cost of Discipleship* (2nd ed.), trans. R. H. Fuller and I. Booth. New York: Macmillan, Inc., 1967.

————, *Creation and Fall,* trans. J. C. Fletcher. New York: Macmillan, Inc., 1965.

————, *Letters and Papers from Prison* (2nd, enlarged ed.), trans. R. H. Fuller and others. New York: Macmillan, Inc., 1975.

————, *Temptation,* trans. K. Downham. London: SCM Press, Ltd., 1955.

BORNKAMM, G. *Jesus of Nazareth,* trans. I. McLuskey and F. McLuskey with J. M. Robinson. New York: Harper & Brothers, Publishers, 1960.

BRIGHT, JOHN, *The Kingdom of God.* New York and Nashville: Abingdon Press, 1953.

BRING, RAGNAR, *How God Speaks to Us.* Philadelphia: Muhlenberg Press, 1962.

BROWN, JAMES, *Subject and Object in Modern Theology.* New York: Macmillan, Inc., 1955.

BROWN, NORMAN O., *Life Against Death.* New York: Random House, Inc., 1959.

————, *Love's Body.* New York: Random House, Inc., 1966.

BROWN, ROBERT M., *The Spirit of Protestantism.* New York: Oxford University Press, Inc., 1961.

BRUNNER, EMIL, *The Christian Doctrine of Creation and Redemption,* trans. O. Wyon. Philadelphia: The Westminster Press, 1952.

————, *The Divine-Human Encounter,* trans. A. W. Loos. Philadelphia: The Westminster Press, 1943.

————, *Revelation and Reason,* trans. O. Wyon. Philadelphia: The Westminster Press, 1946.

BRUNNER, E. AND K. BARTH, *Natural Theology,* trans. P. Fraenkel. London: Centenary Press, 1946.

BUBER, MARTIN, *I and Thou,* trans. W. Kaufmann. New York: Charles Scribner's Sons, 1970.

————, *Two Types of Faith,* trans. N. P. Goldhawk. New York: Macmillan, Inc., 1951.

BULTMANN, RUDOLF, *History and Eschatology*. Edinburgh: The University Press, 1955.

———, *Jesus and the Word*, trans. L. P. Smith and E. H. Lantero. New York: Charles Scribner's Sons, 1934.

———, *Jesus Christ and Mythology*. New York: Charles Scribner's Sons, 1958.

———, *Theology of the New Testament*, trans. K. Grobel. 2 vols. New York: Charles Scribner's Sons, 1955–57.

BURTT, E. A., *The Metaphysical Foundations of Modern Physical Science* (2nd, revised ed.). London: Routledge & Kegan Paul, Ltd. and New Jersey: The Humanities Press, Inc., 1950.

BUTTERFIELD, HERBERT, *Christianity and History*. London: Collins Publishers, (Fontana Books), 1957.

CHESTERTON, G. K., *Orthodoxy*. Westport, Conn.: Greenwood Press, 1974.

CHRISTENSEN, D. E., ed., *Hegel and the Philosophy of Religion*. The Hague: Nijhøff, 1970.

COLLINGWOOD, R. G., *Faith and Reason*, ed. L. Rubinoff. Chicago: Quadrangle Books, Inc., 1968.

———, *The Idea of Nature*. New York: Oxford University Press, Inc., 1960.

CONE, JAMES, *A Black Theology of Liberation*. Philadelphia and New York: J. B. Lippincott Company, 1970.

———, *The Spirituals and the Blues*. New York: The Seabury Press, Inc., 1972.

COPLESTON, FREDERICK, *A History of Philosophy. Volume II: Medieval Philosophy*. Westminster, Md.: The Newman Press, 1950.

CORNFORD, FRANCIS M., *From Religion to Philosophy: A Study in the Origins of Western Speculation*. New York: Harper & Brothers, Publishers, 1957.

COX, HARVEY, *The Feast of Fools*. Cambridge, Mass.: Harvard University Press, 1969.

———, *The Secular City* (rev. ed.). New York: Macmillan, Inc., 1966.

———, *The Seduction of the Spirit*. New York: Simon and Schuster, Inc., 1973.

CULLMANN, OSCAR, *Christ and Time*, trans. F. V. Filson. Philadelphia: The Westminster Press, 1950.

———, *The Christology of the New Testament* (rev. ed.), trans. S. C. Guthrie and C. A. M. Hall. Philadelphia: The Westminster Press, 1964.

———, *Immortality of the Soul or Resurrection of the Dead?* London: Epworth, 1958.

———, *Salvation in History*, trans. S. G. Sowers. New York: Harper and Row, Publishers, Inc., 1967.

CUSHMAN, ROBERT, *Therapeia: Plato's Conception of Philosophy*. New York: Harper & Brothers, Publishers, 1957.

D'ARCY, M. C., *The Mind and Heart of Love* (rev. ed.). New York: Henry Holt & Co., Inc., 1956.

DE UNAMUNO, MIGUEL, *The Tragic Sense of Life*, trans. J. E. C. Flitch. New York: Dover Publications, Inc., 1954.

DEWART, LESLIE, *The Future of Belief*. New York: Herder & Herder, 1966.

DILLENBERGER, JOHN, *Protestant Thought and Natural Science*. Garden City, N.Y.: Doubleday & Co., Inc., 1960.

DODD, C. H., *The Authority of the Bible*. New York and London: Harper & Brothers, Publishers, 1929.

————, *The Bible Today*. Cambridge: Cambridge University Press, 1952.

————, *The Coming of Christ*. Cambridge: Cambridge University Press, 1958.

————, *The Parables of the Kingdom*. London: James Nisbet, 1935.

EICHRODT, W., *Man in the Old Testament. Studies in Biblical Theology*, no. 4. London: SCM Press, Ltd., 1951.

ELIADE, MIRCEA, *Cosmos and History: The Myth of Eternal Return*. New York: Harper & Brothers, Publishers, 1959.

————, *Myth and Reality*. New York: Harper & Row, Publishers, Inc., 1963.

————, *The Sacred and the Profane: The Nature of Religion*, trans. W. R. Trask. New York: Harcourt Brace Jovanovich, Inc., 1959.

ELLWOOD, ROBERT, *Religion from Inside and Outside. An Introduction*. Englewood Cliffs, N.J.: Prentice-Hall, Inc., 1978.

FACKENHEIM, EMIL, *Metaphysics and Historicity*. Milwaukee: Marquette University Press, 1961.

————, *The Religious Dimension in Hegel's Thought*. Bloomington: Indiana University Press, 1967.

FLETCHER, JOSEPH, *Situation Ethics*. Philadelphia: The Westminster Press, 1966.

FRANKFORT, H., et al., *Before Philosophy*. Chicago: University of Chicago Press, 1946.

FRANKL, VIKTOR, *Man's Search for Meaning: An Introduction to Logotherapy*, trans. Ilse Lasch. Boston: Beacon Press, 1963.

GALLOWAY, ALLAN, *The Cosmic Christ*. New York: Harper & Brothers, Publishers, 1951.

GILSON, E., *God and Philosophy*. New Haven, Conn.: Yale University Press, 1941.

GLASSE, JAMES, *Profession: Minister*. Nashville, Tenn.: Abingdon Press, 1968.

GOGARTEN, FRIEDRICH, *Demythologizing and History*, trans. N. H. Smith. London: Camelot Press, 1955.

————, *The Reality of Faith*, trans. C. Michalson and others. Philadelphia: The Westminster Press, 1959.

GRILLMEIER, ALOYS, *Christ in Christian Tradition: Volume One: From the Apostolic Age to Chalcedon* (2nd, rev. ed.), trans. J. Bowden. Atlanta: John Knox Press, 1975.

GUSTAFSON, JAMES, *Christ and the Moral Life*. New York: Harper & Row, Publishers, Inc., 1968.

GUTIERREZ, G., *A Theology of Liberation*, trans. C. Inda and J. Eagleson. Maryknoll, N.Y.: Orbis Books, 1973

HAMMOND, G., *Man in Estrangement: A Comparison of the Thought of Paul Tillich and Erich Fromm*. Nashville, Tenn.: Vanderbilt University Press, 1965.

HART, RAY L., *Unfinished Man and the Imagination*. New York: Herder & Herder, 1968.

HARTSHORNE, CHARLES, *The Divine Relativity: A Social Conception of God*. New Haven, Conn.: Yale University Press, 1964.

————, *Man's Vision of God*. Chicago and New York: Willett-Clark, 1941.

HARVEY, VAN A., *The Historian and the Believer*. New York: Macmillan, Inc., 1966.

HEALEY, F. G., ed., *What Theologians Do*. Grand Rapids, Mich.: Eerdmans, 1971.

HEIDEGGER, MARTIN, *Being and Time*, trans. J. Macquarrie and E. Robinson. New York: Harper & Brothers, Publishers, 1962.

_____, "What Is Metaphysics?" trans. R. F. C. Hull and A. Crick, pp. 325–61 in *Existence and Being*, ed. W. Brock. Chicago: Henry Regnery Company, 1949.

HEILER, FRIEDRICH, *Prayer*, trans. S. McComb. New York: Oxford University Press, Inc., 1958.

HERBERG, WILL, "Biblical Faith as *Heilsgeschichte:* The Meaning of Redemptive History in Human Existence," in *The Christian Scholar*, 39 (1956), 25–31.

_____, *Protestant-Catholic-Jew* (rev. ed.). Garden City, N.Y.: Doubleday & Co., Inc., 1955.

HERZOG, FREDERICK, *Liberation Theology*. New York: The Seabury Press, Inc., 1972.

HICK, JOHN, *Evil and the God of Love*. London: Collins, 1974.

HICK, J. AND A. C. McGILL, eds., *The Many-Faced Argument*. New York: Macmillan, Inc., 1967.

HIERS, RICHARD H., *The Kingdom of God in the Synoptic Tradition*. Gainesville: University of Florida Press, 1970.

HOLBROOK, CLYDE, *Faith and Community*. New York: Harper & Brothers, Publishers, 1959.

HORDERN, WILLIAM, *Christianity, Communism, and History*. Nashville, Tenn.: Abingdon Press, 1954.

JAEGER, WERNER, *Paideia: The Ideals of Greek Culture*. 3 vols., trans. Gilbert Highet. New York: Oxford University Press, Inc., 1939.

JOHNSON, SHERMAN M., *Jesus in His Homeland*. New York: Charles Scribner's Sons, 1957.

JONAS, HANS, *The Gnostic Religion*. Boston: Beacon Press, 1963.

JUNG, C. G., *Modern Man in Search of a Soul*, trans. W. S. Dell and C. F. Baynes. New York: Harcourt, Brace & Co., Inc., 1933.

KANT, IMMANUEL, *Religion within the Limits of Reason Alone*, trans. T. M. Greene and H. H. Hudson. New York: Harper & Brothers, Publishers, 1960.

KAUFMAN, GORDON, *Relativism, Knowledge, and Faith*. Chicago: University of Chicago Press, 1960.

KAZANTZAKIS, NIKOS, *Zorba the Greek*. New York: Simon & Schuster, Inc., 1953.

KEE, H., F. YOUNG AND K. FROEHLICH, *Understanding the New Testament* (3rd ed.). Englewood Cliffs, N.J.: Prentice-Hall, Inc., 1973.

KEEN, SAM, *To a Dancing God*. New York: Harper & Row, Publishers, Inc., 1970.

KELLY, J. N. D., *Early Christian Doctrines* (2nd ed.). New York: Harper & Brothers, Publishers, 1960.

KIERKEGAARD, SØREN, *The Concept of Dread*, trans. Walter Lowrie. Princeton, N.J.: Princeton University Press, 1957.

_____, *Concluding Unscientific Postscript*, trans. D. F. Swenson and W. Lowrie. Princeton, N.J.: Princeton University Press, 1941.

_____, *Fear and Trembling*, trans. W. Lowrie. Princeton, N.J.: Princeton University Press, 1941.

_____, *Philosophical Fragments*, trans. D. F. Swenson. Princeton, N.J.: Princeton University Press, 1936.

———, *The Present Age,* trans. A. Dru. Cambridge, Mass.: Harvard University Press, 1962.

———, *The Sickness unto Death,* trans. W. Lowrie. Princeton, N.J.: Princeton University Press, 1941.

———, *Works of Love,* trans. H. Hong and E. Hong. New York: Harper & Row, Publishers, Inc., 1962.

KNOX, JOHN, *The Church and the Reality of Christ.* New York: Harper & Row, Publishers, Inc., 1962.

KRONER, RICHARD, *Speculation and Revelation in the Age of Christian Philosophy.* Philadelphia: The Westminster Press, 1949.

KÜNG, HANS, *On Being a Christian,* trans. E. Quinn. Garden City, N.Y.: Doubleday & Co., Inc., 1976.

LITTELL, F. H., *The Anabaptist View of the Church.* Boston: Starr King Press, 1958.

———, *The Free Church.* Boston: Starr King Press, 1957.

LONERGAN, BERNARD, *The Way to Nicea,* trans. C. O'Donovan. Philadelphia: The Westminster Press, n.d.

LONG, E. LEROY, *A Survey of Christian Ethics.* New York: Oxford University Press, Inc., 1967.

LOVEJOY, A. O., *The Great Chain of Being.* Cambridge, Mass.: Harvard University Press, 1960.

LÖWITH, KARL, *Meaning in History.* Chicago: University of Chicago Press, 1949.

LUTHER, MARTIN, *The Freedom of a Christian.* (1520)

MACLEISH, ARCHIBALD, *J. B.* Boston: Houghton-Mifflin Company, 1958.

MANSCHRECK, CLYDE C., *A History of Christianity in the World: From Persecution to Uncertainty.* Englewood Cliffs, N.J.: Prentice-Hall, Inc., 1974.

MARCEL, GABRIEL, *Homo Viator,* trans. E. Craufurd. Chicago: Henry Regnery Company, 1951.

MARITAIN, JACQUES, *The Range of Reason.* New York: Charles Scribner's Sons, 1942.

MARTY, MARTIN E., *Varieties of Unbelief.* New York: Holt, Rinehart & Winston, 1964.

MASCALL, E. L., *Christian Theology and Natural Science.* Hamden, Conn.: Archon Books, 1965.

McINTYRE, JOHN, *The Christian Doctrine of History.* Grand Rapids, Mich.: Eerdmans, 1957.

MICHALSON, CARL, *The Hinge of History.* New York: Charles Scribner's Sons, 1959.

———, *The Rationality of Faith.* New York: Charles Scribner's Sons, 1963.

MOLTMANN, JÜRGEN, *Theology of Hope,* trans. J. W. Leitel. New York: Harper & Row, Publishers, Inc., 1967.

MORRIS, H. F., *Scientific Creationism.* San Diego: Creation Life Publishers, 1976.

NIEBUHR, H. R., *Christ and Culture.* New York: Harper & Brothers, Publishers, 1951.

———, *The Meaning of Revelation.* New York: Macmillan, Inc., 1941.

———, *The Responsible Self.* New York: Harper & Row, Publishers, Inc., 1963.

———, *The Social Sources of Denominationalism.* New York: Henry Holt & Co., Inc., 1929.

Niebuhr, Reinhold, *Faith and History*. New York: Charles Scribner's Sons, 1955.

——, *Moral Man and Immoral Society*. New York: Charles Scribner's Sons, 1932.

——, *The Nature and Destiny of Man*. 2 vols. New York: Charles Scribner's Sons, 1941.

——, *The Self and the Dramas of History*. New York: Charles Scribner's Sons, 1955.

Niebuhr, R. R., *Resurrection and Historical Reason*. New York: Charles Scribner's Sons, 1957.

Niesel, Wilhelm, *The Gospel and the Churches*, trans. D. Lewis. Philadelphia: The Westminster Press, 1962.

Nietzsche, F., *The Birth of Tragedy from the Spirit of Music*, trans. W. Kaufmann. Garden City, N.Y.: Doubleday & Co., Inc., 1956.

Nogar, R. J., *The Wisdom of Evolution*. New York: New American Library, 1966.

Novak, Michael, *Ascent of the Mountain, Flight of the Dove*. New York: Harper & Row, Publishers, Inc., 1971.

Nygren, A., *Agape and Eros*, trans. Philip Watson. London, SPCK, 1932–39.

Ogden, Shubert M., *Christ Without Myth*. London: Collins, 1962.

——, *The Reality of God and Other Essays*. New York: Harper & Row, Publishers, Inc., 1963.

Otto, Rudolf, *The Idea of the Holy*, trans. J. W. Harvey. New York: Oxford University Press, Inc., 1958.

——, *The Kingdom of God and the Son of Man* (rev. ed.), trans. F. V. Filson and B. L. Woolf. Boston: Starr King Press, 1957.

Outler, Albert, *The Christian Tradition and the Unity We Seek*. New York: Oxford University Press, Inc., 1957.

Pannenberg, Wolfhart, *Jesus—God and Man*, trans. L. L. Wilkins and D. Priebe. Philadelphia: The Westminster Press, 1968.

——, ed., *Revelation as History*. New York and London: Macmillan, Inc. and Collier-Macmillan, 1968.

——, *Theology and the Kingdom of God*, ed. R. J. Neuhaus. Philadelphia: The Westminster Press, 1969.

Pascal, Blaise, "Pensées," in *Pensées and Provincial Letters*. New York: Random House, Inc., 1941.

Pelikan, Jaroslav, *The Riddle of Roman Catholicism*. New York and Nashville: Abingdon Press, 1959.

——, *The Shape of Death*. Nashville, Tenn.: Abingdon Press, 1961.

Prenter, Regin, *Spiritus Creator*, trans. J. M. Jensen. Philadelphia: Fortress Press, 1953.

Rahner, Karl, *The Priesthood*, trans. E. Quinn. New York: The Seabury Press, 1970.

Ramsdell, E. T., *The Christian Perspective*. Nashville, Tenn.: Abingdon Press, 1950.

Ramsey, Paul, *Basic Christian Ethics*. New York: Charles Scribner's Sons, 1950.

Rauschenbusch, W., *A Theology for the Social Gospel*. New York: Macmillan, Inc., 1917.

RITSCHL, DIETRICH, *A Theology of Proclamation*. Richmond, Va.: John Knox Press, 1960.

ROBINSON, H. W., *The Christian Experience of the Holy Spirit*. London: James Nisbet, 1928.

———, *Corporate Personality in Israel*. Philadelphia: Fortress Press, 1964.

ROBINSON, J. A. T., *The Body: A Study in Pauline Theology. Studies in Biblical Theology*, no. 5. London: SCM Press, Ltd., 1952.

ROLLINS, WAYNE G., *The Gospels: Portraits of Christ*. Philadelphia: The Westminster Press, 1963.

RUPP, GORDON, *The Righteousness of God: Luther Studies*. London: Hodder and Stoughton, 1953.

RUSSELL, BERTRAND, "A Free Man's Worship," in *Mysticism and Logic and Other Essays*. London: George Allen & Unwin, Ltd., 1917.

ST. ANSELM, *St. Anselm: Basic Writings*, trans. and ed. S. N. Deane. LaSalle, Ill.: Open Court Publishing Company, 1951.

ST. AUGUSTINE, *The City of God*. (426)

———, *Confessions*. (ca. 400)

———, *De Trinitate* (On the Trinity). (400–417)

SCHAFF, PHILIP, *The Creeds of Christendom*. 3 vols. New York: Harper & Brothers, Publishers, 1889.

SCHMITHALS, WALTER, *Gnosticism in Corinth*, trans. J. E. Steely. Nashville, Tenn.: Abingdon Press, 1971.

SCHWARZ, HANS, *On the Way to the Future*. Minneapolis, Minn.: Augsburg Publishing House, 1972.

SCHWEITZER, ALBERT, "The Ethics of Reverence for Life," *Christendom*, 1, no. 2 (Winter 1936), 225–39.

———, *The Quest of the Historical Jesus*, trans. W. Montgomery. New York: Macmillan, Inc., 1966.

SEEBERG, REINHOLD, *A Textbook of the History of Doctrines*, trans. C. E. Hay. Grand Rapids, Mich.: Baker, 1952.

SHINN, ROGER, *Christianity and the Problem of History*. New York: Charles Scribner's Sons, 1953.

———, *Tangled World*. New York: Charles Scribner's Sons, 1965.

SMITH, H. SHELTON, *Changing Conceptions of Original Sin*. New York: Charles Scribner's Sons, 1950.

SÖDERBLOM, NATHAN, *The Living God: Basal Forms of Personal Religion*. London: Oxford University Press, Inc., 1933.

STRENG, FREDERICK, CHARLES L. LLOYD, JR., AND JAY T. ALLEN, *Ways of Being Religious*. Englewood Cliffs, N.J.: Prentice-Hall, Inc., 1973.

TAVARD, GEORGE, *Holy Writ or Holy Church*. New York: Harper & Brothers, Publishers, 1959.

TEILHARD DE CHARDIN, PIERRE, *The Future of Man*, trans. N. Denny. New York: Harper & Row, Publishers, Inc., 1964.

———, *The Phenomenon of Man*, trans. B. Wall. New York: Harper & Brothers, Publishers, 1959.

TEMPLE, WILLIAM, *Nature, Man, and God*. London: Macmillan, Inc., 1935.

THOMAS AQUINAS, *Summa Theologiae*. (1265?–1273)

TILLICH, PAUL, *Biblical Religion and the Search for Ultimate Reality*. Chicago: University of Chicago Press, 1955.

———, *Dynamics of Faith*. New York: Harper & Brothers, Publishers, 1958.

———, "Historical and Nonhistorical Interpretations of History: A Comparison," pp. 16–31 in *The Protestant Era* (abridged ed.). Chicago: University of Chicago Press, 1957.

———, *Love, Power, and Justice*. New York: Oxford University Press, 1954.

———, *The New Being*. New York: Charles Scribner's Sons, 1955.

———, "Revelation and the Philosophy of Religion," Vol. II, pp. 46–56, trans. R. A. Wilson, in *Twentieth Century Theology in the Making*, ed. J. Pelikan. New York: Harper & Row, Publishers, Inc., 1971.

———, *The Shaking of the Foundations*. New York: Charles Scribner's Sons, 1948.

———, *Systematic Theology*. 3 vols. Chicago: University of Chicago Press, 1957.

———, *Theology of Culture*. New York: Oxford University Press, Inc., 1959.

TROELTSCH, ERNST, *The Social Teachings of the Christian Churches*, trans. O. Wyon. 2 vols. London: George Allen & Unwin, Ltd., 1931.

UNDERHILL, EVELYN, *Worship*. New York: Harper & Brothers, Publishers, 1937.

VAJTA, VILMOS, *Luther on Worship*, trans. U. S. Leupold. Philadelphia: Muhlenberg Press, 1958.

VAN BUREN, PAUL, *The Secular Meaning of the Gospel*. New York: Macmillan, Inc., 1963.

VAN DER LEEUW, GERARDUS, *Religion in Essence and Manifestation*, trans. J. E. Turner. 2 vols. London: George Allen & Unwin, Ltd. and New York: Harper & Row, Publishers, Inc., 1938.

VOEGELIN, ERIC, *Science, Politics, and Gnosticism*, trans. W. J. Fitzpatrick. South Bend, Ind.: Gateway Editions, Ltd., 1968.

VON RAD, GERHARD, *Genesis: A Commentary*, trans. J. H. Marks. Philadelphia: The Westminster Press, 1961.

WATSON, PHILIP S., *Let God Be God!* Philadelphia: Muhlenberg Press, 1947.

WEBBER, G., *God's Colony in Man's World*. Nashville, Tenn.: Abingdon Press, 1960.

WEBER, MAX, *The Protestant Ethic and the Spirit of Capitalism*, trans. T. Parsons. New York: Charles Scribner's Sons, 1930.

WEIGEL, G. and A. G. MADDEN, *Religion and the Knowledge of God*. Englewood Cliffs, N.J.: Prentice-Hall, Inc., 1961.

WERNER, MARTIN, *The Formation of Christian Dogma*, trans. S. G. F. Brandon. New York: Harper & Brothers, Publishers, 1957.

WHALE, JOHN S., *The Protestant Tradition*. Cambridge: Cambridge University Press, 1955.

WHITE, LYNN, JR., "The Historic Roots of the Ecologic Crisis," *Science*, 155, no. 3767 (March 10, 1967), 1203–1207.

WHITEHEAD, ALFRED N., *Modes of Thought*. Glencoe, Ill.: The Free Press, 1968.

WILLIAMS, J. PAUL, *What Americans Believe and How They Worship* (rev. ed.). New York: Harper & Brothers, Publishers, 1961.

WINGREN, GUSTAV, *Luther on Vocation*, trans. C. C. Rasmussen. Philadelphia: Muhlenberg Press, 1957.

WOLF, W. J., *Man's Knowledge of God*. Garden City, N.Y.: Doubleday & Co., Inc., 1955.

WOLFSON, H. A., *The Philosophy of Spinoza*. 2 vols. in 1. New York: Meridian Books, 1958.

WRIGHT, G. ERNEST, *God Who Acts. Studies in Biblical Theology*, no. 8. London: SCM Press, Ltd., 1952.

WRIGHT, G. E. AND R. H. FULLER, *The Book of the Acts of God*. Garden City, N.Y.: Doubleday & Co., Inc., 1957.

Index

ABELARD, PETER, 27n.
Abraham, 69, 70, 100, 211, 258
  and the faith of Israel, 338
  and Isaac, 109
  and Sarah, 103
Adam, 69, 100, 278
  and Christ, 307–12, 317, 322–23
  hiding from God, 80
  life style as human option, 323
  meaning of name, 54n.
Adam and Eve, 52, 252–53
  commission, 278
  meaning of names, 280
  rejection of responsibility, 282, 303
  their self-deception, 302
  their sin as self-exaltation, 306
Afterlife:
  anxiety regarding, 391
  evokes theological reticence, 390–92
Agape:
  basis, in God, of grace, 377
  Christ's and the Christian's, 377
  criterion of Christian caring, 378
  defined, 376–77
  distinguished from *eros* and *philia,*
    376–77
  Jesus' death as supreme expression, 377
Agnosticism, 136–37, 156–66, 175n.
  absolutizes the fragmentary, 167
  Christian critique of, 159 (*chart*), 160–66
  defined, 136–37
  defines knowledge too narrowly, 160,
    164–66
  and gnosticism compared, 137
  rationalist and empiricist forms distin-
    guished, 157–58, 159 (*chart*)
  types of, 156–58, 159 (*chart*)
Albigensians, 4, 351
Amos, 90, 115, 315

Anath, 35, 38, 296
Anderson, B. W., 59n., 125n.
Anglicanism, 341, 358
Anselm of Canterbury:
  ontological argument, 189–93
  prayer reflecting perplexity, 225–26n.
  theory of atonement, 341
Anthropomorphism, *defined,* 229n.
Antinomianism, 371n., 395n.
Anxiety, 79–80
Apocrypha, definition and composition,
    227n.
Apollinarius of Laodicea, 321nn.
Aquinas, Thomas (*see* Thomas Aquinas)
Arguments, for God's existence (*see* Exis-
    tence of God)
Aristotle, 28n., 42, 325
  on the divine source of motion, 288–89
  on knowing, 129–30
Arius of Alexandria:
  concern for unity of God, 290
  condemnation at Nicea, 319n.
  father of "Arianism," 174n.
  view of Christ, 290–91
Art:
  distinguished from science, 13
  religion as, 13, 17–21, 24
Athanasius:
  and Apollinarius, 321n.
  central concern, 291, 313, 315
  compromise with Greek thought, 291–92
  victory, 292
Atheism:
  inherently irrational (Anselm), 190
  a practical impossibility, 284–85
Atonement, 334, 341, 363n.
Auerbach, Erich, 27n., 109
Augustine of Hippo (Saint Augustine):
  on authority, 342–43

Augustine of Hippo (*cont.*)
  on believing and understanding, 131
  on evil, 271n.
  on evolution (continuous creation), 240,
    270n.
  on the gifts of redemption, 328
  on history, 61, 65, 90–91nn.
  prayer of the restless heart, 286, 317
  on sin as slavery, 300–301
  on the Trinity, 292, 325
Aulén, G., 363n.
Authority:
  of congregation, in sect-churches, 352–53
  of the *magisterium*, in Catholicism, 341–44
  of the *ministerium*, among Protestants,
    348
  of Peter, 341, 363n.
  of the pope, 199, 342–44
  of priests, 345, 346 (*chart*)
  and revelation, 197
Autonomy (*see also* Freedom):
  as Christian desideratum, 56, 275, 337,
    382–83
Averroes, 173n.
Avicenna, 173n.

BAAL, 38, 48 (*chart*), 49, 59n., 296
  meaning of name, 35
Baillie, John, 172n.
  on death and the beyond, 334
Baptism:
  as act of "naming," 220, 345
  of believers only, among sects, 352, 357
    (*chart*)
  distinctive Orthodox rite, 347
  in extremis, 363n.
  of infants, 345, 346 (*chart*), 347, 352
    sectarian disdain for, 352
    significance for corporatists, 345, 352
  as rebirth or resurrection, 220
  reluctance to receive, among ancients,
    363n.
  as rite of forgiveness and reconciliation,
    345
  as way of professing faith, 352, 354
Baptists, 358
Barbour, Ian G., 29n.
Barrett, William, 176n.
Barth, Karl, 268n., 272n.
  as dialogist, 227n.
  on reason and revelation, 172n.

Becker, Ernest, 332
Berdyaev, N., 249
Bettenson, H., 318n., 319nn., 321n.
Bible (*see also* Canon; Scripture; Word of
    God):
  canonization, 204–5
  contents of, 204–5
  and covenant, 217
  interpretive attitudes and approaches,
    205–11
  literary genres in, 102–4
  style compared with that of Homer, 109,
    125n.
  and the Word of God, 204–17, 348
Biblicism (*see also* Textualism):
  defined, 115n.
Bibliolatry, *defined*, 115n.
Body:
  as historical self, 74–76, 393
  as object of redemption, 366
Boman, Thorlief, 50
Bonhoeffer, Dietrich, 318n., 363n.
  on Jesus as "man-for-others," 338
Bornkamm, G., 74–75, 93nn.
Bright, John, 396n.
Brightman, E. S., 249
Bring, R., 172n.
Brother Lawrence, 27n.
Brown, Norman O., 27n., 363n.
  against selfhood, 337
  on symbolism, 15
Brunner, E., 172n., 227n., 268n., 272n.
Bultmann, Rudolf, 74, 93nn., 94n., 397n.
  and demythologizing, 288
  doctrine of Christ as history's "end," 72
Burtt, E. A., 28n.
Byzantine Church (*see also* Eastern Or-
    thodoxy), 2

CAIN AND ABEL, 52, 228n., 253, 303
  Cain's "redemptive" punishment, 59n.,
    218, 230
Calvin, John:
  compared with sectarians, 355
  on the mind as a factory of idols, 284
  on predestination, 391
  sectarian view of, 353
  on Word and Spirit, 205
  on "works," 349
Camus, Albert, 244

Canon (*see also* Bible; Scripture):
  formation and composition, 204–5
  undefined at time of Jesus, 228n.
Care, 80–81
Caring:
  defines Christian love for neighbor, 375
  grounded in God, human nature, time,
    376
Casuistry, *defined*, 369n.
Categorical imperative, 192–93, 223 (*chart*),
    396n.
Cathari, 2, 351
Cathedral, *defined*, 343n.
Catholicism, Roman (*see* Roman Catholi-
    cism)
Celsus, 289
Chesterton, G. K., 274, 318n.
Christ (*see also* Jesus):
  and Adam, 307–12, 322–23
  according to Apollinarius, 321n.
  Arian view, 290–91
  Athanasian view, 291, 313
  attempts to define, 273–74, 289–92
  center of church's authority, 342
  center of history
    in Cullmann, 66–67, 70, 92n.
    in Irenaeus, 64–66
    in Teilhard, 68–69
  Church's exemplar, 360
  and creation, 268n.
  crucifixion and resurrection, 72
  divinity and humanity, 313–14, 321n.
  as "eschatological event," 72
  as eternal *logos*, 225n.
  in the Eucharist, 346, 357
  giver of new law, 356
  as God's act of justification, 303
  in Hegel's system, 150–51
  as "last Adam," 308, 311
  life-pattern *versus* that of Adam, 310–12
  life style as human option, 322–23, 362–
    63n.
  made contemporary by Holy Spirit, 122,
    323, 334, 364n.
  nature of return, 386–87
  as norm of revelation and Scripture,
    216–17
  pioneer of "progress," 72
  proclaimer of the Kingdom, 379
  reason for advent, 278
  as Redeemer, 305–14
  self-emptying, 308–11, 323

Christ (*cont.*)
  significance for history, 64–73, 167
  as Son of Man, 397n.
  and the Spirit, 323–25
  supreme expression of divine will, 154
"Christendom" (Kierkegaard), 335
Christianity:
  affinities with Judaism, 61
  causes of division in, 227n.
  diversity of forms, 60–61
  a historist faith, 61–76, 86, 88–89
  and other faiths, 89
  Western and Eastern compared, 105
Christians, as "little Christs," 202, 349
Christology, central issue in, 273–74, 312–
    14, 318n.
Church (*see also* Community of faith; Sect):
  architecture expresses aim, 350, 364n.
  as body of Christ, 211, 359–60
  as community of reconciliation, 339
  as corporate (constitutional) community,
    340–50
    defined, 340–41
    doctrine of authority, 341–44
    theory of origins, 341
  created and defined by God's Word, 114,
    125n., 339, 348
  defined by two relationships, 366
  as New Israel, 123
  as sect (congregational) community,
    350–56
  as society of the perfect, 351, 364n.
  as world's servant, 360
Churches:
  difficulty of classifying, 357–59
  "high" and "low" distinguished, 356–57
Cicero, 225
Clergy (see *Magisterium; Ministerium;*
    Priests)
Collingwood, R. G., 58n., 176nn., 270n.,
    271n.
  compares religion and science, 27n.,
    176n.
Comedy:
  defined, 53, 59n.
  and history's outcome, 53
Communion of saints, 90n.
Communism, 56–57n., 151
Community of faith (*see also* Church;
    Sect(s)), 338, 356–60
Comte, Auguste, 143, 153
Confirmation, 346, 347

Congregationalism:
  denomination, 358
  principle of church government, 352–55,
    365n.
Conscience, as point of contact with God,
    193, 223 (chart), 354
Constantine, 2, 350, 363n.
  role in subverting Nicene decision, 319n.
Constantinian Edict of Toleration (313), 2
Contingency:
  argument from, 188–89, 192 (chart)
  discloses "createdness," 241–43
  Pascal's experience of, 125–26n.
  significance of experience, 163
Copernicus, 22, 28n.
Copleston, F., 269nn., 270n.
Cornford, F. M., 27n., 28n.
Cosmological arguments (see Existence of
    God)
Council of Chalcedon, 172n., 313–14, 318n.,
    321n.
  decision regarding Christ, 216
Council of Jamnia, canonizes Jewish Bible,
    204–5
Council of Nicea, 172n., 319n.
Counsels of perfection, 349, 355–56
Covenant:
  as divine-human drama, 69
  origin, 50
  reestablished and renewed in Christ,
    122–23
Covenant history, events comprising,
    69–73
Cox, Harvey:
  Christianity and other faiths, 57n.
  definition of religion, 26n.
  desacralization of nature, 244, 271n.
  Exodus as desacralizing event, 71
  on faith and science, 173n.
  on religion and culture, 125n.
Creation:
  as conferral of order, 238–39
  as continuous preservation (creatio con-
    tinua), 239–40, 270nn.
  disclosed through contingency, 241–43
  doctrine's implications for science,
    244–45
  and evolution, 240
  as faith's essential aim, 230–31
  as gift of existence, 238–39

Creation (cont.)
  from nothing (ex nihilo), 233, 269nn.
  political, ecological, and economic impli-
    cations, 245–46
  and redemption, 231, 274–78
  source of world's essential goodness,
    234, 243–46
Creaturehood, 262–63
Cullmann, Oscar, 66–71, 92n.
Culture:
  affinity with intellect, 87
  colored by nature and history, 87–88
  distinguished from nature and history,
    86–87n.
  as "second nature," 86

Dancing, 36, 57n.
  as means to divine communion, 36
D'Arcy, M., 175n.
Darwin, Charles, 22, 240
David, 47, 70, 100
  and Bathsheba, 103
  forebear of the Messiah, 381–82
Death, 262
  American attitudes toward, 332
  Christian and Platonic attitudes com-
    pared, 75, 393
  conquered by Christ, 333–34, 338
  discloses human limitations, 332, 393
  significance of Christ's, 333–34
Deism, 235–36, 268–69n.
Demythologizing, 288n.
Descartes, René, 144, 192 (chart)
Destiny (see Afterlife; Eschatology; Eternal
    life; Predestination; Resurrection)
Determinism (see also Predestination):
  of Spinoza, 145–47
Devil (see also Satan; Tempter)
  as angel of light, 118
Dialogism, 209–11
Dillenberger, John, 29n.
Dionysus, 36, 48 (chart)
Discipleship, price of, 397n.
Ditheism, in gnosticism, 138, 142, 152
    (chart)
Divorce:
  Orthodox view of, 347
  Roman view of, 347, 364n.
Docetism, defined, 140

Dodd, C. H.:
  on biblical inspiration, 227n.
  realized eschatology, 397n.
Dominion (*see also* Image of God), 265–67
  synonym for liberty, 370
  and Western science, 173n.
Donne, John, 396n.
Dostoyevsky, Fyodor, 26n., 335–36, 363n.
Doubt (*see* Agnosticism)
Drama, in the Bible, 103
Dread (*see* Anxiety)
Drugs, as means to divine communion, 36
Dualism:
  gnostic, 138–42, 152 (*chart*)
  Platonic, 44–45, 75, 233, 392–93
  and Platonic attitude toward sex, 233

EASTERN ORTHODOXY (*see also* Byzantine
    Church), 341
  compared with Western Christianity, 105
  concept of regeneration or "deification,"
    347
  distinctive sacramental practices, 347
  theology of sacraments, 347
Ecumenical councils, 172n.
Education, as way of salvation, 18, 44–45
Eliade, Mircea, 59n.
Elijah, 59n., 320n., 396n.
  as forerunner of the Messiah, 380
  at Mt. Horeb, 227n.
  and Queen Jezebel, 115
Elisha, 320n., 396n.
Emotion:
  authentic religious function, 15
  and the problem of knowing God, 203
    (*chart*), 223 (*chart*)
  special role in nature religion, 86, 169
Emotionalism, 113
"Enthusiasm," among sectarians, 352,
    364n.
Eros, 376
Eschatology, 73–76, 375–94
  defined, 93n.
  realized, 397n.
Eternal life, 390 (*see also* Afterlife; Eschatol-
    ogy; Heaven and hell)
Ethics:
  Christian principles debated, 367–75
  deontological, 368
  as essential expression of faith, 117–19

Ethics (*cont.*)
  of historism, 53–54
  of naturism, 33–34
  of reason religion, 42–43
  take form in styles and standards, 104–7
Eucharist (*see also* Lord's Supper), 346–47
  as "medicine of immortality," 347
  three aims of, 346
Euripides, 57n.
Eve, 52–54, 247, 279, 281
  confuses *imago Dei* with divine reality,
    280
  and the original sin, 53–54, 280–81
Evil (*see also* Theodicies):
  its apparent success, eventual demise,
    259–60, 388
  Deuteronomic philosophy regarding,
    255–57
  explanations of, 247–50, 251 (*chart*),
    252–60, 271n.
  in gnosticism, 136, 138–39, 140, 143, 152
    (*chart*)
  in light of Jesus' career, 257–60
  natural distinguished from moral, 247
  origins according to Genesis, 252–53
  as parasitical perversion of good, 247
  result of relative non-being, 248–50
  significance according to *Job,* 254–57
    summarized, 257
  significance for Second Isaiah, 258–59
Evolution, 28n., 270n.
  Augustinian form, 270n.
  and creation, 240
  in Teilhard's thought, 67–69
Existence of God, arguments for:
  cosmological, 183, 185–89, 192 (*chart*)
  critical responses to, 194–97
  moral, 184, 192 (*chart*), 192–94
  ontological, 184, 189–92, 192 (*chart*)
Exodus, 50, 70
  meaning of name, 50
  political significance, 71
  portrays God as historical revolutionary,
    71
Extreme Unction, 347

FACKENHEIN, E. L., 270n., 318n.
Fact(s):
  defined, 9
  and values, 9–11

Faith:
  as activity of the whole person, 155, 175n.
  basis in history, 169–70
  constant features, 99, 119–23
  distinguished from belief, 97–99, 129
  exclusiveness of, 117–18
  expressed through stories, styles, standards, 99–111, 170
  functions of, 81
    forms a world view, 119
    projects a life style, 119
    provides a perspective or "myth," 119–20
  inability to "contain" God, 124n.
  as a project, 95–100, 107
  rooted ultimately in God's love, 394
  social character, 97–99, 338
  three dimensions of, 96–97, 107
  as time-consciousness, 77–81
  as a way of knowing, 168–71
Fall of humankind, 53–54, 69–70, 279–85
Faustus, 271n.
Fletcher, Joseph, 367
Formalism, 113
Form (or shape):
  as clue to value and meaning, 62–63
  as means of "coping," 63
Form criticism, *defined*, 124n.
Fox, George, 354
Francis of Assisi (St. Francis), 263, 286
  founder of Franciscan order, 364n.
  on human worth, 328
Frankfort, Henri, 27n.
Frankl, V., 270n.
Frazer, Sir James, 57n.
Freedom (*see also* Autonomy; Liberty):
  compatible with God's rule, 275–77
  defined, 276
  as enemy of "security" (Grand Inquisitor), 335–36
  essential to love and to moral distinctions, 121–22, 367
  as power to respond to persons, 276, 374
Freud, Sigmund, 58nn., 153
  on the self, 87
Frost, Robert, 28n.
Fundamentalists, views on revelation, 142, 199

Galileo, 22
Galloway, A., 318n.

Gaunilo:
  Anselm's response to, 190–91
  critique of Anselm's argument, 189–90
Gnosticism, 135–56, 172n., 173nn.
  absolutizes the fragmentary, 167
  as Christian heresy, 135, 141–42
  definitive ideas, 136, 152 (*chart*)
  equation of evil with ignorance, 143
  fundamentalist affinities to, 142
  revelationist and rationalist versions distinguished, 135–36, 152 (*chart*)
Gnosticism, rationalist (*see also* Hegel; Marx; Spinoza):
  origins in Descartes, 144
  scorn for traditional religion, 143
Gnosticism, revelationist:
  obscure origins, 135, 137–38
  on sin and salvation, 138–39
  view of Christ, 140–41
  world-picture, 138–39
God (*see also* Christ; Holy Spirit; Trinity; Yahweh):
  according to Aristotle, 288–89
  biblical conception, 294–300
  capable of "becoming" or changing, 314–16
  Creator, 232, 233–34, 236, 238–40, 243–46, 250, 252, 261, 263–65, 267, 295–96, 316, 322
  and evil, 247–50, 251 (*chart*), 252–60
  as Father, 295–300, 316
    special relationship to Christ, 299
  in gnostic theories, 152 (*chart*)
  of gospel *versus* Greek conceptions, 287–92, 314–15
  in Hegel's system, 147–150, 152 (*chart*)
  his "hiddenness," 110
  in history religion, 48 (*chart*), 50–51
  as history's beginning and end, 63, 91n.
  as Judge, 94n., 297, 306–7
  "lives," 287–95
  as Lord of history, 51–53
  in Marx's view, 152 (*chart*)
  in nature religion, 33–35, 48 (*chart*)
  as personal good will or love, 121, 155
  in reason religion, 40–41, 48 (*chart*)
  Redeemer, 298
  as scientific hypothesis, 282, 318n.
  in Spinoza's thought, 144–45, 147, 152 (*chart*)
  transitive powers in, 290–94
  trinitarian, 292–94

God (*cont.*)
  will of, 154
  "within the shadow," 388
Gogarten, Friedrich, 270n.
Golding, William, 107–11
Gospel:
  confers authentic selfhood, 337, and liberty, 369
  of Incarnation, 313
  sacraments as expressions of, 345–46, 354
  theological definition, 106
Grace, *defined*, 377
Graham, Billy, 91
Grillmeier, A., 172n., 318n., 319n.

HEAVEN (*see also* Afterlife; Eternal life; Resurrection):
  defined, 388
Heaven and hell (*see also* Afterlife; Eternal life; Resurrection):
  speculation on, unhealthy, 391–92
Hebrews, significance of name, 49
Hegel, G. W. F., 77, 155, 182n., 192 (*chart*), 240, 248, 271n.
  criticized by Kierkegaard and others, 150–51
  dialectic illustrated, 173–74nn.
  ecological implications of teaching, 150
  on the fluidity of truth, 173n.
  God as Subject, 147
  on logic, 147–48
  and Marx, 151–53
  political influence, 151
  as rational gnostic, 146–50, 152 (*chart*)
  on the tardiness of wisdom, 105–6, 125n.
Heidegger, Martin, 11, 79–80, 124, 269, 396n.
  on "care," 80
  concept of "the They," 335
  defines basic question of metaphysics, 269
  on the "terror" of freedom, 337
Heresy:
  Christian varieties of, 174–75n.
  defined and illustrated, 153–54
Hinduism, 31, 81
Historiolatry (history-worship), 64, 72–73, 91n.
Historians, biblical distinguished from modern, 104
Historism (history religion), 46–56, 88–89

History:
  as arena of redemption, 122
  Christian interpretations, 61–81, 82, 88–89
  as divine-human drama, 52–53, 63, 89
  "lived" and "seen," 78–81
  as medium of revelation, 169–70, 203 (*chart*), 223 (*chart*)
  nature of its value, 64, 91nn.
  sphere of the will, 88–89
  as tragicomedy, 52–53
Holbrook, Clyde, 225n.
Holy Spirit, 122–23
  descent at Pentecost, 386
  as God's holy self-love, 325
  grants and withholds the Word, 348
  as guarantor of participation in Christ, 327, 362n.
  guide "into all truth," 342
  illuminates divine-human drama, 324–25
  Liberator, 328, 331, 337, 338–39
  name for God's mysterious transcendence, 324
  omnipresent, 324, 361n.
  principle of divine vitality, 325
  principle of unity within God, 293, 326
  Reconciler, 295, 326–27, 334
  and sectarian enthusiasm, 352
  source of the "inner Word," 354
  speaks through conscience and consensus, 354
  unites the church, 360
  vital role in sectarian worship, 353
  works through congregation, 352
Homer, 109, 211
Hope:
  authentic *versus* inauthentic, 378
  as child of caring, 378
  as committed and confident expectancy, 379, 389
  grounded ultimately in God's love, 394
  oriented to God's Kingdom, 378–79
  is other-including, 389
  psychological effects, 390
Hosea, 54, 298
Humankind (*see also* Humanness; Image of God):
  defined by relationships, 26n., 84–89, 96, 99, 169–70, 179, 241–43, 261–67
  as inherently religious, 9, 26n., 177–78
  as self-governing (Deism), 236
  sociality of, 267, 396n.

Humanness (*see also* Humankind; Image of God):
  compound of earthly and heavenly, 278
  meaning for historists, 51–52
  meaning for naturists, 33
  meaning for rationalists, 41–43
  means relativity and limitation, 262–63
Hume, David, 93n.

IDOLATRY, 280, 284–85
  defined, 102n., 361n.
  related to self-worship, 301, 308
Ignatius of Antioch, 364n.
Image of God (*imago Dei*), 263–67, 276–77, 322
  as "graven image" or idol, 280, 312
  lost through sin, 264, 281
  as power to love, 276
  situates humans between God and nature, 266–67, 278–79
Immortality (*see* Resurrection)
Incarnation:
  Arius' "angelic" concept, 291
  Church's formulation of, 313–14
  defined, 71, 78
  as "foolishness," 288–90
  implies transitive action, 292
  reestablishes authentic relationship to God, 122, 291, 312–13
  significance for history, 71–73, 78
Individuality (*see also* Autonomy; Self; Selfhood), 94n.
  significance, 74–76, 392–93
Infinitude, beyond reach of the finite, 9–10n., 175n.
Inspiration, of Bible, 206, 227n.
Intellect:
  centrality and fragility within self, 87
  central role in reason (culture) religions, 87
Intention, as life-integrating principle, 170
Interpersonalism, 201–4
  revelation's highest form, 221–24
Irenaeus of Lyons, 68, 69, 91nn.
  against gnosticism, 142
  vision of history, 64–66
Isaiah:
  call to prophesy, 227n.
  on hypocrisy, 329
Israel:
  as covenant community, 122

Israel (*cont.*)
  faith of, 46–56
  meanings of name, 52
  patriotic self-concern, 382
  sources of apocalyptic hope, 380

JACOB:
  and Esau, 59n.
  meanings of name, 52
  renewer of Israel's faith, 338
Jefferson, Thomas, 245, 268n.
Jeremiah, 90n., 115
Jesus (*see also* Christ), 1–2, 74, 77, 98, 122, 178, 210, 211, 226n., 237, 254, 260, 291, 298, 322, 372, 375, 377, 388, 396n., 397nn.
  birth, 1, 70
  as the Christ (Messiah), 2, 64–65, 72–73, 199, 205, 212–13, 215–17, 220, 273–74, 300, 308–12, 315–16, 342, 353
  as Church's center, 342
  on continuous creation, 231–32, 239–40
  crucifixion, 1
  demeanor on the cross, 377
  embodies authentic God-man relation, 122
  encounters with demoniacs, 126n.
  ethical priorities, 368
  on giving alms, 118
  gnostic use of name, 140
  as God incarnate, 71, 122
  on God's unpredictability, 315
  on good works, 116
  on human limits, 130
  on the law's intention and perversion, 329–31
  on life through sacrifice, 390
  on love for the neighbor, 373
  as the "man-for-others," 338
  mystery of his suffering, 109
  and Nicodemus, 219
  "one master only," 117–18
  problem of his identity, 273–74, 288–91, 312–14
  resurrection, 2, 362n., 394
  against the Sabbatarians, 231–32
  significance of his death, 333–34, 363n., 393–94
  in sixteenth-century Seville, 335–36
  special relationship to the Father, 299
  temptations, 379–83

Jesus (*cont.*)
  his use of Scripture, 215–16, 228nn.
  views on God's Kingdom, 382–84, 386–87
  wrestles with evil, 257–260
Job, 109, 182, 255–57, 260, 271n.
Job, Book of, 103, 124–25n., 182, 248
  message regarding evil and suffering,
    254–57
John the Baptist, 181, 379
  deference before Christ, 213
John the Evangelist, 17, 141
  views on God's Kingdom, 386–87
Johnson, Sherman, 259
Jonah, 103, 115
Jonas, Hans, 138, 172n.
Judaism, 104
  Jesus' loyalty to, 1
Judgment of God:
  expressed in the *agape* of Christ, 377
  expressed through the restless heart,
    286–87
  purpose, 218, 230
  rooted in the divine intention, 286
  of self by God (= salvation), 306–7
  of self by self (= sin), 302–6

KANT, IMMANUEL, 24, 76, 77, 79, 93nn., 184,
    192 (*chart*), 195, 223 (*chart*)
  advocate of deontological ethics, 368
  on the categorical imperative, 192–94
  doubts regarding the transcendent, 158
  on good will, 116–17
  on the infinite and the finite, 175n.
  on the nature of religion, 226n.
  phenomenal *versus* noumenal realities,
    79
  views on reason, 184–85, 193–94, 226n.
Kelly, J. N. D., 319n., 364n.
Kerygma, *defined*, 114
Keynes, J. M., 150, 174n.
Kierkegaard, Søren, 26n., 73, 79–80, 94n.,
    211, 363n.
  as critic of Hegel, 150–51
  against "the crowd," 335
  on the "terror" of freedom, 337
Kingdom of God, 366, 379–88
  aim of creation, 275
  anticipated in Eucharist, 346
  compatible with human freedom, 275–77,
    382–83
  cosmic in scope, 378, 384–85

Kingdom of God (*cont.*)
  defined and given by God alone, 388
  divergent interpretations of its advent:
    in modern thought, 385–86
    in New Testament, 386–87
  earthly as well as heavenly, 383–85
  individual *versus* corporate effects, 64,
    383–85
  object of Christian hope, 378–79
  political implications, 382–84
  uncertainty regarding nature and timing,
    379, 383–84, 385–88, 397n.
Knowledge:
  classical theory of, 129
  inadequate as substitute for love, 155
Kroner, Richard, 175n.
Kuhn, T. S., 318n.

LANGUAGE OF RELIGION (*see* Religion, lan-
    guage of)
Laplace, P. S., 318n.
Law (*see also* Legalism):
  as ethical director, 367
    advantages, 367–68
    drawbacks, 368–69
  and gospel, 106, 362n.
  as instrument of self-concern or "tyrant,"
    329
  intention more important than form, 373
  Jesus' views on, 329–31
  as occasion of Paul's downfall, 305–6
  Paul's views on, 106–7, 330–31, 395–96n.
  sacraments as response to, 354–55, 357
    (*chart*)
  theological definitions, 106, 328
Legalism, 329, 367–69, 372–73, 395n.
  versus libertarianism, 372, 375
Legend(s):
  positive significance of, 47n.
  value and perils in, 103
Leibniz, G. W., 248
Liberation (*see also* Autonomy; Freedom;
    Liberty):
  as work of Holy Spirit, 328–38
Libertarianism, 369–75
  biblical, distinguished from modern-
    political philosophy, 371n.
  versus legalism, 371–72, 375
Liberty (*see also* Autonomy; Freedom):
  aim of divine love expressed in creation,
    369–70

Liberty (*cont.*)
  drawbacks in ethic of, 371
  fulfilled and authenticated in love,
    373–75
  mark of authentic existence, 370
  Paul's example, 374
  principal Christian value, 371
  and the "weaker brethren," 374
Lietzmann, H., 173n.
Life, difficulty of defining, 129–30
Life style (*see also* Historism; Naturism;
    Rationalism), 30–55
  of historists, 46–55
  of naturists, 33
  of rationalists, 41–43
Lincoln, Abraham, 392
Literalism (*see also* Textualism):
  dangers in, 102–4, 109
Littell, F. H., 364n.
Liturgy:
  defined, 112n., 363n.
  disdain for, among sects, 353
  esteem for, among corporatists, 344
Logic, Hegelian *versus* Aristotelian, 147–48
Logos, as cosmic principle, 225n.
Lonergan, B., 175–76n.
Lord's Supper (*see also* Eucharist):
  Protestant variation, 317n.
Love:
  as authentic relating, 123
    to God and neighbor simultaneously,
      397n.
  confers freedom from human judgments,
    337
  defined as caring, 366, 375–78
  defined by needs of neighbor, 373
  for enemies, 376–77, 396n.
  expresses law's intention, 373
  fulfills the law, 373
  God's enables the Christian's, 367
  God's for himself, 325, 395n.
  as ground of reality, unity, goodness,
    and freedom, 120–21, 123
  linked closely to freedom, 339
  principal Christian value, 154–55
  priority of love toward God, 368
  three ways of defining: law, liberty,
    neighbor-care, 367–75
  what it is, 373–77
  what it is not, 375
Lowell, James Russell, 368, 388, 398n.

Luke the Evangelist, 65, 71, 257, 397n.
  views on God's Kingdom, 386–87
Luther, Martin:
  on the Church as creature of the Word,
    114
  on demonic "tyrants," 329
  on the divine glory, 270n.
  on faith, 98, 338
  on the gifts of redemption, 328
  on God's "masks," 202, 227n.
  on liberty and love, 375
  on priesthood of all believers, 114,
    201–2
  Reformation of, 5
  compared with sectarians, 355
  sectarian view of, 353
  on sin as slavery, 300
  on the "theological jail," 134
  on "works," 349
Lutheranism, 341, 364n.

McLuhan, Marshall, 166–67
Magisterium, 344–45
  defined, 344
  distinguished from *ministerium,* 348
Man (*see* Humankind)
Manichaeans, 57n.
Marcion of Sinope, 173n.
Maritain, Jacques, 172n.
Mark the Evangelist, view of God's King-
    dom, 386
Marriage:
  as Catholic sacrament, 347
  Roman and Orthodox practices distin-
    guished, 347, 364n.
Marx, Karl, 143, 155
  inverts Hegelian dialectic, 151
  as rational gnostic, 143, 151, 152 (*chart*),
    174n.
  on the source of evil, 252
Mary of Nazareth, 71, 363n.
Mascall, E. L., 269n.
Matter, Christian attitude toward, 246
Meontology:
  defined, 248–49
  and the problem of evil, 248–50, 251
    (*chart*)
Messiah (*see* Christ; Jesus)
Metropolitan Seraphim, 364n.
Michalson, Carl, 228n.

Methodism, 341, 358, 364n.

Milton, John, 247

Ministerium, Protestant counterpart of Catholic *magisterium,* 348–49, 357 (*chart*)

Missions, medieval strategy for, 3

Mitford, Jessica, 362n.

Moltmann, Jürgen, 78, 91n., 94n.

Monasticism, 3n., 344, 349, 351, 356

Montanus, 227n.

Moral argument (*see* Existence of God)

Morris, H. J. 269n.

Moses, 20, 50, 73, 100, 106, 178, 202, 211, 296, 305, 373, 396n.
  as guide for ordinary Christians, 356
  nature of commission, 227n.
  reluctant prophet, 115
  renewer of Israel's faith, 227n., 338

Mt. Sinai, as site of covenant event, 49

Mysticism, 200, 209

Myth(s):
  defined, 9–10n.
  gnostic rationalists' scorn for, 143
  inherent limits of, 9–10n., 124n.
  as life-frame or pattern, 166–67
  as mosaic synthesis, 169
  perils of interpretation, 102
  value for religion, 9–10n., 103

NATURALISM, PHILOSOPHIC, 282
  arbitrary nature of its amoralism, 242

Natural theology (*see also* Existence of God), 181–97
  defined, 181
  distinguished from rationalist gnosticism, 182n.
  special difficulties, 197

Nature:
  history's macrocosmic hero (Teilhard), 67
  as maternal divinity, 33–36, 57n.
  as medium of revelation, 202, 203 (*chart*)

Naturism (nature religion), 32–38
  hostility toward rationalism, 46
  mediated through emotions, 86

Nestorius, 321n.

Neumann, Erich, 28n.

New Covenant, 308, 312

Newton, Sir Isaac, 22

Nicodemus, 12, 219, 228n.

Niebuhr, H. R., 104, 227nn., 318n.
  on faith and history, 78–79, 81

Niebuhr, Reinhold, 59n., 227n.
  on Christianity and the individual, 94n.

Niesel, W., 364nn.

Nietzsche, Friedrich, 18, 26n., 28n., 153
  on religion and philosophy, 18
  on world as a work of art, 226n.

Noah, 297, 320n.

Noah's Ark:
  as image of the Church, 3

Nogar, R. J., 270n.

OGDEN, S. M., 271n.

Ontological argument (Existence of God)

Ontology:
  defined, 249
  etymology of word, 191

Ordination:
  as empowering sacrament, 347
  source of priestly authority, 345

Origen of Alexandria, 227n.

Orthodoxy, Eastern (*see* Eastern Orthodoxy)

PALEY, WILLIAM, 192 (*chart*)

Pannenberg, W., 91n.
  on Christ and the Spirit, 327, 362nn.

Papacy (*see* Pope)

Parmenides, 144

Pascal, Blaise, 94n., 196, 318n., 362n.
  conversion experience, 125–26n.
  on flight from death, 333
  on human worth, 276

Pauck, W., 125n.

Paul of Tarsus, 73, 97, 100, 106, 109, 125n., 211, 259–60, 371, 390, 394, 395n., 398n.
  anguish regarding Israel, 389
  against the antinomians, 371n., 395n.
  on baptism, 220
  on Christian liberty, 370
  on the Church as Christ's body, 211, 359–60
  compared to Eve, 306
  against the Corinthian gnostics, 140–41
  on the cosmic implications of evil, 254
  on cults and cliques, 126n.
  on death, 333

Paul of Tarsus (*cont.*)
on faith *versus* "sight," 168
on the gifts of redemption, 328
on God's rule, 384–85
implicit trinitarianism, 326
on justification, 302–7
before King Agrippa, 176n.
on knowledge and love, 138
on law, liberty, and love, 372–75
on the law's intention and its perversion,
330–31
nature of his hope, 378
on nature's "groaning," 254, 366
on predestination, 398n.
on resurrection of the body, 74–76
on revelation, 226–27n.
on Son and Spirit, 326–27
source of Christian views on sex, 233
spiritual autobiography, 304–5
theology of Christ and Adam, 307–12
on Word and Spirit, 212–13
against works of the law, 349, 395n.
Pelagius, 174–75n.
Pelikan, J., 66, 91–92nn.
Penance, 346–47
Pentecost, 386
Persona, 202
Personhood (*see also* Selfhood), 276–78
Perspective:
Christian, summarized, 119–23, 394
features of Christian, 120–23, 167–70, 394
function defined, 120
Pharisees, 228nn.
Phenomenology, 9
purpose defined, 135n.
Philia (*see also* Love), 376
Philosophy:
and cultural awareness, 125n.
distinguished from religion, 17–18, 25
(*chart*)
Plato, 15, 27n., 28n., 46, 47, 58n., 87, 144,
189, 221
on creation, 233
and demythologizing, 288
on reason's power and divinity, 39–42,
44–45
source of Christian views on sex, 233
sponsor of "intellectual" religion, 18
teaching style compared to that of Jesus,
16
Poetry, in the Bible, 103

Polytheism, 28n., 284–85
Pontius Pilate, 383
Pope:
basis of authority, 199, 226n., 341, 343
conditions of infallibility, 343
necessarily infallible, 199
Pope Gregory VII, 115n.
Pope Leo X, 5
Pope Pius IX, 343
Pope Pius XII, 363n.
Predestination:
Calvin's corollary to, 391
distinguished from determinism, 90–91n.
doctrine affirms mystery of God's rule,
398n.
doctrine's main point, 90–91n., 390–91
empirical basis of doctrine, 124n.
Prenter, Regin, 268, 364n.
Presbyterianism, 341, 358, 364n.
Priesthood of all believers, 114, 201–2
Priests (*see also Magisterium*)
"indelible character" of, 347
powers of, 344–45
ranks among, 344
Proofs (*see* Existence of God)
Project:
defined, 124n.
faith as, 95–99
Prophets:
their reluctance to preach, 115
Protestantism, accent on freedom and resulting diversity, 126n.
Protestant Reformation, 4–5, 348–49,
353–56
Providence, 320n.
Pythagoras, 18, 40, 57–58n.

Quakers, 353–55, 358–59

Rad, Gerhard von, 231, 238, 269nn.
Rall, H. F., 316
Rationalism (reason religion), 38–46
hostility toward naturism, 46
Reason:
Kant's views on, 184–85, 193–94, 226n.
relation to revelation, 132–33, 180–81,
197–98
three conceptions discerned by Tillich,
182–85, 225n.

Reason (*cont.*)
  as way of approaching God, 132–33, 203 (*chart*), 223 (*chart*)
Reasoning, as form of relating, 129
Reconciliation:
  accomplished in Christ, 313–14
  as aim of redemption, 312
  corporate concept *versus* sectarian, 350–51
  defined, 312, 314, 339
  expressed in baptism, 345
  legalist concept *versus* libertarian, 371
  linked closely to liberation, 338
  its three primary effects, 339
  work of Holy Spirit, 338–39
Redemption (*see also* Justification; Liberation; Salvation):
  aim, 316
  and creation, 274–78, 366
  defined, 300
  of historically involved self (body), 366
  unfinished, 366
Regeneration, Orthodox concept of, 347
Reincarnation, 45
Relationship:
  religion as, 9, 11–12, 17, 18–19, 81, 96, 129, 154–55, 167–70, 177–79, 217–20, 222, 241, 267, 307–8, 311–12, 314, 322–23, 327, 339, 350–51, 366, 394
  vital/intellectual contrasted with intellectual, 129–31
Relativism, ethical, 367, 369
Religion (*see also* Faith; Relationship):
  defined, 9–11
  distinguished from philosophy, 17–18, 24, 25 (*chart*)
  distinguished from science, 13–17, 25 (*chart*)
  embraces all of life, 9, 18, 27n., 176n.
  etymology of word, 9
  indefinable elements, 399
  language of, 14–17, 25 (*chart*)
  synthetic function, 9, 26n., 27n.
  theory of origin, 9, 26n.
Religions:
  dissimilarities among, 30–31
  families (naturism, rationalism, historism) compared, 46, 48 (*chart*), 55–56, 81–89
Resurrection:
  of the body, 74–76, 392–94

Resurrection (*cont.*)
  of Christ, 1–2, 78, 220, 334, 338, 362n., 394
  distinguished from immortality, 74–75, 392–93
  faith in expresses faith in God, 394
Revelation (*see also* Holy Spirit; Word of God):
  baptism as analogue, 220
  Bible as medium, 204–11
  Christ as norm, 212–17
  defined, 179–81, 217
  difficulty of defining, 177
  as dynamic, self-correcting process, 202–3
  interpersonal conception most adequate, 221–25
  nature and form, 197–204
  objective, subjective, and interpersonal forms, 198–204
  realigns personal priorities, 219
  as realization of a relationship, 217–20
  relation to reason, 132–33, 180–81, 197–98
  St. Paul's view of, 226–27n.
  as way of knowing God, 132–33
Reverence for life (Schweitzer), 244, 271n.
Roberts, D. E., 226n.
Robinson, Edwin A. 175n.
Robinson, H. W., 27n., 57n.
Robinson, J. A. T., 74–75, 93nn.
Roman Catholicism, 341–50
  concept of authority, 199, 341–45
  and Eastern Orthodoxy, 2, 347, 350
  medieval achievements, 3
  and Protestantism, 4–5, 341, 348–56, 358–59
  theory of revelation, 199
Rousseau, J.-J., 250
Rule of God (*see* Kingdom of God)
Russell, Bertrand, 271n.

SACRAMENTS (*see also* Baptism; Confirmation; Eucharist; Extreme Unction; Marriage; Ordination; Penance):
  evangelical distinguished from empowering, 347
  exceptions from priestly administration, 347, 363n.
  express the gospel (corporate view), 345–46

SACRAMENTS (*cont.*)
  realistic view of corporatists, 345–46, 354, 357
  responses to divine commands, 354–55, 357 (*chart*)
  symbolic view of sectarians, 354–55, 357
  works of God, 345, 346 (*chart*)
  ex opere operato, 364n.
Sadducees, 228n.
Saint Anselm (*see* Anselm of Canterbury)
Saint Augustine (*see* Augustine of Hippo)
Saint Dominic, 364n.
Saint Francis (*see* Francis of Assisi)
Saint John (*see* John the Evangelist)
Saint Luke (*see* Luke the Evangelist)
Saint Mark (*see* Mark the Evangelist)
Saint Matthew, 379–80
Saint Paul (*see* Paul of Tarsus)
Saint Thomas (*see* Thomas Aquinas)
Salvation (*see also* Justification; Reconciliation; Redemption):
  contingent on Incarnation (Athanasius), 291
  and creation, 231–37, 268n., 269n., 274–78
  in gnosticism, 136, 138–39, 145–46, 152 (*chart*), 153, 155
  in history religion, 48 (*chart*), 54–55
  in nature religion, 35–37, 48 (*chart*)
  in reason religion, 43–45, 48 (*chart*)
  of selves, not souls, 268n.
  and sex, 233–34
  as union with God (Athanasius), 291
Sanctification, 356
Satan (*see also* Devil; Tempter), 247, 254–55, 382
Saul, 315
Schaff, P. 319n., 363n.
Schleiermacher, Friedrich, 19, 21, 28n.
Schmithals, W. 172n., 173n.
Schwarz, Hans, 397n.
Schweitzer, Albert, 244, 271n., 386
Science:
  and biblical idea of dominion, 173n.
  distinguished from art, 13
  distinguished from religion, 13–17, 25 (*chart*)
  language of, 14–15, 25 (*chart*)
  method, 14
  "purposelessness," 88
  unseen assumptions of, 26n., 175n.

Scopes, John T., 28n.
Scott, R. B. Y., 57n.
Scribes, 215–16, 228n.
Scripture (*see also* Bible; Canon):
  as interpreted by Jesus, 213, 215–16, 228nn.
Second Isaiah, 258
Sect(s) (*see also* Church; Congregationalism):
  concern for holiness of life, 351, 356
  defined, 351–52
  exclusiveness and discipline as hallmarks, 352–53, 357 (*chart*)
Seeberg, Reinhold, 318n., 319n.
Self:
  and culture, 87–88
  distinguished from things, 80
  and history, 88–89
  history's product, and its producer, 82, 94n.
  and nature, 86
  object of redemption, 366
  powers of, 83–84
  and revelation, 217, 221–24
  its situation, 84–89
  sole mediator of meaning, 82
Selfhood (*see also* Autonomy; Individuality; Personhood; Self):
  accorded intrinsic value, 82
  loss of, 81–82
    in nature religions, 81
    in reason religions, 82
  threatened by "the crowd," 335–37
Sermon(s), 198
  high standing among Protestants, 348, 364n.
  subordinated to sacraments in Catholicism, 345
Sex:
  as power to participate in creation, 234, 267
  sacred cast in paganism, 35–36
  and salvation, 233–34
Shakespeare, William, 94n.
Sheldon, Charles M., 363n.
Silesius, Angelus, 208
Simon Peter, 103, 199, 226n., 343
  as first bishop of Rome, 341
  renaming, 199
Simpson, C. A., 269n., 271n.

Sin (see also Adam and Eve; Eve; Evil;
    Idolatry), 32
  accompanied by self-deception, 302
  as condition and as act, 280
  its effects, 280–82, 284–85
  as idolatry, 280
  meaning for historists, 48 (chart), 53–54
  meaning for naturists, 34, 48 (chart)
  meaning for rationalists, 42–43, 48 (chart)
  origins in self-worship, 280–81, 318n.
  as slavery to self, 300–301
Smith, D. M., Jr., 365n.
Socrates, 16, 28n., 40
  and demythologizing, 288n.
Solomon, 77
Sophocles, 57n.
Spinoza, Benedict de, 155, 182n., 221
  compared to Hegel, 147–53
  God as Substance, 144, 146–47
  harbinger of the new science, 146
  as rational gnostic, 144–46, 152 (chart)
Spirit (see Holy Spirit)
Spiritualism, 207–9
Spivey, R. A., 365n.
Standards:
  danger in slavish conformity to, 106–7
  originate in styles, 105–6
  tend to idealize past and future, 106
Stoics, 48 (chart), 183–84, 225n., 240, 289
Stories, 99–105
  difficulties in interpreting, 100–104
  guidelines for interpreting, 108–10
  value for faith, 100
Style:
  defined and illustrated, 105
  importance in stories, 108–11
  of the "shaper," 46–56, 125n.
  of the "square," 38–46, 125n.
  of the "swinger," 32–38, 125n.
Subject, Hegel's divine Agent, 147
Subjectivism (see Revelation)
Substance, Spinoza's "God," 144, 146–47
Suffering (see also Evil):
  potential significance, 254–60
Suicide:
  as life's central question (Camus), 244
  and life's meaning, 271n.
Symbol(s), functions of, 15, 26n.
Synoptic gospels:
  dated, 387n.
  source of name, 16n.

Taylor, Jeremy, 362n.
T' hom (the "void"), distinguished from
    Tiamat, 269n.
Teilhard de Chardin, P., 19, 27n., 28n.,
    92nn.
  innovative cast of thought, 92n.
  on knowing, 129
  on nature's human bias, 277
  on science and subjectivity, 175n.
  theory of history, 67–69
Temptations (see Jesus)
Tempter (see also Devil; Satan), 380
Tennyson, Alfred Lord, 175n.
Tertullian:
  an ancient textualist, 227n.
  against gnosticism, 142, 173n.
Textualism (see also Biblicism), 206–7, 227n.
Theodicies, 246–60, 251 (chart)
  aesthetic, 248, 251
  biblical, 252–60
  meontological, 249–51
  moral, 250–51
  ontological, 248, 251
  romantic, 250–52
  teleological, 248, 251
Theology (see also Natural theology):
  defined, 114, 134
  as hybrid of religion and philosophy, 25
    (chart)
  limits of, 132–34
  Luther's "theological jail," 134
  necessity for, 134
  origins of, 134, 172n.
Thomas Aquinas, 192 (chart)
  on continuous creation, 270n.
  and cosmological arguments, 225n.
  on God's glory, 269–70n.
  principle of "doing follows being," 116
  on reason and revelation, 133
Tillich, Paul, 26nn., 93n., 97, 175n. 194,
    225n.
  on the centrality of the doctrine of crea-
    tion, 268n.
  concept of evil's source, 249–50
  on content of faith, 124n.
  distinguishes three types of reason,
    182–85, 225n.
  on divine personhood, 277
  doctrine of "dreaming innocence," 10–12
  on ecstatic reason, 133
  idea of "abyss of being," 112, 250

Tillich, Paul (*cont.*)
  on Israel's supra-national God, 94n.
  on revelation, 217
Time, 32, 48 (*chart*)
  Christian perception, 62–69, 76–82
  evokes and compounds care, 378
  in history religions, 46, 47, 48 (*chart*), 49,
    55
  "inner" and "outer," 79
  integrating principle in historism, 169
  mental or extramental?, 76–77, 93nn.
  as mode of relating, 63, 169
  in naturism, 37–38, 48 (*chart*)
  in reason religion, 45–46, 48 (*chart*)
  as religious category, 32, 37
  religious significance, 37, 63, 76
  as "sacrament," 77
  and space, 60, 77, 93n., 93–94n.
Tolstoy, Leo, 389
Torah, 47, 204, 216
Treasury of merit, 341, 347–49
Trinity:
  as affirmation that God lives, 292–94
  classic formulation, 293
  describes modes of divine action, 295
  Hegel's use of the doctrine, 150
  implies divine personality, 293–94
  Truce of God, 3n.

Value(s):
  defined, 9
  role in defining heresies, 154
  significance for religion, 9–12, 14, 17,
    26nn.
Van Buren, Paul, 93n.
  on resurrection, 338–39
Van der Leeuw, G., 28n., 57n.
Voegelin, Eric, 142, 168, 172n., 173n.
Voltaire, F. M. A., 249, 284

Waldensians, 4, 351
Weber, Max, 125n.
Wesley, John:
  advocate of "scriptural holiness," 356
  on the gifts of redemption, 328
  on God and the voice of the people, 336
White, Lynn, Jr., 173n.
Whitehead, A. N., 249

Will:
  defined, 88
  essential to meaningful history, 88–89
  and the problem of knowing God, 203
    (*chart*), 223 (*chart*)
William of Occam, 226n.
Williams, Charles, 395n.
Williams, J. Paul, 58n.
Wingren, G., 364n.
Wittgenstein, 390
Wolfson, H. A., 173n., 319n.
Word of God (*see also* Bible; Christ; Gospel;
    Law; Revelation; Sacraments):
  as Church's ground and substance, 114,
    125n., 339, 348
  as gospel of reconciliation, 339
  its imperious nature, 115
  inseparable from faith, 131
  as *kerygma* and *theologia*, 114
  as love-relation, 154–55
  mainstream Protestant conception, 348
  as new and renewing perspective, 114–15
  Orthodox conception, 347
  and priestly office (corporatism), 345
  Roman Catholic conception, 345–47
  and the sacraments, 345–48
  sectarian conceptions, 353–55
  source of faith, 114
  spoken through conscience and consen-
    sus, 354
  subjective, objective, and projective dis-
    tortions, 115
  transcends word of Church and of Scrip-
    ture, 353, 355
Wordsworth, William, 28n.
Work, as divine vocation, 116–17, 349
Works:
  accord between Orthodox and Protestant
    views, 349–50
  as expressions of reconciliation, 339
  goodness depends on motive, 118
  leftwing Protestant (sectarian) view,
    355–56
  mainstream Protestant view, 117, 349
  necessary expressions of faith, 116–17
  Roman Catholic view, 117, 349
  of supererogation, 349n., 350
World, biblical affirmation of, 112, 141, 222,
    243–46
Worship:
  bases in Christian faith, 111–12

Worship (*cont.*)
  in corporate churches, 344–45
  emotionalism and formalism as distortions, 113
  as expression of reconciliation, 339
  in sectarian churches, 353
  subjective, projective, and objective aspects, 111–13
Wycliffites, 2

YAHWEY (*see also* God), 48 (*chart*)
  definitive qualities, 294
  significance of name, 51, 294
YHWH (*see* Yahweh)

ZÖCKLER, O., 270n.